BIBLIOGRAPHY OF
STRASBOURG IMPRINTS,
1480–1599

BIBLIOGRAPHY OF STRASBOURG IMPRINTS, 1480–1599

MIRIAM USHER CHRISMAN

YALE UNIVERSITY PRESS   NEW HAVEN AND LONDON

Library of Congress Cataloging in Publication Data

Chrisman, Miriam Usher.
  Bibliography of Strasbourg imprints, 1480–1599.
  Includes index.
  1. Strasbourg (France)—Imprints. 2. Incunabula—
Biography. 3. Bibliography—Early printed books—
16th century. I. Title.
Z2184.S83C47   015.44′3835   82-2639
ISBN 0-300-02891-1   AACR2

10   9   8   7   6   5   4   3   2   1

CONTENTS

PREFACE

This bibliography is designed as a tool for scholars working in the six-teenth-century period. The majority of bibliographies for this period are compiled in terms of the work of a particular writer or publisher, or they record books in a library collection listed alphabetically by author. A re-searcher wishing to collate all books published in a given year must work through all the entries in these volumes. It is, furthermore, very difficult to arrive at a sense of the total publication in a given field—all humanist works, for example—and even more difficult to see the relationship of humanist publication to other work published at the same time.

This bibliography attempts to solve some of these problems by listing all surviving books published in Strasbourg between 1480 and 1599 by subject matter and by date. The books were collated from the various sources listed in the Abbreviations below, some thirty catalogues or bibliographies. Nine major divisions were established to denote the major classes of books: Cath-olic; Protestant; Biblical literature; humanism; law and politics; science; classical literature; school texts; and vernacular literature. Each book was then assigned an alphabetic letter based on this primary division, C standing for Catholic; P for Protestant; H for humanism; A for antiquity or editions of the classics; S for science; T for school texts; L for law.

Subject matter categories were then established for each major class based on the books in the study. Some of the categories for Catholic publication, for example, include doctrine and theology, sermons, curate's manuals and other preaching aids, devotionals for private worship and lay manuals of Christian life, missals and breviaries, canon law, and anti-Protestant po-lemic. The subject matter categories for science include medicine, books of distilling, botany and herbals, mathematics and physics, geography, travel and exploration, technical manuals and books on agronomy.

After assignment to the appropriate subject matter category, the books were then sorted by topic. For example, the category missals and breviaries was subdivided into four subtopics: missals; breviaries; sacred music for church worship; books on the administration of the sacraments. All of these books were characterized by the fact that they were compiled for the use of the clergy. The medical category was broken down into the following topics: memory books; gynecology; health rules and regimens; books on plague; books on syphilis; general medical treatises; books on medicinal baths; pharmaceutical texts; books on surgery. The lists of subject matter categories and topics appear at the beginning of each major section of the bibliography, providing a quick introduction to the scope of this particular division of learning or knowledge.

Finally, each book was assigned its place within the appropriate topical division by date. This provides an impression of the historical evolution within each topic or subject-matter category. The major divisions of the bibliography are also presented in order of their chronological appearance. Classes within each division are also listed by date, as are the topics. Each book is listed according to the date of its first publication.

For purposes of reference each book is coded by letter and number based on the classification system described above. The alphabetical letter, as already stated, refers to the major classification. This is followed by an arabic number which designates the subject matter category within that class. The next number, separated by a decimal point, denotes the topic. The final number in the sequence, again separated by a decimal point, denotes the chronological position of the book within the topic. A lower-case letter may follow, which means that the book went through multiple editions. The first edition of any book was automatically designed *a,* although this is not used unless there were subsequent editions. The second edition is then *b,* and so forth. V9.3.7g, for example, means a book from the ninth category of vernacular books (histories). It falls within the third topic (German and imperial histories) and is in the seventh place chronologically. It is the seventh edition of that particular work.

A book appears in the bibliography only once. This created obvious difficulties for school texts prepared by humanists or books which combined theology and humanist commentary. Here it was necessary to make a decision with regard to the primary purpose of the book, decisions which will certainly be questioned by other scholars. Use of the author index, however, should make it possible to find books under their subject-matter listing. An explanation of the major decisions with regard to subject matter classifications and what books were included follows.

For Catholic publication it seemed important to make clear what sources were available and were being used by the theologians in the last decades before the Reformation. Books on theology and doctrine were thus grouped according to three major time periods: (1) works of the Church Fathers and Catholic theologians writing up to 1000 A.D.; (2) works of Catholic theologians active from 1000 to 1400; (3) works of more recent Catholic theologians active from 1400 to 1520. Note that a separate category had to be made for the work of Catholic theologians printed after the Reformation. Another important division in the Catholic literature was that between books written for the clergy and books written for lay use. This led to two categories of books, C4 and C6, for clerical use; one category, C5, for laymen. C9, canon law, was included in Catholic literature because, for quantitative purposes, it was important to have all the books published for and used by the Roman church together. Catholic polemic includes books or treatises written to attack the new faith or to defend the church against Protestant critics. The essential criteria were that the treatise presented an argument or a defense or was controversial in nature.

The designations under Law and Politics are relatively straight forward. Legal texts and legal disputations are included under this rubric, just as scientific texts and scientific disputations are included under science. This was done to place all legal or all scientific work together.

The use of the term science for the next class of books is, as discussed elsewhere, parachronistic. The more correct term, in sixteenth-century language, would be natural philosophy. Since this is unwieldy, it was decided to use the word science to denote all books dealing with the physical or material world. This class covers the full range of medical books and herbals and botanies, mathematical books of all types, and astronomical works, ranging from treatises by learned professors to prognostications and calendars prepared for popular use (sometimes by the same professors). The object was to collect the materials available to all levels of readers and thus gain some insight into how the material world was described and perceived. Pseudo-scientific books—astrology, chiromancy, and alchemy—were also included in this classification, as is common in sixteenth-century bibliographies. Finally, treatises on witchcraft were included in science, since they seemed to fit more with pseudo-science than with any other category. This last was essentially a decision of convenience.

Classical literature (literature of antiquity, to avoid the C used for Catholic) comprises all works by Greek and Roman authors, including editions of Cicero, Homer, and the dramatists, which were prepared for school use. The principle here was to group all work of the ancient writers together, to be able to see what was made available and when. This does mean that a scholar who wants to know what books were used by students must look both here and also under school texts. For scientific and legal texts he must look under those subject-matter classes.

The humanist classification was narrowly defined to cover works by fifteenth- and sixteenth-century writers of a literary nature, namely letters, odes, dialogues, ecologues, orations and poetry. Other works by humanists such as classical editions prepared by them appear under classical literature. The textbooks they wrote are under school texts. In addition to literary works, the humanist class includes dictionaries which are representative of the humanist interest in language. These were dictionaries designed for the use of other scholars in contradistinction to the vocabularies compiled for schoolboys, which are listed under school texts. Humanists works include pedagogical treatises discussing the theory of education and the historical and biographical works of the humanist writers written and published in Latin.

Biblical literature covers all books dealing with the Bible except for the popular biblical tales, which are listed as part of vernacular literature. The biblical class contains all editions of biblical texts and all biblical commentary whether written by humanists, Catholics, or Protestants. The principle here was to group all the work on the Bible over the entire time period.

It is quite clear from the above that school texts are narrowly defined. Law texts are under law, science and mathematics texts under science, editions of classical authors under literature of antiquity. This leaves only the most strictly defined textbooks under school texts: grammars, books on rhetoric, school vocabularies, various types of exercise books. Also included, however, are plays written specifically to be presented by the students of the Gymnasium and the literary and philosophic theses presented by the students of the Academy.

The vernacular classification includes books written in German aimed at a popular audience. For this reason Bible stories in German are listed here rather than under biblical literature, which had a scholarly thrust. Medieval tales, plays presented by the citizens of Strasbourg and other cities, and journalism are important categories in this class. Also included are histories written or translated into German, since they were a particularly important form of popular literature.

The last classification is Protestant literature. Categories similar to those for Catholic literature were used, including the differentiation between books designed for the clergy and those designed for lay use. The most important element, perhaps, is the numerous classifications for polemic works.

The principle of chronological arrangement was used throughout the bibliography, which means that the order of the books was determined by the sixteenth-century writers and publishers, not by a twentieth-century scholar. The bibliography was originally organized according to the importance of the topics to the modern researcher. General medical treatises and surgical manuals seemed to the modern investigator the most important medical works and were placed first. It was then clear that this kind of decision destroyed important evidence. The first medical works published in Strasbourg were memory books, manuals on memory training. That, in itself, was primary data. To preserve the historical evolution of ideas all information in the bibliography is presented chronologically.

These broad directions should make clear the general principles involved in the development of the bibliography. The goal was to make the materials easily available to other scholars to use according to their own interests and to open up the full range of sixteenth-century sources.

ABBREVIATIONS

AMS   Archives Municipales de Strasbourg.

BM   British Museum. *Short-title catalogue of books printed in the German-speaking countries and German books printed in other countries from 1455–1600 now in the British Museum.* London: Trustees of the British Museum, 1962.

B *Cam.*   Benzing, Josef. *Die Drucke Jakob Cammerlander zu Strassburg 1531–1548.* Vienna: Walter Krieg Verlag, 1963.

B *Egen.*   _____. "Christian Egenolff zu Strassburg und seine Drucke (1528–1530)." *Das Antiquariat* IX, no. 8, April 1954, pp. 88–92.

B *Hut.*   _____. *Ulrich von Hutten und seine Drucker, eine Bibliographie der Schriften Huttens in 16. Jahrhundert.* Wiesbaden: O. Harrassowitz, 1956.

B *Luther*   _____. *Lutherbibliographie, Verzeichnis der Gedruckten Schriften Martin Luthers bis zu dessen Tod.* Baden-Baden: Heitz, 1965–66.

B *Ryff*   _____. *Walther H. Ryff und sein literarisches Werk.* Hamburg: Ernst Hauswedell, 1959.

B *SE* 1   _____. "Die Druckerei der Mathias Schürer Erben zu Strassburg (1520–1525)." *Archiv für Geschichte des Buchwesens* II (1969), pp. 173–74.

B *SE* 2   _____. *Jörg Wickram, Die zehn alter der Welt mit einem Nachwort von Josef Benzing.* Wiesbaden: Guido Pressler, 1961.

B *SE* 3   _____. "Die Reformationspresse der Mathias Schürer Erben in Strassburg (1520–1525)." In *Refugium animae bibliotheca, Festschrift für Albert Kolb.* Wiesbaden: Guido Pressler, 1969.

Bosse   Bosse, Friederich. *Illustriertes Wörterbuch der gebräuchlichsten Kunst. Ausdrücke aus dem Gebiete der Architektur, Chromatik, Malerei . . . für den Buchdruck und verwandte Zwiege.* 2 vols. Leipzig: 1888.

Deppermann   Deppermann, Klaus. *Melchior Hoffman. Soziale Unruhen und apokalyptische Visionen im Zeitalter der Reformation.* Göttingen: Vandenhoeck und Ruprecht, 1979.

Fischer   Fischer, Charles. "Ein Beitrag zur Geschichte der Astronomie in Elsass." Strasbourg: Dactylographie, 1975. Copie de Dr. Jean Rott.

Greiner   La revision des catalogues de Ritter de Mlle. Greiner
                        de la Bibliothèque nationale et universitaire de
                        Strasbourg.
Gurlt   Gurlt, Ernst Julius. *Geschichte der Chirurgie und ihrer
                        Ausübung; Volkschirurgie; Altherthum; Mittelalter; Re-
                        naissance.* 3 vols. Berlin: A. Hirschwald, 1898.
Gut. JB   *Gutenberg Jahrbuch,* 1954, pp. 168–70.
Haeser   Haeser, Heinrich. *Grundriss der Geschichte der Medecin.*
                        2 vols. Jena: G. Fischer, 1887.
Haller   Haller, Albrecht von. *Bibliotheca chirurgica qua scripta ad
                        artem chirurgicam facientia a rerum initiis recensentur.* 2
                        vols. Bern: E. Haller, 1774–75.
Harrisse   Harrisse, Henry. *Bibliotheca Americana velustissima: A
                        Description of Works Relating to America Published be-
                        tween the Years 1492 and 1551.* New York: G. P. Philea,
                        1866.
Hellman   Hellman, Clarisse Doris. *The Comet of 1577: Its Place in
                        the History of Astronomy.* London: P. S. King and Sta-
                        ples, Ltd., 1944.
Hirsch   Hirsch, Rudolf. *Preliminary Check-list of Chemical and
                        Alchemical Books Printed 1470–1536.* Philadelphia: 1949.
Hirsch, *PSR*   _____. *Printing, Selling, and Reading, 1450–1550.*
                        Wiesbaden: Otto Harrossowitz, 1967.
Krebs and Rott   Krebs, Manfred, and Rott, Hans Georg. *Elsass I, Stadt
                        Strassburg 1522–1532. Elsass II, Stadt Strassburg
                        1533–1535.* Quellen zur Geschichte der Täufer 7–8.
                        Gütersloh: Gerd Mohn, 1959–60.
Pegg   Pegg, Michael A. *A Catalogue of German Reformation
                        Pamphlets (1516–1546) in Libraries of Great Britain and
                        Ireland.* Bibl. Aureliana XLV, p. 197. Baden-Baden:
                        Valentin Koerner, 1977.
Peter   Peter, Rodolphe. "Les Premiers ouvrages français im-
                        primés à Strasbourg." *L'Annuaire des amis du
                        Vieux-Strasbourg* (1974), pp. 73–93; suite (1979), pp.
                        11–75.
R Bib. Mun.   Ritter, François. *Catalogue des incunables et livres du
                        XVIᵉ siècle de la Bibliothèque municipale de Strasbourg.*
                        Strasbourg: P. H. Heitz, 1948.
R BNU *Inc.*   Ritter, François. *Catalogue des incunables alsaciens de la
                        Bibliothèque nationale et universitaire de Strasbourg.*
                        Strasbourg: Heitz et cie., 1938.
R BNU I–IV   _____. *Répertoire bibliographique des livres imprimés en*

	Alsace au XVIe siècle de la Bibliothèque nationale et univer- *sitaire de Strasbourg.* 4 vols. Strasbourg: Heitz et cie., 1937–55.
R Nfp *Inc.*	_____. *Catalogue des incunables imprimés en Alsace ne* *figurant pas à la Bibliothèque nationale et universitaire de* *Strasbourg.* Strasbourg: P. H. Heitz, 1960.
R Nfp	_____. *Catalogue des livres du XVIe siècle ne figurant pas* *à la Bibliothèque nationale et universitaire de Strasbourg.* Strasbourg: P. H. Heitz, 1960.
R *Imp. Alsc.*	_____. *Histoire de l'imprimerie alsacienne au XVe et* *XVIe siècles.* Strasbourg and Paris: Editions F-X. Le Roux, 1955.
Rott	Rott, Jean. *Bibliographie des oeuvres imprimées du recteur* *Strasbourgeois Jean Sturm (1507–1589). Actes du 95e Con-* *grès National des Sociétés Savantes* (Reims, 1970), pp. 319–404. Paris: Bibliothèque Nationale, 1975.
S	Schmidt, Charles. *Répertoire bibliographique Stras-* *bourgeois jusq'à vers 1530.* 8 vols. Strasbourg: J. H. Ed. Heitz (Heitz und Mündel), 1893–96.
	Volumes and sections of volumes are referred to separately:
S I	Vol. I. Jean Grüninger.
S II A	Vol. II. Martin Schott.
S II B	Vol. II. Jean Schott.
S III A	Vol. III. Jean Prüss I.
S III B	Vol. III. Jean Prüss II.
S IV Eber	Vol. IV. Jacques Eber.
S IV Ans.	Vol. IV. Thomas Anshelm.
S IV. Att.	Vol. IV. Pierre Attendorn.
S IV Dum.	Vol. IV. Frédéric Dumbach.
S IV Kis.	Vol. IV. Barthélemy Kistler.
S IV Sch.	Vol. IV. Guillaume Schaffner.
S IV Bra.	Vol. IV. Matthias Brant.
S IV Wäh.	Vol. IV. Jean Wähinger.
S IV Greff	Vol. IV. Jérome Greff.
S IV Beck	Vol. IV. Reinhart Beck.
S IV Ker.	Vol. IV. Conrad Kerner.
S IV Mor.	Vol. IV. Ulric Morhard.
S V	Vol. V. Matthias Hupfuff.
S VI A	Vol. VI. Martin Flach I.
S VI B	Vol. VI. Martin Flach II.
S VII	Vol. VII. Jean Knobloch.

S VIII	Vol. VIII. Matthias Schürer.
Schottlenloher.	Schottenloher, Karl. *Bibliographie zur deutschen Geschichte im Zeitalter der Glaubensspaltung. 1517–1585.* Leipzig. Stuttgart 1933–66. 7 vols.
Thorndike, *Cat.*	Thorndike, Lynn. *A Catalogue of Incipit of Mediaeval Scientific Writings in Latin.* Cambridge, Mass.: Mediaeval Academy of America, 1913–38.
Thorndike, *Magic*	———. *A History of Magic and Experimental Science,* vol. 5. New York: Macmillan & Co., 1928–58.
Vogeleis	Vogeleis, Martin. *Quellen und Bausteine zu einer Geschichte der Musik und des Theaters im Elsass 500–1800.* Strasbourg: F. X. Le Roux, 1911.
Weber	Weber, Edith. *Musique et théatre dans les pays Rhenanes,* vol. 2, *Le théatre humaniste et scholaire dans les pays Rhenanes.* Paris: Klincksieck, 1974.
Wick	Wick Collection in Zentralbibliothek, Zurich.
Young	Young, William. "Music Printing in Sixteenth-Century Strasbourg." *Renaissance Quarterly* XXIV, no. 4 (1971), pp. 486–501.
Zinner	Zinner, Ernst. *Geschichte und Bibliographie der Astronomischen Literatur in Deutschland zur Zeit der Renaissance.* Stuttgart: Anton Hiersemann, 1964.
Z, PAS	Broadsheets in Graphische Sammlung, Zentralbibliothek, Zurich.

NOTE

Josef Benzing's new volume on Strasbourg imprints came off the press after the final editing and correcting of this volume had been completed. His volume brings together the books printed in Strasbourg from his Luther catalogue, his catalogue of Walther Ryff, and others. It would be wise to refer to this new catalogue before searching his more specialized lists:

Josef Benzing. *Bibliographie Strasbourgeoise, t.* 1, in *Répertoire bibliographique des livres imprimés en France au seizième siècle*. Bibliotheca Bibliographica Aureliana. Baden-Baden: Editions Valentin Koerner, 1981.

Similarly, polemic works and other flugschriften should be checked in the new, comprehensive bibliography now appearing from the Sonderforschungsbereich "Spätmittelalter und Reformation" at Tübingen:

Hans Joachim Köhler, Hildegard Hebenstreit, Andrea Körsgen, Christoph Weismann. *Bibliographie der deutschen und lateinischen Flugschriften des frühen 16. Jahrhunderts. Probedruck zur Erläuterung der Konzeption eines laufenden Forschungsprojekts*. Tübingen: Sonderforschungsbereich "Spätmittelalter und Reformation," 1978.

CATHOLIC LITERATURE

C1. Catholic Doctrine and Theology Printed before the Reform.

   1. Church Fathers and Catholic Theologians before 1000.
   2. Catholic Theologians, 1000–1400.
   3. Catholic Theologians, 1400–1525.

C2. Catholic Doctrine and Theology Printed after the Reform.

C3. Catholic Sermons.

   1. Sermons.
   2. Sermons Preached by Johannes Geiler von Keysersberg.

C4. Catholic Curates' Manuals and Lives of the Saints.

   1. Catholic Curates' Manuals.
   2. Lives of the Saints in Latin.

C5. Catholic Devotionals for Private Worship, Lay Manuals of
     Christian Life, and Popular Religious Music.

   1. Devotionals for Private Worship and Lay Manuals of
       Christian Life.
   2. Popular Religious Music.

C6. Catholic Breviaries, Missals, Sacred Music, and Sacramental
     Books.

   1. Breviaries.
   2. Missals.
   3. Sacred Music for Church Worship.
   4. Books on the Administration of the Sacraments.

C7. Marian Verse, Marian Controversy, and Other Catholic Verse.

   1. Marian Verse and Marian Controversy.
   2. Other Catholic Verse.

C8. Intra-Catholic Controversy.

C9. Canon Law and Ecclesiastical Politics.

C10. Anti-Protestant Polemic.

C1. CATHOLIC DOCTRINE AND THEOLOGY PRINTED BEFORE THE REFORM.

1. CHURCH FATHERS AND CATHOLIC THEOLOGIANS TO 1000.

C1.1.1. Gregorius Magnus (Pope), Dialogi.
J. Eber, 1481 [R Nfp Inc., 301].
No printer, 1496 [R Nfp Inc., 300].

.1.2. Augustinus, Aurelius, Opuscula plurima.
M. Flach I, 1489 [S VI A, 21], 1491 [S VI A, 34].

.1.3. Augustinus, Aurelius, Canones . . . regulam omni statui
modum vivendi prestantes.
M. Schott, 1490 [S II A, 9].

.1.4. Boethius, De consolatione philosophiae.
J. Pruss I, 1491 [R Nfp Inc., 121].
J. Gruninger, 1501 [S I, 57].
J. Knobloch, 1514 [S VII, 89].
J. Schott, 1500 [S II B, 2]. (In German.)

.1.5. Gregorius I. Magnus, Pastorale.
G. Husner, 1496 [R BNU Inc., 194].

.1.6. Gregorius Nazianzenus, Apologeticus, Liber I. De
epiphaniis sive natali domini. De luminibus. De fide
Liber I. De Nicena fide . . . .
J. Knobloch, 1500 [R Nfp Inc., 302], 1508 [R Nfp,
1927], 1508 [S VII, 36; R Nfp, 1036].

.1.7. Dionysius Areopagita, Opera.
No printer, 1502/03 [R BNU I, 655].

.1.8. Avitus, Alcimus, De origine mundi. De originali
peccato. De sententia dei. De diluvio mundi. De
transitu Maria. De virginitate.
J. Gruninger, 1507 [S I, 81].

.1.9. Theodulus, Auctores octo opusculorum cum commentariis
Theodolus cum commentario.
J. Knobloch, ca. 1510 [Greiner].

.1.10. Gregorius Nyssae, Libri VIII. De homine. De anima.
De elementis. De viribus animae. De voluntario et
involuntario. De facto. De libero arbitrio. De
providentia.
M. Schurer, 1512 [S VIII, 72].

.1.11. Nilus (Nilus Ancyranus), Sententiae morales.
M. Schurer, 1516 [S VIII, 194].
J. Pruss II, 1519 [BM 3805.aa.3].

.1.12. Athanasius (Bishop of Alexandria), Opera.
J. Knobloch, 1522 [S VII, 234].

Cl.1.13.   Isidorus, De sectis et nominibus haereticorum. . . .
           Augustinus, Libellus aureus de fide.
           Hieronymus, De perpetua gloriosae Virginitate.
           J. Grüninger, 1523 [S I, 196].

   2.   CATHOLIC THEOLOGIANS, 1000-1400.

Cl.2.1.   Durandus, Guillelmus, Rationale Divinorum Officiorum.
           G. Husner, n.d. [R BNU Inc., 153], 1483 [R Nfp Inc.,
           223], 1484 [R BNU Inc., 154], 1486 [R BNU Inc.,
           156], 1488 [R BNU Inc., 157], 1493 [R BNU Inc.,
           158].
           J. Prüss I, 1486 [R BNU Inc., 155].
           No printer, 1501 [R BNU I, 667].

  .2.2.   Marsilius ab Inghen, Questiones super quattuor libros
           sententiarum.
           M. Flach I, n.d. [R BNU Inc., 301].
           M. Flach II, 1501 [S VI B, 3].

  .2.3.   Petrus Comestor, Historia scholastica.
           G. Husner, n.d. [R BNU Inc., 387], 1485 [R BNU Inc.,
           386].
           J. Grüninger, 1483 [S I, 1].
           J. Prüss I, 1503 [R BNU III, 1851].

  .2.4.   Hugo de S. Victore, De Sacramentis.
           G. Husner, 1485 [R BNU Inc., 244].

  .2.5.   Johannes Gallensis (John of Wales), Communiloquium seu
           Summa collationum.
           G. Husner, 1489 [R BNU Inc., 265].
           J. Knobloch, 1500 [R Nfp Inc., 381].

  .2.6.   Albertus Magnus, Compendium theologicae veritatis.
           J. Prüss I, 1489 [R BNU Inc., 8].

  .2.7.   Bonaventure, Tractatus et libri quam plurimi.
           M. Flach I, 1489 [S VI A, 23].
           G. Husner, 1495 [BM 1.B.1963].

  .2.8.   Thomas de Argentina, Super quattor libros sententiarum.
           M. Flach I, 1490 [S VI A, 33].

  .2.9.   (Guilelmus Ockham), Quodlibeta Septem.
           G. Husner, 1491 [R BNU Inc., 348].

  .2.10.   Bonaventure, Parva Opuscula.
           M. Flach I, 1495 [S VI A, 57].
           G. Husner, 1495 [R BNU Inc., 103].

  .2.11.   Anselmus de Canterbury, Opera.
           G. Husner, 1496 [R Nfp Inc., 78].

C1.2.12.   Alanus de Insulis, De maximis theologiae.
            J. Grüninger, 1497 [R Nfp Inc., 18].

   .2.13.   Albertus Magnus, Tractatus . . . de veris et perfectis
            virtutibus alias, Paradisus anime nuncupatus.
            M. Flach I, 1498 [S VI A, 67].

   .2.14.   Thome de Aquino, Questiones disputate De potentia dei.
            De unione verbi. De spiritualibus creaturis. De
            anima. De virtutibus. De malo.
            M. Flach I, 1500 [S VI A, 76].
            M. Flach II, 1507 [S VI B, 12].

   2.15.   Egidius de Roma (Egidio Colonna Romano), Castigatorium
            . . . in corruptorium librorum sancti Thome de Aquino.
            M. Flach II, 1501 [S VI B, 1].

   .2.16.   Anselmus (Anselm of Canterbury), Opuscula.
            M. Flach II, 1501 [S VI B, 5].

   .2.17.   Robertus Lincolensis (Robert Grosseteste), Commentaria
            in Dionysium Areopagitam.
            No printer, 1502 [R Nfp, 3117].

   .2.18.   Heinricus de Hassia (Heinrich von Langenstein), Secreta
            Sacerdotum.
            M. Hupfuff, 1502 [S V, 19; R BNU II, 1132], 1505
            [S V, 45; R BNU II, 1133].
            J. Knobloch, 1508 [S VII, 43; R BNU II, 1135; BM
            3478.ccc.25.].

   .2.19.   Bernardus (St. Bernardus), In symbolum apostolorum.
            Thomas Wolphius iunior, In Psalmum benedicam.
            J. Knobloch, 1507 [S VII, 26].

   .2.20.   Petrus Hispanus (Pope Joannes XXI), Tractatus duodecim.
            M. Hupfuff, 1511 [R BNU III, 1854], 1515 [S V, 127].
            J. Knobloch, 1514 [R BNU III, 1855].

   .2.21.   Dogma moralium philosophorum, compendiose et studiose
            collectum.
            M. Schürer, 1512 [S VIII, 76], 1513 [S VIII, 106].

   .2.22.   Alanus de Insulis, Liber parabolarum.
            J. Knobloch, 1513 [R Nfp, 774].

   3.   CATHOLIC THEOLOGIANS, 1400-1525.

C1.3.1.   Peraudi, Raimundus (Raimund Pérault; Cardinal),
            Literae indulgentarium.
            J. Grüninger, n.d. [R Nfp, 2867].

   .3.2.   Nicolaus de Blony (Nicolaus de Plove), Tractatus
            sacerdotalis de sacramentis.

          M. Flach I, 1481 [S VI A, 7], 1488 [R BNU Inc., 336],
             1490 [S VI A, 29], 1492 [S VI A, 41], 1493 [S VI A,
             48], 1496 [S VI A, 61], 1499 [S VI A, 73].
          G. Husner, 1495 [R Nfp Inc., 513].
          J. Knobloch, 1500 [S VII, 1], 1508 [S VII, 47; R BNU
             III, 1627], 1512 [S VII, 78; R BNU III, 1628].
          M. Flach II, 1503 [S VI B, 11].

Cl.3.3.   Gerson, Johannes, De arte moriendi.
          J. Knoblochtzer, 1482 [R BNU Inc., 182].

  3.4.   Antichristus.
          No printer, ca. 1482 [R Nfp Inc., 79].

 .3.5.   Nider, Johannes, Praeceptorium divinae legis.
          G. Husner, 1483 [R BNU Inc., 347].

 .3.6.   Antoninus, Florentinus, Confessionale.
          H. Knoblochtzer, 1484 [R Nfp Inc., 82].
          M. Flach I, 1488 [S VI A, 17], 1490 [S VI A, 31],
             1492 [S VI A, 42], 1496 [S VI A, 60], 1499 [S VI A,
             74].

 .3.7.   Hilarius Litomiricensis, Tractatus contra perfidiam
       aliquorum Bohemorum.
          G. Husner, 1485 [R BNU Inc., 233].

 .3.8.   Innocentius VIII, Papa, Copia confirmationis
       indulgentiarum in favorem Hospitalis Sancti Spiritus
       in Sassia de Urbe (Roma).
          J. Prüss I, 1486 [R BNU Inc., 247].

 .3.9.   Johannes Antonius (Gianantonio da Sangiorgio; Cardinal),
       (Letter of indulgence).
          J. Grüninger, 1487 [R Nfp Inc., 378].

 .3.10. Johannes de Turrecremata (Juan de Torquemada; Cardinal),
       Quaestiones evangeliorum.
          G. Husner, ca. 1487 [R BNU Inc., 468].

 .3.11. Speculum exemplorum ab Aegidio Aurifabro collectum.
          G. Husner, 1487 [R BNU Inc., 439], 1495 [R BNU Inc.,
             441].

 .3.12. Bernardinus de Pientinis seu Parentinis, Officii missae
       expositio.
          J. Prüss I, 1487 [R BNU Inc., 83].

 .3.13. Gerson, Johannis (Jean Gerson), Opera et Tractatus.
          J. Prüss I, 1488 [R BNU Inc., 179].
          M. Flach I, 1494 [S VI A, 53].
          M. Flach II, 1502 [S VI B, 7].
          J. Knobloch, 1511 [R Nfp, 1511], 1514 [S VII, 87],
             1517 [S VII, 144].

C1.3.14. Angelicus (Angelus de Clavasio), Summa . . . de casibus
          conscientiae.
              M. Flach I, 1489 [S VI A, 22], 1491 [S VI A, 37],
                 1495 [S VI A, 56], 1498 [S VI A, 66].
              M. Flach II, 1502 [S VI B, 8].
              R. Beck, 1513 [S IV Beck, 7].
              J. Knobloch, 1513 [S VII, 83], 1515 [S VII, 93],
                 1520 [S VII, 195].

  .3.15. Petrus de Alliaco (Pierre d'Ailly), Questiones . . .
          super libros sententiarum.
              M. Flach I, 1490 [S VI A, 28].

  .3.16. Antoninus (Florentinus Antoninus), Summa Antonini.
          4 pars: de anima. de vitiis. de statibus. de virtutibus.
              J. Grüninger, 1490 [S I, 12], 1496 [S I, 24; R BNU
                 Inc., 39].

  .3.17. Antoninus, Florentinus, Tabula Summae theologica.
              J. Grüninger, 1490 [R Nfp Inc., 83].

  .3.18. (Raymond de Sabonde), Theologia naturalis.
              M. Flach I, 1496 [S VI A, 58].
              M. Flach II, 1501 [S VI B, 2; R Nfp, 2053].

  .3.19. Tractatus resolvens dubia circa VII sacramenta
          occurentia.
              J. Grüninger, 1496 [R BNU Inc., 462].

  .3.20. Baldung, Hieronymus, Aphorismi compunctionis
          theologicales.
              J. Grüninger, 1497 [S I, 28; R BNU Inc., 64].

  .3.21. Gresemundus, Theodoricus (Dietrich Gresemund), Oratio
          ad sanctum synodum Moguntinum.
              M. Flach I, 1499 [R Nfp Inc., 302a].

  .3.22. (Bartholomaeus Sibylla), Speculum peregrinarum
          questionum.
              J. Grüninger, 1499 [S I, 44; R BNU Inc., 436].

  .3.23. Nicolaus de Cusa, Opuscula Varia.
              M. Flach I, 1500 [R Nfp Inc., 517].

  .3.24. Johannes Baptista de Gratia Dei, De confutatione
          hebraicae sectae.
              M. Flach I, 1500 [R BNU Inc., 262].

  .3.25. Trebellius, Wigand, Concordia curatorum et fratrum
          medicantium.
              J. Prüss I, 1503 [S III A, 38].

  .3.26. Floretus theologicus carmine descriptum. De fide
          catholica et credendis. De preceptis decem tabularum

Moysi. De peccatorum . . . .
J. Knobloch, 1510 [S VII, 69; R BNU II, 871].

C1.3.27. Mantuanus, Baptista (Joannes Baptista Mantuanus),
Georgius ab Ascensio familiariter explanatus.
M. Schürer, 1510 [S VIII, 41].

.3.28. Mantuanus, Baptista, De patientia. Libri III.
M. Schürer, 1510 [S VIII, 42].

.3.29. (Jacob Wimpheling), Contra turpem libellum Philomusi
defensio theologiae scholasticae et neotericorum.
M. Schürer, 1510 [S VIII, 45].

.3.30. (Joannes Gerson), Alphabetum divini amoris.
M. Schürer, 1511 [S VIII, 64].

.3.31. Bessarion, Cardinalis (Joannes Bessarion; Patriarch of
Constantinople), Oratio de Sacramento Eucharistiae.
M. Schürer, 1513 [S VIII, 116].

.3.32. (Helias Capreolus or Elias Cavriolo), De confirmatione
fidei christianae.
M. Schürer, 1514 [S VIII, 131].

.3.33 Dati, Augustino, De vita beata.
M. Schürer, 1515 [S VIII, 174].

.3.34. (Baptista Trovamala), Summa Roselle de casibus
conscientiae.
J. Knobloch, 1516 [S VII, 109].

.3.35. Dünckelspühel, Nicolaus, Tractatus VIII. De dilectione
dei et proximi. De preceptis decalogi. De oratione
dominica . . . .
J. Schott, 1516 [S II B, 36; R BNU III, 1631].

.3.36. Silvestrinus (Silvestro Mazzolini de Prierio), Summa
summarum.
J. Grüninger, 1518 [S I, 158; R BNU III, 1925].

.3.37. Vipera, Mercurius, De divino et vero nomine
apologeticon.
J. Knobloch, 1520 [S VII, 209].

.3.38. Erasmus, Ratio seu methodus compendio peruenendi ad
veram theologiam.
J. Knobloch, 1521 [S VII, 219; R BNU II, 755], 1522
[S VII, 248], 1523 [S VII, 264].

C2. CATHOLIC DOCTRINE AND THEOLOGY PRINTED AFTER THE REFORM.

C2.1.1. (Conradus de Alemannia), Concordantiae maiores sacrae
bibliae recens auctae.

J. Knobloch, 1526 [S VII, 309].
G. Ulricher, 1529 [BM 3103.e.7].
J. Schott, 1530 [S II B, 115].

C2.1.2. Alcuinus, In Joannis Evangelium commentariorum libri
septem.
J. Herwagen, 1527 [R BNU I, 33].

.1.3. Ignatius Antiochenus, Epistolae undecim.
J. Knobloch (two editions), 1527 [S VII, 319], and
1527 [S VII, 318].

.1.4. Augustinus, Sanctus, III Bücher von Christlicher leer.
B. Beck, 1532 [R BNU I, 110].

.1.5 Smaragdus (Abbott of Saint Mihiel), In Evangelia et
epistolas quae per circuitum anni in templis
legunturcum . . . pia explicatio, ex principibus
Ecclesiae doctoribus.
G. Ulricher, 1536 [R Nfp, 3241].

.1.6. Smaragdus (Abbott of Saint Mihiel), Auszlegung oder
Postilla uber die Evangelia und Episteln des gantzen
jares . . . ausz den heyligen alten Martern und Lerern
der christlichen Kirche.
Cr. Mylius, 1536 [R BNU IV, 2153].

.1.7. Chrysostomus, Johannes, Auszlegung über die Evangelia
sancti Matthei unnd Sancti Johannis.
B. Beck, 1540 [R BNU I, 478].

.1.8. Nilus (Nilus Ancyranus), Sententiae Carmine expressae
(Michael Toxites, ed.)
Cr. Mylius, 1543 [R Nfp, 2773].

.1.9. (Thomas à Kempis), Nachvolgung Christi und verschmähung
aller eitelkeit diser Welt.
J. Prüss II, 1544 [S III B, 52].
W. Köpfel, 1552 [R BNU IV, 2326].

.1.10. Tertullianus, Quintus Septimius Florens, Edel und
Christlich Buch, De Patientia (C. Hedio, ed.).
W. Rihel, 1546 [R BNU IV, 2293].

.1.11. Chrysostomus, Johannes, De Sacerdotio sermones sex.
J. Rihel, 1561 [R BNU I, 480]. (In Greek.)

.1.12. Firmicus Maternus, Julius, De errore profanarum
religionum ad Constantium & Constantem Augustos liber.
P. Messerschmidt, 1562 [R BNU II, 846].

.1.13. Catologus: authorum omnium qui in sacros libros
scripserunt.
N. Wyriot, 1572 [R Nfp, 1321].

C2.1.14. Alanus de Insulis, Dicta Alani.
          No printer, 1582 [R Nfp, 775]. (In German.)

C3. CATHOLIC SERMONS

   1. SERMONS.

C3.1.1.   Sermones parati de Tempore et de Sanctis.
               Printer of Paludanus, n.d. [R Nfp Inc., 551].
               M. Flach I (five editions), n.d. [R Nfp Inc., 552],
                  and n.d. [R Nfp Inc., 553], and n.d. [R Nfp Inc.,
                  554], and n.d. [R Nfp Inc., 555], and 1491 [R Nfp
                  Inc., 557].
               G. Husner, 1487 [R BNU Inc., 368].
               J. Knobloch, 1503 [S VII, 5], 1517 [S VII, 137].

   .1.2.   Hugo Pratensis (Hugo Vinac de Prato Florido), Sermones
            de Tempore.
               G. Husner, n.d. [R BNU Inc., 241].

   .1.3.   Hugo Pratensis (Hugo Vinac de Prato Florido), Sermones
            et epistolae.
               G. Husner, n.d. [R BNU Inc., 239].

   .1.4.   Herolt, Johannes, Sermones super epistolas dominicales.
               G. Husner, n.d. [R BNU Inc., 221].

   .1.5.   Herolt, Johannes, Sermones discipuli de tempore et de
            sanctis.
               A. Rusch, n.d. [R BNU Inc., 222].
               No printer, 1480 [R Nfp Inc., 323], 1483 [R BNU Inc.,
                  223], 1489 [R Nfp Inc., 325].
               Printer of Paludanus, 1487 [R BNU Inc., 224].
               M. Flach I, 1488 [R BNU Inc., 225], 1490 [R Nfp Inc.,
                  326], 1492 [R BNU Inc., 227], 1495 [R BNU Inc.,
                  228], 1499 [S VI A, 71; R BNU Inc., 230].
               M. Flach II, 1503 [S VI B, 10].

   .1.6.   Guilelmus Parisiensis, Postilla super evangelia et
            epistolas de tempore et sanctis.
               G. Husner, 1481 [R Nfp Inc., 309], 1483 [R Nfp Inc.,
                  310], 1485 [R BNU Inc., 207], 1486 [R BNU Inc.,
                  208], 1488 [R BNU Inc., 209], 1489 [R BNU Inc.,
                  210], 1490 [R BNU Inc., 211], 1493 [R BNU Inc.,
                  212].
               J. Prüss I, 1489 [R Nfp Inc., 312].
               M. Flach I, 1500 [S VI A, 77].

   .1.7.   Johannes Junior (Joannes Gobius), Sermones de sanctis.
               No printer, 1481 [R Nfp Inc., 386].

C3.1.8.   Hugo de Campo Florido (Hugo Vinac de Prato Florido),
           Sermones dominicales.
               G. Husner, 1482 [R Nfp Inc., 345].

  .1.9.   Michael de Ungaria, Sermones eximii.
               No printer, 1482 [R Nfp Inc., 482].

  .1.10.   Paludanus, Petrus (Petrus de Palude), Sermones
           Thesauri Novi de Tempore.
               Printer of Vitas Patrum, 1483 [R BNU Inc., 360],
                 1484 [R BNU Inc., 361], 1486 [R Nfp Inc., 549].
               M. Flach I, 1487 [R BNU Inc., 362; S VI A, 11],
                 1488 [R BNU Inc., 363; S VI A, 13], 1490 [R Nfp
                 Inc., 550], 1491 [R BNU Inc., 364; S VI A, 38],
                 1493 [R BNU Inc., 365; S VI A, 46], 1497 [R BNU
                 Inc., 366; S VI A, 62].
               J. Knobloch, 1515 [S VII, 106].

  .1.11.   Jordanus de Quedlinbourg, Opus Postillarum et Sermonum
           de tempore.
               G. Husner, 1483 [R BNU Inc., 274].

  .1.12.   Meffret, Sermones Aestivales et Hiemales.
               G. Husner, 1484 [R Nfp Inc., 459].

  .1.13.   (Jordan de Quedlinbourg), Sermones de sanctis.
               J. Grüninger, 1484 [S I, 3].

  .1.14.   Gritsch, Johannes, Quadragesimale.
               No printer, 1484 [R Nfp Inc., 304].
               Printer of Vitas Patrum, 1486 [R BNU Inc., 196].
               G. Husner, 1490 [R BNU Inc., 197].
               M. Flach I, 1495 [R BNU Inc., 198].

  .1.15.   Martinus Polonus, Sermones de tempore de sanctis.
               No printer (two editions), 1484 [R Bib. Mun., 199],
                 1486 [R Nfp Inc., 452]. Another edition 1486
                 [R Nfp Inc., 451], 1488 [R Bib. Mun., 200].

  .1.16.   Jacobus de Voragine, Sermones de sanctis.
               J. Grüninger, 1484 [R Nfp Inc., 375].

  .1.17.   Conrad von Brundelsheim, Sermones Socci de sanctis.
               J. Grüninger, 1484 [S I, 2], 1484 [S I, 4; R BNU
                 Inc., 140].

  .1.18.   Johannes de Verdena, Sermones Dormi Secure et de
           Sanctis.
               G. Husner, 1485 [R BNU Inc., 270], 1488 [R BNU Inc.,
                 271], 1493 [R Nfp Inc., 396], 1494 [R BNU Inc.,
                 273].
               J. Prüss I, 1489 [R Nfp Inc., 393].

No printer, 1490 [R Bib. Mun., 1727], 1493 [R Bib.
Mun., 1911].
J. Grüninger, 1500 [R Nfp Inc., 397].

C3.1.19. Paludanus, Petrus (Petrus de Palude), Sermones
Thesauri Novi de sanctis.
Printer of Vitas Patrum, 1485 [R BNU Inc., 354],
1486 [R BNU Inc., 355].
M. Flach I, 1488 [S VI A, 14], 1489 [R BNU Inc.,
356], 1491 [R BNU Inc., 357; S VI A, 40], 1493
[R BNU Inc., 358; S VI A, 47], 1497 [R BNU Inc.,
359; S VI A, 63].
J. Knobloch, 1515 [R BNU III, 1751].

.1.20. Paludanus, Petrus (Petrus de Palude), Sermones
Quadragesimales Thesauri Novi.
Printer of Vitas Patrum, 1485 [R Nfp Inc., 543].
M. Flach I, 1487 [R BNU Inc., 351], 1488 [R BNU
Inc., 352; S VI A, 15], 1491 [R Nfp Inc., 544;
S VI A, 39], 1494 [R Nfp Inc., 545], 1497 [R Nfp
Inc., 546].
J. Knobloch, 1508 [S VII, 53], 1508 [S VII supp., 327],
1518 [R BNU III, 1752].

.1.21. Ferrerius Vincentius, Sermones de Tempore, pars
aestivalis.
No printer, 1485 [R Nfp Inc., 268].
G. Husner, 1488 [R BNU Inc., 169], 1493 [R BNU Inc.,
170].

.1.22. Caracciolus, Robertus, Sermones Quadragesimales de
Poenitentia.
M. Schott, 1485 [R BNU Inc., 125].
J. Prüss I, 1490 [R BNU Inc., 123].
J. Grüninger, 1497 [R Nfp Inc., 176].

.1.23. Caracciolus, Robertus, Sermones per Adventum.
M. Schott, 1485 [R BNU Inc., 124].

.1.24. Trithemius, Johannes, Sermones.
J. Knobloch, 1486 [R Nfp Inc., 651].

.1.25. Michael de Ungaria, Sermones Praedicabiles.
G. Husner, 1487 [R BNU Inc., 320], 1490 [R BNU Inc.,
321], 1494 [R BNU Inc., 322].

.1.26. Augustinus, Aurelius, Sermones ad Heremitas.
J. Prüss I, 1487 [R BNU Inc., 58].
G. Husner, 1493/94 [R BNU Inc., 59].

.1.27. Johannes de Verdena, Sermones Dominicales.
G. Husner, 1487 [R Nfp Inc., 392].
No printer, 1489 [R Nfp Inc., 667].

C3.1.28. Paludanus, Petrus (Petrus de Palude), Sermones
          Thesauri Novi Dominicales.
               M. Flach I, 1487 [R Nfp Inc., 540], 1489 [R Nfp Inc.,
               541], 1490 [R Nfp Inc., 542].

   .1.29. Ferrerius, Vincentius, Sermones de tempore, pars
          hiemalis.
               G. Husner, 1488 [R BNU Inc., 169], 1493 [R BNU Inc.,
               171].

   .1.30. Guilelmus Parisiensis, Sermones exquisiti super
          epistolis dominicalibus.
               J. Grüninger, 1489 [BM 1.B.4560.2].

   .1.31. (Wilhelm Lugdunensis), Sermones Exquisiti super
          epistolis per anni Circulum.
               J. Grüninger, 1489 [S I, 9].

   .1.32. Sermones tres de passione Christi.
               M. Flach I, 1490 [R BNU Inc., 434].

   .1.33. Petrus de Alliaco (Pierre d'Ailly), Tractatus et
          Sermones.
               G. Husner, 1490 [R BNU Inc., 383].

   .1.34. Ferrerius, Vincentius, Sermones de sanctis.
               No printer, 1493 [R Bib. Mun., 2065], 1503 [R BNU IV,
               2410].
               G. Husner, 1494 [R Nfp Inc., 269].

   .1.35. Albertus Magnus, Sermones de Eucharistiae Sacramento.
               G. Husner, 1494 [R BNU Inc., 15].

   .1.36. Peregrinus Frater, Sermones de tempore et de sanctis.
               J. Grüninger, 1495 [R Nfp Inc., 565].

   .1.37. Anthonius de Bitonto, Sermones dominicales per totum
          annum.
               J. Grüninger, 1495 [S I, 21], 1496 [S I, 23], 1496
               [S I, 25].

   .1.38. Bonaventura, Saint, Sermones Mediocres de Tempore.
               G. Husner, 1496 [R BNU Inc., 106].

   .1.39. Nicholaus von Dinkelsbühl, Postilla Evangeliorum
          dominicalium.
               J. Grüninger, 1496 [R BNU Inc., 340].

   .1.40. Bernardus (Bernardus Claravallis or Bernard de
          Clairvaux), Sermones . . . super cantica canticorum.
          Gilbertus, Sermones . . . super cantica canticorum.
               M. Flach I, 1497 [S VI A, 64].

   .1.41. Bernardus (Bernardus Claravallis or Bernard de

Clairvaux), <u>Opus sermonum de tempore</u>.
M. Flach I, 1497 [S VI A, 65].

C3.1.42. Caracciolus, Robertus, <u>Sermo de Praedestinato numero</u>
<u>damnatorum</u>.
No printer, 1497 [R Nfp <u>Inc</u>., 177].

.1.43. Chieregatus, Leonellus, <u>Sermones</u>.
J. Pruss I, 1498 [R Nfp <u>Inc</u>., 184].

.1.44. Nicolaus de Blony (Nicolaus de Plove), <u>Sermones de</u>
<u>Tempore</u>.
G. Husner, 1498 [R BNU <u>Inc</u>., 335].

.1.45. Wann, Paulus, <u>Sermones XXIII de praeservatione hominis</u>
<u>a peccato</u>.
No printer, 1500 [R Nfp <u>Inc</u>., 703].

.1.46. Bertrandus de Turre (Bertrandus de Cura), <u>Sermones de</u>
<u>tempore, pars hiemalis</u>.
G. Husner, 1500 [R Nfp <u>Inc</u>., 114], 1501 [R BNU I,
193].

.1.47. Michael de Ungaria, <u>Evagatorium . . . Sermones XIII</u>.
J. Knobloch, 1503 [S VII, 3], 1516 [S VII, 122].

.1.48. Pelbartus de Themeswar, <u>Sermones Pomerii de Sanctis</u>.
J. Knobloch, 1505 [S VII, 9], 1505 [S VII supp., 323],
1505 [S VII supp., 324], 1506 [S VII, 17], 1506 [S
VII supp., 326].

.1.49. Maillardus, Oliverius, <u>Sermones de adventu,</u>
<u>quadragesimales</u>.
J. Knobloch, 1506 [S VII, 18], 1508 [S VII, 48],
1502 [S VII, 77].

.1.50. Morgenstern, Gregorius, <u>Sermones contra omnem mundi</u>
<u>peruersum statum</u>.
W. Schaffner, 1508 [S IV Sch., 2], 1513 [S IV Sch.,
4], 1515 [S IV Sch., 6].

.1.51. <u>Sermones Discipuli de eruditione Christi fidelium</u>.
M. Flach II, 1509 [S VI B, 22].

.1.52. Bossus, Mathaeus, <u>Macarius Mutius eques Camers de</u>
<u>triumpho Christi. . . . Sermo de Passione Jesu Christi</u>.
M. Schurer, 1509 [S VIII, 18].

.1.53. Johannis Effrem Siri, <u>Sermones tam pii quam sancti</u>.
M. Schurer, 1509 [S VIII, 15].

.1.54. Joannis de Gerson, <u>Sermo de passione domini</u>.
M. Schurer, 1509 [S VIII, 12], 1510 [Greiner].

.1.55. Denisse, Nicolas, <u>Sermones</u>.
J. Gruninger, 1510 [S I, 116].

C3.1.56. Icolampadius, Johann, <u>Declamationes de passione et</u>
           <u>ultimo sermone</u>.
             M. Schurer, 1512 [S VIII, 88].

   .1.57. Chrisostomus, Johannes, <u>Ein trostliche predigt</u>.
             J. Gruninger, 1514 [S I, 132].

    1.58. Maillardus, Oliverius, <u>Sermones de sanctis</u>.
             J. Knobloch, 1514 [S VII, 91].

   .1.59. <u>Orationes sacrae ecclesiae</u>.
             J. Knobloch, 1516 [S VII, 110], 1518 [S VII, 167].

   .1.60. Tritemius, Joannes, <u>Sermones et Exhortationes ad</u>
           <u>monachos</u>.
             J. Knobloch, 1516 [S VII, 120].

   .1.61. Krafft, Ulrich, <u>Sermones durch die fiertzigtegigen</u>
           <u>fastenn</u>.
             C. Kerner, 1517 [S IV Ker., 2].

    2. SERMONS PREACHED BY JOHANNES GEILER VON KEYSERSBERG.

C3.2.1. <u>Oratio habita in synodo Argentinensi</u>.
             H. Knoblochtzer, ca. 1482 [R BNU <u>Inc</u>., 177].

   .2.2. <u>Fragmenta passionis domini nostri Jesu Christi</u>.
             M. Schurer, 1508 [S VIII, 7], 1511 [S VIII, 59].

   .2.3. <u>De oratione dominica sermones</u>.
             M. Schurer, 1509 [S VIII, 17].

   .2.4. <u>Passio der vier Evangelisten</u>.
             J. Gruninger, 1509 [R Bib. Mun., 1637].

   .2.5. <u>Navicula sive speculum fatuorum</u>.
             M. Schurer, 1510 [S VIII, 44], 1511 [S VIII, 48].
             J. Knobloch, 1513 [S VII, 80].

   .2.6. <u>Das schon Buch genant der Seelen paradis</u>.
             M. Schurer, 1510 [S VIII, 37].

   .2.7. <u>De oratione dominica sermones</u>.
             M. Schurer, 1510 [BM 852.1.4; S VIII, 39], 1515 [S
             VIII, 170].

   .2.8. <u>Das irrig Schaf, Gebrediget und Gedeutscht</u>.
             M. Schurer, 1510 [S VIII, 43].
             J. Gruninger (two editions), 1514 [R BNU II, 967],
             and 1514 [S I, 136].

   .2.9. <u>Die geistliche Spinnerin</u>.
             J. Knobloch, 1511 [R Nfp, 1855].

   .2.10. <u>Das Buch Granatapfel</u>.
             J. Knobloch, 1511 [S VII, 74], 1516 [S VII, 116].

C3.2.11. Vom Ausgang der Kinder Israel.
          J. Knobloch, 1511 [R Nfp, 1834].

  .2.12. Navicula penitentie . . . predicata.
          M. Schürer, 1512 [S VIII, 73], 1517 [S VIII, 210].

  .2.13. Predig der Himmelfart Mariae.
          J. Grüninger, 1512 [S I, 126].

  .2.14. Das Schiff des heils, auff das aller kürtzest hie
          uszgeleget.
          J. Grüninger, 1512 [S I, 125].

  .2.15. Alphabet in XXIII Predigen.
          No printer, 1512 [R Nfp, 1832].
          J. Grüninger, 1518 [S I, 157].

  .2.16. Passion des Herren Jesu fürgeben und gepredigt.
          J. Grüninger, 1512 [R Nfp, 1846], 1514 [S I, 141].
          J. Schott, 1522 [R Nfp, 1850].

  .2.17. Predig . . . zu bischoff Albrecht von Strasbourg.
          J. Grüninger, 1513 [S I, 131].

  .2.18. Peregrinus.
          M. Schürer, 1513 [S VIII, 96].

  .2.19. Sermones de arbore humana.
          J. Grüninger, 1514 [BM c 136; S I, 135], 1515 [S I,
          146], 1519 [S I, 162].

  .2.20. Pater Noster.
          M. Hupfuff, 1515 [S V, 117].

  .2.21. Das Schiff der penitentz.
          M. Hupfuff, 1515 [R Nfp, 1853].

  .2.22. Das Evangelibuch.
          J. Grüninger, 1515 [BM C 51.g.3; S I, 147], 1517 [S
          I, 156], 1522 [S I, 186].

  .2.23. Die Emeis. Dis ist das büch von der Omeissen . . . in
          eim quadragesimal gepredigt.
          J. Grüninger, 1516 [S I, 149], 1517 [S I, 155].

  .2.24. Herr der Küng.
          J. Grüninger, 1516 [R Nfp, 1845], 1517 [R Nfp, 1839].

  .2.25. Die Brosamlin dort.
          J. Grüninger, 1517 [S I, 154].

  .2.26. Das Buch der Sunden des Munds.
          J. Grüninger, 1518 [S I, 157].

  .2.27. Sermones et varii Tractatus.
          J. Grüninger, 1518 [S I, 159], 1521 [S I, 183].

C3.2.28. Das Narrenschiff.
J. Grüninger, 1520 [S I, 172].

.2.29. Sermon von den dry marien.
J. Grüninger, 1520 [S I, 170].

.2.30. Das Buoch Arbore humana.
J. Grüninger, 1521 [S I, 182].

2.31. Postill.
J. Schott, 1522 [S II B, 66].

C4. CATHOLIC CURATES' MANUALS AND LIVES OF THE SAINTS.

1. CATHOLIC CURATES' MANUALS.

C4.1.1. Melber, Johannes, Vocabularius praedicantium.
G. Husner, n.d. [R BNU Inc., 309], ca. 1500 [R BNU
Inc., 314].
H. Knoblochtzer, 1482 [R BNU Inc., 310].
J. Prüss I, 1486 [R BNU Inc., 311], 1488 [R BNU Inc.,
312; S III A, 22].
M. Flach I, 1492 [S VI A, 43], 1494 [S VI A, 55].
J. Knobloch, 1504 [S VII, 8].

.1.2. Plenarium (Evangelia und Episteln mit der glos).
H. Knoblochtzer, ca. 1480 [R BNU Inc., 396].

.1.3. Plenari nach ordnung der heiligen christlichen Kirchen
in dem man geschriben findet all epistol und ewangeli.
M. Schott, 1481 [S II A, 1], 1483 [S II A, 3].

.1.4. Geiler von Keysersberg, Johannis, Wie man sich halten
sol by eym sterbenden Menschen.
M. Schott, ca. 1482 [S II A, 2].

.1.5. Exhortatio de celebratione Missae.
H. Knoblochtzer, 1482 [R Nfp Inc., 257].

.1.6. Guido de Monte Rotherii, Manipulus Curatorum.
Printer of Legenda Clerici, 1483 [R BNU Inc., 201].
M. Flach I, 1487 [R BNU Inc., 202], 1489 [S VI A, 20],
1499 [R BNU Inc., 206].
G. Husner, 1490 [R BNU Inc., 204], 1493 [R BNU Inc.,
205; R Nfp Inc., 308].

.1.7. Defectus in missa occurentes.
J. Prüss I, 1485 [R Nfp Inc., 201].

.1.8. Balbus, Johannes (Giovanni Balbi), Catholicon.
J. Grüninger, 1485 [R Nfp Inc., 100].

.1.9. Evangeli mit der glos und Epistel teutsch über das gantz
jar . . . .

              T. Anshelm, 1488 [S IV Ans., 1].
              M. Schott, 1491 [S II A, 10; R Nfp Inc., 251].
              J. Grüninger, 1498 [S I, 35], 1500 [S I, 50], 1506
                [S I, 75], 1513 [S I, 130].
              M. Hupfuff, 1512 [S V, 100], 1513 [S V, 110].

C4.1.10.   Antoninus, De arte et vero modo praedicandi libellus.
              M. Flach I, 1488 [S VI A, 18], 1490 [S VI A, 32],
                1499 [S VI A, 75].

  .1.11.   (Johannes Herolt), Discipulus de eruditione cristi
           fidelium cum thematibus dominicalium.
              J. Prüss I, 1490 [S III A, 24].

  .1.12.   Registrum ecclesiae argentinensis.
              J. Prüss I, ca. 1490 [R BNU Inc., 409].

  .1.13.   (Johannes de Lapide or Johann Heynlin), Resolutorium
           dubiorum circa celebrationem missarum.
              M. Flach I, 1493 [S VI A, 49], 1494 [S VI A, 54].

  .1.14.   Epistolae de miseria curatorum.
              J. Prüss I, 1493 [R Nfp Inc., 238].

  .1.15.   Liber Agendorum Rubrice Ecclesie Wratislabiensis.
              F. Dumbach, 1499 [S IV Dum., 2].

  .1.16.   Agenda sive exsequiale sacramentorum.
              J. Prüss I, 1500 [R Nfp Inc., 11], 1500 [R Nfp Inc.,
                13].
              R. Beck, 1513 [R BNU I, 15; S IV Beck, 8].

  .1.17.   Agenda parochialium ecclesiarum Argentinensis diocesis.
              J. Grüninger, ca. 1500 [R BNU Inc., 4].

  .1.18.   Cura Pastoralis pro ordinandorum tentamine collecta.
              M. Hupfuff, 1504 [S V, 36].

  .1.19.   (Ulric Surgant), Manuale Curatorum.
              J. Prüss I, 1506 [S III A, 56].
              J. Schott, 1516 [S II B, 35].
              J. Knobloch, 1520 [S VII, 194].

  .1.20.   Andreas Hispanus (Andres de Escobar), Modus confitendi.
              M. Hupfuff, 1507 [S V, 63; R BNU I, 52].
              J. Knobloch, 1508 [S VII, 42; R BNU I, 53].

  .1.21.   Georgius de Gemmyngen, Annotaciuncula pro Confessoribus
           Spire.
              M. Schürer, 1509 [S VIII, 26].

  .1.22.   (Plenarium).
              J. Grüninger, 1510 [S I, 115].

  .1.23.   Bernonis Abbatis (Berno; Abbott of Reichenau), Libellus

de officio missae.
    M. Schürer, 1511 [S VIII, 62], 1514 [S VIII, 141].

C4.1.24.   Hoest, Stephanus, Modus Predicandi Subtilis et
           Compendiosus . . . .
               J. Prüss II, 1513 [S III B, 5].

   .1.25.   (Jacob Wimpheling), Sermo ad iuvenes qui sacris
           ordinibus iniciari . . . petunt.
               M. Schürer, 1514 [S VIII, 140].
               J. Prüss II, 1519 [S III B, 17].

   .1.26.   Lavacrum conscientie Omnibus sacerdotibus & Clericis
           tam utilis quam necessarius.
               J. Prüss II, 1515 [S III B, 11].

   .1.27.   Nicolaus de Byard, Dictionarius pauperum.
               J. Knobloch, 1516 [S VII, 114], 1518 [S VII, 160; R
               Nfp, 2766].

   .1.28.   Anthonius de Rampegolis, Figurarem Biblie opus
           conducibile et perutile.
               J. Knobloch, 1516 [S VII, 111].

   .1.29.   Teutsch Evangeli und Epistel. Mit sampt vil heilsamer
           leer.
               J. Knobloch, 1519 [S VII, 186], 1522 [S VII, 250].

    2.   LIVES OF THE SAINTS IN LATIN.

C4.2.1.   Jacobus de Voragine, Legenda Aurea. Historia
           Lombardica.
               G. Husner, 1479 [R BNU Inc., 253], 1480 [R Nfp Inc.,
               361], 1483 [R BNU Inc., 254], 1485 [R BNU Inc.,
               255], 1486 [R BNU Inc., 256], 1489 [R BNU Inc.,
               257], 1492 [R BNU Inc., 260], 1496 [R BNU Inc.,
               216], 1498 [R BNU Inc., 258], 1502 [R BNU II, 1256].
               H.Eggestein, 1480 [R Nfp Inc., 360].
               No printer, 1482 [R Nfp Inc., 363], 1487 [R Nfp Inc.,
               365], 1496 [R Nfp Inc., 366].
               J. Grüninger, 1496 [R Nfp Inc., 369], 1497 [R Nfp
               Inc., 372].

   .2.2.   Hieronymus Sanctus, Vitae sanctorum patrum.
               Printer of Vitas Patrum, 1483 [R BNU Inc., 232],
               1485 [R Nfp Inc., 331].

   .2.3.   Legendae.
               No printer, 1486 [R Nfp Inc., 410].

   .2.4.   Viola Sanctorum.
               J. Prüss I, 1487 [S III A, 14], 1499 [R BNU Inc.,
               481].

C4.2.5.   Martyrologium.
          M. Hupfuff, 1492 [R Nfp Inc., 456].
          J. Prüss I, 1500 [R Nfp Inc., 455].

   .2.6.   Petrus Frater, Legenda Sanctae Catharinae.
          J. Grüninger, 1500 [R BNU Inc., 388].

   .2.7.   Nova . . . Legenda ex aliis sex legendis collecta et
          perfecta tractans de origine et vite ordine de conver-
          sione ac magistrali disputatione ac de passione . . .
          sancte Katherine.
          J. Grüninger, 1500 [S I, 48].

   .2.8.   Legenda de Sancta Anna et de universa eius progenie.
          B. Kistler, 1501 [S IV Kis., 16].

   .2.9.   Mantuanus, Giovanni Baptista, De vita beata.
          J. Prüss I, 1504 [R Nfp, 922].

  .2.10.   Vita sanctorum Geruasii et Prothasii cum sermone et
          translatione, Ad oppidum Brisach.
          J. Grüninger, 1505 [S I, 73].

  .2.11.   Wymphelingus, Jacobus, De vita et miraculis Joannis
          Gerson.
          J. Knobloch, 1506 [S VII, 25].

  .2.12.   Vita Sancti Adolphi, patroni Collegii Nouillarensis.
          J. Prüss I, 1506 [S III A, 55].

  .2.13.   Adrianus, Cardinalis (Adriano Castellense),
          S. Chrisogoni venatio.
          M. Schürer, 1512 [S VIII, 81].

  .2.14.   Petrus de Natalibus, Catalogus sanctorum et gestorum.
          M. Flach II, 1513 [S VI B, 37].
          J. Knobloch, 1521 [BM 487.k.20].

  .2.15.   Martyrologium viola sanctorum.
          M. Hupfuff, 1516 [R Bib. Mun., 1469], 1517 [S V, 137].

  .2.16.   Pastoris Nuntii Poenitentiae Visiones quinque Mandata
          duodecim Similitudines vero decem, in quibus apparuit
          & locutus est Hermae discipulo Pauli apostoli. Cui
          etiam in principio apparuit ecclesia in uariis figuris.
          J. Schott, 1522 [S II B, 67].

C5.   CATHOLIC DEVOTIONALS FOR PRIVATE WORSHIP, LAY MANUALS OF
      CHRISTIAN LIFE, AND POPULAR RELIGIOUS MUSIC.

   1.   DEVOTIONALS FOR PRIVATE WORSHIP AND LAY MANUALS OF
        CHRISTIAN LIFE.

C5.1.1.   Farinator, Mathias, Lumen animae.

Printer of the Legenda Clerici, 1482 [R BNU Inc., 167].

C5.1.2.   Ludolphus de Saxonia, Meditationes vitae Jesu Christi. J. Grüninger, 1483 [R BNU Inc., 291].

  .1.3.   (Johannes Junior or Johannes Gobius), Scala Coeli. J. Eber, 1483 [S IV Eber, 1; BM 1.B.1559].

  .1.4.   Johannes de Capua, Directorium humanae vitae. J. Prüss I, 1484/85 [R BNU Inc., 263].

  .1.5.   Herp, Heinrich, Speculum aureum rerum Praeceptorum Dei. No printer, 1486 [R Nfp Inc., 329]. J. Knobloch, 1520 [Greiner].

  .1.6.   (Thomas á Kempis and Johannes Gerson), Tractatus de imitatione Christi cum tractatulo de meditatione cordis. M. Flach I, 1487 [S VI A, 12; BM I.A.2109], 1489 [S VI A, 24]. J. Prüss I, 1489 [R BNU Inc., 457; BM I.A.1663].

  .1.7.   Salicetus, Nicolaus, Antidotarius Anime, Liber meditationum ac orationum devotarum. J. Grüninger, 1489 [S I, 10], 1490 [S I, 13], 1491 [S I, 15], 1493 [S I, 16], 1494 [S I, 18], 1503 [S I, 63], 1513 [R Nfp, 2059].

  .1.8.   Praecordiale Devotorum. J. Prüss I, 1489 [R BNU Inc., 401], 1490 [R BNU Inc., 402].

  .1.9.   Hortulus Animae. J. Grüninger, 1498 [S I, 40], 1500 [S I, 47], 1505 [S I, 72]. W. Schaffner, 1498 [S IV Sch., 1]. J. Wähinger, 1503 [S IV Wäh., 2], 1503 [S IV Wäh., 3]. J. Knobloch, 1507 [R Nfp, 2059a; S VII, 29], 1508 [S VII, 37], 1509 [S VII, 55], 1516 [S VII, 121]. M. Flach II, 1511 [S VI B, 23], 1512 [S VI B, 30]. J. Grüninger, 1501 [S I, 56], 1503 [S I, 64]. (In German.) J. Wähinger, 1502 [S IV Wäh., 1], 1504 [S IV Wäh., 4]. (In German.) J. Knobloch, 1507 [S VII, 27], 1508 [S VII, 328], 1509 [S VII, 58]. (In German.) M. Flach II, 1512 [S VI B, 31], 1513 [S VI B, 35]. (In German.)

 1.10.   Tractatus contra vitia. G. Husner, 1498 [R BNU Inc., 460].

  .1.11. Geiler,Johannes (Johannes Geiler von Keysersberg),

Ein sendtbrief . . . an die würdigen frauwen zu den
Reuwern zu Freiburg . . . , darin sie ermanend zu der
waren evangelischen geystlichkeit.
No printer, 1499 [R Nfp Inc., 285].

C5.1.12. Geiler, Johannes (Johannes Geiler von Keysersberg),
Trostspiegel, so dir vatter, müter, kind od fründ
gestorben synt.
No printer, ca. 1500 [R Nfp, 1856].
J. Knobloch, 1503 [S VII, 4], 1511 [R Nfp, 1858],
1519 [S VII, 184].
M. Schürer, 1510 [S VIII, 37].

.1.13. Albertanus Causidicus Brixiensis (Albertano da Brescia),
Das ist der Brunn des Radts Liber consolationis.
J. Grüninger, ca. 1500 [R Nfp, 776].
M. Flach II, 1508 [R Nfp, 777].

.1.14. Das Büchlin wirt genant die Hymelisch Funtgrüb . . .
betrachten das Lyden Cristi unsers lieben herren.
M. Hupfuff, 1503 [S V, 26], 1507 [S V, 69].
C. Kerner, 1517 [S IV Ker., 1].

.1.15. Von den peinen so den bereyt seind allen denen die do
sterbent in tod sünden.
B. Kistler, 1506 [S IV Kis., 25; R Nfp, 1212], 1509
[S IV Kis., 26; R Nfp, 1213].

.1.16. Rodericus Zamorensis, Speculum Vite Humane.
Papae Paulus II, In theologia, utroque Jure . . . .
J. Prüss I, 1507 [S III A, 59].

.1.17. Heinricus de Hassia (Heinrich von Langenstein),
Speculum animae: seu soliloquium.
J. Knobloch, 1507 [S VII, 31; R BNU II, 1134].

.1.18. Klag eines sündigen sterbenden Menschen.
M. Flach II, 1508 [S VI B, 15].

.1.19. Underichtung eins geistlichen lebens.
J. Prüss I, 1509 [S III A, 77].

.1.20. Von dem kremer Cristi was er guttes zu vorkauffen hat.
M. Hupfuff, 1510 [S V, 81].

.1.21. Das Büch der Selen Wurtzgarten.
M. Hupfuff, 1511 [S V, 83], 1515 [S V, 118].

.1.22. Tractat . . . wie man das hochwurdig heiligthum
verkündt.
J. Knobloch, 1513 [R Nfp, 3360].

.1.23. (Mark von Lindau), Die zehe gebot . . . erclert und

uszgelegt.
  J. Grüninger, 1516 [S I, 152].

C5.1.24. (Mark von Weiden), Ein nützliche leer und underweisung
          waz und wy man betten sol. Und auszlegunge des heiligen
          Pater nosters.
          J. Grüninger, 1516 [S I, 152].

  .1.25. Der beycht spiegel. Ein gar schön tractelin spiegel
          der Bibel . . . von der erkanntnüss der sünden und
          etlicher tugent.
          J. Knobloch, 1517 [S VII, 142].

  .1.26. Vallensis, Joannis, Summa . . . de regimine vite
          humanae.
          J. Knobloch, 1518 [S VII, 158].

  .1.27. Frag und Antwort der Zehen Gebot.
          J. Grüninger, 1520 [S I, 171].

  .1.28. Erasmus Roterodamus, Epistola apologetica . . . de
          interdicto esu carnium.
          J. Knobloch, 1522 [S VII, 245; R BNU II, 764].

  .1.29. Johann von Eck, De Poenitentia et Confessione Secreta
          in Ecclessia Observata.
          U. Morhard, 1522 [BM 3906.d.35].

  .1.30. Erasmus, Desiderius, Epistola nuncupatoria ad Carolum
          Caesarem. Exhortatio ad studium Evangelicae lectionis.
          J. Knobloch, 1523 [S VII, 254].

  .1.31. Erasmus von Roterdam, Vater Unser auszgelegt und
          geteylt in syeben teyl, noch syeben tagen.
          M. Flach II, 1523 [S VI B, 73].

  .1.32. Dietenberger, Johannes, Christliche underweisung, wie
          man gottes heiligen in dem hymmel anrüffen soll.
          J. Grüninger, 1524 [R Nfp, 1507].

  .1.33. Erasmus, Des. Roterdamus, De immensa Dei misericordia.
          J. Knobloch, 1524 [S VII, 280; R BNU II, 776].

  .1.34. Erasmus, Des. Roterdamus, Modus orandi deum.
          J. Knobloch, 1524 [S VII, 284], 1525 [R Nfp, 1607].

  .1.35. Erasmus, Desiderius, Exomologesis sive modus confitendi.
          J. Knobloch, 1524 [Greiner].

  .1.36. Buchstab, Johann, Vier artikel einem cristenliche
          menschen not zethun und zehalten.
          No printer, 1528 [BM 4371.b.32.1].

  .1.37. Erasmus, Christenlicher Ee Institution oder An-

weisung . . . .
    B. Beck, 1542 [R BNU II, 793].

2. POPULAR RELIGIOUS MUSIC.

C5.2.1.   Von dem tod ein geystlich lied zu singen.
      B. Kistler, ca. 1500 [S IV Kis., 12].

.2.2.   Lied wie sich yetz geistlich und auch weltlich halten.
      B. Kistler, 1500 [S IV Kis., 10].

.2.3.   Das ist die hymelfart unser lieben frawen in des regen
   bogen langen don, lied.
      M. Flach II, 1508 [S VI B, 17].

.2.4.   Lied von sant Katerinen liben.
      M. Flach II, 1508 [S VI B, 18].

.2.5.   Lied . . . wie by eynandersassen kluge leyen die redten
   von gott wo er gewesen wer ee er die hymmel het
   beschaffen.
      J. Grüninger, 1510 [S I, 118].

.2.6.   Von dem helgen sacrament . . . lied.
      M. Hupfuff, 1512 [S V, 99].

.2.7.   Lied . . . wie die götlich weisheit und weltliche
   thorheyt wider einander stryten und disputieren.
      M. Hupfuff, 1513 [S V, 106].

.2.8.   Lied von der Siben worten unsers lieben herren die er
   an dem krütz sprach.
      M. Hupfuff, 1515 [S V, 125].

C6. CATHOLIC BREVIARIES, MISSALS, SACRED MUSIC, AND SACRAMENTAL
    BOOKS.

1. BREVIARIES.

C6.1.1.   Breviarium Ratisponense.
      G. Reyser, 1480 [R Nfp Inc., 158].

.1.2.   Breviarium Vratislaviense.
      J. Grüninger, 1485 [R Nfp Inc., 163].

.1.3.   Breviarium Moguntinum.
      J. Grüninger, 1487 [R Nfp Inc., 149].
      J. Prüss I (two editions), 1500 [R Nfp Inc., 151],
        and 1500 [R Nfp Inc., 150].

.1.4.   Breviarium Cisterciense.
      J. Grüninger, 1487 [R Nfp Inc., 143], 1494 [R Nfp
        Inc., 144].

C6.1.5.   Breviarium Constantiense.
          J. Grüninger, 1488 [R Nfp Inc., 146], 1495 [R Nfp
          Inc., 145].

  .1.6.   Breviarium Argentinense.
          J. Grüninger, 1489 [S I, 8].
          J. Prüss I, 1511 [S III A, 85].

  .1.7.   Breviarium Monasteriense.
          J. Grüninger, 1489 [R Nfp Inc., 152], 1497 [R Nfp
          Inc., 153].

  .1.8.   Breviarium Osnabrugense.
          J. Grüninger, 1489 [R Nfp Inc., 155].

  .1.9.   Breviarium Praemonstratense.
          J. Grüninger, 1490 [R Nfp Inc., 156].
          J. Prüss I, 1500 [R Nfp Inc., 157].

  .1.10.   Breviarium Wormatiense.
          J. Grüninger, ca. 1490 [R Nfp Inc., 164].

  .1.11.   Breviarium Hamburgense.
          J. Grüninger, 1490 [R Nfp Inc., 148].

  .1.12.   Breviarium Spirense.
          J. Grüninger, 1491 [R Nfp Inc., 159].
          J. Prüss I, 1500 [R Nfp Inc., 160].

  .1.13.   Breviarium divinorum officiorum . . . Prout in
       Cistertio psallitur.
          J. Grüninger, 1494 [S I, 19].

  .1.14.   Breviarium iuxta ritum ecclesiae Augustiensis dyocesis.
          J. Grüninger, 1495 [S I supp., 1].

  .1.15.   Breviarium et Psalterium.
          J. Grüninger, 1495 [R Nfp Inc., 165].

  1.16.   Breviarium Olomucense.
          J. Grüninger, 1499 [R Nfp Inc., 154].

  1.17.   Breviarium Teutonicorum Dominorum.
          J. Prüss I, 1500 [R Nfp Inc., 162], 1500 [R Nfp Inc.,
          161].

  1.18.   Breviarium Halberstadense.
          J. Prüss I, 1500 [R Nfp Inc., 147].

  1.19.   Officium ex evangelio et probatis doctorum Bernardi:
       Petri de Heliaco: et Johannis Gerson: sententiis absque
       apochrifis collectum de sancto Joseph nutritore Christi.
          J. Wähinger, 1504 [S IV Wäh., 5; R Nfp, 2788].

2. MISSALS.

C6.2.1.   Missale Vratislaviense.
           J. Prüss I, 1487 [R Nfp Inc., 493].
           M. Schott, 1491 [R Nfp Inc., 494].
           M. Flach I, 1491 [R Nfp Inc., 495].

  .2.2.   Missale Cisterciense.
           J. Grüninger, 1487 [S I, 7].

  .2.3.   Missale Argentinense.
           J. Prüss I, 1490 [R Nfp Inc., 490], 1508 [R Nfp Inc.,
           2694].

  .2.4.   Missale Wormatiense.
           J. Prüss I, ca. 1495 [R Nfp Inc., 496].

  .2.5.   Missale Warmiense.
           F. Dumbach, 1497 [S IV Dum., 1].

  .2.6.   Missale speciale.
           J. Prüss I, 1498 [R Nfp Inc., 499], 1508 [Greiner;
           R Nfp, 2706].
           R. Beck, 1512 [S IV Beck, 6], 1514 [R Nfp, 2708].

  .2.7.   Missale Halberstadense.
           J. Grüninger, 1500 [R Nfp Inc., 492].

  .2.8.   Missale speciale Basiliense.
           J. Prüss I, 1500 [R Nfp Inc., 501].

  .2.9.   Missale Moguntinum.
           J. Prüss I, 1500 [R Nfp, 2701], after 1500 [R Nfp,
           2702].

  .2.10.   Missale, Speciale Item Cautele circa defectus vel casus
           in celebratione misse.
           J. Prüss I, 1504 [S III A, 42; R Nfp, 2705], ca. 1504
           [R BNU III, 1361].

  .2.11.   Missale ordinis S. Johannis Hierosolymitani.
           J. Prüss I, 1505 [S III A, 50; R Nfp, 2700].

  .2.12.   Missale Hamburgense.
           J. Prüss I, 1509 [S III A, 76].

  .2.13.   Missale Cracoviense.
           J. Knobloch, 1510 [R Nfp, 2697].

  .2.14.   Missale Ordinis Praemonstratensis.
           R. Beck, 1511 [R Nfp, 2703].

  .2.15.   Missale Bremense.
           R. Beck, 1511 [R Nfp, 2696].

.2.16.   Geiler von Keysersberg, Johannes, <u>Evangelia, Das</u>
         <u>Plenarium und davon gezogen . . . uszlegung der</u>
         <u>evangelien und leren . . . .</u>
         J. Grüninger, 1512 [R Nfp, 1835].

C6.2.17. <u>Missale itinerantium: seu Misse peculiaris.</u>
         No printer, 1517 [R BNU III, 1583; R Nfp, 2700].

.2.18.   Bechoffen, Johann, <u>Quadruplex Expositio. Missalis seu</u>
         <u>officii misse.</u>
         J. Schott, 1519 [R BNU I, 176; S II B, 44].

.2.19.   <u>Missale Speciale noviter impressum.</u>
         R. Beck, 1520 [S IV Beck, 31].

   3. SACRED MUSIC FOR CHURCH WORSHIP.

C6.3.1. <u>Excerpta musices omnis cantus Gregoriani Pytagorici et</u>
         <u>contrapuncti simplicis.</u>
         J. Prüss I, n.d. [R Nfp, 1676].

.3.2.   <u>Flores musice omnis cantus gregoriani.</u>
         J. Prüss I, 1488 [S III A, 21].

.3.3.   <u>Uslegunge der hymbs nach der zitt des gantzen iares.</u>
         J. Grüninger, 1494 [R Nfp <u>Inc.</u>, 97].

.3.4.   <u>Graduale Secundum laudabilem cantum Gregorianum.</u>
         J. Prüss I, 1501 [S III A, 31], 1510 [S III A, 81].

.3.5.   Keinspeck, Michael (Michael Künspeck), <u>Lilium musice</u>
         <u>plane.</u>
         M. Hupfuff, 1504 [R Nfp, 2222].

.3.6.   <u>Psalterium Chorale: secundum morem et consuetudinem</u>
         <u>sancte Romane ecclesie: cum hymnis: antiphonis et</u>
         <u>versiculis.</u>
         J. Prüss I, 1509 [S III A, 75].

3.7.   <u>Hymni de Tempore et de Sanctis in eam formam qua a suis</u>
         <u>autoribus scripti sunt denuo redacti.</u>
         J. Knobloch, 1513 [R BNU II, 1239], 1516 [R BNU II,
         1240], 1519 [S VII, 174].

   4. BOOKS ON THE ADMINISTRATION OF THE SACRAMENTS.

C6.4.1. Guilhelmus de Gouda, <u>Expositio mysteriorum misse et</u>
         <u>verus modus rite celebrandi.</u>
         J. Knobloch, 1500 [R Nfp <u>Inc.</u>, 296], 1508 [S VII, 45],
         1508 [S VII, 46].
         M. Hupfuff, 1507 [S V, 62; R BNU II, 1057].

.4.2.   (Franz Balthasar de Porta), <u>Canon sacratissime misse:</u>

una cum expositione eiusdem.
M. Hupfuff, 1507 [Greiner; R Nfp, 904; S V, 61].

C6.4.3.   Adelphus, Joannes, Sequentiarum luculenta interpretatio:
nedum Scholasticis, sed et ecclesiasticis cognitu
necessaria.
J. Knobloch, 1513 [R BNU I, 6; S VII, 82], 1519 [R
BNU I, 9].

.4.4.   Joannis de Burgo, Pupilla Oculi. De septem sacramentorum administratione.
J. Knobloch, 1514 [S VII, 90], 1517 [S VII, 135],
1518 [S VII, 162].
J. Schott, 1517 [R I, 337].

C7. MARIAN VERSE, MARIAN CONTROVERSY, AND OTHER CATHOLIC VERSE.

1. MARIAN VERSE AND MARIAN CONTROVERSY.

C7.1.1.   Der Rosenkranz von U. L. Frawen unnd Uslegung des
Psalters. Das ist ein . . . Lied von Maria.
No printer, n.d. [R Nfp, 3124].

.1.2.   Bernardinus de Bustis, Mariale.
M. Flach I, 1483 [S VI A, 9], 1492 [S VI A, 44], 1493
[S VI A, 45], 1496 [S VI A, 59], 1498 [S VI A, 68].
M. Flach II, 1502 [S VI B, 9].

.1.3.   Albertus Magnus, Mariale seu de laudibus V. Mariae.
M. Flach I, 1483 [R Nfp Inc., 450], 1493 [R BNU Inc.,
12a].
M. Schott, 1485/89 [R BNU Inc., 12].

.1.4.   Corona Beate Mariae Virginis.
Printer de Vitas Patrum, ca. 1485 [R BNU Inc., 142].
G. Husner, ca. 1488 [R BNU Inc., 143], 1493 [R BNU
Inc., 144].

.1.5.   Pelbartus de Themeswar, Stellarium Coronae benedicte
Virginis Marie.
No printer, 1490 [R Nfp Inc., 560].
J. Knobloch, 1506 [S VII, 21], 1506 [S VII supp.,
325].

1.6.   Bernardus, B., De Planctu Mariae Virg. Textor sermones
de passione Christi.
G. Husner, 1496 [R Nfp Inc., 112].
J. Knobloch, 1508 [S VII, 44].

.1.7.   Trittenheim, Johannes, De immaculata conceptione Beatae
V. Mariae.
M. Hupfuff, 1496 [R Nfp Inc., 652].

C7.1.8.   Brant, Sebastian, Varia Carmina.
          J. Grüninger, 1498 [S I, 36].

 .1.9.   Heinricus de Hassia (Heinrich von Langenstein), Contra
          deceptiones fratrum mendicantium de Conceptione beatae
          Mariae.
              No printer, 1500 [R Nfp Inc., 317].
              R. Beck, 1516 [S IV Beck, 23].

 .1.10.   Maria zum Elend.
              J. Prüss I, 1500 [R Nfp Inc., 449].

 .1.11.   Baptista Mantuanus, Prima parthenice que Mariana
          inscribitur.
              J. Schott, 1501 [S II B, 6].
              J. Knobloch, 1515 [S VII, 95], 1518 [S VII, 151].

 .1.12.   Tractatus de Fraternitate rosarii gloriosae Virginis
          Mariae.
              B. Kistler, 1501 [S IV Kis., 15].

 .1.13.   Bollanus, Dominicus, De conceptione Gloriosissime Dei
          Genetricis Virginis Mariae. Sermo.
              J. Grüninger, 1504 [S I, 65].

 .1.14.   Bertoldus von Hennenberg, De triplici Candore Mariae.
              J. Knobloch, 1505 [S VII, 11].

 .1.15.   De purissima et immaculata conceptione virginis marie.
              M. Hupfuff, 1506 [S V, 57].

 .1.16.   Wimpfeling, Jacob, Soliloquium ad Divum Augustinum de
          Beata Maria.
              No printer, 1511 [R BNU IV, 2488].

 .1.17.   Victor von Carben, Schön . . . Tractat von . . . Marie
          der hymlischen Künigin mütter unsers herren Jesu
          Christi.
              M. Schürer, 1519 [S VIII, 253].

 .1.18.   Murner, Thomas, History von vier ketzern Prediger.
              J. Prüss II, 1521 [R BNU III, 1613].

 .1.19.   (Hieronymus Gebwiler), Beschirmung des lobs und eren
          der hochgelobten hymelischen künigin Marie.
              J. Grüninger, 1523 [S I, 198].

 .1.20.   Cochläus, Johann, Ein christenliche und nutzliche
          Sermon oder Predig sant Bernharts, von unser lieben
          frawen.
              J. Grüninger, 1524 [S I, 215].

 .1.21.   Buchstab, Johann, Von fürbit der mutter gotesz Marie.
              J. Grüninger, 1527 [Pegg, 390].

C7.1.22. Cursus beatae Mariae Virginis.
          Carthusian Press, 1533 [R Nfp, 1472].

    2. OTHER CATHOLIC VERSE.

C7.2.1.   Margarita poetica.
          J. Prüss I, 1503 [S III A, 40].

  .2.2.   Wuolphius, Thomas, Miserere, dum morbo Gallico
          laboraret ad deum none sine lachrymis effusum.
          J. Grüninger, 1508 [S I, 90].

  .2.3.   Paulinus Nolanus (Saint Paulinus), Carmen iambicum
          christianam pietate commendans.
          M. Schürer, 1508 [S VIII, 9].

  .2.4.   Pictorius, Ludoricus Bigus (Ludovico Pittori or Bigi),
          Opusculorum Christianorum libri tres eloquentissimi
          sanctissimique. . . . Pontii Paulini Carmen Jambicum
          Christianam pietatem commendans.
          M. Schürer, 1509 [S VIII, 11].

  .2.5.   Historia thobie cum moralitatibus eiusdem per Matheum
          vin docinensem elegiaco carmine diligenti castigatione
          descripta.
          J. Knobloch, 1510 [S VII, 68].

  .2.6.   (Alanus de Insulis), Libellus metricus, de contemptu
          mundi. Moralitates Faceti.
          J. Knobloch, 1510 [S VII, 65].

  .2.7.   Picus Mirandula, Joannes, Hymni Heroici tres ad
          Sanctissimam Trinitatem, ad Christum, et ad Virginem
          Mariam.
          M. Schürer, 1511 [S VIII, 55], 1521 [R Nfp, 2903].

  .2.8.   Joannis Elius, Odarum Spiritualium Liber.
          Montanus, Jacobus, Cancellerio per Christi sacerdotum.
          M. Schürer, 1513 [S VIII, 97; R Nfp, 1689].

  .2.9.   Baptiste Mantuanus, Secundae Parthenices Opus,
          sacrosanctum divae Virginis Catherinae passionem
          heroico carmini illustrans.
          J. Knobloch, 1515 [S VII, 96], 1518 [S VII, 152].

  .2.10. Baptiste Mantuanus, Parthenice Tertia Divarum
          Margarithae, Agathes, Luciae & Appoloniae Agones
          continens.
          J. Knobloch, 1515 [S VII, 97], 1518 [S VII, 154].

C8. INTRA-CATHOLIC CONTROVERSY.

C8.1.1.   Epistola contra quendam conciliistam archiepiscopum
          videlicet Craynensem et adversus citationem et libellum
          insamen ipsius contra sanctissimum dominum nostrum
          Sixtum papam IV modernum summum Pontificem edidit.
             M. Flach I, 1483 [S VI A, 10].

   .1.2. Barbatia, Andreas, Consilium si Eugenius papa potest
          facere duos episcopus in una dioecesi.
             G. Husner, ca. 1492 [R BNU Inc., 65].

   .1.3. Guilhermus Parisiensis, De collationibus et pluritate
          ecclesiasticorum beneficiorum.
             J. Knobloch, 1500 [R Nfp Inc., 315], 1507 [S VII, 30].

   .1.4. Wimphelingius, Jacobus, Ad Julium II Pontificem max.
          querulosa excusatio . . . ad instantiam Fratrum
          Augustinensium ad curiam Romanam citati: ut propria in
          persona ibidem compareat: propterea quod scripsit diuum
          Augustinum non fuisse monachum vel fratrem mendicantem.
             J. Prüss I, 1507 [S III A, 63].

   .1.5. Vallombrosa, Angelo de, Oratio pro concilio lateranensi
          contra conventiculum pisanum.
             M. Schürer, ca. 1512 [Greiner].

   .1.6. Murner, Thomas (Protest against his removal from the
          guardianship of the Franciscan convent in Strasbourg,
          begins: Allen und yeglichen geistlichen oder weltlichen
          was standts würden und wesens denen dise geschrifft fur
          kompt lesen od hören lesen . . .).
             No printer, 1515 [BM Cup.651.e.74].

   .1.7. Murner, Johannes, Allen und yeglichen geistlichen oder
          weltlichen was stats, wirden und wesens denen dise
          geschrifft für kompt, das ich Hans Murner . . . gegen
          der gemeynen stifft zum Jungen St. Peter . . . mein
          handel . . . für zu tragen.
             No printer, 1520 [R BNU III, 1599].

C9. CANON LAW AND ECCLESIASTICAL POLITICS.

C9.1.1.   Regule Congruitatum. Regimina. Constructiones.
             M. Hupfuff, n.d. [S V, 15].

   .1.2. Andreae, Johannes, Usslegung uber dem boume der
          sypschafft.
             H. Knoblochtzer, 1480 [BM 1.B.1100],
                1483 [R Nfp Inc., 71]. (In Latin: Super
             Arboribus consanguinitatis.)

C9.1.3. Polonus, Martinus (Martinus Strepus; Archbishop of
         Gnesen), Margarita Decreti.
           J. Grüninger, 1484 [S I, 5].
           G. Husner, 1486 [R BNU Inc., 302], 1489 [R BNU Inc.,
             303], 1493 [R Nfp Inc., 453], 1499 [R BNU Inc., 304].

  .1.4. Bernardus Parmensis (Bernardo Bottoni), Casus longi
         super decretales.
           G. Husner, 1484 [R BNU Inc., 79], 1488 [R BNU Inc.,
             80], 1493 [R BNU Inc., 81], 1498 [R BNU Inc., 82].

  .1.5. Accursius, Franciscus, Casus in terminis super novem
         libris Justiniani Codicicis.
           Printer of Vitas Patrum, ca. 1485 [R BNU Inc., 1].

  .1.6. Statuta Provincilia vetera et nova.
           J. Prüss I, 1485 [R BNU Inc., 442].

  .1.7. Michael de Dalen, Casus breves decretalium Sexti et
         Clementinarum libellus.
           G. Husner, 1485 [R BNU Inc., 316], 1493 [R BNU Inc.,
             317].

  .1.8. Regnerius, Elias, Casus longi Sexti et Clementinarum.
           J. Prüss I, 1488 [R BNU Inc., 410].
           G. Husner, 1496 [R BNU Inc., 411].

  .1.9. Gratian, Decretum cum apparatu.
           J. Grüninger, 1489 [R BNU Inc., 192], 1490 [R Nfp
             Inc., 299].

  .1.10. Casus in terminis libri sexti Decretalium.
           M. Flach I, 1490 [S VI A, 30].

   1.11. Clemens V (Pope), Constitutiones et Extravagantes
         Decretales cum apparatu Joh. Andreae.
           J. Grüninger, 1491 [R Nfp Inc., 187].

  .1.12. Alexander VI (Pope), Regulae Cancellariae.
           J. Prüss I, 1492 [R Nfp Inc., 32].

  .1.13. Innocentius VIII, Papa, Regulae cancellariae
         apostolicae.
           J. Prüss I, ca. 1492 [R BNU Inc., 248].

  .1.14. (Knights Hospitlar of the Order of St. John), Registrum
         in privilegia ordinis scti Iohanis.
           J. Prüss I, 1495 [BM IB.9429.2].

  .1.15. Compendium iuris canonici.
           G. Husner, 1499 [R BNU Inc., 138].

  .1.16. Annunciatio Sacri Jubilei instantis Anni Centesimi.
           J. Prüss I, 1500 [S III A, 30].

C9.1.17. Roffredus Beneventanus, Repertorium in Aureum libellare
          opus . . . super utrisque tam Pontificio quam Cesareo
          sacris Juribus, ingeniose editum Necnon ad faustissimas
          Sabbatinas questiones eiusdem.
              J. Grüninger, 1502 [S I, 59].

  .1.18. Hug, Johannes, Quadruvium Ecclesie, Quatuor prelatorum
          officium.
              J. Grüninger, 1504 [S I, 67].
              J. Grüninger, 1504 [S I, 68]. (In German.)

  .1.19. Raymundus de Penna Forti, Summula . . . De sortilegiis:
          simonia: furto: rapina: usura: atque variis casi-
          bus . . . .
              J. Knobloch, 1504 [R BNU III, 1974], 1518 [S VII,
              155].

  .1.20. Paul de Citadinis, Tractatus juris patronatus et
          summaria distinctionum: ac questionum causarum decreti.
              J. Grüninger, 1506 [S I, 76].

  .1.21. Lectura Abbatis Antiqui super quinque libris
          Decretalium.
              J. Schott, 1510 [S II B, 16].

  .1.22. Lupus, Johannes (Juan López), De Libertate ecclesiastica.
              J. Schott, 1511 [S II B, 18].

  .1.23. Hostiensis (Henricus de Segusia), Lectura sive apparatus
          domini Hostiensis super quinque libris Decretalium.
              J. Schott, 1512 [S II B, 20].

  .1.24. Flores, Petrus, De summo pont. aligendo Julii II,
          Pontific. Maxi sucessore.
              M. Schürer, 1513 [S VIII, 101].

   1.25. Cyntholtz, Johannes (Joannes Lyndholz), Arbores
          Consanguinitatis. Affinitatis. Cognationis Spiritualis
          atque Legalis.
              J. Schott, 1516 [R Nfp, 1475].

  .1.26. Erasmus Roterodamus, In leges Pontificias et Caesareas.
          De Haereticis . . . De re Evangelica et Haeriticorum
          poenis . . . .
              C. Egenolff, 1529 [R Nfp, 1559].

  .1.27. Index Expurgatorius Librorum.
              L. Zetzner, 1599 [R BNU II, 1244].

C10.   ANTI-PROTESTANT POLEMIC.

C10.1.1. Murner, Thomas, Christenliche und briederliche ermanung
          zu dem hoch gelerten Doctor Martino luter Augustiner

order zu Wittemburg.
J. Grüninger, 1520 [S I, 174], 1521 [S I, 179].

C10.1.2.   Murner, Thomas, Vom Doctor Martinus luters leren und
           predigen. Das sie argwenig seint, und nit gantzlich
           glaubwirdig zu halten.
           J. Grüninger, 1520 [S I, 175].

.1.3.   Murner, Thomas, Von dem babstenthum das ist von der
           höchsten oberkeyt Christlichs glauben wyder doctor
           Martinum Luther.
           J. Grüninger, 1520 [S I, 177].

.1.4.   Murner, Thomas, An den Groszmechtigsten und Durch-
           lüchtigsten adel tütscher nation das sye den christ-
           lichen glauben beschirmen wyder den zerstörer des
           glaubens christi Martinum luther einen verfierer der
           einfeltigen christen.
           J. Grüninger, 1520 [S I, 178].

.1.5.   Alveld, Augustin, Libellus quo ostendere conatur
           diuino iure institutum hoc esse ut totius ecclesiae
           caput romanus sit pontifex.
           No printer, 1520 [BM 4051.ee.3.I].

.1.6.   Modestus, Joiannis Antonius, Oratio ad Carolum Caesarem
           contra Martinum Lutherum.
           J. Grüninger, 1521 [S I, 180].

.1.7.   Murner, Thomas, Wie doctor M. Luther usz falschen
           ursachen bewegt Daz geistlich recht verbrennet hat.
           J. Grüninger, 1521 [S I, 181].

.1.8.   Murner, Thomas, Protestation D. Thome Murner das er
           wider Doc. Mar. Luther nichts unrechts gehandelt hab.
           J. Grüninger, 1521 [BM Cup.651.e.2].

.1.9.   Murner, Thomas, Ob der künig uss Engelland ein lügner
           sey oder der Luther.
           J. Grüninger, 1522 [S I, 191].

.1.10.   Murner, Thomas, Antwort und klag mit entschuldigung
           wider Michel Stifel.
           J. Grüninger, 1522 [BM 3905.d.106].

.1.11.   Murner, Thomas, Von dem grossen Lutherischen Narren.
           J. Grüninger, 1522 [S I, 193].

.1.12.   Henricus Rex Anglie, Assertio Septem Sacramentorum
           adversus Martinum Lutherum.
           J. Grüninger, 1522 [S I, 188].
           J. Grüninger, 1522 [S I, 189]. (In German; T.
           Murner, trans.)

C10.1.13.   Henricus VIII, Hoc libello continentur Articuli D.
            Mart. Luther ex eiusdem captivitate babilonica excerpti
            per Henricum Angliae . . . in assertionum libro pro
            maiori parte improbati.
                J. Grüninger, 1522 [R Nfp, 1986].

    .1.14. Cochlaeus, Johannes, De gratia sacramentorum liber
            unus . . . adversus assertionem Marti. Lutheri.
                J. Grüninger, 1522 [S I, 192].

    .1.15. Erasmus, Desiderius, Von walfart. Vermanung Wo
            Christus und sein Reych zu suchen ist.
                M. Schürer Erben, 1522 [B SE 1, 4].

    .1.16. Cochleus, Johannes, Glos und Comment auff den xiii
            Artickel von rechtem Mesz halten widr Luterische
            zwispalt.
                J. Grüninger, 1523 [S I, 207].

    .1.17. Cochleus, Johannes, Glos und Comment . . . uff CLIIII.
            Articklen gezogen usz einem Sermon Doc. mar. Lutersz
            von der heiligen mesz und nüem Testament.
                J. Grüninger, 1523 [S I, 200].

    .1.18. Cochlaeus, Johannes, Adversus cucullatum Minotaurum
            Wittembergensem.
                J. Grüninger, 1523 [R Nfp, 1403].

    .1.19. Cochlaeus, Johannes, De Baptismo parvulorum.
                J. Grüninger, 1523 [S I, 195].

    .1.20. Cochläus, Johannes, Spiegel der Ewangelischen freyheit,
            wie die Christus warhafftiklich gelert, und Martin
            Luther yetz in unseren zeyten die selbigen unnützlich
            fürgeben hat.
                J. Grüninger, 1523 [S I, 206], 1524 [R BNU I, 552].

    .1.21. Dietenberger, Joannes, Wider CXXXIX Schluszreden Mar.
            Luthers, von gelübdniss und geistlichem leben der
            Klosterlüt . . . vertütscht durch Jo. Cochleum.
                J. Grüninger, 1523 [S I, 205].

    .1.22. Dietenberger, Joannes, Obe die christen mügen durch
            iere guten werck dz hymelreich verdienen.
                J. Grüninger, 1523 [S I, 202].

    .1.23. Dietenberger, Joannes, Antwurt, das Junckfrawen die
            Klöster und Klosterliche glübd nümmer götlich ver-
            lassen mögen.
                J. Grüninger, 1523 [S I, 201].

    .1.24. Johannes von Roffa (John Fisher; Bishop of Rochester),
            CXXXIX artickel wider M. Luther (J. Cochläus, trans.).
                J. Grüninger, 1523 [S I, 204].

C10.1.25.   Albert, Cardinal, Archbishop, <u>Ein mandat widder die</u>
            <u>Luttherische lere. Item ein ander mandat der gemeynen</u>
            <u>Leyen.</u>
                R. Beck Erben, ca. 1523 [Pegg, 41].

  .1.26.   Krantz, Albertus, <u>Hystoria von den alten hussen zu</u>
            <u>Behemen</u> (J. Dobneck, trans.).
                J. Grüninger, 1523 [Pegg, 1622].

  .1.27.   Dietenberger, Johannes, <u>Von Menschen ler widerlegung</u>
            <u>des Lutherischen büchlins von menschen leren zu meiden.</u>
                J. Grüninger, 1523 [S I, 203], 1524 [R BNU I, 650].

  .1.28.   Bartholomaeus de Usingen, <u>Concertatio haud inelegans</u>
            (Johannis) Culsameri Lutherani et F. Bartholomei.
                J. Grüninger, 1523 [S I, 194; R Nfp, 3387].

  .1.29.   Felbaum, Sebastian, <u>Ein nutzliche rede, frag und ant-</u>
            <u>wort von dreyen personen sich uben in lutrischen</u>
            <u>sachen.</u>
                J. Grüninger, 1524 [Pegg, 1101; R Bib. Mun., 971].

  .1.30.   Cochläus, Johannes, <u>Ob sant Peter zu Rom sey gewesen.</u>
                J. Grüninger, 1524 [BM 3906.f.30].

  .1.31.   Cochläus, Johannes, <u>Antwort auff Martin Luth.</u>
            <u>freueliche Appellation, Anno 1520 von babst uff ein</u>
            <u>zukunfftig Concilium.</u>
                J. Grüninger, 1524 [S I, 217], 1525 [S I, 224].

  .1.32.   Cochleus, Johannes, <u>De fomite peccati.</u>
                J. Grüninger, 1524 [S I, 209].

  .1.33.   <u>Ein heilsamer Tractat S. Cypriani von einfaltigkeit</u>
            <u>der Prelaten und einigkeit der Kirchen. wider die</u>
            <u>Ketzerey und zertrennung</u> (J. Cochläus, trans.).
                J. Grüninger, 1524 [S I, 216].

  .1.34.   (Johannes Dietenberger), <u>Der leye. Obe der gelaub</u>
            <u>allein selig macht.</u>
                J. Grüninger (two editions), 1524 [S I, 213], and
                    1524 [R BNU I, 651].

  .1.35.   Dietenberger, Johannes, <u>Der Bauer, Obe die Christen</u>
            <u>mügen durch iere güten werck das hymelreich verdienen.</u>
                J. Grüninger, 1524 [S I, 212].

  .1.36.   Dytenberger, Jo., <u>Christliche underweisung wie man</u>
            <u>gotes heiligen in dem hymmel an ruffen, und das heil-</u>
            <u>thum auff erden Eeren soll.</u>
                J. Grüninger, 1524 [S I, 218].

  .1.37.   (Jerome Emser), <u>Missae Christianorum contra Lutheranam</u>

missandi formulam Assertio.
J. Grüninger, 1524 [S I, 219].

C10.1.38. Johannes von Roffen (John Fisher; Bishop of Rochester),
Zwey artikel verteuscht von Doctor Jo. Cochleus.
J. Grüninger, 1524 [S I, 214].

.1.39. Hugo, Bischoffen zu Constantz, Christenlich underrichtung . . . die Bildnüssen und das opfer der Mess
betreffend.
J. Grüninger, 1524 [S I, 220].

.1.40. Tectonus, Theophilus, Compendiosa Boemice seu
Hussitane Hereseos ortus et euisdem damnatorum
Articulorum descriptio.
J. Grüninger, 1524 [S I, 210].

.1.41. Treger, Conrad, Ad Episcopum Lausanensem paradoxa
Centum . . . de ecclesiae Conciliorumque auctoritate.
J. Grüninger, 1524 [S I, 211].

.1.42. Erasmus, Roteroda, De Libero Arbitrio.
J. Knobloch, 1524 [S VII, 279].

.1.43. Erasmus, Spongia adversus aspergines Hutteni.
J. Knobloch, ca. 1525 [Pegg, 1067].

.1.44. Cochleus, Johannes, Antwort auf XCI artickelen usz
dreien sermonen M. Luth. gezogen.
J. Grüninger, 1525 [S I, 226].

.1.45. Buchstab, Johannes, Von dem Hochwirdigen Sacrament des
leibs und bluts Christi.
J. Grüninger, 1527 [Pegg, 389].

.1.46. Buchstab, Johannes, Das nit alle Cristglöbige menschen
gleich priester seyend.
J. Grüninger, 1527 [R BNU I, 321].

.1.47. Buchstab, Johannes, Von becleidunge der priester gesang
und bildnussen in der christlichen kilhen.
J. Grüninger, 1527 [R BNU I, 322].

.1.48. Buchstab, Johannes, Von dem fegfëur.
J. Grüninger, 1527 [R BNU I, 323].

.1.49. Erasmus, Contra Quosdam qui se falso iactant evangelicos epistola.
No printer, 1529 [BM 847.c.10].

.1.50. Bchüstab, Johannes, Dasz die Biblischen geschrifften
müssen ein geystliche usslegung han.
J. Grüninger, 1529 [S I, 244].

.1.51. Erasmus, Epistola nuper missa ad legatum apposto.

Auguste Agentem.
W. Köpfel, 1530 [Pegg, 785].

C10.1.52. Erasmus, Epistel wider etliche die sich fälschlich
rühmen evangelisch zu sein.
No printer, ca. 1532 [R Nfp, 1600].

.1.53. Erasmus, Von der kirchen lieblichen vereinigung.
M. Apiarius, 1533 [R BNU II, 786].

.1.54. Pole, Reginaldus, Consilium delectorum Cardinalium, de
emendanda Ecclesia.   Epistola Joannis Sturmi de eadem
re ad Cardinales . . . ad eam consultationem delectos.
Cr. Mylius, 1538 [R BNU III, 1903].

.1.55. Sadoletus, Jacobus, Cardinalis, Epistola ad Senatum
populumque Genuensem, qua in obedientiam Romani
Pontificis eos reducere conatur.
W. Rihel, 1539 [R BNU IV, 2057].

.1.56. Latomus, Bartholomaeus, Scripta duo adversaria D.
Barthol. Latomi et Martini Buceri.
W. Rihel, 1544 [R BNU III, 1337].

.1.57. Erasmus a Limburg, Bischof von Strassburg (Einberufung
zu der 2 April 1549 . . . Synode).
No printer, 1549 [R BNU II, 794].

.1.58. Carapha, Joh. Petrus (Gian Pietro Carafa or Pope Paul
IV), Consilium de emendanda ecclesia . . . olim
Cardinali Theatino nunc sub Pauli quarti nomine
Pontifice Romano.
T. Rihel, 1555 [R Nfp, 1291].

.1.59. Lutz, Reinhardus, Verzaichnus . . . der Kätzerischen,
und verdampten Leer Martin Steinbachs, der verfluchten
Gotslesterers.
Chr. Mylius I, 1566 [R Bib. Mun., 1442].

.1.60. Rabus, Jacobus, Adversus Theses contra S. Reliquiarum
miracula.
No printer, 1574 [R BNU III, 1961].

LEGAL TREATISES AND DOCUMENTS

L1. Legal Treatises and Documents.

     1. Imperial Politics, Letters, and Ordinances.
     2. Law in Latin.
     3. Law in German.
     4. Statutes and Ordinances of Cities other than Strasbourg.
     5. Political and Military Treatises.
     6. External Political Matters involving Strasbourg.
     7. Edicts and Treaties.
     8. Legal Disputations.

L2. Municipal Ordinances.

L3. Notarial Manuals.

L1. LEGAL TREATISES AND DOCUMENTS.

1. IMPERIAL POLITICS, LETTERS, AND ORDINANCES.

L1.1.1.   Charles VIII, Roi de France, Botschaft und Werbung an
           Kaiser Friedrich III.
                J. Grüninger, n.d. [R Nfp, 1331].

  .1.2.   Kynig Maximiliani Cronung und Gemeiner Landfride.
                J. Prüss I, 1486 [BM 1A.1574].

  .1.3.   Friedrich III, Achtbrief gegen die Stadt Regensburg.
                No printer, 1491 [R Nfp Inc., 276].

  .1.4.   Maximilian I, Ad Leonem Papam Maximiliani Caesaris
           Responsio.
                J. Prüss II, 1517 [BM 1312.c.58].

  .1.5.   Leo X (Pope), Bäbstlicher heilikeit sampt Römscher
           Keiserlicher Maiestat anschlag wider die Türcken.
                J. Grüninger, 1518 [Pegg, 3510].

  .1.6.   Carolus Ro. Rex. Elect. Oratio Legationis Francisci
           Regis Franciae.
                J. Schott, 1519 [S II B, 47].

  .1.7.   Sigismund (Emperor of Germany), Ein Reformation des
           geistlichen und weltlichen stands durch Keyser Sigmundum
           furgenummen.
                M. Schürer, 1520 [BM 3906.r.29.2].

  .1.8.   (Proclamation of the Landfriede).
                No printer, 1521 [BM D.C. 4/1.7].

  .1.9.   Ordenung und sundere gesatz des heiligen römischen
           reichs hofgericht zu rotweil.
                J. Grüninger, 1523 [S I, 199; R BNU III, 1673].

  .1.10.   Sendtbrief so die Romisch Keyserlich Maiestat ires
           erlangten sygs gegen dem Barbarossa in Königreich
           Thunis seiner . . . Brüder dem Römischen König . . .
           zugeschriben hat.
                J. Prüss II, 1535 [BM G.6204.1].
                W. Rihel, 1535 [R Nfp, 3216].

  .1.11.   Der Nider Osterreichischer Land Ussschuss und Gesandten
           an Röm. Kun. Mt. Ferdinandum Christliche Religion sach
           belanged supplication.
                J. Schott, 1542 [BM 9325.b.29].

  .1.12.   Copey und Abdruck der Römischen Kayserlichen Maiestat
           Freyheit, den Erfindern der Holtzsparungskunst.
                No printer, 1557 [BM 9325.b.24].
                T. Rihel, 1572 [R BNU I, 585].

41

L1.1.13.   Verzeychnus aller Potentaten, Chur und Fürsten, Geyst-
           lich und Weltlich, auch derselben Gesandten: Item,
           Graffen, Freyen, und deren von der Ritterschafft . . .
           zu Frankfurt MDLXII persönlich gewesen und erschinen
           sind.
               Chr. Mylius I, 1562 [R BNU IV, 2402].

  .1.14.   Rhegius, Ernestus, De Hominis Politici Persona et
           Officio. Ad Juniorem Borussiae principem.
               S. Emmel, 1568 [R BNU III, 2009].

  .1.15.   Wir Sebastian Mueg . . . und der Raht . . . Straszburg,
           Thus zuwisen . . . des Heil. Reichs Policey und Pein-
           lichen halszgerichts Ordnung bey hohen straffen und
           Poenen verbotten . . . So gebietten wir allen Das sich
           keiner . . . gelusten lasse, dergleichen Pasquillos,
           Famosschrifften, Schandgedicht . . . zudichten zu-
           schreiben.
               No printer, 1590 [R BNU III, 1729].

     2.   LAW IN LATIN.

L1.2.1.   Vocabularius utriusque juris.
               G. Husner, 1486 [R BNU Inc., 485], 1490 [R Nfp Inc.,
               696], 1494 [R Nfp Inc., 697], 1500 [R BNU Inc.,
               486].

  .2.2.   Modus legendi abbreviaturas cum aliis tractatibus
           juridicis.
               G. Husner, 1488 [R Nfp Inc., 504], 1490 [R Nfp Inc.,
               327], 1494 [R BNU Inc., 328].
               M. Flach I, 1499 [S VI A, 72].

  .2.3.   Directorium Statuum. Seu verius. Tribulatio seculi.
               P. Attendorn, 1489 [S IV Att., 1].

  .2.4.   Cepolla, Bartholomaeus (Bartolemeo Cipolla), Cautelae.
               J. Prüss I, 1490 [R Nfp Inc., 181].

  .2.5.   Corpus juris civilis. Justiniani Institutiones.
               J. Grüninger, 1491 [R Nfp Inc., 196].

  .2.6.   Berberius, Johannes, Viatorium utriusque juris.
               J. Prüss I, 1493 [R BNU Inc., 70].

  .2.7.   Nicolaus Tudeschis (Niccoló de Tudeschi), Processus
           judiciarius.
               J. Grüninger, ca. 1495 [R BNU Inc., 464].

  .2.8.   Flores legum.
               J. Grüninger, 1496 [R BNU Inc., 173].

  .2.9.   Exceptiones Legum Romanorum cum tractatu actionum:

earundemque longinquitate.
> J. Schott, 1500 [S II B, 3].

L1.2.10. Sequuntur aliqua Avisamenta ad quae Caesar et illus-
trissimi principes praelati et civitates Imperii
attendere debent.
> No printer, ca. 1505 [R Nfp, 894].

.2.11. Leopoldus de Bebenburg (Lupold von Bebenburg), De
Iuribus et Translatione Imperii. Hexastichon Seb. Brant.
Ad lectorem. Beatus Arnoaldus.
> M. Schürer, 1508 [S VIII, 3].

.2.12. Refugium Advocatorum. Contenta in hoc opusculo. Summa
Odofredi de formandis libellis. Summa Hermanni, centum
libellorum In arborem iudiciariam Joannis de Grassis
scriptum domesticum.
> J. Schott, 1510 [S II B, 17].

.2.13. Stynna, Johannes de, Speculator abbreviatus . . . cum
variis libellorum . . . tam in judiciis, quam in con-
tractionibus . . . .
> J. Schott?, 1511 [R BNU IV, 2243].

.2.14. Concordata principum nationis Germanicae cum argumentis
sive summariis iam additis.
> R. Beck, 1513 [Greiner].

.2.15. Alzati, Andree (Andrea Alciati), In tres posteriores
Codices Justiniani Annotationes.
> J. Schott, 1515 [S II B, 30].

.2.16. Spiegel, Jacob, Lexicon Juris Civilis.
> J. Schott, 1538 [S II B, 138], 1539 [R BNU IV, 2184],
> 1541 [R BNU IV, 2185].

.2.17. Tancretus (Tancredus Bononiensis), Tractatus, hucusque
neque in Germania, neque alibi uisus, . . . ad universa
fere veterum Practicorum scripta . . . .
> Cr. Mylius, 1545 [R BNU IV, 2266].

.2.18. Zasius, Johann Ulric, Catalogus legum antiquarum.
> W. Köpfel, 1551 [Rott, 67].

.2.19. Winkel, Johannes, Varia opuscula. De exercitatione
iurisconsultorum. De vera et compendiaria ratione
docendi, et discendi Iura. . . . Disputationes et
alia . . . .
> W. Rihel, 1554 [R BNU IV, 2499].

.2.20. Oelinger, Paul, Ethicorum Legalium Liber Primus . . .
ex verbis Aristotelis.
> B. Fabricius, 1555 [R BNU III, 1669].

L1.2.21. Gremp von Freundenstein, Ludwig, Analysis. Resolutio
          Dialectica IV. Librorum Institutionum Imperialium.
              S. Emmel, 1567 [R BNU II, 1039].

  .2.22. Bebio, Ludovicus, In Institutionum imperialium libros
          IV. Erotemata dialectica. Nunc primum edita opera et
          studio Johannis Richardii (alias Winkel).
              T. Rihel, 1571 [R Nfp, 969].

  .2.23. Schneidewin, Johannes, In quatuor Institutionum
          Imperialium D. Justiniani libros Commentarii . . . cum
          multis libellorum et actuum iudicalium formis.
              T. Rihel, 1571 [R Nfp, 3179], 1575 [R Nfp, 3180],
              1580 [R BNU III, 2084], 1583 [R BNU III, 2085],
              1584 [BM c.74.f.7], 1585 [R Nfp, 3181], 1586 [R
              BNU III, 2086], 1592 [BM 5305.e.5], 1597 [R Nfp,
              3182], 1599 [R BNU III, 2087].

  .2.24. Obrecht, Georgius, Oikonomia. Qua diffusa et perplexa
          Pignorum Materia Breviter et Perspicue explicata con-
          tinentur.
              A. Bertram, 1591 [R BNU III, 1650].

  .2.25. Beuther, Michael, Animadversionum sive Disceptationum
          tam Historicarum quam Chronographicarum.
              B. Jobin, 1593 [R BNU I, 196].

  .2.26. Obrecht, Georgius, Oikonomia Donationis Simplicis et
          relatae . . . .
              A. Bertram, 1595 [R BNU III, 1653].

  .2.27. Coler, Christophorus, Sententiae ex utroque iure denvo
          Collectae . . . Iuris studiosis optatissimus et
          aptissimus.
              A. Bertram, 1595 [R BNU I, 559].

  .2.28. Backer, Nicolaus, Privatarum disputationum, ex quatuor
          Institutionum libris, . . . partes 2.
              J. Martin, 1595 [R Nfp, 895].

  .2.29. Pegius, Martinus, De jure protomiseos congrui vel
          Retractus . . . .
              L. Zetzner, 1596 [R BNU III, 1808].

   2.30. Obrecht, Georgius, Brevis explicatio singularum legum
          Tituli D. de Officio eius, cui Mandata est Iurisdictio.
              A. Bertram, 1597 [R BNU III, 1654].

  .2.31. Speculum Aulicarum atque Politicarum observationum
          libelli quatuor: I. De consiliis et consiliariis
          primcipum Fridericus Furius. II. Consiliarius Hippoliti
          à Collibus. III. Aulicus Politicus Duri de Pascolo.
          IV. Hypomneses Politicae Francisci Guiceiardini.
              L. Zetzner, 1599 [R Nfp, 3263].

3. LAW IN GERMAN.

L1.3.1.   Clag antwort und uszgesprochne urteyl gezogen uss
            geystlichen und weltlichen rechten. Dodurch sich eyn
            jeder, er sey clager. antworter. oder richter vor un-
            rechter that. handelung. und fürnemen hüten mag.
              J. Grüninger, 1500 [S I, 45].

 .3.2.   Keyserlich und künigliche Lant und lehenrecht nach
            gemeinen sitten und gebruch der rechten.
              M. Hupfuff, 1505 [S V, 38].

 .3.3.   Ordenunge des Gerichts kürtz begriffen, Dardurch sich
            ein yeglicher vor dem gericht behelffen und verdedingen
            mag.
              M. Hupfuff, 1507 [S V, 67].

 .3.4.   Tengler, Ulrich, Layenspiegel. Von rechtmässigen
            ordnungen in Burgerlichen und peinlichen regimenten.
            Mit allegation und Bewerungen ausz geschribnen rechten
            unnd gesatzen.
              M. Hupfuff, 1510 [S V, 78], 1511 [S V, 82], 1514 [S
                V, 115].
              No printer, 1513 [R Nfp, 3314], 1515 [R Nfp, 3316],
                1516 [R Nfp, 3317].
              J. Knobloch, 1518 [R BNU IV, 2276], 1527 [S VII, 315].
              H. Knobloch, 1530 [R BNU IV, 2278], 1532 [R BNU IV,
                2279].
              J. Albrecht, 1536 [R BNU IV, 2280], 1538 [R BNU IV,
                2281].
              W. Rihel & G. Messerschmidt, 1544 [R BNU IV, 2282].
              J. Rihel & G. Messerschmidt, 1560 [R Bib. Mun., 2052].

 .3.5.   Brant, Sebastian, Der Richterlich Clagspiegel . . . wie
            man . . . formieren sol nach ordenung der rechten ein
            yede clag, antwort und urteilen, gezogen uss geist-
            lichen und weltlichen rechten . . . .
              M. Hupfuff, 1516 [S V, 134].
              J. Knobloch, 1518 [S VII, 159].
              M. Flach II, 1521 [R BNU I, 243].
              J. Albrecht, 1533 [R BNU I, 245], 1536 [R BNU I, 246].
              J. Albrecht & W. Rihel, 1538 [R BNU I, 247].
              W. Rihel & G. Messerschmidt, 1553 [R Bib. Mun., 739].

 .3.6.   Murner, Thomas, Der Keiserlichen stat rechten ein
            ingang und wares fundament. Meister und Rädten tütscher
            nation.
              J. Grüninger, 1521 [S I, 185].

 .3.7.   Gerichts Ordenung und Prozess ietzlauffiger übungen.
            Mit Rechtmässiger deren Gründ und klarer anzeyg in

Keyserlichen unnd Geystlichen Rechten.
　　C. Egenolff, 1530 [R Nfp, 1878].

L1.3.8.　　Gail, Andreas, Tractatus von Pfändungssachen, wie es
　　　　　mit denselben an den Kais. Cammergericht vermög der
　　　　　Ordnung und des Gerichts Practick, gehalten, und
　　　　　geurtheylt werde . . . .
　　　　　　B. Jobin, 1585 [R BNU II, 930].

　.3.9.　　Boterus, Johannes (Giovanni Botero), Gründlicher
　　　　　Bericht, Von Anordnung Guter Policeyen und Regiments:
　　　　　auch Fürsten und Herren Stands. Sampt Gründlicher
　　　　　Erklärung der Ursachen wadürch Stätt zu auffnemen und
　　　　　hochheiten kommen mögen.
　　　　　　L. Zetzner, 1596 [R BNU I, 232].

　.3.10.　　Cepolla, Bartolemeus (Bartolomeo Cipolla), Tractat de
　　　　　Servitutibus der in Stätten und auff dem Land gelegener
　　　　　Gebäw und Feldguter Dienstbarkeiten sampt gründlichem
　　　　　Bericht.
　　　　　　L. Zetzner, 1596 [R Bib. Mun., 710].

　　4.　STATUTES AND ORDINANCES OF CITIES OTHER THAN STRASBOURG.

L1.4.1.　　Der stat Worms Reformation und statuten ordenung.
　　　　　Satzung die allen Stetten. communen. Regimenten.
　　　　　　M. Hupfuff (two editions), 1507 [Greiner], 1509
　　　　　　[Greiner], and 1509 [S V, 76].

　.4.2.　　Der marggraffschafft Badrn statuten und Ordenungen in
　　　　　Testamenten Erbfellen und Vormundschafften.
　　　　　　R. Beck, 1511 [S IV Beck, 2].

　.4.3.　　Reformation, Ordnung und Satzungen einer Ersamen Rhats
　　　　　des Heiligen Reichs Cammer, und Statt Hagenaw.
　　　　　　No printer, 1571 [R BNU III, 1978].

　.4.4.　　Underthenigiste Klag und Trewhertzige Erinnerung der
　　　　　Ritterschaft in Lottringen und Hertzogthumb Barr: An
　　　　　die Königlich Maj. in Franckreich wegen der inn Lott-
　　　　　ringen eingewurtzelter Spanischer bedrengus in Schat-
　　　　　zungen und zugenöttigen Kriegswesen.
　　　　　　No printer, 1593 [R BNU II, 1312].

　　5.　POLITICAL AND MILITARY THEORY.

L1.5.1.　　Porria Jacobus, Comes Purliliarum, De re militari
　　　　　Libri II. Iam recens editi.
　　　　　　J. Knobloch, 1521 [S VII, 317].

　.5.2.　　Ferrandus, Fulgentius, Paraeneticus qualis esse debeat

dux religiosus in actibus militaribus.
J. Herwagen, 1526 [Pegg, 1103].

L1.5.3. Ordnung: Namen, unnd Regiment, alles Kriegsvolcks. Von
Geschlechten. Namen und Zal aller Büchsen . . . ausz
dem Kriegs Rahtschlag Jacoben Preussen.
C. Egenolff, 1530 [R Nfp, 2798].

.5.4. Johannes von Morsheim, New Kriegsrustung.
J. Cammerlander, 1534 [R Nfp, 2727].

.5.5. (Gentillet, Innocent), Regentenkunst oder Fürsten-
spiegel geschriben wider . . . Nicolaum Machiavellum.
B. Jobin, 1580 [Greiner; R Nfp, 1872].

.5.6. Guicciardini, Franciscus, Hypomneses Politicae.
L. Zetzner, 1599 [R Nfp, 1942].

6. EXTERNAL POLITICAL MATTERS INVOLVING STRASBOURG.

L1.6.1. Ordnung Keyserlicher Mandat delegierten Cammerrichtern
in der Stadt Strassburg.
No printer, n.d. [R BNU III, 1672].

.6.2. Sleidanus, Johannes, Oration an Keiserl. Maiestat. Von
dem, Das der ietzige Religions handel, kein menschlich,
sonder Gottes werck . . . sei . . . .
G. Messerschmidt, 1544 [R BNU IV, 2127].

.6.3. Sleidanus, Johannes, Orationes Duae. Una ad Carolum V.
Caesar. Altera ad Germaniae Principes.
Cr. Mylius, 1544 [R BNU IV, 2128].

7. EDICTS AND TREATIES.

L1.7.1. Friedens Articul . . . zwischen Hertzogen von Anjou
. . . und . . . König von Navarre (as Deputies of the
Reformed Religion).
B. Jobin, 1581 [R Bib. Mun., 1020].

.7.2. Henri II, Roi de France, Edict (on Catholic Churches).
No printer, 1584 [R Bib. Mun., 1185].

.7.3. Alexandre de Parme (Alessandro Farnese; Duke of Parma
and Piacenza), Sendbrief desz Printzen von Parma an
Bürgermeister, Scheffen und Obrigkeit . . . und Zünften
der Stadt Antorff. Auch Antwort der Herren Bürgermeister, Scheffen, Rentmeister und Raht der Staff
Antorff.
A. Bertram, 1585 [R Nfp, 806].

.7.4. Accort et capitulation faict entre le Roy de Navarre

et le Duc du Cazimir pour la levé de l'Armee de
Reistres venus en France en l'année 1587.
   G. le Pords, 1587 [R Nfp, 734].

8. LEGAL DISPUTATIONS.

Ll.8.1. Obrecht, Georgius, Disputatio de Patrocinio Pupillorum.
         A. Bertram, n.d. [R BNU III, 1642], 1586 [R BNU III,
         1646].

.8.2.   Obrecht, Georgius, Exercitium Juris Practicum.
         A. Bertram, 1585 [R BNU III, 1643].

.8.3.   Obrecht, Georgius, Disputatio de Furto, Delicto gravi
         et quotidiano.
         A. Bertram, 1586 [R BNU III, 1644].

.8.4.   Obrecht, Georgius, Disputatio de Patrimonio Mulierum.
         A. Bertram (two editions), 1586 [R BNU III, 1645],
         and 1586 [R BNU III, 1644].

.8.5.   Obrecht, Georgius, Disputatio de Praescriptionibus.
         A. Bertram, 1590 [R BNU III, 1648].

.8.6.   Obrecht, Georgius, Disputationes II. Juridicae: Prior
         De Principiis Belli et eius Constitutione . . .
         Posterior De Militari. Disciplina.
         A. Bertram, 1590 [R BNU III, 1649].

.8.7.   Obrecht, Georgius, Disputatio de Forma Actionis et
         Libelli.
         A. Bertram, 1590 [R BNU III, 1647].

.8.8.   Schad, Johann Jacob, Propositiones aliquot Juridicae.
         A. Bertram, 1592 [R Bib. Mun., 1882].

.8.9.   Obrecht, Georgius, Disputatio de Militari Disciplina
         quae Administrationis Belli Primam et praecipuam partem
         continet.
         A. Bertram, 1592 [R BNU III, 1651].

.8.10.   Gothofredus, Dionysius (Denis Godefroy), Disputatio de
         Iureiurando eiusque speciebus causis atque effectibus.
         A. Bertram, 1592 [R BNU II, 1023].

.8.11.   Praetorius, Martinus, De principatu Salutariter
         administrando opusculum, cum praeceptis politicis.
         B. Jobin, 1594 [R BNU III, 1921].

.8.12.   Obrecht, Georgius, Disputatio prima . . . de judiciis.
         A. Bertram, 1594 [R BNU III, 1652].

.8.13.   Obrecht, Georgius, Disputatio Feudalis prima.
         A. Bertram, 1597 [R BNU III, 1655].

L1.8.14. Obrecht, Georgius, <u>Disputatio Feudalis secunda.</u>
          A. Bertram, 1597 [R BNU III, 1656].

  .8.15. Obrecht, Georgius, <u>Disputatio Feudalis Tertia.</u>
          A. Bertram, 1597 [R BNU III, 1657].

  .8.16. Beck, Andreas, <u>Thesium decades quinque. De Testamentis</u>
          <u>eorum qui iustis natalibus laborant et quando fiscus</u>
          <u>intestatis succedat.</u>
          J. Rihel or T. Rihel, 1597 [R Nfp, 971].

  .8.17. Beck, Andreas, <u>Thesium decades sex . . . De non capace</u>
          <u>Haerede legatorio et successore.</u>
          J. Rihel or T. Rihel, 1598 [R Nfp, 970].

  .8.18. Borkowski, Petrus, <u>Disputatio XL. De legum necessitate</u>
          <u>ad rectam institutionem ac perfectionem bonorum morum.</u>
          A. Bertram, 1598 [R Nfp, 1035].

  .8.19. Obrecht, Georgius, <u>Exercitia II. Juridica publice</u>
          <u>Argentinensi in Academia instituta. I. De commodati</u>
          <u>actione . . . II. Exercitium juridicum de poema</u>
          <u>militis . . . .</u>
          A. Bertram, 1599 [R BNU III, 1659].

  .8.20. Pontanus, Melchisedech, <u>Disputatio de Praescriptionibus.</u>
          A. Bertram, 1599 [R BNU III, 1914].

  .8.21. Lontzen, Johannes, <u>Disputatio de dominio et modo</u>
          <u>acquirendi naturalibus.</u>
          A. Bertram, 1599 [R BNU III, 1386].

  .8.22. Obrecht, Georgius, <u>Selectissimae Disputationes ex Iuris</u>
          <u>Civilis Materiis . . . .</u>
          A. Bertram, 1599 [R BNU III, 1658].

L2. MUNICIPAL ORDINANCES.

L2.1.1. <u>Gesatz und ordenunge der . . . Freyen statt Straszburg</u>
          <u>. . . wider Eebruch, concubinerei und Hurerei.</u>
          M. Hupfuff, 1501 [S V, 14].

  .1.2. <u>Ordinanz . . . wider Eebruchen, üppigkeit und anderere</u>
          <u>süntliche werck.</u>
          No printer, 1514 [AMS R/3, 47].

  .1.3. (Proclamation of the ban of the Empire against all
          Germans taking service with the King of France).
          No printer, 1515 [BM D.C.4/1.1], 1516 [BM D.C.4/1.2],
            1521 [BM D.C.4/4.4], 1521 [BM D.C.4/1.5], 1521 [BM
            D.C.4/1.6], 1523 [BM D.C.4/1.8].

  .1.4. <u>Müntzordung wider Lothringische müntz.</u>

No printer, 1515 [AMS R/3, 54], 1517 [AMS R/3, 64],
1589 [AMS R/5, 159].

L2.1.5.   Verbot der lystlis spiel und Schwüre, Gotslesterung
ouch des zudrincken.
No printer, 1516 [AMS R/3, 53], 1526 [AMS R/3, 131],
1526 [AMS R/3, 147], 1529 [BM 5510.ee.6.52],
1529 [R BNU III, 1675], 1533 [AMS R/3, 217], 1549
[R BNU III, 1677], 1568 [BM 5510.ee.6.57].

.1.6.   Ordnung . . . wider vogel schiessen.
No printer, 1516 [AMS R/3, 57].

.1.7.   (Proclamation . . . to prevent the making of self-
firing guns).
No printer, 1518 [BM D.C.4/1.3].

1.8.   Verbot den Wein vor dem Herbst zu verkaufen.
No printer, 1518 [BM 1853.c.2.1], 1580 [AMS R/5, 121],
1588 [AMS R/5, 150], 1591 [AMS R/5, 177].

.1.9.   Des Verschribung und Verwilligung des Herren Karle
gegen dem Heyligen Reich.
R. Beck, 1519 [BM 1193.1.49].

.1.10.   Ordnung des Fridbruchs halb.
No printer, 1519 [AMS R/3, 84].

.1.11.   Burger artickel (Fixing a tax to support the expedition
against the Turks).
No printer, 1522 [BM 1853.c.2.3].

.1.12.   Niemans . . . uff den gassen oder vor den hüsern zo
betteln . . .
No printer, 1523 [R BNU III, 1682].

.1.13.   Constitution von Ablosung der ewigen, ehrschätzigen und
Fürbietigen Zinss.
No printer, 1523 [AMS R/3, 115].

.1.14.   Prediger, Das . . . alle die so sich Predigens, in
unser Statt . . . nicht anders dann das heylig Evangelium, und die leer Gottes verkünden sollen.
No printer, 1523 [R BNU III, 1683].

.1.15.   Ordnung der Censur. Unsern malern, büchtruckern, büch-
fürern . . . furthyn kein schmach oder laster büch
oder geschrifften (schreiben oder drucken).
No printer, 1524 [R BNU III, 1684].

.1.16.   So inn diszer sorgveltigen zeit, alle burgers frauwen
und kinder, des gleichen alle mann und frauwen personen
in iren häuszern und herberger blieben unnd nit under
die thuren, noch auff dis ganz gan sollen.
No printer, 1525 [R BNU III, 1685].

L2.1.17. Allen Burger, Angehörigen und Inwonern diser Statt,
          Geystlichen oder Weltlichen . . . so mit argwenig in
          Concubinen . . . haushalten das sie all . . . solchs
          ungebürlichen beysitz . . . entschlahen und in eynen
          erlichen standt . . . schicken.
          No printer, 1525 [AMS R/3, 126].

  .1.18. Alle Straszburg Burger aller uffrürischen und schmach
          worten sich enthalten solten.
          No printer, 1526 [R BNU III, 1681].

  .1.19. Nach dem sich . . . vil Secten und irrigen leere
          erheben ereügen, mit ettlichen personen die wider-
          teuffer genant, gepieten wir unser Bürgern das sy sich
          solgen bey inen husern herbergen etzen oder trencken
          noch underschleyff geben.
          No printer, 1527 [R BNU III, 1687], 1535 [AMS R/3,
              233].

  .1.20. Jungfrawe auf kein Chor gehen sollen . . . und hinden
          inn der kirchen bleiben sollen.
          No printer, 1527 [AMS R/3, 145].

  .1.21. Einladung zum Büchsenschutzen.
          No printer, 1528 [AMS R/3, 147].

  .1.22. Markt Ordnung. Wein and Fruchten sollen nicht vor
          Herbst und vor der Ernd verkaufft werden . . .
          Früchten, weyn, korn . . . nicht kauffen dweil die noch
          uff dem velde gestanden und gewachsen.
          No printer, 1529 [AMS R/30, 160], 1529 [R BNU III,
              1690], 1531 [AMS R/30, 199], 1532 [AMS R/30, 203],
              1533 [AMS R/3, 223], 1539 [R BNU III, 1703], 1546
              [R BNU III, 1714], 1552 [AMS R/5, 28], 1594 [AMS
              R/5, 192].

  .1.23. Burgeren und Burgers sünen keinen hern zu dienst zu
          ziehen, reiten oder von yemant sich bestellen lassen
          sollen, es sey zu rosz oder füsz.
          No printer, 1530 [R BNU III, 1692], 1530 [R
              BNU III, 1691], 1531 [R BNU III, 1694], 1535 [R BNU
              III, 1699], 1539 [R BNU III, 1702], 1542 [R BNU III,
              1707], 1543 [R BNU III, 1708], 1545 [R BNU III,
              1711], 1547 [R BNU III, 1718].

  .1.24. Unsern Burgern von kein Juden . . . nichts entlehen
          oder auffnemen.
          No printer, 1530 [AMS R/30, 178], 1539 [AMS R/3, 270],
              1570 [AMS R/5, 71].

  .1.25. Die Huszfuerer hinfurter keyn meel meer beuttelen,
          sonder eyn jeden syn gebeuttelt oder ungebeutelt meel

zu gutem brot bachen.
No printer, 1531 [R BNU III, 1693], 1532 [R BNU III, 1695].

L2.1.26. Hochziet Ordinanz . . . der arbeitenden mann . . . von der uberflüssig kosten zu schirmen . . . kein hochzeit bei keinem würt, gasthalter in oder ausserhalb in der Statt verdingen soll.
No printer, 1531 [AMS R/3, 187], 1544 [R BNU III, 1709], 1547 [R BNU III, 1717], 1550 [R BNU III, 1719], 1573 [AMS R/5, 94-101], 1586 [AMS R/5, 145], 1589 [AMS R/5, 155-57], 1595 [AMS R/5, 198-201].

.1.27. Das die verkauffer uber das geordnet kauffgeldt ein sonderlich beschwerlich fürlon und meszgeldt darauff geschlagen und one dasselbig die fruchte nit verkauffen.
No printer, 1532 [R BNU III, 1696].

.1.28. Büsstag . . . Samstag letzten dieses monats umb acht oren vor mittag zuhalten . . . andechtig Gebett in der kirchen Gottes . . . alles in kirche zu gehen . . . .
No printer, 1532 [AMS R/30, 208].

.1.29. Sontags Ordinanz . . . der Sontag in der Statt Straszburg keinerly handarbeit thun solle bey peen dreissig schilling . . . niemantz spazierung zu zeit der predig im Munster.
No printer, 1534 [AMS R/3, 227].

.1.30. Was die Alten herren . . . den zünfften daselbst uff iren stuben für gehalten haben. I. Mandat von dem Sontag. II. Mandat das sich die Burger der secten und fürnemlich der Widertäuffer entschlahen sollen. III. Mandat das die Burger ijre Kinder am sontag zu predig füren. IIII. Mandat von den Kirchen flagern und irem ampt . . . (im ganzen 10 verordnung).
J. Prüss II, 1535 [R BNU II, 1161].

.1.31. Ordinanz . . . das sich villerlai irrige Secten und Stritige meinung des Glaubens halb, erhaben . . . Darumb so vermanen wir alle das sie bei dem h. Evangelio bestendlich bleiben.
No printer, 1535 [R Bib. Mun., 556].

.1.32. Weinmarcks ordnung . . . alle wein vom land auff wagen oder kerchen herinn zu Marckt kommen, an kein ander ort dann auff den Weinmarckt gefüret werden.
No printer, 1535 [R BNU III, 1698], 1572 [R BNU III, 1724].

.1.33. Hochzeit in der statt zu halten wann der Kirchgang auszer der Statt gehalten worden verbot.

No printer, 1537 [R BNU III, 1701], 1570 [AMS R/5, 75].

L2.1.34. Hinfüro keyn Wurt noch Gasthalter uff den stuben in diser Statt und dem burckbann kein geschelschafft in iren heüsern oder uff den stuben annemen sollen.
No printer, 1537 [R BNU III, 1700].

.1.35. Widertauffer Mandaten . . . hinfüro alle die so solcher secten seind an leib und leben je nach gstalt der sachen thün straffen.
No printer, 1540 [R BNU III, 1705].

.1.36. Handtbüchs Ordinanz . . . Kein burger . . . zu fuss, oder zu Ross in burgbann statts Straszburg dheiner fewr oder handtbuchs abschiessen solle.
No printer, 1541 [R BNU III, 1706], 1587 [AMS R/5, 147].

.1.37. An Sontag . . . kein Gasthalter, Würt oder Hauptkann weden visch noch fleisch, gesotten noch gepraten, sonder allein wein, brot, kasz and obs geben sollen.
No printer, 1545 [R BNU III, 1710].

.1.38. Wie zu unser notturfft etlich Kriegsvolk zubewerben abfertigt. Ist darumb an jede was Stands oder Wesens die seind . . . sie wollen ihne an sollichem nit verhinderen.
No printer, 1546 [R BNU III, 1712].

.1.39. Allen und jeder Hauptkannen Gasthaltern und Offnen Würten verbotten und gebotten das sie durch sich selbs keine junge Spanferlin auff den Zunfftstuben in den Herbergen und Würtzheusern brüen sonder dieselben in das Gemein Brühausz tragen.
No printer, 1547 [R BNU III, 1713].

.1.40. Nach dem der Allmechtig das vergangen jar die Tëutsche Nation mit ganz schweren Kriegen heimgesücht hat . . . Der halben so gebieten von keinem burger weder bei den hochzeiten noch sonsten kein dantz gehalten werden.
No printer, 1547 [R BNU III, 1715].

.1.41. Hinfüro keiner harnasch, handtgewehr oder iehtzig anders so zu Kriegsgeschafften gehörig oder zu den-selben gebraucht werden mocht, auff keinen Musterplatz hinfüren.
No printer, 1547 [R BNU III, 1716].

.1.42. Als in dieser Statt offtermals zugetragen, das etliche Hëuser taufft, und etwa zwey, drey oder mehr zusammen brochen worden . . . so setzen und ordnen wir, kein

Hausz von niemanden zusammen grbrochen oder zu einem
Hausz gesesz gericht und gemacht werden sollen.
   No printer, 1552 [R BNU III, 1720], 1582 [AMS R/5,
     134b].

L2.1.43. Auff Romischer Keiserlicher Maiestet und der Stenden
des Heiligen Reich aussgangen Policey . . . in vergang-
nem Augsburgischen Reichs und Wormbsischen Reinischen
kreis abschieden.
   W. Rihel, 1552 [AMS R/5, 8–26].

.1.44. Constitution und satzung . . . wie es mit dem
ungeerbten ussgohn hinfürer gehalten werden soll.
   No printer, 1552 [AMS R/5, 34–36].

.1.45. Allen und jeden unsere Burgern und Einwonern . . . das
sie solliche ire eigene oder gelehenete Hëuser oder
Hofe . . . keinem Frembden man oder Weibs personen die
nit Burger und Zünfftig sein.
   No printer, 1554 [AMS R/5, 38], 1575 [AMS R/5, 103].

.1.46. Hinfürther alle Karcher so Stein, Ziegel, Kalck, Sandt,
Grundt, Leimen und Gerör in die Statt oder auss der
Statt füren werden Nachfolgende belonung . . . .
   No printer, 1555 [AMS R/5, 42].

.1.47. Ordnung der Statt Straszburg inn wölchen grad die ehe
der Blütfreundschafft oder Schwagerschafften halben
zugelassen oder verboten sein soll.
   No printer, 1560 [R BNU I, 623].

.1.48. Zu wissen . . . der Kornfrüchten erschinen so hat man
doch bishero nit allein kein abschlag sonder mehrere
und weitere Theurung und Auffschlag gespürt. Das die
oberkeit disz Lands under Elsass mit ringer deren
enderung entschlossen.
   No printer, 1562 [R BNU III, 1721], 1571 [AMS R/5,
     82].

.1.49. Der Steinmetzen Brüderschaft Ordnungen und Articul.
   No printer, 1563 [R Bib. Mun., 1592].

.1.50. Decret der Ehe belangend.
   No printer, 1565 [R Nfp, 1498].

.1.51. Neuwe Ordnung wider die Heimlichen Eheverlobnüssen.
   Chr. Mylius I, 1565 [R Bib. Mun., 1591].

.1.52. Durch die unerhörte langwirige harte Kelte . . . hinfüro und so lang wir solches nit wider auffthün und
erlauben, einich wein, es sey lützel oder vil, auff
Mehrschatz widerumb zu verkauffen.
   No printer, 1565 [R BNU III, 1722].

L2.1.53. Der Pfarrherr . . . dem Volck oder Gemein auff der
          Cantzel fürhalten . . . der grausam und erschrocklich
          des Christlichen Namen und Glaubens Erbfeind der Turck.
          No printer, 1566 [AMS R/5, 59-60].

 .1.54.   Hinfüro alle unsere Burger . . . niemands aussgenommen,
          keinen Studenten der komme gleich frembd her . . .
          zubehausung bringe ihn zuvor . . . bei dem Rectors
          inschreiben lassen.
          No printer, 1568 [AMS R/5, 62].

 .1.55.   Demnach der Allmechtige güttige Gott vätterliche straff
          der erschrockenlichen Kranckheit der Pestilenz . . . so
          haben wir gebieten Das hinfüro wider bey Hochzeiten
          noch sonsten keinen dantz halten.
          No printer, 1569 [R BNU III, 1723].

 .1.56.   Junge döchter nicht allein vor dem ehelichen offentlich
          Kirchengang, sonder zu zeitten auch zuvor sie ehelichen
          verlobt worden . . . ire Jungfrawschafft verloren . . .
          So Mandieren wir allen das sie sich enthalten nach
          unserer Constitution und Ordnungen in der heyligen Ehe.
          No printer, 1570 [AMS R/5, 73].

 .1.57.   Verzeichnus was vermög des Heyligen Romischen Reichs
          Müntzordnung von 1559, 1566, und 1570 Jarn für Silberin
          ung Guldine Müntz, auch in welchem Preis und Werth die
          hinfüro zu nemen und geben zugelassen.
          No printer, 1571 [AMS R/5, 76-80].

 .1.58.   Markt Ordinanz . . . Niemand zu kauffen sonder was sie
          für die woche bedürfen.
          No printer, 1573 [AMS R/5, 87].

 .1.59.   Gemeine Ständ und oberkeiten dises Land under Elsass,
          . . . bey einander . . . ein gleichmessige ordnung
          zugeben . . . einer gemeinen Landsmetzger oder Fleisch-
          ordnung einhelliglich verglichen.
          No printer, 1574 [R BNU III, 1725].

 .1.60.   Bevelch gegeben, Das an dem Ein und Aussfluss der
          Wasser disser Statt ein jeder bey den geordneten
          Wachten zuvor anfahren . . . .
          No printer, 1575 [AMS R/5, 105].

 .1.61.   Wir mit beschwerden zusehen . . . mit was unbescheiden-
          heit frembde Leüt, auch etwann Hohes Stands in diser
          Statt allhie. Wir auff allen Zünfften anzukunden . . .
          Wann die Frembden hohes oder niders Stand personen
          ankommen, Ihnen nach eines jeden Stand und gelegenheit
          alle Ehr, Freundschafft . . . erzeigen und beweisen.
          No printer, 1576 [AMS R/5, 107].

L2.1.62. Reben . . . etwas schaden empfangen . . . allen wein
          verkaufft von xx tag April bis Johannis des Teuffers
          tag . . . allher inn dise Statt bringen und lüffern
          lassen.
          No printer, 1576 [AMS R/5, 109].

   .1.63. Müntzordnung . . . Niderlandische Thaler vil zü ring
          befunden . . . virwarnung da einer dem andern inn
          bezalung . . . straff nicht allein mit Confiscation.
          No printer, 1578 [AMS R/5, 111].

   .1.64. Kurtzer Ausszug . . . so hinfürter Jarlich auff den
          Zunften neben anderen Constitutionen und ordnung für-
          gelesen werden.
          No printer, 1579 (AMS R/5, 112-16].

   .1.65. Müntzordnung. Dieweil . . . vil andere mehr neuwe
          Guldene und Silberne ungerechte Müntsorten
          eingeschleifft werden, so allen unsern Burgern so bald
          solche neuwe Müntzsorten zur hand komen, eyn stuck oder
          zwei darvon unsern geordneten des Pfennigthurm liefere,
          proben darvon zu machen.
          No printer, 1580 [AMS R/5, 123].

   .1.66. Verbieten allen das sich des Pulvermachens understehn
          noch annemmen soll.
             No printer, 1581 [R Nfp, 1025], 1581 [R BNU III,
             1726].

   .1.67. Constitution . . . Ehebruchs . . . erinnert, Straff
          gescherpfft.
          No printer, 1581 [AMS R/5, 129].

   .1.68. Zwischen etlichen under euch . . . strietige Religions
          Puncten . . . schrifften inn Lateinischer und Teutsch-
          ersprach auff den gassen gefunden worden . . . lassen
          wir obgemelt der solche Schmach schrifft findet . . .
          das er den selben dem regierenden Ammeister anzeigen
          . . . darzu 100 Thaler zu verehrung gegeben werden.
          No printer, 1581 [AMS R/5, 127].

   .1.69. Als unsere Burger und Handelsleut so mit dem Häring
          handlen supplicando fürgebracht Wie das ein falsch
          erdicht geschrey auszgebrachtet als ob der Häring nicht
          gerecht und gut, sonder kleine schlangen darinne das
          man dessen ohne gefahr und schaden nit möchte geniessen.
          So ist und newlicher tagen von unsern güten freunden
          Burgermaister und Raht der Stat Cöllen eben dises
          gescheffts halben zugeschriben.
          No printer, 1582 [R BNU III, 1727].

   .1.70. Gebietten unsern Burgern, Burgersonen, Studiosen,

Inwohnern, angehörigen, aussheischens aussforderns und (solches) sich gentzlich enthalten.
No printer, 1583 [AMS R/5, 137].

L2.1.71. Gebieten allen das die hiezwischen dato und nechtskünfftigem Sanct Johans des Teuffers tag . . . (den) ausstand auff dem Stall richtig machen und bezalen sollen.
No printer, 1585 [R Nfp, 1026].

.1.72. Allen unsern Burgern, Angehörige . . . weib, kind, Dienstknecht, Lehrjungen . . . auff die Sontag und gewohnliche Bettag beiden Predigten besuchen.
No printer, 1585 [AMS R/5, 141].

.1.73. Acta und Handlung der Kais. Commissarien belangend der Evang. Capitularn . . . .
R. Freyen, 1586 [R Bib. Mun., 352].

.1.74. Dass sie das kupffer weiss . . . und solche Arbeyt von Geschirren, Schawpfennig, Beschlag machen . . . Dass es das ansehen als ob es just und gut silber were.
No printer, 1587 [AMS R/5, 148].

.1.75. Hinfüro kein frembden Metzger auff dem allhieigen Marckt, weder Kölben, Schaaf, Böck, . . . einzukauffen macht haben.
No printer, 1588 [R BNU III, 1728], 1593 [AMS R/5, 181].

.1.76. Wie die Sonntag und Monatliche Grosse Bettag soll gehalten werden.
No printer, 1589 [AMS R/5, 160-62].

.1.77. Erkandtnusz, das Ganthausz und Stattgericht belangend.
No printer, 1590 [R BNU II, 795].

.1.78. Famoslibell . . . Keiner, er sey was stands, ansehens . . . Pasquillos, Famosschrifften, Schandgedicht . . . zumachen, zudichten.
No printer, 1590 [AMS R/5, 167], 1592 [AMS R/5, 179].

.1.79. Falliment undt Frönungs Ordnanz . . . Dasz dann alle Gläubiger auff den angesetzten Termin durch sich selbst oder ihre gevollmächtigte Anwälte erscheinen bey verlust ihrer forderung.
No printer, 1591 [R BNU III, 1730].

.1.80. Niemand . . . einige Müntzen, es seyen Reichs oder andere aussländische Sorten auff oder einwechseln, trahieren, brechen, granalieren.
No printer, 1593 [AMS R/5, 182], 1593 [AMS R/5, 183], 1596/97 [AMS R/5, 203].

L2.1.81.   Ordnung welchermassen hinfüro frembde mannspersonen mit
           witwen und ledigen töchtern veheürath werden sollen.
           No printer, 1594 [R BNU III, 1679].

  .1.82.   Constitution und Satzung wie der Ehebruch und andere
           Unzucht hinfüro gestrafft werden sollen.
           No printer, 1594 [AMS R/5, 186-90; R BNU I, 584].

  .1.83.   Verordnet. Auch unserm Hauszherrn im Kauffhausz
           aufferlegt und bevolhen die Handelsleute Frembd und
           Heymische so Zollbare Wahren allher bringen allhie
           kauffen oder durchführen wöllen zubefragen was es für
           wahren und in was priesz dieselbige verhandelt worden
           seien.
           No printer, 1594 [R BNU III, 1732].

  .1.84.   Der arme Burgerschafft zum handarbeit gewinnen . . .
           wir haben vor wenig jahren das Barchant weben auff ein
           versuchens zubestellen angefangen. Haben wir ermelten
           solchen Barchant zu continuiren und in ein recht wesen
           zubringen. Niemands anders Barchant zu machen . . . .
           No printer, 1594 [AMS R/5, 194; R BNU III, 1731].

  .1.85.   Müntzordnung für Weiynachten Mess.
           No printer, 1597 [AMS R/5, 204].

  .1.86.   Ernewerte Ordnungen . . . von Gerichten und Gericht-
           lichen Processen.
           No printer, 1598 [AMS R/5, 206-29].

L3. NOTARIAL MANUALS.

L3.1.1.   Mennicken, Carolus, Formulae Epistolarum.
               J. Grüninger, 1485 [R Nfp Inc., 473], 1486 [R Nfp
               Inc., 474], 1490 [R Nfp Inc., 477].
               M. Schott, 1487 [R BNU Inc., 295].
               G. Husner, 1493 [R Nfp Inc., 478].

  .1.2.   Formulare Instrumentorum Nec non Ars Notariatus cum
           Tabulis subiunctis.
               J. Knobloch, 1504 [S VII, 7], 1516 [S VII, 124].

  .1.3.   Hertzog, Samson, Notariats Gemeine Eynleitung, sampt
           dem Formular und zweyen unterschiedlichen Register.
               L. Zetzner, 1597 [R Bib. Mun., 1205].

  .1.4.   Hertzog, Samson, Notariats von Contracten auszfürliche
           und in Geistlichen und Weltlichen Rechten gegründte
           Underrichtung.
               L. Zetzner, 1599 [R Bib. Mun., 1207].

L3.1.5.   Hertzog, Samson, <u>Notariats von Testamentum unnd andern</u>
           <u>letsten Willen unterrichtung</u>.
                L. Zetzner, 1599 [R Bib. Mun., 1206].

LITERATURE OF ANTIQUITY

A1. Latin Classics.

      1. Catonis Disticha.
      2. Quintus Horatius Flaccus.
      3. Publius Vergilius Maro.
      4. Other Latin Poets.
      5. Other Latin Authors.
      6. Marcus Tullius Cicero.
      7. Publius Ovidius Naso.

A2. Greek Classics.

      1. Aesopus.
      2. Other Greek Authors.
      3. Homerus.
      4. Plato.
      5. Aristotles.

A3. Greek and Latin Classics in German.

A4. Classical Drama.

      1. Publius Terentius Afer.
      2. Titus Maccius Plautus.
      3. Other Dramatists.
      4. Classical Plays in German.

A5. Classical Historians.

      1. Historical Works in Latin or Greek.
      2. Translations of Classical Historians.

A1. LATIN CLASSICS.

1. CATONIS DISTICHA.

A1.1.1. Maralissimus cum commento Roberti de Euromodio, vulgo
Disticha Catonis.
M. Flach I, 1487 [R BNU Inc., 129].
J. Grüninger, 1488 [R Nfp Inc., 179].

.1.2. Libri morales cum expositione alemanica.
J. Prüss I, 1499 [S III A, 28].

.1.3. Praecepta moralia recognita atque interpretata ab
Erasmo Roterodamo. Mimi Publiani. Septem sapientum
illustres sententiae. Institutio hominis christiani
uersib. hexametris. per Erasm. Roterodamum.
M. Schürer, 1515 [S VIII, 167], 1516 [S VIII, 184],
October 1516 [R Nfp 1313; S VIII, 196], November
1517 [R Nfp, 1314; S VIII, 222], September 1518 [S
VIII, 234], 1519 [S VIII, 251].
J. Knobloch, 1520 [S VII, 196].

.1.4. Moralia cum scholiis auctis Erasmi Roteroda.
Apophthegmata Graeciae sapientum interprete Erasmo.
J. Knobloch, 1523 [S VII, 262].
C. Egenolff, 1530 [R Nfp, 1317].
Chr. Mylius II, 1574 [R Nfp, 1318], 1578 [R Nfp,
1319].

.1.5. De Moribus nomine Catonis inscripta (M. Corderius, ed.).
G. Messerschmidt, 1540 [BM 827.d.36.6].

.1.6. Ethica. Una cum Lemmatibus et praefatione Joannis
Joannis Sturmii scholis Argentinensibus.
J. Rihel, 1565 [Rott, 92].
No printer, 1587 [Rott, 92a].

2. QUINTUS HORATIUS FLACCUS.

A1.2.1. Opera cum quibusdam Annotationibus Imaginibusque
pubcherrimis aptisque ad Odarum concentus et sententias.
J. Grüninger, 1498 [S I, 34].

.2.2. Liber Epistolarum eiusdem de arte poetica.
M. Schürer, 1514 [S VIII, 128], 1520 [S VII, 199].

.2.3. Sermonum seu Satyrarum Libri Duo.
M. Schürer, 1514 [S VIII, 142], 1517 [S VIII, 207].

.2.4. Epodon Liber. Eiusdem, de arte Poetica. Item
Epistolarum Libri Duo.

M. Schürer, 1515 [S VIII, 151], 1516 [S VIII, 202],
        1520 [S VIII, 255].

A1.2.5. Odarum. Libri IV.
        M. Schürer, 1516 [S VIII, 182], 1517 [S VIII, 209],
        1520 [S VIII, 261].

   .2.6. Collinus, Matthaeus (Matous Kollin Z. Choteriny),
        Harmoniae univocae in odas Horatianas . . . collectae
        et moris piorum versuum exemplis illustratae.
        No printer, 1568 [R Nfp, 1419].

   3. PUBLIUS VERGILIUS MARO.

A1.3.1. Opera.
        J. Grüninger, 1502 [S I, 60].
        J. Knobloch, 1520 [S VII, 200], 1527 [R BNU IV, 2422].

   .3.2. Bucolica cum commento Hermanni Torrentini.
        J. Knobloch, 1508 [S VII supp., 329; R Nfp, 3425],
        1510 [S VII, 71], 1512 [S VII, 79], 1516 [S VII,
        117].
        M. Schürer, 1517 [S VIII, 220].
        B. Fabricius, 1556 [R BNU IV, 2423].

   .3.3. Georgicorum . . . cum novo commentario Hermanni
        Torrentini.
        J. Knobloch, 1508 [S VII, 51], 1509 [S VII, 63],
        1513 [R BNU IV, 2416], 1513 [S VII, 86a; R BNU IV,
        2417].
        M. Schürer, 1515 [S VIII, 172].

   .3.4. Aeneis cum familiari expositione.
        J. Knobloch, 1509 [S VII, 57], 1515 [S VII, 92],
        1525 [S VII, 305].
        M. Schürer, 1515 [S VIII, 159], 1520 [S VIII, 258].

   .3.5. Opuscula cum familiari expositione. Culex, Dire,
        Aethna, Cyris . . . .
        J. Knobloch, 1509 [S VII, 56].

   .3.6. Bucolicorum Libellus.
        M. Schürer, 1515 [S VIII, 158], 1520 [S VII, 259].

   4. OTHER LATIN POETS.

A1.4.1. Juvenalis, Decimus Junius, Liber Moreti docens mores
        in supplementum illorum . . . per Sebastianum Brant.
        J. Knobloch, 1508 [S VII, 50].

   .4.2. Lucanus, Marcus Annaeus, Pharsaliae seu belli civilis

libri.
 J. Prüss I, 1509 [S III A, 71].

A1.4.3.   Juvenalis, Decimus Junius, Inter Latinos satyrographos
           consummatissimi Satyrae: emaculatius impressae.
            J. Knobloch, 1513 [S VII, 86], 1518 [S VII, 150],
              1527 [S VII, 320].

  .4.4.   Martialis, Marcus Valerius, Epigrammata (Ottmar
           Nachtigall, ed.).
            J. Knobloch, 1515 [S VII, 99].

  .4.5.   Persius Flaccus, Aulus, Satyrarum opus.
            J. Knobloch, 1517 [S VII, 145].

  .4.6.   Lucanus, Marcus Annaeus, Epitaphium.
            J. Knobloch, 1520 [S VII, 198].

  .4.7.   Martialis, Marcus Valerius, Epigrammaton, Libri XV.
            L. Zetzner, 1595 [R BNU III, 1493].

   5. OTHER LATIN AUTHORS.

A1.5.1.   Seneca, Lucius Annaeus, Proverbia (actually by
           Publilius Syrus).
            J. Prüss I, n.d. [R BNU Inc., 431].

  .5.2.   Symmachus, Quintus Aurelius, Epistolae familiares,
           Item Laudini Equitis hierosolymitani in epistolas Turci
           magni traductio.
            J. Schott, 1510 [S II B, 15].
            J. Grüninger, 1510 [S I, 117].

  .5.3.   Plinius Secundus, C., Epistolarum libri decem.
            M. Schürer, 1514 [S VIII, 125; R BNU III, 1890].
            U. Morhard, 1521 [S IV Mor., 5].

  .5.4.   Statius, Publius Papinius, Achilleidos, Libri Duo.
           Item. Vita Authoris a Petro Crinito descripta.
            M. Schürer, 1515 [S VIII, 157].

  .5.5.   Apuleius, Lucius, Floridum Libri IV. De Dogmate
           Platonis.
            M. Schürer, 1516 [S VIII, 193].

  .5.6.   Gellius, Aulus, Noctium Atticarum libri undeviginti.
            J. Knobloch, 1517 [S VII, 140], 1521 [S VII, 213].
            M. Schürer, 1517 [S VIII, 214].

  .5.7.   Valerius Flaccus, Caius, Argonauticon. Libri Octo, à
           Philippo Engentino emendati.
            J. Knobloch, 1525 [S VII, 296].

Al.5.8.   Sallustius Crispus, C., and Curtius Rufus, Quintus,
           Flores, selecti per Huldericum Huttenum equidem
           eiusdemque scholiis non indoctis illustrati.
           J. Herwagen, 1528 [R BNU IV, 2112].

   .5.9.   Asconius Pedianus, Quintus, Fragmentum Commentariorum
           . . . in orationes aliquot M. Tullii Ciceronis.
           J. Albrecht, 1535 [R BNU I, 89].

   .5.10. Quintilianus, Marcus Fabius, Epitome seu compendium
           institutionum oratoriarum.
           No printer, 1568 [R Nfp, 3060].

   .5.11. Aurelius Antoninus, Marcus, De vita sua Lib. XII. Ad
           animi tranquillitatem fortuna tam secunda quam adversa
           parandam per quam utiles. Antonini liberalis
           metamorphoseon collectanea. Phlegontis Tralliani de
           rebus miris.
           L. Zetzner, 1590 [R BNU I, 69].

   .5.12. Caesar, C. Julius, Omnia quae extant. Ex Bibliotheca
           olim Fulvii Ursinii.
           L. Zetzner, 1596 [Greiner].

     6.   MARCUS TULLIUS CICERO.

Al.6.1.   Questionum Libri Quinque.
           M. Schürer, 1511 [S VIII, 65], 1514 [S VIII, 144],
             1516 [S VIII, 188].
           U. Morhard, 1522 [S IV Mor., 8].

   .6.2.   De Officiis, Libri tres, Cum Indice Auctorum,
           adagiorumque suo loco citatorum.
           M. Schürer, 1512 [R BNU I, 490], 1516 [S VIII, 201],
             1521 [S VIII, 264].
           J. Knobloch, 1521 [S VII, 212], 1522 [S VII, 240].

   .6.3.   Epistole Familiares cum Ascensianis introductiunculis
           recognitis et auctis & argumentis illustratis.
           M. Schürer, 1512 [S VIII, 68], 1515 [S VIII, 149],
             1519 [S VIII, 247].
           J. Knobloch, 1525 [R BNU I, 498].

   .6.4.   Opera. De Officiis. Libri tres. De amicitia. Liber
           unus. De Senectute. Liber unus. Item. Paradoxa.
           M. Schürer, 1512 [S VIII, 78].
           M. Schürer, 1519 [S VIII, 244]. (Erasmus, ed.)

   .6.5.   De Amicitia. De Senectute. Paradoxa.
           M. Schürer, 1513 [S VIII, 112], 1515 [S VIII, 156],
             1516 [S VIII, 192], 1521 [R Nfp, 1345].
           J. Knobloch, 1520 [S VII, 203], 1522 [S VII, 242].

A1.6.6.   Rhetoricorum Libri IV ad Herennium.
          M. Schürer, 1515 [S VIII, 168], 1518 [S VIII, 226].
          J. Knobloch, 1527 [S VII, 313].

.6.7.   Ad Quintum Fratrem Dialogi de oratore. Eiusdem Orator
         ad Brutum.
          J. Knobloch, 1524 [S VII, 278].

.6.8.   Orationum volumen primum.
          J. Knobloch, 1524 [S VII, 274].

.6.9.   Orationum volumen secundum.
          J. Knobloch, 1524 [S VII, 275].

.6.10.   Ad C. Trebatium Topica. Item, De participatione
         oratoria Dialogus. Item De optimo Genere oratorum.
          J. Knobloch, 1527 [S VII, 314].

.6.11.   Oratio pro A. Cecinna cum enarrationibus Bartholomaei
         Latomi nunc primum aeditis.
          Cr. Mylius, 1539 [R BNU I, 502].

.6.12.   In hoc volumine haec continentur. Rhetoricorum ad C.
         Herenneum lib. IIII. De inventione lib. II. Eiusdem de
         oratore ad Quintum fratrem lib. IIII. . . . Post
         Naugerianam & Victorianam correctionem emandati (J.
         Sturm, ed.).
          W. Rihel, 1540 [R BNU I, 504], 1548 [R Nfp, 1384].
          J. & T. Rihel, 1557 [R BNU I, 514].
          J. Rihel, 1564 [R BNU I, 523], 1568 [R BNU I, 528],
            1570 [Rott, 42g], 1574 [Rott, 42h], 1578 [R BNU I,
            535].

6.13.   Orationum Volumina tria. Post postremam Naugerianam, &
         Victorianam (J. Sturm, ed.).
          W. Rihel, 1540 [R BNU I, 503], 1544 [R BNU I, 507],
            1550 [R BNU I, 511].
          J. Rihel, 1558 [R BNU, 516], 1563 [R BNU I, 521],
            1569 [R BNU I, 529], 1574 [R BNU I, 531], 1578 [R
            BNU I, 534].

.6.14.   Orationum Volumen Secundum (J. Sturm, ed.).
          W. Rihel, 1540 [Rott, 41], 1550 [Rott, 41b].
          J. Rihel, 1558 [R BNU I, 516], 1563 [Rott, 41e].

.6.15.   Orationum Volumen Tertium (J. Sturm, ed.).
          W. Rihel, 1540 [Rott, 41], 1544 [R BNU I, 508], 1550
            [Rott, 41b].
          J. Rihel, 1558 [R BNU I, 516], 1564 [Rott, 41e],
            1569 [R BNU I, 529], 1578 [Rott, 41h].

.6.16.   Epistolarum Volumen Primum (J. Sturm, ed.).
          W. Rihel, 1541 [Rott, 49; R Nfp, 1347], 1543 [Rott,

49a], 1549 [R BNU I, 509].
J. Rihel, 1559 [R BNU I, 517], 1563 [Rott, 49f],
1565 [R BNU I, 524], 1574 [Rott, 49j], 1575 [R Nfp,
1355].

A1.6.17. Alterum epistolarum volumen (J. Sturm, ed.).
W. Rihel, 1541 [Rott, 49; R BNU I, 505; R Nfp, 1348],
1543 [Rott, 49a], 1550 [R BNU I, 509].
J. Rihel, 1558 [R BNU I, 515], 1563 [Rott, 49f],
1568 [R BNU I, 526], 1572 [R Nfp, 1354], 1574 [Rott,
49j], 1575 [R BNU I, 533], 1582 [R Nfp, 1356].

.6.18. Librorum philosophicorum volumen primum post
Naugerianam et Victorianam (J. Sturm, ed.).
W. Rihel, 1541 [R BNU I, 506], 1549 [R BNU I, 510].
J. Rihel, 1558 [Rott, 46c], 1564 [Rott, 46d], 1569
[R BNU I, 530], 1574 [R BNU I, 532].

.6.19. Librorum philosphicorum volumen secundum (J. Sturm,
ed.).
W. Rihel, 1541 [R BNU I, 506], 1549 [R BNU I, 510].
J. Rihel, 1558 [Rott, 46c], 1564 [Rott, 46d], 1569
[R BNU I, 530], 1574 [R BNU I, 532].

.6.20. De Officiis Libri III. Cato major, sive de senectute.
Laelius, sive de amicitia. Somnium Scipionis, Paradoxa,
Sylloge lib. de Repub. (J. Sturm, ed.).
W. Rihel, 1541 [R BNU I, 486; Rott, 47], 1545 [Rott,
47c; Greiner], 1553 [R BNU I, 513].
J. Rihel, 1559 [Rott, 47h], 1564 [R BNU I, 522],
1574 [Greiner; Rott, 47j], 1575 [Rott, 47k], 1579
[Rott, 471], 1582 [Rott, 47m].

.6.21. Opus de Officiis, cum commentariis Viti Amerbachii.
Cr. Mylius, 1545 [R Nfp, 1368].
J. Rihel, 1582 [R Nfp, 1369].

.6.22. Duae orationes, altera pro M. Caelio, altera pro T.
Annio Milone, ad puerilem ac scholasticum usum selectae,
cum scholiis Joachimi Camerarii.
W. Rihel, 1550 [R Nfp, 1376].

.6.23. Pro A. Cluentio habita Oratio.
W. Rihel, 1550 [R Nfp, 1372].

.6.24. Epistolarum libri tres (J. Sturm and Val. Eyrthraeus,
eds.).
J. Frölich, 1550 [R Nfp, 1351; Rott, 33b].
Chr. Mylius I, 1560 [R BNU I, 518; Rott, 33e].
J. Rihel, 1596 [Rott, 33j].

.6.25. Epistolarum libri quatuor . . . puerili educationi
confecti (J. Sturm, ed.).

J. Rihel, 1560 [R Nfp, 1352], 1562 [R Nfp, 1353], 1572 [Rott, 33h].

A1.6.26. Epistolarum Familiarum Libri XVI. ex eloquentissimorum oratorum castigationibus recogniti (Paul Manutius, ed.).
J. Rihel & S. Emmel, 1560 [R BNU I, 519].

.6.27. Epistola scripta ad Q. fratrem, pro schola Argentoratensi.
J. Rihel, 1560 [R Nfp, 1383].

.6.28. Orationes tres elegantissimae, pro Q. Ligario, Lege Manilia, & Rege Deiotaro, pro Schola Argentinensi selectae.
J. Rihel, 1562 [R BNU I, 520].

.6.29. Verrina sexta (J. Sturm, ed.).
J. Rihel, ca. 1565 [Rott, 88], ca. 1570 [R Nfp, 1392].

.6.30. Orationes duo.
J. Rihel, 1567 [R Nfp, 1377].

.6.31. M.T. Scipionis ex sexto libro de Repub. Scipionis Somnium, una cum argumento Lud. Vivis & Scholiis brevibus.
S. Emmel, 1567 [R Nfp, 1388].

.6.32. Oratio pro P. Sextio, in usum Academiae Argentinensis separatim excusa (Paul Manutius, ed.).
S. Emmel, 1567 [R Nfp, 1373].

.6.33. Epitheta, antitheta et adiuneta.
T. Rihel, ca. 1570 [R Bib. Mun., 721].

.6.34. Philosophicorum librorum pars prima (D. Lambinus, ed.).
J. Rihel & J. Dupuys, 1572 [R Nfp, 1381].

.6.35. Philosophicorum librorum pars secunda (D. Lambinus, ed.).
J. Rihel & J. Dupuys, 1572 [R Nfp, 1381].

.6.36. Opera omnia quae exstant . . . Fragmenta omnia quae exstant (D. Lambinus, ed.).
Volume II, Orationum Volumen primum.
Volume IV, Orationum Volumen III.
Volume V, Epistolarum ad Familiareis, Libri XVI.
Volume VI, Epistolarum ad Atticum, Libri XVI. Eiusdem Epistolarum ad Q. Fratrem, Lib. IIII.
Volume VII, Philosophicorum Librorum pars prima.
Volume VIII, Philosophicorum pars secunda.
Volume IX, Philosophicorum pars tertia, . . . De Officiis libros tres.
J. Rihel & J. Dupuys, 1581 [R BNU I, 536].

A1.6.37.   Ex . . . Orationibus Loci aliquot Communes, eum in
            finem selecti atque explicati ut eorundem tractandi
            ratio appareat (Melchior Junius, ed.).
            L. Zetzner, 1594 [R BNU I, 537].

   .6.38.   Resolutio brevis orationum . . . secundum causarum
            genera, Orationum partes, materias in eloquentiae
            studiosorum gratiam ea potissimum de causa instituta
            (Melchior Junius, ed.).
            J. Rihel, 1594 [R BNU I, 538].

   .6.39.   Selectarum Epistolarum . . . Familiaribus, volumen
            primum (Melchior Junius, ed.).
            J. Rihel, 1597 [R Nfp, 1357].

   .6.40.   Selectarum Epistolarum . . . Familiaribus, et aliis:
            Volumen II (M. Junius, ed.).
            J. Rihel, 1597 [R Nfp, 1358].

   .6.41.   Selectarum Epistolarum . . . Familiaribus et aliis:
            Volumen III (M. Junius, ed.).
            J. Rihel, 1597 [R Nfp, 1359].

     7.   PUBLIUS OVIDIUS NASO.

A1.7.1.   De Remedio amoris, Libri Duo. De Philomela, Elegia.
            M. Schürer, n.d. [S VIII, 267; R BNU III, 1740], 1514
            [R BNU III, 1742].

   .7.2.   Heroidum Epistolae. Auli Sabini Epistolae tres.
            M. Schürer, 1514 [S VIII, 135], 1518 [S VIII, 229],
            1520 [S VIII, 257].

   .7.3.   Metamorphoseon, libri XV.
            J. Schott, 1515 [S II B, 29].
            M. Schürer, 1515 [S VIII, 161].
            J. Knobloch, 1519 [S VII, 179], 1522 [S VII, 235],
            1525 [S VII, 295].

   .7.4.   Fastorum. Libri Sex. Vita authoris.
            M. Schürer, 1515 [S VIII, 160], 1519 [R BNU III,
            1745].

   .7.5.   De tristibus Libri Quinque.
            M. Schürer, 1515 [R BNU III, 1744], 1520 [S VIII,
            256].

   .7.6.   De Ponto. Liber IV.
            M. Schürer, 1515 [S VIII, 154].

   .7.7.   Heroidum Epistolae. Amorum Libri (J. Hervagius, ed.).
            J. Knobloch, 1522 [BM 237a.15].

A2. GREEK CLASSICS.

  1. AESOPUS.

A2.1.1.   Vita et Fabulae.
          H. Knoblochtzer, 1481 [R Nfp Inc., 7].

  .1.2.   Moralisatus cum bono commento et glosa interlineari.
          J. Prüss II, after 1500 [R Nfp, 759], ca. 1505 [BM
             12304.ee.41; R Nfp, 761], 1516 [BM G.7721.1],
             1517 [BM 12305.f.9].
          J. Knobloch, 1508 [R Nfp, 760].

  .1.3.   Esopi vatis ingeniosissimi fabulae adamussim
          moralisatae: commentariolo & familiari cum glossemate
          nuper elimatius exaratae.
          No printer, 1513 [R BNU I, 92].

  .1.4.   Fabellae quaedam Aesopi Graecae ad puerilem educationem
          in gymnasio Argentoratense selectae.
          W. Rihel, after 1535 [R BNU I, 91], 1541 [R BNU I,
             101], 1543 [R BNU I, 102].

  .1.5.   Fabulae Iam denuo multo emandatius quam antea aeditae.
          Autore Joach. Camerario Pabergensi.
          J. Frölich, 1558 [R Nfp, 756].
          Chr. Mylius I, 1562 [R Nfp, 757].

  .1.6.   Fabellae . . . quaedam notiores et in Scholis usitate.
          Chr. Mylius II, 1572 [R BNU I, 103].

  2. OTHER GREEK AUTHORS.

A2.2.1.   Xenocrates, De morte. Interprete Marsilii Ficini.
          J. Knobloch, 1507 [S VII, 33].

  .2.2.   Subnotata hic continentur. Magni Athanasii in psalmos
          opusculum. Enchiridion Epicteti stoici. Basilii oratio
          de inuidia. Plutarchus de differentia inter odium et
          inuidiam. Tabula Cebetis Thebani (Preface by T. Wolf).
          M. Schürer, 1508 [S VIII, 1].

  .2.3.   In decem Ethicorum Libros Aristotelis. . . . Leonardi
          Aretini Dialogus de Moribus. . . . Xenophontis Dialogus
          de Economia (Jacques Le Fèvre d'Etaples, ed.).
          J. Grüninger, 1511 [S I, 120].

  .2.4.   Pythagoras, Hieroclis stoici in aurea Pythagorae
          carmina commentarius.
          M. Schürer, 1511 [S VIII, 50].

  .2.5.   Plutarchus, Stoici ac viri clarissimi De his qui tarde

umine corripiuntur Libellus.
M. Schürer, 1514 [S VIII, 132].

A2.2.6.   Isocrates, Ad Demonicum Eiusdem oratio de gubernando regno ad Nicoclem.
J. Knobloch, 1515 [S VII, 102].

.2.7.   Fabulae Graecarum (Aleander, ed.).
M. Schürer, 1515 [S VIII, 173].

.2.8.   Collectanea sacrosancta, graece discere cupientibus non aspernanda (Ottmar Nachtigall [Luscinus], ed.).
J. Schott, 1515 [S II B, 32].

.2.9.   Senarii Graecanici quingenti et eo amplius versi (Ottmar Nachtigall [Luscinius], ed.).
J. Knobloch, 1515 [S VII, 101].

.2.10.   In hoc opere continentur. Hesiodi ascraei duo libri Georgicon . . . Catonis Romani moralia instituta. Tabula Cebetis Thebani (Ottmar Nachtigall, ed.).
J. Knobloch, 1515 [S VII, 103].

.2.11.   Lucianus Samosatensis, Deorum dialgoi numero. 70. una cum interpretatione e regione latina: nusquam antea impressi.
J. Schott, 1515 [S II B, 31].

.2.12.   Plutarchus, De Philosophorum Placitis.
M. Schürer, 1516 [S VIII, 191].

.2.13.   Palaephatus, Opusculum de non credendis fabulosis narrationibus.
M. Schürer, 1517 [S VIII, 206].

.2.14.   Lucianus Samosatensis, Ex Luciano quaedam iam recens traducta. Somnium. Adversus eum qui inquit etc. Nigrinus. Caucasus.
J. Knobloch, 1517 [S VII, 139].

.2.15.   Lucianus Samosatensis, Piscator Sev Reviviscentes, Bilibaldo Prickhyemero . . . interprete.
M. Schürer, 1518 [R BNU III, 1390].

.2.16.   Lucianus Samosatensis, Omnes Dialogi iucundis salibus et impendio festivis iocis referti.
J. Schott, 1519 [S II B, 50].

.2.17.   Plutarchus, Problema, Num in convivio philosophandi sit locus? (Ottmar Nachtigall, ed.).
J. Schott, 1519 [S II B, 51].

.2.18.   Graece et Latine Senarii Proverbiales ex diversis Poetis graecis (Ottmar Nachtigall, ed.).
J. Knobloch, 1521 [S VII, 224].

A2.2.19. Progymnasmata Graecae Literaturae, . . . Epistola de
          utilitate graecarum Literarum (Ottmar Nachtigall, ed.).
          J. Knobloch, 1521 [S VII, 225], 1523 [S VII, 269].

  .2.20. Plutarchus, Aliquot commentarii iam recens . . . De eo
          quod docenda sit virtus (Ottmar Nachtigall, trans.).
          J. Knobloch, 1522 [S VII, 239].

  .2.21. Lucianus Samosatensis, Gallus, Latinus factus per
          Rudolphum Agricolam Frisum. Eiusdem Vitarum auctio,
          Iudicium Vocalium. Infernorum Dialogus: Charontis,
          Mercurii & Menippi.
              C. Egenolff, 1530 [R BNU III, 1397].

  .2.22. Pythagoras and Phocylides, Poemata.
              Cr. Mylius, 1539 [R BNU III, 1960], 1545 [R Nfp,
              3054].
              Chr. Mylius I, 1561 [R Bib. Mun., 1768], 1565 [R Bib.
              Mun., 1768a].

  .2.23. Porphyrius, Homericarum quaestionum liber. euisdem De
          nympharum antro in Odyssea, opusculum.
              W. Rihel, 1539 [R BNU III, 1918].

  .2.24. Aeschines, Praestantissimorum Graeciae Oratorum . . .
          et Demosthenis orationes.
              W. Rihel, 1545 [R BNU I, 87], 1550 [R BNU I, 88].

  .2.25. Demosthenes, de Falsa Legatione contra Aeschinem
          Oratio.
              W. Rihel, 1550 [R BNU I, 631].

  .2.26. Xenophon, In Laudem Agesilai Lacedaemoniorum regis
          Oratio. Item: Hieron sive Tyrannus.
              W. Rihel, 1553 [R BNU IV, 2504].

  .2.27. Lucianus Samosatensis, Dialogi selectiores: Coelestes,
          Marini & Inferni . . . Prometheus sive Caucasus,
          Menippus, sue Necromantia. Timon sive osor hominum.
              P. & P. Köpfel, 1554 [R BNU III, 1400].
              J. Rihel, 1563 [R BNU III, 1401].

  .2.28. Epictetus, Moralis Philosophiae Medulla.
              W. Rihel, 1554 [R BNU II, 696].

  .2.29. Xenophon, Oichonomichos logos A.
              W. Rihel, 1554 [R BNU IV, 2505].

  .2.30. Xenophon, De Cryi Expeditione, libri VII, in usum
          scholarum seorsim excusi.
              J. Rihel, 1561 [R BNU IV, 2506].

  .2.31. Demosthenes, Orationes Olynthiacae tres et quatuor
          Philippicae.

J. Rihel, 1561 [BM 834.c.b.].
T. Rihel, 1564 [Greiner], ca. 1570 [BM G.8888],
   ca. 1575 [BM 1131.b.12].

A2.2.32.   Pindar, Oda prima . . . & secunda oda.
           Chr. Mylius I, 1564 [Rott, 85].
           N. Wyriot, 1584 [Rott, 85a].

   .2.33.   Xenophon, Cyri Paediae Libri Quatuor priores In usum
            scholarum seorsim excusi.
            T. Rihel, 1565 [R BNU IV, 2507].

   .2.34.   Isocrates, Epistolae aliquot.
            S. Emmel, 1568 [R Nfp, 2135].

   .2.35.   Xenophon, Cyri Paediae Libri primi Latina conversio &
            Thematum omnium, phrasiumquae difficiliorum, quae in
            eo continentur, investigatio & explicatio.
            N. Wyriot, 1575 [R Nfp, 3573].

   3. HOMERUS.

A2.3.1.   Odyssea, Eiusdem Batrachomyomachia, Hymni, aliaque
           eius opuscula, seu catalecta.
           T. Rihel, n.d. [R BNU II, 1186].

   .3.2.   Odyssea de erroribus Ulyxis.
            J. Schott, 1510 [S II B, 12].

   .3.3.   Iliados.
            J. Schott, 1516 [S II B, 37].

   .3.4.   Ilias (Wuolf Cephal, ed.).
            W. Köpfel, 1525 [R BNU II, 1189], 1542 [R BNU II,
               1195], 1550 [R BNU II, 1197].

   .3.5.   Odyssea (Johannes Lonicerus, ed.).
            W. Köpfel, 1525 [R BNU II, 1190], 1542 [R BNU II,
               1194], 1550 [R BNU II, 1198].

   .3.6.   Illias/Odyssea (in Greek).
            W. Köpfel, 1534 [R BNU II, 1191].

   .3.7.   Iliados (Joachim Camerarius, ed.).
            Cr. Mylius, 1538 [R BNU I, 419; R BNU II, 1192], 1540
               R BNU I, 420].

   .3.8.   Homeri Interpres cum indice locupletissimo Illias/
            Oddyssea (in Greek; J. Bedrot, ed.).
            W. Rihel, 1539 [R BNU II, 1193].

   .3.9.   Illias, sev Potius omnia eius quae extant opera.
            T. Rihel, 1572 [R BNU II, 1199].

4. PLATO.

A2.4.1. Alcibiades posterior et Menexenus.
          W. Rihel, 1538 [R Nfp, 2933].

  .4.2.   Apologia Socratis Graece.
          W. Rihel, 1540 [R Nfp, 2934].

  .4.3.   Crito. Graece.
          W. Rihel, 1540 [R Nfp, 2935].

  .4.4.   Georgias aut de Rhetorica, Socratis Apologia, Crito
          aut quid Faciendum sit. Graece (J. Sturm, ed.).
          W. Rihel, 1541 [R Nfp, 2936].

  .4.5.   Theatetus vel de scientia Pro schola Argentinensi,
          Graece.
          No printer, 1567 [R Nfp, 2937].

  .4.6.   Pro Socrate defensio graece et latine, addita oratione
          Boschii atque praefatione de vita Platonis (M.
          Boschius, ed.).
          A. Bertram, 1592 [R Nfp, 2939].

  .4.7.   Crito graece et latine cum praefatione Mich. Boschii.
          A. Bertram, 1592 [R Nfp, 2939].

  5. ARISTOTLES.

A2.5.1. De moribus ad Nicomachun Libri decem.
          W. Rihel, 1540 [Greiner], 1545 [R BNU I, 75].
          W. Rihel Erben, 1556 [R BNU I, 78].
          J. Rihel, 1563 [R BNU I, 80], 1597 [R Nfp, 852],
          1598 [R Nfp, 851].

  .5.2.   Politicorum Libri Octo (J. Bedrot, ed.).
          W. Rihel, 1540 [R BNU I, 74], 1549 [R BNU I, 76].

  .5.3.   De Virtutibus. Michaelis Pseli Hominis Doctissimi
          Iambi . . . . Definitiones Platonis.
          J. Rihel, 1560 [R BNU I, 79].

A3. GREEK AND LATIN CLASSICS IN GERMAN.

A3.1.1. Aesopus, Vita et fabulae (in German; Heinrich Steinhöwel,
          trans.).
          H. Knoblochtzer, 1482 [R Nfp Inc., 8], 1483 [R Nfp
          Inc., 9].

  .1.2.   Ovid, Hie hebt sich an das buch Ovidii die liebe zu
          erwerben. Und auch die liebe zu verschmehen (Johann

Hartlieb, trans.).
M. Schott, 1484 [S II A, 5].

A3.1.3.   Apuleius, Lucius, Ein hübsche history von lucius
apuleius in gestalt eines esels verwandelt und verkerd
wardt und langer wan ein gantzes ior dar in pleybe
(Niclas von Wyl, trans.).
B. Kistler, 1499 [S IV Kis., 6].
J. Knobloch, 1506 [S VII, 16], 1509 [S VII, 54].

.1.4.   Terentius Afer, Publius, Terentius . . . von Latin zu
Tütsch transferiert. nach dem text und nach der gloss.
In sinen VI büchern. Uss dem ein yeglicher mensch
erkennen die sitten und gemut der andren menschen.
J. Grüninger, 1499 [S I, 43].

.1.5.   Boethius, Von dem Trost der Weiszheit (Peter von
Kastel, trans.).
J. Schott, 1500 [S II B, 2].

.1.6.   Catho in Latin durch Sebastianum Brant getützschet.
M. Hupfuff (two translations), 1501 [S V, 16] and
1504 [S V, 31].
J. Knobloch, 1508 [S VII, 49], 1509 [S VII, 64].

.1.7.   Aesopus, Ersten teils: das leben und fabel Esopi;
Aviani, Doligani, Adelfonsi: Disciplina clericalis mit
schimpffreden Pogii. Des andern theils usszüge schöner
fabeln und exempelen (Sebastian Brant, ed.).
J. Prüss I, 1508 [S III A, 69].

.1.8.   Lucianus Samosatensis, Palinurus usz kriechischer
sprach durch das latyn in tütsch transferiert Sagen von
geferlichkeit und trübsal in allen ständen der welt
(Johann Gallinarius, trans.).
M. Hupfuff, 1512 [S V, 93].

.1.9.   Vergilius Maro, Publius, Dryzehen aeneadische Bucher
von Troianischer zerstörung, und ussgang des Römischen
Reiches (T. Murner, trans.).
J. Grüninger, 1515 [S I, 144].

.1.10. Cicero, Marcus Tullius, Spiegel der waren Rhetoric
. . . Mit iren Glidern clugen reden. Sendtbrieffen und
formen mencher contract.
J. Knobloch, 1517 [S VII, 136].

.1.11. Plinius Secundus, C., Lobsagung: zu Zeiten er zu Rom
das Consulat ampt eingetretten hat vor offem Radt und
zuhörender Gemaind vom Heyligen Kayser Traiano
warhafftigklich, on schmeicheley gantz zierlichen und

wolgespräch, aussgesagt (Dietrich von Plenigen, trans.).
M. Flach II, 1520 [S VI B, 41].

A3.1.12. Plutarchus, Kurtz weise und höfliche sprüch (Heinrich
von Eppendorf, trans.).
J. Schott, 1534 [S II B, 129], 1554 [R Nfp, 2960].

.1.13. Plutarchus, Guter Sitten einundzwentzig Bücher (Michael
Herr, trans.).
J. Schott, 1535 [S II B, 133; R BNU III, 1895].

.1.14. Seneca, Lucius Annaeus, Zuchtbücher vast dientlich und
nutzlich zu lesen (Michael Herr, trans.).
B. Beck, 1536 [R BNU IV, 2115], 1540 [R BNU IV,
2116], 1545 [R Nfp, 3219].

.1.15. Pseudo-Cicero (J. Vielfeld), Fines Bonorum et malorum
F. T. C. Von der alten philosophen seligkait paradoxa
sechsz, sampt ihrer probierung und schussreden von der
Seligkait.
J. Cammerlander, ca. 1539 [R BNU I, 501].

.1.16. Plutarchus, Guoter Sytten. XXI Bücher, nammlich disze,
von Burgerlicher Polizey unnd Leben anzurichten. Von
der leer und Weiszheit der Fürsten (Hieronymus Boner,
trans.).
J. Schott, 1544 [R BNU III, 1897].

.1.17. Lucianus Samosatensis, Spigel der menschlichen
blödigkeit. Warhafftige Abcontrafactur aller
menschlichen ständen (J. Vielfeldt, trans.).
J. Cammerlander, 1545 [R Nfp, 2433].
W. Rihel, 1549 [R BNU III, 1399].
J. Rihel, 1564 [BM 8405.ccc.20.2].

.1.18. Plutarchus, Tugendspiegel der Hoch und weltweisen von
löblichen guten Sitten und handel. XXI Bücher
(Heinrich von Eppendorf, trans.).
No printer, 1551 [R Nfp, 2959].

.1.19. Vergilius Maro, Publius, Dreyzehen Eneadische Bücher.
Chr. Mylius I, 1559 [Greiner].

.1.20. Aesopus, Hundert Fabeln . . . Sampt einer schönen
Vorrede D. Martin Luth. vom rechten Nutz und Brauch
desselben Buchs (Luther and Mathesio, trans.).
No printer, 1572 [R Nfp, 758].

A4. CLASSICAL DRAMA.

1. PUBLIUS TERENTIUS AFER.

A4.1.1.   Comediae cum Commentariis (Johann Curtus, ed.).
           J. Grüninger, 1496 [S I, 26], 1499 [S I, 42], 1503
           [S I, 61].

  .1.2.   Comedie: cum annotationibus Petri Marsi et Pauli
         Malleoli in singulas scenas.
           J. Prüss I, 1503 [S III A, 37], 1506 [R Nfp, 3319].
           M. Flach II, 1511 [S VI B, 25].
           J. Knobloch, 1513 [S VII, 81], 1514 [S VII, 88],
              December 1516 [S VII, 125], 1516 [S VII, 129],
              1519 [S VII, 177].

  .1.3.   Comediae cum brevi vocabulorum difficilium
         interpretatione pro puerulis (Thomas Aucuparius, ed.).
           J. Grüninger, 1511 [S I, 119].

  .1.4.   Andria. Eunuchus. Heautontimorumenos. Adelphi. Phormio.
         Ecyra. Recognitae nuper, & castigatissime impressae.
           M. Schürer, 1516 [S VIII, 177].

  .1.5.   Comediae sex omnes summo labore exquisitaque
         diligentia.
           M. Schürer, 1521 [S VIII, 265].

  .1.6.   Comoediae VI nuper adantiquum exemplar collotae (L.
         Victor Fausto, ed.).
           J. Knobloch, 1522 [S VII, 231], 1523 [S VII, 270].

  .1.7.   Ex Terentii Comoediis Latinissimae Colloquiorum
         Formulae, ordinae selectae: Una cum eiusdem Poetae
         insignioribus Sententiis.
           C. Egenolff, 1530 [R BNU IV, 2290].

  .1.8.   P. Terentius A Philippo Melanchthone iam nouissime
         restitutus.
           J. Albrecht, 1533 [R BNU IV, 2291].

  .1.9.   Comoediae Sex. Ad Vetusta Exemplaria diligentissime
         emendatae. Cum Castigatione Duplici Ioannis Riuii &
         Georgii Fabricii.
           W. Rihel, 1548 [R BNU IV, 2292].

   2.   TITUS MACCIUS PLAUTUS.

A4.2.1.   Poeta Comicus (Johann Adelphus, ed.).
           J. Grüninger, 1508 [S I, 88].

  .2.2.   Aulularia Plautina, Comediarum Lepidissima (Cordus
         Urceus, ed.).
           J. Prüss I, ca. 1510 [S III A, 84].
           M. Schürer, 1511 [S VIII, 52], 1517 [S VIII, 208].

J. Knobloch & P. Gotz, 1520 [S VII, 204].
No printer, 1520 [R Nfp, 2943].

A4.2.3.   Continentur in hoc libello quattuor comoediae:
Amphtruo: Aulularia: Duo Captivi: & Menech.
J. Grüninger, 1511 [S I, 122].

.2.4.   Comoediae quinque 1 Amphitryo. 2 Asinaria. 3 Aulularia.
4 Captivi duo. 5 Curculio (Pylade Brixianus, ed.).
M. Schürer, 1514 [S VIII, 137].

.2.5.   Aulularia a mendis vindicata et doctissimis scholiis
. . . illustrata (Stephanus Riccius, ed.).
No Printer, 1537 [R Nfp, 2944].

.2.6.   Comoediae sex. Aulularia, Menaechmi, Trinummus, Captivi,
Miles gloriosus, Amphitruo (preface by J. Sturm).
J. Rihel, 1566 [R Nfp, 2945].

3. OTHER DRAMATISTS.

A4.3.1.   Seneca, Luscius Annaeus, Hercules Furens Tragoedia.
J. Knobloch, 1521 [S VII, 218].

.3.2.   Lucianus Samosatensis, Tragoedia Luciani cui Titulus
est, Podagra. A Quodam Graece latineque erudito,
eursibus reddita. Podagrae Laus, Bilibaldo Pirckeymhero
Authore.
H. Seybold, 1529 [R BNU III, 1396].

.3.3.   Sophocles, Aiax flagellifer et Philoctetes.
No printer, 1552 [R Nfp, 3243].

.3.4.   Sophocles, Oedipus Tyrannos pro schola Argentinensi
(in Greek).
Chr. Mylius I, 1567 [Greiner].

.3.5.   Euripides, Alcestis (George Buchanan, trans.).
J. Rihel, 1567 [R BNU II, 820], 1568 [R Nfp, 1659].

.3.6.   Euripides, Hecuba et Iphigenia in Aulide, Graece pro
Schola Argentinensi.
J. Rihel, 1567 [R BNU II, 819].

.3.7.   Lucianus Samosatensis, De Podagrae Laudibus, doctorum
. . . lusus. I. Bilibaldi Brickheymeri Norici. II.
Luciani Tragedia. III. Christophori Balistae (Michael
Toxites, ed.).
Chr. Mylius II, 1570 [R BNU III, 1416].

.3.8.   Euripides, Medea. Graece cum versione Buchanan.
J. Rihel, 1576 [R Nfp, 1662].

A4.3.9.   Euripides, Phoenissae. Graece et Lat. (C. Calaminus,
          ed.).
          N. Wyriot, 1577 [R Nfp, 1663], 1577 [R Nfp, 1664].

.3.10.   Euripides, Troades cum interpretatione lat. . . . Phil
          Melanchthonis.
          N. Wyriot, 1578 [R Nfp, 1665].

.3.11.   Euripides, Cyclops (Phil. Melanchton and C. Martiani,
          trans.).
          N. Wyriot, 1582 [R Nfp, 1660].

.3.12.   Sophocles, Aiax lorarius stylo tragico (Joseph
          Scaligerus, trans.).
          A. Bertram, 1587 [R Nfp, 3245].

.3.13.   Euripides, Medea Graeca Tragoedia: Cum Latina Versione
          (George Buchanan, trans.).
          J. Rihel, 1598 [R BNU II, 821].

.3.14.   Seneca, Luscius Annaeus, Hercules Furens.
          A. Bertram, 1599 [R Imp. Alsc., 573].

   4. CLASSICAL PLAYS IN GERMAN.

A4.4.1.   Plautus, Titus Maccius, Menaechmi (Jonas Bitner, trans.).
          T. Berger, 1570 [R Nfp, 2946].

.4.2.   Euripides, Medea (George Buchanan, trans.).
          No printer, 1571 [R Nfp, 1661].

.4.3.   Sophocles, Tranchiniai, die Tranchinierinnen.
          No printer, 1584 [R Nfp, 3244].

.4.4.   Euripides, Teutsche Argumenta, samt der Vorrede und
          Beschlusz in die griechische Tragoedi Euripides, Medea
          genantt, und in die zugegebene Choros ausz dem Pindaro
          (Aegidius Hunnius, ed.).
          J. Rihel Erben, 1598 [R Nfp, 2085].

A5. CLASSICAL HISTORIANS.

   1. HISTORICAL WORKS IN LATIN OR GREEK.

A5.1.1.   Hic subnotata continentur. Vita M. Catonis. Sextus
          Aurelius de Vitis Caesarum. Benevenutus de eadem re.
          Philippi Beroaldi & Thomae Vuolphii Junioris
          disceptatio de nomine imperatorio. Epithoma rerum
          Germanicarum usque ad nostra tempora. Thomae Aucuparii
          Distichon.
          J. Prüss I, 1505 [S III A, 49].

A5.1.2.   Nepos, Cornelius, <u>Vitae Excellentium imperatorum.</u>
           M. Schürer, 1506 [BM 609.e.2.1.], 1511 [S VIII, 51].

  .1.3.   Plinius, Secundus, C., <u>Liber illustrium Vororum. C.</u>
           <u>Plinii . . . vita per Angelum Tiphernatem. C. Suetonii</u>
           <u>Tranquilli de grammaticis et rhetoribus claris</u>
           <u>libellus.</u>
           M. Schürer, 1510 [S VIII, 31; R Nfp, 874; R BNU III,
              1889].

  .1.4.   Suetonius Tranquillus, C., <u>Illustres viri.</u>
           J. Knobloch, 1510 [S VII, 70; R Nfp, 875; R BNU IV,
              2244].

  .1.5.   Suetonius Tranquillus, C., <u>Liber illustrium virorum.</u>
           M. Schürer, 1512 [S VIII, 70; R BNU IV, 2245], 1513
              S VIII, 111; R Nfp, 877; R BNU IV, 2246], 1517 [S
              VIII, 212; R Nfp, 879; R BNU IV, 2248].

  .1.6.   Plinius Secundus, C., <u>De viris illustribus.</u>
           M. Schürer, 1512 [S VIII, 93; R Nfp, 876].

  .1.7.   Sallustius Crispus, C., <u>Bellum Catilnarium.</u>
           M. Schürer, 1512 [S VIII, 82], 1517 [S VIII, 219].
           U. Morhard, 1521 [S IV Mor., 4].

  .1.8.   Herodianus, <u>Historici Graeci. Libri VIII</u> (Angelo
           Politiano, ed.).
           M. Schürer, 1513 [S VIII, 113].

  .1.9.   Sallustius Crispus, C., <u>De conjuratione Catilnae.</u>
           M. Schürer, 1513 [S VIII, 114].

  .1.10.   Plinius Secundus, C., <u>De viris illustribus in re</u>
           <u>militari, & administranda rep. Suetonii Tranquilli:</u>
           <u>De claris grammaticis et rhetoribus. Julii</u>
           <u>Obsequentis: Prodigiorum Liber.</u>
           M. Schürer, 1514 [S VIII, 133].
           U. Morhard, 1521 [S IV Mor., 6; R Nfp, 880; R BNU
              III, 1892].

  .1.11.   Suetonius Tranquillus, C., <u>De vita duodecim Caesarum,</u>
           <u>Libri XII.</u>
           M. Schürer, 1515 [S VIII, 153], 1521 [S VIII, 263].
           J. Prüss II, 1520 [S III B, 22].

  .1.12.   Philostratus, Flavius, <u>De Vitis Sophistarum Libri duo</u>
           (Antonio Bomfino, ed.).
           M. Schürer, 1516 [S VIII, 183].

  .1.13.   Curtius Rufus, Quintus, <u>De rebus gestis Alexandri Magni</u>
           <u>Regis Macedonum</u> (Erasmus, ed.).
           M. Schürer, 1518 [S VIII, 231].

A5.1.14. Consulum Romanorum Elenchus. Cum privilegio Caesareo.
          W. Kopfel, 1534 [R Nfp, 1539].

   .1.15. Jospehus, Flavius, Historia belli Iudaici . . .
          translata per Davidem Kyberum.
          J. Frölich, 1550 [R BNU II, 1274].

   .1.16. Herodotus, Omeroy Bios (in Greek).
          W. Köpfel, 1550 [R Nfp, 1995; R BNU II, 1196].

   .1.17. Thucydides, Bellum Siculum . . . Pro Schola
          Argentoratensi.
          J. Rihel, 1561 [R BNU IV, 2327].

   .1.18. Epistolae regum, principum, rerumpublicarum ac
          sapientum vivorum: Ex antiquis & recentioribus, tam
          Graecis, quam Latinis Historiis & Annalibus collectae.
          L. Zetzner, 1593 [R BNU II, 701].

   .1.19. Tacitus, Cornelius, De Situ, Moribus & Populis
          Germanorum (Michael Beuther, ed.).
          B. Jobin Erben, 1594 [R BNU I, 197].

   2. TRANSLATIONS OF CLASSICAL HISTORIANS.

A5.2.1.   Caesar, C. Julius, Von seinen Kriegen. erstmals usz dem
          Latin in Tütsch bracht. (M. Ringmann, trans.).
          J. Grüninger, 1507 [S I, 78], 1508 [S I, 91].

   .2.2.   Livius, Titus, Römsche history (Bernard Schöfferlin
          and Yvon Wittig, eds.).
          J. Grüninger, 1507 [S I, 79].
          J. Rihel, 1562 [R BNU III, 1373], 1563 [R BNU III,
          1374].

   .2.3.   Sallustius, Crispus, C., Bellum Catilnarium (J.
          Vielfeld, trans.).
          No printer, 1530 [R Nfp, 3159].

   .2.4.   Josphus, Flavius, Historici. Zwentzig bücher von den
          alten geschichten . . . Siben bücher von dem Jüdischen
          krieg und der zerstörung Jierusalem (Caspar Hedio,
          trans.).
          B. Beck & M. Meyer, 1531 [R BNU II, 1270].
          B. Beck, 1535 [R BNU II, 1271], 1539 [R BNU II,
          1272], 1544 [R BNU II, 1273].
          S. Emmel, 1553 [R BNU II, 1275], 1556 [R BNU II,
          1276], 1562 [R BNU II, 1277], 1564 [R BNU II,
          1278].

   .2.5.   Hegesippus, Fünff historische bücher . . . Von dem
          Jüdischen Krieg. Von der zerstörung Jierusalem. Von

grausammer straff der Juden die sich an Christo und
Apostlen versündigt (Caspar Hedio, trans.).
  B. Beck, 1532 [R BNU II, 1111], 1537 [R BNU II,
    1112].

A5.2.6. Valerius Maximus, Von geschichten der Römer und aussers
         volcks, Perser, Medier, Griechen, Aphern, Flemming und
         Teutschen (Peter Selbet, trans.).
           J. Cammerlander, 1533 [R BNU IV, 2377], 1535 [R BNU
             IV, 2378], 1541 [B Cam., 133].

  .2.7. Sallustius, Crispus, C., Chronica von dem römischen
         Buntschuch, Rottung oder Empörung wider eyn oberkeyt
         und Gemainen Nutz zu Rom under dem ersten
         Burgermaisterthumb Marci Tullii Ciceronis, durch Lucium
         Catilinam angestifft und practicirt.
           J. Cammerlander, 1534 [R BNU IV, 2065].

  .2.8. Nepos, Cornelius, Vom ursprung des Römischen Reichs,
         den Sieben künigen, wie die regiert, auch wie sie
         zuletst vertrieben seind worden und das
         Burgermaisterthumb angefangen.
           J. Cammerlander, ca. 1535 [R BNU III, 1623; R Nfp,
             881], after 1535 [R Nfp, 882].

  .2.9. Suetonius Tranquillus, C., Von Geburt, Leben, Thaten
         und Todt Julii, Augusti, Tyberiti, Caligule, Claudii,
         Neronis, Galbe, Othonis, Vitelii, Vespasiani, Titi,
         und Domitiani der XII. ersten Römischen keyser (Conrad
         Weidman, trans.).
           J. Cammerlander, 1536 [R BNU IV, 2251].

  .2.10. Von der Zerstörung der Stat Jerusalem und dem
         grausamen erschröckenlichen jamer, so sich darinnen
         verlauffen. Gezogen ausz Josepho (Hans Ragel, ed.).
           J. Frölich, ca. 1540 [R Nfp, 3071].

  .2.11. Florus, Lucius Annaeus, Compendio de las Catorze
         decadas de Tito Liuio Paduano principe de la historia
         Romana . . . y al presente traduzido en lengua
         Castellana.
           A. Fries, 1550 [R BNU II, 873].

  .2.12. Plutarchus, Von den Leben und Ritterlichen thaten, der
         aller durchleüchtigsten Männer, Griechen und Römer,
         Künig, Bürgermeister, und Hauptleüten, als namlich
         Tesei Künig zu Athen, Romuli und Remi &c (Hieronymus
         Boner, trans.).
           A. Fries, 1555 [R BNU III, 1898].

  .2.13. Livius, Titus, Von Ankunfft und Ursprung des Römischen
         Reichs . . . . (Conrad Lautenbach, trans.).

          T. Rihel, 1574 [R BNU III, 1375], 1575 [R BNU III,
          1376], 1576 [R BNU III, 1377], 1587 [R BNU III,
          1378], 1590 [R BNU III, 1379], 1596 [R BNU III,
          1380], 1598 [R BNU III, 1381].

A5.2.14. Hegesippus, Fünff Bücher: Vom Jüdischen Krieg, und
          endlicher zerstörung der Heyligen und gewaltigen Statt
          Jerusalem (Conrad Lautenbach, trans.).
            T. Rihel, 1574 [R BNU II, 1113], 1575 [R BNU II,
            1114], 1576 [R Nfp, 1976], 1581 [R BNU II, 1115],
            1587 [R BNU II, 1116], 1595 [R BNU II, 1117], 1597
            [R BNU II, 1118].

 .2.15. Josephus, Flavius, Historien und Bücher, Von alten
          Jüdischen Geschichten, zwentzig, sambt eynem von
          seinem Leben (Conrad Lautenbach, trans.).
            T. Rihel, 1574 [R BNU II, 1279], 1576 [R Bib. Mun.,
            1306], 1578 [BM 4516.g.5.1.], 1581 [R BNU II, 1280],
            1587 [R BNU II, 1281], 1590 [R BNU II, 1282],
            1595 [R BNU II, 1283], 1597 [R BNU II, 1284].

BIBLICAL LITERATURE

B1. Entire Bibles.

B2. Psalters.

B3. Bible Stories in Latin.

B4. Psalms set to Music.

B5. The New Testament and Parts Thereof.

B6. The Old Testament and Parts Thereof.

B7. Biblical Commentary in Latin.

    1. Catholic Biblical Commentary.
    2. Desiderius Erasmus.
    3. Philipp Melanchton.
    4. Martin Luther.
    5. François Lambert.
    6. Other Reformers and Theologians.
    7. Strasbourg Reformers.
    8. Otto Brunfels.

B8. Biblical Commentary in the Vernacular.

    1. Commentary by Martin Luther.
    2. Vernacular Commentary by Erasmus and Other German and Swiss Reformers.
    3. Commentaries by Laymen.
    4. Commentaries by Strasbourg Reformers.
    5. Commentaries by Anabaptists.
    6. Commentaries by Cyriacus Spangenberg.

B1.   ENTIRE BIBLES.

B1.1.1.   Biblia Latina.
              A. Rusch for A. Koberger, 1481 [R BNU Inc., 87].
              J. Grüninger, 1483 [R Nfp Inc., 117], 1492 [R BNU
                 Inc., 89], 1497 [S I, 29].
              Printer of the Vitas Patrum, 1485 [R Nfp Inc., 118].
              J. Prüss I, 1486 [R BNU Inc., 88], 1489 [R Nfp Inc.,
                 119].

   .1.2.   Biblia Germanica.
              J. Grüninger, 1485 [R BNU Inc., 92].

   .1.3.   Biblia Divinae Scripturae, veteris novaque omnis.
              W. Köpfel, 1526 [R BNU I, 198].

   .1.4.   Biblia veteris et novi Testamenti iuxta vulgatem
           editionem ad hebraicam veritatem candori pristino
           restituta.
              J. Schott, 1535 [S II B, 134].

   .1.5.   Luther, Martin, Biblia. Das ist: die gantz Heylige
           Schrift Deütsch.
              W. Köpfel, 1535 [R BNU I, 200], 1537 [R Nfp, 1004],
                 1544 [R Nfp, 1005], 1547 [R Nfp, 1006].
              W. Rihel, 1535 [R Nfp, 1003], ca. 1540 [R Imp. Alsc.,
                 276], ca. 1542 [R Imp. Alsc., 276].

   .1.6.   Biblia.
              T. Rihel, ca. 1595 [R Imp. Alsc., 276].

B2.   PSALTERS.

B2.1.1.   Psalterium ad usum ecclesiae argentinensis.
              J. Grüninger, 1489 [R Nfp Inc., 589].

   .1.2.   Psalterium.
              J. Prüss I, 1500 [BM 1B.1748].

   .1.3.   Psalterium correctum et hymni.
              J. Prüss I, 1502 [S III A, 35].

   .1.4.   Psalterium cum apparatu vulgari firmiter appresso.
              M. Hupfuff, 1506 [S V, 51].
              J. Knobloch, 1508 [S VII, 41].

   .1.5.   Psalterium . . . Carthusiensium.
              R. Beck, 1519 [S IV Beck, 30].

   .1.6.   Psalterium (in Greek).
              W. Köpfel, 1524 [R BNU III, 1946], 1545 [R BNU III,
                 1953].

B2.1.7.   Luther, Martin, Der Psalter Teutsch.
          J. Knobloch, 1524 [S VII, 285], 1526 [S VII, 312].
          J. Prüss II, 1526 [S III B, 38].

  .1.8.   Psalterium Davidis, Cunradi Pelicani opera elaboratum.
          W. Köpfel, 1527 [R BNU III, 1947].

  .1.9.   Der siben und dreyssigst psalm Davids: Noli emulari in
          malignantibus, Von dem urteyl Gottes uber der welt
          tyrannen.
          W. Köpfel, 1527 [R Nfp, 2998].

  .1.10. Bucer, Martin, Sacrorum Psalmorum Libri Quinque ad
          Ebraicam ueritatem genuina uersione in Latinum
          traducti.
          G. Ulricher, 1529 [R Nfp, 1168], 1532 [R BNU I, 363].

  .1.11. Bucer, Martin, The Psalter of David in Englishe purely
          and faithfully translated after the text of Felin
          every Psalme havynge his Argument before declaring
          brefly thentente and Substance of the whole Psalme
          (Martin Bucer, trans.).
          F. Foxe, 1530 [R Nfp, 3034; R Nfp, 1171].

  .1.12. Psalterium impressum cum aliis correquisitis ordinis
          Carthusiani.
          No printer, 1531 [R Nfp, 3046].

  .1.13. Psalterium Davidis carmine redditum per Eobanum Hessum.
          Cr. Mylius, 1539 [R BNU III, 1949], 1540 [R Nfp,
             3047], 1541 [R BNU III, 1950], 1542 [R BNU III,
             1951], 1543 [R Nfp, 3048], 1544 [R BNU III,
             1952], 1545 [R BNU III, 1954], 1546 [R Nfp, 3049].

  .1.14. Liber Psalmorum cum translationibus quatuor.
          G. Messerschmidt, 1545 [R BNU III, 1955].

  .1.15. Spangenberg, Conradus, Der Heylige Psalter des
          Königklichen Propheten Davids in gewisse und
          ordentliche Hauptartikel verfasset.
          S. Emmel, 1560 [R BNU IV, 2166].

  .1.16. Buchanan, Georgius, Psalmorum Davidis paraphrasis
          poetica.
          J. Rihel, 1566 [R Nfp, 1189], 1568 [R Nfp, 1190],
             1575 [R Nfp, 1191], 1578 [R Nfp, 1192].

  .1.17. Portus, Aemilius, Davidis regis Prophetae Psalmi omnes
          noviter conversi.
          B. Jobin, 1582 [R Nfp, 2974; R Nfp, 3031].

  .1.18. Maior, Georgius, Psalmi Davidis iuxta translationem

veterem iam postremo ad Hebraicam veritatem repurgati.
J. Rihel, 1584 [Greiner], 1594 [R BNU III, 1464].

B3.   BIBLE STORIES IN LATIN.

B3.1.1.   Nicolaus de Hanapis (Nicolas de Hannapes; Patriarch of
          Jerusalem), Biblia Pauperum.
          J. Grüninger, 1490 [R Nfp Inc., 520].
          J. Prüss I, 1490 [R Nfp Inc., 521].

   .1.2.   Biblia aurea veteris ac novi testamenti vocitatus.
           J. Grüninger, 1495 [S I, 22], 1496 [S I, 27], 1515
           [S I, 143].
           M. Schürer, 1509 [S VIII, 24].

   .1.3.   Chelidonius, Benedictus, Passio Jesu Christi
           saluatoris mundi.
           J. Knobloch, 1506 [S VII, 23].

   .1.4.   Passionis Christi unum ex quattuor evangelistis textum.
           J. Knobloch, 1506 [S VII, 22], 1507 [S VII, 34],
             1508 [S VII, 40].
           M. Hupfuff, 1513 [S V, 109].

   .1.5.   Pictorale Dominice Passionis.
           J. Knobloch, 1509 [R BNU III, 1805].

   .1.6.   Montanus, Jacobus, De Passione ac Morte christi.
           M. Schürer, ca. 1513 [S VIII, 98].

   .1.7.   Keller, Bruckhard, Historia Passionis ac Mortis Domini
           Salvatoris Nostri Iesu Christi.
           J. Martin, 1599 [R BNU II, 1305].

B4.   PSALMS SET TO MUSIC.

B4.1.1.   Psalterium Davidicum. Cantica et hymni. Cum carmine
          Joh. Gallinarii.
          J. Prüss I, 1504 [S III A, 48].
          J. Prüss II, 1512 [S III B, 1].
          R. Beck, 1520 [S IV Beck, 32].

   .1.2.   (Greiter, Matthaeus), Der LI Psalm Davids Miserere mei
           deus hoch zu singen da der prophet Nathan zu ihm kam.
           W. Köpfel, 1525 [R Nfp, 1930].

   .1.3.   Greiter, Matthaeus, Die zwen Psalmen: In exitu . . .
           und Domine probasti me.
           W. Köpfel, 1527 [R Nfp, 1931], 1543 [R Nfp, 3007].

   .1.4.   Psalmen und geystliche Lieder, die man zu Straszburg,

und auch die man in andern kirchen pflegt zu finden.
   J. Prüss II, 1537 [S III B, 46].
   W. Köpfel, 1539 [B Luther, 3617], 1543 [B Luther,
     3615], 1557 [R Nfp, 3012].
   G. Messerschmidt, 1541 [R BNU III, 1937].
   No printer, 1543 [R Nfp, 3010].

B4.1.5.   Psalterium. Das seindt alle Psalmen Davids mit iren
        Melodien.
          W. Köpfel, 1538 [R BNU III, 1948].

.1.6.   Aulcuns Pseaulmes et cantiques mys en chant.
          No printer, 1539 [R Nfp, 3051].

.1.7.   Das ander teyl aller Psalmen Davids. Auch geystliche
        Lieder, wölche im Ersten teyl nit begriffen.
          W. Köpfel, 1544 [R Nfp, 3011].

.1.8.   Marot, Clément, Cinquante Psaumes de Marot par
        Guillaume Franck.
          No printer, 1545 [R Nfp, 2602a].

.1.9.   Marot, Clément, Pseaumes de David Traduictz en rithme
        francoise.
          R. Guédon, 1548 [Peter, 14].

.1.10. Psalmen und Geystliche Gesäng, so in der Gemein Gottes
        fürnemlich geübt.
          Chr. Mylius I, 1568 [R BNU III, 1938].

.1.11. Luther, Martin, Psalmen, geystliche Lieder und Gesänge,
        sambt etlichen Gebetten.
          T. Rihel, 1569 [R Nfp, 3014], 1569 [R Nfp, 3015],
            1571 [R Nfp, 3016], 1573 [R Nfp, 3017], 1575 [R
            BNU III, 1939], 1578 [R Nfp, 3023], 1581 [R Nfp,
            3024], 1589 [R BNU III, 1940].
          B. Jobin, 1573 [R Nfp, 3018], 1575 [R Nfp, 3019],
            1576 [R Nfp, 3020], 1589 [R Nfp, 3027].
          A. Bertram, 1587 [R Nfp, 3026].

.1.12. Psalmbüchlein von den gepraüchlichsten Kirchengesängen,
        Psalmen und Lidern.
          B. Jobin, 1577 [R Nfp, 3028], 1577 [R Nfp, 2999],
            1591 [R Nfp, 3000].
          A. Bertram, 1597 [R Nfp, 3001].

.1.13. Psalmen mit vier Stimmen in Kirchen und Schulen zu
        singen.
          No printer, 1577 [R Nfp, 3021].

.1.14. Psalmen und Geistliche Lieder welche in Kirchen und

Schulen gesungen werden.
   N. Wyriot, 1578 [R Nfp, 3022].

B4.1.15. Psalterium Davidis: integrum carmine redditum a Frid.
       Widebramo.
         T. Rihel, 1578 [R Nfp, 3050].

 .1.16. Omnes Psalmi Davidis in Graecum Carmine Heroico
       conversi.
         B. Jobin, 1581 [BM 1407.c.13].

 .1.17. Wolkenstein, David, Psalmen für Kirchen und Schulen
       auff die gemeine Melodeyen . . . .
         N. Wyriot, 1582 [R Nfp, 3554].
         No printer, 1583 [R Nfp, 3555].

 .1.18. Spangenberg, Cyriacus, Der gantze Psalter Davids . . .
       Gesangweise gefasset.
         B. Jobin, 1582 [R Nfp, 3037].

 .1.19. Wolkenstein, David, Harmonia Psalmorum Davidis quatuor
       vocum.
         N. Wyriot, 1583 [R Nfp, 3556].

 .1.20. Lobwasser, Ambrosius, Psalmen Davids nach Frantzösicher
       Melodey und Reimen.
         B. Jobin, 1586 [R Nfp, 2412], 1589 [R Nfp, 2413],
           1596 [R Nfp, 2414], 1597 [R Nfp, 2415].

 .1.21. Psalmen und Geistliche Lieder welche in Kirchen und
       Schulen des Fürstenthumbs Zweibrücken gesungen werden.
         B. Jobin, 1587 [R Nfp, 3025].

B5. NEW TESTAMENT AND PARTS THEREOF.

B5.1.1. Erasmus Roterodamus, Ex novo Testamento Quatuor
       Evangelia.
         U. Morhard, 1520 [S IV Mor., 2].

 .1.2. Paulus Apostolus, Epistolae Pauli Apostoli ad Graecum
       Veritatem . . . fidem recognitae per erasmum
       Roterodamum.
         U. Morhard, 1521 [R Imp. Alsc., 306], 1522 [R BNU
           III, 1803].

 .1.3. Erasmus Roterodamus, Testamentum Novum latinum.
         U. Morhard, 1521 [S IV Mor., 3], 1522 [S IV Mor.,
           12].
         J. Knobloch, 1522 [S VII, 236], 1523 [S VII, 259],
           September 1523 [R BNU IV, 2302].

J. Herwagen, 1523 [R BNU IV, 2300].
T. Rihel 1559 [R BNU IV, 2304], 1567 [R BNU IV, 2305].

B5.1.4. Luther, Martinus, Evangelium Johannes verdeütscht.
J. Prüss II, 1522 [S III B, 32].

.1.5. Jhesus, Das neuw Testament Deutsch (Martin Luther,
ed.).
J. Schott, 1522 [S II B, 69].
J. Knobloch, 1524 [S VII, 287], 1525 [S VII, 300],
1528 [S VII, 321].
J. Grüninger, 1527 [S I, 236], 1529 [R BNU IV, 2310],
1532 [R Nfp, 3337].
G. Ulricher, 1533 [R Nfp, 3338].
W. Köpfel, 1538 [R Nfp, 3339].

.1.6. (Lonicer, Johann, or Lonitzer, Johann), Novum
Testamentum Graece.
W. Köpfel, 1524 [R BNU IV, 2303].

.1.7. Das Neüwe Testament . . . .
W. Köpfel, 1537 [R BNU IV, 2311].

.1.8. Das Newe Testament Mart. Luth. .
W. Rihel, 1542 [R BNU IV, 2312].
T. Berger, 1576 [R BNU IV, 2314].
T. Rihel, 1588 [R BNU IV, 2315].

.1.9. Das Newe Testament mit schonen Figuren.
W. Rihel, 1549 [R BNU IV, 2313].

.1.10. Erasmus Roterodamus, De. Testamentum Novum Graece et
Latine.
T. Rihel, after 1554 [R BNU IV, 2298].

.1.11. Erasmus Roterodamus, D. Testamentum Novum Iesu Christi,
Filii Dei.
T. Rihel, after 1554 [R BNU IV, 2297].

.1.12. Testamentum Novum (in Hebrew).
No printer, 1592 [R BNU IV, 2316].

B6. THE OLD TESTAMENT AND PARTS THEREOF.

B6.1.1. Luther, M., Das alte Testament Deutsch nach
urspringlicher Hebreischer warheit.
J. Knobloch, 1524 [S VII, 283].

.1.2. (Luther, Martin), Biblia Sacrae Scripturae veteris
omnia . . . voluminibus sex.
J. Knobloch, 1524 [S VII, 241].

B6.1.3.   Luther, Martinus, Der Hiob teutsch.
           J. Knobloch, 1525 [S VII, 304].

  .1.4.   Bucer, Martin, Tzephaniah quem Sophoniam vulgo vocant,
           prophetarum epitomographus ad ebraicam veritatem
           versus et commentario explanatus.
           J. Herwagen, 1528 [R Nfp, 1178].

  .1.5.   Jud, Leo, Apocryphi. Biblische Bücher so wiewol bey
           den Alten under Biblischer Schrifft nit gezelt, yedoch
           bewerdt . . . und in hohem brauch.
           H. Knobloch, 1530 [R BNU II, 1288].

  .1.6.   Joye, Georgius, Translation of the Prophet Essay.
           B. Beck, 1531 [R Nfp, 2165].

  .1.7.   Luther, Martin, Die Propheten alle Teutsch.
           J. Albrecht, 1533 [R Nfp, 2541].

  .1.8.   Proverbia Kohelet, Canticum (in Hebrew).
           No printer, 1591 [R BNU III, 1934].

B7. BIBLICAL COMMENTARY IN LATIN.

  1. CATHOLIC BIBLICAL COMMENTARY.

B7.1.1.   Nicolaus de Lyra, Moralia super Bibliam.
           G. Husner, n.d. [R BNU Inc., 344].

  .1.2.   Johannes de Turrecremata (Juan de Torquemada;
           Cardinal), Expositio Psalterii.
           Printer of the Legenda Aurea, 1482 [R BNU Inc.,
             465].
           G. Husner, 1485 [R BNU Inc., 466], 1487 [R BNU Inc.,
             467].

  .1.3.   Marchesinus, Joannes, Mammotrectus Super Bibliam.
           Printer of the Vitas Patrum, 1483 [R BNU Inc., 296].
           M. Flach, 1487 [R BNU Inc., 298], 1494 [R BNU Inc.,
             300].
           No printer, 1489 [Sélestat, 319].
           J. Grüninger, 1489 [R BNU Inc., 299].

  .1.4.   Rampegolo, Antonio, Compendium Bibliae.
           Printer of the Vitas Patrum, 1486 [R Nfp Inc., 594].

  .1.5.   Pelbartus de Themeswar, Expositio Libri Psalmorum.
           No printer, 1487 [R Nfp Inc., 559].

  .1.6.   Beets, Johannes, Compendium super decem praeceptis
           decalogi.
           No printer, 1489 [R Nfp Inc., 108].

B7.1.7.   Arator, In Actus Apostolorum.
           J. Grüninger, 1507 [S I, 82].

  .1.8.   Volphius, Thomas Iunior., In Psalmum. Domine quis
           habitabit in tabernaculo tuo.
           J. Grüninger, 1508 [S I, 89; R Nfp, 3553].

  .1.9.   Aureolus, Petrus (Abbot of Aix), Compendium Biblie
           totius, hoc est Epitomasacrae scripturae.
           J. Schott, 1514 [S II B, 26].

  .1.10.   Druthinarus, Christianus (Christianus, Druthmar),
           Expositio in evangelium secundum Matteum Divini
           Sermonis Preconibus commodissima.
           J. Grüninger, 1514 [S I, 138].

  .1.11.   Gregorianus (Gregorius the Great), Super novum
           testamentum.
           J. Knobloch, 1516 [S VII, 119].

  .1.12.   Haymonis (Haymo, Bishop of Halberstadt), In divi Pauli
           epistolas expositio.
           R. Beck, 1519 [S IV Beck, 29].

   2.   DESIDERIUS ERASMUS.

B7.2.1.   Paraphrasis in epistolam Pauli ad Romanos.
           No printer, 1519 [R Nfp, 1620].

  .2.2.   In epistolam Pauli ad Galatas.
           J. Prüss II, 1520 [S III B, 19].

  .2.3.   Arnobius Afer the Elder, Commentarii pii iuxta ac
           sinceriter eruditi in omnes psalmos sermone latino
           (Erasmus, ed.).
           J. Knobloch, 1522 [S VII, 247].

  .2.4.   Commentarius in psalmum quare fremuerunt gentes.
           J. Knobloch, 1522 [R Nfp, 1621].

  .2.5.   Paraphrasis in Evangelium Mathaei.
           J. Knobloch, 1523 [R Nfp, 1603].

  .2.6.   Paraphrases in epistolas Pauli Apostoli . . . ad
           Hebraeos.
           J. Knobloch, 1523 [S VII, 255].

  .2.7.   Paraphrases in epistolas Pauli ad Timotheum . . . .
           J. Knobloch, 1523 [S VII, 256; R BNU II, 771].

  .2.8.   Paraphrases in Evangelium Marci.
           J. Knobloch, 1524 [S VII, 286].

B7.2.9.   Paraphrasis in Acta Apostolorum.
          J. Knobloch, 1525 [S VII, 289].

  .2.10. Paraphrasis in evangelium secundum Johannem.
          J. Knobloch, 1525 [S VII, 292].

   3. PHILIPP MELANCHTHON.

B7.3.1.   Declamatiunculae duae in Divi Pauli doctrinam.
          J. Herwagen, 1522 [R BNU III, 1506].

  .3.2.   Annotationes . . . in Epistolam Pauli ad Romanos unam
          et ad Corinthios duas.
          J. Herwagen, 1523 [R BNU III, 1508], May 1523 [R BNU
          III, 1509], September 1523 [R BNU III, 1510],
          6 September 1523 [B Luther, 1257], 1524 [B Luther,
          1259], 1525 [R BNU III, 1520].

  .3.3.   In Evangelium Matthaei annotationes inque historiam
          passionis Domini.
          J. Herwagen, 1523 [R Nfp, 2618], 1524 [R BNU III,
          1516].

  .3.4.   Commentarii in Epistolam Pauli ad Romanos.
          Cr. Mylius, 1540 [R BNU III, 1537], 1544 [R Nfp,
          2626].

   4. MARTIN LUTHER.

B7.4.1.   Luther et Annémond de Coct, Pro Sequentibus
          Commentariis Epistolae.
          J. Knobloch, 1523 [S VII, 272].

  .4.2.   Praefatio methodica totius scripturae in Epistolam
          Pauli ad Romanos.
          J. Knobloch, 1523 [S VII, 267].

  .4.3.   In Epistolam Pauli ad Galatas . . . Commentarius.
          J. Herwagen, 1523 [R BNU III, 1421].

  .4.4.   Savonarola, Hieronymus, Meditatio pia et erudita . . .
          super Psalmos Miserere mei (Luther, ed.).
          J. Herwagen, 1524 [R BNU III, 1422].

  .4.5.   Enarrationes in Epistolas D. Petri duas & Iudae unam.
          J. Herwagen, 1524 [R BNU III, 1422], 1525 [R BNU
          III, 1428].

  .4.6.   Deuteronomion Mose cum Annotationibus.
          J. Knobloch, 1525 [R BNU III, 1427].

B7.4.7.   Super magnificat commentarii.
          J. Herwagen, 1525 [B Luther, 865].

 .4.8.   In septimum primae ad Corinthios caput, Exegesis.
          No printer, 1525 [R Nfp, 2499].

 .4.9.   Ioannis Huss Locorum aliquot ex Osee et Ezechiele
          Prophetis, cap. V et VII.
          J. Schott, 1525 [B Luther, 2215].

 .4.10.   Habacuc Propheta cum Annotationibus.
          J. Knobloch, 1526 [S VII, 308].

 .4.11.   Ionah Propheta . . . Lutheri commentariolo explicatus.
          J. Herwagen, 1526 [B Luther, 2284].
          J. Knobloch, 1526 [S VII, 310].

 .4.12.   In divae virginis Mariae Zachariaeque odas
          commentarii.
          J. Herwagen, 1526 [B Luther, 866].

 .4.13.   Enarratio in Tres Prophetas, Iohelem, Amos, & Abdiam.
          J. Albrecht, 1536 [R BNU III, 1446].

 .4.14.   Enarratio Psalmi LI Miserere Mei Deus et Psalmi CXXX
          de profundis clamaui.
             Cr. Mylius, 1538 [B Luther, 3273], 1539 [R BNU III,
             1447].

 .4.15.   In Quindecim Psalmos Graduum commentarii ex
          pralectionibus.
             Cr. Mylius, 1540 [R BNU III, 1448], 1542 [R Nfp,
             1545].

    5. FRANÇOIS LAMBERT.

B7.5.1.   In Iohelem prophetam.
          J. Herwagen, n.d. [R BNU III, 1322].

 .5.2.   In divi Lucae Evangeliumm commentarii.
          J. Herwagen, 1524 [R BNU III, 1325], 1525 [R BNU
          III, 1328].

 .5.3.   In Cantica canticorum Salomonis.
          J. Herwagen, 1524 [R BNU III, 1324].

 .5.4.   In primum duodecim prophetarum, nempe Oseam.
          J. Herwagen, 1525 [BM 843.h.8].

 .5.5.   In Amos, Abdiam et Ionam prophetas, comentarii.
          J. Herwagen, 1525 [R BNU III, 1327].

 .5.6.   In quator ultimos prophetas, nempe Sophoniam, Aggeum,

Zachariam et Malachiam.
J. Herwagen, 1526 [R BNU III, 1330].

B7.5.7.   Commentarii de prophetia, eruditione et linguis deque
litera et spiritu.
J. Herwagen, 1526 [R BNU III, 1329].

6.   OTHER REFORMERS AND THEOLOGIANS.

B7.6.1.   Bugenhagen, Johannes, Annotationes . . . in X
Epistolas Pauli.
J. Herwagen, 1524 [R BNU I, 325].

.6.2.   Bugenhagen, Johannes, Annotationes in Deuteronomium,
in Samuelem prophetam.
J. Knobloch, 1524 [S VII, 282].

.6.3.   Bugenhagen, Johannes, In librum Psalmorum
interpretatio.
J. Knobloch, 1524 [S VII, 277].

.6.4.   Bugenhagen, Johannes, Annotationes . . . in epistolas
Pauli ad Galatas, Ephesios, Philippenses, Colossenses,
Thessalonicenses primam et secundam, Timotheum primam
et secundam, Titum, Philemonem, Hebraeos.
J. Knobloch, 1525 [S VII, 294].

.6.5.   Bugenhagen, Johannes, In Regum duos ultimos libros
annotationes.
J. Knobloch, 1525 [Pegg, 419].

.6.6.   Knopken, Andreas, In epistolam ad Romanos.
J. Knobloch, 1525 [S VII, 306].

.6.7.   Jonas, Justus, Annotationes in acta Apostolorum.
J. Knobloch, 1525 [S VII, 301].

.6.8.   Althamerus, Andreas, and Brenzius, Johannes,
Annotationes in Epistolam Beati Jacobi.
J. Schott, 1527 [S II B, 102].

.6.9.   Pellicanus, Conradus, In Psalmos Paraphrasis.
W. Köpfel, 1527 [R Nfp, 2865].

.6.10.   Cratoaldus, Valentinus (Valentin Crautwald), In Tria
Priora Capita Libri Geneseos annotata.
P. Schaefer, 1530 [R BNU I, 595].

.6.11.   Oecolampadius, Johannes, In Hieremiam Prophetam
Commentariorum.
M. Apiarius, 1533 [R BNU III, 1663].

B7.6.12. Oecolampadius, Johannes, In Epistolam ad Hebraeos.
          M. Apiarius, 1534 [R BNU III, 1664].

  .6.13. Oecolampadius, Johannes, In Prophetam Ezechielem
          Commentarius.
          M. Apiarius, 1534 [R BNU III, 1665].

  .6.14. Robertus Regiensis (Robertus Retenensis[?]), Ex sacris
          literis observationes de mensuris liquidorum &
          leguminum.
          M. Apiarius, 1534 [R BNU III, 2020].

  .6.15. Westheimer, Bartholomaeus, Collectanae troporum,
          sacrae scripturae . . . ex Hebraeorum, quam
          Ecclesiasticorum commentariis.
          J. Albrecht, 1535 [R BNU IV, 2455].

  .6.16. Calvin, Joannis, Commentarii in Epistolam Pauli ad
          Romanos.
          W. Rihel, 1540 [R BNU I, 405].

  .6.17. Cruciger, Caspar, In Epistolam Pauli ad Timotheum.
          Cr. Mylius, 1540 [R BNU I, 598], 1542 [R BNU I,
          599].

  .6.18. Willichius, Jodocus, Commentaria in utramque ad
          Timotheum Pauli Epistolam.
          Cr. Mylius, 1542 [R Nfp, 3522].

  .6.19. Aepinus, Johannes, In Psalmum XV Davidis Commentarius.
          J. Cammerlander, 1543 [R Nfp, 745].

  .6.20. Willichius, Jodocus, In Pauli epistolam ad
          Thessalonicenses utramque Commentarii.
          Cr. Mylius, 1545 [R Nfp, 3523].

  .6.21. Onkelos, Targum. Paraphrasis in Sacra Biblia.
          G. Messerschmidt, 1546 [R BNU IV, 2270].

  .6.22. Cruciger, Caspar, In Evangelium Johannis Apostoli.
          Cr. Mylius, 1546 [R BNU I, 600].
          S. Emmel, 1557 [R BNU I, 601], 1564 [R Nfp, 1465].

  .6.23. Brentius, Johannes, Auszlegung des Predigers
          Salomonis.
          S. Emmel, 1560 [R BNU I, 269].

  .6.24. Zacharias Propheta Carmine Elegiaco Redditus a S.
          Culingio.
          J. Rihel, 1562 [BM c.65.e.10].

  .6.25. Wigand, Johannes, Catechisticae Explicationes,
          breviter et methodice recitatae in Catechismi

Lutheri Accessit explicatio Psalmi CXLV & CXLVII.
B. Jobin, 1576 [R Nfp, 3520].

B7.6.26. Strigelius, Victorinus, Orationes XXX. De praecipuis
patriarchis, prophetibus et regibus.
B. Jobin, 1583 [R BNU IV, 2194].

.6.27. Hemmingsen, Niels, Commentaria in omnes Epistolas
Apostolorum Pauli, Petri, Iudae, Johannis, Jacobi.
T. Rihel, 1586 [R BNU II, 1124].

.6.28. Cubicularius, Ulricus, Cerva matutina, hoc est Psalmi
XXII Deus meus Paraphrasis.
A. Bertram, 1590 [R Nfp, 1470].

7. STRASBOURG REFORMERS.

B7.7.1. Capito, Wolfgang, In Habakuk Prophetam.
W. Köpfel, 1526 [R BNU I, 441].

.7.2. Bucer, Martin, Epistola D. Pauli ad Ephesios . . . in
eamdem Commentarius.
J. Herwagen, 1527 [R Nfp, 1157].

.7.3. Bucer, Martin, Enarrationum in Evangelia Matthaei,
Marci et Lucae.
J. Herwagen, 1527 [R BNU I, 354].

.7.4. Capito, Wolfgang, In Hoseam Prophetam Commentarius.
J. Herwagen, 1528 [R BNU I, 442a].

.7.5. Bucer, Martin, Commentaria in Librum Job.
No printer, 1528 [R Nfp, 1164].

.7.6. Butzer, Martin (Martin Bucer), Enarratio in Evangelion
Iohannis.
J. Herwagen, 1528 [R BNU I, 356].

.7.7. Bucer, Martin, Aretii Felini Exposftio in Psalms.
No printer, 1530 [R Nfp, 1169].

.7.8. Bucer, Martin, Commentarius in Ecclesiasten.
No printer, 1532 [R Nfp, 1154].

.7.9. Butzer, Martin (Martin Bucer), Metaphrases et
Enarrationes perpetuae Epistolarum D. Pauli Apostoli.
W. Rihel, 1536 [R BNU I, 371].

.7.10. Bucer, Martin, Enarratio in Evangelium Matthaei VI.
Tu es Petrus.
No printer, 1555 [R Nfp, 1155].

.7.11. Marbach, Erasmus, Commentariorum in Pentateuchum,

Tomus I, II.
  B. Jobin, 1597 [R Nfp, 2596].

8. OTTO BRUNFELS.

B7.8.1. Catalogi virorum illustrium Veteris et Novi
          Testamenti.
          J. Schott, 1527 [S II B, 101], 1528 [R BNU I, 281].

.8.2.   Pandectarum Veteris et Novi Testamenti, Libri XII.
          J. Schott, 1527 [S II B, 100].

.8.3.   Loci Omnium fere capitum Evangelii secundum Mathaeum,
          Marcum, Joannem, Actorum item apostolicorum.
          J. Schott, 1527 [S II supp., 13], 1528 [S II supp.,
          15], 1529 [S II B, 106], 1534 [S II B, 128].

.8.4.   Pandectarum libri XXIII de tropis, figuris et modis
          loquendi Scriptararum.
          J. Schott, 1528 [R Nfp, 1119; S II supp., 18].

.8.5.   Pandectarum veteris et novi Testamenti, Libri XXII.
          J. Schott, 1528 [S II B, 103], 1529 [S II B, 107],
          1530 [S II supp., 19], 1532 [R BNU I, 292].

.8.6.   Precationes Bibliae Sanctorum Patrum, illustrium
          virorum et mulierum utriusque Testamenti.
          J. Schott, 1528 [S II B, 104].

.8.7.   Annotationes in quatuor Evangelia et acta Apostolorum
          ex Orthodoxis Sacrarum Literarum Scriptionibus
          congestae.
          G. Ulricher, 1535 [R BNU I, 299].

B8. BIBLICAL COMMENTARY IN THE VERNACULAR.

1. COMMENTARY BY MARTIN LUTHER.

B8.1.1. Die syben Büss Psalmen mit teütscher auszlegung.
          J. Knobloch, 1519 [S VII, 183].

.1.2.   Der sechssundreissigest Psalm.
          M. Schürer Erben, 1521 [B SE 1, 13].
          J. Prüss II, 1522 [BM 3090.c.18].

.1.3.   Evangelium von den Zehen auszsetzigen verdeutscht und
          auszgelegt.
          W. Köpfel, 1522 [B Luther, 991].

.1.4.   Uszlegung der Epistel und Ewangeli des Advents.
          M. Schürer Erben, 1522 [B SE 2, 21].

B8.1.5.   Das Jesus Christus eyn geborner Jud sey.
           J. Prüss II, 1523 [B Luther, 1539].

  .1.6.   Das Siebendt Capitel Sancti Pauli zu den Corinthern
           auszgelegt.
           W. Köpfel, 1523 [R Nfp, 2532].
           M. Schürer Erben, 1523 [B SE 3, 14].

  .1.7.   Der 127 Psalm ussgelegt an die Christen zu Rigen.
           J. Schwann, 1524 [B Luther, 1953].

  .1.8.   Glossen über die schwersten örter das Neuen
           Testaments.
           W. Köpfel, 1524 [B Luther, 1994].

  .1.9.   Verzeichnungen über das Fünfft Buch Mose,
           Deuteronomium genandt.
           No printer, 1525 [R BNU III, 1431].

  .1.10.   Von der Christlichen Hoffnung ein leer . . . über on
           ein den letsten verss des fünfften Psalmen.
           M. Schürer Erben, 1525 [B SE 2, 71].

  .1.11.   Der Prophet Jona, ausgelegt.
           H. Knobloch, 1526 [S VII, 310].

  .1.12.   Der Prophet Habacuc aussgelegt.
           J. Knobloch, 1526 [B Luther, 2303].

  .1.13.   Epistel aus dem Propheten Jeremia, von Christus reich
           und Christlicher freyheit.
           J. Prüss II, 1527 [S III B, 39].

  .1.14.   Prophetie de Iesaie de l'enfant nouveau ne Jesus
           Christ avec les annotations du docteur de Clermont.
           J. Prüss II, 1527 [BM 3901.a.3].

  .1.15.   Vorrede inn gemein uber das gantz Newe Testament.
           G. Ulricher, 1533 [B Luther, 2906a].

  .1.16.   Jesus Syrach.
           J. Prüss II, 1540 [S III B, 49].

  .1.17.   Auszlegung über die fünfzehen Psalmen.
           Cr. Mylius, 1541 [R Nfp, 2546].

  .1.18.   Comment, oder Auszlegung uber den CXXVII Psalm.
           Chr. Mylius I, 1563 [R BNU III, 1452].

   2.   VERNACULAR COMMENTARY BY ERASMUS AND OTHER GERMAN AND
        SWISS REFORMERS.

B8.2.1.   Erasmus von Roterdam, D. Auslegung des ersten Psalmen.
           J. Knobloch, 1520 [S VII, 208].

B8.2.2.   Styfel, Michael, Evangelium von den zehen Pfunden,
          Matthei am XXV.
             J. Schott, 1522 [S II B, 73].

  .2.3.   Styfel, Michael, Das Evangelium von dem verlornen Sun.
          Luce XV . . . .
             M. Schürer Erben, 1524 [R Nfp, 3279a].

  .2.4.   Concordantz des Newen Testaments zu Teütsch.
             J. Schott, 1524 [S II B, 85].

  .2.5.   Keller, Andreas, Ausslegung des evangelischen
          Lobgsangs Benedictus.
             J. Schwann, 1524 [BM T.2165.7].

  .2.6.   Keller, Andreas, Ein shone auslegung des XXIII
          capitels in Matheo.
             J. Schwann, 1524 [BM T.2165.6].

  .2.7.   Keller, Andreas, Auslegung des vierden Capitels in der
          geschichte(n) der Apostel.
             M. Schürer Erben, 1525 [B SE 2, 70].

  .2.8.   Rhegius, Urbanus, Ob das new Testament yetz recht
          verteuscht sey.
             M. Schürer Erben, 1525 [BM T.2165.5].

  .2.9.   Bugenhagen, Johannes, Annotationes uber die zehen
          epistel S. Pauli.
             J. Knobloch, 1525 [S VII, 288].

  .2.10. Melanchthon, Phillip, Ein kleyne Auslegung über das XX
          Capital Exodi, der zehen Gebot.
             W. Köpfel, 1525 [R Nfp, 2639].

  .2.11. Toltz, Johannes, Der Heyligen geschrifft Ardt, Weise
          und gebrauch.
             J. Knobloch, 1527 [R BNU IV, 2332].

  .2.12. Brunner, Lienhart, Concordantz und zeyger der sprüch
          und historien aller Biblischen bücher alts und news
          Testaments.
             W. Köpfel, 1530 [R BNU I, 308].

  .2.13. Corvinus, Antonius, Auszlegung der herlichen Historien
          Josephs aus dem Ersten büch Mose.
             W. Köpfel, 1541 [R BNU I, 594].

  .2.14. Link, Wenceslaus, Das erst teyl des alten Testaments.
             B. Beck, 1543 [R BNU III, 1369], 1545 [R BNU III,
             1370].
             S. Emmel, 1555 [R BNU III, 1371].

3.   COMMENTARIES BY LAYMEN.

B8.3.1.   Ziegler, Clemens, <u>Ain Kurtz Register und ausszug der</u>
<u>Bibel in wölchem man findet was Abgöterey sey.</u>
W. Köpfel, 1524 [R BNU IV, 2522].
J. Schwann, 1524 [R BNU IV, 2523].

.3.2.   Wurm von Geudertheim, Mathias, <u>Jesus, auszlegung der</u>
<u>geschrifft im andere capitel S. Jacobs Epistel.</u>
J. Schwann, 1524 [R Nfp, 3568].
M. Schürer Erben, 1525 [B <u>SE 2</u>, 76].

.3.3.   Goldschmidt, Sebastian, <u>Ein underweisung etzlicher</u>
<u>artickel so bruder Mattis Prior des prediger closters</u>
<u>zu Worms . . . offentlich gepridiget hat.</u>
M. Schürer Erben, 1525 [B <u>SE 1</u>, 30].

4.   COMMENTARIES BY STRASBOURG REFORMERS.

B8.4.1.   Bucer, Martin, <u>Das Martin Bucer, sich in verteütschung</u>
<u>des Psalters Johann Pommers, getrewlich und Christlich</u>
<u>gehalten.</u>
No printer, 1527 [R Nfp, 1172].

.4.2.   Brunnfels, Otho, <u>Pandect Büchlin, Beylauffig aller</u>
<u>Sprüch beyder Testament uszugk.</u>
J. Schott, 1529 [S II B, 109].

.4.3.   (Brunfels, Otto), <u>Helden Büchlin . . . von der hohen</u>
<u>Gottserwölten Männern und Weibern . . . beyder</u>
<u>Testament.</u>
J. Schott, 1529 [S II B, 110].

.4.4.   Butzer, Martin (Martin Bucer), <u>Der CXX Psalm, Ein</u>
<u>danck und Betpsalm wider die falschen zungen, und</u>
<u>stehte widerfechter Christlicher Religion.</u>
G. Messerschmidt, 1546 [R BNU I, 386].

.4.5.   Specker, Melchior, <u>Von der Herrlichen Zukunfft Jesu</u>
<u>Christi, zum Jüngsten Gericht . . . alles was hievon</u>
<u>im H. Neüwen Testament geoffenbart.</u>
S. Emmel, 1555 [R Bib. Mun., 1961].

.4.6.   Specker, Melchior (Melchior Spener), <u>Auslegung des</u>
<u>Evangelii Matthei am XXV Capitel.</u>
T. Rihel, 1568 [R Bib. Mun., 1962; R Nfp, 3264].

.4.7.   Florus, Nicolaus, <u>Auslegung des 91. Psalmen.</u>
T. Berger, 1576 [R Bib. Mun., 1002].

.4.8.   Pappus, Johannes, <u>Biblische Historia, von den Königen</u>

unnd Propheten in Juda und Israel. Ausz den Büchern
Samuelis, der Könige und Chronica. Auch den Psalmen
und Propheten.
    B. Jobin, 1586 [R Nfp, 2816].

B8.4.9.   Florus, Nicolaus, Der CXXXVII Psalm. An den Wassern zu
           Babel.
               K. Kieffer, 1587 [R BNU II, 874].

   5.   COMMENTARIES BY ANABAPTISTS.

B8.5.1.   Buenderlin, Johann, Ein gemeyne einlaytung in
           aygentlichen Verstand Mose und der Propheten.
               B. Beck, 1529 [Gut. Jb., 99].

  .5.2.   Hoffman, Melchior, Weissagung usz heiliger göttlicher
           geschrift. Von den trübsalen diser letsten zeit.
               B. Beck, 1529 [Depperman bibliog., 9].

  .5.3.   Hoffman, Melchior, Joannis und des Heiligen Apostels
           und Evangelisten.
               B. Beck, 1530 [R BNU II, 1179].

  .5.4.   Hoffman, Melchior, Der leuchter des alten Testament
           usz gelegt, welcher im heylge stund der hütten Mose,
           mit seinen siben lampen, blumen, knöppfen und köpffen,
           liechtschneützen und Leschnepff.
               B. Beck, 1530 [R BNU II, 1178].

           Also listed as:

           Hoffman, Melchior, Ausslegung der heimlichen
           Offenbarung Joannis.
               B. Beck, 1530 [Deppermann bibliog., 11].

  .5.5.   Hoffman, Melchior, Das ware trostliche unnd
           freundenreiche Evangelien.
               H. Knobloch, 1531 [Pegg, 1313].

  .5.6.   Hoffman, Melchior, Warhafftige erklerung aus heyliger
           Biblischen schrifft, das der Satan . . . nit aus gott,
           sundern alleyn auss eygenem will erwachsen sei.
               J. Cammerlander, 1531 [Deppermann bibliog., 15].

  .5.7.   Denck, Johann, Micha der Prophet wie den Hans D. uff
           diese zeit verglichen hat.
               J. Cammerlander, 1532 [Krebs and Rott I, 411].
               No printer, 1532 [Krebs and Rott I, 411].

  .5.8.   Eisenburgk, Johannes (probably with Melchior Hoffman),
           Die Epistel dess Apostels S. Jacobs erklärt.
               J. Cammerlander, 1534 [Depperman bibliog., 26].

6.   COMMENTARIES BY CYRIACUS SPANGENBERG.

B8.6.1.   Der weyse und Gerechte Knecht Gottes, das ist Das
          LIII Capital Essaie.
          S. Emmel, 1560 [R BNU IV, 2167].

  .6.2.   Die Epistel des Heyligen Apostels S. Pauli an Titum.
          S. Emmel, 1562 [R BNU IV, 2168], 1564 [R Nfp, 3252].

  .6.3.   Die ander Epistel Pauli an die Corinthier.
          S. Emmel, 1562 [R Nfp, 3250].

  .6.4.   Die erste Epistel Pauli an Timotheum.
          S. Emmel, 1564 [R Nfp, 3251], 1569 [R BNU IV, 2170].

  .6.5.   Die erste und ander Epistel des heyligen Apostels S.
          Pauli Thessalonicher.
          S. Emmel, 1564 [R Nfp, 3253].

  .6.6.   Auszlegung der Ersten Acht Capitel der Episteln S.
          Pauli an die Römer.
          S. Emmel, 1566 [R Nfp, 3247].

  .6.7.   Die erste Epistel Pauli an die Corinthier.
          S. Emmel, 1569 [R BNU IV, 2170].

  .6.8.   Auszlegung der letsten acht Capitel der Episteln S.
          Pauli an die Römer.
          S. Emmel, 1569 [Greiner].

SCHOOL TEXTS

T1. School Texts in Latin.

    1. Grammars.
    2. Rhetoric Texts.
    3. Oratorical Texts.
    4. School Vocabularies.
    5. Poetics.
    6. Dialectics and Logic.
    7. Musical Theory and Texts.
    8. Writing Exercises, Letters, and Dialogues.
    9. Song Books for the Gymnasium and Academy.
  10. Miscellaneous Texts.

T2. School Texts in Greek or in Greek accompanied by Latin or German.

    1. Greek Grammars.
    2. Greek Oratorical Texts and Examples.

T3. Plays for the School.

    1. Latin Plays for the School Theater.
    2. Biblical Plays in Latin for the Gymnasium.

T4. Academic Disputations and Theses.

    1. Theses, Disputations, and Poems of Congratulation.
    2. Orations Given at the Academy.

T1.   SCHOOL TEXTS IN LATIN.

   1.   GRAMMARS.

T1.1.1.   Manuale Scholarium.
          M. Flach I, 1481 [S VI A, 8].

   .1.2.   Donatus, Aelius, Ars minor.
           H. Knoblochtzer, ca. 1483 [R Nfp Inc., 212].
           J. Prüss I, 1487 [R Nfp Inc., 213], 1500 [R Nfp
           Inc., 218].
           B. Kistler, 1498 [R Nfp Inc., 215].
           M. Schürer, 1500 [R Nfp, 1521].
           M. Hupfuff, 1505 [R Nfp, 1520], 1511 [S V, 90].

   .1.3.   Joannes de Garlandia, Verba deponentalia.
           J. Prüss I, ca. 1485 [BM 1.A.4760.c.4].

   .1.4.   Alexander de Villa Dei (Alexandre de Villedieu),
           Doctrinale.
           Pars I et II.
              J. Prüss I, 1485 [R Nfp Inc., 33], 1499 [R Nfp
              Inc., 54].
              M. Flach I, 1488 [S VI A, 16].
           Pars I.
              M. Schott, 1487 [R Nfp Inc., 35].
              M. Flach I, 1488 [S VI A, 19], 1490 [R Nfp Inc.,
              43], 1493 [R Nfp Inc., 47; S VI A, 51].
              J. Prüss I, 1490 [R Nfp Inc., 45].
              M. Hupfuff, 1506 [R Nfp, 800].
           Pars II.
              M. Schott, 1487 [R Nfp Inc., 36].
              M. Flach I, 1490 [S VI A, 25], 1491 [S VI A, 35],
              1493 [S VI A, 52].
              J. Prüss I, 1490 [R Nfp Inc., 40], 1507 [R Nfp,
              801].
              J. Grüninger, 1500 [R Nfp Inc., 51].
           Pars III et IV.
              M. Flach I, 1490 [S VI A, 26].
           Pars III.
              M. Flach I, 1491 [S VI A, 36], 1493 [S VI A, 50].
           Pars I-IV.
              J. Prüss, ca. 1495 [R Nfp Inc., 50].

   .1.5.   Perotti, Niccolo, Rudimenta Grammatica (Bernardo
           Perger, trans.).
              J. Grüninger, 1486 [R Nfp Inc., 569].
              M. Flach II, 1501 [S VI B, 6].
              W. Schaffner, 1510 [S IV Sch., 3].
              J. Knobloch, 1510 [Greiner].

T1.1.6.   Composita Verborum.
           J. Grüninger, 1486 [S I, 6], 1490 [S I, 14].

  .1.7.   Helius, Petrus, Grammatica.
           M. Flach I, 1490 [S VI A, 27], 1499 [S VI A, 70].

  .1.8.   Ebrardus, Udalricus, Modus latinitatis.
           J. Prüss I, 1490 [R Nfp Inc., 224], 1491 [R Nfp
           Inc., 225], 1493 [R Nfp Inc., 226].
           M. Flach I, 1498 [R Nfp Inc. 227; S VI A, 69].
           M Flach II, ca. 1501 [Greiner].

  .1.9.   Lindelbach, Michael, Praecepta Latinitatis.
           J. Prüss I, ca. 1490 [R Nfp Inc., 427].

  .1.10.   Grammatellus cum glossa Germanica.
           No printer, 1493 [R Nfp Inc., 297].

  .1.11.   Exercitium puerorum grammaticale.
           G. Husner, 1494 [R Nfp Inc., 254], 1495 [R Nfp Inc.,
           255], 1498 [R Nfp Inc., 256], 1502 [R Nfp, 1677].

  .1.12.   Synthen, Johannis, Dicta super prima parte Alexandri.
           J. Prüss I, 1499 [S III A, 29].

  .1.13.   Regule Grammaticales Antiquorum.
           M. Hupfuff, 1502 [S V, 17].

  .1.14.   Zenders de Werdt, Guilhelmus, Lilium grammatice.
           M. Hupfuff, 1503 [R BNU IV, 2517].

  .1.15.   Augustinus (Saint), Dathus nonus denuo correctus et
           in Elangantiis per litteras capitales perpulcre
           distinctus.
           M. Hupfuff, 1504 [S V, 30].

  .1.16.   Donatus, Aelius, Figure . . . continens
           interpretationem Donati minoris.
           J. Grüninger, 1505 [BM 12933.bb.10].

  .1.17.   Perottus, Nicolaus, Cornucopiae ad lectorem . . .
           opus commentariorum linguae latinae.
           J. Prüss I, 1506 [S III A, 57].

  .1.18.   Es tu scholaris.
           M. Hupfuff, 1507 [S V, 65].

  .1.19.   Torrentinus, Hermannus, Opusculum aureum omnibus
           studentibus perutile et necessarium.
           M. Hupfuff, 1507 [S V 64; R BNU IV, 2336].

  .1.20.   Torrentinus, Hermannus, Commentaria in primam partem
           doctinalis Alexandri.
           J. Prüss I, 1507 [S III A, 65].

                    J. Prüss II, 1513 [S III B, 4].
                    M. Hupfuff, 1516 [S V, 135].

T1.1.21.   Augustinus, Aurelius (Saint), De arte grammaticae
           libellus nitidissimus.
                    J. Grüninger, 1508 [S I, 100].

   .1.22. Brassicanus, Joannis, Institutiones grammaticae.
                    J. Prüss I, 1508 [S III A, 66], 1509 [S III A, 74].
                    J. Prüss II, 1512 [S III B, 3], 1513 [R BNU I, 253].
                    M. Schürer, 1512 [S VIII, 83], 1519 [S VIII, 248].
                    R. Beck, 1517 [S IV Beck, 25].

   .1.23. Heinrichmannus, Jacobus, Grammaticae institutiones.
                    J. Prüss I, 1509 [S III A, 79].
                    J. Prüss II, 1512 [S III B, 2].
                    U. Morhard, 1522 [S IV Mor., 11].

   .1.24. Wimpheling, Jacob, Elegantiae majores.
                    M. Hupfuff, 1511 [R Nfp, 3533], 1515 [S V, 120].
                    J. Knobloch, 1513 [S VII, 85], 1516 [S VII, 130].

   .1.25. Guarna, Andreas, Grammaticale Bellum.
                    M. Schürer, 1512 [R BNU II, 1051; S VIII, 84], 1516
                    [S VIII, 185].

   .1.26. Corvinus, Laurentius, Hortulus elegantiarum.
                    M. Flach II, 1512 [S VI B, 28], 1516 [Greiner].
                    J. Knobloch, 1516 [S VII, 113], 1518 [S VII, 163].

   .1.27. Cochleus, Johannes, Grammatica.
                    R. Beck, 1513 [S IV Beck, 13], 1514 [S IV Beck, 16].
                    J. Prüss II, 1515 [S III B, 14].
                    J. Knobloch, 1519 [S VII, 176].

   .1.28. Erasmus Roterodamus, Desiderius, De duplici copia rerum.
                    M. Schürer, 1513 [S VIII, 94], 1514 [S VIII, 145],
                    1516 [S VIII, 180], 1516 [S VIII, 195], 1518 [S
                    VIII, 239].
                    U. Morhard, 1519 [S IV Mor., 1].
                    J. Knobloch, 1521 [S VII, 230], 1522 [R BNU II,
                    761], 1523 [S VII, 261], 1524 [S VII, 276], 1525
                    [S VII, 291].

   .1.29. Aventinus, Joannis, Grammatica.
                    M. Hupfuff, 1515 [S V, 126].

   .1.30. Glogoviensis, Joannis (Jan Glogowyck), Exercitium
           veteris artis . . . secunde partis Alexandrei.
                    J. Knobloch, 1517 [S VII, 148].

   .1.31. Curius Lancilotus Pasius, De arte grammatica.
                    M. Schürer, 1518 [S VIII, 238].

T1.1.32. Formula declinandi et coniugandi.
          J. Knobloch, 1519 [S VII, 185].
          M. Flach II, 1521 [S VI B, 63].

   .1.33. Murmellius, Joannis, Pappa quae grammaticis rudimenta
          affectantibus, impendio conducibilis.
          M. Flach II, 1521 [S VI B, 62].

   .1.34. Donatus, Aelius, Methodus Grammatices.
          J. Knobloch, 1522 [BM c.40.b.64.2].

   .1.35. Bathodius, Lucas, Paedia grammatices.
          W. Köpfel, 1525 [R Nfp, 940].

   .1.36. Rutilius, Lupus, De figuris sententiarum ac verborum
          . . . Petri Mossellani Tabulae de schematibus et
          tropis.
          W. Köpfel, 1539 [R Nfp, 3132].

   .1.37. Bitner, Jonas, De grammatica.
          W. Köpfel, 1550 [R Nfp, 1016].

   .1.38. Bitner, Jonas, De syntaxi et ratione conjugendarum
          vocum.
          W. Köpfel, 1550 [R Nfp, 1017].

   .1.39. Sussanneau, Hubert, Connubium adverbiorum.
          J. Rihel, 1576 [R BNU IV, 2261], 1585 [R BNU IV,
          2262].

   .1.40. Golius, Theophilus, Educationis puerilis linguae
          Latinae.
          J. Rihel, 1578 [R BNU II, 1018].

   .1.41. Sturm, Johannes, Linguae Latinae resoluendae ratio.
          N. Wyriot, 1581 [R BNU IV, 2235; R Nfp, 3101].

   .1.42. Caucius, Antonius, Grammaticae Gallicae Libri III.
          B. Jobin, 1586 [R BNU I, 473].

     2. RHETORIC TEXTS.

T1.2.1. Poncius, magister, Rhetorica.
          J. Grüninger, 1486 [R BNU Inc., 399].

   .2.2. Locher, Jacobus, Compendium rhetorices ex Tulliano.
          R. Beck, 1514 [S IV Beck, 19], 1518 [S IV Beck, 27].

   .2.3. Valerius Maximus, Dictorum et factorum meorabilium.
          M. Schürer, 1514 [S VIII, 136], 1516 [S VIII, 190],
          1518 [S VIII, 230].
          J. Knobloch, 1521 [S VII, 215], 1524 [S VII, 273].

   .2.4. Melanchthon, Philippus, Institutiones Rhetoricae.
          J. Herwagen, 1523 [R BNU III, 1512].

T1.2.5.   Melanchthon, Philippus, De Rhetorica libri tres.
           J. Knobloch, 1524 [R BNU III, 1519].

   .2.6.   Melanchthon, Philippus, Elementorum Rhetorices.
            C. Egenolff, 1529 [R Nfp, 2658].
            Cr. Mylius, 1542 [R BNU III, 1540], 1543 [R Nfp,
               2659], 1546 [R BNU III, 1545].

   .2.7.   Mosellanus, Petrus, Tabulae de schematibus et tropis,
            In Rhetoricum Philippi Melancthon.
            C. Egenolff, 1529 [B Egen., 11].

   .2.8.   Hermogenes Tarsensis, Partitionum Rhetoricarum liber
            unus (J. Sturm, ed.).
            J. Rihel, 1547 [R BNU II, 1147].

   .2.9.   Sturm, Johannes, Libri duo . . . de periodis unus.
            Dionysii Hallicarnassaei, de collocatione verborum
            alter.
            W. Rihel, 1550 [R BNU IV, 2208].

   .2.10.   Sturm, Johannes, Liber unus de periodis explicatus
            non tam scholiis quam scholis a Valentino Erythraeo
            Lindauensi.
            J. Rihel, 1567 [R BNU IV, 2216].

   .2.11.   Sturm, Johannes, Scholae in libros IIII Hermogenis de
            inventione.
            J. Rihel, 1570 [R BNU IV, 2219], 1570 [R BNU IV,
               2220].

   .2.12.   Aristotle, Rhetoricorum Libri III (J. Sturm, ed.).
            T. Rihel, 1570 [R BNU I, 81], 1570 [Greiner].

   .2.13.   Hermogenes Tarsensis, De ratione inveniendi oratorias
            (J. Sturm, ed.).
            J. Rihel, 1570 [R BNU II, 1148].

   .2.14.   Sturm, Johannes, Ad Philippum Lippianum. De
            exercitationibus Rhetoricis.
            N. Wyriot, 1575 [R BNU IV, 2225].

   .2.15.   Sturm, Johannes, De Universa ratione elocutionis
            Rhetoricae.
            B. Jobin, 1576 [R BNU IV, 2230].

   .2.16.   Reusner, Nicolas, Elementorum artis Rhetoricae.
            N. Wyriot, 1578 [R Nfp, 3100].

   .2.17.   Junius, Melchior, Scholae Rhetoricae, De Contexendarum
            Epistolarum Ratione.
            L. Zetzner, 1597 [R BNU II, 1297].

   3.   ORATORICAL TEXTS.

T1.3.1. Wimpfelingius, Jacobus, Elegantiarum medulla:
         Oratoriaque precepta.
         M. Brant, n.d. [S IV Bra., 2].
         J. Grüninger, 1498 [S I, 37].
         M. Hupfuff, 1506 [S V, 55].
         J. Knobloch, 1508 [S VII, 52].

  .3.2. Bebelius, Henricus, Opusculum de institutione
         puerorum . . . oratio de utilitate eloquentiae.
         M. Schürer, 1513 [S VIII, 102; R Nfp, 956].

  .3.3. Absolutissimus de octo orationis partium constructione
         libellus.
         M. Schürer, 1515 [S VIII, 169].
         J. Prüss II, 1515 [S III B, 13].

  .3.4. Erasmus Roterodamus, De octo orationis partium
         constructione libellus.
         J. Knobloch, 1522 [S VII, 251], 1523 [R BNU II,
             766].
         No printer, 1524 [R Nfp, 1611].
         J. Frölich, 1540 [R Nfp, 1612].

  .3.5. Pellisson, Johannes, Modus Examinandae Constructionis
         in Oratione.
         J. Albrecht, 1533 [R BNU III, 1846].

  .3.6. Riccius, Bartholomeaus (Bartolomeo Ricci), Apparatus
         Latinae Locutionis.
         M. Apiarius, 1535 [R BNU III, 2015].

  .3.7. Latomus, Bartholomaeus, Oratio pro Cecinna cum
         enarrationi.
         Cr. Mylius, 1539 [R Nfp, 2274].

  .3.8. Sturm, Johannes, In partitiones oratorias Ciceronis
         dialogi duo.
         Cr. Mylius, 1539 [R BNU IV, 2201], 1540 [Rott, 34b],
             1545 [Rott, 34f].

  .3.9. Melanchthon, Philippus, Liber Selectarum Declamationum
         . . . Adiecta sunt eiusdem Praefationes in aliquot
         illustres autores.
         Cr. Mylius, 1541 [R BNU III, 1538], 1544 [R BNU III,
             1543], 1544 [R BNU III, 1542], 1558 [R BNU III,
             1548].
         No printer, 1566-1569 [R Nfp, 2631]. (7 volumes.)
         Tomus tertius.
         S. Emmel, 1559 [R BNU III, 1550], 1562 [R BNU III,
             1552], 1567 [R BNU III, 1555].
         T. Rihel, 1570 [R BNU III, 1543].

Tomus secundus.
   S. Emmel, 1564 [R BNU III, 1553], 1569 [R BNU III,
     1557].
   T. Rihel, 1570 [R BNU III, 1559].
Tomus quartus.
   S. Emmel, 1566 [R BNU III, 1554].
Tomus primus.
   S. Emmel, 1567 [R BNU III, 1556].
   T. Rfhel, 1570 [R BNU III, 1558].

T1.3.10.   Erythraeus, Valentinus, Tabulae quaedum partitionum
          oratoriarum Ciceronis.
            Cr. Mylius, 1547 [R BNU II, 797].
            Chr. Mylius I, 1560 [R Nfp, 1640].

.3.11.   Schorus, Antonius (Antonius van Schore), De Ratione
          Discendae Docendaeque Linguae Latinae & Graecae.
            W. Rihel, 1549 [R BNU IV, 2091].
            J. Rihel, 1575 [R Nfp, 3189], 1596 [R BNU IV, 2095].

.3.12.   Sturm, Johannes, In partitiones oratoriae Ciceronis
          dialogi quattuor.
            No printer, 1549 [Rott, 341].
            B. Fabricius, ca. 1552 [Rott, 34p].
            T. Rihel, ca. 1557 [Rott, 34t], 1563 [R BNU IV,
              2198], 1565 [Rott, 34w].
            P. Messerschmidt, 1558 [Rott, 34u], 1559 [Rott,
              34v].

.3.13.   Sturm, Johannes, and Toxites, Michael, Commentarius
          in orationem M.T. Ciceronis Pro Cn. Plancio ex
          scholis Joannis Sturmii.
            W. Rihel, 1551 [Rott, 62].

.3.14.   Sturm, Johannes and Toxites, Michael, Commentarius
          . . . in orationem M.T. Ciceronis primam contra
          Verrem . . . .
            W. Rihel, 1551 [Rott, 63].

.3.15.   Sturm, Johannes, and Toxites, Michael, Commentarius
          . . . pro P. Quintio . . . .
            W. Rihel, 1551 [Rott, 64].

.3.16.   Sturm, Johannes, and Toxites, Michael, Commentarius
          . . . in Philippicam M.T. Ciceronis primam.
            W. Rihel, 1552 [Rott, 68].

.3.17.   Sturm, Johannes, and Toxites, Michael, Commentarius
          . . . in Philippicam . . . Alteram.
            W. Rihel, 1552 [Rott, 69].

.3.18.   Sturm, Johannes, and Toxites, Michael, Commentarius

            . . . in Philippicam . . . Septimam.
            W. Rihel, 1552 [Rott, 70].

T1.3.19.   Goniaeus, Joannes, Selectarum declamationum
            professorum academiae Jenensis tomus primus.
            B. Fabricius, 1554 [R Nfp, 1920].

  .3.20.   Erythreaus, Valentinus, In Orationem M.T.C. pro lege
            Manilia de Pompeii laudibus Annotationes . . . Una
            cum oratione Ciceroniana emendate.
            Chr. Mylius I, 1556 [R BNU II, 799].

  .3.21.   Sturm, Johannes, Neanisci Dialogus.
            J. Rihel, 1565 [Rott, 91]. (Volumes I-IV.)
            J. Rihel, 1566 [Rott, 91a], 1579 [Rott, 91e].
            (Volume II.)
            J. Rihel, 1570 [Rott, 91b]. (Volumes I-V.)
            J. Rihel, 1573 [Rott, 91d]. (Volume VI.)

  .3.22.   Erythraeus, Valentinus, De elocutione libri tres.
            J. Rihel, 1567 [R BNU II, 805].

  .3.23.   Vives, Johannes Ludovicus (Juan Luis Vives) De
            disputatione.
            Chr. Mylius I, 1568 [R Nfp, 3433].

  .3.24.   Sturm, Johannes, Scholae in libros duos Hermogenis de
            formis orationum seu Dicendi Generibus.
            J. Rihel, 1571 [R BNU IV, 2222].

  .3.25.   Sturm, Johannes, De imitatione oratoria libri tres.
            B. Jobin, 1574 [R BNU IV, 2224], 1576 [R BNU IV,
            2229].

  .3.26.   Sturm, Johannes, Commentarii in M.T. Ciceronis
            Tusculanam primam confecti ex scholis.
            B. Jobin, 1575 [R BNU IV, 2226].

  .3.27.   Junius, Melchior, Methodus eloquentiae comparandae,
            scholis Aliquot.
            L. Zetzner, 1585 [R BNU II, 1292].

  .3.28.   Junius, Melchior, In Oratorem M. T. Ciceronis ad M.
            Brutum.
            A. Bertram, 1585 [R Nfp, 2170].

  .3.29.   Bentzius, Johann, Erotemata in M. T. Ciceronis libros
            III De Officiis. Itemque de Senectute et de Amicitia
            Dialogos.
            A. Bertram, 1589 [R BNU I, 181].

  .3.30.   Junius, Melchior, Artis dicendi praecepta secundum
            oficii oratorii partes breviter ex Platone,

Aristotele, Hermogene, Cicerone.
   A. Bertram, 1590 [R Nfp, 2171], 1594 [R BNU II, 1296].

T1.3.31. Junius, Melchior, Methodus eloquentiae comparandae, scholis rhetoricis tradita.
   L. Zetzner, 1592 [R BNU II, 1294], 1598 [R Nfp, 2174].

.3.32. Sturm, Johannes, Epitome partitionum oratoriarum M. T. Ciceronis . . . in usum scholae argentinensis.
   J. Rihel, 1593 [Rott, 34x], 1597 [Rott, 34y].

.3.33. Junius, Melchior, Resolutio brevis Orationum M. T. Ciceronis secundum causarum genera.
   J. Rihel, 1594 [R Nfp, 2173].

.3.34. Bentzius, Johann, Epitome partitionum oratoriarum M. T. Ciceronis et Ioannis Sturmii recognita et perspicuis exemplis illustrata.
   J. Rihel, 1594 [Greiner].

.3.35. Junius, Melchior, Orationum ex Historicis.
   L. Zetzner, 1598 [R BNU II, 1298].

4. SCHOOL VOCABULARIES.

T1.4.1. Niavis, Paulus, Dialogus paruulis scolaribus ad latinum ydeoma perutilissimus.
   M. Hupfuff, 1502 [S V, 18].
   J. Prüss I, 1504 [S III A, 46].

.4.2. Corvinus, Laurentius, Latinum Idioma.
   M. Hupfuff, 1506 [S V, 49].

.4.3. Grapaldi, Franciscus Maius (Francisco Mario Grapaldi), De partibus aedium Dictionarius.
   J. Prüss I, 1508 [S III A, 68].

.4.4. Altenstaig, Joannis, Vocabularius.
   J. Prüss I, 1509 [S III A, 73].
   J. Prüss II, 1515 [S III B, 10].

.4.5. Calepinus, Ambrosius, Dictionum latinarum e greco . . . dirivantium earundemque interpretaionus collector . . . omniumque Cornucopie vocabulorum insertor.
   J. Grüninger, 1512 [S I, 128].

.4.6. Cocleus, Joannis (Johann Cochlaus), Vocabulorum in Grammaticum Collectaneum.
   J. Prüss II, 1515 [S III B, 12].

T1.4.7. Cingularius, Hieronymus (Hieronymus Gurtler),
         Synonymorum Collectanea.
         R. Beck, 1518 [S IV Beck, 28].
         M. Flach II, 1522 [R BNU II, 1067].

 .4.8.   Dasypodius, Petrus, Lexicon Graecolatinum in usum
         iuuentutis Graecarum literarum studiosae, diligenter
         congestum.
         W. Rihel, 1539 [R BNU I, 619].

 .4.9.   Schorus, Antonius (Antonius van Schore), Apparatus
         verborum linguae latinae.
         W. Rihel, 1551 [Greiner].

 .4.10. Schorus, Antonius (Antonius van Schore), Thesaurus
         Verborum Linguae Latinae, Ciceronianus.
         J. Rihel, 1557 [R BNU IV, 2092], 1570 [Rott, 66c],
            1580 [R BNU IV, 2093], 1586 [R BNU IV, 2094],
            1597 [R BNU IV, 2096].

 .4.11. Sturm, Johannes, Onomasticon puerile argentinense II.
         J. Rihel, 1566 [Rott, 94], 1571 [Rott, 94a].

 .4.12. Golius, Theophilus, Onomasticon Latino-Germanicum in
         usum scholae argentoratensis.
         J. Rihel, 1578 [R Nfp, 1918], 1579 [Rott, 128],
            1582 [R BNU II, 1020].

 .4.13. Bentzius, Johannes, Thesaurus pure loquendi, et
         scribendi Graeco-Latinus.
         L. Zetzner, 1594 [R Nfp, 975], 1596 [R BNU I, 82].

   5. POETICS

T1.5.1. (Ringmann, Matthias), Hemistichia poetarum
         sentenciosiora pro pueris.
         J. Knobloch, 1505 [S VII, 13].

 .5.2.   Wimpfelingius, Jacobus, De arte metrificandi.
         Libellus.
         M. Hupfuff, 1505 [S V, 40].

 .5.3.   Jacobus, Gaudensis (Jacobus von Gouda), Aerarium
         aureum poetarum.
         J. Schott, 1515 [R Nfp, 2137; S II B, 34].

 .5.4.   Sturm, Johannes, and Crusius, Martin, Scholia in
         primam, secundam ac tertiam Virgilii eclogam
         sturmiana.
         B. Fabricius, 1556 [Rott, 76].

 .5.5.   Sturm, Johannes, Poeticum volumen.

J. Rihel, 1565 [R BNU IV, 2212], 1584 [Rott, 90h;
R BNU IV, 2236]. (Volume I.)
J. Rihel, 1573 [Rott, 90b], 1580 [Rott, 90g].
(Volume VI.)
J. Rihel, 1574 [Rott, 90c], 1580 [Rott, 90g], 1587
[R BNU IV, 2239]. (Volume IV.)
J. Rihel, 1575 [Rott, 90d], 1588 [R BNU IV, 2240].
(Volume V.)
J. Rihel, 1577 [Rott, 90e], 1586 [Rott, 90i], 1597
[R BNU IV, 2241]. (Volume III.)
J. Rihel, 1578 [Rott, 90f; BM R 2015], 1587 [R BNU
IV, 2238]. (Volume II.)

T1.5.6. Sturm, Johannes, Commentarii in artem poëticam
         Horatii confecti ex scholis.
         N. Wyriot, 1576 [R BNU IV, 2228].

   6. DIALECTICS AND LOGIC.

T1.6.1. Eccius, Johann (Johannes Eck), Bursa Pavonis,
         Logices exercitamenta appellata parva logicalia.
         M. Hupfuff, 1507 [S V, 66].

  .6.2. Petrus Hispanus (Pope Joannes XXI), Tractatus
         duodecim.
         M. Hupfuff, 1511 [R BNU III, 1854].
         J. Knobloch, 1514 [R BNU III, 1855].

  .6.3. Michaelis de Vratislavia, Introductorium dyalectice.
         J. Knobloch, 1515 [S VII, 105].

  .6.4. Petrus Hispanus (Pope Joannes XXI), Exercitium super
         omnes tractatus parvorum logicalium.
         J. Knobloch, 1517 [S VII, 147].

  .6.5. Agricola, Rudolphus, De inventione Dialectica Libri
         tres.
         J. Knobloch, 1521 [S VII, 226].

  .6.6. Melanchthon, Philippus, Compendiaria dialectices
         ratio.
         J. Herwagen, 1523 [R BNU III, 1511].
         No printer, 1536 [R BNU III, 1502].
         Cr. Mylius, 1538 [R Nfp, 2633], 1539 [R BNU III,
         1536], 1545 [R BNU III, 1544].

  .6.7. Neobarius, Conradus, Compendiosa facilisque artis
         Dialecticae ratio in puerorum gratiam nunc primum
         conscripta.
         W. Rihel, 1536 [R Nfp, 2754].

T1.6.8.   Sturm, Johannes, Partitionum dialecticarum.
          Libri II.
            W. Rihel, 1539 [Rott, 35].
          Libri IV.
            W. Rihel, 1543 [Rott, 35b], 1549 [R BNU IV, 2207].
            No printer, 1548 [Rott, 35e].
            J. Rihel, ca. 1557 [Rott, 35i], 1560 [R BNU IV,
              2111], 1566 [R BNU IV, 2214], 1571 [R BNU IV,
              2221], 1582 [Rott, 35n], 1591 [R Nfp, 3297;
              Rott, 35o].
          Epitome primi et secundi libri.
            W. Rihel, 1555 [Rott, 35q].
          Epitome Recognita.
            J. Rihel, 1593 [Rott, 35r], 1597 [R BNU IV, 2242].

  .6.9.   Erythraeus, Valentinus, Tabulae duorum librorum
          partitionum dialecticarum.
            J. Frölich, 1541 [R Nfp, 1638].
            Chr. Mylius I, 1551 [Rott, 61], 1555 [R Nfp, 1637],
              1561 [R BNU II, 801], 1565 [R BNU II, 803].

  .6.10. Erythraeus, Valentinus, Commentarii Notationis
          Artificii Rhetorici, ac Dialectici, in Orationem
          M.T. Ciceronis, . . . pro Archia.
            W. Rihel, 1550 [R Nfp, 1636].

  .6.11. Erythraeus, Valentinus, De Usu Decem Categoriarum in
          simplici quaestione.
            Chr. Mylius I, 1566 [R BNU II, 804].

  .6.12. Rodolphus, Chaparus (Caspar Rodolph), Dialectica.
            Chr. Mylius I, 1568 [R Nfp, 1329].

  .6.13. Hermogenes Tarsensis, De Dicendi Generibus sive
          formis orationum Libri II.
            J. Rihel, 1571 [R BNU II, 1149].

  .6.14. Schorus, Henricus (Heinrich Schor), Specimen et forma
          legitime tradendi sermonis et orationis disciplinas ex
          P. Rami scriptis collecta.
            J. Rihel, 1572 [R BNU IV, 2097].

  .6.15. Reusner, Johannes, Elementorum artis Dialecticae
          libri quatuor.
            N. Wyriot, 1578 [R Nfp, 3098].

  .6.16. Bentzius, Johann (Johann Benz), Partitionum
          dialecticarum Ioannis Sturmii epitome recognita.
            J. Rihel, 1594 [Greiner].

7. MUSICAL THEORY AND TEXTS.

T1.7.1.   Nachtgall, Othmar (Ottmar Luscinius Nachtigall),
          Institutiones Musicales.
             J. Knobloch, 1515 [S VII, 100].

  .7.2.   Philomates, Wenceslaus (Wenceslaus Philomates de Novo
          Domo), Musicorum libri quatuor.
             No printer, 1533 [R Nfp, 2898].
             J. Frölich, 1543 [R Nfp, 2897].

  .7.3.   Frosch, Johann, Rerum Musicarum Opusculum Rarum ac
          Insigne.
             P. Schaeffer, 1535 [R BNU II, 925].

  .7.4.   Luscinius, Othomaras (Ottmar Luscinius Nachtigall),
          Musurgia, seu praxis Musicae.
             J. Schott, 1536 [S II B, 137], 1542 [S II B, 142].

  .7.5.   Greiter, Matheus, Elementale Musicum.
             J. Frölich, 1544 [R Nfp, 1932], 1546 [R Nfp, 1933].

  .7.6.   Fabricius, Georgius, Disticha de quibusdam musicis
          et septem sapientibus.
             No printer, 1546 [R Nfp, 1680].

  .7.7.   Claudius, Sebastianes, Bellum Musicale, inter Plani
          et Mensuralis cantus Reges.
             P. Messerschmidt, 1563 [R Nfp, 1397], 1568 [R Nfp,
             1398].

8. WRITING EXERCISES, LETTERS, AND DIALOGUES.

T1.8.1.   Johannes de Lapide (Johann Heynlin), Dialogus de arte
          punctuandi.
             No printer, 1495 [R Nfp Inc., 407].

  .8.2.   Erasmus, Familiarium colloquiorum formulae in gratiam
          iuventutis recognitae.
             J. Knobloch, 1520 [R Nfp, 1568], 1521 [S VII, 214],
             1522 [S VII, 244].
             J. Prüss II, 1520 [R BNU II, 743].
             W. Köpfel, 1529 [R BNU II, 785].
             J. Frölich, 1537 [R BNU II, 792].

  .8.3.   Erasmus Roterodamus, De conscribendis epistolis.
             J. Knobloch, 1522 [S VII, 243].
             J. Herwagen, 1525 [R BNU II, 778].
             C. Egenolff, 1529 [R BNU II, 784].
             J. Albrecht, 1534 [R BNU II, 787].

T1.8.4.   Erasmus, Quotidiani Sermonis Formulae Communiores ex
          . . . Colloquiis, cum aliis in puerorum usum
          decerptae.
              J. Frölich, 1549 [R Nfp, 1628].

  .8.5.   Schreppeler, Jörg, Libellus valde doctus, elegans et
          utilis . . . . scribendarum literarum genera
          complectens.
              T. Berger, 1564 [R Nfp, 3194].

  .8.6.   Hawenreuter, Johann Ludwig, Adagia classica.
              J. Rihel, 1573 [R BNU II, 1076].

  .8.7.   Erythraeus, Valentinus, De ratione legendi explicandi
          & scribendi Epistolas.
              B. Jobin, 1576 [R Bib. Mun., 917].

  .8.8.   Chytraeus, David, Catechesis Recens Recognita et
          multis definitionigus aucta.
              J. Rihel, 1596 [R BNU I, 484].

    9. SONG BOOKS FOR THE GYMNASIUM AND ACADEMY.

T1.9.1.   Christianae Cantiones et precationes partim Graecae,
          partim Latinae usitatae in classibus Gymnasii
          Argentinensis.
              B. Fabricius, 1555 [R BNU I, 425].

  .9.2.   Selectae cantiones octo et septem vocum in usum
          Academiae Reipublicae Argentoratensis.
              N. Wyriot, 1578 [R Nfp, 1277].

  .9.3.   Wolkenstein, David, Primum musicum volumen Scholarum
          Argentoratensium. Quartae editionis.
              A. Bertram, 1585 [R Nfp, 3557].

  .9.4.   Faber, Henricus, Compendium Musicae cum compendiolo
          recognito . . . in usum Academiae Argentoratensis.
              No printer, 1596 [R Nfp, 1679].

   10. MISCELLANEOUS TEXTS.

T1.10.1. Camerarius, Joachim, Disputatio de piis et Catholicis
          atque orthodoxis precibus ad usum . . . institutionis
          puerilis.
              J. Rihel, 1560 [R BNU I, 422].

  .10.2. Chytraeus, David, De lectione historiarum recte
          instituenda. Et historiarum ferè omnium, et
          argumenta . . . .

Chr. Mylius I, 1563 [R Nfp, 1337], 1565 [R BNU I, 482].

T1.10.3. Sturm, Johannes, Scholae in librum Hermogenis de ratione tractandae gravitatis occultae.
J. Rihel, 1571 [R BNU IV, 2223; R BNU II, 1150].

.10.4. Oelinger, Albertus, Underricht der Hoch Teutschen Sprach, Grammatica seu Institutio Verae Germanicae linguae.
N. Wyriot, 1573 [R Bib. Mun., 1581], 1574 [R BNU III, 1668].

.10.5. Schadaeus, Elias, Grammatica Linguae Sanctae (in Hebrew).
J. Martin, 1591 [R BNU IV, 2077].

.10.6. Pappus, Johannes, Germaniae Veteris Descriptiones ex Probatissimis Authoribus . . . in usum Scholarum Historicarum Academiae Argentoratensis.
A. Bertram, 1591 [R BNU III, 1762].

.10.7. Bentius, Johannes, De Figuris libri duo.
J. Rihel, 1594 [R Nfp, 974].

.10.8. Schickfuss, Jacobus, Synopsis Philosophiae tam contemplativae quam practicae.
A. Bertram, 1597 [R Nfp, 3176].

.10.9. Lullus, Raymundus, Opera ea quae ad adinventam ab ipso artem universalem, scientiarum artiemque omnium brevi compendio . . . . De audita Kabbalistico. XII principia philosophica Lulliani. Dialectica seu Logica. Rhetorica.
L. Zetzner, 1598 [R Nfp, 2442].

T2. SCHOOL TEXTS IN GREEK OR IN GREEK ACCOMPANIED BY LATIN OR GERMAN.

1. GREEK GRAMMARS.

T2.1.1. Ebrardus Bethunienis (Eberhard of Bethune or Graecista), Graecismus cum commentario.
J. Prüss I, 1489 [R Nfp Inc. 228].

.1.2. Elementale Introductorium In Nominum et Verborum declinationes Graecas.
M. Schürer, 1512 [S VIII, 90], 1513 [S VIII, 100], 1514 [S VIII, 130], 1515 [S VIII, 166], 1517 [S VIII, 211].
J. Knobloch, 1523 [S VIII, 271].

T2.1.3.   Chrysoloras (Manuel Chrysoloras), <u>Erotemata</u>.
           J. Knobloch, 1516 [S VII, 123].

.1.4.   Luscinius, Ottomarus (Ottmar Luscinius Nachtigall),
           <u>Progymnasmata Graecae lituraturae . , . qua ratione</u>
           <u>citrà praeceptoris operam graece discere possis</u>.
           J. Knobloch, 1517 [S VII, 138], 1521 [S VII, 225].

.1.5.   Golius, Theophilus, <u>Educatio Puerilis Linguae</u>
           <u>Graecae Aesopi Fabellae</u>.
               W. Rihel, 1541 [R BNU II, 1015], 1543 [R BNU II,
               1016], 1549 [R BNU II, 1017].
               J. Rihel, 1572 [R Bib. Mun., 1130], 1578 [R BNU
               II, 1018], 1580 [R BNU II, 1019], 1593 [R Bib.
               Mun., 1131], 1596 [R BNU II, 1021], 1597 [R
               BNU II, 1022].

.1.6.   Erythraeus, Valentinus, <u>Libri Duo: unus de</u>
           <u>Grammaticorum figuris . . . alter . . . de modis</u>.
               W. Köpfel, 1549 [R BNU II, 798].
               Chr. Mylius I, 1561 [R BNU II, 800].

.1.7.   Rulandus, Martinus, <u>De emendata linguae Graecae</u>
           <u>structura, Libri II</u>.
               J. Rihel, 1559 [R Nfp, 3129].

.1.8.   Fabricius, Georg, <u>Syntaxis Graeca</u>.
           J. Rihel, 1576 [R Bib. Mun., 965].

.1.9.   Frischlin, Nikodemus, <u>Demonstratio, Graecos non</u>
           <u>carere Ablativo</u>.
               A. Bertram, 1586 [R BNU II, 907].

   2.   GREEK ORATORICAL TEXTS AND EXAMPLES.

T2.2.1.   Demosthenes, Πρὸϛ Λεπτίνην λόγοϛ (<u>Contra Legem</u>
           <u>Leptinae oratio</u>).
               W. Rihel, 1539 [Greiner].

.2.2.   Fabricius, Georg, <u>De syntaxi partium orationis apud</u>
           <u>graecos</u>.
               W. Rihel, 1551 [R BNU II, 836].

.2.3.   Hermogenes Tarsensis (rhetorician), <u>De formis</u>
           <u>orationum</u>.
               J. Rihel, 1555 [R BNU II, 1146].

T3.   PLAYS FOR THE SCHOOL.

   1.   LATIN PLAYS FOR THE SCHOOL THEATER.

T3.1.1.   Locher, Jacob, Historia de rege francia.
            No printer, 1495 [Weber].

  .1.2.   Wimpheling, Jacob, Stylpho.
            J. Grüninger(?), 1495 [Weber].

  .1.3.   Reuchlin, Johann, Scenica progymnasmata.
            J. Grüninger, 1497 [R Nfp Inc., 603], 1498 [Weber].

  .1.4.   Stymelius, Christophorus, Studentes. Comoedia de
            vita studiosorum.
            No printer, 1562 [R Nfp, 3299].

  .1.5.   Frischlin, Nikodemus, Priscianus Vapulans, Comedia
            Lepida . . . in qua demonstrantur soloecismi et
            barbarismi.
            B. Jobin, 1580 [R BNU II, 904], 1580 [R BNU II,
                905].

  .1.6.   Gnaphaeus, Guilielmus, Commediae aliquot.
            No printer, 1581 [R Nfp 1913].

  .1.7.   Holonius (Gregorius Holonius), Laurentias.
            No printer, 1584 [R Nfp 2038a].

  .1.8.   Frischlin, Nikodemus, Operum Poeticorum . . .
            Comediae quinque, Rebecca, Susanna, Hildegarde,
            Julius Redivivus, Priscianus Vapulans, Tragoediae
            Duae, Venus, Dido.
            No printer, 1584 [Weber].
            B. Jobin, 1585 [R BNU II, 906], 1587 [R BNU II,
                911].

  .1.9.   Frischlin, Nikodemus, Helvetio-Germani Comoedia nova.
            B. Jobin, 1589 [R BNU II, 913].

  .1.10.   Hospeinius, Michael, Equus Troianus sive de eversione
            Ilii tragoedia nova ex libris II. Aeneid. Virgilii
            confecta.
            A. Bertram, 1590 [R Nfp, 2078].

  .1.11.   Hospeinius, Michael, Dido tragoedia nova ex libris
            IV prioribus Virgilianae Aeneidos.
            B. Jobin, 1591 [R Nfp, 2079].

  .1.12.   Frischlin, Nikodemus, Phasma: Comedia posthume nova
            et sacra. De variis haerisebus et Haeresiarchis.
            B. Jobin Erben, 1592 [R BNU II, 914], 1598 [R BNU
                II, 923].

  .1.13.   Frischlin, Nikodemus, Operum Poeticorum pars scenica,
            Comediae Sex . . . Tragoediae Duae.

           B. Jobin Erben, 1592 [Greiner], 1598 [R BNU II,
           920].

T3.1.14.   Calaminus, Georgius, Rudolphottocarus: Austriaca
           Tragoedia nova.
              J. Rihel, 1594 [R BNU I, 399].

.1.15.   Frischlin, Nikodemus, Operum Poeticorum pars scenica,
           Comediae septem.
              B. Jobin Erben, 1595 [R BNU II, 917].

.1.16.   Junius, Samuel, Lucretia: Tragoedia Nova.
              A. Bertram, 1599 [R BNU II, 1299].

   2. BIBLICAL PLAYS IN LATIN FOR THE GYMNASIUM.

T3.2.1.   Sapidus, Johannes, Anabion sive Lazarus redivivus,
           comoedia nova et sacra.
              Cr. Mylius, 1539 [R BNU IV, 2071], 1540 [R BNU IV,
              2072].

.2.2.   Crocus, Cornelius, Comoedia sacra cui titulus Joseph
           ad christianae iuventutis institutionem.
              J. Frölich, 1542 [R Nfp, 1456].

.2.3.   Kirchmeier, Thomas (Thomas Naogeorgus), Judas
           Iscariotes, tragoedia nova et sacra.
              No printer, 1552 [R Nfp, 2243].

.2.4.   Gnaphaeus, Guilielmus, Acolastus, De filio prodigo
           comoedia.
              Chr. Mylius I, 1561 [R Nfp, 1912].

.2.5.   Gwalther, Rudolphus (Rudolph Walter), Nabal,
           Comoedia.
              Chr. Mylius I, 1561 [R BNU II, 1068].

.2.6.   Schoepperus, Jacobus, Ectrachelistis, sive Decollatus
           Joannes, tragoedia sacra.
              Chr. Mylius I, 1565 [R Nfp, 3185].

.2.7.   Dasypodius, Petrus, Philargyrus (sive ingenium
           avaritiae) Comoedia.
              No printer, 1565 [R Nfp, 1493].

.2.8.   Schonaeus, Cornelius, Tobaeus, comoedia sacra.
              N. Wyriot, 1572 [R Imp. Alsc. 571], 1583 [R Nfp,
              3187].

.2.9.   Calaminus, Georgius, Carmius sive Messias in praesepi
           . . . Ecloga. Ad Ioannem Schenckbecherum
           Tredecemvirum acta in Scholis Argentorati.
              N. Wyriot, 1576 [R Nfp, 1256].

T3.2.10.   Hunnius, Aegidius, <u>Josephus venditus. Comoedia</u>
           <u>sacra . . . Pro Argentinensi Theatro.</u>
                A. Bertram, 1584 [R Nfp, 2084a], 1597 [R BNU II,
                1217], 1597 [R BNU II, 1216].

   .2.11.   Birck, Sixtus, <u>Judith, Drama Comico Tragicum.</u>
                A. Bertram, 1585 [R BNU I, 205].

   .2.12.   Birck, Sixtus, <u>Susanna.</u>
                No printer, 1585 [Weber].

   .2.13.   Calaminus, Georgius, <u>Helis Tragoedia Sacra, Eiusdem</u>
           <u>de casu nuptiali Freidekiano Austriaco.</u>
                A. Bertram, 1591 [R BNU I, 398].

   .2.14.   Laurimanus, Cornelius, <u>Esthera Regina Comedia Sacra.</u>
                A. Bertram, 1596 [R BNU III, 1341].

T4.   ACADEMIC DISPUTATIONS AND THESES.

   1.   THESES, DISPUTATIONS, AND POEMS OF CONGRATULATION.

T4.1.1.   Jacobeaus, Nikolaus, <u>Declamatio . . . de laudibus</u>
           <u>artium et disciplinarum.</u>
                Chr. Mylius I, 1558 [R BNU II, 1252].

   .1.2.   Specker, Melchior, <u>Disputatio ex XI cap. ad Rom. de</u>
           <u>Gratia et Operibus.</u>
                No printer, ca. 1560 [R BNU IV, 2174].

   .1.3.   Hawenreuter, Johann Ludwig, <u>Theses artium.</u>
                J. Rihel, 1573 [R Bib. Mun., 1166].

   .1.4.   Beuther, Michael, <u>Themata historica de quibus</u>
           <u>disputabitur X. cal. Junii.</u>
                J. Rihel, 1573 [R Nfp, 1000].

   .1.5.   Freinshemius, Wolfgangus, <u>Disputatio in quinque</u>
           <u>vocibus, quae a dialecticis praedicabilia dicuntur.</u>
                J. Rihel, 1575 [R Bib. Mun., 1018].

   .1.6.   Dietrich, Hulderich, <u>Theses de usucapione et</u>
           <u>praescriptionibus temporum.</u>
                J. Rihel, 1575 [R Bib. Mun., 831].

   .1.7.   Boschius, Michael, <u>Oratio de militia scholastica.</u>
                N. Wyriot, 1578 [R BNU I, 229].

   .1.8.   Pappus, Johannes, <u>De autoritate patrum sive</u>
           <u>scriptorum ecclesiasticorum capita disputationis</u>
           <u>ordinariae.</u>
                N. Wyriot, 1579 [R BNU III, 1755].

T4.1.9.   Cargius, Stephanus, Isaac immolandus carmine
          descriptus.
          N. Wyriot, 1580 [R Nfp, 1293].

.1.10.   Reppusius, Caspar, Conversio D. Pauli Apostoli carmine
          conscripta.
          N. Wyriot, 1581 [R BNU III, 1988].

.1.11.   Carmina gratulatoria Michael Salzensis.
          N. Wyriot, 1583 [R BNU I, 453].

.1.12.   Carmina gratulatoria Math. Stolbergi Salzensis.
          N. Wyriot, 1583 [R BNU I, 454].

.1.13.   Carmina gratulatoria Joh. Jac. Braun.
          N. Wyriot, 1583 [R BNU I, 450].

.1.14.   Carmina gratulatoria Christ. Vualdis prima lauria.
          Chr. Mylius II Erben, 1583 [R BNU I, 451].

.1.15.   Carmina Gratulatoria Iuuenis Johannes Rigelii
          Meiningensis Hennenbergiaci.
          N. Wyriot, 1583 [R BNU I, 452].

.1.16.   Carmina Gratulatoria Friderico Docandro, accipientis
          insignia magisterii.
          A. Bertram, 1584 [R BNU I, 453].

.1.17.   Carmina gratulatoria Helfreci Emmelii.
          No printer, 1584 [R BNU I, 449].

.1.18.   Vakius, Cosmas, Theses. de progressione
          demonstrationis ex libro primo posteriorum
          analyticorum Aristotelis.
          A. Bertram, 1584 [Greiner].

.1.19.   Carmina gratulatoria Philippo Nagelio Winssemio.
          N. Waldt, 1585 [R BNU I, 457].

.1.20.   Carmina gratulatoria Ioannis Hofmanii cum ei
          Magisterii.
          A. Bertram, 1585 [R BNU I, 458].

.1.21.   Carmina gratulatoria Melchisedeci Pontani Austrii.
          A. Bertram, 1585 [R BNU I, 456].

.1.22.   Marbach, Erasmus, Theses, de Evangelio.
          A. Bertram, 1586 [R BNU III, 1478].

.1.23.   Frischlin, Nikodemus, Disputatio Grammaticae.
          A. Bertram, 1586 [R BNU II, 908].

.1.24.   Heinerer, Adam, Disputatio de patrimonio mulierum.
          A. Bertram, 1586 [R Bib. Mun., 1211].

T4.1.25.   Berchtoldus, Stephanus, <u>Actio Reivindicationis, Ad</u>
           <u>usum fori communem accomodata.</u>
               A. Bertram, 1586 [R BNU I, 183].

  .1.26.   Pappus, Johannes, <u>De Monarchis sive quatuor summis</u>
           <u>Imperiis. Capita Disputationis Publicae in Scholis</u>
           <u>Theologorum Academiae argentoratensis.</u>
               A. Bertram, 1586 [R BNU III, 1758].

  .1.27.   Hawenreuter, Johann Ludwig, <u>Analysis libri tertii</u>
           <u>politicorum Aristotelis.</u>
               A. Bertram, 1589 [R BNU II, 1080].

  .1.28.   Graseccius, Paulus, <u>De Tertia principali Personarum</u>
           <u>divisione</u> . . . <u>disputatio.</u>
               A. Bertram, 1589 [R BNU II, 1025].

  .1.29.   Hawenreuter, Johann Ludwig, <u>Ψυχολογία</u>   , <u>sive</u>
           <u>philosophica de Animo ex libris tribus Aristotelis</u>
           . . . <u>excerpta ad disputandum.</u>
               A. Bertram, 1591 [R BNU II, 1083].

  .1.30.   Graseccius, Paulus, <u>Disputatio de obligationibus in</u>
           <u>genere earumque speciebus, natura et causis.</u>
               A. Bertram, 1591 [R BNU II, 1026].

  .1.31.   Graseccius, Paulus, <u>Theses de verborum obligatione</u>
           <u>sive de stipulationibus.</u>
               A. Bertram, 1591 [R BNU II, 1027].

  .1.32.   Deczius, Johannes, <u>Synopsis philosophiae in privatum</u>
           <u>memoriae subsidium thesibus.</u>
               A. Bertram, 1591 [R BNU I, 624].

  .1.33.   Bader, Matthaeus, <u>Σνγχαριοτικὸν Πρόγραμμα</u>   in <u>laudem</u>
           <u>et honorem trium eximie doctorum juvenum.</u>
               A. Bertram, 1591 [R Nfp, 901].

  .1.34.   Schadaeus, Elias, <u>Theses de nominum impositione et</u>
           <u>dulcissimo nomine Jesu.</u>
               S. Meyer, 1592 [R BNU IV, 2078].

  .1.35.   Graseccius, Paulus, <u>Conclusiones de societate.</u>
               A. Bertram, 1592 [R BNU II, 1025].

  .1.36.   Hawenreuter, Johann Ludwig, <u>Theses ex praecipuis</u>
           <u>philosophiae partibus.</u>
               A. Bertram, 1593 [R Nfp, 1957].

  .1.37.   Hawenreuter, Johann Ludwig, <u>Aristotelis philosophorum</u>
           <u>omnium principis de iuventute et senectute</u> . . .
           <u>Theses.</u>
               A. Bertram, 1593 [R BNU II, 1089].

T4.1.38.   Mollinger, Ernestus Fridericus, Disputatio XXIX.
           Ethica, ex libro septimo Ethicorum Nicomachiorum
           Aristotelis.
               A. Bertram, 1597 [R Bib. Mun., 1504].

   .1.39.   Prechter, Bernardus, Fridericus, Disputatio XXVI
           Ethica.
               A. Bertram, 1597 [R Bib. Mun., 1756].

   .1.40.   Plesch, Maximilianus, Disputatio XXIII Ethica.
               A. Bertram, 1597 [R Bib. Mun., 1721].

   .1.41.   Plesch, Maximilianus, Disputatio XXXII Ethica.
               A. Bertram, 1597 [R Bib. Mun., 1722].

   .1.42.   Kullman, Petrus, Disputatio XXVIII Ethica.
               A. Bertram, 1597 [R Bib. Mun., 1350].

   .1.43.   Kefelius, Samuel, Disputatio XXX Ethica.
               A. Bertram, 1597 [R Bib. Mun., 1334, 1335, 1336].

   .1.44.   Bernerdin, Daniel, Disputatio XXXI Ethica.
               A. Bertram, 1597 [R Nfp, 989].

   .1.45.   Bernerdin, Daniel, Disputatio XXI Ethica.
               A. Bertram, 1597 [R Nfp, 988].

   .1.46.   Borkowski, Petrus, Disputatio XXII Ethica.
               A. Bertram, 1597 [R Nfp, 1034].

   .1.47.   Ritter, Sebastianus, Disputatio XXVII Ethica.
               A. Bertram, 1597 [R Bib. Mun., 1823].

   .1.48.   Borkowski, Petrus, Disputatio XXI Ethica.
               A. Bertram, 1597 [R Nfp, 1033].

   .1.49.   Borkowski, Petrus, Disputatio XXXI Ethica.
               A. Bertram, 1597 [R Bib. Mun., 573].

   .1.50.   Borkowski, Petrus, Disputatio XXXII Ethica.
               A. Bertram, 1597 [R Bib. Mun., 574].

   .1.51.   Borkowski, Petrus, Disputatio XL Ethica.
               A. Bertram, 1598 [R Bib. Mun., 575].

   .1.52.   Foeckler, Christophorus, Disputatio XXXIV Ethica.
               A. Bertram, 1598 [R Bib. Mun., 1003].

   .1.53.   Carmen et oratio Gratulationis recitata ab Zdenkone
           Brtniezensi Barone à Walstein.
               J. Rihel, 1598 [R Nfp, 3460].

   .1.54.   Prechter, Bernardus Fridericus, Disputatio XXXV
           Ethica.
               A. Bertram, 1598 [R Bib. Mun., 1757].

T4.1.55. Mollinger, Ernstus Fridericus, Disputatio XXXIX
          Ethica.
             A. Bertram, 1598 [R Bib. Mun., 1505].

  .1.56. Ritter, Sebastianus, Disputatio XXVI Ethica.
             A. Bertram, 1598 [R Bib. Mun., 1824].

  .1.57. Schwartz, Abraham, Disputatio de furto delicto gravi
          et quotidiano.
             A. Bertram, 1599 [R BNU IV, 2104].

  .1.58. Bökel, Guilelmus, Disputatio de substitutionibus.
             A. Bertram, 1599 [R BNU I, 226].

  .1.59. Mortiz, Erasmus, Disputatio de usucapionibus, materia
          utili et quotidiana.
             A. Bertram, 1599 [R BNU III, 1594].

  .1.60. Greventhal, Martin, Themata de rerum divisione et
          qualitatibus.
             A. Bertram, 1599 [R BNU II, 1046].

  .1.61. Funck, Johann, Disputatio de forma actionis.
             A. Bertram, 1599 [R BNU II, 929].

  .1.62. Selmnitz, Johannes Philippus, Disputatio de
          institutione heredum.
             A. Bertram, 1599 [R BNU IV, 2111].

  .1.63. Reusner, Bartholomaeus, Disputatio de traditionibus
          modo adquirendi Dominii naturali et frequenti.
             A. Bertram, 1599 [R BNU III, 1997].

  .1.64. Schelhase, Stephanus, Disputatio ex difficili et
          quotidiana L.N.C. de rescindo vendo.
             A. Bertram, 1599 [R BNU IV, 20B1].

  .1.65. Hornmold, Johannes Sebastian, Disputatio de
          compensationibus in Inclyta Argentoratensium Academia
          publici exercitii causa proposita à Georgio Obrechto
          I.C..
             A. Bertram, 1599 [R BNU II, 1203].

     2. ORATIONS GIVEN AT THE ACADEMY.

T4.2.1. Erythraeus, Valentinus, Oratio de honoribus academicis
          et eorum gradibus.
             N. Wyriot, 1574 [R BNU II, 806].

  .2.2. Ostrorog, Johannes, Oratio . . . cum . . . valediceret.
             N. Wyriot, 1581 [R BNU III, 1735].

  .2.3. Orationes quinque de certo genere vitae homini

nobili deligendo.
A. Bertram, 1586 [R Nfp, 2792].

T4.2.4. Chytraeus, David, De tribus nostrae aetatis
Caesaribus Augustis Carolo V, Ferdinando I, Maximi
Maximiliano II, Orationes.
K. Kieffer, 1587 [R Nfp, 1338].

.2.5. Frischlin, Nicodemus, Dialogus II, Pro sua Latina
grammatica adversus Martini Crusii.
B. Jobin, 1587 [R BNU II, 909].

.2.6. Frischlin, Nicodemus, Pro sua Grammatica, Dialogus
III.
B. Jobin, 1587 [R BNU II, 910].

.2.7. Schadaeus, Elias, Oratoria de linguae sanctae.
J. Martin, 1591 [R Bib. Mun., 1884].

.2.8. Boschius, Michael, Oratio de vellere aureo scholastico.
A. Bertram, 1591 [R BNU I, 230].

.2.9. Junius, Melchior, Orationum quae Argentinensi in
Academia exercitii gratia scriptae et recitatae.
(Parts I-V).
L. Zetzner, 1592-1596 [R BNU II, 1295].

.2.10. Marbach, Philippus, Orationes quinque.
B. Jobin, 1596 [R BNU III, 1486].

.2.11. Rantzow, Joachim, Oratio de nobilitate ed ad quodnam
honorum genus illa referenda sit.
A. Bertram, 1596 [R Nfp, 3074].

.2.12. Junius, Melchior, Orationum quae Argentinensi in
Academia, pars sexta.
L. Zetzner, 1597 [R BNU II, 1295].

.2.13. Goll, Theophilus, Epitome doctrinae moralis, ex decem
libris Ethicorum Aristotelis, . . . pro Academia
Argentinensi.
J. Rihel, 1597 [R Nfp, 1919].

.2.14. Junius, Melchior, Orationum quae Argentinensi in
Academia, pars septima.
L. Zetzner, 1598 [R BNU II, 1295; R Nfp, 2175].

HUMANIST WORKS

H1.   Humanist Works in Latin.

      1.   German and Swiss Humanists.
      2.   Alsatian Humanists.
      3.   Italian Humanists.
      4.   Dutch Humanists.
      5.   French Humanists.
      6.   Other Humanists.

H2.   Humanist Collections.

H3.   Pedagogical Treatises.

H4.   Dictionaries and Vocabularies.

H5.   Historical Works in Latin.

      1.   Ancient History.
      2.   Ecclesiastical History.
      3.   German and Imperial History.
      4.   Other Historical Works.

H1. HUMANIST WORKS IN LATIN.

   1. GERMAN AND SWISS HUMANISTS.

H1.1.1. Hemmerlin, Felix, De nobilitate et rusticitate
         dialogus.
         J. Prüss I, n.d. [R BNU Inc., 216].

  .1.2. Hemmerlin, Felix, Variae oblectationis Opuscula et
         Tractatus.
         J. Prüss I, n.d. [R BNU Inc., 215].
         G. Husner, 1497 [R Nfp Inc., 321].

  .1.3. Urbanus Prebusinus, Oratio mordacissima ostendens
         damnum quod omnibus se colentibus afferant virtutes
         et laudans vicia.
         J. Grüninger, n.d. [R Nfp, 3384; S I, 39].

  .1.4. Schottenius, Hermann, Confabulationes tyronum
         literariorum ad amussim Colloquiorum Erasmi
         Roterodami.
         No printer, n.d. [R Nfp, 3192].

  .1.5. Albertus von Eyb, Margarita Poetica.
         Printer of Vitas Patrum, 1484 [R Nfp Inc., 266].
         J. Prüss I, 1503 [S III A, 40].

  .1.6. Libri Philomusi. Panegyricus ad Maximilianum.
         Tragoedia de Turcis et Soldano. Dialogus de
         heresiarchis.
         J. Grüninger, 1497 [S I, 32].

  .1.7. Beroaldus, Philippus, Declamatio de tribus fratribus
         ebrioso, Scortatore et lufore.
         Wimpffelingius, Jacobus, Germania ad Rempublican
         Argen.
         J. Prüss I, 1501 [S III A, 32].
         W. Köpfel, 1542 [BM 1080.h.19.22].

  .1.8. Günther, Petrus, Defensio Germaniae.
         J. Grüninger, 1502 [R BNU II, 1064].

  .1.9. Badius Ascensius, Jodocus, Stultiferae nauiculae seu
         scaphae, Fatuarum mulierum . . . .
         J. Prüss I, 1502 [S III A, 36].

  .1.10. Bebelius, Henricus, Commentaria epistolarum
         conficiendarum . . . contra Epistolandi modos Pontii
         et aliorum. Contra epistolas Caroli. Commentaria de
         abusione linguae latinae apud Germanos et proprietate
         eiusdem.

J. Grüninger, 1503 [S I, 62], 1506 [S I, 79].
M. Schürer [S VIII, 109], 1513 [S VIII, 119], 1516
[S VIII, 179].

H1.1.11. Vehus, Hieronymus, Deo auspice pro divo Maximi. Ro.
Re. . . . Boemicus Triumphus.
J. Grüninger, 1504 [S I, 69].

.1.12. Kratwol, Heinrich, Oracio . . . habita in con-
secracione Georgii . . . Episcopi Babenbergensis.
J. Schott, 1505 [R BNU II, 1318].

.1.13. Hartlieb, Jacob, De fide meretricu in suos amatores.
M. Hupfuff, 1505 [S V, 39].

.1.14. Locher, Jacob, Apologia Philomusi contra Georgium
Zingel.
J. Grüninger, ca. 1505 [BM 11824.e.25.].

.1.15. Peutingerus, Conradus, Sermones Convivales: de
mirandis Germaniae antiquitatibus.
J. Prüss I, 1506 [S III A, 54].
C. Egenolff, 1530 [R Nfp, 2855].

.1.16. Bebelius (Heinrich Bebel), Ars versificandi et
carminum condendorum.
J. Prüss I, 1507 [S III A, 64], 1513 [R Nfp, 959].
M. Schürer, June 1513 [S VIII, 103], 1513 [S VIII,
104].
U. Morhard, 1522 [R BNU I, 175].

.1.17. Bebeliana (Heinrich Bebel), Opuscula Nova.
J. Grüninger, 1508 [S I, 96], 1509 [S I, 102].
M. Schürer, 1512 [S VIII, 87], 1514 [S VIII, 138].

.1.18. Zasius, Udalricus (Ulrich Zasius), Questiones de
paruulis Iudeorum Baptisandis.
J. Grüninger, 1508 [S I, 98].

.1.19. Motis, Joannis, Apologia mulierum in viros probrosos.
R. Beck, 1511 [S IV Beck, 3].

.1.20. Gresemundus, Theodoricus (Dietrich Gresemund), Carmen
de Historia Violatae Crucis.
R. Beck, 1512 [S IV Beck, 4], 1514 [S IV Beck, 15].

.1.21. Celtis, Conradus, Libri odarum IV, cum epodo et
saeculari carmine.
M. Schürer, 1513 [S VIII, 99].

.1.22. Engelbrecht, Philippus, Friburgica--florentissimae
urbis Friburgi apud Brisgoicos, descriptionem
complectens.
J. Schott, 1515 [S II B, 33].

H1.1.23. Emser, Hieronymus, Opuscula: . . . Epistola.
          Tetrastichon . . . . Epistolaria progymnasmata
          epistoliis centum numero. Epistola Philippi Beroaldi
          ad Hieronymum Emser . . . .
                J. Knobloch, 1516 [S VII, 112].

    .1.24. Hutten, Ulrich, Epistolae Obscurorum Virorum.
                J. Grüninger, ca. 1517 [R, Nfp, 2106].

    .1.25. Ludi Literarii Magistris: Vultis Auditoribus vestris
            (Joannes Alexandrus Brassicanus, ed.).
                J. Knobloch, 1519 [S VII, 175].

    .1.26. Latomus, Bartholomeus, Nenia in Obitum Divi
            Maximiliani Caesaris.
                J. Knobloch, 1519 [S VII, 181].

    .1.27. Aegidius, Petrus, Lamentatio . . . in obitum
            Caesaris Maximiliani.
                J. Schott, 1519 [S II B, 46].

    .1.28. Brassicanus, Joannes, Huschelini Testamentum.
                J. Knobloch, 1520 [S VII, 205].

    .1.29. Latomus, Bartholomaeus, Epistola Austriae.
                J. Knobloch, 1521 [S VII, 222].

    .1.30. Eobanus, Hessus Helius (Helius Eobanus Hessus),
            Exhortatorium. Carmine elegant . . . . ad
            Huldericum Huttinum ut Christianae veritatis, caussam
            et Lutheri iniuriam . . . .
                J. Schott, 1521 [R Nfp, 1546].

    .1.31. Brassicanus, Joannes, Hymnus in Appollinem Studiorum
            pariter ac studiosorum omnium Exemplar.
                J. Knobloch, 1523 [S VII, 258].

    .1.32. Rivius, Johannes, In Andriam Terentii ad Lectorum.
                W. Köpfel, 1529 [R BNU III, 2019].

    .1.33. Bolerus, Martinus, Scholia in orationem M. T.
            Ciceronis pro A. Licinio . . . .
                C. Egenolff, 1530 [R Nfp, 1028].

    .1.34. Bolerus, Martinus, Epicedion illustrissimi principis
            George Palatini Rheni.
                C. Egenolff(?), 1530 [R Nfp, 1029; B Egen., 17].

    .1.35. Eobanus, Hessus Helius (Helius Eobanus Hessus),
            Bonae valetudinis conservandae praecepta.
                H. Seybold, 1530 [R Nfp, 1549].

    .1.36. Melanchton, Philipp, Oratio ducta cum decerneretur
            gradus magisterii D. Andreae Vuinclero.
                J. Frölich, 1535 [Pegg, 3115].

H1.1.37. Agrippa, Henricus Cornelius (Heinrich von Nettesheim),
          *Epistola Apologetica ad Clarissimum urbis Coloniae
          Senatum, contra insaniam Conradi Cölin de Ulma* . . . .
              P. Schöffer, 1535 [R BNU I, 22].
              P. Schöffer, 1535 [R Nfp, 773]. (In German).

  .1.38. Eobanus, Hessus Helius, (Helius Eobanus Hessus), *In
          funera Erasmi Roterdami epicedion.*
              J. Frölich, 1537 [R Nfp, 1550].

  .1.39. Melanchthon, Philipp, *Philosophiae moralis epitome.*
              Cr. Mylius, 1538 [R Nfp, 2653], 1541 [R Nfp, 2654],
                  1544 [R BNU III, 1540], 1546 [R BNU III, 1546].
              P. Messerschmidt, 1559 [R BNU III, 1549].
              B. Fabricius, 1561 [R BNU III, 1560].

  .1.40. Amerbach, Vitus (Veit Amerbach), *Commentaria in
          Ciceronis tres libros de Officiis.*
              Cr. Mylius, 1538 [R Nfp, 815].

  .1.41. Sabinus, Georgius, *Poemata.*
              No printer, 1538 [R Nfp, 3144].
              Cr. Mylius, 1544 [R BNU IV, 2051].

  .1.42. Hutten, Ulrich, *Opera Poetica ex diversis monumentis
          collecta.*
              Cr. Mylius, 1538 [R Nfp, 2089].

  .1.43. Heldelin, Kaspar, *Paraphrasis in XVI Orationes
          Vergilii, quae quidem prima Aeneidos libro
          continentur.*
              Cr. Mylius, 1538 [R BNU II, 1121].

  .1.44. Willichius, Jodocus, *Commentaria in artem poeticam
          Horatii.*
              Cr. Mylius, 1539 [R BNU IV, 2465a], 1545 [R BNU
                  IV, 2468].

  .1.45. Tappius, Eberhardus, *Germanicorum Adagiorum Cum
          Latinis ac Graecis collatorum, Centuriae septem.*
              W. Rihel, 1539 [R BNU IV, 2268], 1545 [R BNU IV,
                  2269].

  .1.46. Latomus, Bartholomaeus, *Enarrationes in Topica
          Ciceronis.*
              Cr. Mylius, 1539 [R BNU III, 1336].

  .1.47. Schottenius, Hermann, *Ludus Martius sive bellicus.*
              No printer, ca. 1540 [R Nfp, 3192a].

  .1.48. Willichius, Jodocus, *Erotematum Dialectices libri
          tres.*
              Cr. Mylius, 1540 [R Nfp, 3521].

H1.1.49. Tatius, Marcus (Marcus Tatius Alpinus), Ad Ferdinandum
          Caesarem . . . Carmen.
          W. Rihel, 1540 [R BNU IV, 2271].

.1.50.   Camerarius, Joachim, Elegiae et carmen.
          Cr. Mylius, 1541 [R BNU I, 421].

.1.51.   Amerbach, Veit, Antiparadoxa.
          Cr. Mylius, 1541 [R BNU I, 47].

.1.52.   Polychorius (pseud.) or Vielfeldt, Jocorum
          Facetiorumque silva.
          J. Cammerlander, 1542 [R Nfp, 2968].

.1.53.   Amerbach, Vitus (Veit Amerbach), IV libri de Anima.
          Cr. Mylius, 1542 [R BNU I, 48].

.1.54.   Amerbach, Vitus (Veit Amerbach), In Artem Poeticam
          Horatii commentaria.
          Cr. Mylius, 1543 [R Nfp, 816], 1547 [R BNU I, 49].

.1.55.   Faustus, Gerardus; Fabricius, Georg; Hessus, Helius
          Eobanus, Poetae Historici Germani aliquot celebres
          singulis Distichis descripti.
          J. Schott, 1546 [R BNU III, 1899].

.1.56.   Melanchthon, Philippus, Commentarius de Anima.
          Cr. Mylius, 1548 [R BNU III, 1547].

.1.57.   Fabricius, Georg, Explicatio Castigationum in
          Terentii comoedias.
          W. Rihel, 1548 [R BNU II, 835].

.1.58.   Fabricius, Georgius, Antiquitatis aliquot monimenta
          insignia ex aere, marmoribus membranisque, veteribus
          descripta atque collecta.
          B. Fabricius, 1549 [R Nfp, 1681].

.1.59.   Fabricius, Jakob, Ad Urbem Memmingam Oda.
          S. Emmel, 1554 [R BNU II, 837].

.1.60.   Sidel Andreas, Praecepta morum ac vitae Isocratis ad
          Demonicum.
          B. Fabricius, 1555 [R Nfp, 3225].
          P. Messerschmidt, 1559 [R Nfp, 3226].

.1.61.   Siber, Adam, Ludus litterarum apud Chemnicium Misniae.
          B. Fabricius, 1555 [R Nfp, 3223].

.1.62.   Gildeleianus, Isaac Mauritius (Isaac Mauritius),
          Propemptikon Ad nobiles et optimarum artium studiis
          eruditos viros Andream et Guilielmum Dresselberg.
          S. Emmel, 1558 [R Nfp, 1905].

H1.1.63. Hutten, Ulrich, <u>Aula Dialogus.</u>
          T. Berger, 1559 [R Nfp, 2092].

  .1.64. Eobanus Hessus, Helius, <u>In P. Vergilii Maronis</u>
          <u>Bucolica Annotationes.</u>
          Chr. Mylius I, 1561 [R BNU II, 693].

  .1.65. Stainingerus, Gallus, <u>Carmen funebre in mortem C.</u>
          <u>Herlin.</u>
          Chr. Mylius I, 1562 [BM 837.h.3.25].

  .1.66. <u>Epistolae aliquot consolatoriae piae et utiles. Cum</u>
          <u>Praefatione Cyriaci Spangenberg.</u>
          S. Emmel, 1566 [R BNU II, 700].

  .1.67. Jociscus, Andreas, <u>Oratio de Ortu, Vita, et Obitu</u>
          <u>Ioannis Oporini Basiliensis, Typographicorum Germaniae</u>
          <u>Principis . . . .</u>
          T. Rihel, 1569 [R BNU II, 1259].

  .1.68. Premer, Johann, <u>Epithalamion scriptum in honorem</u>
          <u>Nuptiarum Clarissimi Viri D. Israelis Achatii . . .</u>
          <u>et Margaretae Gybshornin.</u>
          J. Rihel, 1570 [Greiner].

  .1.69. Rasarius, Johannes Baptista, <u>De Victoria Christianorum</u>
          <u>ad Echinadas, Oratio.</u>
          J. Rihel, 1572 [R BNU III, 1970].

  .1.70. Frischlin, Nikodemus, <u>Oratio de praestantia P.</u>
          <u>Virgilii Aeneidos.</u>
          B. Jobin, 1574 [R BNU II, 902; R Nfp, 1788].

  .1.71. Premerus, Johannes, <u>Carmen Elegiacum in Nuptias</u>
          <u>Principis . . . Ludovicii Wirtembergici.</u>
          N. Wyriot, 1575 [R BNU III, 1923].

  .1.72. Calaminus, Georg, <u>Thyrsis . . . in abitum M. Chiliani</u>
          <u>Passaveri Landaviensis amici sui.</u>
          N. Wyriot, 1575 [R BNU I, 394], 1583 [R Nfp, 1257].

  .1.73. Lossius, Lucas, <u>Fabulae versibus latinis expressae.</u>
          No printer, 1575 [R Nfp, 2426].

  .1.74. Calaminus, Georg, <u>Epithalamia in honorem nuptiarum</u>
          <u>Georgii Popii Gotthani.</u>
          N. Wyriot, 1575 [R BNU I, 393].

  .1.75. Calaminus, Georg, <u>Abitus viri doctissimi . . .</u>
          <u>Ioannis Memhardi.</u>
          N. Wyriot, 1576 [R BNU I, 396].

  .1.76. Crato a Grafftheim (Johannes Crato von Krafftheim),

Oratio funebris de divo Maximiliano II imperatore.
N. Wyriot, 1577 [R Nfp, 1452].

H1.1.77. Calaminus, Georg, Daphnis seu Christus patiens,
ecologa.
N. Wyriot, 1580 [R Nfp, 1256a].

.1.78. Holtzwart, Mathias, Emblematum tyrocinia, sive Picta
poesis latino Germanica (J. Fischart, ed.).
B. Jobin, 1581 [R Nfp, 2039].

.1.79. Calaminus, Georg, Liber vel epistole Mnemosynes ad
Eugeniam, de literarum origine et propagatione.
N. Wyriot, 1583 [R BNU I, 397].

.1.80. Epigrammata in Honorem doctissimi . . . Conradi
Wolffii.
No printer, 1584 [R BNU II, 697].

.1.81. Frider, Petrus, Hasma Thrêmêtikon in obitum Annae
sororis . . . suae prudentissimi viri Jacobi Hugonis
conjugis.
A. Bertram, 1584 [Greiner].

.1.82. Frischlin, Nicodemus, Strigilis Grammatica.
B. Jobin, 1585 [R Nfp, 1790].
B. Jobin Erben, 1594 [R BNU II, 915], 1595 [R BNU
II, 918], 1596 [R BNU II, 919], 1599 [R Bib.
Mun., 1029].
No printer, 1594 [R BNU II, 916].

.1.83. Frenzel, Salomon, Poemata Sacra et Nova.
A. Bertram, 1585 [R BNU II, 885].

.1.84. Euphemiai . . . Honori Leonhardi Weihemaieri.
C. Mylius Erben, 1585 [R BNU II, 818].

.1.85. Gamelia sive Symbola Nuptialia clarorum Germaniae
virorum virtuti et honori nobilium conjugum
Jeremiae Reusneri . . . et Elisabethae Wilandinae.
K. Kieffer, 1586 [R Nfp, 1810].

.1.86. Macropedius, Georgius, Hecastus Macropodii. Fabula non
minus pia quam iucunda.
A. Bertram, 1586 [R Nfp, 2579].

.1.87. Salm (Julius Comes Salm; Julius Graf von Salm),
Anathema sive arae sepulcrales inclytae familiae
Salmensis.
A. Bertram, 1586 [R Nfp, 3150].

.1.88. Crusius, Martinus, Libri duo ad Nicodemum Frischlinum.
I. Animadversionum in Grammaticen eius. II. Ad

eiusdem strigilim grammaticam antistrigilis.
  J. Rihel, 1586 [R BNU I, 602].

H1.1.89. Hunger, Wolfgang, Linguae Germanicae Vindicatio contra
          Exoticas quasdam, quae complurium vocum et dictionum,
          mere Germanicarum, etymologias ex sua petere sunt
          conati.
            B. Jobin, 1586 [R BNU II, 1215].

  .1.90. Epicedia in obitum honestissimae . . . Ursulae
          Beinheimin, Didymi Obrechti . . . coniugis scripta ab
          amicis.
            A. Bertram, 1586 [Greiner].

  .1.91. Disdorpius, Mauritius, Carmen de Auspicata Foederis
          Vetusti inter Tres Principes ac . . . Civitates,
          Tigurinam, Bernensem, et Argentinensem.
            A. Bertram, 1588 [R BNU I, 660].

  .1.92. Hiemeier, David, Carmen de Iesu Christo.
            A. Bertram, 1589 [R BNU II, 1165].

  .1.93. Lauterbach, Johannes, Aenigmata . . . ad Henricum
          Ranzouium, Regium Holsatiae Vicarium . . . .
            A. Bertram, 1589 [R BNU III, 1342].

  .1.94. Epitaphia generosi adolexcentis Chr. Megzinii
          Kvrozwekii haeredis.
            A. Bertram, 1590 [Greiner].

  .1.95. Coler, Christophorus (Christophorus Colerus),
          Daphnis transalpinus, carmen pastorale.
            J. Martin, 1592 [R Nfp, 1418].

  .1.96. Praetorius, Berhardus, Acclamatio Gratulatoria, ad
          . . . Episcopum Argentinensem Johannen Georgium.
            A. Bertram, 1592 [R BNU III, 1920].

  .1.97. Epicedia in obitum . . . Erasmi Marbachii.
            No printer, 1593 [R Nfp, 1552].

  .1.98. Zwinger, Theodosius, Methodus Apodemica in eorum
          gratiam qui . . . in quocumque . . . vitae genere
          peregrinari cupiunt.
            L. Zetzner, 1594 [R BNU IV, 2531].

  .1.99. Frischlin, Nikodemus, Operum Poeticorum.
            B. Jobin Erben, 1595 [R Bib. Mun., 1035], 1598
              [R Bib. Mun., 1036], 1598 [R BNU II, 921].
            No printer, 1596 [R Nfp, 1789a].

  .1.100. Scultetus, Tobias, Strenae.
            A. Bertram, 1595 [R BNU IV, 2107].

H1.1.101.   Agricola, Johann (Johann Agricola von Nuremberg),
            Disputatio XXV de modis tellendarum obligationum
            principalioribus desumpta.
               J. Martin, 1597 [R Nfp, 772].

   .1.102. Frischlin, Nikodemus, Orationes Insigniores Aliquot.
               B. Jobin Erben, 1598 [R BNU II, 922; R Nfp, 1791].

   .1.103. Engelhard, Joseph, Disputatio de Commodato.
               A. Bertram, 1599 [R BNU II, 687].

   2. ALSATIAN HUMANISTS.

H1.2.1.   Murner, Thomas, Hoc Epulum Comede.
               No printer, n.d. [R BNU III, 1601].

   .2.2.   Wimpheling, Jacob, Laudes Ecclesiae Spirensis.
               No printer, 1486 [R Nfp Inc., 713].

   .2.3.   Brant, Sebastian, De Monstruoso partu apud Wormatiam.
               J. Prüss I, 1495 [R BNU Inc., 113].

   .2.4.   Wynpfelingius, Jacobus, Ad Illustrissimum Principem
            Eberardum: Wyrtenbergensem.
               J. Prüss I, 1495 [S III A, 26].

   .2.5.   Brant, Sebastianus, Stultifera Navis. Narragonice
            profectionis nunquam satis laudata Nauis.
               J. Grüninger, 1497 [S I, 30].

   .2.6.   Brant, Sebastianus, Varia Carmina.
            Joannis Röchlin Phorcensis, Scenica Progymnasmata.
               J. Grüninger, 1498 [S I, 36].

   .2.7.   Wuimpfelin, Jacob, Agatharchia Id est bonus
            Principatus.
               M. Schott, 1498 [S II A, 16].

   .2.8.   Schottus, Petrus, Lucubraciunculae ornatissimae.
               M. Schott, 1498 [S II A, 13].

   .2.9.   Wuimpflingus, Jacobus, Philippica . . . in laudem &
            defensionem Philippi Comitis Rheni Palatini Bauariae
            Ducis &c.
               M. Schott, 1498 [S II A, 15].

   .2.10.   (Schott, Peter), De mensuris Syllabarum epithoma
            sicuti succinctissimum ita et fructuosissimum.
               J. Schott, 1500 [S II B, 4].

   .2.11.   Wimpheling, Jacobus, Germania . . . ad Rempublicam
            Argen.
               J. Prüss I, 1501 [R Nfp, 3540].

H1.2.12. Gresemundus (Dietrich Gresemund); Murner, Thomas;
          Wolff, Thomas; Wimphelingus, Jacobus, In hoc libello
          haec continentur: Versicli Theodorici Gresmundi.
          Epistola Thome Wolffi. Tetrastichon Jacobi
          Wimphelingi. Epistola Thome Murner.
          J. Knobloch, 1502 [S VII, 2].

  .2.13. Pellicanus, Conrad, De modo legendi et intelligendi
          Hebraeum.
          No printer, 1504 [R Nfp, 2864].

  .2.14. Wimphelingus, Jacobus, De Integritate Libellus.
          J. Knobloch, 1505 [S VII, 12], 1506 [S VII, 19],
             1515 [S VII, 108].

  .2.15. Wimphelingius, Jacobus, Soliloquium . . . Pro pace
          christianorum et pro Helvetiis ut resipiscant.
          J. Knobloch, 1505 [S VII, 14].

  .2.16. Wimphelingius, Jacobus, Appologetica declaratio.
          J. Knobloch, 1505 [S VII, 15].

  .2.17. (Wimpheling, Jacob), Epistola excusatoria ad Suevos.
          M. Hupfuff, 1506 [S V, 54].

  .2.18. Schottus, Petrus, Epithoma De sillabarum quantitate
          ac versuum connexione.
          M. Hupfuff, 1506 [S V, 53].

  .2.19. Murner, Thomas, Logica memorativa. Chartiludium
          logice, sive totius dialectice memoria.
          J. Grüninger, 1509 [S I, 108].

  .2.20. Murner, Thomas, De augustiniana hieronymianaque
          reformatione poetarum.
          J. Schott, 1509 [S II B, 11], 1519 [R Nfp, 2744].

  .2.21. Rhenanus, Beatus, Ad Lectorem Paraenesis.
          Michaelis Tarchaniotae, (Michael Marulic),
          Epigrammata et Hymni.
          M. Schürer, 1509 [S VIII, 20], 1509 [S VIII, 23].

  .2.22. Rhenanus, Beatus, Johannis Geileri . . . vita.
          M. Schürer, 1510 [R BNU I, 163].

  .2.23. Murner, Thomas, De syllabarum quantitatibus et arte
          carminandi facilima praxis.
          S. Murner, 1510 [R BNU III, 1605].

  .2.24. Wuimpfelfngius, Jacobus, Castigationes locorum in
          canticis ecclesiasticis et divinis officiis
          depravatorum.
          J. Schott, 1513 [S II B, 24].

H1.2.25. Vuimphelingius, Jacobus, <u>Ad Leonem Decimum</u>
          <u>Pontificem Maximum Carmen</u>.
          M. Schürer, 1514 [S VIII, 148].

  .2.26. Wimpheling, Jacobus, <u>Elegantiae maiores</u>.
          J. Knobloch, 1516 [R BNU IV, 2496].

  .2.27. Brant, Sebastianus, <u>Ad Divum Maximilianum Caesarem</u>
          <u>Invictissimum, cunctosque Christiani nominis</u>
          <u>principes et populos, Naenia . . . In Thurcarum</u>
          <u>Nyciteria</u>.
          J. Schott, 1518 [S II B, 41].

  .2.28. Murner, Thomas, <u>Chartiludium Institute summarie . . .</u>
          <u>Justinianus Cesar in prohemio digestorum</u>.
          J. Knobloch, 1518 [S VII, 168].
          J. Prüss II, 1518 [S III B, 15].

  .2.29. Gebuilerius, Hieronymus (Hieronymus Gebwiler),
          <u>Libertas Germaniae</u>.
          J. Schott, 1519 [S II B, 52].

  .2.30. Brant, Sebastianus, <u>In Laudem divi Maximiliani</u>
          <u>Caesaris</u>.
          J. Schott, 1520 [S II B, 53].

  .2.31. Gebuilerus, Hieronymus (Hieronymus Gebwiler),
          <u>Panegyris Carolina continens Hecatosthicon elegiacum</u>
          <u>carmen</u>.
          J. Prüss II, 1521 [S III B, 27], 1529 [R Nfp,
          1827].

  .2.32. Luscinius, Ottomarus (Othmar Nachtigall), <u>Grunnius</u>
          <u>sophista sive Pelagus humanae miseriae</u>.
          J. Knobloch, 1522 [S VII, 232].

  .2.33. Capito, Wolfgang Fabricius, <u>Institutionum Hebraicarum,</u>
          <u>Libri Duo</u>.
          W. Köpfel, 1525 [R BNU I, 437].

  .2.34. Luscinius, Ottomar (Othmar Nachtfgall), <u>Seria</u>
          <u>Jocique . . . literarum mecoenati D. Ant.</u>
          <u>Fuggero. . . .</u>
          No printer, 1529 [R Nfp, 2452].

  .2.35. Wimpheling, Jacobus, <u>De fide concubinarum</u>.
          J. Schott, ca. 1530 [R Nfp, 3529].

  .2.36. Sturm, Johannes, <u>De Amissa dicendi ratione . . .</u>
          <u>libri duo</u>.
          W. Rihel, 1538 [R BNU IV, 2199], 1543 [R BNU IV,
          2205].

H1.2.37.   Toxites, Michael, Querela Anseris vel de ingratitudine
           hominum elegia.
              No printer, 1540 [R BNU IV, 2348].

   .2.38.   Sturm, Johannes, Epistolae duae duorum amicorum
           Bartholomaei Latomi et Ioannis Sturmij, de dissidio
           periculoque Germaniae.
              Cr. Mylius, 1540 [R BNU IV, 2203].
              S. Emmel, 1567 [R BNU IV, 2215].

   .2.39.   Sapidus, Johann and Sturm, Johannes, Bucolicae
           querelae. Eucharii Synesii Romulus. Baptistae Persii
           Thyrsis.
              J. Frölich, 1540 [Rott, 39].

   .2.40.   Sturm, Johannes, Gymnasii Argentoratensis luctus ad
           Jacob Camerarium.
              W. Rihel, 1542 [R BNU IV, 2204].

   .2.41.   Sapidus, Johannes, Epitaphia sive gymnasii
           Argentoratensis luctus.
              W. Rihel, 1542 [R BNU IV, 2073].

   .2.42.   Sapidus, Johannes, Paraclesis sive consolatio de
           morte Alberti Marchionis Badensis.
              Cr. Mylius, 1543 [R Nfp, 3165].

   .2.43.   Hedio, Caspar, Paraphrasis in XVI orationes Vergilii.
              Cr. Mylius, ca. 1548 [R Nfp, 1968].

   .2.44.   Sturm, Johannes, Ad Werteros fratres nobilitas
           literata, liber unus.
              W. Rihel, 1549 [R BNU IV, 2206; R Nfp, 3290],
                 1556 [Rott, 56a], 1557 [Rott, 56a].

   .2.45.   Sturm, Johannes, Consolatio ad senatum Argentinensem,
           de morte Jacobi Sturmii nobilissimi uiri.
              W. Rihel, 1553 [R BNU IV, 2209].

   .2.46.   Toxites, Michael, Epicedion in funere Jacobi
           Sturmii.
              No printer, 1554 [R BNU IV, 2349].

   .2.47.   Marbach, Johannes, Consolatio funebris . . . J.
           Sapidus. Item, Adiecta Est Elegia Studiosi
           adolescentis.
              No printer, 1561 [R BNU III, 1479].

   .2.48.   Sturm, Johannes, De morte reverendissimi principis
           domini Erasmi Argentinensis episcopi.
              J. Rihel, 1569 [R BNU IV, 2218].

H1.2.49. Hawenreuter, Johann Ludwig, <u>Epistolarum Ioannis</u>
          <u>Sturmii . . . schematismoi.</u>
              J. Rihel, 1571 [R BNU II, 1075].

  .2.50. Sturm, Johannes, <u>De statibus causarum civilium</u>
          <u>universa doctrina Hermogenis Graeci Rhetoris.</u>
              B. Jobin, 1575 [R BNU IV, 2227].

  .2.51. Sturm, Johannes, <u>Consolatoria . . . epistola, ad</u>
          <u>virum clarissimum D. Bernhardum Botzemium . . . .</u>
              N. Wyriot, 1577 [R BNU IV, 2231].

  .2.52. <u>Epistola Musarum ad d. Johannem Sturmium.</u>
              No printer, 1581 [R BNU II, 699].

  .2.53. Hawenreuter, Johann Ludwig, <u>Oratio.</u>
              N. Wyriot, 1581 [R Nfp, 1956].

  .2.54. Reusner, Nicolaus, <u>Icones seu imagines virorum</u>
          <u>literis illustrium.</u>
              No printer, 1581 [R Nfp, 3102].
              B. Jobin, 1593 [R Nfp, 3103].

  .2.55. Reusner, Nicolaus, <u>Agalmatum Aureolorum emblematum,</u>
          <u>liber singularis.</u>
              B. Jobin, 1587 [Greiner], 1589 [R BNU IV, 2007],
                 1591 [R Nfp, 3105].

  .2.56. Reusner, Nicolaus, <u>Anagrammata de nomine magnifici</u>
          <u>et illustris viri, D. Henrici Ranzovii.</u>
              A. Bertram, 1588 [R BNU IV, 2006].

  .2.57. Rhenanus, Beatus, <u>Rerum germanicarum libri tres.</u>
              L. Zetzner, 1590 [R Nfp, 3108].

  .2.58. <u>Manes Sturmiani sive Epicedia.</u>
              J. Rihel, 1590 [R BNU III, 1473].

  .2.59. Beuther, Michael, <u>In Pub. Corn. Taciti Eq. Romani</u>
          <u>De situ, Moribus et Populis Germanorum . . .</u>
          <u>Libellum commentarii . . . nostris temporibus</u>
          <u>accomodati.</u>
              B. Jobin Erben, 1594 [R BNU I, 197].

  .2.60. Langius, Jospehus (Jospeh Lang), <u>Adagia sive</u>
          <u>sententiae proverbiales: Graecae, Latinae,</u>
          <u>Germanicae.</u>
              J. Rihel, 1596 [BM 1070.i.11].

  .2.61. Lang, Josphus, <u>Loci communes sive Florilegium Rerum</u>
          <u>et Materiarum Selectarum.</u>
              J. Rihel Erben, 1598 [R BNU III, 1333].

3. ITALIAN HUMANISTS.

H1.3.1.   Bartolini, Riccardo, Carmen geniale . . . de Carolo
           Hispaniorum rege nuper in Romanorum regem
           Francofordiae electo.
               J. Schott, n.d. [R Nfp, 935].

.3.2.   Gasparinus (Gasparini Barzizza), Epistolae.
               J. Prüss I, 1486 [S III A, 11].

.3.3.   Philelphus, Franciscus (Francesco Filelfo),
           Epistolae breviores et elegantiores.
               No printer, 1495 [R Nfp Inc., 575].
               J. Knobloch, 1509 [S VII, 61], 1511 [S VII, 75],
                   1515 [R BNU III, 1862].
               M. Schürer, 1512 [R Nfp, 2887], 1514 [S VIII, 134],
                   1518 [S VIII, 235].
               J. Prüss II, 1513 [S III B, 7], 1520 [S III B, 20].

.3.4.   Ficinus, Marcilius, Epistolae.
               G. Husner, 1497 [R Nfp Inc., 270].

.3.5.   *Basilius Magnus (Saint Basilius the Great), De
           legendis antiquorum libris opusculum divinum.
               J. Knobloch, ca. 1500 [R Nfp, 937].
               M. Hupfuff, 1507 [S V, 60].

.3.6.   Mancinellus, Antonius, Elegantiae portus. Laurentii
           Vallensis Lima quedam . . . .
               No printer, 1502 [R BNU III, 1469].

.3.7.   Baptista Mantuanus, Calamitates.
               J. Schott, 1502 [S II B, 7].
               J. Knobloch, 1515 [S VII, 98], 1518 [S VII, 157].

.3.8.   Baptista, Mantuanus, Contra poetas impudice loquentes
           carmen.
               J. Schott, 1502 [R Nfp, 920].

.3.9.   Baptista Mantuanus, Bucolica.
               J. Prüss I, 1503 [S III A, 39], 1504 [S III A, 45],
                   1505 [R Nfp, 908], 1506 [S III A, 58], 1507 [S
                   III A, 62], 1510 [S III A, 83].
               J Prüss II, 1513 [S III B, 6], 1514 [S III B, 9],
                   1520 [S III B, 18].
               R. Beck, 1515 [S IV Beck, 22], 1517 [S IV Beck, 26].
               J. Knobloch, 1515 [R BNU I, 140].
               Also listed as:
               Baptista Mantuanus, Georgius.
                   J. Schott, 1510 [S II B, 14].
     *Basil the Great's treatise was used by the humanists to
justify reading the classics.

H1.3.10. Joannis Picus Mirandule Comitis (Giovanni Pico della
          Mirandola), Opera . . . novissime accurate revisa.
          J. Prüss I, 1504 [S III A, 43].

   .3.11. Garson, Joannes (Giovanni Garzoni), De Miseria
          Humana.
          J. Grüninger, 1505 [S I, 70].

   .3.12. Beroaldus, Philippus, Oratio Proverbiorum.
          M. Hupfuff, 1505 [S V, 37].

   .3.13. Johannis Franciscus Picus Mirandulae (Giovanni Pico
          della Mirandola), De fide et ordine credendi.
          Theoremata . . . .
          J. Knobloch, 1506 [S VII, 20].

   .3.14. Eneas Silvius (Aeneas Silvius Piccolomini; Pope
          Pius II), De Prauis Mulieribus.
          J. Grüninger, 1507 [S I, 83], 1507 [S I, 84].

   .3.15. Joannis Franciscus Picus Mirandulae (Giovanni Pico
          della Mirandola), De Rerum Praenotione, libri novem.
          J. Knobloch, 1507 [S VII, 28].
          J. Grüninger, 1509 [S I, 106].

   .3.16. Ficinus, Marcilius, De religione christiana et fidei
          pietate opusculum.
          J. Knobloch, 1507 [S VII, 33].

   .3.17. Bossus, Matheus, De immoderato mulierum cultu ad
          Bessarionem cohortatio.
          M. Schürer, 1508 [S VIII, 8].

   .3.18. Sabellicus, Marcus, Antonius Coccius, Exemplorum
          Libri X ordine elegantia et utilitate
          praestantissimi.
          M. Schürer, 1508 [S VIII, 10], 1509 [S VIII, 16],
             1511 [S VIII, 61], 1518 [S VIII, 237].

   .3.19. Andrelinus, Publius Faustus, Epistolae proverbiales
          et morales.
          M. Schürer, 1508 [S VIII, 6], 1510 [S VIII, 38],
             1513 [S VIII, 118], 1516 [S VIII, 178], 1517
             [S VIII, 215], 1519 [S VIII, 243].
          J. Prüss II, 1520 [S III B, 24].
          M. Hupfuff, 1522 [R Nfp, 822].

   .3.20. Landinus, Christophorus, Libri Quatuor. I. De vita
          activa et contemplativa. II. De summo bono. III. IV:
          In . . . Virgilii . . . allegorias.
          M. Schürer, 1508 [S VIII, 5].

H1.3.21. Joannis Franciscus Picus Mirandulae (Giovanni Pico
          della Mirandola), De Providentia contra
          Philosophastros.
          J. Grüninger, 1509 [S I, 105].

  .3.22. Bossus, Mathaeus, Contenta . . . De veris et
          salutaribus animi guadiis . . . De instituendo
          sapientiae animo . . . de tolerandis aduersis . . . de
          Gerendo Magistratu iustitiaque.
          M. Schürer, 1509 [S VIII, 25].

  .3.23. Andrelinus, Publius Faustus, De virtutibus cum
          moralibus tam intellectualibus, Carmen dignissimum.
          M. Schürer, 1509 [S VIII, 14].

  .3.24. Trapezontius, Georgius, Dialectica . . . .
               M. Schürer, 1509 [S VIII, 19], 1509 [S VIII, 28],
               1513 [S VIII, 115; R BNU II, 996], 1516 [S VIII,
               189], 1519 [S VIII, 252].

  .3.25. Vergilius, Polydorus, De inventoribus rerum, Libri
          III.
               M. Schürer, 1509 [S VIII, 27], 1512 [S VIII, 74],
               1515 [S VIII, 175].

  .3.26. Nicolas von Wyle, Transzlatzion oder tutschungen
          . . . etlicher bücher Enee Silvii: Pogii florentini:
          felicis hemerlin: mit sampt andern schrifften.
          J. Prüss I, 1510 [S III A, 80].

  .3.27. Mancellinus, Antonius, Sermonum decas: ad Angelum
          Colotium.
          M. Schürer, 1510 [S VIII, 32].

  .3.28. Mancinellus, Antonius, De parentum cura in liberos et
          de filiorum erga parentes obedientia, honore et
          pietate.
               M. Schürer, 1510 [S VIII, 46], 1512 [S VIII, 80],
               1516 [S VIII, 203].

  .3.29. Modestus, Joannis Antonius, Carmen ad invictissimum
          Caesarem Maximilianum.
          M. Schürer, 1510 [S VIII, 33].

  .3.30. Helianus Ludovicus, De bello suscipiendo adversus
          Venetianos & Turcas oratio.
          M. Schürer, 1510 [S VIII, 34].

  .3.31. Vergilius, Polydorus, Proverbiorum liber.
          M. Schürer, 1510 [S VIII, 30], 1516 [S VIII, 205].

  .3.32. Poggius (Poggio Bracciolini), Historiae Convivales

Disceptativae, Orationes Investivae, Epistolae
Descriptiones Quaedam et Faceciarum Liber.
J. Knobloch, 1510 [S VII, 66; R BNU III, 1900],
1511 [R BNU III, 1901].
M. Schott, 1513 [R BNU III, 1902; S II A, 22].

H1.3.33. Pomponius Laetus (Giulio Pomponio Leto), Opera . . .
Epistolae aliquot familiares . . . Romanae historiae
compendium . . . .
M. Schürer, 1510 [S VIII, 29], 1516 [S VIII, 197].

.3.34. Landinus, Epistolae.
J. Knobloch, 1511 [S VII, 76].

.3.35. Collenucius, Pandulphus, (Pandolfo Collenuccio),
Apologi Quatuor.
M. Schürer, 1511 [S VIII, 63].

.3.36. Ziraldus, Lilius Graegorius (Lilio Gregoria Giraldi),
Syntagma de musis.
M. Schürer, 1511 [S VIII, 54], 1512 [S VIII, 77].

.3.37. Pasius, Curius Lancilotus, Non Vulgaris literaturae
Lib. VIII.
M. Schürer, 1511 [S VIII, 49].

.3.38. Zambertus, Barthol., Comoedia quam lepidissima
Dolotechne.
M. Schürer, 1511 [S VIII, 60].

.3.39. Calentius, Elisius Croacus (Eliseo Calenzio), De
bello ranarum in quo adolexcens iocatus est.
M. Schürer, 1511 [S VIII, 67], 1512 [S VIII, 91].

.3.40. Mancinellus, Antonius, Epigrammatum.
M. Schürer, 1512 [R BNU III, 1471].

.3.41. Faustus, P. (Publius Faustus Andrelinus), Aegloga
moralissima. Euisdem Hecatodistichon.
M. Schürer, 1512 [S VIII, 86], 1513 [S VIII, 117].

.3.42. Cimbriacus (Quintus Aemilianus), Encomiastica ad
divos Caess. Foedericum imperatorem et Maximilanum
regem ro.
M. Schürer, 1512 [S VIII, 71].

.3.43. Joannis Franciscus Mirandulae (Giovanni Pico della
Mirandola), De expellendis Venere et Cupidine.
J. Schott, 1513 [S II B, 23].

.3.44. Politianus, Angelus et aliorum virorum illustrium,
Epistolarum libri XII.
M. Schürer, 1513 [S VIII, 108].

H1.3.45. Piattino de Piatti, Libellus de Carcere.
          M. Schürer, 1513 [R Nfp, 2902].

   .3.46. Enchiridion poeticum . . . Epitheta . . . Vergilii
          ac aliorum.
          J. Schott, 1513 [S II B, 25], 1514 [S II B, 28].

   .3.47. Cantalycius, Pinnensis (Giovanni Battista Cantalicio),
          De Parthenope Bis Recepta, Gonsalvia. Liber IV.
          M. Schürer, 1513 [S VIII, 105].

   .3.48. Pontanus, Joannis Jovianus, Amorum Libri II.
          J. Knobloch, 1515 [S VII, 104].

   .3.49. Bartholinus, Riccardus, Ad divum Maximilianum
          Caesarem Augusti et bello Norico Austriados Libri
          duodecim.
          M. Schürer, 1516 [S VIII, 181].

   .3.50. Eneas Silvius (Aeneas Silvius Piccolomini; Pope
          Pius II), Dis büchlin sagt und meldet . . . von
          fraw Glück.
          J. Grüninger, 1516 [S I, 150].

   .3.51. Valla (Lorenzo Valla), Elegantiae, libri VI.
          M. Schürer, 1517 [S VIII, 225].

   .3.52. Platina (Bartolomeo Platina), De honesta voluptate et
          valetudine vel de obsoniis et arte Coquinaria libri
          decem.
          J. Knobloch, 1517 [S VII, 146].

   .3.53. Baptista Mantuanus, Fastorum libri XII.
          M. Schürer, 1518 [S VIII, 233].
          M. Hupfuff, 1520 [S V, 140].

   .3.54. Vallae, Laurentius, Elegantia linguae Latinae . . .
          et apologia in Poggium.
          U. Morhard, 1521 [S IV Mor., 7].

   .3.55. Vallensis, Laurentius (Lorenzo Valla), Calumnia
          Theologica.
          U. Morhard, 1522 [S IV Mor., 9].

   .3.56. Abstemius, Laurentius (Lorenzo Astemio), Hecatomythium
          alterum.
          No printer, 1522 [R Nfp, 732].

   .3.57. Montanus, Petrus, Satyrae . . . I. De Poetis . . .
          II. De Medicis . . . III. De principibus . . .
          IIII. De vita beata.
          C. Egenolff, 1529 [R BNU III, 1592].

H1.3.58. Valerianus Pierius, Johannes (Giovanni Pierio
          Valeriano Bolzani), Apologia . . . pro sacerdotum
          barbis.
             J. Albrecht, 1534 [R BNU IV, 2370].

   .3.59. Mirandula, Octavianus, Illustrium Poetarum flores
          per Octavianum Mirandulum collecti.
             W. Rihel, 1538 [R BNU III, 1577], 1544 [R BNU III,
             1578], 1549 [R BNU III, 1579].
             J. Rihel, 1559 [R BNU III, 1580], 1567 [R BNU III,
             1581].

   .3.60. Manutius, Paulus (Paolo Manuzio), Scholia, quibus et
          loci familiarium epistolarum difficiliores
          explicantur.
             W. Rihel, 1549 [R BNU III, 1477].

   .3.61. Castiglione, Balthasar de, Aulicuse. Accessit de Aula
          dialogus.
             No printer, 1563 [R Nfp, 1302].

   4. DUTCH HUMANISTS.

H1.4.1.   Hervicus de Amsterdamis (Gysbertus zoom Herwych),
          Oratio funebris in Fridericum Bavariae ducem.
             J. Grüninger, 1498 [R Nfp Inc., 330].

   .4.2.   Erasmus, Desiderius, Collectanea Adagiorum Veterum.
             M. Schürer, 1509 [S VIII, 22], 1510 [S VIII, 40],
             1511 [S VIII, 66], 1512 [S VIII, 75], 1513 [S
             VIII, 110], 1515 [S VIII, 155], 1516 [S VIII,
             187], 1517 [S VIII, 218], 1518 [S VIII, 227],
             1519 [S VIII, 250], 1520 [S VIII, 260], 1521 [R
             Nfp, 1566].

   .4.3.   Erasmus Roterodamus, Moriae Encomium.
             M. Schürer, 1511 [S VIII, 56], 1512 [S VIII, 85],
             1514 [S VIII, 143].

   .4.4.   Despauterius Joannis (Jean van Pauteren), Ars
          versificatoria.
             M. Schürer, 1512 [S VIII, 89].

   .4.5.   Erasmus Roterodamus, Parabolarum sive similium liber.
             M. Schürer, 1514 [S VIII, 146], 1516 [S VIII, 198],
             1518 [S VIII, 232], 1521 [S VIII, 262].
             J. Knobloch, 1521 [S VII, 216], 1522 [S VII, 246],
             1523 [S VII, 263], 1525 [S VII, 293].

   .4.6.   Erasmus, Roterodamus, Lucubrationes.

M. Schürer, 1516 [R BNU II, 722], 1517 [S VIII, 221].

H1.4.7. Erasmus Roterodamus, <u>Apologia ad eximium virum Jacobum Fabrum Stapulensem</u>.
M. Schürer, 1517 [S VIII, 224].

.4.8. Erasmus Roterodamus, <u>Stultitiae laus . . . Epistola Apologetica ad Martinum Dorpium</u>.
M. Schürer, 1517 [S VIII, 223], 1519 [S VIII, 246].
J. Knobloch, 1521 [S VII, 227], 1522 [S VII, 249], 1523 [S VII, 268].

.4.9. Erasmus Desiderius, <u>Encomium Matrimonii</u>.
M. Schürer, 1518 [R BNU II, 731].
J. Prüss II, 1522 [BM 8415.d.2].

.4.10. Erasmus, <u>Paraclesis id est adhortatio ad Christianae Philosophiae studium</u>.
J. Prüss II, 1519 [R Nfp 1618; BM 1351.a.11.2].
M. Flach, 1520 [Pegg, 1005]. (In German.)
J. Prüss II, 1522 [Pegg, 1006]. (In German.)

.4.11. Erasmus, Roterodamus, <u>Auctarium Delectarum aliquot Epistolarum</u>.
M. Schürer, 1519 [S VIII, 242].

.4.12. Erasmus Roterodamus, <u>Aliquot Epistolae sane quam elegantes</u>.
M. Schürer, 1519 [S VIII, 241].

.4.13. Erasmus, Desiderius, <u>Enchiridion militis Christiani</u>.
M. Schürer, 1519 [S VIII, 240].
J. Knobloch, 1521 [S VII, 217], 1522 [S VII, 237], February 1522 [R BNU II, 762], 1523 [S VII, 257], 1523 [S VII, 265], 1524 [S VII, 281].
U. Morhard, 1522 [Pegg, 947].

.4.14. Erasmus, D. Roterodamus, <u>Antibarbarorum, liber unus</u>.
J. Knobloch, 1520 [S VII, 206], 1521 [R BNU II, 750], 1522 [S VII, 238].

.4.15. Erasmus, Des. Roterodamus, <u>Bellum</u>.
J. Prüss II, 1520 [S III B, 23].
M. Schürer Erben, 1520 [B SE 1, 2]. (In German.)
J. Knobloch, 1523 [S VII, 266].

.4.16. Erasmus, <u>Scarabeus</u>.
J. Knobloch, 1522 [R Nfp, 1627].

.4.17. Erasmus Roterodamus, <u>In Jacobum Lopim Stunicam non admodum circumspectum calumniatorem Apologia</u>.
U. Morhard, 1522 [S IV Mor. 10].

H1.4.18. Erasmus Roterodamus, Querela pacis.
          J. Knobloch, 1522 [S VII, 233], 1523 [R BNU II,
             772].
          M. Schürer Erben, 1522 [B SE 1, 13]. (In German.)

   .4.19. Erasmus, Modus orandi Deum.
          J. Knobloch, 1525 [Pegg, 974].

   .4.20. Erasmus, Epistola cum amico expostulans.
          J. Knobloch, ca. 1525 [Pegg, 799].

   .4.21. Erasmus, Dialogus de vanitate scientiarum et ruina
          christiane religionis.
          No printer, 1534 [BM 4372.aa.20].

   .4.22. Bucoldianus, Gerardus, De inventione et amplifacatione
          Oratoria: Libri III.
          J. Albrecht, 1534 [R BNU I, 324].

   .4.23. Erasmus, De civilitate morum puerilium.
          No printer, 1552 [R Nfp, 1625].

     5. FRENCH HUMANISTS.

H1.5.1.   Budé, Guillaume, De contemptu rerum fortuitarum libri
          tres.
          G. Ulricher, 1529 [Greiner].

   .5.2. Baudouin, François, Cato sive commentarius ad
          Regulam Catonianam.
          Chr. Mylius I, 1555 [R Nfp, 947].

   .5.3. Crespin, Jean, Τὰ Σωζόξενα vetutissimorum authorum
          georgica bucolica et gnomica poemata quae supersunt.
          No printer, 1565 [R Nfp, 1454], 1567 [R Nfp, 1455].

   .5.4. Estienne, Henri, Carmen de senatulo foeminarum . . . .
          A. Bertram, 1596 [R Nfp, 1648].

   .5.5. Estienne, Henri, Carmen gratulatorium ad nobilissimum
          . . . Senatum Argent.
          A. Bertram, 1596 [R BNU II, 807].

     6. OTHER HUMANISTS.

H1.6.1.   Mallinius, Casparus Polonus, Iatrotheologonomicomachia
          Carmen Quo medicinae excellentia . . . .
          B. Jobin, 1575 [R BNU III, 1467].

   .6.2. Buchanan, Joh. (George Buchanan), Baptistes sive
          calumnia.
          N. Wyriot, 1579 [R Nfp, 1194].

H2. HUMANIST COLLECTIONS.

H2.1.1.   Margarita Facetiarum--Alfonsi Aragonum Regis
           vafredicta. Proverbia Sigismundi & Friderici tertii
           Ro. Imperatorum. Scomata Ioannis Keisersberg. Marsilii
           Ficini Florentini de Sole opusculum. Hermolai Barbari
           Orationes. Facetiae Adelphinae (Johannes Adelphus
           Mühling, ed.).
              J. Grüninger, 1508 [S I, 97], 1509 [S I, 112].

   .1.2.   Gregorii Thipherni poetae opuscula. Francisci Octavii
           poetae elegiae. Eiusdem epistolae amorum ad Juliam.
           Sulpitiae carmina LXXX. Georgii Merulae opera in
           lucem edita. Cornelii Galli poetae . . . elegiarum
           fragmenta. Pomponii Gauricii Neapol elegiacon.
              M. Schürer, 1508 [S VIII, 4], 1509 [S VIII, 21].

   .1.3.   De fortuna Francisci Marchionis Mantuae. F. Baptistae
           Mantuani Carmen elegantissimum . . . ad Caesarem
           Maximilianum. Epistola Elegiaca Fausti Andrelini . . .
           Antonii Syluioli Parisiensis Chilias. Petri de ponte
           Brugensis de abitu & reditu pacis Carmen. Domini
           Zachariae abbatis ad Venetos Elegia.
              M. Schürer, 1510 [S VIII, 36].

   .1.4.   Laurentii Valle Elegantiarum libri sex. Antonii
           Mancinelli lima suis locis apposita. Jodoci Badii
           Ascentii epitomatis singulis capitibus antepositis.
           Adnotationes eiusdem in Antonium Raudensem. Apologus
           seu actus scaenicus in Pogium florentinum.
              M. Schürer, 1512 [S VIII, 69], 1517 [S VIII, 216].

   .1.5.   Pierii Valeriani de Honoribus illustrissimo ac
           reuerendissimo Gurcensi Caesareo . . . Epistola.
           Panegyris Th. D. Mathei Episcopi Gurc. Per Just.
           Fran. Vitalem Panormium. Hieronymi Nogaroli Comitis
           ad Maximilianum Aug. pro Vicentinis habita Oratio.
              M. Schürer, 1513 [S VIII, 95].

   .1.6.   In hoc libello Amice Lector, iamprimum in lucem edita
           continentur, Isocrates, De Regno Gubernando . . .
           Divo Friderico III. Dicatus. ad Dominum Jacobum de
           Bannissis. Quintii Haemiliani Cimpriaci Poetae &
           Comitis Palatini Epicoedion Tetracolon in diuum
           Fridericum. III. Imperatorem. ad Maximilianum Ro.
           Regum, cum Epistola liminari Jacobi Spiegel ad
           Sebastianum Sperantium, Aloisii Marliani Mediolanensis
           ad Jacobum de Banissis . . . .
              J. Prüss II, 1514 [S III B, 8].

H2.1.7.   Aesopus, <u>Fabularum quae hoc libro continentur</u>
           <u>interpretes atque authores. Guilielmus Goudanus,</u>
           <u>Hadrianus Barlandus, Erasmus Roterodamus, Aulus</u>
           <u>Gellius, Angelus Politianus, Petrus Crinitus, Joannes</u>
           <u>Antonius Campanus, Plinius Secundus Nouocomensis,</u>
           <u>Aesopi Vita ex Max. Planude excerpta.</u>
               M. Schürer, ca. 1514 [R BNU I, 90], 1514 [S VIII,
                  147], 1515 [S VIII, 171], 1516 [S VIII, 199],
                  1516 [R BNU I, 95], 1517 [S VIII, 213], 1518 [S
                  VIII, 236], 1519 [S VIII, 249].
               J. Knobloch, 1520 [S VII, 207], 1521 [R BNU I, 98],
                  1522 [S VII, 253], 1523 [S VII, 260].
               J. Prüss II, 1523 [R Nfp, 753].

  .1.8.   <u>Contenta in hoc opere sunt haec. Catonis praecepta</u>
           <u>moralia recognita atque interpretata ab Erasmo</u>
           <u>Roterodamo. Mimi Publiani. Septem sapientum illustres</u>
           <u>sententiae. Institutio hominis christiani versi--</u>
           <u>hexametris. per Erasmum Roterodamum. Isocratis</u>
           <u>Paraensis ad Demoniacum Rudolpho Agricola interprete,</u>
           <u>recognita per Martinum Dorpium.</u>
               M. Schürer, 1516 [S VIII, 196], 1517 [S VIII, 222],
                  1518 [S VIII, 234], 1519 [S VIII, 251].

H3.   PEDAGOGICAL TREATISES.

H3.1.1.   Herolt, Johannes, <u>De eruditione christifidelium.</u>
               J. Eber, 1481 [R Nfp <u>Inc.</u>, 328].

  .1.2.   Boethius (pseud.), <u>De disciplina scholarium.</u>
               G. Husner, 1491 [R BNU <u>Inc.</u>, 99], 1495 [R BNU <u>Inc.</u>,
                  100].

  .1.3.   Vympfelingus, Jacobus, <u>Isidoneus Germanicus.</u>
               J. Grüninger, 1496 [R Nfp <u>Inc.</u>, 708], 1497 [S I,
                  33], 1498 [S I, 38].

  .1.4.   Wympfelingius, Jacobus, <u>Adolescentia.</u>
               M. Flach I, 1500 [S VI A, 78].
               J. Knobloch, 1505 [S VII, 10], 1515 [S VII, 94].
               M. Hupfuff, 1506 [S V, 56], 1514 [S V, 114],
                  1515 [S V, 119].
               M. Flach II, 1511 [S VI B, 24].

  .1.5.   Purliliarum, Jacobus, <u>De liberorum educatione.</u>
               J. Schott, 1510 [S II B, 13].

  .1.6.   Erasmus Roterodamus, <u>De ratione studii ac legendi.</u>
               M. Schürer, 1512 [S VIII, 79], 1513 [S VIII, 107],
                  1514 [S VIII, 139], 1516 [S VIII, 186], 1518 [S

VIII, 228], 1519 [S VIII, 245].
J. Prüss II, 1520 [S III B, 21].
J. Knobloch, 1521 [S VII, 220].

H3.1.7.   Bebelius, Henricus, De institutione puerorum quibus
          artibus et preceptoribus instituendi et tradendi sint.
          M. Schürer, 1513 [S VIII, 102].

.1.8.   Guarinus, Baptista, De Modo et Ordine, Docendi ac
          Discendi.
          M. Schürer, 1514 [S VIII, 129].

.1.9.   Brunnfelsius, Othonis (Otto Brunfels), De Corrigendis
          studiis severioribus Praeceptiunculae.
          J. Schott, 1519 [S II B, 49].

.1.10.   Othones B. (Otto Brunfels), Aphorismi Institutionis
          Puerorum.
          J. Schott, 1519 [S II B, 48].

.1.11.   Aretinus, Leonardus (Leonardo Bruni Aretino),
          De bonis studiis Epistola ad Baptistam de Malatesta.
          J. Knobloch, 1521 [S VII, 228], November 1521 [S
            VII, 221].

.1.12.   Mosellanus, Petrus, Paedologia . . . in puerorum
          usum conscripta et aucta.
          J. Knobloch, 1521 [S VII, 223].

.1.13.   Luther, Martinus, An die Radherren aller stedte
          Teütscheslands das sie Christliche Schülen uffrichten
          und halten sollen.
          M. Schürer Erben, 1524 [B Luther, 1880].
          J. Prüss II, 1524 [S III B, 37; B Luther, 1881].

.1.14.   Brunfels, Otto, Von der Zucht und Underweisung der
          Kinder.
          W. Köpfel, 1525 [R Nfp, 1109].

.1.15.   Melanchthon, Philippus, Ein büchlin für die leyen
          unnd kinder . . . wie mann die kinder zu der schrifft
          und lere halten soll.
          J. Prüss II, 1527 [R BNU III, 1525].

.1.16.   Erasmus, De Puerius statim ac liberaliter instituendis
          libellus et novus et elegans.
          C. Egenolff, 1529 [R Nfp, 1623].

.1.17.   Brunfels, Otto, Catechesis puerorum in Fide, in
          literis et in Moribus. Ex Cicerone, Quintiliano,
          Plutarcho, Angelo Politiano, Rudolpho Agricola,
          Erasmo, Philippo Melanch. atque aliis probatissimis
          Authoribus.

                J. Schott, 1529 [R BNU I, 283; S II B, 108].
                C. Egenolff, 1529 [R Nfp, 1103].

H3.1.18.   Sadoletus, Jacobus, De liberis recte instituendis.
                J. Albrecht, 1535 [R BNU IV, 2056].

.1.19.   Sturm, Johannes, De literarum ludis recte aperiendis.
                W. Rihel, 1538 [R BNU IV, 2200], 1539 [R BNU IV,
                   2202], 1543 [Beinecke, Lba 14.543s].
                J. & T. Rihel, 1557 [R BNU IV, 2210].
                J. or T. Rihel after 1557 [Rott, 29e].

.1.20.   Quotidiani sermonis formulae communiores ex Erasmi
        Roterodami Colloquiis.
                J. Frölich, 1542 [R BNU II, 876].

.1.21.   Heresbach, Konrad, De laudibus Graecarum literarum
        oratio.
        Joan Sturmius, De Educatione Principum.
                W. Rihel, 1551 [R BNU II, 1141].

.1.22.   Dasypodius, Petrus, De schola urbis Argentoratensis.
                W. Rihel, 1556 [R BNU I, 621].

.1.23.   Knaust, Heinrich, Agapetus Scholasticus praedo
        factus   conversus. Comoedia de Recta Institutione
        et è contra.
                P. Messerschmidt, 1562 [R BNU II, 1313].

.1.24.   Sturm, Johannes, Classicarum epistolarum, libri III.
                J. Rihel, 1565 [R BNU IV, 2213], 1573 [R Bib.Mun.,
                   2007].

.1.25.   Coelestinus, Johann Friedrich, Von Schulen.
                S. Emmel, 1568 [R Nfp, 1415].

.1.26.   Sturm, Johannes, Academicae epistolae urbanae.
                J. Rihel, 1569 [R BNU IV, 2217].

.1.27.   Boschius, Michael, Actus tres, Academiae . . .
        Argentoratensis, I. Classicorum, II. Baccalaureorum,
        III. Magistrorum.
                N. Wyriot, 1578 [R BNU I, 228].

.1.28.   Sturm, Johannes, Epistola ad illustrissimum principem
        ac Dominum Alexandrum Ducem Slucens em. Eiusdem de
        educatione principum.
                N. Wyriot, 1581 [R Bib.Mun. 2022].

H4.   DICTIONARIES AND VOCABULARIES.

H4.1.1.   Brack, Wenceslaus, Vocabularius Rerum.
                J. Grüninger, ca. 1485–1487 [R BNU Inc., 109].

J. Prüss I, 1489 [S III A, 23], 1495 [S III A,
   27].
M. Schott, 1489 [R Nfp Inc., 129].
G. Husner, 1491 [R BNU Inc., 110].
M. Flach II, 1512 [S VI B, 27].

H4.1.2.   Vocabularius Exquo.
           J. Prüss I, 1487 [S III A, 16], ca. 1488 [R
              BNU Inc., 684].
           M. Flach, 1490 [R Nfp Inc., 686].
           G. Husner, 1498 [R Nfp Inc., 687].

   .1.3.   Reuchlin, Johannes, Vocabularius Breviloquus.
           G. Husner, 1488 [R BNU Inc., 413], 1491 [R Nfp
              Inc., 601], 1493 [R BNU Inc., 414], 1495 [R Nfp
              Inc., 602], 1496 [R BNU Inc., 415].
           J. Prüss I, 1504 [S III A, 44].

   .1.4.   Vocabularius de partibus indeclinabilibus.
           G. Husner, 1491 [R Nfp Inc., 679].

   .1.5.   Vocabularius Variorum terminorum, ex poetis et
           historiographis congestus.
           J. Prüss I, 1502 [S III A, 33].

   .1.6.   (Torrentinus, Hermann), Elucidarius carminum et
           hystoriarum. Vel vocabularius poeticus.
           J. Prüss I, 1505 [S III A, 52], 1510 [S III A,
              82].
           R. Beck, 1514 [S IV Beck, 14], 1516 [S IV Beck,
              24].
           M. Hupfuff, 1515 [S V, 121].
           J. Knobloch, 1520 [S VII, 201].

   .1.7.   Vocabularius Gemmagemmarum.
           J. Prüss I, 1505 [S III A, 51], 1508 [S III A, 67].
           R. Beck, 1511 [S IV Beck, 1], 1513 [S IV Beck, 9;
              R BNU IV, 2435], 1514 [S IV Beck, 18].
           W. Schaffner, 1514 [S IV Sch., 5].
           J. Knobloch, 1518 [S VII, 164], 1520 [S VII, 202].

   .1.8.   Nestoris Novariensis, Vocabula suis locis: et
           secundum Alphabeti ordinem collocata.
           J. Prüss I, 1507 [S III A, 60].

   .1.9.   Calepinus, Ambrosius, Dictionarium copiosissimum: ex
           variis Lingue . . . Congregatis Latinis: grecis.
           M. Schürer, 1515 [S VIII, 176], 1516 [S VIII, 200].
           J. Schott, 1537 [S II B, 137a].

   .1.10. Polyanthea; hoc est Opus suavissimis floribus
           celebriorum sententiarum tam Graecarum quam Latinarum

exornatum (Nanus Mirabellius, ed.).
    M. Schürer, 1517 [S VIII, 217].

H4.1.11. Pinicianus, Joh., Promptuarium Vocabulorum.
          J. Knobloch, 1520 [S VII, 210].

  .1.12. Dasypodius, Petrus, Dictionarium voces propemodum
          Vniuersas in autoribus latinae linguae germanice
          explicans.
          W. Rihel, 1535 [R BNU I, 617].

  .1.13. Dasypodius, Petrus, Dictionarium Latino Germanicum
          Voces Propemodum uniuersas in autoribus Latinae
          linguae probatis explicans.
          W. Rihel, 1536 [R BNU I, 618].

  .1.14. Dasypodius, Petrus, Dictionarium Latino germanicum
          et germanicum latinum.
              W. Rihel, 1537 [R Nfp, 1488], 1539 [R Nfp, 1489],
              1543 [R Nfp, 1490], 1547 [R Nfp, 1491], 1554 [R
              BNU I, 620].
              T. Rihel, 1569 [R Nfp, 1492], 1596 [R BNU I, 622],
              1596 [R BNU I, 616], 1599 [R BNU I, 615].

  .1.15. Kyber, David, Lexicon rei Herbarjae trilingue.
          W. Rihel, 1553 [R BNU II, 1321].

  .1.16. Lexicon trilingue, ex Thesauro Roberti Stephani et
          Dictionario Joannis Frisii Summa fide ac diligentia
          collectum.
              T. Rihel, 1587 [R Bib. Mun., 1377], 1588 [R BNU III,
              1353], 1590 [R BNU III, 1354].

  .1.17. Emmel, Helferich, Nomenclator Latinus Propriorum
          Vocabulorum . . . Regionum, Insularum, Marium . . . .
              T. Rihel, ca. 1592 [R BNU II, 680].

  .1.18. Emmel, Helerich, Nomenclator Quadrilinguis,
          Germanico Latino-graeco gallicus.
              T. Rihel, ca. 1592 [R BNU II, 681].

  .1.19. Emmel, Helferich, Nomenclator Quadrilinguis, Latino
          Germanico Greco Gallicus.
              T. Rihel, ca. 1592 [R BNU II, 682].

  .1.20. Emmel, Helferich, Sylva quinquelinguis vocabulorum et
          phrasium Germanicae, Latinae, Graecae, Hebraicae,
          Gallicae linguae.
              T. Rihel, ca. 1592 [R BNU II, 683].

  .1.21. Lang, Joseph, Index omnium vocabulorum quae in
          omnibus . . . Martialis poematum libris reperiuntur.
              L. Zetzner, 1595 [R III, 1332].

H4.1.22.   Spach, Israel, Nomenclator Scriptorum Philosophicorum
           atque Philologicorum.
           A. Bertram, 1598 [R BNU IV, 2165].

H5.   HISTORICAL WORKS IN LATIN.

   1.   ANCIENT HISTORY.

H5.1.1.   Guido de Columna (Guida delle Colonne), Historia
           destructionis Trojae.
               Printer of Vitas Patrum, ca. 1485 [R BNU Inc., 134].
               G. Husner, 1486 [R BNU Inc., 135], 1489 [R BNU Inc.,
                   136], 1494 [R BNU Inc., 137].

  .1.2.   (Rolewink, Werner), Fasciculus temporum omnes
           antiquorum cronicas complectens.
               J. Prüss I, 1487 [S III A, 13], 1488 [S III A, 18].

  .1.3.   Baptista Mantuanus, Libri Tres de vita Dionysii.
           M. Schürer, 1508 [S VIII, 2].

  .1.4.   Huttichius, Johannes, Imperatorum Romanorum Libellus.
           Una cum imaginibus ad uiuam effigiem expressis.
               W. Köpfel, 1525 [R BNU II, 1235], 1534 [R BNU II,
                   1237], 1537 [R Nfp, 2118], 1540 [R Nfp, 2119].

  .1.5.   Boccacio, Giovanni, Compendium Romanae Historiae.
           J. Frölich, 1535 [BM 803.c.1.1].

  .1.6.   Thomas, Hubertus, De Tungris et Eburonibus aliisque
           inferioris Germaniae populis . . . commentarius,
           utilis ommibus qui Caesaris de bello Gallico
           historam Recte intelligere cupiunt.
               W. Rihel, 1541 [R BNU IV, 2323].

  .1.7.   Velcurio, Johannes, Explicationes in T. Liuii
           Patauini historiarum ab urbe condita libros, primum
           et secundum . . . .
               W. Rihel, 1545 [R BNU IV, 2390].

  .1.8.   Huttichius, Johannes, Romanorum Principum effigies:
           cum historiarum annotatione (Johannes Sambucus, ed.).
               W. Köpfel, 1551 [BM 811.c.3.1], 1552 [R BNU II,
                   1238].

  .1.9.   Hedio, Caspar, Vita Flavii Josephi.
               S. Emmel, 1556 [R Imp. Alsc. 567].

  .1.10.   Sleidanus, Johannes, De quatuor summis imperiis,
           libri tres. (Babylonico, Persico, graeco et romano).
               J. & T. Rihel, 1556 [R Nfp, 3235].
               J. Rihel, 1557 [Greiner].

H5.1.11. Chytraeus, David, <u>Chronologia Historiae Herodoti,</u>
          <u>et Thucydidis.</u>
              Chr. Mylius I, 1563 [R BNU I, 481].

   .1.12. Schubert, Clemens, <u>Libri Quatuor de Scrupulis</u>
          <u>Chronologorum in quibus non solum Calculus Sacrae</u>
          <u>scripturae cum Serie quatuor Monarchiarum et</u>
          <u>Olympiadibus Graecorum, atque Annis ab Urbe Roma</u>
          <u>condita pulcherrima harmonia conciliatur.</u>
              B. Jobin, 1575 [R BNU IV, 2100].

   .1.13. Frischlin, Nikodemus, <u>Hebraeis. Continens duodecim</u>
          <u>libros: quibus tota Regum Judaicorum et Israeliticorum</u>
          <u>historia ex sacris litteris desumpta . . . .</u>
              B. Jobin Erben, 1599 [R BNU II, 924].

   2. ECCLESIASTICAL HISTORY.

H5.2.1.   Cassiodorus, M. Aurelius (Flavius Magnus Aurelius
          Cassiodorus; Senator), <u>Historia ecclesiastica</u>
          <u>tripartita.</u>
              J. Prüss I, ca. 1500 [R BNU <u>Inc.</u>, 126].

   .2.2.   Eusebius, Pamphilius, <u>Ecclestica historia et</u>
          <u>Ecclesiastica historia gentis Anglorum</u>
          <u>Venerabilis Bede.</u>
              G. Husner, 1500 [R BNU <u>Inc.</u>, 161; R Nfp <u>Inc.</u>, 244].
              No printer, 1500 [R BNU II, 823].
              M. Schott, 1500 [R Nfp <u>Inc.</u>, 245].

   .2.3.   (Wimpheling, Jacob), <u>Argentinensium Episcoporum</u>
          <u>Cathalogus cum eorundum vita atque certis historiis:</u>
          <u>rebusque gestis.</u>
              J. Grüninger, 1508 [S I, 92].

   .2.4.   Heinrich von Haguenau, <u>De vita et moribus episcoporum</u>
          <u>aliorumque prelatorum et principum libellus, etiam</u>
          <u>privatis personis utilis lectuque jucundus.</u>
              R. Beck, 1512 [S IV Beck, 5].

   .2.5.   Richardus (Richard of St. Victor), <u>De Duodecim</u>
          <u>Patriarchis.</u>
              J. Knobloch, 1516 [S VII, 128].

   .2.6.   Pappus, Johannes, <u>Historiae Ecclesiasticae, de</u>
          <u>Conversionibus Gentium, Persecutionibus Ecclesiae,</u>
          <u>Haeresibus, et Conciliis oecumenicis Epitome.</u>
              B. Jobin, 1584 [R BNU III, 1757].
              B. Jobin Erben, 1596 [R BNU III, 1765].

   .2.7.   Schorus, Henricus (Heinrich Schor), <u>Breviarium</u>

            Romanorum Pontificum Qui Romanam Rexerunt Ecclesiam.
            B. Jobin, 1588 [R BNU IV, 2098].

H5.2.8.   Sten, Simon, Vita Ignatii Lojolae, Qui religionem
          Clericorum Societatis Iesu instituit, Ante aliquot
          annos descripta à Petro Ribadeneira.
            J. Rihel(?), 1598 [R IV, 2190].

    3. GERMAN AND IMPERIAL HISTORY.

H5.3.1.   Sopher, Gervasius, Henrici Quarti Ro. Imperato bellum
          contra Saxones.
            J. Grüninger, 1508 [S I, 99].

  .3.2.   Ottonis Phrisigensis (Otto, Bishop of Freising),
          Rerum aborigine mundi ad ipsius usque tempora
          gestarum, Libri Octo. Eiusdem De gestis Friderici
          primi Aeno-barbi Caes. Aug. Libri Duo.
          Radevicus Phrisingen, Libri duo, prioribus additi,
          de eiusdem Friderici Imp. gestis. (Joannes
          Cuspinianus, ed.).
            M. Schürer, 1515 [S VIII, 152].

  .3.3.   Enees Silvius (Aeneas Silvius Piccolomini; Pope Pius
          II), Germania.
            R. Beck, 1515 [S IV Beck, 21].

  .3.4.   Gebwiler, Hieronymus, Epitoma Regii ac Vetustissimi
          Ortus . . . Maiestatis . . . Ferdinandi Boemiae regis.
            J. Grüninger, 1527 [S I, 232].

  .3.5.   Gunther (Gunther of Pairis), Ligurinus seu Opus
          de Rebus gestis Imp. Caesaris Frederici, I Aug.
          Lib. X absolutum.
            J. Schott, 1531 [S II B, 118].

  .3.6.   Burchardus, Urspergensis, Chronicum . . . a Nino
          Rege Assyriorum Magno, usque ad Fridericum II,
          Romanorum Imperatorem.
            Cr. Mylius, 1537 [R BNU I, 331], 1540 [R BNU I,
              332].

  .3.7.   Cuspinianus, Johannes Spiesshaymer, De Caesaribus
          atque Imperatoribus Romanis opus insigne. Dedicatio
          Operis ad . . . Carolum Quintum per Christophorum
          Scheurle. Vita Joannis Cuspiniani, et de utilitate
          huius historiae per D. Nicolaum Gerbelium.
            Cr. Mylius, 1540 [R BNU I, 606].
            No printer, 1550 [R Nfp, 1474].

  .3.8.   Cuspinianus, Johannes, and Gerbelius, Nicolaus,

Icones Imperatorum et breves vitae.
Cr. Mylius, 1544 [BM 803.c.1.2].

H5.3.9. Ausonius, Jac. Micyllus, and Velius, Ursinus,
Icones Imperatorum, et Breves vitae, atque rerum
cuiusque gestarum indicationes.
Cr. Mylius, 1544 [R BNU I, 115].

.3.10. Sleidanus, Johannes, De statu religionis et Reipublicae,
Carolo Quinto, Caesare, Commentarii.
W. Rihel, 1555 [R BNU IV, 2129], 1555 [R BNU IV,
2131].
W. Rihel Erben, 1555 [R BNU IV, 2130].
T. Rihel, 1556 [R Bib. Mun., 1928], after 1557 [R
BNU IV, 2132], after 1557 [R BNU IV, 2133], after
1557 [R BNU IV, 2134], 1566 [Greiner], 1566 [R
BNU IV, 2144], 1568 [R BNU IV, 2145], 1576 [R BNU
IV, 2148].
J. Rihel, 1558 [R BNU IV, 2139], 1559 [R BNU IV,
2142], 1561 [R BNU IV, 2143].

.3.11. Sleidanus, Johannes, Tabulae in libros historiarum
De Religione & Republica.
J. Rihel, 1558 [R BNU IV, 2140].

.3.12. Beuther, Michael, Commentariorum de rebus in Europa
et aliis . . . orbis terrarum . . . illustioribus
regnis Carolo V. Imperatore gestis Libri VIII.
T. Rihel, 1568 [R Bib. Mun., 532].

.3.13. Holtzwart, Mathias, Eikones cum descriptionibus
duodecim primorum veteris Germaniae Heroum.
B. Jobin, 1573 [BM 555.a.1].

.3.14. Cilicius, Christian (Henricus Rantzau), Belli
Dithmarsici ab Inclyto Daniae rege Friderico II et
illustrissimis Holsatiae Ducibus, Johanne et Adelpho
fratribus, gesti anno . . . 1559.
B. Jobin, 1574 [R Nfp, 1393; R BNU IV, 1968].

.3.15. Paracelsus, Testamentum.
Chr. Mylius II, 1574 [R Bib. Mun., 1631].

.3.16. Calaminus, Georg, Vita Clarissimi Joannis Guintherii
Andernaci Medici celeberrimi.
No printer, 1575 [R BNU I, 395].

.3.17. Reusner, Nicolaus, Gamelia sive Symbola Nuptialia
clarorum Germaniae virorum.
K. Kieffer, 1586 [R BNU III, 2003].

.3.18. Reusner, Nicolaus, Anathemata sive Arae Sepulcrales
inclytae Familiae Salmensis Auspiciis inclyti et

        magnanissimi Herois O. Iulii Comitis Salmoe et
        Neoburgi ad Oenum &c. Sacr. Maiest. Imperial . .
            A. Bertram, 1586 [R BNU III, 2002].

H5.3.19. Reusner, Nicolaus, Icones sive Imagines virorum
          literis illustrium . . . in Germania praesertim.
              B. Jobin, 1587 [R BNU III, 2005], 1590 [R BNU, III,
              2008].
              B. Jobin Erben, 1590 [R Bib Mun., 1808].

  .3.20. Candidus, Pantaleon, Bohemais hoc est de ducibus
          Bohemicis libri duo, de regibus Bohemiae: libri V.
              No printer, 1587 [R Nfp, 1274].

  .3.21. Chytraeus, David, Cronici Saxoniae et vicini Orbis
          Arctoi.
              B. Jobin, 1590 [R BNU I, 483].

  .3.22. Frischlin, Jakob, Nicodemus Frischlinus . . . factus
          Redivivus.
              B. Jobin Erben, 1599 [R BNU II, 900].

    4. OTHER HISTORICAL WORKS.

H5.4.1.   Burlaeus (Walter Burleigh), Vita Philosophorum et
          Poetarum: cum auctoritatibus et sententiis aureis
          eorundem annexis.
              J. Knobloch, 1516 [S VII, 115; R BNU I, 340].

  .4.2.   Geldenhauer, Gerardus, Pompa exequiarum Hispaniarum
          Regis Ferdonandi . . . .
              M. Schürer, 1516 [BM 9930.f.68].

  .4.3.   Geldenhauer, Gerardus, Vita clarissimi principis
          Philippi à Burgundia, boni Philippi Burgundionum
          Ducis filii, in qua non paucis locis Christiani
          Principis exempla proponumtur.
              C. Egenolff, 1529 [R BNU II, 990].

  .4.4.   Barletius, Marinus, De vita moribus ac rebus
          praecpive adversus Turcas, Gesti, Georgii Castrioti,
          clarissimi Epirotarum principis. Alexander Magnus
          . . . libri Tredecem.
              Cr. Mylius, 1537 [R BNU I, 152].

  .4.5.   Jovius, Paulus, Turcicorum rerum commentarius . . .
          Origo Turcici Imperii. Vitae omnium Turciorum
          imperatorum.
              W. Rihel, 1537 [R Nfp, 2163].

  .4.6.   Gassarus, Achilles P. (Achilles Pirmin Gasser),
          Historiarum et Chronicorum totius mundi Epitome.
              Cr. Mylius, 1538 [R Nfp, 1816].

H5.4.7.　Capella, Gallaecius, <u>Commentarii de rebus gestis pro</u>
<u>restitutione Fransisci Sfortiae II. Mediolani Ducis</u>.
Cr. Mylius, 1538 [R BNU I, 429].

.4.8.　Durand, Nicolas (Nicolaus Durand de Villegagnon),
<u>Caroli V. Imperatoris expeditio in Africam ad</u>
<u>Argieriam</u>.
W. Rihel, 1542 [BM T.1929.6].

.4.9.　Comines, Philippe de, <u>De Rebus Gestis Ludovici, eius</u>
<u>nominis undecimi, Galliarum Regis, et Caroli,</u>
<u>Burgundiae Ducis, . . . Commentarii</u>.
Cr. Mylius, 1545 [R BNU I, 562].

.4.10.　Phillipe de Comines and Johannes Sleidanus, <u>De Carolo</u>
<u>Octavo, Galliae rege & bello Neapolitano, commentarii</u>.
W. Rihel, 1548 [R Nfp, 1424].

.4.11.　Krantz, Albrecht, <u>Chronica Regnorum Aquilonarium</u>;
<u>Daniae, Svetiae, Norvagiae</u>.
J. Schott, 1548 [R BNU II, 1317].

.4.12.　Drechsler, Wolfgang, <u>De Saracenis et Turcis</u>
<u>Chronichon</u>.
J. Frölich, 1550 [R Bib. Mun., 859].

.4.13.　Jovius, Paulus, <u>Historiarum sui Temporis</u>.
A. Fries, 1556 [R BNU II, 1285].

.4.14.　Reusner, Nicolaus, <u>Januarius sive Fastorum Sacrorum</u>
<u>et Historicorum. Liber primus</u>.
B. Jobin, 1584 [R BNU III, 1999].

.4.15.　Reusner, Nicolaus, <u>Partitio, sive Oeconomia Iuris</u>
<u>Utriusque, civilis et Canonici</u>.
B. Jobin, 1585 [R BNU III, 2001].

.4.16.　Reusner, Nicolaus, <u>Februarius, sive Fastorum sacrorum</u>
<u>et historicorum Liber secundus</u>.
A. Bertram, 1586 [R BNU III, 2004].

.4.17.　Candidus, Pantaleon, <u>Gotiberis Hoc est De Goticis</u>
<u>per Hispaniam Regibus e Teutonica Gente Originem</u>
<u>Trahentibus: Libri VI</u>.
A. Bertram, 1587 [R BNU I, 423].

.4.18.　Beuther, Michael, <u>Animadversionum sive discerptationum</u>
<u>tam historicarum quam chronographicarum liber</u>
<u>singularis</u>.
B. Jobin, 1593 [R Bib. Mun., 536].

.4.19.　Patricius, Franciscus (Francesco Patrizi), <u>De</u>
<u>institutione reipublicae Libri IX</u>.
L. Zetzner, 1594 [R BNU III, 1796].

H5.4.20. Patricius, Franciscus (Francesco Patrizi), <u>De</u>
          <u>regno et regis institutione. Libri IX.</u>
            L. Zetzner, 1594 [R BNU III, 1797].

   .4.21. Candidus, Pantaleon, <u>Tabulae chronologicae.</u>
          <u>continentes seriem annorum mundi, et brevem</u>
          <u>annotationem ab initio mundi usq. ad presentem annum</u>
          <u>MDXCVI Christi concinnatae.</u>
            J. Rihel, 1597 [R Nfp, 1273].

   .4.22. Bodin, Jean, <u>Methodus ad facilem historiarum</u>
          <u>cognitionem.</u>
            L. Zetzner, 1599 [R BNU I, 224].

VERNACULAR LITERATURE

V1.   Bible Stories in German.

V2.   Medieval Tales and Romances.

       1. Chivalric Tales.
       2. Monastic and Clerical Tales.
       3. Tales Based on Greek and Roman Sources.
       4. Ghost Stories.

V3.   Lives of the Saints in German.

V4.   Popular Textbooks and German ABC's.

V5.   Moral Treatises.

       1. On Marriage and Women's Position in Society.
       2. On Good Morals and Moral Advice.
       3. On Drunkenness and Gluttony.
       4. On Gambling.
       5. On Raising Children.
       6. On Charity and Justice.
       7. On Court Life.

V6.   Popular Stories, Poems and Joke Books.

       1. Joke Books.
       2. Satire.
       3. Novels, Stories, and Poems.

V7.   Music, Including Popular Songs.

       1. Popular Songs.
       2. Collections of Latin and German Songs for Group Singing.
       3. Instrumental Music.

V8.   Plays.

       1. Biblical Plays in German.
       2. Plays on Other Themes.

V9.   History in the Vernacular.

       1. General History and Chronicles.
       2. Ancient History.
       3. German and Imperial History.
       4. Ecclesiastical History.

V10. Popular Journalism.

    1.   Accounts of Prophecies, Heresies, Religious Executions, and Other Religious Occurrences.
    2.   Accounts of Natural Disasters.
    3.   Accounts of Marvelous and Monstrous Births.
    4.   Accounts of Murders.
    5.   Accounts of Wonderful or Exceptional Plants.
    6.   Accounts of Marvelous and Miraculous Apparitions.
    7.   Accounts of Marvelous and Remarkable Events.
    8.   Portrait Broadsheets.
    9.   Accounts of Comets.
  10.   Anti-Semitic Broadsheets.
  11.   Local Events in Strasbourg, Festivals, and Celebrations.
  12.   Accounts of Floods.
  13.   Broadsheets Illustrating Coinage.
  14.   Anti-Catholic Polemical Broadsheets.
  15.   Historical Broadsheets.

V11. Accounts of Recent Events.

    1.   Imperial Politics, Neighboring Events, and Knights' and Peasant Wars.
    2.   The War against the Turks.
    3.   The Revolt of the Netherlands.
    4.   The Wars of Religion in France.
    5.   The Bishops' War.

V1. BIBLE STORIES IN GERMAN.

V1.1.1.   Johannes Hildeshemiensis (Joannes of Hildesheim), Buch
           der Heiligen drei könige.
           J. Prüss I, ca. 1480 [R BNU Inc., 268].

   .1.2.   Jacobus de Theramo, Buch Belial.
           H. Knoblochtzer, 1481 [R Nfp Inc., 359], 1483 [R
           BNU Inc., 250].
           J. Prüss I, 1508 [S III A, 70].

   .1.3.   Job. Dieses büchlin sagt von dem heiligen Job.
           B. Kistler, 1498 [R Nfp Inc., 376].

   .1.4.   Dis biechlin halt yn die ausslegung der treüm Danielis.
           M. Hupfuff, 1500 [R Nfp Inc., 200], 1511 [S V, 85].

   .1.5.   Die heimlich offenbarung johannis.
           H. Greff, 1502 [S IV Greff, 1].

   .1.6.   Der Text des passions oder lidens christi, usz den
           vier evangelisten zusammen inn eyn syn bracht mit
           schönen figüren.
           J. Knoblock, 1506 [S VII, 24], 1507 [S VII, 35],
           1509 [S VII, 60].
           J. Grüninger, 1509 [S I, 110].
           M. Hupfuff, 1513 [S V, 108].

   .1.7.   Das leben Jesu Christi gezogen ausz den vier Evangelis-
           ten.
           J. Knoblock, 1508 [S VII, 39].

   .1.8.   Mennel, Jacob (Manlius), Der Passion in form eines
           gerichthandels.
           J. Grüninger, 1514 [S I, 134; R Nfp, 2843].

   .1.9.   Krafft Ulrich, Das ist die arch Noe.
           C. Kerner, 1517 [S IV Ker., 3].

   .1.10.   Klinger, Bernhard, Gulden Paradies Apfel mit dem Vall
           Adam und Eva.
           M. Flach II, 1520 [S VI B, 56].

   .1.11.   Pambst, Paul, Loosbuch, zu ehren der Römischen,
           Ungerischen unnd Bohëmischen Künigen (Accounts of
           Biblical Personages).
           B. Beck, 1546 [R BNU III, 1753].

   .1.12.   Heyden, Sebald, Der Passion ausz den vier Evangelisten
           gezogen.
           T. Berger, ca. 1560 [R Nfp, 2013].

   .1.13.   Historia des Leidens, Aufferstehung und Himmelfahrt

          unsers Herren Jesu Christi.
             Chr. Mylius I, 1566 [R Nfp, 2025].

V1.1.14. Fischart, Johann, and Stimmer, Tobias, Novae Tobiae
          Stimmeri sacrorum bibliorum figurae versibus latinis
          et germanicis.
             B. Jobin, 1590 [B M 1110.c.21].

  .1.15. Testament der zwölff Patriarchen, der söne Jacobs.
             B. Jobin Erben, 1596 [R Bib. Mun., 2060].

  .1.16. Negelin, Matthaeus, Historia Von der aller Heyligsten
          Empfengnuss unnd Geburt Jhesu Christi, sampt der
          selbigen Erklerung.
             J. Martin, 1598 [R BNU III, 1622].

V2. MEDIEVAL TALES AND ROMANCES.

  .1. CHIVALRIC TALES.

V2.1.1. Dass oventurlich buch beweiset . . . von einer frouwen
          genant Melusina.
             H. Knoblochtzer, n.d. [R BNU Inc., 315].
             J. Prüss I, ca. 1480 [S III A, 1].
             M. Hupfuff, 1506 [S V, 447].
             J. Knobloch, 1516 [S VIII, 332].
             Chr. Mylius II, 1577 [R Nfp, 2666].

  .1.2. Die gantz warlich legend von dem . . . ritter genandt
          her Peter Diemringer.
             M. Schott, n.d. [S II A, 19].
          Also listed as:
          Egenolf von Staufenberg, Geschichte von Peter Diemeringer.
             J. Prüss I, 1483 [R Nfp Inc., 229].
             M. Schott, 1490 [R Nfp Inc., 231].
             B. Jobin, 1588 [R Nfp, 1534] (Joh. Fischart, ed.).

  .1.3. Hie fahet an der Helden buch das man nennet den Wolf
          Dieterich.
             J. Prüss I, n.d. [S III A, 2].
             J. Knobloch, 1509 [S VII, 59].

  .1.4. Büchlin . . . von einer verzuckten selen eines Ritters
          genant Tundalus.
             B. Kistler, n.d. [R Nfp Inc., 655].
             M. Hupfuff, 1500 [R Nfp Inc., 656].
             J. Knobloch, 1519 [S VII, 193].

  .1.5. L. Brunus Arentinus (Leonardo Bruni Aretino), De duobus
          amantibus (N. Wyle, trans.).
             H. Knoblochtzer, 1482 [R Nfp Inc., 168].

V2.1.6.   Petrarch, Historia Griseldis.
             H. Knoblochtzer, ca. 1482 [R BNU Inc., 379].
             No printer, 1520 [R Nfp, 2871].
             J. Frölich, 1534 [R Nfp 2872], 1538 [R Nfp, 2873],
               1540 [R Nfp 2874], 1554 [R Nfp 2875].

.1.7.   Andreas Capellanus (Andrè le Chapelain), De amore et
           de amoris remediis (J. Hartlieb, trans.).
             M. Schott, 1484 [R Nfp Inc., 74].

.1.8.   Die historien von dem ritter beringer.
             M. Hupfuff, 1495 [S V, 2].

.1.9.   Das dis büchlin werd bekant. Amor die lieb ist es
           genant. . . .
             M. Hupfuff, 1499 [S V, 5].

.1.10.   Dis büchli seit Künig Salomon und seiner hauszfrawn
           Salome.
             M. Hupfuff, 1499 [R Imp. Alsc., 146].
             J. Knobloch, 1510 [S VII, 72; R Nfp 3154].
             Chr. Mylius I, after 1555 [R Nfp, 3155].

.1.11.   Büchlin von dem rosengarten künig Laurin. . . .
             M. Hupfuff, 1500 [S V, 10], 1509 [S V, 75].

.1.12.   Hans vom Bühel, History von eines küniges tochter von
           Frankreich ein hübsches lesen.
             J. Grüninger, 1500 [S I, 54], 1500 [R BNU Inc., 120],
               1508 [S I, 94].

.1.13.   History von Hug Schäpler . . . ein gewaltiger küng
           zu Frankreich.
             J. Grüninger, 1500 [S I, 53], 1508 [S I, 93].
             B. Grüninger, 1537 [R BNU II, 1210].

.1.14.   Historie von dem wilde Dracole . . . wie er die leut
           gespist hat. . . .
             M. Hupfuff, 1500 [R Nfp Inc., 335].

.1.15.   Das ist Herr Egken ussfart wie er von dreyen künigin
           ward ussgesant nach Herr Dietrich von Bern. . . .
             M. Hupfuff, 1503 [S V, 27].

.1.16.   Sigenot.
             B. Kistler, 1503 [R Nfp, 3230], 1510 [R Nfp, 3231].
             Chr. Mylius, I, ca. 1560 [R Nfp, 3232], 1577(?)
               R Nfp, 3234].
             T. Berger, ca. 1560 [R Nfp, 3233].

.1.17.   Walther von der Vogelweide, Der Freidanck (S. Brant,
           ed.).
             J. Grüninger, 1508 [S I, 95].

V2.1.18. History von Tristrant und der schönen Isolden von
          Irlande.
          No printer, 1510 [R Nfp, 3371].
          J. Frölich, 1557 [R Nfp, 3372].

   .1.19. Von dem aller könsten weygant Herr Dietrich von Bern
          und von Hiltibrant . . . wie sy wider die Risen
          stritent.
          B. Kistler, 1510 [S IV Kis., 27].
          T. Berger, 1560 [R Nfp, 1509].

   .1.20. Herman von Sachszenheim, Die Mörin, Ein schon
          Kürtzweilig lesen.
          J. Grüninger, 1512 [S I, 127].

   .1.21. Der weis Ritter wie er so getruwlich bestund ritter
          Leuwen, des Hertzogen sun von Burges. . . .
          J. Grüninger, 1514 [S I, 140].

   .1.22. Lurcker, Erhart, Hüpsche historie von einem Ritter
          genant herr Thorelle . . . wie er vom grosan Soldan
          gefanger wardt.
          J. Grüninger, 1515 [R Nfp, 2445].

   .1.23. Ein history . . . Wie ein junckfraw genant Giletta,
          den Künig von Frankreich einer seiner Krankheit
          gesundt machet.
          J. Knobloch, 1519 [S VII, 192].

   .1.24. History von dem Edelen herren Wigolais vom Rade. Ein
          ritter von der Tafelrunde.
          J. Knobloch, 1519 [S VII, 191].

   .1.25. Geoffroy de La Tour de Landry, Der Ritter vom Turn
          Oder der Spiegel der Tugent und Ersamkeyt. . . .
          J. Knobloch, 1519 [S VII, 172].
          J. Cammerlander, 1538 [R BNU III, 1339].

   .1.26. Von einer Grefinn von Anhalt, die hatt ein Grafen von
          Schwartzenburg gehabt aus Schwedien. . . .
          M. Flach II, 1522 [S VI B, 67].

   .1.27. History . . . wonn Herren Florio des küniglichen fürsten
          und Biacessora, ein dochter des römers Lelio genant.
          Wie grosse lieben die zweizüsammen hetten. . . .
          J. Grüninger, 1530 [S I, 247].
          A. Farckal, 1530 [R BNU II, 869].

   .1.28. Kurtz viler Historien Handbuchlin.
          J. Schott, 1536 [R Nfp, 1951].

   .1.29. Thym, Georg (Georg Klee), Des Edlen und Streitbaren
          heldes Thedel Unvorferden von Walmoden, manlicher und

Ritterlicher thaten.
   P. Messerschmidt, 1558 [R BNU IV, 2328], 1560 [R
   Nfp, 2247].

V2.1.30. History . . . von dem Ritter Herren Policarpen von
   Kirrlarissa. . . .
      Chr. Mylius I, ca. 1560 [R Nfp, 2032].

 .1.31. Hertzog Heynrichs, genannt Lewen in das Heylig Landt
   fürgenommener verren Reysz . . . .
      Chr. Mylius I, 1561 [R Nfp, 2033].

 .1.32. Die Schön Magelona, . . . eines Künigs tochter von
   Neapel, und einem Ritter genannt Peter. . . .
      No printer, ca. 1562 [R Nfp, 2582].

 .1.33. Tageweiss von eines Künigs Tochter, wie es ihr mit
   einem Zwerglein erginge.
      T. Berger, 1570 [R Nfp, 3310].

 .1.34. Mexia, Pedro, Historischer Geschichts-Natur-und
   Wunderwald allerhand merkwürdigen Erzählungen.
      No printer, 1570 [R Nfp, 2676].

 .1.35. Das Lalebuch. Wunderseltzame, Abentheurliche . . .
   und bisher unbeschriebene. Geschichten und Thaten
   der Lalen zu Lalenburg.
      B. Jobin, 1597 [R Nfp, 2262].

 .2. MONASTIC AND CLERICAL TALES.

V2.2.1. Amis der Pfaffe, Von dem Stricker.
      J. Prüss I, 1483 [R Nfp Inc., 70a].

 .2.2. Wunderbarliche geschichten, die da geschehen synt von
   geystlichen wybs personen in disen Joren.
      B. Kistler, 1502 [S IV Kis., 21].

 .2.3. Dis buechlin saget von Bruder Rauschen und was er
   wunders getriben hat in einem Closter. . . .
      M. Flach II, 1508 [S VI B, 19].
      B. Kistler, 1509 [R Nfp, 1217].
      M. Hupfuff, 1510 [R Nfp, 1218], 1515 [S V, 131].

 .2.4. Geschichte des Pfarres von Kalenberg.
      J. Grüninger, ca. 1515 [R Nfp, 1898].

 .3. TALES BASED ON GREEK AND ROMAN SOURCES.

V2.3.1. Gesta Romanorum (in Latin).
      M. Schott, n.d. [R BNU Inc., 183].
      J. Grüninger, 1488 [R BNU Inc., 184], 1489 [S I,

11], 1499 [S I, 41].
    G. Husner, 1489 [R BNU Inc., 185], 1493 [R BNU Inc.,
       186], 1499 [R BNU Inc., 187].
    J. Herwagen, 1528 [R Nfp, 1739] (Lucius Annaeus
       Florus, ed.).
Also listed as:
Die sieben weisen Meister. . . .
    M. Hupfuff, 1512 [S V, 102].
    J. Knobloch, 1520 [R Nfp, 2609].
    J. Frölich, 1539 [R Nfp, 2608], 1540 [R Nfp, 2610].
Die Alten Römer. Historien und Zuchtgleichnussen der
Alten Römer.
    J. Cammerlander, 1536 [R Nfp, 2607], 1538 [R BNU II,
       1012], 1546 [R Nfp, 2611].
Gleichnussen der sieben weisen Meister.
    W. Rihel, 1549 [R Nfp, 2612].
    Chr. Mylius I, 1558 [R Nfp, 2613].
    Chr. Mylius II, 1572 [R Nfp, 2614], 1577 [R Nfp,
       2615].

V2.3.2.   Der Alten Weissen exempel sprüch, mit vil schönen
          Beyspilen und Figuren er Lëuchtet. Darinnen fast
          aller menschen wesen, Händel, Untrew . . . Geschwindig-
          keyt . . . angezeygt werden.
              M. Schott, n.d. [Selestat, 123].
              J. Grüninger, 1501 [S I, 55], 1525 [R Nfp, 1186],
                 1529 [S I, 243].
              No printer, 1512 [R Nfp, 1184].
              B. Grüninger, 1536 [R BNU I, 314].
              J. Frölich, 1539 [R BNU I, 315]', 1545 [R Nfp, 1188].

  .3.3.   Leo Archipresbyter, Historia Alexandri Magni. (in
           Latin)
              G. Husner, 1488 [R BNU Inc., 281], 1489 [R BNU Inc.,
                 282], 1494 [R BNU Inc., 283].
           Also listed as:
           Das buch der geschicht des grossen Alexanders.
              M. Schott, 1488 [S II A, 6], 1489 [S II A, 8], 1493
                 [S II A, 11; Beinecke].
              B. Kistler, 1503 [S IV Kis., 22].
              M. Hupfuff, 1509 [R Nfp, 798], 1514 [S V, 112].
           Alexandri Magni . . . vita per Gaultherum . . .
           scripta.
              R. Beck, 1513 [S IV Beck II],
              No printer, 1513 [R Nfp, 1286].

  .3.4.   Ein hubsche histori von der kunigelichenn stat troy
           wei si zerstorett wartt.

      M. Schott, 1489 [S II A, 7], 1499 [S II A, 17].
      J. Knobloch, 1510 !S VII, 67].

V2.3.5. Hie in diesem buchlin vindet man die grossen wunder
      werck, der heyligen stat Rome wie sie gebawet wart
      und von dem ersten Kunig und Keyser.
      M. Hupfuff, 1500 [S V, 11].
      J. Prüss I, 1500 [R Nfp Inc., 488].

.3.6. Eyn rhumreich zierlich und fast fruchtbar Histori von
      dem Edlen Ritter Ponto . . . Auch von der schonen
      Sidonia. . . .
      M. Flach II, 1509 [S V B, 21].
      S. Bund, 1539 [R BNU III, 1916].

.3.7. Appolonius . . . hie nach folget gar eine Schöne
      histori von dem künig appoloni. Wie lang er vor
      Christ Geburt geregirt hat.
      M. Hupfuff, 1516 [S V, 136].

.3.8. Sabellicus, Marcus Antonius Coccius, Exempelbuch von
      wunderbarlichen Geschichten. Und gleichsan eyn zeyger
      aller Historien, der Juden, Christen und Heyden . . .
      lustig auch nutzlich der jetzigen Welt zu lesen.
      J. Cammerlander, 1535 [R BNU IV, 2050].

.3.9. Ein schone . . . Histori von dem Keyser Octaviano,
      seinem weib und zweyen sunen, wie die in das ellend
      verschickt unnd wunderbarlich in Franckreich bey dem
      frummen Kunig Dagobert Wiederumb zusamen komen sind.
      B. Gruninger, 1535 [R Nfp, 2779].
      J. Frölich, 1548 [R Nfp, 2780], 1557 [R Nfp, 2781].
      No printer, ca. 1560 [R Nfp, 2782].

.3.10. Pius II, (Pope), Histori von zweyen Liebhabenden
      Menschen Euriolo und Lucretia (N. Wyle, trans.).
      No printer, 1550 [R Nfp, 2917].

.3.11. Heliodorus (Heliodorus of Emesa), Aethiopica Historia
      . . . . Histori von . . . Helden aus Griechenland und
      einer uberschonen Junckfrawen, eines Konigs dochter
      der schwartzen Moren . . . Aus dem griechischen ins
      Latin und yetzundt newlich ins Teutsch bracht von
      Joh. Zschorn.
      P. Messerschmidt, 1559 [R Nfp, 1978].

.3.12. Frey, Jakob, Von den drey und viertzig alten,
      nohtvesten unnd starcken helden, wie die ihre leib,
      leben, gut unnd blut . . . fur den gemeinen nutz
      dargestreckt . . . aus den alten Romischen und
      Griechischen historien zusamen gesucht.
      P. Messerschmidt, 1562 [R BNU II, 887].

V2.3.13. Eustachius (Eustathius Macrembolites), Ismenius.
          Histori von der Lieb des Junglings Ismeni und der
          Jungfrawen Ismene (Johann Fischart, trans.).
          B. Jobin, 1573 [R Nfp, 1666], 1594 [R BNU II, 864].

    .4. GHOST STORIES.

V2.4.1.   Wie Arent Bosman ein Geist erschien.
          M. Hupfuff, 1500 [R Nfp Inc., 127], 1505 [S V, 46],
          1515 [S V, 132].

V3. LIVES OF THE SAINTS IN GERMAN.

V3.1.1.   Ein Büch gesetzet in eren unseres Herren Jhesu cristi
          und seiner muter marien und der heyligen dreyen
          kunige wirdikeit. . . . (Johann von Hildescheim,
          trans.).
          J. Prüss I, n.d. [S III A, 4].

    .1.2. Otto von Passau, Büch . . . die vier und twenzig
          Alten, oder der guldin tron. . . .
          J. Prüss I, n.d. [S III A, 3].
          M. Schott, 1483 [S II A, 4], 1483 [R BNU Inc., 349].
          J. Schott, 1500 [S II B, 1].
          J. Knobloch, 1508 [S VII, 38].

    .1.3. Passional oder Leben der Heiligen.
          J. Prüss I, ca. 1480 [R BNU Inc., 369].

    .1.4. Hieronymus Sanctus (Saint Hieronymus), Leven der
          hilligen Oldvaderen.
          No printer, 1482 [R Nfp Inc., 332].

    .1.5. Martirologium der heiligen nach dem Kalendar.
          J. Prüss I, 1484 [S III A, 9].

    .1.6. (Nider, Jean), Die vier und zwenzig gulden harpfen.
          M. Schott, 1493 [S II A, 12].

    .1.7. Lesen von sant Brandon was wunders er uff dem mer
          erfaren hat.
          M. Hupfuff, 1494 [R Nfp Inc., 131], 1499 [R Nfp Inc.,
          133], 1510 [S V, 80], 1514 [S V, 116].
          J. Knobloch, 1518 [S VII, 170].

    .1.8. Von Sant Ursulen schifflin.
          B. Kistler, 1497 [S III Kis. 3].

    .1.9. Leben, das ist sant Pauls Leben.
          B. Kistler, 1498 [R BNU Inc., 279].
          J. Knobloch, 1517 [S VII, 149].

V3.1.10. Leben Sankt Wolfgangs.
                No printer, 1500 [R Nfp Inc., 717].
                M. Hupfuff, 1502 [S V, 23].

   .1.11. Petrus Frater, Legende der sant Katherinen.
                J. Grüninger, April 1500 [R BNU Inc., 388], July
                1500 [R BNU Inc., 389].

   .1.12. Legende von sant Annan.
                B. Kistler, ca. 1500 [S IV Kis. 17].
                No printer, 1509 [R BNU III, 1350].

   .1.13. Das leben des heiligen bischoff Eucharii, Valerii und
                Materni di do disze tutzland zu den cristen glauben
                haben bekort.
                B. Kistler, 1500 [R Nfp Inc., 242].

   .1.14. Brant, Sebastian, Der heiligen Leben nüw mit vil me
                Heiligen.
                J. Grüninger, 1502 [S I, 58], 1508 [R Nfp, 1044],
                1510 [S I, 114], 1514 [S I, 139].

   .1.15. Der Heiligen Altväter leben nüw getruckt.
                J. Grüninger, 1507 [S I, 80], 1516 [S I, 151].
                M. Hupfuff, 1508 [S V, 73], 1513 [S V, 103].

   .1.16. Der heiligen leben neüw getruckt. Der hohen
                unteilbarlichen drivaltigkeit zu lob. Marie der
                wurdigsten Junckfranwen und mutter gottes zu eeren.
                M. Hupfuff, 1513 [S V, 104].
                J. Knobloch, 1517 [S VII, 141].
                M. Flach II, 1521 [S VI B, 61].

   .1.17. Das seind die allerandechtigsten ermanungen unnd gebet
                sant Brigitten von dem heiligen leyden unsers selig
                machers.
                J. Prüss II, ca. 1518 [S III B, 16].

   .1.18. Gebwiler, Hieronymus, Ein schöne wahrhafftig und
                hievor üngehorte hystorie des Fürstlichen stammens
                und härkommens der heiligen junckfrawen Otilie.
                No printer, 1521 [R Nfp, 1826].

V4. POPULAR TEXTBOOKS AND GERMAN ABC'S.

V4.1.1.   (Gessler, Heinrich), Formulare und tutsch Rethorica.
                J. Prüss I, 1483 [S III A, 7], 1486 [S III A, 12],
                1502 [S III A, 34].
                J. Knobloch, 1511 [S VII Suppl. 331], 1519 [S VII,
                171].
                P. Götz, 1514 [R BNU II, 988].

Also listed as:
Wie man einem jeglichen was stads wurde und eren der
ist schriben sol. New regel der rhetoric.
J. Prüss I, 1493 [S III A, 25].

V4.1.2.   Stephanus Fliscus de Sontino, Formulae Loquendi (in
German and Latin).
J. Prüss I, 1487 [S III A, 15].

.1.3.   Biechlin . . . wie man einem jeglichen Tütschen
Fürsten und Herren schriben sol. Auch Ritter und
Knechten, Stetten und Dörffern, Geystlichen und
Weltlichen stat eins yeglichen Brieffs anfang und
beschlus.
M. Hupfuff, 1499 [S V, 6], 1504 [S V, 35].

.1.4.   ABC guter ler und underwysung wie man soll Gutes tun.
B. Kistler, 1500 [R Nfp Inc., 1].

.1.5.   (Riedrer, Friederich,) Spiegel der waren Retoric uss
Mario Tulio Cicerone. und andern getutscht. Mit iren
glidern Clüger reden, Sandtbrieffen und Formen mencher
Contract, seltzam, Reguliertz Tütsch und nutzbar
Exempliert. . . .
J. Prüss I, 1505 [S III A, 53], 1509 [S III A, 78].
J. Knobloch, 1517 [S VII, 136; R BNU III, 2018].

.1.6.   In disem büchlin vindet man gar clarlichen Die Titel
oder die Oberschriffte aller stende Anfang und
Beschluss der Briefe.
M. Hupfuff, 1507 [S V, 68].

.1.7.   Cantzley Büchlein. Wie man schriben sol: eim yeden
in was würden: stadt: oder wesens er ist. . . .
M. Hupfuff, 1513 [S V, 105], 1515 [S V, 130].
J. Knobloch, 1520 [S VII, 211], 1522 [R BNU I, 426].

.1.8.   Vocabularius: primo ponens dictiones theutonicas. in
lingua vernacula. . . . Ein ordenliche anzeygung: wie
man ein yeglichs teutsch wort zu latyn reden mag.
Einem yeden leyen des verstand, des latyns begierig:
vast nutzlich.
M. Hupfuff, 1515 [S V, 122].

.1.9.   Vocabularius Latinis Gallicis et Theutonicus Verbis
scriptus (A dictionary and phrase book for merchants).
M. Flach II, 1521 [S VI B 64].
W. Köpfel, 1535 [R BNU I, 640; Peter, 5b].
N. Wyriot, 1575 [Peter, 38].
A. Bertram, 1590 [Peter, 41].
See Peter, Vol. 2, p. 14.

V4.1.10.   Agricola, Johann, <u>Hundert und LVI gemeyner Fragstucke</u>
<u>für die jungen Kinder in der teütschen kinder Schüle.</u>
No printer, 1528 [R Nfp, 768].

.1.11.   <u>Notariat und Schreiber Kunst.</u> Wes sich ein Notarius
oder Schreiber in Seinem Ampt mit allen Cautelen,
Gebräuchen und Regeln . . . zu halten hab.
C. Egenolff, 1529 [R Nfp, 2774].

.1.12.   Fruck, Ludwig, <u>Teutsch Formular, wie man in</u>
Gerichtsachen . . . handeln mag . . . Mit einem Titel
Büchlin, wie man an jeden Hohen und Nidern schreiben
soll.
C. Egenolff, 1529 [R Nfp, 1796].

.1.13.   Vogtherr, Heinrich, <u>Eyn schone und Gotselige kurtzweil</u>
<u>eines Christlichen Lossbuchs, nach ordnung eines</u>
<u>Alphabets oder ABC.</u>
H. Vogtherr, 1539 [R BNU IV, 2443].

.1.14.   Franck, Fabian, <u>Orthographia, Haimliche und verborgne</u>
<u>Cancellei, wie man recht grüntlich teütsch schreiben</u>
<u>soll. . . .</u>
J. Cammerlander, 1539 [B <u>Cam.</u>, 30], 1540 [R BNU II,
881].

.1.15.   Schreppeler, Jörg, <u>Ein künstlich Alphabet sampt der</u>
<u>selben Reimen. . . .</u>
T. Berger, 1554 [R Nfp, 3195], 1568 [R Nfp, 3196].

.1.16   <u>ABC: Ein jeder schüler Christi sold Disz ABC gantz</u>
<u>kene wol.</u>
T. Berger, ca 1560-1562 [R Nfp, 721].
See also S5. 4.10.

V5.   MORAL TREATISES.

1.   ON MARRIAGE AND WOMEN'S POSITION IN SOCIETY.

V5.1.1.   Boccaccio, Giovanni, <u>Von den Erlychten Frauen.</u>
J. Prüss I, 1488 [R BNU <u>Inc.</u>, 95].

.1.2.   Murner, Johann, <u>Von Eelichs Stadts nutz und</u>
<u>beschwerden.</u>
M. Hupfuff, ca. 1512 [R BNU III, 1600].

.1.3.   <u>Der frawen Spiegel in welchem spiegel sich das</u>
<u>weyblich byld, jung oder alt beschawen oder lernen,</u>
<u>zu gebrauchen, die woltat gegen irem eelichen gemahel.</u>
M. Flach II, 1520 [S VI B, 60].

.1.4.   Erasmus, Desiderius, <u>Wie ein weyb iren man ir</u>

freüntlich sol machen gesprech. Eulalia und Xantippen.
> M. Schürer Erben, 1524 [B SE 3, 29].

V5.1.5.   Guevara, Antonio, Missive an den Edlen, Herrn Moises
Pusch von Valentz, in welcher, wie und was gestalt,
sich die Ehepersonen, gegen einander verhalten sollen.
> B. Jobin, after 1572 [R BNU II, 1050].

.1.6.   Fischart, Johann, Das Philosophisch Ehzuchtbüchlein. .
. . Des berümtesten . . . Griechischen Philosophi, . .
. und Lehrers Plutarchi . . . Eheliche Gesaz . . .
Sammt auch Bericht von . . . Kinder Zucht. Darzu eyn
schönes Gespräch, von Klag des Ehestands, oder wie
man eyn ruhig Ehe gehaben mag.
> B. Jobin, 1578 [R BNU II, 854], 1591 [R BNU II, 863],
> 1597 [B M 84515.aa.Z].

.2.   ON GOOD MORALS AND MORAL ADVICE.

V5.2.1.   Ein schöner spruch wie sich ein mensch bey seinem
leben soll schicken zum sterben.
> T. Berger, n.d. [R Nfp, 3270].

.2.2.   Dis sind die vier Angeltugent. Wysheit,
Gerechtigkeit, Stercke und Mässigkeit. . . .
> P. Attendorn, ca. 1492 [R Nfp, 76].
> M. Hupfuf, 1515 [S V, 128].

.2.3.   Ackermann, Johann, Schöne red und widerred eins acker-
mans und des todes mit scharpffer entscheidung irs
kriegs eim jegklichen vast kurtzweilig und nutzlich zu
lessen.
> J. Schott, 1500 [S II B, 5].
> M. Hupfuff, 1502 [R Nfp, 735].
> M. Flach II, 1520 [S VI B, 59].
> No printer, ca. 1520 [R Nfp, 736].
> M. Schürer Erben, 1521 [B SE 2, 12].

.2.4.   Hie noch folgen . . . schöne leren wie man sol guts
thun und von besöm sich kerren. . . .
> B. Kistler, 1500 [S IV Kis., 8].

.2.5.   Diss ist der Brunn des radts uss welichem ein bekü-
merter oder ein betrüpter mensch trost radt und
wysheit . . . empfahet.
> J. Grüninger, 1500 [S I, 46].
> M. Hupfuff, 1504 [S V, 34].
> M. Flach II, 1508 [S VI B, 20].

.2.6.   Hye hebt sich an des Endkrist leben und regierung
durch Verhengnis gottes, Wieer die welt dut verkeren

         mit siner falschen ler und Rat des tüfels. . . .
           M. Hupfuff, 1503 [S V, 28], after 1503 [S V, 29].

V5.2.7.   Pico della Mirandella, Sendtbrieff des . . . Graven
         Joannis Pici von Mirandel zu seinem vettern yn zu
         ermanen zu christenlichen leben und zu lere der
         Heiligen geschrifft unangesehen ergernuss.
           M. Hupfuff, 1509 [S V, 77].

 .2.8.   Kartenlossbuch darinnen ausz Heilige Schrifft vil
         laster gestrafft und heylsamer leeren angezeygt
         werden.
           J. Cammerlander, 1543 [R Nfp, 2218].

 .2.9.   Kern, Matthias, Militia Humana, Der Menschliche
         Streit, in teutsche Rymen transfertiert.
           J. Frölich, 1545 [R Nfp, 2226].

 .2.10. Brammer, David, Reiszbuch. . . I. Den Wanderstab und
         Leytung des lieblichen Reisens unnd Wanderens. . . II.
         Die Pilgerschafft und Wahlfahrt der frommen Christen.
           B. Jobin, 1584 [R BNU I, 235].

 .3.   ON DRUNKENNESS AND GLUTTONY.

V5.3.1.   Beroaldus, Phillip, Ein hüpsche subtyliche
         Declamation . . . von dreyen Brüdern, der erst ist
         ein drunckner boss, der ander ein hurer, der dritt
         ein spyler.
           R. Beck, 1513 [S IV Beck, 12], 1521 [R Nfp, 993].

 .3.2.   Altenstaig, Johann, Von der Füllerery, ein müter aller
         übel . . . auch arzeneien darwider.
           J. Grüninger, 1525 [S I, 225].

 .3.3.   Schertlin, Leonhard, Künstlich Trincken. Eyn Dialog
         von Künstlichem und höflichem, Auch vihischem und
         unzüchtigem trincken. . . .
           J. Cammerlander, 1538 [R Nfp, 3173].

 .3.4.   Franck, Sebastian, Von den grewlichen laster der
         trunckenheit, So inn disen letsten zeyten: erst
         schier mit den Frantzosen auffkommen. . . .
           J. Prüss II, 1539 [R BNU II, 883].

 .3.5.   Bock, Hieronymus, Der Vollen Brüder Orden, Diss
         Buchlein zeyget an was der Wein wurcke inn denen so
         ihn missbrauchen.
           W. Rihel, 1540 [BM T.2167(4)].

 .3.6.   Wickram, Georg, Ein schoner und nützlicher Dialogus,
         in welchem angezogen wirt, das mechtig heuptlaster,

der trunckenheit, durch vil und mancherley Biblische
. . . Historien anzeigt.
P. & P. Köpfel, 1555 [R BNU IV, 2460].
J. Frölich, 1555 [R Imp. Alsc., 563].

.4. ON GAMBLING.

V5.4.1. Klinger, Bernhard, In disem büchlin findest du Wie
man sich hüten sol vor dem Spiel.
M. Flach II, 1520 [S VI B, 57].

.5. ON RAISING CHILDREN.

V5.5.1. Ad patrem pro juvenibus (in Latin and German).
M. Hupfuff, 1506 [S V, 48].

.5.2. Erasmus, Paraclesis Teütsch.
M. Flach, 1520 [R Nfp, 1619].
J. Prüss II, 1522 [BM 3906.b.62].

.5.3. Erasmus, Zuchtiger Sitten Zierlichen wandels und
höflicher Geberden der jugent.
J. Frölich, 1536 [R Nfp, 1624].

.6. ON CHARITY AND JUSTICE.

V5.6.1. Disses büchlin seit von den geschwinden nuwen finden,
Unnd gebruch der Rechten, domit der arm gemein beladen
auch was bruch und mangel dar uss entstott.
B. Kistler, 1502 [S IV Kis., 19].

.6.2. Vives, Johannes (Jaun Luis Vives), Von Almusen geben.
. . . durch D. Casparn Hedio verteutscht und eim
Ersamen Radt und frummer burgerschafft zu Straszburg
zugeschriben.
B. Beck(?), 1533 [R BNU IV, 2429].

.7. ON COURT LIFE.

V5.7.1. Johannes von Morssheim, Aulica Vita- -Hoffleben. Und
sunst der gantzen welt händel.
J. Cammerlander, 1539 [R BNU III, 1595].

.7.2. Guevara, Antonio, Der Hofleut Wecker . . . welcher
massen sich eyn Hofman gegen meniglich erzeygen soll
und durch was mittel er seinen Fursten und Herren,
so er dieselbe erlangt, behalten moge.
B. Jobin, 1582 [R BNU II, 1053], 1593 [R BNU II, 1054].

V6.   POPULAR STORIES, POEMS, AND JOKE BOOKS.

.1.   JOKE BOOKS.

V6.1.1.   Wickram, Jörg, <u>Kurzweiliges Loos-oder Dreh Büchlein</u>
          <u>. . . Glücks-Rad</u>.
                No printer, n.d. [R Nfp, 3500], 1534 [R Nfp, 3501],
                    1539 [R Nfp, 3502].
                J. Cammerlander, 1543 [B <u>Cam.</u>, 140].
                Also listed as:
                <u>Das Weltlich Loszbuch</u>.
                No printer, 1557 [R Nfp, 3503], 1559 [R Nfp, 3504].
                A. Bertram, 1594 [R Nfp, 3507].

.1.2.   <u>Rätterbüchlin</u>.
                T. Berger, n.d. [R Nfp, 3069].

.1.3.   <u>Wölchem an kürtzweill thet zerriden Mag woll diss</u>
          <u>büchlein durchgrynden Er findet darin vile kluger ler</u>
          <u>Von Rettelsch gedicht und vile nüwer mer</u>.
                M. Hupfuff, 1505 [S V, 42], ca. 1511 [S V, 87],
                    1519 [S V, 139].
                J. Cammerlander, ca. 1540 [R Nfp, 3070], 1545
                    [B <u>Cam.</u>, 141].

.1.4.   <u>Facetus</u> (in Latin and German; Seb. Brant, trans.).
                J. Knobloch, 1508 [R Nfp, 1685].

.1.5.   <u>Ein Narr gab seinem herren ain guten rat. . . .</u>
                J. Knobloch, 1510 [S VII, 73].

.1.6.   Pauli, Johannes, <u>Schimpf und Ernst. . . .</u>
                J. Grüninger, 1522 [S I, 190].
                B. Grüninger, 1533 [R BNU III, 1798], 1535 [R BNU
                    III, 1799], 1538 [R Nfp, 2849].
                J. Knobloch, 1525 [R Nfp, 2848].
                Chr. Mylius II Erben, 1528 [R Nfp, 2850].

.1.7.   Ritter, Hans, <u>Welcher gern wissen well/Von armutz</u>
          <u>nott und ungefell</u>.
                J. Prüss II, 1525 [BM 11517.d.29].

.1.8.   <u>Wuerfelbuch</u>.
                C. Egenolff, 1529 [R BNU IV, 2502].

.1.9.   Wickram, Jörg, <u>Das Rollwagenbüchlein</u>.
                No printer, 1555 [R Nfp, 3509], 1591 [R Nfp, 3512].
                Chr. Mylius I, 1563 [R Nfp, 3511].

.2.   SATIRE.

.2.1.   Brant, Sebastian, <u>Das nüw Schiff von Narrogonia</u>.

(Das neue Narrenschiff).
> J. Grüninger, 1494 [S I, 20], 1496 [R Nfp Inc., 136],
> 1497 [R Nfp Inc., 137].
> M. Hupfuff, 1512 [S V, 96].
> J. Cammerlander, 1540 [R Nfp, 1051], 1545 [R Nfp,
> 1052].
> W. Rihel, 1549 [R BNU I, 249].

V6.2.2. (Boccaccio, Giovanni), Cento Novella, Das Buch der
hundert nüwer Historien.
> J. Grüninger, 1509 [S I, 107], 1519 [S I, 163].
> G. Messerschmidt, 1547 [R BNU I, 208], 1551 [R BNU
> I, 209], 1557 [R Nfp, 1021].
> P. Messerschmidt, 1561 [R BNU I, 210].

.2.3. Mürner, Thomas, Ein andechtig geistlich Badenfart.
> J. Grüninger, 1511 [R Nfp, 2737a], 1514 [S I, 137],
> 1518 [R Nfp, 2738].

.2.4. Murner, Thomas, Narrenbeschwerung.
> M. Hupfuff, 1511 [S V, 95], 1512 [R BNU III, 1606].
> J. Knobloch, 1518 [S VII, 161], 1522 [R Nfp, 2743].
> G. Messerschmidt, 1556 [R BNU III, 1618], 1558
> [R BNU III, 1619].

.2.5. Murner, Thomas, Der schelmen zunfft.
> M. Hupfuff, 1512 [S V, 94].
> J. Knobloch, 1516 [S VII, 133].
> J. Cammerlander, ca. 1540 [R Nfp, 2747].
> No printer, 1568 [R Nfp, 2746], 1574 [BM 11517.a.15].

.2.6. Gengenbach, Pamphilius, Der Bundt Schuh.
> No printer, 1514 [BM 11515.b.25].

.2.7. Murner, Thomas, Ein kurzwillig lessen von Dyl
Ulenspiegel. . . .
> J. Grüninger, 1515 [S I, 145], 1519 [S I, 164].

.2.8. Murner, Thomas, Die Mülle von Swyndelssheym . . . .
> M. Hupfuff, 1515 [S V, 123].

.2.9. Wunderbarliche . . . historyen Tyll Ulenspiegel.
> J. Frölich, 1529 [R Nfp, 1655], 1543 [R Nfp, 1656],
> 1551 [R Nfp, 1657].
> C. Grüninger(?), 1531 [R Nfp, 1654].
> B. Jobin, 1572 [R Nfp, 1658].

.2.10. Otthenthaler, Paulus, Schmorotzer Trost.
> Chr. Mylius I, 1569 [R BNU III, 1737].

.2.11. Fischart, Johann, Flöh Hatz Weiber Tratz.
> B. Jobin, 1573 [R Nfp, 1710], 1577 [R Nfp, 1711],

1578 [R BNU II, 853].
B. Jobin Erben, 1594 [R Nfp, 1712].

V6.2.12. Fischart, Johann, Affenteurliche Naupenge heurliche
Geschichtklitterung Von Thaten . . . Gargantua und
Pantagruel. . . .
B. Jobin, 1575 [R Nfp, 1713], 1582 [R BNU II, 857],
1590 [R BNU II, 862], 1594 [R Nfp, 1716].

.2.13. Fischart, Johann, Podogrammisch Trostbüchlin . . . zwo
. . . Reden . . . des zarten Fraülins Podagra.
B. Jobin, 1577 [R Nfp, 1724a].

.2.14. Fischart, Johann, Catalogus Catalogorum perpetuo
durabilis . . . Newlich . . . erditricht, abgelöst
und an Tag gebracht.
B. Jobin, 1590 [R Nfp, 1706].

.2.15. Amadis de Gaulis, (Amadis von Frank Reich),
Schatzkammer: Schöner und zierlicher Orationen,
Sendbrieffen, Gesprächen und dergleichen. . . .
L. Zetzner, 1596 [R Nfp, 3171], 1597 [BM
12410.bbb.2G].

.3. NOVELS, STORIES, AND POEMS.

V6.3.1. Hie in finstu zu einem nuwen Jar Einen Hussrat den hon
ich dir fürwar.
M. Hupfuff, 1511 [S V, 88].

.3.2. History von eines Reichen Burgers sun usz . . .
Cippern geborn. . . .
J. Grüninger, 1516 [S I, 153].

.3.3. Wickram, Jörg, Der Ritter Galmy.
J. Frölich, 1539 [R Nfp, 3489], 1540 [R Nfp,
3490], 1548 [R Nfp, 3491], 1550 [R Nfp, 3492],
1554 [R Nfp, 3493].
No printer, 1588 [R Nfp, 3494].

.3.4. Wickram, Jörg, Ein schöne History, Von zweien jungen
Rittern . . . (Gabriotto und Reinhard).
J. Frölich, ca. 1540 [R Nfp, 3497], ca. 1551
[R Nfp, 3487], 1551 [R Nfp, 3488].

.3.5. Wickram, Jörg, Eine Warhafftige History, von einem
ungerahtnen Son, in ein Dialogum gestellet,
zweyer guten freundt, Georgius, Casparus.
J. Frölich, ca. 1540 [R Nfp, 3495].

.3.6. Brentel, Jorgen, Allen Christen wunnsche ich zwar

geduldt in creutz zum neuwen jar.
J. Frölich, 1548 [BM 11517.ee.16].

V6.3.7.   Wickram, Georg, Der Jungen Knaben Spiegel.
J. Frölich, 1554 [R BNU IV, 2459].
No printer, 1555 [R Nfp, 3499].

.3.8.   Vegius, Mapheus, Gespräche von einem waldtmann,
Philatthes, welchem die Junckfraw Veritas . . .
begegnet. . . .
G. Messerschmidt, 1555 [R BNU IV, 2389a].

.3.9.   Wickram, Georg, Der Irr Reitend Bilger.
G. Messerschmidt, 1556 [R BNU IV, 2461].

.3.10   Wickram, Georg, Die Siben Hauptlaster.
G. Messerschmidt, 1556 [R BNU IV, 2461a], 1558
[R BNU IV, 2461d].

.3.11.   Wickram, Georg, Von Guten und Bösen Nachbaurn.
G. Messerschmidt, 1556 [R BNU IV, 2461b], 1557
[R BNU IV, 2461c].

.3.12.   Wickram, Jörg, Die Narrenbeschwerung . . . auff ein
newes überlesen und an vil orten corrigiert.
G. Messerschmidt, 1556 [R Nfp, 3508].

.3.13.   Frey, Jakob, Die Garten Gesellschaft . . . Schimrff-
reden, Spaywerck . . . von Historien und Fabulen
gefunden.
G. Messerschmidt, 1557 [R BNU II, 886].

.3.14.   Wickram, Jörg, Der Goldfaden.
J. Frölich, 1557 [R Nfp, 3496].

.3.15.   Georgievicz, Bartholomaeus (Bartholomaeus
Gjorgjevic), Türckenbüchlein . . . unnd ein Disputaz
eines Christen und Türcken vom Glauben.
No printer, 1558 [R Nfp, 1873].

.3.16.   Wickram, Jörg, Der Trew Eckart.
Chr. Mylius I, 1559 [R Nfp, 3485].

.3.17.   Montanus, Martinus, Das ander theyl der Garten
gesellschafft. . . .
P. Messerschmidt, 1560 [R Nfp, 2716].

.3.18.   Montanus, Martinus, Hystori vonn zweyenn Jungen
gesellen, wie die liebe zu zweyen Jungfrawen
truogen. . . .
P. Messerschmidt, ca. 1560 [R Nfp, 2719].

.3.19.   Montanus, Martinus, Hystoria, von zweyen liebhabenden

Menschen wie die bey einander gefunden worden. . . .
P. Messerschmidt, ca. 1560 [R Nfp, 2720].

V6.3.20.   Montanus, Martinus, Theobaldus . . . Hystoria von dem
. . . Ritter Theobaldo.
P. Messerschmidt, ca. 1560 [R Nfp, 2718].

.3.21.   Holtzwart, Matthias, Lustgart Newer deuttscher Poëteri
in funff Buchern. . . .
J. Rihel, 1568 [R BNU II, 1184].

.3.22.   (Fischart, Johann), Definitiva oder Endlicher
Auszspruch desz Esels, in strittigen sachen der
Nachtigaln, an einem, wider der Guckguck. . . .
(B. Jobin), before 1575, [WJ, 34].

.3.23.   (Die menschlichen Alterstufen).
(B. Jobin), ca. 1575-1577 [WJ, 44].

.3.24.   Wirry (Heinrich Wirrich), Lobspruch auf Straszburg.
No printer, 1576 [R Nfp, 3551].

.3.25.   Fischart, Johann, Bewärung und Erkiärung des Uralten
gemeynen Sprüchwortes. Die Gelehrten Die
Verkehrten. . . .
B. Jobin, 1584 [R BNU II, 858].

V7.   MUSIC, INCLUDING POPULAR SONGS.

.1.   POPULAR SONGS.

V7.1.1.   Ein hübsches schimpfliches Lied von einem reichen
Baur.
No printer, n.d. [R Nfp, 2323].

.1.2.   Lied von den rosz teütschern.
U. Morhard, n.d. [R Nfp, 2317].

.1.3.   Buttermilchlied: Eins bawren son hat sich vermessen
er wolt ein gute buttermilch essen.
J. Frölich, n.d. [R Nfp, 1253].

.1.4.   Buxbaumlied: Der Buxbaum und Felbinger.
J. Frölich, n.d. [R Nfp, 1254].

.1.5.   Der Engelisch Grusz . . . Ein ander neüw Geistlich
Lied. Der unfal reit mich gantz und gar. . . .
T. Berger, n.d. [R Nfp, 1935].

.1.6.   Das Lied von dem Ritter Ausz Steürmarck.
T. Berger, n.d. [R Nfp, 2288].

.1.7.   Lied vonn dem zug wider die Kron ausz Franckreich.
T. Berger, n.d. [R Nfp, 2360].

.1.8.   Der Christen Bilgerschaft . . . Ein ander Geistlich
         Lied. Ein schöne Tageweysz. . . .
                  T. Berger, n.d. [R Nfp, 2909].

.1.9.   Lied von dem fürnempsten Hauptmann.
                  T. Berger, n.d. [R Nfp, 2355].

.1.10.   Lied, der Margraff schiffet über den Rhein. Das ander
         Lied, Von der belägerung Schwinfurt. . . .
                  T. Berger, n.d. [R Nfp, 2356].

.1.11.   Lied. Von einer Junckfrawen die da Trew jagt. . . .
                  T. Berger, n.d. [R Nfp, 2354].

.1.12.   Lidt, von der zerstörung Jerusalem.
                  T. Berger, n.d. [R Nfp, 2359].

.1.13.   Lied, von dem Künig Laszala.
                  T. Berger, n.d. [R Nfp, 2344].

.1.14.   Lied, von der Statt Callis.
                  T. Berger, n.d. [R Nfp, 2325].

.1.15.   Lied von dem Tode und einem jungen Mann.
                  T. Berger, n.d. [R Nfp, 2327].

.1.16.   Klag und Dank-Lied, der Gemein zu Heydelberg. Uber der
         gewesenen Churf. G. tödtlichem abgang.
                  T. Berger, n.d. [R Nfp, 2246].

.1.17.   Nun wöll wir aber singen . . . (das Fraülein von
         Britania).
                  Chr. Mylius I, n.d. [R Nfp, 2287].

.1.18.   Von Kaiser Karls recht. Wie er ein Kauffman und ein
         juden macht schlecht . . . Gar ein hüpsch lied. . . .
                  M. Hupfuff, 1498 [S V, 3].

.1.19.   Hüpsch Lied von den schönen frowen.
                  B. Kistler, 1500 [S IV Kis. 11; R Nfp Inc., 419].

.1.20.   Ein hübsch lied vun des brembergers end und todt.
                  B. Kistler, 1500 [S IV Kis. 13].

.1.21.   Ein hübsch Lied zu singen im Schwartzen ton von den
         schonen frauer.
                  B. Kistler, 1500 [S 4 Kis., 11].

.1.22.   Schiller, Jörg, Lied von eynem Wirt und eynem
         Gesellen.
                  M. Hupfuff, 1505 [S V, 44].

.1.23.   Schiller, Jörg, Lied vor Frawen und Jungfrawen zu
         singen genant des Meyen Zyt.
                  M. Hupfuff, 1505 [S V, 43].

V7.1.24. Lied wie ein Münch tzwey zuzamen koppelt on sein
          wissen.
          M. Hupfuff, 1515 [S V, 133].

  .1.25. (Binder, Ludwig), Lied . . . von Lucretia.
          No printer, ca. 1520 [R Nfp, 1014].

  .1.26. Lied von eym Schneyder unnd Schumacher wie sie rechten
          umd die Geyss.
          M. Schürer Erben, 1520 [B SE 2, 2].

  .1.27. Lied . . . von einer kron, Welch die küngin von Afion
          wol zwölff küngen het machen lon.
          M. Schürer Erben, 1521 [B SE 2, 24].

  .1.28. Lied von dem Hammen von Reystett wie in der Peter von
          Zeytenen gefangen hat.
          M. Schürer Erben, 1521 [B SE 1, 10].

  .1.29. Eyn schön reygenlied . . . neulich geschmidet durch
          Meyster Hemerlin in berg Ethna.
          M. Schürer Erben, 1524 [B SE 1, 24].

  .1.30. Fünff und seczig teütscher Lieder.
          P. Schöffer & M. Apiarius, 1536 [Young, 492].

  .1.31. Lied wie der König von Franckreich inn das Teutschland
          mit höres macht ist gezogen.
          T. Berger, 1552 [R Nfp, 2318].

  .1.32. Lied von der schlacht so zwischen Hertzog Moritzen
          von Sachsen . . . und Margraff Albrechten von
          Brandenburg gehalten wurden.
          T. Berger, 1553 [R Nfp, 2331].

  .1.33. Lied von den geschichten so sich zu Frona in Zibbs,
          im Ungerischen kreis zugetragen im Monat May 1557.
          T. Berger, 1557 [R Nfp, 2333].

  .1.34. Lied, vonn der Schlacht so sich zwischen dem Künig
          ausz Engellant unnd Künig inn Franckreich zugetragen
          . . . Anno 1557.
          T. Berger, 1557 [R Nfp, 2332].

  .1.35. Lied . . . des . . . glücks so Gott den Steyerischen
          unnd den selben Reuttern in Wündisch Landen wider den
          Türcken, der Christenheit zu gutem bewisen hat . . .
          1557.
          T. Berger, 1557 [R Nfp, 2372].

  .1.36. Lied von der Statt Dietlenhoffen wie sie in 1558 .
          . . von den Franzosen belägert.
          T. Berger, 1558 [R Nfp, 2361].

V7.1.37. Hertzog Ernst. In gesangs weyse.
          T. Berger, 1560 [R Nfp, 1635].

  .1.38. Der Hürnen Seyfrid . . . ein schönes lied.
          T. Berger, 1563 [R Nfp, 3227].
          Chr. Mylius II Erben, 1580 [R Nfp, 3228], after
          1580 [R Nfp, 3229].

  .1.39. Lied von der Schlacht . . . zwischen dens Hertzog von
          Conde und dem Hertzog von Guiss geschehen am Weynacht
          abend, 1562.
          T. Berger, 1563 [R Nfp, 2334].

  .1.40. Lied Ausz der Histori Eusebii . . . Von den . . .
          zerstörung des Christenthums.
          T. Berger, 1565 [R Nfp, 2335].

  .1.41. Lied: Wie man umb ein Krantz singt.
          T. Berger, ca. 1570 [R Nfp, 2362].

  .1.42. Vier hübsche Weltliche Lieder.
          T. Berger, ca. 1570 [R Nfp, 2404].

  .1.43. Drey schöne neüwe Lieder. Das erst, Ein hüpsche
          Tagweisz von einem truwen Wächter. . . .
          T. Berger, ca. 1570 [R Nfp, 2402].

  .1.44. Lied, von ihren vieren vom Adel . . . Wie dieselben
          Mörderischer weiss, durch einen Burgundischen
          angriffen und wie es inen ergangen.
          P. Hugg, ca. 1570 [R Nfp, 2373].

  .1.45. Lied von dem grausamen . . . Mord, so ein junger
          Gesell, ein meil wegs von Franckfurt am Meyn . . .
          an eines . . . Pfarrherrs Tochter . . . begangen hat.
          T. Berger, 1570 [R Nfp, 2336].

  .1.46. Vier schöne newe Lieder, Das vierdt von Art und
          eigenschafft der gesellen der löblichen Kunst, der
          Buchtruckerey.
          T. Berger, 1570 [R Nfp, 2405].

  .1.47. Es steht ein lind in jenem Thal.
          T. Berger, ca. 1570 [R Nfp, 2301].

  .1.48. Lied vom Malers Töchterlein.
          T. Berger, ca. 1570 [R Nfp, 2300].

  .1.49. Lied von dreyen lieben Frauen.
          T. Berger, ca. 1570 [R Nfp, 2299].

  .1.50. Lied von Alexander von Metz wie er in der
          Heidenschafft gefangen . . . und durch sein Frauw

. . . erlöst ward.
T. Berger, ca. 1570 [R Nfp, 2298].

V7.1.51. Ich zeunt mir nechten einen Zaun.
T. Berger, ca. 1570 [R Nfp, 3569].

.1.52. Lied: Winter! du must urlaub han.
T. Berger, ca. 1570 [R Nfp, 2297].

1.53. Lied, Ich weiss ein leines waldvögelein.
T. Berger, ca. 1570 [R Nfp. 2296].

1.54. Lied, einmal thet ich spatzieren. . . .
T. Berger, ca. 1570 [R Nfp. 2295].

1.55. Lied, Ich stund an einem Morgen.
T. Berger, ca. 1570 [R Nfp, 2294].

.1.56. Lied von dem Erschröcklichen wasser geschehen in
Frankreich . . . M.D. LXX.
P. Hugg, 1571 [R Nfp, 2337].

.1.57. Lied von der erschröckelichen geschicht . . . zu
Magdeburg . . . 1571.
T. Berger, ca. 1571 [R Nfp, 2363].

.1.58. Drey schöne newe Lieder, Das erst von der Statt
Magdeburg . . . Das ander, Ein Klaglied der
Huchgebornen Frawen Sybillen Hertzogin von Sachsen.
T. Berger, ca. 1571 [R Nfp, 2401].

.1.59. Lied von der Tyranney so der Moscoviter mit der Stat
Reffel in Lieffland getriben hat.
P. Hugg, 1571 [R Nfp, 2324].

.1.60. Neüwer Bergreyen vom Künig Ludwig ausz ungern . . .
Ein ander new Lied, ausz der Römer History gezogen.
T. Berger, 1571 [R Nfp, 978].

.1.61. Puschman, Adam, Ein Ander kurtze Beschreibung des
Schönen Münsters zu Strasburg. In der Stumpfen
Lirchenweis.
No printer, 1571 [R Nfp, 3053].

.1.62. Lied von dem Wunderzeichen, wölche Gott zu Roschell
erscheinen lassen . . . 1573.
No printer, 1573 [R Nfp, 2374].

.1.63. Lied von der grossen schlacht und Niderlag des Königs
aus Poln in Frackreich im 1576.
B. Jobin, 1576 [R Nfp, 2364].

.1.64. Eckenlied.
No printer, ca. 1577 [R Nfp, 1533].

V7.1.65. Lied vom Riesen Sigenot.
          No printer, 1577 [R Nfp, 2302].

   .1.66. Lied von dem Kampff . . . zwischen dem Roraffen
           Welcher unter der Orglen im Münster zu Strassburg
           ist und dem Hanen, so auff den Alten Uhren war.
           N. Wyriot, 1580 [R Nfp, 2303].

   .1.67. Philipp, Freiherr zu Winneberg der Jungere,
           Christliche Reuter Lieder.
           No printer, 1580 [R Nfp, 2894].
           B. Jobin, 1582 [R Nfp, 2893], 1586 [R Nfp, 2895].

   .1.68. Ein new Lied, von dem jetzigen zug, so beschen in 83.
           Jar im obern Elsess.
           No printer, 1583 [R Nfp, 2338].

   .1.69. Lied . . . von dem zug für Mülhausen. . . .
           B. Jobin, 1587 [R Nfp, 2339].

   .1.70. Klaglied der Bauren in dem undern Elsass und
           Kochersberg, über den tyrranischen Durchzug von einem
           armen verbrenten verdorben Baurenfreund gedicht.
           N. Kuffer, 1587 [R Nfp, 2340].

   .1.71. Lied, von der Statt Mülhausen. . . .
           B. Jobin, 1587 [R Nfp, 2375].

   .1.72. Lied von der Edlen Statt Strassburg unnd Bistumb da
           selbs im jetzigen Kriegswesen.
           B. Jobin, 1592 [R Nfp, 2350].

   .1.73. Lied . . . von der Lothringischen Bezalung . . . Allen
           Teutchen zu trewer Warnung.
           No printer, 1592 [R BNU III, 1363].

   .1.74. Lied von der Wunderküh, so die Jesuiten zu Moltzheim
           Weyssagen gelehrt.
           No printer, 1592 [R BNU III, 1364].

   .1.75. Lied uff das geschrey so man uff des Bischoffs Grab
           soll hören.
           No printer, 1592 [R BNU III, 1365].

   .1.76. Lied an alle Strasburgische Reutter unnd Knechte
           ausz trewem Teutschen Hertzen.
           No printer, 1592 [R BNU III, 1366].

   .1.77. Lied von dem Elsazsischen Kreig, und was dardurch
           gesucht und understanden würt.
           No printers, 1593 [R BNU III, 1367].

   .1.78. Spangenberg, Cyriacus, Von der kunst der musica, auch

von aufkommen der meistersänger.
No printer, 1598 [R Nfp, 3257].

.2.   COLLECTIONS FOR GROUP SINGING (SONGS OFTEN IN THE
      VERNACULAR).

V7.2.1.   Cantiones quinque vocarum . . . Germaniae inferioris,
          Galliae et Italiae musices magistris editae.
          P. Schöffer, 1529 [R Nfp, 1276], 1539 [Young, 492].

.2.2.   Viginti Cantiunculae gallicae quatuor vocum.
          P. Schöffer, 1530 [R Nfp, 1280].

.2.3.   Motetarum quatuor vocum.
          P. Schöffer, 1535 [Young, 492].

.2.4.   Theatrum Musicum.
          No printer, 1580 [Young, 493].

.2.5.   Sex vocum cantiones.
          N. Wyriot, 1580 [Young, 493].

.2.6.   Arietulus, Kilianus, Cantilena sex vocum.
          N. Wyriot, 1581 [BM, 61].

.2.7.   Paix, Jacobus, Thesaurus Motetarum.
          B. Jobin, 1589 [R Nfp, 2813].

.3.   INSTRUMENTAL MUSIC.

V7.3.1.   Heckel, Wolfgang, Tenor Lautenbuch.
          U. Wyss, 1556 [R Nfp, 1962].
          Chr. Mylius I, 1562 [R Nfp, 1965].

.3.2.   Heckel, Wolfgang, Discant-Lautenbuch.
          No printer (U. Wyss?), 1556 [R Nfp, 1963].
          Chr. Mylius I, 1562 [R Nfp, 1964].

.3.3.   Heckel, Wolfgang, Lauten Buch von mancherley schönen
          und lieblichen stücken. . . .
          U. Wyss, 1556 [R Nfp, 1961].

.3.4.   Das Erste Buch newerleszner Kunstlicher Lautenstück.
          B. Jobin, 1572 [R Nfp, 2146].

.3.5.   Das Ander Buch Newerleszner Kunstlicher Lautenstück.
          B. Jobin, 1573 [R Nfp, 2147].

.3.6.   Neusidler, Melchior, Teutsch Lautenbuch.
          B. Jobin, 1574 [R Nfp, 2760], 1596 [R Nfp, 2761].

.3.7.   Kaergel, Sixt, Novae elegantissimae gallicae . . .
          cantilenae Mutetae et Passomezo, adiuncti suis

Saltarelis, mira dulcedine in Testudine canenda in
Tabulaturam pertranslatae.
    B. Jobin, 1574 [R Nfp, 2201].
    No printer, 1580 [Young, 495].

V7.3.8.   Schmid, Bernhard, Zwey Bücher Einer Neuen Kunstlichen
           Tabulatur auff Orgel und Instrument.
               No printer, 1577 [Young, 493].

  .3.9.   Kaergel, Sixt, Renovata Cythara. . . .
           B. Jobin, 1578 [R Nfp, 2202].

  .3.10. Kaergel, Sixt, Toppel Cythar . . . Neue künstliche
           Tablatur auf der Lauten gemäss Toppel Cythar mit 6
           Cohren.
               B. Jobin, 1578 [R Nfp, 2203].

  .3.11. Barbetta, Giulio Cesare, Novae Tabulae Musicae
           testudinariae Hexachordiae et Haptachordiae New
           Lautenbuch.
               B. Jobin, 1582 [R Nfp, 925].

  .3.12. Kaergel, Sixt, Lautenbuch viler newerlessner . . .
           Lautenstück.
               B. Jobin, 1586 [R Nfp, 2204].

  .3.13. Neusidler, Melchior, Sex Motetten von Josquin de
           Prés à six parties en tablature de Luth.
               No printer, 1587 [R Nfp, 2762].

V8. PLAYS.

  .1. BIBLICAL PLAYS IN GERMAN.

V8.1.1.   Vogel, Nicolas, Ein hubsch lied von dem Verlorenen
           Son.
               J. Frölich, n.d. [R Imp. Alsc., 563].

  .1.2.   Adelphus, Johann, Passion des Herren Jesu in Tütsch
           sprach.
               J. Grüninger, 1513 [Weber].

  .1.3.   Gengenbach, Pamphilus, Die Zehen Alter: nach gemeynem
           lauff der Welt, Ausz der Bibel gezogen, von newem
           gespilt, gemert und gebessert worden, durch eine
           Ersame burgerschafft ein löblichen statt Colmar.
           (George Wickram, arrang.).
               J. Frölich, 1533 [R Nfp, 1865].

  .1.4.   Gnapheus, Guilielmus, Acolastus . . . Der verlorner
           Sohn (in German; Georg Binder, trans.).
               J. Frölich, ca. 1535 [R Nfp, 1911].

V8.1.5.   Wickram, Georg, Ein hüsch new Fasznacht Spil, ausz
          heyliger Biblischer geschrifft gezogen, der trew
          Eckart genant.
              J. Frölich, 1538 [R Nfp, 3484].
              Chr. Mylius I, 1559 [R Nfp, 3485].

  .1.6.   Wickram, Georg, Das Narren giessen. Ein kurtzweilig
          Fasznachtspyl so zu Colmar von einer Burgerschafft
          gespylt worden ist. . . .
              J. Frölich, 1538 [R BNU IV, 2457].

  .1.7.   Seitz, Alexander, Ein Tragedi, das ist, ein Spile . .
          . vom grossen Abentmal und den zehen
          Junckfrawen. . . .
              J Knobloch, 1540 [Weber].
              Also listed as:
              G. Messerschmidt (?), 1560 (?) [R Nfp, 3215].

  .1.8.   Gart, Thiebold, Joseph, eine schöne und fruchtbare
          comedy. . . .
              S. Bundt, 1540 [R Nfp, 1813], 1546 [R BNU II, 934].
              Chr. Mylius I, 1559 [R Nfp, 1815].

  .1.9.   Frey, Jacob, Spil von König Salomon.
              T. Berger, 1541 [Weber].

  .1.10. Wickram, Georg, Ein recht schön christlich
          Burgerspiel, Tobias genant.
              J. Frölich, 1541 [R Nfp, 3514], 1551 [R BNU IV,
                 2458].
              T. Berger, 1562 [R Nfp, 3513].

  .1.11. Ein holdselige Evangelisch History, gantz kurtweilig
          zu spilen Luce am X cap von der liebe des Nechsten
          . . . da ein mensch von Jerusalem gen Jericho
          ging. . . .
              J. Frölich, 1550 [R Nfp, 2029], 1555 [R Imp. Alsc.,
                 563].

  .1.12. Ein schön spil . . . von Tobia.
              J. Frölich, 1551 [R Imp. Alsc., 563].

  .1.13. Sunnentag, Thomas, Ein . . . Spil, von dem
          Ehebrüchigen Weib, Auch von Christo, wie in die Juden
          wolten versteynigen. . . .
              J. Frölich, 1552 [R Nfp, 3306].

  .1.14. Wickram, Georg, Ein Schönes und Christenliches Spyl
          aus den Geschichten der Aposteln gezogen.
              J. Frölich, 1552 [Wickram, 272].

  .1.15. Frey, Jacob, Von dem armen Lazaro, und dem reichen

Mann.
    P. Messerschmidt, 1556 [R Nfp, 1769].

V8.1.16. Kirchmeier, Thomas (Thomas Naogeorgus), <u>Judas</u>
        <u>Icharioth</u> (in German; J. Mercur Moerszheymer trans.).
        W. Köpfel, 1556 [R Nfp, 2244].

  .1.17. Frey, Jakob, <u>Ein Andächtig, Biblisch . . . spiel, wie</u>
        <u>Abraham Issac seinen sun auffopffern solte . . . Auch</u>
        <u>von der verderbung Sodome und Gomorre.</u>
        P. Messerschmidt, 1556 [R Nfp, 1770].

  .1.18. Ruof, Jacobus (Jacob Rueff), <u>Ein schön nützlich Spil</u>
        <u>von dem frommen . . . Job . . . welche von einer</u>
        <u>löblichen Burgerschafft zu Straszburg im . . . 1558</u>
        <u>gespilt worden ist.</u>
        T. Berger, 1558 [R Nfp, 3131].

  .1.19. Birck, Sixte, <u>Judith, eine schöne History, in</u>
        <u>Spielweiss. . . .</u>
        Chr. Mylius I, 1559 [R Nfp, 2167].
        A. Bertram, 1586 [R BNU I, 206].

  .1.20. Hoppenrod, Andreas, <u>Das Gulden Kalb, Ein Spil.</u>
        S. Emmel, 1563 [R Nfp, 2041].

  .1.21. (Frey, Jacob), <u>Ein schön biblisch Spyl . . . Judith</u>
        <u>gennennt, Neulich zu Strassburg durch eine junge</u>
        <u>Burgersscafft . . . offentlich gespilt.</u>
        T. Berger, 1564 [R Nfp, 3268].

  .1.22. <u>Ein schön new Spyl von . . . König Salomon zu Anfang</u>
        <u>seines Reiches über zwo Hüren samt ihren Kindern</u>
        <u>gestellet hat. . . .</u>
        T. Berger, 1566 [R Nfp, 3153].

  .1.23. Buchanan, Georgius, <u>Jephtes oder Gelübd, eine schöne,</u>
        <u>nützliche Tragedi. . . . </u>(J. Bitner, trans.).
        J. Rihel, 1567 [R Nfp, 1192a].
        N. Wyriot, 1569 [R Nfp, 1193].

  .1.24. Walliser, Christoph Thomas (L'ainé), <u>Ein schön . . .</u>
        <u>Spyl, nemlich die schöne History Esther . . . gespilt</u>
        <u>zu Strassburg . . . September 1568.</u>
        Chr. Mylius I, 1568 [R Nfp, 3461].

  .1.25. Sachs, Hans, <u>Spyl von dem Urteil so Kunig Salomon zum</u>
        <u>Anfang seines Reiches uber zwei Hüren samt ihren</u>
        <u>Kinder.</u>
        T. Berger, 1570 [Weber].

  .1.26. Zyrl, Christian, <u>Rebecca, Ein schöne hochzeit Comedia.</u>
        T. Berger, 1572 [R BNU IV, 2533].

V8.1.27.   Zyrl, Christian, <u>Die gantze Historia vom Joseph in</u>
           <u>eine schöne christliche Comediam gefasset. . . .</u>
           No printer, 1572 [Weber], 1573 [R Nfp, 3626].

   .1.28. Meyenbrunn, Andreas, <u>Tragoedia. Johannis des heiligen</u>
           <u>Vorläuffers und Täuffers Jesu Christi . . . gespilt</u>
           <u>durch ein Ehrsame Burgerschafft zu Colmar . . . 1573.</u>
           N. Wyriot, 1575 [R Nfp, 2677].

   .1.29. Schütz, Hieronymus, <u>Vom Abgott Bel zu Babel.</u>
           N. Wyriot, 1576 [R <u>Imp. Alsc.</u>, 571].

   .1.30. <u>Comoedia und Lehrbaffte History von dem Verlornen</u>
           <u>Sohn, Luce am 15. Cap. Spielweise.</u>
           Chr. Mylius II, 1578 [R Nfp, 1426].

   .1.31. Crocus, Cornelius, <u>Joseph in Egypten, eine schöne . .</u>
           <u>. Comödie ans lateinischer Sprach in die Teutsche</u>
           <u>verdolmetshet</u> (J. Bitner, trans.).
           N. Wyriot, 1583 [R Nfp, 1457].

   .1.32. Colb, Adam, <u>Ein schön Wyhenachten Spil gestelt. . . .</u>
           Chr. Mylius II, 1583 [R Nfp, 1417].

   .1.33. <u>Ein schön . . . Spil vom Reichen Mann und Armen</u>
           <u>Lazarus.</u>
           J. Martin, 1590 [R <u>Imp. Alsc.</u>, 575].

   .1.34. Zyrl, Christian, <u>Urteil Salomons, ein . . . comedia.</u>
           No printer, 1592 [R Nfp, 3627].

   .1.35. <u>Comoedia von König David.</u>
           <u>Gespräch von dreyen Personën, einem Wucherer, Bawrsman</u>
           <u>und Doctor gestelt durch Joh. Beuchter.</u>
           A. Bertram, 1598 [R Nfp, 1427].

   .1.36. Kenier, Johannes, <u>Teutsche Reimen des Predigers</u>
           <u>Solomonis mit der auslegung Joan. Claij.</u>
           No printer, 1599 [R Nfp, 2225].

   .2.   PLAYS ON OTHER THEMES.

V8.2.1.   Manuel, Nicolaus, <u>Das Barbeli, Ein gespräch.</u>
           Chr. Mylius I, n.d. [R Nfp, 2594].

   .2.2.   Frey, Jacob, <u>Vater, Müter, . . . wie sie ihre Kinder</u>
           <u>zu Schul tun.</u>
           J. Frölich, 1534 [Weber].

   .2.3.   Erasmus, <u>Ein hübsch lutspyl d'Weiber Reichstag genant</u>
           <u>ausz den Colloquiis Erasmus genummen. . . .</u>
           J. Frölich, 1537 [R Nfp, 1574].

V8.2.4. Wickram, Georg, Ein schöne unnd fast schimpflich
         kurtzweil so durch Umtreiben eyner scheiben Allten
         und Jungen Mann und weiblichen Personen . . . die
         traurigen schlaferigen Gemuter widerumb zu lachenden
         Freyden zu bewegen.
              No printer, 1539 [Weber].

  .2.5. Gengenback, Pamphilius, Der alt und new bruder Nolhard
         . . . zu Basel von einer jungen Burgerschafft gespielt.
              J. Cammerlander, 1545 [R Nfp, 1866].

  .2.6. Von Fortunatus und seinem Seckel auch Wünschhütlein.
              No printer, 1546 [R Nfp, 1755], ca. 1570 [R Nfp,
                 1757].
              Chr. Mylius I, 1558 [R Nfp, 1756].

  .2.7. Ein schön Spil von . . . Lucretia. . . .
              J. Frölich, 1550 [R Nfp, 2439].

  .2.8. Wickram, Georg, Der Jungen Knaben Spiegel, ein schönes
         Spyl von zwei Jungen Knaben.
              J. Frölich, 1554 [Wickram, 273].

  .2.9. (Frey, Jacob), Ein schönes und kurtzweiliges Fasznacht
         Spil . . . von einem Krämer und zwei Mägden. . . .
              No printer, 1556 [R Nfp, 1768].

  .2.10. Montanus, Martin, Ein untrew Knecht.
              P. Messerschmidt, 1560 [R BNU III, 1590].

  .2.11. Montanus, Martin, Von zweien Römern, Tito Quinto
         Fulvio und Gisippo, Ein newes lustiges, . . . Spiel.
              P. Messerschmidt, 1560 [R BNU III, 1591].

  .2.12. Montanus, Martin, Ein newes . . . Spil von einem
         Graven.
              P. Messerschmidt, 1560 [R BNU III, 1589].

  .2.13. Sachs, Hans, Ein hüpsch Spil vonn einen alten
         Wittling.
              T. Berger, 1565-1570 [R Nfp, 3145].

  .2.14. Ein schön . . . Spyl von einem Vatter und einer
         Mutter, wie sie ihre Kinder zur Schul thun.
              T. Berger, 1566 [R Nfp, 3269], 1570 [Weber].

  .2.15. Rasser, Johann, Ein schön Christlich new Spil von
         Kinderzucht.
              T. Berger, 1574 [R BNU III, 1971].

  .2.16. (Gengenback, Pamphilus), Die Gauchmatt. Ein . . .
         Fasznachtspiel, gedicht zu ehren dem Ehestand, wider
         die sünd des Ehebruchs, und Unkeuschheit, . . .

gespielt von . . . Burgern einer . . . Statt Basel.
   Chr. Mylius II, 1582 [R Nfp, 1871].

V8.2.17. Macropedius, Georgius, Hecastus verteutscht (J.
          Schreckenberger, trans.).
          A. Bertram, 1589 [R Nfp, 2580].

  .2.18. Comoedia von Künig Dario.
          A. Bertram, 1598 [R Imp. Alsc., 573].

  .2.19. Frischlin, Nicodemus, Ein schöne Comedien von Fraw
          Hildegardin Hertzog Hildebrandts in Schwaben Tochter,
          Keysers Caroli Nagni Gamahlin.
          A. Bertram, 1599 [R Nfp, 1792].

  .2.20. Junius, Samuel, Teudsche Argumenta Oder Innhalt der
          Tragoediae Lucretia genant.
          A. Bertram, 1599 [R BNU I, 73].

V9. HISTORY IN THE VERNACULAR.

  .1. GENERAL HISTORY AND CHRONICLES.

V9.1.1. Rolewinck, Werner, Ein Cronica von Anfang der Welt.
         J. Prüss I, 1492 [R. BNU Inc., 420].

  .1.2. Caoursin, Guilelmus (Guillaume Caoursin), Der
         vermaledigsten unfromen Türggen anschleg und fürnemen
         wider die heilige Cristenheit.
         B. Kistler, 1502 [S IV Kis., 20].

  .1.3. Müling, Johannes Adelphus, Die Türkish Chronica
         von irem ursprung anefang und regiment biss auff dise
         zeit, sampt yren Kriegen und Streyten mit den
         christen begangen.
         M. Flach II, 1513 [S VI B, 36].
         J. Knobloch, 1516 [S VII, 126].

  .1.4. Caoursin, Guilelmus (Guillaume Caoursin), Historia
         Von Rhodis wie ritterlich sie sich gehalten mit dem
         Tyrannischen Keiser Machomet uss Türckyen.
         M. Flach II, 1513 [S VI B, 32].

  .1.5. Brant, Sebastian, Von dem Anfang und Wesen der haligen
         Statt Jerusalem. . . .
         J. Knobloch, 1518 [S VII, 156; R BNU I, 241].

  .1.6. Türkei. Chronica, Glaube, Gesatz, Sitten, Herkommen
         . . . Im 1436 Jar beschriben.
         C. Egenolff, January 1530 [R Nfp, 1335], May 1530
         [B Egen., 28].

V9.1.7.   Franck, Sebastian, <u>Chronica, Zeytbuch und Geschycht</u>
            <u>bibel von anbegyn bisz inn disz gegenwertig MDXXXI</u>
            <u>jar.</u>
            B. Beck, 1531 [R BNU II, 882].

  .1.8.   Vives, Johannes Ludovicus (Juan Luis Vives), <u>Wie der</u>
            <u>Türck die Christen haltet so under im leben</u> (C. Hedio,
            trans.).
            B. Beck, 1532 [R BNU IV, 2428].

  .1.9.   Hedio, Kaspar, <u>Ein auszerleszne Chronick von</u>
            <u>angang der Welt bis auff das jar nach Christi unsers</u>
            <u>eynigen Heylands geburt MDXXXIX.</u>
                Cr. Mylius, 1539 [R BNU II, 1097], 1543 [R BNU II,
                1098].
                Second edition goes to MDXLIII.

  .1.10.   Heinrich von Eppendorf, <u>Türkischer Keyser Ankunfft,</u>
            <u>Kryeg und Handlung gegen und wider die Christen, bitz</u>
            <u>ynschlyesslich uff den yetzt regyerenden Solymannum.</u>
                J. Schott, 1540 [S II B, 140].

  .1.11.   <u>Alchoran, Das ist des Mahometischen Gesatzbuch und</u>
            <u>Turckischen Aberglaubens ynnhalt und ablänung.</u>
                J. Schott, 1540 [S II B, 141].

  .1.12.   Schott, Johann, <u>Das weltlich Layenbuch.</u>
            No printer, 1541 [R Nfp, 3191].

  .1.13.   Krantz, Albert, <u>Swedische Chronick</u> (Heinrich von
            Eppendorf, trans.).
                J. Schott, 1545 [R BNU II, 1316].

  .1.14.   Krantz, Albert, <u>Norwägische Chronick</u> (H. von Eppendorf,
            trans.).
                J. Schott, 1545 [R BNU II, 1315].

  .1.15.   Krantz, Albert, <u>Dennmärkische Chronick</u> (H. von
            Eppendorf, trans.).
                J. Schott, 1545 [S II B, 145; R BNU II, 1314].

  .1.16.   Burchardus Ursbergensis (Burchardus, Provost of
            Ursperg), <u>Ein Ausserlessne Chronik von Anfang der</u>
            <u>Welt bis auff das jar MDXLIII</u> (C. Hedio, trans.).
                Chr. Mylius I & B. Fabricius, 1549 [BM 9007.i.I].

  .1.17.   Philippes de Comines, <u>History, Ursprung und Ursach</u>
            <u>des Burgundischen Kriegs.</u> (C. Hedio, trans.).
                W. Rihel, 1551 [R BNU I, 564].
                No printer, 1561 [R Nfp, 1425].

  .1.18.   Phillipes de Comines, <u>History von könig Carle aus</u>

Frankreich, . . . und von dem krieg zu Napels.
W. Rihel, 1552 [R BNU I, 565].

V9.1.19.   Du Chene, François (pseud.) or Francisco de Enzinas,
Histoire de l'estat du País Bas et de la Réligion
d'Espagne.
F. Perrin, 1558 [Peter, 17].

.1.20.   Philipes de Comines, Historia. Sachen und Handel, so
sich bey der Fürsten und Herren, Ludwig des Eylfften,
Königs von Frankreich, Herren Carles Hertzogen zu
Burgend . . . haben verlauffen und zugetraffen.
J. Rihel, 1566 [R BNU I, 566], 1580 [R BNU I, 567].

.1.21.   Recueil des choses mémorables faites et passées pour
le faict de la religion en estat de ce royaume depuis
la mort du roi Henry II, jusques au commencement des
troubles en 1565.
P. Estiart, 1566 [R Nfp, 3077].

.1.22.   Beuther, Michael, Chronica das ist eyn Auszerlesen
zeitbuch darinn allerley namhaffte Händel
beschribenen.
T. Rihel, 1566 [Greiner].

.1.23.   Messias, Petrus (Pedro Mexia), Schöne Historie,
Exempel, Underweisungen, Auch viler naturlicher dingen
Ursachen, Herrlicher Philosophen Sententz,
Disputationes und Argumenta (Hans B. Grass [Vay],
trans.).
T. Berger, 1570 R. Bib. Mun., 1487].

.1.24.   Jovius, Paulus (Paolo Giovio; Bishop of Nocera),
Berümter fürtrefflicher Leut Leben, handlung und
Thaten . . . Historien und Geschichten Insonderheyb,
der . . . Zuge urd Kriege im Mayland . . . und
Neaples. Darzwisechen die Statt Rom mit gewalt
erobert, geplündert . . . Welches alles durch
dapffere Ritter Thaten des Teutschen Kriegsvoloks
verrilhtet worden . . . Ander theyl: Darinnen das
Epicurisch, ünpich und Sodomitisch Wesen des
Romischen Hofes und entwichten New Römischen . . .
Klar an tas gibt (G. Klee, trans.).
    B. Jobin, 1580 [R Nfp, 2164].
    B. Jobin, 1589 [R BNU II, 1286]. (Part I.)
    B. Jobin, 1589 [R BNU II, 1287]. (Part II.)

.1.25.   Sigonius, Carolus, Von Geschichtenn des Königreichs
Italie . . . von Jar Christi 570 bisz ins Tausetest
zweyhunderst Jar (G. Nigrinus, trans.).
    B. Jobin, 1584 [R BNU IV, 2125].

V9.1.26.   Reusner, Nicolaus, <u>Aureolorum Emblematum Liber</u>
           <u>singularis Tobiae Stimmeri iconibus effictis exornatus</u>
           (in Latin and German).
               B. Jobin, 1587 [BM 96.a.6].

  .1.27.   Steger, Tobias, <u>Unpostreuterische Geschicht schriften</u>
           <u>so sich in dem mehrerteil Europa zugetragen</u>.
               No printer, 1590 [BM 8610.bb.48.5].

  .2.   ANCIENT HISTORY.

V9.2.1.   Lirer, Thomas, <u>Chronica von allen Künig und Kaiseren</u>
           <u>von Anfang Rom</u>.
               J. Knobloch, 1500 [R Nfp <u>Inc</u>., 429].

  .2.2.   <u>Cronica von allen kunig und Keisern: von anfang Rom</u>.
               B. Kistler, ca. 1500 [S IV Kis. 9].

  .2.3.   Coccinius, Michaelis, <u>De Imperii a Graecis ad Germanos</u>
           <u>tralatione. In quo etiam disseritur. qui Galliae</u>
           <u>populi spectent ad ius & ditionem imperii. Item de</u>
           <u>Francorum origine, ac de duplici Francia</u>. . . .
               J. Grüninger, 1506 [S I, 77].

  .2.4.   <u>In das leben und tugendtliche geschichten Keyser Tyti</u>
           <u>Vespasiani des miltenn</u> (S. Brant, trans.).
               M. Flach II, 1520 [S VI B, 42].

  .2.5.   Huttich, Johannes, <u>J.H. Römische kayser abcontraveyt,</u>
           <u>vom ersten Caio Julio an untz uff den ietzigen H.K.</u>
           <u>Carolum. Mit kurtzer anzeygung ires Lebens dapffer</u>
           <u>thaten und historien</u>.
               W. Köpfel, 1526 [R Nfp, 2116].

  .2.6.   Heinrich von Eppendorf, <u>Römischer Historien</u>
           <u>Bekürtzung</u>.
               J. Schott, 1536 [S II B, 135].

  .2.7.   Cuspinianus, Johannes, <u>Chronicka von C. Julio Cesare</u>
           <u>dem ersten, bisz auff Carolum quintum diser zeit</u>
           <u>Rhömischen Keyser, auch von allen Orientischen oder</u>
           <u>Griechischen und Türckischen Keysern</u> (C. Hedio,
           trans.).
               Cr. Mylius, 1541 [R BNU I, 607].

  .2.8.   Floridus, Franciscus Sabinus (Franciscus
           Floridus), <u>Kreigsübung desz fürtrefflichsten und</u>
           <u>streitbarsten ersten Römischen Kaisers Julii</u>. . . .
           <u>Die wunderbarliche Histori von der Christen auszug,</u>
           <u>under Kaiser Heinrichen dem vierdten zu des haligen</u>
           <u>lands, und der darinn Christliches namens gefanger</u>

errettung. Die belegerung und eroberung der
Kaiserlichen statt Constantinoplis, welche Mahomet
der Turck . . . dem Kaiser Constantino abgegrunden.
G. Messerschmidt, 1551 [R BNU II, 872].

V9.2.9.   Sleidanus, Johannes, Trois Livres des Quatre Empires
Souverains, Assauoir, De Babylone, Perse, Grece, Rome.
No printer, 1558 [R BNU IV, 2138].
J. Rihel, 1568 [R Nfp, 3240].

.2.10.   Zschorn, Johann, Chronica, oder Keyser Büchlin. Darinn
alle Römische Keyser von dem ersten Keyser Julio biss
auff den yetzt regierenden Keyser Ferdinancum . . .
gfunden werden.
P. Messerschmidt, 1559 [R BNU IV, 2530].

.2.11.   Spangenberg, Cyriacus, Chronicon Corinthiacum.
Historien und Geschicht der Stadt Corinth.
S. Emmel, 1569 [R Nfp, 3254].

.3.   GERMAN AND IMPERIAL HISTORY.

V9.3.1.   Ein schöne warhafftige Hystory von Keiser Karolus
sun genant Loher oder Lotarius. . . .
J. Grüninger, 1513 [R Nfp, 2422], 1514 [S I, 133].

.3.2.   Adelssus, Johannes (Johannes Adelphus Müling),
Barbarossa . . . beschreibung des lebens und der
geschichten Keiser friderichs des ersten genant
Barbarossa.
J. Grüninger, 1520 [S I, 173], 1520 [R Nfp, 2731],
1530 [S I, 248].

.3.3.   Gebweiller, Heronymus, Keiserlich und Hispanischer
Maiestat auch Fürstlicher durchlüchtigkeit und aller
hievor, Ertzhertzogen und hertzogen von Österreich,
Darzu der fürstlichen grauen von Habsburg, alt
künglich harkummen mit namen, gar nahe off
zweitusent jar.
J. Grüninger, 1527 [S I, 230].

.3.4.   Sachs, Hans, Der Fürsten Schatz. Ebenbildt auss
Göttlicher und Heydnischer geschrifft wess sich eyn
jeder Keyser, König, Furst, Herr etc. Halten soll.
J. Cammerlander, 1536 [B Cam., 108], 1538 [B Cam.,
109].

.3.5.   Sturm, Caspar, Die Kleyn Fürstlich Chronica . . .
Abkürtzung der vier Monarchien.
J. Cammerlander, 1544 [B Cam., 125].

V9.3.6.   Accolti, Benedetto, Die wunderbarliche Histori von
           der Christen Auszug under Kaiser Heinrichen den
           vierdten zu des heiligenlands errettung (H. von
           Eppendorf, trans.).
           No printer, 1551 [R Nfp, 733].

  .3.7.   Sleidanus, Johannes, Beschreibung . . . Geistlichen
           und Weltlichen sachen so sich under der regierung des
           Groszmechtigsten Keysers Caroli disz namens des V.
           verlauffen (Marc Stamler, trans.).
           No printer, 1557 [R BNU IV, 2135].
           No printer, 1558 [R BNU IV, 2137]. (In French.)
           J. Rihel, 1558 [R BNU IV, 2136], 1559 [R BNU IV,
              2141], 1568 [R Nfp, 3239].
           T. Rihel, 1568 [R Bib. Mun., 1936], 1570 [R Bib.
              Mun., 1937], 1574 [R BNU IV, 2146], 1575 [R BNU
              IV, 2147], 1579 [R BNU IV, 2149], 1588 [R BNU IV,
              2150], 1593 [R BNU IV, 2151], 1598 [R BNU IV,
              2152].

  .3.8.   Sleidanus, Johannes, Sommaire de l'histoire de Jean
           Sleidan disposé par tables en tel ordre et facilité
           que le lecteur pourra aisément et sans travail
           comprendre par iceluy tout le long narre de ladite
           histoire.
           No printer, 1558 [Greiner].

  .3.9.   Rantzau, Heinrich, Verzeychnisz des Krieges, in
           welchem König Friderich zu Dänemarck . . . alle
           Hertzogen Holsteyn . . . im 1559 wider die Dietmarsen
           geführt.
           T. Rihel, 1569 [R BNU III, 1969].

  .3.10.   Hoppenrod, Andreas, Stammbuch Oder Erzölung aller
           namhaffter unnd inn Teütschen Historien berümpter
           Fursten, Graffen unnd Herren Geschlechter, wölche
           ungefehrlich innerhalb Tausent unnd weniger jaren,
           ihre Herrschaften inn den Sächsischen Landen, zwischen
           der Elbe unnd dem Rhein, vom Hartzwald bisz an die
           West Sehe, und Danische Grentz, besessen, und volgends
           ihren nachtkommenden bisz auff jetzige zeit mit Rhum
           zu besitzen haben hinderlossen.
           J. Rihel, 1570 [R BNU II, 1200].

  .3.11.   Sigonius, Carolus, Deutschen Römischen Reichs Hoch
           Achtung und dessen von Teutschen Keysern, Königen und
           verwesen rühmlicher Regierung und Verwaltung nothwen-
           dige stattliche Ehren Rettung, wider etliche
           offentlich auszkommene partheiliche Italianische
           Scribenten und bevorab den sonst vil berümbten

historicum Carolum Sigonium (G. Nigrinus, ed.).
B. Jobin, 1584 [R BNU IV, 2124].

V9.3.12. Spangenberg, Cyriacus, Sächsische Chronik.
No printer, 1585 [R Nfp, 3255].

.3.13. Reusner, Christophorus, Contrafacturbuch. Ware und
lebendige Bildnussen etlicher weitberhümbten und
Hochgelehrten Männer in Teütschland.
B. Jobin, 1587 [R BNU III, 1998].

.3.14. Hertzog, Bernhard, Chronicon Alsatiae. Elsässer
Cronick unnd auszfürliche beschreibung des unterm
Elsasses am Rheinstrom.
B. Jobin, 1592 [R BNU II, 1162].

.3.15. Spangenberg, Cyriacus, Hennebergische Chronica.
B. Jobin Erben, 1599 [R BNU IV, 2173].
See also V9.2.10.

.4. ECCLESIASTICAL HISTORY.

V9.4.1. Hedio, Kaspar, Chronica der Altenn Christlichen Kirchen
ausz Eusebio, Ruffino, Sozomeno, Theodoreto,
Tertulliano, Justino, Cypriano und Plinio (C. Hedio,
ed. and Trans.).
G. Ulricher, 1530 [R BNU II, 1093].
W. Köpfel, 1545 [R BNU II, 1099], 1558 [R BNU II,
1100].

.4.2. Platina, Baptista, Historia von der Bäbst und Keiser
Leben (C. Hedio, trans.).
W. Rihel, 1546 [R BNU III, 1881].
J. Rihel, 1565 [R Nfp, 2930].

.4.3. Jean de Hainaut, L'Estat de l'Eglise dez le temps des
Apostres, jusques a l'an present. Avec un recueil de
troubles avenus en France sous le Roy Francoys II.
et Charles IX.
No printer, 1564 [Peter, 28], 1565 [R BNU II, 1069].

.4.4. Panvinius, Onuphrius (Onofrid Panvinio), Accuratae
Effigies Pontificum Maximorum (in Latin and German).
B. Jobin, 1573 [R BNU III, 1754].

.4.5. Gloccer, Georg, Warhafftige Historia. Und grundlicher
Summarischer Bericht von der Lehr, Leben, Beruff und
seligen Abschiedt Doctoris Martini Lutheri.
A. Bertram, 1586 [R Nfp, 1910].

V10.   POPULAR JOURNALISM.

V10.1.   ACCOUNTS OF PROPHECIES, HERESIES, RELIGIOUS EXECUTIONS,
           AND OTHER RELIGIOUS OCCURENCES.

           All titles are abbreviated.

V10.1.1.   Warhaftig sag . . . von dem Rock Jesu cristi Neulich
           in der heiligen stat Trier erfunden.
           M. Hupfuff, 1512 [S V, 98].

    .1.2. Adelphus, Joannes, Declaration unnd erclerung der
           warheit des Rocks Jesu Christi, newlich zu Trier
           erfunden.
           M. Flach II, 1513 [S VI B, 33].

    .1.3. Ein schöner spruch von zweyen Junckfrawen Bericht von
           der Verbrennung der adeligen und reformiert gesinnten
           Maria und Ursula von Becken in Delden . . . in der
           Niederlanden, 1546.
           J. Frölich, ca. 1546 [Z, PAS II, 1/2].

    .1.4. Verzeichness un kurtzer begriff . . . Martin Rainbach
           . . . der verfluchte, glotlossen red.
           Chr. Mylius I, 1566 [Wick].

    .1.5. Fischart, Johann, Ein Wunderlässliche Zeitung von
           einem Newen Propheten, so newlicher zeit zu Einsidelen
           . . . ist erstanden.
           B. Jobin, 1573 [Z, PAS II, 10/10], 1575 [R Nfp, 3606].

    .1.6. Ins Hailand Jesu Christ; Namen, Bigen sich die Knig
           allesamen . . . (Christ as the Conqueror of the world,
           death, and the devil.).
           B. Jobin, ca. 1575-1580 [WJ, 45].

    .1.7. Chassanion, Jean, La réfutation des erreurs étranges
           et blasphèmes horribles d'un . . . malhereux qui pour
           telles impiétez a esté . . . bruslé en la cité de
           Metz, le 29 juin 1582.
           N. Wyriot, 1583 [R Nfp, 1332].

    .1.8. Klägliche newe Zeitung. Wie zu Theuren zwen
           Evangelische prediger . . . enthaupt worden.
           N. Waldt, 1583 [R Nfp, 3612].

    .1.9. Franzelius, Salomon, Germania Suplex, Jesu Christo
           suo redemptori et Conservatori unico.
           T. Berger, 1585 [Z PAS II, 22/12; R Nfp, 1767].

.2. ACCOUNTS OF NATURAL DISASTERS.

V10.2.1. Eisslinger, Balthasar, <u>Der erschrocklichen Erdbidem</u>
<u>in der Statt Heydelberg . . . M.D. XXXIIII Jar.</u>
J. Prüss II, 1534 [S III B, 44].

.2.2. Moibanus, Ambrosius, <u>Von eim erschrecklichen</u>
<u>Ungewitter inn der Slesien zu Olse . . . begeben</u>
<u>haben.</u>
J. Prüss II, 1536 [S III B, 45].

.2.3. <u>Von dem erschrocklichen . . . ungewitter zu Mechlin.</u>
J. Prüss II, 1546 [S III B, 54].

.2.4. <u>Zeittung von Sieben Stetten . . . in den grentzen von</u>
<u>Frankreich versuncken und undergegangen.</u>
P. Hugg, 1566 [R Nfp, 3592].

.2.5. <u>Erschröckliche geschicht von einem fall eines Bergs</u>
<u>in Saffoy.</u>
T. Berger, 1567 [R Nfp, 3593].

.2.6. <u>Von einem erschröcklichen Brandt auff der Insel Pyru</u>
<u>. . . M.D.LXVII.</u>
P. Hugg, 1567 [R Nfp, 3595].

.2.7. <u>Von den Erdbidemen inn der Statt Ferrar.</u>
P. Hugg, 1570 [BM 1393.b.38(4)].

.2.8. <u>Erschröckliche Geschicht . . . welche sich . . . in</u>
<u>der. Reichsstatt Magdenburg verlauffen . . . hat.</u>
P. Hugg, 1571 [R Nfp, 1901].

.2.9. <u>Von dem erschrecklichen Feuerzeichen und Erdbidem . .</u>
<u>. im Schweitzerland.</u>
T. Berger, 1584 [R Nfp, 3614].

.3. ACCOUNTS OF MARVELOUS AND MONSTROUS BIRTHS.

V10.3.1. <u>Ein wunderbare geburt und veranderung der natur von</u>
<u>einer hennen in Thoma Eherlin's Bursar zu Kolmar</u>
<u>hauss.</u>
J. Frölich, 1538 [Z, PASS II, 1/7].

.3.2. <u>Contrafactur einer Wunderbarlichen geburt so zu</u>
<u>Bischen bei Roszen . . . geschehen.</u>
P. Hugg, 1563 [Z, PAS II, 4/7; R Nfp, 1436].

.3.3. Goelitzsch, Johannes, <u>Ein erschröckliche Geburt und</u>
<u>Augenscheinlich Wunderzeichen des Allmechtigen Gottes.</u>
T. Berger, 1564 [R Nfp, 1915].

210   Popular Journalism

V10.3.4. Beschreibung einer Wundergeburt.
          T. Berger, 1565 [Z, PAS II, 6/7; R Nfp, 994].

   .3.5. Zeittung von einer abschewlichen Geburt zu Renchen
          . . . zu sonderlicher Warnung von Gott.
          P. Hugg, 1569 [Z, PAS II, 7/5; Z PAS II, 12/71].
          No printer, 1569 [Z, PASS II, 8/10].

   .3.6. Warhaftige und schrockliche Bildnuss und gestalt
          zwoer . . . ungewonlicher Missgeburt . . . im Land
          Wirtenberg. Sampt der beschreibung des Erbarmlichen
          Wassergusses . . . in Land Wirtenberg. . . .
          (B. Jobin ?), 1578 [Z, PAS II, 15/33].

   .4. ACCOUNTS OF MURDERS.

V10.4.1. Bekantnüs der Mörderischen . . . ungehörter
          Usbelthaten durch Hansen von Berstatt an einem
          fünffthalb Järigen Kindlin.
          No printer, 1540 [Z, PAS II, 12/26].

   .4.2. Der grewlich Cains mordt den ein Römischen Hispanien
          . . . an seinem lieblichen und einigen Christlichen
          bruder umb des heiligen Evangelions Willen.
          J. Cammerlander, 1546 [Z, PAS II, 12/35].

   .4.3. Ein grausamlich mord so geschehen ist in dem
          Minsterthal . . . da ein pfaff ein schwangere frawen
          gemordt die in kindsnöten gelegen ist.
          No printer, 1556 [Z, PAS II, 12/50].

   .4.4. Ein erschreckenlich, greusam, unerhört mordt . . .
          geschehen zu Obernahen . . . ein Burger seiner Rechten
          . . . Kinder . . . umbracht. . . .
          A. Fries, 1556 [R Nfp, 2723; Z, PAS II, 12/53].

   .4.5. Anzeigung welcher massen der beschehen Mordt zu Ober
          Hasel . . . sich zugetragen.
          T. Berger, 1557 [R Nfp, 831; Z, PAS II, 2/8; Z, PAS
          II, 12/58].

   .4.6. Zeittung von etlichen Mördern . . . wie sie sich dem
          Teuffel ergeben.
          No printer, 1583 [BM 8630.d.12].

   .4.7. Seltzam unerhorte Zeytung, Wz gestalt Georg Hanober
          Von Olmitz, vermeinter Alchemist, mit dem Strang ist
          hingerichtet worden.
          No printer, 1597 [R Nfp, 3619].

.5. ACCOUNTS OF WONDERFUL OR EXCEPTIONAL PLANTS.

V10.5.1. Von unerhörte Figur unnd gewachs so zu Albersweiler
         bey Landauw . . . erfonden worden.
            (H. Vogtherr), 1541 [Z, PAS II, 12/25].

  .5.2. Ein wunderbar doch fröliche . . . gewechs eines halmen
         . . . mit funffzehen Eehern . . . bey Malsch am
         Bruckrein. . . .
            (H. Vogtherr), 1541 [Z, PAS II, 1/11].

  .5.3. Abbildung des wunderbaren schönen Weitzenstocks von
         LXXII halmen.
            T. Berger, 1563 [R Nfp, 720; Z, PAS II, 12/69].

  .5.4. Heubner, Mathias, Effigies duarum et septuaginta spi-
         carum, refertarum tritico, quae singulis culmis
         insistentes ex uno grano, unaque radice enatae, ad
         maturitatem omnes pervenerunt. . . .
            T. Berger, 1563 [R Nfp, 2081].

  .5.5. Zwey seltzam Wundergewechs . . . diseit und jhenseit
         des Rheins gefunden.
            T. Berger, 1563 [R Nfp, 3559; Z, PAS II, 4/10].

  .5.6. Zwey seltzam Wundergewechs . . . diseit und jhenseit
         des Rheins gefunden.
            T. Berger, 1563 [R Nfp, 3560].

  .5.7. Wunderbarliche Gewächss auff den Eychbeumen.
            T. Berger, 1582 [R Nfp, 3610].

  .6. ACCOUNTS OF MARVELOUS AND MIRACULOUS APPARITIONS.

V10.6.1. Ain wunderbarlich erschrockenlich gesicht so auff den
         vierdten tag des Mayens disen xxxxiii jahrs in dem
         Dorff Zessenhausen . . . gesehen worden.
            J. Cammerlander, 1543 [Z, PAS II, 12/32].

  .6.2. Wunderbarlich Gesicht erschienen 1547 auf den Tag
         Maria Magdalen.
            J. Frölich, 1547 [Z, PAS II, 12/5].

  .6.3. Wunderbarlich . . . Geschicht . . . gesehen . . . in
         der Churfürstliche Staat Wittemberg.
            J. Frölich, 1547 [Z, PAS II, 12/36].

  .6.4. Newe Zeittung am Himmel ist gesehen worden zwischen
         Nürmberg, Feüchtwangen und Anoltzpach.
            J. Prüss II, ca. 1550 [R Nfp, 3584].

  .6.5. Wunderwerck Korn von dem Hymmel wie ein regen gefallen

                      ist, . . . warhafftig geschehen.
                      W. Köpfel, 1550 [R Nfp, 3561; Z, PAS II, 2/23].

V10.6.6.   New Zeyttung von vilen Menschen zu Ingolstandt zu
            Regensburg und zu Nürnberg am Himmel gesehen worden.
                      T. Berger, 1554 [R Nfp, 3585; Z, PAS II, 12/46].

    .6.7.   Abcontrefactur dreyer steinen die in einem wasser
            Thösz gefunden worden sind.
                      A. Fries, 1556 [R Nfp, 723; Z, PAS II, 1/5].

    .6.8.   Zeitung, eines wunderbarlichen gesichts, gesehen durch
            ein Burger zu Schonauw.
                      J. Frölich, 1557 [R Nfp, 3587; Z, PAS II, 12/59].
                      No printer, 1557 [Z, PAS II, 4/1].

    .6.9.   Wunderzeichen und gesicht so zu Gengenbach . . . an
            dem Firmament des Himmels . . . gesehen ist.
                      T. Berger, 1563 [R Nfp, 3562; Z, PAS II, 4/9; Z, PAS
                      II, 12/65].

    .6.10. Gesicht oder zeychen zum Blech . . . von vilen
            menschen gesehen wurden.
                      T. Berger, 1564 [R Nfp, 1903; Z, PAS II, 12/6].

    .6.11. Wundergesicht am Himmel gesehen worden in einem thal
            auf dem Schwartzwald.
                      T. Berger, 1566 [R Nfp, 3558; Z, PAS II, 12/73; Z,
                      PAS II, 6/10].

    .6.12. Newe Zeittung von der Grossen . . . Schlacht . . .
            zwischen dem Konig in Denmarck und Schweden. . . .
            Andere Zeitung von Zweien Gewappneten Männern so am
            Himmel mit zweien fewrigen schwerten . . . über Calis
            gesehen.
                      P. Hugg, 1567 [R Imp. Alsc., 570], 1568 [R Nfp,
                      3594].

    .6.13. Wunderzeichen . . . zu Gniessen im landt zu Polen.
                      Chr. Mylius II, 1571 [R Nfp, 3602; Z, PAS II, 8/11].

    .6.14. Zeitung von dreien mercklichen Himelszeichen . . . zu
            Eltzach.
                      N. Faber, 1575 [R Nfp, 3605].

    .6.15. Von schrecklichen Wunderzeichen . . . am Himmel in
            Vielen Landen gesehen.
                      N. Faber, 1575 [R Nfp, 3604].

    .6.16. Wunderzeichen . . . in dem Land Würtemberg gesehen.
                      B. Jobin, 1578 [R Nfp, 3609; Z, PAS II, 15/1].

    .6.17. Irsamer, Andreas, Beschreibung . . . die frembden und

unbekandten Vögel im Westerreich mit einem unmensch-
lichen hauffen geflogen sein.
  No printer, 1584 [R Nfp, 2128].

.7.   ACCOUNTS OF MARVELOUS AND REMARKABLE EVENTS.

V10.7.1. Wirry, Heinrich, Wunderbarlich geschicht so geschehen
          ist in dem Schwytzerland by einer statt heist Willisaw
          . . . von dryen gesellen, die mit einander gespilt
          habend.
            A. Fries, 1553 [R Nfp, 3550; Z, PAS II, 12/56].
            No printer, 1553 [Z, PAS II, 2/27].

   .7.2. Abzaichnus der fremden Ehrenbegrabnus des neulich
          verstorbenen Turkischen Kaisers Selymi und seiner fünf
          son die von ältern pruder Murat . . . sint gewürget
          worden.
            No printer, 1575 [Z, PAS II, 12/3].

   .7.3. Merkliche Beschreibung sampt eygenlicher Abbildung
          eynes frembden unbekanten Volcks einer neuerfundenen
          landschaft . . . vom Martin Frobiser . . . erkundiget.
            B. Jobin, 1578 [Z, PAS II, 15/32], 1578 [Z, PAS II,
            15/33].

   .7.4. History . . . ein magdlin siben jar lang weder gessen
          noch getruncken.
            (B. Jobin ?), 1585 [Z, PAS II, 22/3].

.8.   PORTRAIT BROADSHEETS.

V10.8.1. Stigelius, Johannes, Warhafftiger Bericht, wie . . .
          Hans Friedrich, der Elter. Hertzog zu Sachsen, und
          geborner Churfürst von diser welt abgescheyden.
            J. Frölich, 1554 [R Nfp, 3280].

   .8.2. Conterfehtung des Fürnemen, Ersamen, Weisen und umb
          ein löbliche Statt Strassburg wolverdieten Herrn
          Mathis Pfarrers . . . diesen 1568 Jars Seliglich
          verschieden, Seines alters nahe bey 7 jahren.
            B. Jobin, 1568 [WJ, 2].

   .8.3. Fischart, Johann, Vera Effigies Reverendi Viri D.
          Heynrichi Bullyngeri (in Latin; portrait by Tobias
          Stimmer).
            B. Jobin, 1570 [Z, PAS II, 25/16; R Nfp, 1703].

   .8.4. Vera Effigies Clarissimi Viri Ioannis Sturmii.
            B. Jobin, 1570 [WJ, 6].

V10.8.5. Effigies nobilissime atque clarissimi ac praetorii
          viri D. Jacobi Sturmii civis Argentinensis . . . ali-
          quot virorum huius urbis, in obitium ipsius
          luctuosissimum.
              B. Jobin, ca. 1570-1571 [WJ, 7], 1577 [WJ, 52].

  .8.6.   Bildnusz des weiland Edlen Herrn Jacob Sturmen,
          Staetsmeisters zu Strasburg. . . .
              B. Jobin, ca. 1570-1571 [WJ, 8].

  .8.7.   Fischart, Johann, Eigenliche Conterfahtung Heinrichen
          Bullingers.
              B. Jobin, 1571 [Z, PAS II, 12/11; R Nfp, 1704], after
              1571 [WJ, 5].

  .8.8.   Effigies Reverendi Viri, D. Rodolphe Gualtheri:
          Tigurinae Nune Ecclesiae Pastoris et Antistitis
          Vigilantissime.
              B. Jobin, 1571 [WJ, 13].

  .8.9.   Ware Bildnüs des Ehrwürdigen Herrn Rudolph Gwalthers
          Kirchendieners zu Zürich.
              B. Jobin, 1571 [WJ, 14].

  .8.10. Fischart, Johann, Ware Bildnus des Erwürdigen Herrn
          Mathie Flaccii Illyrici diener des Worts Gottes.
              B. Jobin, 1571 [WJ, 15].

  .8.11. Fischart, Johann, Waare Conterfehtung Bernhardi
          Schmidt, Organisten zu Straszburg.
              B. Jobin, 1571 [WJ, 16], 1592 [WJ, 67].

  .8.12. Abcontrefeitung des Karl Mieg, alten Ammeisters zu
          Strassburg.
              B. Jobin, 1572 [R Nfp, 724; WJ, 17].

  .8.13. Fischart, Johann, Vera Effigies Generosissimi
          Fortissimique Herois D. Gaspardi Collignii, Domini in
          Castillon. . . .
              B. Jobin, 1573 [WJ, 23], 1577 [WJ, 51].

  .8.14. Effigies . . . Principis ac Domini D. Henrici Valesii,
          Henrici Galliarum quondam Regis Filii, modo in Regem
          Poloniae, Lithuaniaeque Ducem . . . electi.
              B. Jobin, 1574 [Z, PAS II, 11/1; R Nfp, 1989].

  .8.15. Der Grosnächtig König Hainrich der III dises Namens
          inn Frankreich.
              B. Jobin, 1574 [WJ, 25].

  .8.16. Ioan: Christoffel Stimmer.
              B. Jobin, 1574 [WJ, 26].

V10.8.17. Effigies D. Stephani Bretelii, Mathematicarum
disciplinarum, Arithmetices comprimis peritissimi,
qui anno Christi M.D. LXXIIII . . . ex hac vita
excessit, annum agens LI.
B. Jobin, 1574 [WJ, 27].

.8.18. Fischart, Johann, Effigies Accuratissima . . . D.
Ottonis Heinrici Comitis Schwarzenburgensis, Domini
in Hohen Landspergen etc. Gubernatoris, modo Badensis.
B. Jobin, 1574 [WJ, 28].

.8.19. Fischart, Johann, Der Wolgeborn Herr, Herr Otto
Hainrich, Grave von Schwarzenburg und Kerr zu Hohen
Landsperg.
B. Jobin, 1574 [WJ, 53].

.8.20. Melchior Newsidler, Aetatis Suae XXXXIII.
B. Jobin, 1574 [WJ, 33].

.8.21. Divy. Impp. ac Caess: Augg: Ferd: I Et: Maximi. II
Consul . . . Iacobus Taurelius, alias Ooechse,
Selestad.
B. Jobin, 1575 [WJ, 40].

.8.22. Der Hochberunt Edel, und Christlich Held Herr Caspart
von Cologni, Herr zu Castillon, Weilund Ammiral inn
Frankreich.
B. Jobin, 1577 [WJ, 50].

.8.23. Contrafait des Durchleuchtigen Fursten und Herrn Johan
Casimirs, Pfaltzgraf bei Rhein.
B. Jobin, 1578 [Z, PAS II, 16/3].

.8.24. Contrafaicte Bildnusz desz Wolgebornen Herrn . . .
Lazarus von Schwendi. Freiherrn zu Hohan Landsperg,
Rc. Roen. Kays. Maiestat Raht und Feldobersten.
B. Jobin, 1579 [WJ, 62].

.8.25. Bildnusz Antonii Franckenpoint aus Gellern, Welcher
einer ungewonlichen hie unden verzeichneten groese und
Laenge halben ist gegenwertiger gstalt angezeygt.
B. Jobin, 1583 [WJ, 63].

.8.26. Abcontrafactur des Ehrwürdigen und hochgelehrten
Herren, Martin Butzer, Diener des Evangelions Jhesu
Christi zu Straszburg.
(B. Jobin), 1586 [WJ, 65].

.8.27. Bildnusz Desz Edlen Ehrenvesten und Hochweisen Herrn
Friderich von Gottesheim . . . desz Reichs freyen
Statt Straszburg Herren Dreizehnern.
(B. Jobin), 1592 [WJ, 66].

.9.   ACCOUNTS OF COMETS.

V10.9.1.   Verzeichnuss des Cometen so im anfang des Mertzens
           erschinen ist, 1556.
               T. Berger, 1556 [Z, PAS II, 12/52].

   .9.2.   Warhafftige beschriebung was auff einen jeden
           sollichen Cometen geschehen sey.
               A. Fries, 1556 [Z, PAS II, 12/56; Z, PAS II, 2/15].

   .9.3.   Beschreibung und Deutung des Newn Sternes von 1572.
               B. Jobin, 1572 [Fischer, 661].

   .9.4.   Bericht über den Wundersternen oder besondern Cometen
           . . . aus 72 und 73 Jahre zu sonderem warnung zeichen
           dieser letzten zeit ist erschienen.
               B. Jobin, 1573 [Z, PAS II, 10/8].

   .9.5.   Corporis Luminosi . . . 1572/73.
               B. Jobin, 1573 [Z, PAS II, 10/5].

   .9.6.   Beschreibung des grossen Wunderzeichens, welches den
           13 januar 1580 am Himmel gesehen ist.
               T. Berger, 1580 [Fischer, 662].

   .10.   ANTI-SEMITIC BROADSHEETS.

V10.10.1. Schroetter, Heinrich, Etliche wenige . . .
           Ertzbubenstücke, der von Gott verblendten Juden in
           gemein. Item, wie sie uns Christen . . . alle
           Sabatstag in Ihren Synagogen greülich verfluchen.
               T. Berger, 1563 [R Nfp, 3200].

   .10.2. Dasselbige Blüt das blendet mich . . . Mit Christi
           blut uberwind ich dich . . . (with illustrations of the
           Synagogue and the Church from the Strasbourg
           cathedral).
               (B. Jobin), ca. 1572 [WJ, 18].

   .10.3. (Fischart, Johann), Ain gewisse Wunderzaitung von
           einer Schwangeren Judin zu Binzwangen . . . an statt
           zwaier kinder zwei leibhafte Schweinlin gepracht hat.
               No printer, after 1574 [R Nfp, 1732].
               B. Jobin, 1575 [R Nfp, 3563].

   .11.   LOCAL EVENTS IN STRASBOURG, FESTIVALS, AND CELEBRATIONS.

V10.11.1. Specklin, Daniel, Verzeichnisz des Strasburger
           Münsters.
               B. Jobin, 1566 [Musée de L'Oeuvre Notre Dame, Salle
               X].

V10.11.2. Fischart, Johann, <u>Eygentliche Fürbildung und</u>
<u>Beschreibung des Newen Künstreichen Astronomischen</u>
<u>Urwerck zu Straszburg</u> (long version).
    B. Jobin, 1574 [R BNU II, 851; WJ, 29].

.11.3. Fischart, Johann, <u>Eygentliche Fürbildung und</u>
<u>Beschreibung, des Newen Künstlichen Astronomischen</u>
<u>Uhrwerck</u>, (short version).
    B. Jobin, 1574 [R BNU II, 852; WJ, 30], 1574 [WJ, 31],
        after 1574 [WJ, 32].

.11.4. <u>Verzeichnus des berümten Strasburgischen</u>
<u>Hauptschiessens.</u>
    B. Jobin, 1576 [R Nfp, 3405; Z, PAS II, 13/5-6].
    No printer, 1590 [R BNU IV, 2404].

.11.5. Fischart, Johann, <u>Das Glückhafft Schiff von Zürich.</u>
<u>Ein Lobspruch . . . auff das auszgeschriben Schiessen</u>
<u>gen Straszburg den 21. Juni des 76 jars.</u>
    B. Jobin, 1576 [R Nfp, 1717a], 1577 [R Nfp, 1718],
        1577 [R Nfp, 1719].

.11.6. Fischart, Johann, <u>Ordenliche Beschreibung welcher</u>
<u>gestalt die Nachbarliche Bündnusz und Verain der</u>
<u>dreyen Löblichen Freien Stätt Zürich, Bern und</u>
<u>Straszburg . . . 1588.</u>
    B. Jobin, 1588 [R BNU II, 860].

.11.7. <u>Verzeichnusz Aller und jeder Gaben, so in Leonhard und</u>
<u>Friderich Krugen . . . Gluckhaffen kommen</u> (Prizes
offered for a local lottery).
    N. Waldt, 1590 [R BNU IV, 2403].

.11.8. Schmidt, Bernhard, <u>Eygentliche unnd ordentliche</u>
<u>Beschreibung desz löblichen Ubungschiessens . . . der</u>
<u>Statt Straszburg.</u>
    B. Jobin, 1590 [R BNU IV, 2083].

.12. ACCOUNTS OF FLOODS.

V10.12.1. <u>Von dem grossen und gewaltigen zulauff des</u>
<u>Wasserflussz der Statt Dieterich Bern . . . und von</u>
<u>dem grossen schaden zu Vincentz, Padua, Triendt und im</u>
<u>gantzen Thal . . . 1567.</u>
    T. Berger, 1568 [R BNU IV, 2519].

.12.2. <u>Zeyttung aus Niderland, Braband, Holland . . . von dem</u>
<u>schedlichen . . . undergang vieler Land, Stedte,</u>
<u>Flecken und Dörffer.</u>
    P. Hugg, 1570 [R Nfp, 3599].
    T. Berger, 1571 [R Nfp, 3600].

V10.12.3. I. Von dem schrecklichen Gewasser, welchs zu Pariss
. . . ist urplötzlich eingefallen . . . II. Von der
Ernsten Belägerung der Wehrhafften Statt Mastricht.
B. Jobin, 1579 [R Nfp, 3564].

.12.4. Stephani, Clement, Erbarmliche Newezeitung der
Wassernot in Keiser Karls Bad.
N. Faber, 1582 [BM 9340.c.14].

.13. BROADSHEETS ILLUSTRATING COINAGE.

V10.13.1. Verzeychnus, was vermög des Heyligen Römischen Reichs
Müntzordnungen und Abschied vom 1559, 1566, unnd 1570
Jaren, für Silberin unnd Guldine Müntz Sorten.
No printer, 1571 [R BNU IV, 2405].

.14. ANTI-CATHOLIC POLEMICAL BROADSHEETS.

V10.14.1. Fischart, Johann, Gorgonkopf . . . warnung vor der
Frucht des Papsten.
B. Jobin, ca. 1570-1571 [Z, PAS II, 25/17], ca. 1570-
1571, [Z, PAS II, 13/8], 1577 [Z,PAS II, 25/18].

.14.2. (Die Pfaffenmühle).
B. Jobin, before 1573 [WJ, 19], 1573 [WJ, 57].

.14.3. Fischart, Johann, Malchopapo.
B. Jobin, 1577 [Z, PAS II, 14/8].

.14.4. Fischart, Johann, Von Römischen Abgotsdienst . . . in
Munster zu Strasburg gegen dem Predigstul.
(B. Jobin?), 1576 [WJ, 47], ca. 1576-1577 [WJ, 48],
after 1576 [WJ, 47a].

.14.5. Wunder newe Zeitung . . . von der Nunnen heiligkeit
und reinigkeit . . . in einem Kloster im Etschlandt
gelegen.
B. Jobin, 1583 [R Nfp, 3613].

.15. HISTORICAL BROADSHEETS.

V10.15.1. Histori der Stadt Biberach.
B. Jobin, 1579 [Z, PAS II, 16/10-12].

V11. ACCOUNTS OF RECENT EVENTS.

.1. IMPERIAL POLITICS, NEIGHBORING EVENTS, AND KNIGHTS' AND
PEASANT WARS.

V11.1.1. Die verschribung und verwilligung . . . Herren Karle

Römischen und Hispanischen Künig gegen dem heyligen
Reich.
No printer, 1519 [R Nfp, 2205].

Vll.1.2. Von der Chür und Woll des groszmächtigsten Königs
Karolum.
J. Knobloch, 1519 [R Nfp, 1336].

.1.3. Sturm, Caspar, Wie die drey Kriegsfursten . . .
Frantzen von Sickingen überzogen
No printer, 1523 [R BNU IV, 2197].

.1.4. Doering, J., Neuw Zeytung so kürtzlich disz Jars zu
Kyngsburg in Pruessen fürgangen.
J. Schwann, 1524 [R Nfp, 1518].

.1.5. Abrede . . . zwischen den Samlungen zweyer hauffen in
Ortnau vor Offenburg und zwischen Bühel und Steinbach.
W. Kopfel, 1525 [R Nfp, 730].

.1.6. Underricht wie die Düringschen buwern vor
Franckenhausen, unb ir misshandlung gestrafft, und bei
der stett. Mülhusen und Franckenhausen erobert worden.
J. Grüninger, 1525 [S I, 223].

.1.7. Die Summa unnd Namen der schloss . . . so durch
versammlung der Bawern in stifften, Bamberg, Würtzburg
und Brandenburgisch Margraffschafft verbrandt und
verhört sindt.
J. Grüninger, 1525 [S I, 227].

.1.8. Melanchthon, Phillip, Wider die Bauernschaft.
W. Köpfel, 1525 [R Nfp, 2622].

.1.9. Artickel so yetzund vorgewendt von der gemeynen
bauwerschafft die sich allenthalben zusammen rottet.
M. Schürer Erben, 1525 [B SE 3, 36].

.1.10. Luther, Martin, Newe Zeytung von den Widertauffern zu
Munster.
J. Prüss II, 1535 [B. Luther, 3145].

.1.11. Zanobius, Ceffinus, Triumphliche einzug dess aller
durchleuchtigsten, Grossmechtigsten Römischen Keysers,
Caroli des Funfften . . . in Rom.
J. Frölich, ca. 1536 [R Nfp, 3575].

.1.12. Du Boulay, Edmond, Les dialogues des trois estatz de
Lorraine sus la nativité de Charles de Lorraine . . .
le 15 févirer 1543.
G. Messerschmidt, 1543 [Peter, XIa].

V11.1.13. Der Chürfürsten, Fürsten, Grauen und Stende der
          Christlichen Einung wahraffter Bericht von wegen der
          rechtmessigen Defension welche jre Churf. F.G.G. und
          Sie wider Heinrichen von Braunschweig fürzunemmen
          gedrungen.
               W. Rihel(?), 1544 [Pegg, 1224].

    .1.14. Erzelung wie und was sich Hertzog Heinrich von
           Braunschweigs und seiner anhangende gesellschaft
           halben des 1544 Jars zugetragen.
               S. Bundt, 1545 [R Nfp, 1642].

    .1.15. Neüwe Zeytung des Christlichen Glaubens auff dem
           Landtag zu Piotrkow durch die gesandten des
           Kunigreichs Polen.
               T. Berger, 1555 [R Nfp, 3586].

    .1.16. Zeitung von der Kirchen im eussern Morenlandt.
               T. Berger, 1561 [R Nfp, 3588].

    .1.17. Beschreibung . . . welcher gestalt die Königliche
           Wirde Maximilian, und Fräwlin Maria, geborne Königin
           ausz Hispanien, dero Gemahel zu Böhemischen König und
           Königin in Prag . . . gekrönet worden seind.
               Chr. Mylius I, 1562 [R BNU I, 194].

    .1.18. Audientz. Des aller Grosmechtigsten Durch Leüchtigsten
           . . . Romischen Keysers Maximilian des Andern unsers
           aller gnaedigsten Herren, wie die durch ihr Maiestet
           zu Speyer auff dem Reychstag ist gehalten worden in
           Jar 1570.
               B. Jobin, 1570 [WJ, 12].

    .1.19. Beschreibung des Lotringischen und Guisischen
           Feindlichen einfals in die Graveschafft Mümpelgart.
               B. Jobin, 1588 [R Nfp, 995].

    .2. THE WAR AGAINST THE TURKS.

V11.2.1. Histori wie die Statt Wien . . . dem Turkischen Keiser
         belägert ist.
               R. Beck, 1529 [R Nfp, 2024].

    .2.2. Zeyttung . . . wie die streiffend rott des Türkischen
          Tyrannen . . . durch die unsern erlegt und umgebracht,
          Andere Newe Zeyttung.
               No printer, 1532 [Wick].

    .2.3. Newe Zeitung des Ratschlags und Reyss der
          Kriegsrustung so der Turck newlich wider Karolus den

Römischen Keyser und die Christen furgenommen.
W. Rihel, 1536 [Wick].

V11.2.4. Köbel, Jakob, Der Türckisch Trach. Zerstörung des
Dürckischen Kaiserthumgs.
J. Cammerlander, 1542 [B. Cam., 57].

.2.5. Türcken Buchlin. . . . beschreibung von den pein . . .
so die Türcken den Christen . . . anlegen.
P. Messerschmidt, ca. 1560 [R Nfp, 3375].

.2.6. Türkischer botschafft Ebrahim Strotschen . . .
anbringen . . . in Schlavonischer sprach Gethan.
Chr. Mylius I, ca. 1562 [R Nfp, 3281].

.2.7. Fransciscus von Guevara, (Fransisco de Guevara), Neuwe
Zeitung und Abschrifft eines Brieffs so letzlich von
Malta kommen ist in welchem angezeigt wirdt wie . . .
des erbfeinds des Turckens erlediget sey worden.
T. Berger, 1565 [Wick].

.2.8. Ein dritt New Zeitung vom XXI, Tag Augusti auss Wien,
wie Jula wiederumb von den Türcken hefftig belegert.
P. Hugg, 1566 [R Nfp, 3589].

.2.9. Die vierdt new Zeittung. . . . Ertzhertzog Ferdinanden
zu Osterreich . . . wieder den Türckischen Feind
ausgezogen.
T. Berger, 1566 [R Nfp, 3590].

.2.10. Die sext neüw Zeitung welchermassen Herr Lazarus von
Schwendi die die Türcken . . . erledigt.
T. Berger, 1566 [R Imp. Alsc., 365].

.2.11. Die sibend new zeittung aus der Kay. Mayest. Feldleger
in Ungarn.
P. Hugg, 1566 [R Nfp, 3591].

.2.12. Zeitung. Wie der Türck die Statt Nicosiam . . .
eingenommen.
Chr. Mylius II, 1571 [R Nfp, 3601].

.2.13. Zeytung ausz Constantinopel von dem Auflauff der
Janitschaer und Spachen wider den Turckischen Keyser.
No printer, 1589 [Wick].

.2.14. Zeytung von dem Türcken, Wie er die Stadt Molach
eingenommen, Auch alle Christen darinnen ermordet.
N. Waldt, 1591 [R Nfp, 3617].

.3. THE REVOLT OF THE NETHERLANDS.

V11.3.1. Newe . . . unchristliche Spannisch Zeitung . . . Wie

. . . der könig von Hispanien durch sein inquisitoren
. . . unversehener weisz vil gute leüt mit glatten und
guten worten bereden . . . und in hafftung gezogen
wurden, auch wie iren gütern gehandelt würt.
    P. Hugg, 1563 [R Bib. Mun., 2263], ca. 1567 [BM
       9180.d.24].
    T. Berger, 1568 [Wick].

Vll.3.2. Zeittung aus den Niederlanden. Wie . . . Herr . . .
Grave zu Nassaw und des Printzen von Oranigen . . .
mit dem Spaniern in Friesland . . . glückliche
Schlacht begangen und verbracht hat.
    T. Berger, 1568 [R Bib. Mun., 2264].

.3.3. Von dem Abfall etlicher Evangelischer Stend in
Niderland, so sich dem Printz von Uranien
ergeben. . . .
    T. Berger, 1572 [R Nfp, 3603].

.3.4. Antorfische Zeitung . . . Beschreibung der Ursachen
der Niderländischen Empörungen.
    B. Jobin, 1577 [R Nfp, 3607].

.3.5. Le Vray Patriot, Das ist: Getreues Ermanen und
Auszschreiben deren in den Niderlanden . . . Darinnen
. . . das . . . verleumden vermeynter Stände der
Niderlanden widerlegt, und unschuld der Flandrischen
. . . offentlich dargethan wird.
    B. Jobin, 1578 [R Nfp, 2845], 1579 [R Nfp, 2844].

.3.6. Von der ernsten Belagerung der . . . Statt Mastricht.
    B. Jobin, 1579 [R Nfp, 3564].

.3.7. Von der grossen Blutstürtzung, so zu Andorff . . .
geschehen.
    N. Faber, 1583 [R Nfp, 3611].

.3.8. Alexander von Parma (Alessandro Farnese; Duke of Parma),
Sendbrieff des Printzen von Parma an Burgermeister
Sheffen und Obrigkeit . . . der Stadt Antorff. Auch
Antwort der Herren Bürgermeister, Scheffen und Raht
der Statt Antdorff.
    A. Bertram, 1585 [R Bib. Mun., 384].

.3.9. Wie die mächtig . . . Spanische Armada zu end
verschienenen.
    B. Jobin, 1588 [R Nfp, 1730].

.3.10. Ein ausz Meyland uberschribener Bericht, inn was
gestalt der Schweitzerischen Catholischen Sechs Ortten
Gesanten von des Königs ausz Spanien Legaten zu

Meyland . . . stattlich seind empfangen und . . .
Bündnisse vollzogen. . . .
    B. Jobin, 1588 [R Nfp, 1699].

.4.   THE WARS OF RELIGION IN FRANCE.

V11.4.1.   (Hotman, Francois), L'histoire du tumalte d'Amboyse.
    J. Nesle (pseud.), 1560 [Peter, XXIV], 1560 [Peter,
    XXV].

.4.2.   Von der Schlacht in Frankreich zwischen dem Hertzog
von Condé und . . . von Guiss.
    No printer, 1563 [Wick].

.4.3.   Zeytung auss Frankreich . . . was sich zwischen dem
Hertzogen von Guise Connastebel und den Marschalk von
St. André mit dem Hertzog von Condé. . . .
    T. Berger, 1563 [Wick].

.4.4.   Beschreibung der Zug im Frankreich von dem . . .
Printzen und Herrn Johann Casimirs Pfaltzgraf bei Rhein.
    B. Jobin, 1570 [Wick].

.4.5.   (Estienne, Henri), Ausschreiben, der ubelbefridigten
Stand inn Frankreich, die Sich Mal Content nennen
(J. Fischart, trans.).
    B. Jobin, ca. 1572 [R BNU II, 848], 1575 [R Nfp,
    1645], 1575 [R Nfp, 1646], 1576 [R Nfp, 1647].

.4.6.   Bericht von der unerhörten, verräterischen Mordery zu
Paris . . . 24 Augusti 1572.
    No printer, 1572 [R Nfp, 998; Z, PAS II, 10/13].
    No printer, 1572 [Z, PAS II, 10/14].

.4.7.   Henri I de Condé, Déclaration de Henry de Bourbon
aujourd'hui troisième prince du sang de France.
    No printer, 1574 [R Nfp, 1429].

.4.8.   (Barnaud, Nicolas), Reveille matin oder Wacht früe
auf. Das ist Summarischer und warhafter Bericht von
den verschinen . . . händeln in Franckreich (Ausebius
Philadelphus, trans.).
    B. Jobin(?) 1575 [R Nfp, 928], 1575 [R Nfp, 929],
    1593 [R Nfp, 930].
    See Peter, II, p. 44, fn. 149.

.4.9.   Declaration et protestation de monseigneur de
Dampville.
    No printer, 1575 [Peter, XXXVII].

.4.10.   Neuwe Zeitung auss Frankreich.
    No printer, 1576 [Wick].

Vll.4.11. Zeitung von . . . Handelungen mit Kön. Maj. inn
          Frankreich durch die deputirte Abgesandte, von wegen
          Johann Casimir, Pfalzgrafen bei Rein.
             B. Jobin, 1577 [R Nfp, 3608].

  .4.12. Frankreichische Zeitungen: I. Die Apologie . . . der
         Reformirten Kirchen in Frankreich auf des Koniglichen
         Gesanten . . . fürgeben. II. Wie des Königs Bruder die
         Stät Charite und Lissoire hat eingenommen. III. Kurze
         verzaichnus der neulich Niderländischen Händel.
            B. Jobin, 1577 [R Nfp, 3620].

  4.13. Merckliche Frantzösische Zeitung, von den herrlichen
        Ceremonien, so bei dem Neuen Ritterlichen Orden vom
        H. Geyst Gebraucht und gehalten.
           B. Jobin, 1579 [R Nfp, 3579], 1579 [R Nfp, 3580].

  4.14. Zeitungen . . . was sich jüngsthin beyderzeits
        zugetragen, als sie den König zu Franckreich
        zuziehende Eydgenossen den Hertzog von Savoi
        angriffen. . . .
           B. Jobin, 1579 [R Imp. Alsc., 558], 1589 [R Nfp, 3621].

  .4.15. Zeitung von dess Königs Navarra auss Frankreich
         gesandten, Herrn Jacobi Segurii Pardelliani Schreiben,
         an etliche Chur und Fürsten.
            N. Waldt, 1587 [R Nfp, 3615].

  4.16. (Fischart, Johann), Discours. Ein . . . Bedencken und
        wol erwogenes Urtheil von heutigem zustand
        Franckreichs.
           B. Jobin, 1589 [R Nfp, 1708].

  .4.17. Beschreibung: Wolbedenckliche, Des, an dem König in
         Frankreich newlich verrhäterlich begangenen
         Meuchelmords von einem Mönch Prediger Ordens.
            B. Jobin, 1589 [R Nfp, 997].

  .4.18. (Arnauld, Antoine), Antihispanus, das ist Widerlegung
         spanischer unart, angemaszter der Kron Franckreich
         unzeitigen beherrschung.
            B. Jobin, 1590 [R Nfp, 855], 1590 [R Nfp, 856].

  .4.19. Declaration oder Erklärung Kon. Maj. zu Frankreich und
         Navarren.
            B. Jobin, 1590 [R Nfp, 1707].

  .4.20. Bericht von der Herrlichen Victori so die Königliche
         Maj. in Frankreich wider den Hertzog von Mayne und die
         Ligischen . . . erhalten.
            B. Jobin, 1590 [R Nfp, 1709].

V11.4.21. Antimartyrion: Das ist Gegenzeugnusz . . . das Jacob
          Clemens . . . König Heinrichen dritten . . . ermordet,
          und keins wegs für ein Heiliger zuhalten sonder für
          ein Rebellen.
               B. Jobin, 1590 [R Nfp, 828].

    .4.22. Schreiben von eines catholischen Edelmannes uber des
           elend in Paris. Das ander aus dem Leger von Pariss an
           etliche Herren in Holland.
               No printer, 1590 [R Nfp, 725], after 1590 [R Nfp,
               726].

    .4.23. Gruntliche Entdeckung der Kron Franckreich gegen ihren
           Inwohnern, unnd besonders den Parisern.
               B. Jobin, 1590 [Greiner].

    4.24. Newe Zeitung auss Franckreich. Was Schrecklichen
           Jamers zu Pariss zugetragen.
               B. Jobin, 1591 [R Nfp, 3616].

    .5.   THE BISHOPS' WAR.

V11.5.1. Pappus, Johannes, Bericht von dem Rechten Anfang und
          warhafften Ursachen der jetzigen Unruhe im Bistumb und
          Stifft Straszburg.
               J. Martin, 1592 [R Bib. Mun., 1626; R BNU III, 1764].

    .5.2. Baldus, Elias, Straszburgische Kriegs Sachen Kurtze
           und doch warhaffte Erzehlung.
               E. Baldus, 1592 [R BNU I, 125].

    .5.3. Baldus, Elias, Strassburger Augustus. Oder,
           Beschreibungen des Jhenigen, so sich in dem
           Kriegswesen . . . zwischen den Strasburgern dem
           Newpostulierten Bischoff . . . und dem Cardinal von
           Lotringen . . . verlauffen hat.
               E. Baldus, 1592 [R BNU I, 126].

    .5.4. Franz von Kriechingen, Erklerung. . . . belangendt die
           Bischoffliche Election zu Straszburg.
               No printer, 1592 [R Nfp, 1764].

    .5.5. Bericht von Ubergebung . . . der Statt Moltzheim, Auch
           Abzug der Lothringischen Garnison daselbst.
               A. Bertram, 1592 [R BNU I, 185].

    .5.6. Zwo Warhaffte Newe Zeittung. . . . Das jetzige
           Strassburgische Kriegswesen betreffende . . . Die
           ander Zeitung auss Reussen und Lifflandt, was sich
           alda mit dem Wütterischen Moscoviter zugetragen hat.
               J. Martin, 1592 [R Nfp, 3618].

V11.5.7.   <u>Statt Straszburg Gegenerklärung</u> (A statement by the
           city in regard to the Bishop Charles of Strasbourg
           and Metz).
              No printer, 1592 [R Bib. Mun., 1073].

SCIENTIFIC WRITINGS
(MEDICINE, NATURAL SCIENCE, PSEUDO-SCIENCE, AND TECHNOLOGY

S1. Medicine.

     1. Memory Books.
     2. Gynecology.
     3. Health Rules and Regimens.
     4. Plague.
     5. Surgery.
     6. Syphilis.
     7. General Medical Treatises.
     8. Baths.
     9. Pharmaceutical Books.
    10. Anatomies.
    11. Medical Treatises based on Greek Sources.
    12. Specific Medical Treatises.
    13. Medical Treatises Based on Arabic Sources.
    14. Works by Theophrastus Bombastus Paracelsus.
    15. Medical Theses.

S2. Books on Distilling.

S3. Botany and Herbals.

S4. Astronomy.

     1. Traditional Astronomical Texts.
     2. Planetary Theory.
     3. Eclipses.
     4. Meteors, Comets, and Bright Stars.
     5. Astronomical Techniques.
     6. Meteorology.
     7. Treatises on the Strasbourg Clock.
     8. Debate over the Gregorian Calendar.

S5. Mathematics and Physics.

     1. Traditional Encyclopedias.
     2. Books on Scientific Measurement.
     3. Physics.
     4. Applied Mathematics.
     5. Geometry.
     6. Orations on Studying Mathematics.
     7. Arithmetic.
     8. Mathematical Texts.
     9. Scientific Theses.

S6.   Geography, Travel, and Exploration.

    1. Traditional Voyages and Descriptions.
    2. Descriptions of Voyages to the New World and East
        Indies.
    3. General Geographies and Cosmographies.
    4. Maps, Itineraries, and How to Use Them.
    5. Descriptions of Particular Regions.

S7.   Natural History.

S8.   Agronomy.

S9.   Veterinary Texts.

S10.   Hunting Manuals.

S11.   Technical Manuals.

    1. Cookbooks.
    2. Fencing and Boxing.
    3. Gunpowder.
    4. Mining and Metalworking.
    5. Textile Dyes.
    6. Models for Design.
    7. Making and Preserving Wine.
    8. Sundials.
    9. Architecture.
   10. Surveying.
   11. Embroidery.

S12.   Calendars and Prognostications for Popular Use.

S13.   Astronomical Calendars.

S14.   Ecclesiastical Calendars.

S15.   Astrology and Chiromancy.

    1. Astrology.
    2. Chiromancy and Physiognomy.
    3. Dream Books.

S16.   Alchemy.

S17.   Witchcraft.

S1. MEDICINE.

1. MEMORY BOOKS.

S1.1.1.   Matheoli Perusinus (Mattrolo Mattrolii, De Memoria
          augenda.
               H. Knoblochtzer, 1480 [R BNU Inc., 306].

  .1.2.   Phrisius, Laurentinus (Lorenz Fries), Ars Memorativa.
               J. Prüss I, 1497 [R Nfp Inc., 277].
               J. Grüninger, 1523 [S I supp., 3].
               J. Grüninger, 1523 [S I, 197]. (In German.)

  .1.3.   Matheoli Perusinus, Artis Memorative Matheio
          Perusini medici Doctoris Praestatissimi.
               M. Schott, 1498 [S II A, 14].

  .1.4.   Ryff, Walter, Memoria Artificialis quam memorativam
          Artem vocant.
               B. Beck, 1541 [B Luther, 99].

2. GYNECOLOGY.

S1.2.1.   Albertus Magnus, De secretis mulierum et virorum.
               H. Knoblochtzer, 1483 [R BNU Inc., 14].
               M. Hupfuff, 1510 [S V, 79].

  .2.2.   Rösslin, Eucharius, Der Schwangeren Frauen
          Rosengarten.
               M. Flach II, 1507 [S VI B, 14], 1513 [S VI B, 34],
                  1522 [S VI B, 69].
               B. Beck, 1529 [R BNU III, 2026].

  .2.3.   Bonaciuli, Lodovico (Luigi Bonacciuoli), De
          Conceptionis indiciis nec non maris foemineique
          partus significatione. Eiusdem quae utero gravibus
          accidant et eorum medicinae prognostica causaque
          effluxionum et abortuum proceritatis
          improceritatisque partuum causae Heinrich Sybold, ed.).
               H. Seybold, 1530 [R Nfp, 1031].

  .2.4.   Bonaciuli, Lodovico (Luigi Bonacciuoli), De uteri
          partiumque eius consecutione. Eiusdem quonam usu in
          absentibus etiamnum Venus citetur. Quid, quale,
          undeque prolificum semen unde menstrua.
               H. Seybold, 1530 [R Nfp, 1030].

  .2.5.   Brunfels, Otto, Weiber und Kinder Apotheck.
               J. Cammerlander, 1534 [R BNU I, 298].

  .2.6.   Dunus, Thaddäus, Muliebrium Morborum omnis Generis
          Remedia ex Dioscoride, Galeno, Plinio, Barbarisque

et Arabibus studiose collecta et disposita.
J. Rihel, 1565 [R BNU I, 666].

S1.2.7.   De Partu Caesareo das ist von der im fall eussersten
notwunderbarlicher und vor nie erhorten noch bewusten
kunstlicher lösoung dedirung und scheidung eines
Kinds auss von Mutterleib.
B. Jobin, 1583 [Bosse II, 265].

•2.8.   Spach, Israel, Gynaeciorum sive de Mulierum communibus.
L. Zetzner, 1597 [R BNU IV, 2164].

3.   HEALTH RULES AND REGIMENS.

S1.3.1.   Valla, Georgius, De Tuenda Sanitate.
H. Seybold, n.d. [R BNU IV, 2379].

•3.2.   Arnoldus de Villa Nova, Regimen Sanitatis Salernitanum.
G. Husner, 1491 [R BNU Inc., 40].

•3.3.   Carmina de Sanitatis Regimine que quondam Schola
Salernis Anglicorum Regi Conscripsit.
M. Hupfuff, 1499 [S V, 9].

•3.4.   Regimen Sanitatis.
M. Brant, 1500 [S IV Bra., 1].
M. Hupfuff, 1506 [S V, 52], 1513 [S V, 107].

•3.5.   Magninus, Regimen Sanitatis.
J. Prüss I, 1503 [S III A, 41].

•3.6.   Paulus Aeginetae, Praecepta Salubria Guilelmo Copo
Basileiensi interprete.
M. Schürer, 1510 [S VIII, 47], 1511 [S VIII, 54],
1511 [S VIII, 53].

•3.7.   Iste est Tractatus Medicinalis quem Doctores
Parisienses miserunt Regi Anglie.
M. Hupfuff, 1519 [S V, 138].

•3.8.   Hessus, Helius Eobanus, Bonae valetudinis
conservandae praecepta medicinae laus.
H. Seybold, 1530 [Gut. Jb., 168–70].

4.   PLAGUE.

S1.4.1.   Jung Ambrosius, De pestilentia.
No printer, 1491 [R Nfp Inc., 403].

•4.2.   Brunswig, Hieronymus (Hieronymus Brunschwig), Liber
Pestilentialis de venenis epidemie.
J. Grüninger, 1500 [S I, 52].

S1.4.3.   Ein Tractat contra pestem, preservative und regiment.
          B. Kistler, 1500 [S IV Kis., 7].

  .4.4.   Hie in disem büchlin vindest du ein gut regiment für
          die Pestilenz.
          M. Hupfuff, 1502 [S V, 20].

  .4.5.   Beroaldus, Phillipus, Opusculum de Terraemotu et
          Pestilentia cum Anno tamentis Galeni.
          M. Schürer, 1510 [S VIII, 35].

  .4.6.   Wydman, Johann, Regimen . . . Wie man sich in
          pestilentzischem lufft halten soll.
          M. Schürer, 1511 [S VIII, 57], 1519 [S VIII, 254].
          J. Knobloch, 1519 [S VII, 189].

  .4.7.   Stromer Aurbachius, Henricus, Adversus pestilentiam
          observationes.
          J. Grüninger, 1518 [S I, 161].

  .4.8.   Melbrey, Hans, Ordnung und Regimint deren sich in der
          Schweys sucht, das Englisch Bad ganannt, zu halten sey.
          J. Schott, 1529 [S II B, 113].

  .4.9.   Nidepontanus, Johannes (Johannes Neidbruck) and
          Fries, Laurentius, Sudoris Anglici Exitialis
          pestiferique ratio et cura.
          J. Knobloch, 1529 [R Nfp, 2769].

  .4.10. Fettich, Theobald, Ordenung und regiment sich vor der
          überscharpffen und gifftigen Kranckheit der
          Pestilenz zu enthalten.
          C. Egenolff, 1531 [Greiner].

  .4.11. Guentherius, Johann (Johann Guenther von Andernach),
          De victu et medicinae ratione.
          W. Rihel, 1542 [R Nfp, 1939].

  .4.12. Guentherius, Johann (Johann Guenther von Andernach),
          Instruction . . . se maintenir en . . . santé au
          temps de peste comme en autre temps.
          R. Guédon, 1547 [R Nfp, 1940].

  .4.13. Alexander, Trallianus, Libri Duodecim, Razae de
          Pestillentia Libellus.
          R. Guédon, 1549 [R BNU I, 36].

  .4.14. Guinterius, Johannes Andernacus, Kurtzer Auszug des
          Buchlins vonn der Pestilenz.
          J. Rihel, 1564 [R BNU II, 1061].

  .4.15. Guinterius, Johannes Andernacus, Bericht, Regiment
          und Ordnung wie bei diesen sterbenden leuffen die

232Medicine

Pestilenzzichen fieber zuerkennen . . . .
  J. Rihel, 1564 [R BNU II, 1060].

S1.4.16. Guinterius, Johannes Andernacus, <u>De Pestilentia,
Commentarius in IV Dialogus distinctus.</u>
  Chr. Mylius I, 1565 [R BNU II, 1062].

.4.17. Comeandenus, Balthasar, <u>Undericht wie ein jeder sein
hausss vor der Ungerishen sucht und auch
Schweissauchten hirntoben hals und lungengeschwer
auch Seitenwehe und Breune unnd dergleichen halten
und regieren sol.</u>
  No printer, 1574 [Bosse II, 252].

.4.18. Droetus, Petrus, <u>Consilium novum de pestilentia.</u>
  B. Jobin, 1576 [R BNU I, 663].

.4.19. Imsser, Philipp, <u>Pestilentzbüchlin, für die armen
Handwercks und Baurs Leut</u> . . . .
  Chr. Mylius II Erben, 1582 [R BNU II, 1243].
  <u>See also</u> S1.14.21; S1.14.27.

5. SURGERY.

S1.5.1. Brunschwig, Hieronymus, <u>Das Buch der Cirurgia,
Hantwirchung und Wundartzney.</u>
  J. Grüninger, 1497 [S I, 31], 1513 [S I, 129].

.5.2. Hans von Gersdorff, <u>Feddtbuch der Wundartzney.</u>
  J. Schott, 1517 [S II B, 40], 1526 [S II B, 99],
  1528 [R BNU II, 1000], 1530 [R BNU II, 1001],
  1535 [S II B, 132], 1540 [R BNU II, 1002].
  No printer, 1524 [Haeser II, 162], 1542 [Gurlt II,
  222-23].

.5.3. Lanfrancus (Lanfranco of Milan), <u>Kleine Wundartzney</u>
(O. Brunfels, trans.).
  J. Schott, 1528 [S II B, 105].
  Also listed as:
  C. Egenolff, 1528 [B <u>Egen.</u>, 4].

.5.4. Charetanus, Joannes (Johannes de Ketham), <u>Wundartzney.</u>
  C. Egenolff, 1530 [R Nfp, 1330].

.5.5. Albucasis (Abu al-Qāsim Khalaf ibn 'Abbas al-Zahrāwi),
<u>Chirurgicorum Libri III.</u>
  J. Schott, 1532 [R Nfp, 2989].

.5.6. Johann von Paris (Jean de Paris), <u>Eyn new Wund Artznei.</u>
  J. Cammerlander, after 1538 [B Cam., 48].

.5.7. Ryff, Walter, <u>Die kleine Chirurgi.</u>

          B. Beck, 1542 [B Luther, 112].
          B. Beck Erben, 1551 [R BNU III, 2041].

S1.5.8.   Fluguss, Georg, Experimenta Chirurgica et unguenta.
          No printer, 1578 [Haller I, 176].

   6. SYPHILIS.

S1.6.1.   Widmann, Johannes, Tractatus de pustulis.
          J. Grüninger, 1497 [R Nfp Inc., 704].

  .6.2.   Hock, Vuendelinus, Mentagra sive tractatus de causis
          . . . et cura morbi Gallici.
          J. Schott, 1514 [S II B, 27].

  .6.3.   Ulrichen von Hutten, Von der Wunderbarlichen artzney
          des Holtz Guaiacum genant, und wie man die Frantzosen
          oder blatteren heilen sol.
          J. Grüninger, 1519 [S I, 166].

  .6.4.   Ulrich von Hutten, Ein clarer bericht wie man alte
          schaden heylen soll mit dem holz Guaico.
          No printer, 1525 [BM C.31.e.17].
          J. Grüninger, 1529 [S I, 242]. (Paracelsus, ed.).

  .6.5.   Friesen, Laurentius (Lorenz Fries), Ein grüntlich und
          bestendig heilung alter schäden . . . mit dem tranck
          des holtzes Guiaco.
          J. Prüss II, 1539 [S III B, 47a].

  .6.6.   Gratarolus, Guilelmus, Petri Abani de Veneris
          eorumque remedis Item . . . curatio sudoris anglici
          in Germania experta . . . .
          No printer, 1566 [Bosse II, 334].
          See also S1.14.26.

   7. GENERAL MEDICAL TREATISES.

S1.7.1.   Valla, Georgius, De inventa Medicina.
          H. Seybold, n.d. [R BNU IV, 2381].

  .7.2.   Valla, Georgius, De Physicis quaestionibus.
          H. Seybold, n.d. [Gut. Jb. 1954, 168-70].

  .7.3.   Johannes Tollat von Vochenberg, Margarita Medicinae.
          B. Kistler, 1500 [R BNU Inc., 458].
          M. Hupfuff, 1508 [S V, 74], 1515 [S V, 124].
          M. Flach II, 1512 [S VI B, 29].
          No printer, 1518 [R BNU IV, 2331].

  .7.4.   Marsilius Ficinus, de Triplici Vita . . . cum textu
          seu regimine sanitatis Salerni (J. Adelphus, ed.).
          J. Schott, 1511 [S II B, 19].

S1.7.5.   Versehung beyder seel und leibs des menschen durch
          geistliche und leibliche artzneyung.
              J. Knobloch, 1518 [S VII, 169].

  .7.6.   Fries, Lorenz, Spiegel der Artzny des geleichen
          vormals nie von keinen doctor in tütsch uszgangen ist
          nützlich und gut allen denen so der artzet radt
          begerent, auch der gestreiffelten leyen welche sich
          underwinden mit artzney umb zegon.
              J. Grüninger, 1518 [R BNU II, 888], 1519 [R BNU II,
                  889], 1526 [R Nfp, 1785], 1529 [R Nfp, 1786].
              B. Beck, 1529 [R BNU II, 894], 1532 [R BNU II,
                  896].
              No printer, 1537 [R Nfp, 1784].

  .7.7.   Manardus, Johannes (Giovanni Manardo), Medicinales
          Epistolae.
              J. Schott, 1529 [S II B, 112].

  .7.8.   Brunnfelsius, Ot., Catalogus illustrium Medicorum
          sive de primis Medicinae Scriptoribus.
              J. Schott, 1530 [S II B, 116].

  .7.9.   Brunfels, Otto, Theses seu communes loci totius rei
          medicae.
              G. Ulricher, 1532 [R BNU I, 293].

  .7.10. Brunfels, Otto, Iatrion Medicamentorum Simplicium
          Libri IV.
              G. Ulricher, 1533 [R BNU I, 294].

  .7.11. Brunfels, Otto, Neoticorum aliquot medicorum in
          medicinam practicam introductiones.
              J. Albrecht, 1533 [R Nfp, 1118].

  .7.12. Brunfelsius, Othonis, Onomaetikon Medicinae.
              J. Schott, 1534 [S II B, 130], 1544 [S II B, 144].

  .7.13. Burgawer, Dominicus, Ein notwendiger bericht . . . so
          die artzney . . . brauchen sollen.
              M. Apiarius, 1534 [R BNU I, 333].

  .7.14. Fuchs, Leonhart, Compendiaria in Artem Medendi
          introductio.
              J. Albrecht, 1534 [R BNU II, 926].

  .7.15. Scholl, Jacobus, Astrologiae ad Medicinam Adplicatio
          Brevis.
              J. Cammerlander, 1537 [R BNU IV, 2090].

  .7.16. Ryff, Walter Hermann, Manual Buchlein von allerhandt
          Gifft, Wunden und Feld Krankenheyten.
              J. Cammerlander, 1538 [R BNU III, 2030].

S1.7.17. Ryff, Walter, Magen-Büchlein, von allerley gebresten
          desz Magens, Miltzes und lebern.
             J. Cammerlander, 1540 [R BNU III, 1459], 1546 [R
               Nfp, 3136].

   .7.18. Ryff, Walter, New erfundne Heylsame und bewärte
          artzney gewisse hilff unnd radt nit allein die
          Frantzosen oder bösen blatern zu vertreiben, heylen
          und Curieren mit . . . gebrauch des Indianischen
          holtz Guiaiacum . . . sondern auch andere schwere
          Kranckheit zu vertreiben.
             B. Beck. 1541 [R Nfp, 3135].
             S. Emmel, 1559 [B Luther, 110].

   .7.19. Ryff, Walter, Handtbüchlin gemeyner Practick der
          ganzten leibartzney.
             B. Beck, 1541 [R BNU III, 2034], 1541 [B Luther,
               115], 1541 [R BNU III, 2035], 1552 [B Luther, 116].

   .7.20. Baviera, Giovanni, Consiliorum de re medica . . .
          liber (Gualth. H. Ryff, ed.).
             B. Beck, 1542 [R Nfp, 953], 1543 [R Nfp, 1543; R
               BNU III, 2039].

   .7.21. Guentherius, Johannes (Johann Guenther von Andernach),
          De victu et medicinae ratione.
             J. Rihel, 1542 [R Nfp, 1939].

   .7.22. Ryff, Walter Hermann, Medicinae Theoricae et Practicae.
             G. Messerschmidt, 1542 [R BNU III, 2037].

   .7.23. Albertus Magnus, Naturalia . . . VI Buchlin von
          haimligkaiten der Natur. . . . Von Weibern und
          Geburten der Kinder. . . . Abcontrafactur ettlicher
          Kreuter . . . der Sieben Planeten Kreuter genant
          eygenschaften und tugenten . . . .
             J. Cammerlander, 1545 [R BNU I, 30], 1548 [R BNU I,
               31].
             W. Rihel, 1549 [R Nfp, 785], 1551 [B Ryff, 10].

   .7.24. Hollerius, Blasius, Medice artis Theorica, Libris
          Duobus succincte compraehensa, atque medicinae
          studiosis apprimè necessaria.
             J. Rihel, 1565 [R BNU II, 1183].

   .7.25. Toxites, Michael, Spongia stibii adversus Lucae
          Stenglini medicinae doctoris et physici Augustani
          aspergines.
             Chr. Mylius I, 1567 [R Nfp, 3352].

   .7.26. Ryff, Walter, Kurzes Handtbüchlin und Experiment
          vieler Artzneyen.

J. Rihel, 1567 [B <u>Luther</u>, 50], 1571 [B <u>Luther</u>, 53],
1575 [B <u>Luther</u>, 54], 1578 [B <u>Luther</u>, 56], 1583
[B <u>Luther</u>, 58], 1589 [R Nfp, 3141], 1594 [R BNU
III, 2045], 1596 [B <u>Luther</u>, 62], 1599 [R BNU III,
2046].

S1.7.27. Nonnus, Theophanes, <u>De Omnium Particularium Morborum</u>
<u>Curationne.</u>
J. Rihel, 1568 [R BNU III, 1640].

.7.28. Seltzame Felle, <u>Fragen und Historien aus was Ursach</u>
<u>unsere ersten Vätter zu einem höheren Alter kommen</u>
<u>und langer als die Menschen jetzt bey unseren Zeiten</u>
<u>Gelebt haben.</u>
T. Berger, 1570 [R Bib. Mun., 968].

.7.29. Carrichter, Bartholomaeus, <u>Practica</u>. I. <u>Von allerhand</u>
<u>Leibs kranckheiten; II. Von Ursprung der Offenen</u>
<u>Schäden</u> . . . .
Chr. Mylius II, 1575 [R BNU I, 459], 1579 [R BNU I,
461].
A. Bertram, 1589 [R Nfp, 1300], 1590 [R BNU I, 463].

.7.30. Degen, Jacob (Jacob Degin Schegk), <u>De Plastici</u>
<u>seminis</u> . . . <u>Libri III.</u>
B. Jobin, 1580 [R BNU I, 625].

.7.31. Taurellus, Nicolaus, <u>Medicae praedictione methodus.</u>
B. Jobin, 1581 [R BNU IV, 2272].

8. BATHS.

S1.8.1. Foltz, Hans, <u>Eine gute Lehre von allen willtbaden.</u>
B. Kistler, 1504 [R Nfp, 1746].

.8.2. Foltz, Hans, <u>Püchlin</u> . . . <u>von allen Paten die von</u>
<u>Natur Heiss sein.</u>
B. Kistler, 1504 [S IV, Kis., 24].

.8.3. Wintperger, Wollfgang, <u>Ein Tractat der Badenfart.</u>
M. Flach II, 1507 [S VI B, 13], 1512 [S VI B, 26].

.8.4. Fries, Lorenz, <u>Tractat der Wildbeder Natuer</u> . . .
<u>auch wie man baden, und ettliche züfell der badenden</u>
<u>wenden sol.</u>
J. Grüninger, 1519 [R BNU II, 891].

.8.5. Brunfels, Otto, <u>Ein Newe Badenfart.</u>
J. Cammerlander, 1537 [R BNU I, 300].

.8.6. Fries, Lorenz, <u>Eyn New Badenfart.</u>
J. Cammerlander, 1537 [R BNU II, 898], ca. 1540 [BM

1170.p.43], 1548 [R Nfp, 1777].
B. Grüninger, 1538 [R Nfp, 1776].

S1.8.7.   Eynn nützlich Bad und Artzney, den Bruch . . .
          Zuheylen.
              H. Vogtherr, 1538 [R BNU I, 122].
              H. Vogtherr, 1539 [R Nfp, 1802]. (Leonard Fuchs,
              ed.)

   .8.8. Guinterius, Johannes Andernacus, De Balneis et aquis
          medicatis.
              T. Rihel, 1565 [R BNU II, 1063].

   .8.9. Etschenreuter, Gallus, Aller heilsamen Bäden und
          Brunnen Natur Krafft tugendt und würckung so in
          Teutschlanden bekandt und erfahen.
              Chr. Mylius II, 1571 [R BNU II, 808].
              Chr. Mylius II Erben, 1580 [R BNU II, 809].
              J. Martin, 1599 [R BNU II, 810].

   .8.10. (Tabernaemontanus, Jakob Theodor), Des deux fontaines
          dites de Greysbach et de Sainct-Pierre.
              A. Bertrand, 1590 [Peter, 42].

   9. PHARMACEUTICAL BOOKS.

S1.9.1.   Nicolaus (Nicolaus de Metri), Antidotarius
          Medicinalis.
              J. Prüss I, n.d. [S II A, 6].

   .9.2. Brunfels, Otto, Iatrionices Medicamentorum, Liber II.
              G. Ulricher, n.d. [R Nfp, 1108].

   .9.3. Brunfels, Otto, Von allerhandt apothekischen
          Confectionen, Lattwergen, Oel, Pillulen, wie, wann
          und warzu man jedes brauchen soll.
              J. Cammerlander, n.d. [R Nfp, 1100].

   .9.4. Ficinus, Marsilius, Medicinarius Das buch der
          Gesuntheit. Liber de arte distillandi simplicia et
          composita.
              J. Grüninger, 1509 [R BNU II, 840].

   .9.5. Phrysius Argentarie (Lorenz Fries), Synonoyma und
          gerecht uszlegung der wörter so man in der artzny,
          allen krütern wurtzeln blümen somen gesteinen
          safften und anderen dingen zu schreiben ist . . . .
              J. Grüninger, 1518 [S I, 169], 1519 [R BNU II, 890].
              B. Grüninger, 1535 [R BNU II, 897].

   .9.6. Valla, Georgius, De Simplicium natura-liber unus.
              H. Seybold, 1528 [R Nfp, 2383].

S1.9.7.   (Brunschwig, H. and Schrick, M.), <u>Apotek für den</u>
          <u>gemeinen man der die artzet zu ersuchen am gut nicht</u>
          <u>vermag oder sunst in der not, nit erreichen kan</u>.
              B. Beck, 1529 [Greiner].

   .9.8.   Brunfels, Otto, <u>Pharmacorum Simplicium, Libri VIII</u>.
              No printer, 1529 [R Nfp, 1123].

   .9.9.   Dioscoridae, P., <u>Pharmacorum simplicium reique</u>
          <u>Medicae Libri VIII</u> (J. Ruellio [Jean Ruel], ed.).
              J. Schott, 1529 [S II B, 111].

   .9.10. Valla, Georgius, <u>De Universi corporis purgatione</u>.
              H. Seybold, 1529 [R BNU IV, 2384].

   .9.11. Paulus Aeginetae, <u>Pharmaca, Simplicia, Othone</u>
          <u>Brunfels Interprete</u>.
              G. Ulricher, 1531 [R BNU III, 1801].

   .9.12. Brunfels, Otto, <u>De Simplicibus medicinis opus praeclarum</u>.
              No printer, 1531 [R Nfp, 1124].

   .9.13. S. Hildegardis, <u>Physica Elementorum</u>;
          Oribassius, <u>De Simplicibus, Libri V</u>.
          Aesculapius, <u>De Morborum Infirmitatum Passionumque</u>
          <u>corporis humani caussis, descriptionisbus et cura</u>.
              J. Schott, 1533 [S II B, 126].

   .9.14. Brunfels, Otto, <u>Reformation der Apothecken</u>.
              W. Rihel, 1536 [R BNU, 303].

   .9.15. Brunfels, Otto, <u>Appendix de usu et administratione</u>
          <u>simplicium</u>.
              J. Schott, 1539 [R Nfp, 1125].

   .9.16. Ryff, Walter, <u>Die kleine deutsche Apotheke, Alle</u>
          <u>Latwergen, Confect, Conserven einbeitzungen und</u>
          <u>einmachungen</u>.
              B. Beck, 1540 [R BNU III, 2031], 1542 [R BNU III,
                 2038].
              B. Beck Erben, 1552 [R Nfp, 3137].
              S. Emmel, after 1552 [R BNU III, 2043].

   .9.17. Ryff, Walter, <u>Der Drit theyl der kleynen Teütschen</u>
          <u>Apoteck von rechten gebrauch . . . aller Laxativen,</u>
          <u>purgierender oder treibender Artzney</u>.
              B. Beck, 1541 [R BNU III, 2033].
              B. Beck Erben, 1552 [R Nfp, 3138].

   .9.18. Dioscorides, <u>Hoc est de curationibus morborum per</u>
          <u>medicamenta paratu facilia</u>.
              J. Rihel, 1565 [R BNU I, 659].

S1.9.19.   Rulandus, Martin, <u>Medicina Practica recens et nova</u>.
           J. Rihel, 1567 [BM 547.b.10].

  .9.20.   Ryff, Walter, <u>Reformierte Deutsche Apotek</u>.
           J. Rihel, 1573 [R BNU III, 2044].

  .9.21.   Toxites, Michael, <u>De tinctura Physicorum libellus</u>.
           Chr. Mylius II, 1574 [R Nfp, 3354].

  .9.22.   Bauderon, Brice (Brigon Bauderon), <u>Teutsche Apotheck</u>
           <u>erstlich in Frantzösicher sprach . . . jetzt durch</u>
           <u>Olaum Sudenum verdeutschet</u>.
           L. Zetzner, 1595 [R Nfp, 946].

   10. ANATOMIES.

S1.10.1.   Mundinus (Mondino dei Luzzi), <u>De omnibus humani</u>
           <u>corporis interioribus menbris Anathomia</u> (J. Adelphus
           Muleng, ed.).
           M. Flach II, 1513 [S VI B, 38; R Nfp, 2734; YML].

  .10.2.   Benedictus, Alexander, <u>Anatomice sive de Hystoria</u>
           <u>corporis humani libri quinque</u> (Otto Brunfels, ed.).
           J. Herwagen, 1528 [R BNU I, 180; R Nfp, 1098].

  .10.3.   Berengario, Jacopo, <u>Isagoge breves in Anatomiam</u>
           <u>humane corporis</u>.
           H. Seybold, 1530 [R Nfp, 976].

  .10.4.   Vogtherr, Heinrich, <u>Anathomia oder abconterfeitung</u>
           <u>eines Weibs leib</u>.
           H. Vogtherr, 1537 [R Nfp, 3442].
           J. Frölich, 1544 [R BNU I, 51].

  .10.5.   Vogtherr, Heinrich, <u>Ein newes Hochnuczlichs Büchlin</u>
           <u>von erkantnus der Krankheyten der Augen. Sampt einer</u>
           <u>figur oder Anathomia eines augs</u>.
           H. Vogtherr, 1538 [R Nfp, 3445; R BNU I, 319], 1539
              [R BNU I, 320].

  .10.6.   Vogtherr, Heinrich, <u>Anathomia, oder abconterfeitung</u>
           <u>eines Mans leyb, wie er innwendig gestaltet</u>
           <u>ist. . . . Anathomia eines Weybs leyb, wie er</u>
           <u>innwendig gestaltet ist</u>.
           H. Vogtherr, 1539 [R Nfp, 3443]. (Folio edition)
           H. Vogtherr, 1539 [R BNU I, 114].
           J. Frölich, 1551 [R Nfp, 3444]. (In Latin.)

  .10.7.   Ryff, Walter, <u>Anatomie sampt Contrafactur aller</u>
           <u>Glieder, Das Menschen (oder dein selbst) Anatomie</u>.
           B. Beck, 1541 [B <u>Luther</u>, 90].

S1.10.8.   Ryff, Walter, Des aller . . . höchsten unnd
           adelichsten geschöpffs . . . von Gott . . . Das ist
           der menschen . . . warhafftige beschreibung oder
           Anatomi.
               B. Beck, 1541 [R BNU III, 2032].

  .10.9.   Ryff, Walter, Omnium humani corporis partium
           descriptio seu Anatomia.
               B. Beck, 1541 [B Luther, 91].

  .10.10. Willichius, Joducus, Commentarius anatomicus.
               Cr. Mylius, 1544 [R BNU IV, 2467].

  .10.11. Kobenhaupt, Johannis Sebaldus, De partium humani
           corporis natura.
               K. Kieffer, 1598 [R Imp. Alsc., app. n. 400].

    11.   MEDICAL TREATISES BASED ON GREEK SOURCES.

S1.11.1.   Ein hüpsch biechlin das durch die natürlichen meister
           Aristotilem, Avicennam, Galieneum, Albertum und
           anderen natürlichen meistern, von Mancherley
           seltzamen fragen beschribenn unnd der Menschlichen
           natur gar nutzlichen zu wissen; Propleumata
           Aristotelis.
               M. Hupfuff, 1515 [S V, 129].
               M. Flach II, 1520 [S VI B, 58].

  .11.2.   Horatianus, Octavius (Theodorus Priscianus), Rerum
           Medicarum Libri IV.
               J. Schott, 1532 [R Nfp, 2043; R Nfp, 2989].

  .11.3.   Sebastianus, Rubeacensis (Sebastianus Austrius), De
           Secunda valetudine tuenda in Pauli Aeginetae Medici
           . . . librum explanatio.
               J. Schott, 1538 [R BNU IV, 2108; R Nfp, 890].

  .11.4.   Paulus Aegineta, Compendium Libri VII.
               W. Rihel, 1542 [R Nfp, 2853].

  .11.5.   Problemata Aristotelis, Avicenne, Galeni und Alberti
           Magni, darinn menschlicher und thierlicher natur
           eygenschafften durch fragstück begriffen.
               J. Cammerlander, 1543 [R BNU III, 1929], 1545 [R
                 BNU III, 1930].

  .11.6.   Priscianus, Theodorus, De curationibus omnium ferme
           morborum homini accidentium . . . Libri IV.
               No printer, 1544 [R Nfp, 2990].

  .11.7.   Lusitanus, Amatus, In Dioscoridis Anazarbei de
           Medica.

W. Rihel, 1554 [R BNU III, 1415].
No printer, 1561 [R Nfp, 2454].

S1.11.8.   Galenus, Claudius, De Humoribus Liber nunquam
antehac typis excusus . . . .
B. Fabricius, 1557 R Nfp, 1808]. (In Greek.)
S. Emmel, 1558 [R BNU II, 932].

.11.9.   Hollerus, Blaise (Blaise Hollier), In Hippocratis
Librum de natura hominis commentarius.
No printer, 1558 [R Nfp, 2038].

.11.10.   Cordus, Valerius Eberwein, Annotationes in Pedacii
Dioscoridis Anazarbei de Medica materia Lib. V. Val.
Cordi Historiae Stirpium Lib. IIII.
J. Rihel, 1561 [R BNU I, 587].

.11.11.   Massarius, Hieronymus, Hippocratis, De natura Hominis.
P. Messerschmidt, 1564 [R BNU III, 1497].

12.   SPECIFIC MEDICAL TREATISES.

S1.12.1.   Valla, Georgius, De Corporis commodis et incommodis.
H. Seybold, n.d. [R Nfp, 2380].

.12.2.   Galen; Theophilus; Diocles, De Urinae significatione
Quaestiones in Hippocratem, Diocles epistola . . .
Galeni, De Bona valetudine tuenda (Georgius Valla,
ed.).
H. Seybold, ca. 1528 [BM 957.k.28.2].

.12.3.   Valla, Georgius, de Natura Oculorum.
H. Seybold, 1529 [R Nfp, 3390].

.12.4.   Valla, Georgius, De Urinae Significatione.
H. Seybold, 1529 [BM 714.a.15].

.12.5.   Burgawer, Dominicus, Ob das Podagra möglich zü
generen oder nit.
M. Apiarius, 1534 [R BNU I, 334].

.12.6.   Fuchs, Leonhard, Eyn künstreichs . . . urteil und
Sekret büchlein des harns.
H. Vogtherr, 1538 [R Nfp, 1801].

.12.7.   Eyn künstreichs . . . urteil und sekret büchlin des
Harns . . . .
H. Vogtherr, 1538 [R BNU IV, 2368].

.12.8.   Büchlein, den Erbgrind . . . an alten und jungen von
grund ausz zuheylen.
H. Vogtherr, 1538 [R BNU I, 317], 1539 [R BNU I,
318].

S1.12.9.   Fuchs, Leonhard, <u>Alle Kranckhet der Augen</u> . . . <u>allen</u>
            <u>augenartzen hochnöttig zuwissen</u>.
                H. Vogtherr, 1539 [R BNU II, 927].

   .12.10. <u>Podagra. Wie Doctor Laurin eym Edalman das Podargram</u>
            <u>mit seltzamen artzneien zuvertreiben</u>.
                J. Cammerlander, ca. 1540 [B <u>Cam</u>., 93].

   .12.11. Willich, Jodocus, <u>Observationes in libellum</u>
            <u>lanctantii firmiani</u>, . . . <u>Item: Hippocratis libellus</u>
            <u>de genitura</u>.
                Cr. Mylius, 1542 [Greiner].

   .12.12. Ryff, Walter, <u>Recht gründtliche bewerte Cur des</u>
            <u>Steins, Sandt und Griesz in Nieren, Blasen und</u>
            <u>Lenden</u>.
                G. Messerschmidt, 1543 [R BNU III, 2040].

   .12.13. (Bock, Hieronymus), <u>Kurtz Regiment für das grausam</u>
            <u>Hauptweh und Breune für die gemeine und armes</u>
            <u>heuflin</u>.
                G. Messerschmidt, 1544 [R Nfp, 3083].

   .12.14. Augurellus, Joannes Aurelius (Giovanni Aurelio
            Augurello), <u>Chrysopoeiae Libri III</u>.
                Chr. Mylius I, 1565 [BM 1213.c.2].

   .12.15. Toxites, Michael, <u>De Podagrae laudibus doctorum</u>
            <u>hominum lusus</u>.
                Chr. Mylius II, 1570 [R Nfp, 3353].

   .12.16. Arnoldus de Villanova, <u>Herliche Medicinische Tractat</u>
            <u>vor nie in truck kommen, von Cur des Podagrams</u>
            (H. Wolf, ed.)
                B. Jobin, 1576 [R BNU IV, 2409; R Nfp, 3552].

   .12.17. Schopff, Philippe, <u>Kurtzer aber doch ausführlicher</u>
            <u>Bericht von dem Aussatz, auch dessen Ursachen,</u>
            <u>Zeychen und Curationen</u>.
                B. Jobin, 1582 [R Nfp, 3188].

    13. MEDICAL TREATISES BASED ON ARABIC SOURCES.

S1.13.1.   Fries, Lorenz, <u>Defensio Medicorum principis</u>
            <u>Avicennae, ad Germaniae Medicos</u>.
                J. Knobloch, 1530 [R BNU II, 895].

   .13.2.   <u>Tacuini Sanitatis Elluchasem Elimathan, Medici de</u>
            <u>Baldath, De sex Rebus non naturalibus, Alben Gnefit,</u>
            <u>De virtutibus Medicianarum. Jac. Alkindus, De Rerum</u>
            <u>Gradibus</u> (Gerardus Cremonensis, trans.).
                J. Schott, 1531 [S II B, 119].

S1.13.3.   Serapion, Johannes (Serapion, the younger), In hoc
            volumine continentur Ioan. Serapionis Arabis de
            Simplicibus Medicinis praeclarum . . . Averrois, De
            eisdem Liber eximus. Rasis . . . Opusculum perutile.
                G. Ulricher, 1531 [R BNU IV, 2119; R Nfp, 729].

   .13.4.   Aboul Kasim al Zahravi (Abu al-Qasim Khalaf ibn
            'Abbas al-Zahrawi), Theoricae nec non Practicae
            Liber.
                No printer, 1532 [R Nfp, 727].

   .13.5.   (Ibin Botlam or Ibn Butlan), Tacuini Aegritudlnum et
            Morborum ferme omnium Corporis humani.
                J. Schott, 1532 [S II B, 124].

   .13.6.   Elluchasem Elimathar (Abul Hafsan al Mukhtar),
            Tacuini Sanitatis.
                J. Schott, 1533 [R Nfp, 1540].
                J. Schott, 1533 [S II B, 127]. (In German; Michael
                Herr, trans.; Schachtafeln der Gesuntheit.)

   .13.7.   Johannitius (Hunayn ibn Ishaq), Tractatus Medicinae.
                J. Cammerlander, 1534 [R BNU II, 1269].

   14. WORKS BY THEOPHRASTUS BOMBASTUS PARACELSUS.

            See Also S1.6.46.; S3.1.2.

S1.14.1.   Holtzbuchlein, Von dem Vitriol (M. Toxites, ed.).
                Chr. Mylius I, 1564 [BM 546.b.13(1)].

   .14.2.   Corpus chirurgicum.
                No printer, 1564 [R Nfp, 2820].

   .14.3.   Zwei Bücher . . . von der Pestilentz und ihren
            zufällen.
                P. Messerschmidt, 1564 [R BNU III, 1770].

   .14.4.   Drey Bucher Paracelsi. Das Holtz Buchlin; Von dem
            Vitriol; Ein Kleyne Chyrurgy (M. Toxites, ed.).
                Chr. Mylius I, 1565 [BM 957.c.18(3)].

   .14.5.   Libri duo . . . I. Defensiones septem; II. De
            tartaro sive de morbis tartareis.
                No printer, 1566 [R Nfp, 2824].

   .14.6.   Libellus . . . de Urinarum ac pulsuum iudiciis (M.
            Toxites, ed.).
                S. Emmel, 1568 [R BNU III, 1771].

   .14.7.   Trei Tractat . . . I. Von offnung der Haut; II. Von
            heylung der Wunden; III. Von Schlangen, Spinnen,

Krotten, Krepsen . . . und ihrer tugent (Preface by
M. Toxites).
    T. Rihel, 1570 [R BNU III, 1774].

S1.14.8. Von dem Bad Pfeffers, gelegen in Oberschweitz.
    No printer, 1571 [R Nfp, 2819].

.14.9. Tractat, von Eygenschafften, eines Volkommen
Wundtartzets (M. Toxites, ed.).
    Chr. Mylius II, 1571 [R BNU III, 1775].

.14.10. De Lapide Philosophorum Drei Tractat, I. Manuale de
Lapide medicale, II. de Tunctura Physicorum, III. de
Tinctura Planetarum (M. Toxites, ed.).
    N. Wyriot, 1572 [BM 8632.b.25(4)].

.14.11. Schreiben praeparationum oder von Zubereitung
etlicher dinger, notwendig, . . . zu wüssen den
Medicis.
    No printer, 1572 [R Nfp, 2837].

.14.12. Zwen Tractatus, I. De viribus membrorum spiritualium;
II. De Electro (M. Toxites, ed.).
    B. Jobin, 1572 [R BNU III, 1776].

.14.13. Chirurgia Magna, in Duos Tomos. I. De Vulnerib. Et
Fracturis. II. De Ulceribus. III. De Tumoribus . . . .
    No printer, 1573 [R BNU III, 1778].

.14.14. Chirurgia Minor.
    B. Jobin, 1573 [R BNU III, 1777].

.14.15. Fünff Bücher von dem Langen Leben.
    B. Jobin, 1574 [BM 7305.a.3].

.14.16. Gründliche Erklärung in allerlei Sprachen . . . der
Philosophischen, Medizinischen und Chimischen Namen.
    B. Jobin, 1574 [R Nfp, 2830].

.14.17. Onomastica, I. Philosophicum, Medicum, Synonymum, ex
variis vulgaribusque linguis. II. Theophrasti
Paracelsii hoc est earum vocum, quarum in scriptis
eius solet usus esse, explicatio (M. Toxites, ed.).
    B. Jobin, 1574 [R BNU IV 2350; R Nfp, 1724].

.14.18. Das Buch Paramirum, item von Fundament der Künsten,
der Seelen und leibes Krankheiten durch Adam von
Bodenstein.
    No printer, 1575 [R Nfp, 2833].

.14.19. Libri XIII, Paragraphorum Philosophi Summi, à Toxite
. . . Restituti.
    Chr. Mylius II, 1575 [R BNU III, 1779].

S1.14.20. Schreiben von den Krankheiten, so den Menschen der Vernunft natürlich berauben, sammt ihren Kuren.
No printer, 1576 [R Nfp, 2838].

.14.21. De Peste . . . vorhin nie getruckt (M. Toxites, ed.).
N. Wyriot, 1576 [R BNU III, 1781].

.14.22. Von den offenen Scheden und geschweren.
No printer, 1577 [R Nfp, 2836].

.14.23. Drey Tractatus de generatione hominis, massa corporis humani . . . secretis creationis.
No printer, 1577 [R Nfp, 2825].

.14.24. Von der Wundtartzney, Vier Bücher (M. Toxites, ed.).
Chr. Mylius II, 1577 [R BNU III, 1782].

.14.25. Pharmacandi Modus. Was der Artzt in dem Menschen zu Purgieren habe. (M. Toxites, ed.).
Chr. Mylius II, 1578 [R BNU III, 1783].

.14.26. De Morbo Gallico, warhaffte Cur der Frantzosen . . . .
Chr. Mylius II, 1578 [R Nfp, 2829].

.14.27. Bericht von der jetzt regierenden Pestilentz.
No printer, 1583 [R Nfp, 2835].

15. MEDICAL THESES.

S1.15.1. Planerus, Andreas, Theses Medicae Physicae De differentiss humanae valetudinis . . . .
N. Wyriot, 1574 [R Bib. Mun., 1712].

.15.2. Planerus, Andreas, Theses . . . de divine et miranda formatione humani foetus.
N. Wyriot, 1576 [Bosse II, 307].

.15.3. Hawenreuter, Johann Ludwig, Disputatio de Mente Intelligenti.
K. Kieffer, 1586 [R BNU II, 1079].

.15.4. Frid, Johann Sebastian, Theses medicae. De Iis Rebus Quae in principio artis medicae Galeni traduntur.
A. Bertram, 1586 [Greiner].

.15.5. Spach, Israel, Theses medicae, De partium humani corporis natura; ex libro Galeni.
K. Kieffer, 1590 [R BNU IV, 2158].

.15.6. Spach, Israel, Disputatio medica. De elementis.
A. Bertram, 1590 [R BNU IV, 2156].

.15.7. Spach, Israel, Progymnasma ad agonismata medica

celebranda in Argentinensi medicorum gymnasio.
A. Bertram, 1590 [R BNU IV, 2157].

S1.15.8.   Spach, Israel, Themata Medica, De animae facultibus,
earundemque Functionibus.
A. Bertram, 1591 [R BNU IV, 2160].

.15.9.   Hawenreuter, Johann Ludwig, Theses Physicae, De somno
et vigilia, insomniis et divinatione, ex libris
Aristotelis.
A. Bertram, 1591 [R BNU II, 1084].

.15.10.   Spach, Israel, D.N.A. Disputatio Medica De Humoribus.
A. Bertram, 1591 [R BNU IV, 2159].

.15.11.   Burgower, Johannes, Theses Physicae, Ex libro
Aristotelis De sensu et sensili desumptae.
A. Bertram, 1592 [R BNU I, 338].

.15.12.   Pappus, Johann Sigismund, Themata medica de animae
facultatibus earundemque functionibus.
A. Bertram, 1592 [Bosse I, 328].

.15.13.   Agerius, Nicolaus, Theses medicae de dysenterio.
A. Bertram, 1593 [R Nfp, 765].

.15.14.   Agerius, Nicolaus, Theses medicae physicae, de homine
sano.
A. Bertram, 1593 [R Nfp, 764].

.15.15.   Sebitz, Melchior, Theses medicae De dyssenteria . . . .
A. Bertram, 1593 [R BNU IV, 2109].

.15.16.   Hawenreuter, Johann Ludwig, Favente Altissimo
Themata Medicae Physica; De Facultatibus sive
Potentiis Naturalibus.
A. Bertram, 1593 [R BNU II, 1088].

.15.17.   Spach, Israel, Theses medicae physicae de homine
sano, hoc est, de partibus humanum corpus
constituentibus . . . .
A. Bertram, 1593 [R BNU IV, 2161].

.15.18.   Feuchter, Johann, Theses Physicae. De somno et
vigilia somnique affectionibus.
A. Bertram, 1594 [Greiner].

.15.19.   Spach, Israel, Theses Medicae. De Aere.
J. Martin, 1594 [Greiner].

.15.20.   Spach, Israel, Theses medicae de cibo ac potu.
A. Bertram, 1594 [R BNU IV, 2162].

.15.21.   Spach, Israel, Theses medicae De motu, sive

exercitiis et quiete.
A. Bertram, 1595 [R BNU IV, 2163].

S1.15.22.   Spach, Israel, Theses medicae . . . De somno et
vigilia.
A. Bertram, 1597 [Greiner].

.15.23.   Sebitz, Melchior, Disputatio Medica de quatuor
humoribus naturalibus.
J. Martin, 1599 [Greiner].

.15.24.   Spach, Israel, Propositiones medicae de vesica
humana.
A. Bertram, 1599 [Greiner].

S2.   BOOKS ON DISTILLING.

S2.1.1.   Schrick, Michael, Von den ausgebrenten und
Distillierten Wassern.
M. Schott, 1481 [R Nfp Inc., 615].
No printer, 1483 [Hirsch, 140], 1505 [Hirsch, 140],
1518 [Hirsch, 140].
M. Hupfuff, 1502 [S V, 22].
J. Knobloch, 1519 [S VII, 182].
C. Egenolff, 1530 [R Nfp, 3199].

.1.2.   Arnoldus de Villa Nova, Tractat von der bereytung der
Wein (Wilhelm von Hirnkofen, trans.).
H. Knoblochtzer, 1483 [R Nfp Inc., 88].
M. Schott, 1484 [R Nfp Inc., 89].
J. Schott, after 1500 [R Nfp, 860].
M. Hupfuff, 1506 [R Nfp, 861], 1512 [R Nfp, 863].
J. Knobloch, 1519 [S VII, 173].
M. Flach II, 1522 [R Nfp, 865].

.1.3.   Brunschwygk, Hieronymus (Hieronymus Brunschwig),
Liber de arte distillandi, Distillierbuch.
J. Grüninger, 1500 [S I, 49], 1505 [S I, 71], 1508
[S I, 86], 1509 [S I, 111].

.1.4.   Brunschwick, Hieronymus (Hieronymus Brunschwig),
Liber de arte Distillandi de Compositis. Das buch
der waren kunst zu distillierin (or Das nüwe
distillier buch).
J. Grüninger, 1512 [S I, 123], 1514 [R Nfp, 1132],
1515 [S I, 148], 1517 [S I supp., 2], 1519 [S I,
167], 1521 [S I, 184], 1528 [S I, 237], 1531 [S
I, 250].
B. Grüninger, 1531 [B Luther, 16], 1532 [R Imp.
Alsc., 416], 1537 [R Nfp, 1137].

S2.1.5.   Dise Tractat helt yn von bereytung der wein zü
           gesuntheyt unnd nützbarkeit der menschen.
               M. Hupfuff, 1512 [S V, 101].
               M. Flach II, 1522 [R Nfp, 865; S VI B, 68].

   .1.6.   Arnoldus de Villa Nova, Opera quae edita sunt
           hactenus omnia . . . per Gualtherum H. (W. Ryff,
           ed.).
               Cr. Mylius, 1541 [R Nfp, 859].
               B. Beck, 1541 [BM 775.f.1].

S3.   BOTANY AND HERBALS.

S3.1.1.   Ortus Sanitatis, De herbis et plantis, De animalibus
           reptilibus, De lapidibus in terre . . . De Urinis et
           earum speciebus Tabula medicinalis cum directorio
           generali per omnes tractatus.
               J. Prüss I, n.d. [S III A, 5], 1510 [BM c.14.b.9;
               BM 546.c.1.].
               R. Beck, 1510 [BM 449.1.3].
               J. Grüninger, 1517 [R Nfp, 2075].
               B. Beck, 1527 [R Nfp, 2076], 1529 [R BNU II, 1205].
               M. Apiarius, 1536 [R BNU II, 1206].

   .1.2.   Theophrastus (Theophrastus Paracelsus), De
           Suffructibus, Herbisque, ac Frugibus.
               H. Seybold, n.d. [R BNU IV, 2321], 1529 [R BNU IV,
               2322].

   .1.3.   Albertus Magnus, Liber secretorum de virtutibus
           Herbarum et animalium quorundam . . . de mirabilibus
           mundi.
               J. Grüninger, 1493 [S I, 17].

   .1.4.   In disem Buch ist der Herbary: oder Kruterbuch
           genannt der Gart der gesuntheit: mit merern figuren
           et registern.
               J. Prüss I, 1507 [S III A, 61], 1509 [S III A, 72].
               R. Beck, 1515 [S IV Beck, 20], 1521 [S IV, Beck,
               33].
               B. Beck, 1528 [R BNU II, 1139], 1530 [R BNU II,
               1140].
               J. Grüninger, 1529 [S I, 241].

   .1.5.   Albertus Magnus, Das Buch der Versamlung, oder das
           buch der Heymlichkeiten . . . von der tugenden der
           Krüter und edelgestein und von etlichen thieren.
               M. Flach II, 1508 [S VI B, 16], 1519 [S VI B, 40].
               J. Knobloch, 1516 [S VII, 131].

           .

S3.1.6.   Fiera, Baptista, <u>De Herbarum Medicae et ea Medicae</u>
                <u>Artis parte</u>.
                C. Egenolff, 1529 [R BNU II, 843].

 .1.7.   <u>Lustgärten und Pflantzungen . . . allerhand Bäum</u>,
                <u>Kreutter, Blumen und Früchten . . . .</u>
                C. Egenolff, 1530 [R Nfp, 2456].

 .1.8.   Brunf., Oth. (Otto Brunfels), <u>Herbarum Vivae Icones</u>
                <u>ad naturae imitationem . . . cum Effectibus earundem</u>.
                J. Schott, 1530 [S II B, 117], 1539 [R BNU I, 304).
                   Volume I.)
                J. Schott, 1532 [S II B, 122]. (Volume II.)
                J. Schott, 1536 [S II B, 136]. (Volume III;
                   Michael Herr, ed.)
                J. Schott, 1537 [BM 449.k.2]. (Volumes I-III.)

 .1.9.   Brunnfelsz, Oth. (Otto Brunfels), <u>Contrafayt</u>
                <u>Kreüterbuch Nach rechter vollkommer art, unnd</u>
                <u>Beschreibungen der alten, besstberümpten ärtzt . . . .</u>
                   Vol. I, J. Schott, 1532 [S II B, 125], 1534 [S II
                   B, 131]. <u>Ander Teyl</u> (Michael Herr, transl.).
                J. Schott, 1537 [R Nfp, 1111].

 .1.10.   Bock, Hieronymus, <u>New Krëuter Buch. Darin</u>
                <u>underscheid, würckung und namen der kreüter so in</u>
                <u>Deutschen landen wachsen. Auch der selbigen . . .</u>
                <u>gebrauch in der Artznei . . . .</u>
                   W. Rihel, 1539 [R BNU I, 211], 1546 [R BNU I, 128],
                   1550 [R <u>Imp. Alsc</u>., app. n. 294], 1551 [R BNU I,
                   215].
                   W. Rihel, 1552 [R I, 216]. (In Latin.)
                   J. Rihel, 1556 [R Nfp, 1022], 1560 [R BNU I, 218],
                   1572 [BM 448.k.3], 1577 [Greiner], 1580 [R Nfp,
                   1023], 1587 [R BNU I, 219], 1595 [R BNU I, 220].

 .1.11.   Dioscorides, <u>Historia Herbarum</u>.
                J. Schott, 1543 [R Nfp, 1515].

 .1.12.   Bock, Hieronymus, <u>Teütsche Speiszkammer</u>.
                W. Rihel, 1550 [R BNU I, 214], 1555 [R BNU I, 217].

 .1.13.   Kyber, David, <u>Lexicon Rei Herbariae, Trilingue ex</u>
                <u>variis; . . . qui de Stirpium historia scripserunt</u>,
                <u>authoribus concinnatum</u>.
                W. Rihel, 1553 [R BNU II, 1321].

 .1.14.   Bock, Hieronymus, <u>Verae atque ad viuum expressae</u>
                <u>imagines omnium herbarum quarum nomenclaturam</u>.
                W. Rihel, 1553 [BM 452.a.16].

S3.1.15.   Cordus, Valerius, <u>De Hortis Germaniae Liber Recens</u>
            <u>una cum descriptione Tulipae Turcorum</u>.
                J. Rihel, 1561 [R <u>Imp. Alsc</u>., app. n. 294].

    .1.16.   Cordus, Valerius, <u>Stirpium descriptionis liber</u>
            <u>quintas qua in Italia sibi uisas describit</u>.
                J. Rihel, 1563 [R BNU I, 588].

    .1.17.   Carrichter, Bartholomaeus (Martinus Pegius),
            <u>Kreutterbuch</u> (M. Toxites, ed.).
                Chr. Mylius II, 1575 [BM 546.b.14.c2], 1576 [R BNU
                    III, 1806], 1577 [R BNU I, 460].
                A. Bertram, 1589 [R BNU I, 462], 1595 [R BNU III,
                    1807], 1597 [BM 957.k.31].
                L. Zetzner, 1596 [R Nfp, 2899].

    .1.18.   Jacob von Ramingen, <u>Von den Aromaten und</u>
            <u>wolschmäckenden, gantz drefftigen und hailsamen</u>
            <u>Specereyen so ausz frembden lander, zu uns Teutschen,</u>
            <u>gebracht werden</u>.
                Chr. Mylius II, 1580 [R BNU III, 1965].

    .1.19.   Schoenfeldt, Melchior, <u>Kreuterbuch</u>.
                A. Bertram, 1595 [R Bib. Mun., 1888].

S4. ASTRONOMY.

    1. TRADITIONAL ASTRONOMICAL TEXTS.

S4.1.1.   <u>Ain lieblichs Biechlin zu lesen von dem hochgelerten</u>
            <u>Meister Lucidarius. Der do sagt von den wunderbaren</u>
            <u>Sachen der Welt und des hymels</u>.
                No printer, n.d. [S II A, 18].
                H. Knoblochtzer, ca. 1482 [R BNU <u>Inc</u>., 288].
                M. Hupfuff, 1499 [S V, 8], 1506 [S V, 59], 1511
                    [S V, 89], 1514 [S V, 113].
                B. Kistler, 1503 [S IV Kis., 23].
                J. Knobloch, 1519 [S VII, 187].
                J. Cammerlander, ca. 1535 [R BNU III, 1404], 1539
                    [R Nfp, 2438].

    .1.2.   Joannis de Sacrobusto (Sacro Bosco or John of
            Holywood), <u>Introductorium in Tractatum Sphere</u>
            <u>Materialis</u>.
                J. Knobloch, 1518 [S VII, 165].
                J. Cammerlander, 1533 [R BNU IV, 2408], 1539 [BM
                    8561.aaaa.47].

    .1.3.   Hyginus (Caius Julius Hyginus), <u>Higini Astronomi von</u>
            <u>den bildern der zwölff zaychen am himel mit ihren</u>

sternen und aygenschaften.
J. Cammerlander, 1531 [R Nfp, 2120].

2. PLANETARY THEORY.

S4.2.1.   Regiomontanus, Johannes (Johann Müller von
           Königsberg), Naturlicher Kunst der Astronomei.
               C. Egenolff, 1528 [R Nfp, 3084], 1529 [R BNU II,
               1268].

.2.2.   Von natur, eigenthumb und wirkung der siben Planeten
           unnd zwöllf Zeychen des Himmels.
               J. Cammerlander, 1535 [R Nfp, 2752].

.2.3.   Der Newen Welt Gattung Schlag und eygenschafft. Von
           der Weltlauff.
               J. Cammerlander, 1539 [R Nfp, 1819].

.2.4.   Proclus Diadochus, De circulis spherae astronomiam
           discere.
               W. Rihel, 1539 [R BNU III, 1932].

.2.5.   Eisenmenger, Samuel, De usu partium coeli.
               No printer, 1567 [Zinner, 2415].

.2.6.   Dasypodius, Conrad, Compendium Theoriae Planetarum.
               No printer, 1567 [Hellman, 236-40].

.2.7.   Dasypodius, Conrad, Hypotyposes orbium coelestium
           congruentes cum tabulis Alfonsis et Copernici.
               T. Rihel, 1568 [BM 1485.Cw.26].
               Also listed as:
               Peucer, Kaspar, Hypotyposes orbium coelestium
               congruentes . . . .
               T. Riehl, 1568 [R Nfp, 2884].

.2.8.   Dasypodius, Conrad, Sphericae doctrinae propositiones
           graecae et latinae.
               Chr. Mylius II, 1572 [R Nfp, 1487].

.2.9.   Finck, Thomas, Ephemerides Caelestium Motuum.
               No printer, 1581 [Zinner, 2976; Bosse I, 559].

3. ECLIPSES.

S4.3.1.   Regiomontanus, Joh. (Johann Müller von Königsberg),
           New und Volmon, des tags leng, finsternisz der Sonnen
           und des Mons . . . bisz auff das 1556 jar erlengt.
               J. Cammerlander, 1532 [R Nfp, 3086].

.3.2.   Pruckner, Nocolaus (Nicolaus Prugner), Von den dreien

Finsternissen, 1547.
  J. Cammerlander, 1548 [Zinner, 1917].

S4.3.3.   Dasypodius, Conrad, Tabula eclipsium solis et lunae,
           1573-1605.
             No printer, 1572 [Zinner, 2579].

   4. METEORS, COMETS, BRIGHT STARS.

S4.4.1.   Prugner, Nicolaus, Was eine Comet sey, woher er komme
           und sein Ursprung habe.
             J. Albrecht, 1532 [Fischer, 438].

  .4.2.   Sabinus, Georg, Poemata (on the comet of 1531).
             Cr. Mylius, 1538 [Zinner, 1700].

  .4.3.   Pontanus, Joh. Jovianus (Giovanni Gioviano Pontano),
           Liber de Meteoris.
             No printer, 1539 [R Nfp, 2971].
             Cr. Mylius, 1545 [R Nfp, 2972].

  .4.4.   Camerarius, Joachim, Von den Cometen, ihren
           schrecklichen Bedeutungen, historien und exempeln,
           ein schon büchlein . . . .
             P. Messerschmidt, 1561 [R Nfp, 1271].

  .4.5.   Dasypodius, Conrad, Descriptio corporis luminosi.
             B. Jobin, 1572 [R Nfp, 1480].
             B. Jobin, 1572 [R Nfp, 1481]. (In German.)

  .4.6.   Ein Richtiger und kurtzer Bericht über den
           Wundersternen oder besonderen Cometen, so nun manche
           Monatszeit disz 72. und 73. Jar zu sonderem
           Warnungszeichen dieser letzten Zeit ist erschienen.
             B. Jobin, 1573 [R Nfp, 982].

  .4.7.   Dasypodius, Conrad, Von Cometen und ihrer würckung.
             N. Wyriot, 1578 [R Nfp, 1478].

  .4.8.   Dasypodius, Conrad, Brevis doctrina de Cometis et
           Cometarum effectibus.
             N. Wyriot, 1578 [R Nfp, 1479].

  .4.9.   Roeslin, Helisaeus, Theoria Nova Coelestium
           Meteoron. In qua ex plurium Cometarum phaenomenis.
             B. Jobin, 1578 [Fischer, 463].

   5. ASTRONOMICAL TECHNIQUES.

      See also S5.2.1. and S6.4.2.

S4.5.1.   Curio, Jacobus, Erudita iuxta pia confabulatio de

honestarum artium studiis, praecipue de Numerorum,
figurarum et astronomices necessario . . . .
    Chr. Mylius I, 1555 [R BNU I, 604].

S4.5.2.   Beuther, Michael, De Globo astronomico et circulis.
    No printer, 1580 [Zinner, 2916].

.5.3.   Reimarus, Ursus Nicolaus, Fundamentum astronomicum
id est nova doctrina sinuum et traangulorum eaque
absolutissima et perfectissima eiusque usus in
astronomica calculatione et observatione.
    B. Jobin, 1588 [R Nfp, 3090].

.5.4.   Reimarus, Ursus, Nicolaus, Metamorphosis Logicae, in
qua rationes et clarissima ars ab omnibus
supervacaneis et superfluis imputatur.
    No printer, 1589 [Bosse I, 530].

6. METEOROLOGY.

S4.6.1.   Aristoteles, Meteorologicorum lib. I. graece et
latine (C. Dasypodius, ed.).
    J. Rihel, 1566 [R Nfp, 850].

.6.2.   Bader, Matthaeus, Praedictiones meteorologicae et
physicae: von dem 1579 Jar.
    N. Wyriot, 1578 [R Nfp, 900].

7. TREATISES ON THE STRASBOURG CLOCK.

S4.7.1.   Frischlin, Nikodemus, Vera Effigies ac Descriptio
Astronomici Horologii Argentinensis.
    B. Jobin, 1574 [R BNU II, 901].

.7.2.   Frischlin, Nikodemus, Carmen de Astronomico Horologio
Argentoratensi.
    N. Wyriot, 1575 [R BNU II, 903].

.7.3.   Dasypodius, Conradus, Auszlegung und Beschreybund des
Astronomischen Urwercks zu Strassburg.
    N. Wyriot, 1578 [R BNU I, 611], 1580 [R BNU I,
      612].

.7.4.   Dasypodius, Conradus, De Mechanicis artibus, atque
disciplinis. Eiusdem Horologiii astronomici
Argentorati in summo Templo erecti . . . .
    N. Wyriot, 1580 [R BNU I, 613].

8. THE DEBATE OVER THE GREGORIAN CALENDAR.

S4.8.1.   Plieninger, Lambertus Floridus, Kurtz Bedencken. Von

der Emendation desz Jars durch Bapst Gregorium den
XIII. fürgenommen, und von seinem Kalendar, nach ihm
Kalendarium Gregorianum perpetuum intituliert. Ob
solcher den Protestierenden Ständen anzunemen seie
oder nicht . . . .
>   J. Rihel, 1582 [R Bib. Mun., 1723], 1583 [R BNU
>   III, 1886], 1584 [R Nfp, 2949].

S4.8.2.   Beuther, Michael, De Correctione novi calendarii
           Gregoriani.
>   No printer, 1583 [Zinner, 3065].

S5. MATHEMATICS AND PHYSICS.

1. TRADITIONAL ENCYCLOPEDIAS.

S5.1.1   Bartholomaeus Anglicus (Bartholomaeus Glanville),
           Liber de proprietatibus rerum.
>   G. Husner, 1485 [R BNU Inc., 66], 1491 [R BNU Inc.,
>   67], 1505 [R BNU I, 156].

.1.2.   Anianus, Compotus Manualis metricus cum commento Et
           algorismus.
>   J. Prüss I, 1488 [S III A, 17].

.1.3.   (Gregorius Reisch), Margarita Philosophica.
>   J. Schott, 1503 [S II B, 8], 1504 [S II B, 9],
>   1508 [S II B, 10].
>   J. Grüninger, 1504 [S I, 66], 1508 [S I, 87], 1512
>   [S I, 124], 1515 [S I, 142].

2. BOOKS ON SCIENTIFIC MEASUREMENT.

S5.2.1.   Messahala (Māshā' allah), Tractatus de compositione
           astrolabii.
>   J. Grüninger, 1512 [R Nfp, 2668].

.2.2.   Nicolaus de Cusa, De staticis.
>   G. Messerschmidt, 1543 [R BNU III, 1061], 1550 [R
>   BNU III, 1061].

3. PHYSICS.

S5.3.1.   Stapulensis, Jacobus (Jacques Le Fèvre d'Étaples),
           Introductio in Physicam paraphrasim (J. Gebwiler,
           ed.).
>   R. Beck, 1514 [S IV Beck, 17].

.3.2   Aristoteles, De Naturali Auscultatione, seu de
           principiis (in Greek; introduction by Hieronymus

Zanchius).

> W. Rihel, 1553 [Rott, 71], 1554 [R BNU I, 77].

S5.3.3.   Frosch, Johannes, __De origine et principiis naturalium__
          __impressionum in singulis aëris regionibus nascentium.__
          No printer, 1562 [R Nfp, 1794].

.3.4.   Guilielmus de Conchis (Guillaume de Conches),
        __Dialogus de substantiis physicis.__
        J. Rihel, 1567 [BM 536.a.6].

.3.5.   Hawenreuter, Johann Ludwig, __Compendium Physicae . . .__
        __ex libris Aristotelis.__
        A. Bertram, 1589 [R BNU II, 1081].
        J. Rihel, 1593 [BM 520.a.22].

4.   APPLIED MATHEMATICS.

S5.4.1.   __Rechenbüchlein. In disem Biechlin seind die Rechenung__
          __gesetzt und vahet die erst von eim halben gülden__
          __gelts an . . . .__
          J. Knobloch, 1518 [R Nfp, 1220].

.4.2.   Rudolff von Jauer, Christoph, __Behend und Hübsch__
        __Rechnung durch die Kunstreichen Regeln Algebre so__
        __gemeinlich die Cosz genennt werden.__
        W. Köpfel, 1525 [R Nfp, 3128].

.4.3.   __Gerechnet Büchlin worin Müntz, Gewicht. Elen und Mass__
        __Aller Land . . . .__
        C. Egenolff, ca. 1528-30 [B __Egen.__, 1].

.4.4.   __Dem würdt gross weissheyt derechnet zu . . . Diss__
        __Täflin gantz zeyt an alle wurf . . . .__
        C. Egenolff, 1529 [B __Egen.__, 5].

.4.5.   Kern, Ulrich, __Eyn new Kunstlichs wolgegrundet__
        __Visierbuch . . . ausz rechten art der Geometria,__
        __Rechnung und Circelmessen.__
        P. Schaeffer, 1531 [R BNU II, 1307].

.4.6.   Waelckl, Georg, __Die Wälsch Practica, gezogen ausz der__
        __kunst der Proportion.__
        M. Apiarius, 1536 [R BNU IV, 2444].

.4.7.   Stiltz, Christophorus, __Eyn new Rechenbuch. Wie mann__
        __eyn ordenliche Raittung oder Rechnung . . . auch über__
        __eyn gantze Amptsverwaltigung, oder Schaffneien,__
        __stellen soll.__
        J. Cammerlander, 1542 [B __Cam.__, 124].

.4.8.   __Rechenbüchlin.__
        J. Prüss II, 1546 [S III B, 53].

S5.4.9.   Flinsbach, Kunemann, <u>Confirmatio Chronologiae atque</u>
           <u>locorum difficilium qui in tota computatione occurunt</u>
           <u>expositio una cum coniecturis extremis.</u>
           W. Rihel, 1552 [R BNU II, 868].

  .4.10.   Eschenburg, Nicolaus, <u>Ein seer schön und Recht wohl</u>
           <u>geordnet Fundument buch.</u>
           P. Hugg, 1571 [R Nfp, 1644].

  .4.11.   Caesar, Julius, <u>Gewisse erinnerung einer allgemeinen</u>
           <u>arithmetischen Practick sampt erklarung die zuffer</u>
           <u>der Arithmetic zu verstehen . . . .</u>
           No printer, 1582 [Bosse II, 356].

  .4.12.   Caesar, Julius, <u>Practica welche dienstlich ist durch</u>
           <u>alle Welt zu kauffen verkauffen.</u>
           No printer, 1583 [Bosse II, 356].

  .4.13.   Höflin, Georg, <u>Rechenbüchlin mit der Ziffer und</u>
           <u>Zalpfennigen, von allerley gemeinen gebräuchlichen</u>
           <u>nützlichen Hausz und Kauffmanns Rechnungen.</u>
           A. Bertram, 1586 [R BNU II, 1177].

    5. GEOMETRY.

S5.5.1.   <u>Regulae congruitatum: Regimina. Constructiones.</u>
           M. Hupfuff, n.d. [R Nfp, 3088].

  .5.2.   Voegelin, Johannes, <u>Elementale Geometricum, Ex</u>
           <u>Euclidis Geometria . . . .</u>
           C. Egenolff, 1529 [R BNU IV, 2442].

  .5.3.   <u>Euclides,</u>
           W. Rihel, 1538 [R NfP, 1649].
           No printer, 1539 [R Nfp, 1650].

  .5.4.   Finaeus, Orontius (Oronce Fine), <u>De Geometria</u>
           <u>Practica . . . ex demonstratis Euclidis.</u>
           G. Messerschmidt, 1544 [R BNU II, 844], 1558 [R BNU
           II, 845].

  .5.5.   Euclides, <u>Catoptrica id est Elementa ejust scientiae,</u>
           <u>qua universa speculorum vis atque natura explicatur</u>
           (Conrad Dasypodius, trans.).
           No printer, 1557 [R Nfp, 1651].

  .5.6.   Herlinus, Christianus, <u>Analyseis Geometricae sex</u>
           <u>librorum Euclidis</u> (C. Herlin and C. Dasypodius, eds.).
           J. Rihel, 1564 [BM 8532.g.4], 1566 [R BNU II,
           1142].

  .5.7.   Euclides, <u>Quindecim Elementorum Geometriae primum: ex</u>
           <u>Theonis Commentariis Graece et Latine Cui</u>

accesseaunt Scholia . . . authore cunrado Dasypodio.
  Chr. Mylius I, 1564 [R BNU II, 811].
  Chr. Mylius II, ca. 1573 [Blumhoff, 22].

S5.5.8.   Id est, Euclides Quindecim elementorum Geometriae
          secundum: ex Theonis commentariis . . . Item Barlaam
          monachi Arithmetica demonstratio eorum, quae in
          secundo libro elementorum sunt in lineis et figuris
          planis demonstrata . . . per Conradum Dasypodium.
            Chr. Mylius I, 1564 [R BNU II, 812].

  .5.9.   Euclides, Propositiones reliquorum Librorum
          Geometriae Euclidis, . . . in usum eorum, qui
          volumine Euclidis carent . . . per Cunradum
          Dasypodium.
            Chr. Mylius I, 1564 [R BNU II, 813].

  .5.10. Euclides, Elementorum, Liber Primus. Heronis
          Alexandrini vocabula geometrica (Conrad Dasypodius,
          ed.).
            Chr. Mylius I Erben, 1570 [R BNU II, 814], 1571 [R
              BNU II, 816].

  .5.11. Euclides, Propositiones. Elementorum. 15. Opticorum.
          Catoptricorum. Harmonicorum. Et Apparentiarum per
          Conradun Dasypodium.
            Chr. Mylius I Erben, 1570 [R BNU II, 815].

  .5.12. Euclides, Euclidis Omnes Omnium Lobrorum
          Propositiones . . . editae per Cunradum Dasypodium.
            Chr. Mylius I Erben, 1571 [R BNU II, 817].

  .5.13. Isaacus, Monachus, Scholia in Euclidls Elementorum
          geometriae sex priores libros (Conrad Dasypodius, ed.).
            No printer, 1579 [R Nfp, 2129].

  .5.14. Reusner, Nicolaus, Agalmatum Aureolorum emblematum
          liber, singularis Thobiae Stimmeri iconibus
          exornatus.
            B. Jobin, 1591 [R Nfp, 3104].

  6. ORATIONS ON STUDYING MATHEMATICS.

S5.6.1.   Melanchthon, Philippus, Mathematicarum disciplinarum
          tum etiam astrologiae encomium.
            No printer, 1536 [Zinner, 1634]. (In German.)
            No printer, 1536 [Zinner, 1634].
            Cr. Mylius, 1537 [R Nfp, 2637; Zinner, 1670].

  .6.2.   Velsius (Velsius Medicus or Justus Velsius), De
          mathematicarum disciplinarum vario usu dignitateque.
            Cr. Mylius, 1544 [R Nfp, 3397].

S5.6.3.   Dasypodius, Conradus, <u>Oratio de disciplinis</u>
           <u>Mathematicis . . . .</u>
               N. Wyriot, 1579 [R Nfp, 1482].

  .6.4.   Virdung, Paulus, <u>De fato studiosorum cum primis</u>
           <u>Mathematicorum . . . .</u>
               J. Martin, 1594 [R Nfp, 3419].

   7. ARITHMETIC.

S5.7.1.   Wolf, Johannes, <u>Rudimenta Arithmetices</u>.
               G. Messerschmidt, 1539 [R BNU IV, 2500].

  .7.2.   Willichius, Jodocus, <u>Arithmeticae, libri tres</u>.
               Cr. Mylius, 1540 [R BNU IV, 2466].

   8. MATHEMATICAL TEXTS.

S5.8.1.   Dasypodius, Conradus, <u>Volumen primum mathematicum,</u>
           <u>prima et simplicissima mathematicarum disciplinarum</u>
           <u>principia complectens: geometriae, logisticae,</u>
           <u>astronomiae, geographiae. . . . Volumen secundum</u>
           <u>mathematicum, complectens praecepta mathematica,</u>
           <u>astronomica, logistica.</u>
               J. Rihel, 1567 [R Nfp, 1484].
               J. Rihel, 1570 [R BNU I, 610]. (<u>Volumen secundum</u>.)

  .8.2.   Dasypodius, Conradus, <u>Dictionarium mathematicum</u>.
               N. Wyriot, 1573 [R Nfp, 1483].

  .8.3.   Dasypodius, Conradus, <u>Institutionum mathematicarum,</u>
           <u>volumen Primum Erotemata</u>.
               J. Rihel, 1593 [R Nfp, 1485].

  .8.4.   Dasypodius, Conrad, <u>Protheoria Mathematica . . .</u>
           <u>Brevis corporis Math. in III volumine</u>.
               J. Martin, 1593 [R BNU I, 614].

  .8.5.   Dasypodius, Conradus, <u>(Institutionum Mathematicarum.)</u>
           <u>. . . Appendix Elementorum. Arithmeticae--Geodaesiae.</u>
           <u>Opticae--Catoptricae. Seenographiae . . .</u>
           <u>Astronomicae, Astrologiae, Musicae, Mechanicae</u>.
               J. Rihel, 1596 [R Nfp, 1486].

   9. SCIENTIFIC THESES.

S5.9.1.   Planer, Andreas, <u>Analysis libri primi physicorum</u>
           <u>Aristotelis in disputationem ab eodem proposita</u>.
               No printer, 1571 [Bosse I, 435].

  .9.2.   Cellarius, Georg, <u>Themata physica de infinito ex</u>

altera parte tertii libri physicarum auscultationum
Aristotelis.
J. Rihel, 1574 [Greiner].

S5.9.3.　　Hawenreuter, Johann Ludwig, De Inani physica
disquisitio ex secunda parti quarti. Libri Physicorum
Aristotelis.
J. Rihel, 1576 [R BNU II, 1078].

.9.4.　　Hawenreuter, Johann Ludwig, Theses quae complectuntur
Προλεγομενα λογιχὰ　propos…
J. Rihel, 1576 [R BNU II, 1077].

.9.5.　　Theses physicae de natura universe, ex libro primo
Aristotelis.
No printer, 1579 [Bosse I, 558].

.9.6.　　Theses physicae de coelo ex libro secundo Aristotelia
de Coelo.
No printer, 1580 [Bosse I, 558].

.9.7.　　Jacobus, Mathias, Theses de mutatione elementorum
qua loco feruntur.
N. Wyriot, 1582 [Greiner].

.9.8.　　Beuther, Johannes Michael, Theses de igneis Meteoris
ex libro primo Meteorologicorum Aristotelis.
A. Bertram, 1584 [Greiner].

.9.9.　　Hawenreuter, Johann Ludwig, Theses de fluminum ortu,
ex libro primo meteorologicorum Aristotelis.
K. Kieffer, 1589 [R BNU II, 1082].

.9.10.　　Hawenreuter, Johann Ludwig, Theses Physicae, De
desumptae Mundi partibus, ex IV Aristotelis de
collo libris.
J. Martin, 1591 [R BNU II, 1085].

.9.11.　　Uffenbach, Peter, Disp. physica ex duobus de
generatione . . . libris desumpta.
A. Bertram, 1591 [Bosse I, 541].

.9.12.　　Hauwenreuter, Johann Ludwig, Theses physicae ex
quarto meteorologicorum Aristostotelis libro desumptae.
A. Bertram, 1592 [R BNU II, 1087].

.9.13.　　Hauwenreuter, Johann Ludwig, De Mari. Theses ex
libro II.
A. Bertram, 1592 [R BNU II, 1086].

S6.　GEOGRAPHY, TRAVEL, AND EXPLORATION.

1.　TRADITIONAL VOYAGES AND DESCRIPTIONS.

S6.1.1.   Caoursin, Guilelmus, <u>Obsidionis Rhodine Urbis</u>
           <u>Descriptio</u> (in German).
               No printer, n.d. [R Nfp, 1284].
           Also listed as:
           Petrus de Aubusson, <u>Relatio de obsidione urbis</u>
           <u>Rhodiae</u>.
               H. Knoblochtzer, 1480 [R BNU <u>Inc</u>., 45].

  .1.2.   Tucher, Hans, <u>Reise zum heiligen Grabe</u>.
               H. Knobloch, 1484 [R Nfp <u>Inc</u>., 653].

  .1.3.   Johannes von Montivilla (John of Mandeville), <u>Von</u>
           <u>der erfarung des strengen Ritters Johannes von</u>
           <u>Montivilla</u>.
               J. Prüss I, 1484 [S III A, 8], 1488 [S III A, 19].
               B. Kistler, 1499 [S IV, Kis., 4].
               M. Hupfuff, 1501 [S V, 12].
               J. Knobloch, 1507 [S VII, 32].

  .1.4.   <u>Die ritterlich und lobwürdig reiss des . . . erfanen</u>
           <u>Ritters . . . Herren Ludovico Vartomans von Bolonia</u>.
               J. Knobloch, 1515 [S VII, 107], 1516 [S VII, 132].

    2. DESCRIPTIONS OF VOYAGES TO THE NEW WORLD AND EAST INDIES.

S6.2.1.   <u>Ein schön hübsch lesen von etlichen inszlen die do</u>
           <u>in kurtzen zyten funden synd durch den künig von</u>
           <u>hispania . . . .</u>
               B. Kistler, 1497 [S IV, Kis., 1].

  .2.2.   (Ringmann, M.), <u>De Ora Antarctica per regem</u>
           <u>Portugallie Pridem Inventa</u>.
               M. Hupfuff, 1505 [S V, 41; R BNU IV, 2406 ; R Nfp,
               3407].

  .2.3.   (Ringmann, M.), <u>Von den nüwen Insulen und landen so</u>
           <u>yetz kürtzlich erfunden synt durch den Künig von</u>
           <u>Portugall</u>.
               M. Hupfuff, 1506 [S V, 50; R BNU IV, 2407; R Nfp,
               3408].

  .2.4.   Vespucci, Americo, <u>Diss Büchlin saget wie die zwen</u>
           <u>durchlüchtigsten Herren Her Fernandus. Künig zu</u>
           <u>Castilien und Herr Emanuel. Künig zu Portugal haben</u>
           <u>das weyte mör ersüchet unnd funden vil Insulen unnd</u>
           <u>eine Nüwe welt von wilden nackenden Leüten, vormals</u>
           <u>unbekannt</u>.
               J. Grüninger, 1509 [S I, 101].

  .2.5.   Emanuel, King of Portugal, <u>Epistola de victoria</u>
           <u>habita in India et Malacha. Triumphus de infidelibus</u>

acquisitus Leoni X conscriptus.
J. Grüninger, 1513 [BM C.32.f.15].

S6.2.6.   Emanuel, King of Portugal, Abdruck eines
Lateinischen Sendtbrieves an Bapstliche Heiligkeit
von der Eroberten Stat Malacha.
M. Hupfuff, 1513 [BM C.32.f.12].

.2.7.   Grynaeus, Simon, Die new welt der landschaften unnd
Insulen, so bis hie her allen Altweltbeschrybern
unbekant, Sambt den sitten und gebreuchen . . . der
Inwonenden völcker. Auch was Gütter oder waren man
bey jnen funden und jhn unsere Landt bracht hab
(Michael Herr, trans.).
G. Ulricher, 1534 [R BNU II, 1048].

.2.8.   Huttich, Johann, Novus orbis regionum germanice,
. . . Die new Welt der Landschaften und Insulen.
G. Ulricher, 1534 [R Nfp, 2117].

3.   GENERAL GEOGRAPHIES AND COSMOGRAPHIES.

S6.3.1.   (Waldseemüller, Martin), Cosmographiae introductio:
cum quibusdam Geometriae ac astronomiae principiis
. . . Universalis Cosmographia secundum Ptolomaei
traditionem et Americi Vespucii aliorumque
lustrationes.
No printer, 1507 [R Nfp, 3455].
J. Grüninger, 1509 [S I, 109].

.3.2.   Lud, Gantier (Gaulterus Ludd), Speculi orbin
succinctiss. Sed neque poenitenda neque inelegans
declaratio et canon.
J. Grüninger, 1507 [S I, 85].

.3.3.   (Waldseemüller, Martin), Globus Mundi, Declaratio
sive descriptio mundi et totius orbis terrarum,
globulo rotundo comparati ut sphera solida.
J. Grüninger, 1509 [S I, 104].

.3.4.   Müling, Johann Adelphus, Der welt kugel, Beschrybung
der welt und dess gantzen Ertreichs hie angezögt und
vergleicht einer Rotunden Kuglen . . . .
J. Grüninger, 1509 [S I, 103].

.3.5.   Ptolemaeus, Claudius, Geographiae opus novissima
traductione e Graecorum (Waldseemüller & Ringmann,
eds.).
J. Schott, 1513 [R BNU III, 1957].

.3.6.   Ptolemaeus (Claudius Ptolomaes), Auctus restitutus

Emaculatus Cum Tabulis Veteribus Ac Novis (Georg
Ubelin, ed.).
   J. Schott, 1520 [S II B, 54].

S6.3.7.   Ptolemaeus, Claudius, Opus Geographiae noviter
castigatum et emaculatum additionibus. Rari et
inuisis. (L Fries, ed.).
   J. Grüninger, 1522 [S I, 187; R BNU III, 1958].

.3.8.   Ptolemaeus, Claudius, Geographicae Enarrationis
Libri Octo (Bilibald Pirckheimer, ed.).
   J. Grüninger, 1525 [S I, 222; R BNU III, 1959].

.3.9.   Ptolemaeus, Claudius, Tabulae Geographicae.
P. Schäffer, 1532 [Harrisse, 285].

.3.10.   Cellarius, Martinus (Martin Borrhaus), Elementale
cosmographicum.
   Cr. Mylius, 1539 [R Nfp, 1324].

.3.11.   Hildensaemus, Franciscus, Mundi Catholica sive
Cosmographiae praecepta universalia.
   N. Wyriot, 1581 [R BNU II, 1169].

4. MAPS, ITINERARIES, AND HOW TO USE THEM.

S6.4.1.   (Waldseemüller, Martin), Instructio Manuductionem
Prestans in Cartam Itinerariam Martini Hilaco . . . .
   J. Grüninger, 1511 [S I, 121].

.4.2.   Fries, Lorenz, Expositio Astrolabii.
   J. Grüninger, 1522 [R BNU II, 893].

.4.3.   Europa seu Chartae Itinerariae quo pacto intelligi
debeat summaria instructio una cum indice.
   J. Grüninger, 1527 [S I, 234].

.4.4.   Underweisung und usslegung der Mercarthen oder Der
Cartha Marina Darin man sehen mag, wo einer in der
welt sy . . . .
   J. Grüninger, 1527 [R Nfp, 3458; S I, 233], 1530
   [S I, 246].

.4.5.   Gratarolo, Guglielmo, Regimen omnium iteragentium,
postromo editum.
   W. Rihel, 1563 [R BNU II, 1030].

5. DESCRIPTIONS OF PARTICULAR REGIONS.

S6.5.1.   Saracenisch, Türkisch und Mahometisch glaub, Gesatz,
Gotsdienst, . . . alle Gebräuch, Ordnungen,
Disciplinen in Kriegs und Friedenszeiten.
   C. Egenolff, 1530 [R Nfp, 1906].

S6.5.2.   Ziegler, Jacob, Quae intus continentur: Syria . . . ,
           Palestina . . . Arabia . . . Petraea . . .
           Aegyptus . . . .
               P. Schöffer, 1532 [R BNU IV, 2525; R Nfp, 3309].

   .5.3.   Ziegler, Jacobus, Terra sanctae quam Palestinam
           nominant, Syriae, Arabiae, Aegypti et Schondiae . . . .
               W. Rihel, 1536 [R BNU IV, 2526].

   .5.4.   Magnus, Olaus, Beschreibung allerley Gelegenheyte,
           Sitten, Gebräuchen und Gewonheyten der Mitnächtigen
           volcker in Sueden, Ost unnd Westgthen, Norwegen
           unnd andern Landen.
               T. Rihel, 1567 [R Nfp, 2583].

   .5.5.   Crusius, Georg, Descriptio Bredenbergae, quae est
           arx in Holsatia sita . . . novis aedificiis
           eleganter instaurata ornataque. Cum praefatione
           Joachimi Camerarii.
               B. Jobin, 1573 [R Nfp, 1466].

   .5.6.   Turler, Hieronymus, De peregrinatione et agro
           neapolitano Libri II.
               B. Jobin, 1574 [R BNU IV, 2364].

   .5.7.   Crusius, Martinus, Salomoni Schweigkero Sultzensi,
           qui Constantinopoli in aula legati Imperii Romani
           aliquot annos ecclesiasta fuit:et in Aegypto,
           Palestina, Syria peregrinatus est: gratulatio. Cum
           descriptionis illus peregrinationis.
               N. Wyriot, 1582 [R Nfp, 1468].

   .5.8.   Reusner, Nicolaus, De Italia, Regione Europae
           Nobilissima. Libri Duo.
               B. Jobin, 1585 [R BNU III, 2000].

   .5.9.   Deidricius, Georgius, Hodoeporicon Itineris,
           Argentoratensis Insigniumque Aliquot Locorum et
           Urbium cum Ungariae vero . . . Germaniae
           descriptiones.
               K. Kieffer, 1589 [R BNU I, 626].

   .5.10. Rosslin, Helisaeus, Der Elsäsz und gegen Lotringen
           grentzenden Waszgawischer Gebirgs gelegenheit, und
           Commoditeten inn Victualien und Mineralien.
               B. Jobin, 1593 [R BNU III, 2027].

S7. NATURAL HISTORY.

S7.1.1.   Albertus Magnus, Liber Aggregationis seu secretorum
           de mirabilibus mundi.
               J. Grüninger, 1493 [BM I.A.1419].

S7.1.2.   Marsilius (Marsilius ab Inghen), <u>Questiones</u>
            <u>exquisite clarissimi Marsilii in libros</u>
            <u>Aristotelis de generatione et corruptione</u>.
            M. Flach II, 1501 [S VI B, 4].

  .1.3.   Petrus de Eliaco (Pierre d'Ailly), <u>Tractatus</u> . . .
            <u>super Metheororum de impressionibus aeris</u>.
            J. Prüss I, 1504 [S III A, 47; R BNU III, 1850].

  .1.4.   Albertus Magnus, <u>De natura locorum</u> . . .
            <u>Cosmographica vel Physica</u>.
            M. Schürer, 1515 [S VIII, 150; R BNU I, 29].

  .1.5.   Albertus Magnus, <u>Philosophia pauperorum</u>.
            No printer, 1520 [Hirsch, 126].

  .1.6.   Albertus Magnus, <u>Philosophia naturalis Isagoge</u>.
            U. Morhard, 1520 [R Nfp, 784].

  .1.7.   Virdung, Johannes, <u>Ausslegung der Coniunction aller</u>
            <u>Planeten in den Fischen</u>.
            No printer, 1525 [Zinner, 1310].

  .1.8.   Valla, Georgius, <u>De natura partium animalium</u>.
            H. Seybold, 1529 [BM 954.b.9].

  .1.9.   Oppianus, <u>Alieuticon sive De Piscibus</u>.
            Plinius, C., <u>Naturalis Historiae</u>.
            Jovius, Paulus, <u>De Piscibus</u>.
            J. Cammerlander, 1534 [R BNU III, 1670].

  .1.10.   Gaius Plinius Secundus, <u>Natürlicher History Fünff</u>
            <u>Bücher</u>.
            J. Schott, 1543 [S II B, 143].

  .1.11.   Herr, Michael, <u>Gründtlicher underricht, und</u>
            <u>beschreibung, wunderbarlicher seltzamer art, natur,</u>
            <u>kraft und eygenschafft aller vier füssigen thier,</u>
            <u>wild und zam</u> . . . .
            B. Beck, 1546 [R BNU II, 1160].

  .1.12.   Aristoteles, <u>De natura aut de rerum principiis libri</u>
            <u>VIII</u>.
            S. Emmel, 1549 [R Nfp, 849].
            No printer, 1568 [Bosse I, 440].

  .1.13.   Guillaume de Conches, <u>Pragmaticon</u>.
            No printer, 1557 [Thorndike, <u>Magic</u>, 600].

  .1.14.   Aristoteles, <u>De Mundo</u>.
            No printer, 1565 [Zinner, 2360].

  .1.15.   Aristoteles, <u>De anima libri tres</u>.
            S. Emmel, 1568 [R Bib. Mun., 423].

S7.1.16.   Paracelsus, Theophrastus, Ettliche Tractatus . . .
            I. Von Natürlichen dingen, II. Beschreibung etlicher
            Kreüter, III. Von Metallen, IV. Von Edlen gesteinen
            (M. Toxites, ed.).
                Chr. Mylius II, 1570 [R BNU III, 1773], 1582 [R
                BNU III, 1784].

  .1.17.   Rasch, Johann, De Terrae Motibus et terrae hiatibus.
                B. Jobin, 1581 [Guntner, Jb. Münch. Gesch. 4 1890].

  .1.18.   Paracelsus, Theophrastus, De Natura Rerum IX Bücher
            (L. Bathodius, ed.).
                B. Jobin, 1584 [R BNU III, 1785].

  .1.19.   Aristoteles, Florum Illustriorum ex Universa eius
            Philosophia Collectorum libri tres.
                L. Zetzner, 1598 [R BNU I, 82].

  .1.20.   Bruno, Giordano, De Luilliano specierum scrutinio.
            De Lampade combinatoria Lulliana. De progressa
            logicae venationis.
                No printer, 1598 [R Nfp, 1129].

S8. AGRONOMY.

S8.1.1.   Bauernpraktik In diesem Biechlin wirt funden der
            Pauren Practick.
                No printer, n.d. [R Nfp, 950], 1579 [R Nfp, 952].
                M. Schürer, n.d. [R Nfp, 951].

  .1.2.   Crescentius, Petrus de, Opus Ruralium Commodorum.
                G. Husner, 1486 [R BNU Inc., 145].

  .1.3.   Petrus de Crescentiis (Pietro de Crescenzi), Von dem
            nutz der ding die in äckern gebuwet werden.
                No printer, 1512 [R Nfp, 1453].
                J. Knobloch, 1518 [S VII, 153].
                J. Knobloch II, 1531 [R BNU I, 597].
                J. Schott, 1518 [S II B, 42].

  .1.4.   Columella, Lucius, Das Ackerwerk . . . allen
            veldbaw, von getreyd, wein, früchten, allerley
            kreütern. Und allerley gartenwerk.
                W. Rihel, 1538 [R BNU I, 561].

  .1.5.   Bassus, Cassianus, Der Veldbaw oder das buch von der
            veld arbeyt (Michael Herr, trans.).
                B. Beck, 1545 [R BNU I, 160].
                T. Rihel, 1551 [R BNU I, 161].
                S. Emmel, 1561 [R BNU I, 162].
                No printer, 1563 [R Nfp, 1301], 1566 [R Nfp, 1302].

  .1.6.   Gratarolo, Gugliemo, Oratio luculenta, in qua sunt

laudes Agriculturae eiusque cum urbana vita
collatio. Item. Leges de re Rustica . . . Dialysis
IV librorum Vergeli in Georgicis. Accedunt
experimenta multa Rei Rusticae et hortensis.
   No printer, 1563 [R BNU II, 1029].

S8.1.7.   Libaltus, Johannes (Jean Liebault), Siben Bücher von
dem Feldbau und volkomnenner Bestellung eynes
ordenlichen Mayerhofs oder Landguts.
     B. Jobin, 1579 [R BNU III, 1355], 1580 [R BNU III,
       1356], 1592 [R BNU III, 1357], 1598 [R BNU III,
       1358].

S9. VETERINARY TEXTS.

S9.1.1.   Albrecht (Meister), Arzneibuch der Rosse.
     M. Hupfuff, 1499 [R Nfp Inc., 24].
     J. Frölich, after 1535 [R Nfp, 792].

.1.2.   Dis büchlin sagt wie man pferd artzneyen und
erkennen soll.
     M. Hupfuff, 1502 [S V, 21], 1511 [S V, 91].

.1.3.   Erziehung, Gebrauch, Lernung, Artznei in . . .
kranckheyten aller zahmen, dem menschen
gebraüchlichen . . . Thier. Als nämlich pferd, Esel,
Ochsen, Küe, Säuwe, Schaaf . . . Hüner Gans . . . .
     C. Egenolff, 1530 [R Nfp, 1643].

.1.4.   (Wyriot, Nicolaus), Ein newe und bewerte Rossartzney
. . . .
     N. Wyriot, 1583 [R Nfp, 3571].

.1.5.   Reuschel, Caspar, Hippiatra. Gründlichter un
eigentlicher Bericht . . . von Art und Eygenschafft
der Pferde, . . . Kranckheiten, und deroselbigen
bewehrten Curation und heilsamen Artzneyung.
     B. Jobin, 1593 [R BNU III, 1995], 1599 [R BNU III,
       1996].

.1.6.   Ross Artzney Buch. Darinnen zu finden, wie
allerhand zufälliger Kranckheiten unnd Gebrechen der
Pferd zu erkennen.
     L. Zetzner, 1599 [R BNU III, 2024].

S10. HUNTING MANUALS.

S10.1.1.   Buchlein wie man visch und vogen fahen soll mit den
henden und auch sonst mit vil bewerten recepten:und
ist geteilt in xxvii capitel.

M. Hupfuff, 1498 [R Nfp Inc., 171], 1499 [R Nfp Inc., 172], 1508 [S V, 72], 1511 [S V, 86].

S10.1.2. Ein schons Buchlin von dem beyssen mit dem habich und eim Hund, alle bresten unnd geschicklicheyte des federspiels trewlich underrichtend unnd lernend.
J. Knobloch, 1510 [S VII supp., 330].

.1.3. Weydtwergk: Vögel zufahen mit Raubvögeln. Netzen. Stricken. Leime. Geschosz. Wildt fahen mit Netzen, Reusen, Angeln, Kasten.
C. Egenolff, 1530 [R Nfp, 3479].

.1.4. Tappe, Eberhard, Waidwerck Federspiel. Von der Häbichen unnd Falcken natur, art unnd eygenthumb.
J. Cammerlander, 1542 [B Cam., 127].

.1.5. Jacques de Fouilloux, New Jägerbuch . . . Von Jäger, der Jagte Anfang, des Jägers Horn und Stimm, auch von Laid, Jagt, Hetz und allerley Hunden . . . .
B. Jobin, 1590 [R BNU II, 879].

.1.6. Johann von Clamorgan (Jean de Clamorgan), Wolffsjagt . . . inn welcher begrieffen und dargethon ist desz Wollffs Natur und Eygenschafft . . . .
B. Jobin, 1590 [R BNU I, 541].

S11. TECHNICAL MANUALS.

1. COOKBOOKS.

S11.1.1. Kuchenmeistery.
M. Hupfuff, 1507 [S V, 71].
J. Knobloch, 1516 [S VII, 134], 1519 [S VII, 190].

.1.2. Platina, Bartholomaeus, Von allen Speisen und Gerichten. Wie man sie allerhandt art, künstlich und wol, kochen, einmachen und bereytten sol.
C. Egenolff, January 1530 [R Nfp, 2931], July, 1530 [B Egen. 31].

2. FENCING AND BOXING.

S11.2.1. In diesem büchlin findt man die rechte kunst und art des Ringens.
M. Hupfuff, 1512 [R Nfp, 1222].

.2.2. Meyer, Joachin, Gründliche Beschreibung der Kunst des Fechtens.
No printer, 1520 [R Nfp, 2679].

3. GUNPOWDER.

S11.3.1.   Büchsenmeisterei; von Geschosz, Büchsen, Pulver,
            Saltpeter und Feuerwerk.
                C. Egenolff, 1529 [R Nfp, 1225].

4. MINING AND METALWORKING.

S11.4.1.   Probier-Büchlin, Auff Goldt, Silber, Alle Ertz und
            Metall. Mit vil Kostbarlichen Alchimeiischen Künsten.
            Sampt allem Zugehör und Instrumenten dar zu dienlich.
            Die Bergknamen, für die newen, angehnde Bergkleut.
                C. Egenolff, 1530 [R BNU III, 1926].

   .4.2.   Von Stahel und Eisen, die kunstlich waich und herrt
            zumachen. Allen Waffenschmiden, Goltdschmiden,
            Gürtlern, Sigil und Stempffel. Schneidern . . . zu
            wissen.
                J. Cammerlander, 1539 [R BNU IV, 2187].
                Chr. Mylius II, 1583 [R Nfp, 2261].

   .4.3.   Probier-Büchlein auff Gold, Silber, Kupffer, und
            Bley.
                J. Frölich, 1549 [R Nfp, 2991].

5. TEXTILE DYES.

S11.5.1.   Mangmeistery Mancherlei Farben.
                No printer, ca. 1530 [Hirsch, 136].
                J. Cammerlander, ca. 1540 [B Cam., 66].

   .5.2.   Artliche Künste mancherley weise Dinten, Goldt und
            allerhand Farben zu bereyten.
                H. Grimm, 1545 [R Imp. Alsc., 329].

6. MODELS FOR DESIGN.

S11.6.1.   Vogtherr, Heinrich, Ein frembds und wunderbars
            kunstbüchlein allen Molern, Bildschnitzern,
            Goldschmieden hochnützlich zu gebrauchen.
                H. Vogtherr, 1537 [R Nfp, 3446], 1538 [R Nfp,
                3447], 1539 [R Imp. Alsc., 284].
                J. Frölich, 1543 [R Imp. Alsc., 284], 1545 [R
                Imp. Alsc., 284].
                Chr. Mylius I, 1559 [R Imp. Alsc., 284].
                Chr. Mylius II, 1572 [R Nfp, 3451].

   .6.2.   Vogtherr, Heinrich, Kunstbuchlein; Libellus
            artificiosus.
                H. Vogtherr, 1540 [R Nfp, 3450].

S11.6.3.   Eyn news Kunstbüchlin. Allen Malern, Bildtschnitzern,
            Goldschmieden, Steinmetzen, Schreinern, Waffen und
            Messerschmieden vast dienstlich.
                J. Cammerlander, 1543 [B Cam., 53].

    .6.4.   Dasypodius, Conradus, Heron Mechanicus, Seu de
            Mechanicis artibus, atque disciplinis . . . Eiusdem
            Horologii astronomici . . . descriptio.
                N. Wyriot, 1580 [R BNU I, 613].

      7. MAKING AND PRESERVING WINE.

S11.7.1.   Grundlicher Bericht wie man alle Wein Teutscher und
            Welscher landen vor allen zufällen bewaren, die
            bresthaften widerbringen medt, bier, essig machen
            sol.
                No printer, 1538 [R Nfp, 981].

S11.7.2.   Greulich, Martin, Ein Newe und hübsche bewerte
            kunst, wie man die wein erhalten soll. Und dem
            bresthafftigen abgefallnen Wein wider helffen.
                J. Frölich, 1549 [R Nfp, 1934], 1555 [R BNU II,
                1045].
                Chr. Mylius II, 1572 [Greiner].

    .7.3.   Gratarolo, Guilielmo, De Vini natura, artificio et
            uso deque de omni potabili.
                T. Rihel, 1565 [R BNU II, 1031].

      8. SUNDIALS.

S11.8.1.   Vogtherr, Georg, Sumari Büchlein aller Sonnen uhr.
                H. Vogtherr, 1539 [R Imp. Alsc., 285], 1540 [R
                Nfp, 3448], 1544 [R Nfp, 3449].

    .8.2.   Ein wolgegründs . . . Summari Büchlin, aller Sonnen
            Uhr.
                Chr. Mylius I, 1559 [R BNU IV, 2252].
                Chr. Mylius I Erben, 1568 [R BNU IV, 2253].
                Chr. Mylius II Erben, 1582 [R BNU IV, 2254].

      9. ARCHITECTURE.

S11.9.1.   Alberti, Leone Battista, De re aedificatoria, libri
            X.
                J. Cammerlander, 1541 [R Nfp, 778].

    .9.2.   Vitruvius, M. Pollio, De Architectura, libri X.
                G. Messerschmidt, 1543 [R BNU IV, 2424]., 1550
                [R Nfp, 2425].

S11.9.3.   Specklin, Daniel, Architectura Von Vestungen.
            B. Jobin, 1589 [R BNU IV, 2176].
            L. Zetzner, 1599 [R BNU IV, 2177].

   .9.4.   Dietterlin, Wendelinus, Architecturen unnd
            Ausstheilung der V. Seüln.
            B. Jobin Erben, 1593 [R BNU I, 653].

      10. SURVEYING.

S11.10.1.   Conrad von Ulm, Johann, Geodaisia. Das ist: Von
            gewisser und bewährter Feldmessung.
            B. Jobin, 1580 [R Nfp, 1432].

      11. EMBROIDERY.

S11.11.1   New Künstlichs Modelbuch von Mödeln auff der laden
            zu wircken oder mit der zopffnot, creutz und
            Judenstich, und anderer gewonlicher weiss zumachen.
            B. Jobin Erben, 1596 [BM C.31.h.6].
            J. Martin, 1599 [R Nfp, 2710].

S12. CALENDARS AND PROGNOSTICATIONS FOR POPULAR USE.

S12.1.1.   Kalendar.
            J. Knoblochtzer, 1482 [Fischer, 604].

   .1.2.   Kalendar für 1484.
            J. Grüninger, 1483 [Fischer, 605].

   .1.3.   Kalendar für 1484.
            J. Prüss I, 1483 [Fischer, 606].

   .1.4.   Kalendar für 1487.
            J. Prüss I, 1486 [Fischer, 607].

   .1.5.   Kalendar für 1487.
            J. Prüss I, 1486 [Fischer, 608].

   .1.6.   Schrotbanck, Hans, Practica auf das Jahar 1490.
            J. Grüninger, 1490 [R Nfp Inc., 61].

   .1.7.   Kalendar für 1493.
            J. Grüninger, 1492 [Fischer, 609].

   .1.8.   Kalendar für 1494.
            J. Prüss I, 1493 [Fischer, 610].

   .1.9.   Kalendar für 1497.
            J. Prüss I, 1496 [Fischer, 612].

   .1.10.   Kalendar für 1497.
            J. Grüninger, 1496 [Fischer, 611].

S12.1.11.   Lichtenberger, Johann, Prenosticatio zu teutsch für
            1496 und sagt von wunderbarlichen dyngen.
               B. Kistler, 1497 [S IV Kis., 2].

     .1.12. (Lichtenberger, Johann), Prognosticatio . . . de
            present. anno et sequentibus quam plurimus
            annis . . . .
               B. Kistler, 1499 [R Nfp Inc., 417].

     .1.13. Kalendar für 1500.
               J. Grüninger, 1499 [Fischer, 613].

     .1.14. Dyse Practica ist gemacht uff das fünffzehen hundert
            und eyn jar. unnd saget von wunderlichen dingen die
            zeit geschehen sollen in der welt.
               B. Kistler, 1500 [S IV Kis., 14].

     .1.15   Dise Practica ist gemacht uff das funffzehen hunderd
            und ein jar nach Christi.
               M. Hupfuff, 1501 [S V, 13].

     .1.16. Practica dütsch anfohen.
               M. Hupfuff, 1502 [S V, 24].

     .1.17. Prattica dütsch anfahen.
               B. Kistler, 1502 [S IV Kis., 18].

     .1.18. Hans Virdung von Hasfurt, Prattica teütsch etlich
            jar werende . . . uss der grossen coniunction der
            dryen öbersten Planeten Saturni Jovis und Martis
            gezogen.
               M. Hupfuff, 1503 [S V, 25], 1504 [S V, 33].
               J. Cammerlander, 1542 [R Nfp, 3415], 1544 [R Nfp,
                  3416], 1545 [R Nfp, 3417].

     .1.19. Kalendar für 1504.
               M. Hupfuff, 1503 [Fischer, 614].

     .1.20. Henrichmann, Jacobus, Prognostica alioquin barbare
            practica nuncupata.
               J. Grüninger, 1504 [S I, 113].

     .1.21. Kalendar für 1511.
               M. Hupfuff, 1511 [Fischer, 615].

     .1.22. Kalendar für 1513.
               M. Hupfuff, 1512 [Fischer, 616].

     .1.23. Kalendar für 1515.
               M. Hupfuff, 1514 [Fischer, 617].

     .1.24. Kalendar für 1518.
               M. Hupfuff, 1518 [Fischer, 618].

     .1.25. Gallianus, Conradus, Practica uff drey jar namlich

des XXII XXIII und XXIIII.
    J. Schott, 1521 [S II B, 65].
    J. Schott, 1521 [Fischer, 255]. (In Latin.)

S12.1.26. Schrottentreck, Johann, Vorhersage für 1523.
    No printer, 1522 [Fischer, 518].

.1.27. Fries, Laurent, Prognosticatio . . . Ein zusammen
gelesen urteyl aus den alten erfarnen meistern der
astrology.
    J. Grüninger, 1523 [S I, 208], 1525 [S I, 228; R
      Nfp, 1781], 1530 [S I, 249; R Nfp, 1782].
    J. Knobloch, 1530 [S VII, 322; R Nfp, 1783].

.1.28. Prognosticon auf die Jahre 1530-34.
    C. Egenolff, 1529 [R Nfp, 2992].

.1.29. Paracelsus, Wunnderbar und mercklicher Geschichten.
Prognostication.
    C. Egenolff, 1530 [R Nfp, 2826].

.1.30 Künigsberger, Johann (Johann Muller von Konigsberg;
Regiomontanus), Kalendrium . . . bis auff den 1556
jar (mit vorrede des Martin Polydorius).
    J. Cammerlander, 1532 [Fischer, 370].

.1.31. Eckart der trew sagt dir verwar, Wie es im MDXXXiiii
Iar, Sol erghan auff erd durch alle Ständ.
    J. Cammerlander, 1533 [B Cam., 26].

.1.32. Muller von Köngsberg, Johann (Regiomontanus),
Kalendarius . . . dess tags leng, finsternuss der
Sonnen and Monds . . . zuerlernen. Von den zwölff
Zeychen, XXXvi Bildern des himmels.
    J. Cammerlander, 1534 [B Cam., 74], 1535 [B Cam.,
      76].

.1.33. Lichtenberger, Johann, Die Gross Practica warhafftig
bis man zelt MDLxxxi jar.
    J. Cammerlander, 1535 [BM 8610.bbb.4].

.1.34. Muller von Königsberg, Johann (Regiomontanus), Ein
newer Kalendar, Von allerley Artzney durch alles
himmelische Gestirn.
    J. Cammerlander, 1536 [B Cam., 77].

.1.35. Pruckner, Nicolaus, Der grossen und grausamen
Fynsternüsz der Sonnen uff das 1540 jar Prognosticon.
    J. Schott, 1539 [R Nfp, 2995].

.1.36. Alle alten Propheceien von Keyserlich Maiestat.
Keyserliche Practica und Prognostication, ausz allen
alten Weissagungen, von CCC jaren her

zusammengeschreiben.
    J. Cammerlander, ca. 1540 [R BNU III, 1919].

S12.1.37. Das Grosse Planeten Buch sampt der Geomanci,
         Physiognomi und Chiromanci.
           J. Cammerlander, 1541 [Zinner, 1781a], 1544 [R Nfp,
             2921; Zinner, 1856], 1546 [R Nfp, 2922].
           W. Rihel, 1549 [Zinner, 1964], 1550 [Zinner, 1996].
           No printer, 1570 [Zinner, 2527].
           J. Rihel, 1572 [R Nfp, 2923], 1575 [R BNU III,
             1879], 1578 [Zinner, 2842], 1578 [Zinner, 2843],
             1581 [R Nfp, 2926], 1584 [R Nfp, 2927], 1590 [R
             Nfp, 2928], 1593 [R Nfp, 2929].

.1.38. Salamon, Magister, Vorhersage für 1543, deutsch.
           J. Cammerlander, 1541 [Fischer, 489].

.1.39. Prugner, Nicolaus, Practica Teutsch uff das 1543 jar.
           No printer, 1542 [Fischer, 43].

.1.40. Practica auffs MDXLIV Jar. Darinnen werden
         erschröckliche Finsternussen durch den Schreiber
         Esdram an Tag bracht.
           J. Cammerlander, 1543 [R Nfp, 2979].

.1.41. Carion, Johann and Mag. Salomon, Practica und
         Prognostication.
           J. Cammerlander, 1543 [R Nfp, 1294], 1544 [R Nfp,
             1296], 1545 [R Nfp, 1295].

.1.42. Ryff, Walter, Vorhersage für 1544.
           No printer, 1543 [Fischer, 482].

.1.43. Prugner, Nicolaus, Vorhersage für 1548.
           J. Cammerlander, 1547 [Fischer, 441]. (In Latin.)
           No printer, 1548 [Fischer, 436].
           W. Köpfel, 1551 [Fischer, 445], 1552 [Fischer,
             437].

.1.44. Kalendar für 1549.
           No printer, 1548 [Fischer, 620].

.1.45. Carion, Johann, Auszlegung der verborgenen wiessagung.
           W. Rihel, 1549 [R BNU I, 448].

.1.46. Kalendar für 1552.
           No printer, 1551 [Fischer, 621].

.1.47. Kalendar für 1560.
           No printer, 1559 [Fischer, 622].

.1.48. Kalendar für 1563.
           No printer, 1562 [Fischer, 619].

S12.1.49. Simitz, Theodor, <u>Vorhersage . . . für 1563-1566</u>.
           No printer, 1562 [Fischer, 530].

   .1.50. <u>Prognosticon . . . Practica . . . geprakitziert inn</u>
           <u>der Hochberümptet universitet, da man mit</u>
           <u>streugabeln schreibt (Spott-Vorhersage)</u>.
           No printer, 1563 [Fischer, 519].

   .1.51. <u>Kalendar für 1564</u>.
           No printer, 1563 [Fischer, 623].

   .1.52. Fabricius, Georg, <u>Vorhersage für 1565, deutsch</u>.
           T. Berger, ca. 1564 [Fischer, 212].

   .1.53. Hebenstreit, Johann Vorhersage. <u>Prognosticon</u>
           <u>historicum und physicum für 1566</u>.
              Chr. Mylius I, 1565 [R Nfp, 1960].

   .1.54. Dasypodius, Conrad, <u>Vorhersage für . . . .</u>
              T. Berger, 1569 [Fischer, 174], 1577 [Fischer,
              177], 1581 [Fischer, 178].
              N. Wyriot, 1574 [Fischer, 175], 1576 [Fischer,
              176].

   .1.55. Fischart, Johann, <u>Aller Practick Grossmutter</u>.
              B. Jobin, 1572 [R Nfp, 1725], 1573 [R Nfp, 1726],
              1574 [R Nfp, 1727], 1593 [R Nfp, 1728], 1598 [R
              BNU II, 865].

   .1.56. Carrichter, Bartholomaeus, <u>Practica . . . .</u>
              No printer, 1574 [Fischer, 163], 1578 [Fischer,
              164].

   .1.57. Starkenfelser, Henricus, <u>Practica für 1578</u>.
              N. Wyriot, 1577 [R Nfp, 3272].

   .1.58. Ursinus, Georgius and Weisse, Nicolaus, <u>Duo</u>
           <u>prognostica</u>.
              N. Wyriot, 1577 [R Nfp, 3385].

   .1.59. Weiss, Nicolaus, <u>Kalendar für 1578</u>.
              N. Wyriot, 1577 [Fischer, 593].

   .1.60. Weiss, Nicolaus, <u>Practica auf das Jahr 1578</u>.
              No printer, 1577 [Fischer, 594].

   .1.61. Schawjnsland, Urban, <u>Newe Zeit und Prophecy</u>.
           <u>Practica die best auss Himmels und Erden abgemerckt,</u>
           <u>geschriben und ausgelegt zu gut dem Menschen</u>.
              N. Wyriot, 1581 [R BNU IV, 2080].

   .1.62. <u>Kalendar für 1585</u>.
              No printer, 1584 [Fischer, 624].

   .1.63. Bathodius, Lucas, <u>Prognostication</u>.

N. Waldt, 1586 [R <u>Imp. Alsc.</u>, 347], 1587 [R <u>Imp.</u>
<u>Alsc.</u>, 347], 1588 [R Nfp, 941].
J. Martin, 1591 [R Nfp, 942], 1592 [R <u>Imp. Alsc.</u>,
575], 1593 [R Nfp, 943], 1594 [R Nfp, 944].
A. Bertram, 1595 [R Nfp, 945].

S12.1.64. <u>Prognosticon Theologicum, das ist, gaistliche grosse</u>
<u>practica ausz hailiger biblischer schrifft und</u>
<u>historien von der welt nahe und garausz. Inhaltend</u>
<u>die verwunderlichsten veränderungen im Kirchenstand.</u>
B. Jobin(?), 1588 [R Nfp, 2493].

.1.65. <u>Kalendar für 1589.</u>
No printer, 1588 [Fischer, 625].

S13. ASTRONOMICAL CALENDARS.

S13.1.1. <u>In diszen teütschen Kalendar findet man . . . die</u>
<u>zwelff zeichen. und die syben Planeten. Wie ein</u>
<u>itlicher regieren sol.</u>
M. Hupfuff, 1504 [S V, 32], 1511 [S V, 92], 1513
[S V, 111].

.1.2. Weber, Johann, <u>Lasz tafel auff das tausent</u>
<u>Fünffhundert und Dreyssiggest jar.</u>
No printer, 1530 [R BNU IV, 2452].

.1.3. <u>Kalendar new geordnet, mitt vielen underweisungen</u>
<u>der himmelischen Leuff.</u>
J. Cammerlander, 1534 [R Nfp, 2188].

.1.4. <u>Kalendarius der siben Planeten . . . Von dem</u>
<u>weitberhümpten Joanne Königsberger ausz dem Hyginio.</u>
J. Cammerlander, 1535 [R Nfp, 2189], 1536 [R Nfp,
2190], 1537 [R Nfp, 2191], 1538 [R Nfp, 2192],
1540 [R Nfp, 2193].

.1.5. Fink, Thomas, <u>Ephemeris caelestium motuum anni 1582.</u>
<u>Supputata ex Prutensis.</u>
N. Wyriot, 1582 [R Nfp, 1695].

.1.6. Malleolus, Isak, <u>Kalender.</u>
J. Martin, 1599 [R Nfp, 2588].

S14. ECCLESIASTICAL CALENDARS.

S14.1.1. <u>Kalendar. So man zalt nach Christi geburt MCCCCC</u>
<u>und XIII jar ist die gulden zal XXIII zal I. . . . .</u>
<u>Der Heyligen christlichen ordenung eins gemeinen</u>
<u>Kalendars Römischer X Sonntag buchstab B. Römischer</u>
<u>Kirchen.</u>
J. Schott, 1513 [R Nfp, 2187; S II B supp., 1].

S14.1.2.   Sequentie de tempore et sanctis per totum annum
            1516.
            J. Knobloch, 1516 [S VII, 118].

   .1.3.   Brunfels, Otto, Almanach ewig werend, Teütszch und
            Christlich Practick Von dem XXVI jar an, bitz zu
            endt der welt aller welt.
            J. Schött, 1526 [R BNU I, 278].

   .1.4.   Conrad von Dankrotzheim, Das Heilige Namenbuch.
            No printer, 1530 [R Nfp, 1431].

   .1.5.   Kalender der Strassburger Domherren.
            H. Preussen, 1548 [R Nfp, 2194], 1551 [R Nfp,
               2195].
            T. Berger, 1559 [R Nfp, 2196], 1562 [R Nfp, 2197].
            N. Waldt, 1584 [R Nfp, 2198].
            A. Bertram, 1584 [R Nfp, 2199].

S15. ASTROLOGY AND CHIROMANCY.

   1. ASTROLOGY.

S15.1.1.   Niphus, Augustinus (Agostino Nifo), De Diebus
            Criticis.
            H. Seybold, n.d. [R BNU III, 1637].

   .1.2.   Murner, Thomas, Investiva contra Astrologos.
            M. Hupfuff, 1499 [S V, 7].

   .1.3.   Fries, Laurentz, Schirmred der Kunst Astrologie
            . . . auch etliche antwurt uff die reden Luthers.
            J. Grüninger, 1520 [S I, 176].

   .1.4.   Tanstetter, Georgius Collimitius (Georg Tanstetter
            von Thannau), Artificium de Applicatione Astrologiae
            ad Medicinam.
            G. Ulricher, 1531 [R BNU IV, 2267].

   .1.5.   Geomanci eyn verborgene Kunst, der Astronomi
            anhengig, daraus der mensch durch dess gestirns
            influentz, alle seine anschleg . . . erlernen mag.
            J. Cammerlander, 1531 [B Cam., 40].

   .1.6.   Geomanci. Die viertzehen Weisen Meyster in der
            Geomanci.
            J. Cammerlander, ca. 1533 [B Cam., 41].

   .1.7.   Gruenbeck, Joseph (Joseph Gruenpeck), Practica der
            gegenwertigen grossen trübsaln so am himel
            erscheinen.
            J. Cammerlander, 1540 [BM 8610.b.b.].

S15.1.8.   Ryff, Walter, Iatromathematicae, hoc est,
           medicationis accommodatae ad Astrologicam rationem
           Enchiridion, de Crisi, deque investigatione et
           inventione dierum Criticorum, Indicativorum,
           Intercadentium, sive provocativorum, et Vacuorum,
           rationali modo et plane astrologico.
              G. Messerschmidt, 1542 [R BNU III, 2036].

   .1.9.   Eisenmenger, Samuel, Oratio de methodo
           iatromathematicae conjunctionis in qua astrologiae
           fundamenta certissima indicantur.
              J. Rihel, 1563 [R Nfp, 1537].

   .1.10. Roeslin, Helisaeus, Theoria nova Coelestium
           METEORON, in qua ex plurium cometarum phaenomenis
           epilogisticos quaedam afferuntur, de novis tertiae
           cuiusdam miraculorum Sphaerae circulis et
           regularissimo ad superioribus annis conspectam
           Stellam.
              B. Jobin, 1578 [R Nfp, 3123].

   .1.11. Ranzovius, Henricus (Henrik Rantzau), Methodus
           apodemica horoscopum.
              A. Bertram, 1581 [Fischer, 447].

   .1.12. Ranzovius, Henricus (Henrik Rantzau),
           Horoscopographia continens fabricus cardium
           coelestium . . . .
              A. Bertram, 1585 [Fischer, 446].

   .1.13. Astrologische Wahrsagung und Betrachtung des newen
           Kometen 1596.
              No printer, 1596 [Fischer, 663].

   .1.14. Astrologica Divinatio des Newen Cometen im Monat
           Julio dieses 1596 jars erschinen.
              J. Martin, 1596 [R Nfp, 1517].

   .1.15. Rösslin, Helisaeus, Tractatus
           Meteorastrologiphysicus. Das ist, Ausz richtigem
           lauff der Cometen, zusammenleuchtung der Planeten,
           etlicher Herrn Nativiteten, Natürliche Vermutungen
           und ein Weissagung.
              B. Jobin Erben, 1597 [R BNU III, 2028].

   2. CHIROMANCY AND PHYSIOGNOMY.

S15.2.1.   Chiromantia.
              J. Grüninger, 1500 [R Nfp Inc., 185].

   .2.2.   In diesem biechlein wirt erfunden von complexion der
           menschen zu erlernen leiblich unnd menschliche natur

ir siten, geberden und nayglichayt zu erkennen und
urtaylen.
    M. Hupfuff, 1511 [S V, 84].
    J. Knobloch, 1516 [S VII, 127].
    M. Flach II, 1519 [S VI B, 39; R Nfp, 1205].

S15.2.3. Ioanne Indagine (Johannes ab Indagine), Chiromanti.
    J. Schott, 1522 [S II B, 68], 1523 [S II B, 84],
      1531 [S II B, 120], 1534 [Fischer, 344], 1540
      [Zinner, 4748].
    J. Schött, 1540 [Fischer, 345]. (In Latin.)

.2.4. Coclitus, Barth. (Bartolommeo Cocles), Physionomey
und Ciromancey.
    J. Grüninger, 1524 [S I, 221].
    C. Egenolff, 1530 [B Egen., 19].
    J. Albrecht, 1533 [R BNU I, 555], 1534 [R BNU I,
      556], 1536 [R BNU I, 557].
    No printer, 1537 [Thorndike, Magic, 64-65].
    J. Cammerlander, 1541 [B Cam., 19].
    G. Messerschmidt, 1551 [R Nfp, 1412], 1544 [R Nfp,
      1413], 1555 [R BNU I, 558].

.2.5. Cocles Barth. (Bartolommeo Cocles), Phisionomei.
Eins ieden menschen Art, Natur und complexion . . . .
    C. Egenolff, 1530 [R Nfp, 1409].

.2.6. Ein newes Complexion Büchlin, Der menschen natur,
geburt, sitten . . . ausz der phisionomi der siben
Planeten, xii zichen unnd den xxxvi Bildern des
himmels.
    J. Cammerlander, ca. 1535 [B Cam., 20], 1537 [B
      Cam., 21], before 1539 [R BNU I, 571], 1540 [B
      Cam., 23].

.2.7. Creutzer, Peter, Das Kleyn Planeten Büchlin . . .
Ein jeden menschen Art, Natur und Complexion.
    J. Cammerlander, 1536 [B Cam., 25].

3. DREAM BOOKS.

S15.3.1. Ein newes Traum Büchlein, Von allerhandt Treumen
ausz heidnischen und götlichen geschrifften.
    J. Cammerlander, n.d. [R BNU IV, 2355].

.3.2. Ryff, Walter, Underweisung von den Träumen,
Erscheinungen und nächtlichen Gesichten.
    B. Beck, 1551 [R Nfp, 3139].

.3.3. Ryff, Walter, Troumbüchlin, Darinn warhafftig ausz
Natürlichen ursachen auch der alten und Weissagern

der Heyden . . . alle Tröum, . . . erfaren unnd
erlernet werden.
>S. Emmel, 1558 [R BNU III, 2042], 1566 [R Nfp,
>3140].

S16. ALCHEMY

>See also T1.10.8.

S16.1.1.   Hermes Trismegistus, Pimander.
>No printer, ca. 1500 [Hirsch, 133].

.1.2.   Ulstadius, Phillipus, Coelum Philosophorum Seu de
Secretis Naturae Liber.
>J. Grüninger, 1526 [S I, 229], 1527 [S I, 231],
>1528 [S I, 238].
>J. Cammerlander, 1536 [R BNU, 2366].

.1.3.   Geberus (Jabir ibn Haiyān), De Alchimi Libri Tres.
>J. Grüninger, 1529 [S I, 239], 1530 [S I, 245],
>1531 [S I, 251].
>L. Zetzner, 1598 [R BNU II, 938].

.1.4.   Kertzenmacher, Petrus, Alchimia wie man alle farben,
wasser, olea, salia und alumina machen soll.
>J. Cammerlander, 1538 [B Cam., 54], 1539 [R Nfp,
>2228], 1544 [R Nfp, 2227].

.1.5.   De Chemia Senioris Antiquissimi Philosophi Libellus,
ut Brevis, Ita artem discentibus, et exercentibus,
utilissimus et verè aureus . . . .
>S. Emmel, 1560 [R BNU III, 1360].

.1.6.   Ars chemica quod sit licita recte exercentibus . . .
VII Tractutus seu capitula Hermetis Trismegisti.
>S. Emmel, 1566 [R Nfp, 866].

.1.7.   Bernardus, Comes Treverensis (Bernardus Trevisanus),
(De alchimia) opus historicum et dogmaticum . . . . .
>S. Emmel, 1567 [R Nfp, 987].

.1.8.   Etschenreuter, Gallus (pseud.), or Bernardus
Trevisanus, Drachmolepton et Drachmotomiani.
>No printer, 1569 [Sitzmann I, 462].

.1.9.   Paracelsus, Theophrastus, Archidoxa. Von
heymlichkeyten der Natur. Item I De Tinctura
Physicorum. II. De occulta Philosophia.
>T. Rihel, 1570 [R BNU III, 1772].
>Chr. Mylius II, 1574 [R BNU III, 1778a].

.1.10. Paracelsus, De lapide philosophorum drey tractat.
>N. Wyriot, 1572 [BM 8632.b.25(4)].

S16.1.11.   Bernardus, Trevisanus, Von der Hermetischen
             Philosophia, das ist, von dem Gebenedeiten Stain der
             Weisen.
                  Chr. Mylius II, 1574 [R BNU I, 188].
                  Chr. Mylius II Erben, 1582 [R Nfp, 985].
                  A. Bertram, 1586 [R Nfp, 986].

    .1.12.   Paracelsus, Theophrastus, De Secretis Creationis.
             Von Heimligkeiten der Schöpfung aller dingen.
                  Chr. Mylius II, 1575 [R BNU III, 1780; R Nfp
                       3355].

    .1.13.   Ricardus Anglicus, I. Correctorium Alchymiae
             Richardi Anglici. Das ist Reformierte Alchimy.
                  B. Jobin, 1581 [R BNU III, 2014].

S17. WITCHCRAFT.

S17.1.1.   (Wecker, Johann Jacob), Hexen Büchlein, das ist,
             ware entdeckung und erklärung, oder Declaration
             fürnämlicher artickel der Zauberey, und was von
             Zauberern, Unholden, Hengsten, Nachtschaden,
             Schützet. . . . Allen Vögten, Schultheyssen,
             Amptleüten oder Amptsverwaltern, und Regenten des
             weltlichen Schwerdts und Regiments nutzlich zu lesen.
                  No printer, n.d. [R BNU II, 1164], 1575 [Greiner].

    .1.2.   Molitor, Ulrich, De Lamiis et phitonicis mulieribus.
                  M. Flach, 1489 [R BNU Inc., 330].

    .1.3.   Murner, Thomas, Tractatus de phytonico contractu.
                  M. Hupfuff, 1499 [R BNU Inc., 332].

    .1.4.   Nider, Johannes, Formicarius.
                  J. Knobloch, 1517 [S VII, 143].
                  J. Schott, 1517 [S II B, 39].

    .1.5.   Molitor, Ulrich, Hexen Meystery. [Blättchen] Deb
             . . . Hertzog Sigmunds von Osterreich mit D. Ulrich
             Molitoris und herr Conrad Schatz . . . ein schön
             gesprech von den Onholden . . . .
                  J. Cammerlander, 1545 [B Cam., 70].

    .1.6.   Molitoris, Ulricus, Von Hexen und Unholden. Ein
             Christlicher, nutzlicher . . . notwendiger Bericht,
             ausz Gottes wort, geistlichen und weltlichen
             Rechten auch sonst allerley historien gezogen.
                  Chr. Mylius II, 1575 [R Bib. Mun., 1501].

    .1.7.   Bodin, Johann (Jean Bodin), De Daemonomania Magorum,
             Vom Ausgelasznen Wütigen Teuffelsheer der Besessenen

Unsinnigen Hexen und Hexenmeyster . . . .
   B. Jobin, 1581 [R BNU I, 221], 1586 [R BNU I,
     222], 1591 [R BNU I, 223].

S17.1.8.   Fischart, Johann, Malleus maleficarum.
          L. Zetzner, 1582 [R Nfp, 1723].

  .1.9.   Warhaffte . . . Zeyttung. Von Hundert und vier und
dreyssig Unholden. So umb jrer Zaubery halben disz
verschinen 1582. Jars zu gefencknus gebracht, und
den 15. 19. 24. 29. October auff jhr unmenschliche
thaten und gräwliche auszag unnd Bekandtnus, mit
rechtem Urtheyl, zum Fewer verdampt und verbrennet
worden.
     N. Wyriot, 1583 [R BNU IV, 2520].

PROTESTANT LITERATURE

P1. Protestant Doctrine and Theology.

   1. Martin Luther.
   2. The Eucharist.
   3. Philipp Melanchthon.
   4. Other Protestant Theology.
   5. Religious Councils and Attempts at Religious Settlement.
   6. Catechisms and Other Books of Instruction.
   7. Marriage.
   8. Strasbourg Theologians.
   9. Confessions of Faith.

P2. Protestant Sermons.

   1. Martin Luther.
   2. Local Reformers.
   3. Other Sermons.
   4. Funeral Sermons.

P3. Anti-Catholic Polemic.

   1. Martin Luther.
   2. Ulrich von Hutten.
   3. Laymen.
   4. English Polemic and Statements of Faith.
   5. General Polemic by Other German and Swiss Reformers.
   6. Anti-Papal Polemic.
   7. Marriage of the Clergy.
   8. Appeals to the German Nation for Ecclesiastical Reform.
   9. Defenses of Martin Luther.
  10. Philipp Melanchthon and Other Wittenberg Theologians.
  11. Strasbourg Reformers.
  12. Otto Brunfels.
  13. Polemic against Episcopal Authority.
  14. French Polemical Tracts and Treatises.
  15. Polemic against the Council of Trent.
  16. Johann Fischart.
  17. The Bishop's War.

P4. Intra-Protestant Controversy and Anabaptism.

   1. Anabaptist, Spiritualist, and Sectarian Tracts.
   2. Polemic against Anabaptists and Sectarians.
   3. Reports on the Anabaptists.

    4.   The Sturm-Pappus Controversy and the Spangenberg-Pistorius
       Controversy.

P5. Protestant Devotionals, Prayerbooks, and Service Books for
      Lay Use.

P6. Protestant Hymnals and Devotional Songs.

    1.   Collections of Hymns for Congregational Singing.
    2.   Church Music for Choirs.
    3.   Popular Spiritual Songs.

P7. Protestant Manuals for the Clergy.

    1.   Protestant Postils.
    2.   Liturgies.

P8. Protestant Martyrologies.

P1. PROTESTANT DOCTRINE AND THEOLOGY.

   1. MARTIN LUTHER.

P1.1.1.   Theologia teütsch (Preface by Martin Luther).
           J. Knobloch, 1519 [S VII, 178], 1520 [S VII, 197].

   .1.2.   Ein heilsams Büchlein . . . von der Beycht gemacht.
           J. Knobloch, 1520 [B Luther, 626].

   .1.3.   Von der Freyhayt Aines Christenmenschen.
           J. Prüss II, 1520 [B Luther, 740], 1521 [S III B, 28].
           R. Beck, 1520 [R Nfp, 2501].
           J. Knobloch, 1521 [R Nfp, 2502].
           M. Schürer Erben, 1522 [B SE 3, 7].
           W. Köpfel, 1524 [B Luther, 749].

   .1.4.   Von der Beycht, ob die der Bapst macht hab zu gebieten.
           J. Prüss II, 1522 [R Nfp, 2471].
           W. Köpfel, 1522 [R Nfp, 2472].

   .1.5.   Ein treü ermanung zu allen Christen. Sich zu verhuten
           vor auffrur und Emporung.
           J. Knobloch, 1522 [B Luther, 1051].

   .1.6.   De Abroganda Missa Privata.
           U. Morhard, 1522 [B Luther, 998].

   .1.7.   Von weltlicher Oberkeit, wie weit man ir gehorsam
           schuldig sey.
           J. Prüss II, 1523 [R Nfp, 2525].

   .1.8.   Vom Glauben und Wercken.
           J. Knobloch, 1523 [B Luther, 1602].

   .1.9.   Ordenung eyns gemeynen kastens. Radschlag wie die
           geystlichen gütter zu handeln sind.
           J. Knobloch, 1523 [B Luther, 1611].

   .1.10. Meynen lieben Herren und fründen, in Christo allen
           Christlichen burgern zu Esslingen.
           J. Prüss II, 1523 [S III B, 35].

   .1.11. Ein Sendbrieff über die frag, ob auch yemant On glauben
           verstorben, selig werden mug.
           M. Schürer Erben, 1523 [B Luther, 1271].

   .1.12. Von weltlicher Oberkeit wie weit mannyhr gehorsam
           schüldig sey.
           W. Köpfel, 1523 [B Luther, 1513; Pegg, 2874].

   .1.13. Von zweyerley menschen, wie sie sich in dem glauben
           halten sollen und was der sey.
           M. Schürer Erben, 1523 [B SE 2, 37].

Pl.1.14. Ein brieff an die Christen im Nyderland.
          M. Schürer Erben, 1523 [B SE 3, 13].

   .1.15. Von ordenung gottes dienst in der gemeyne.
          M. Schürer Erben, 1523 [B SE 2, 38].

   .1.16. Von Kauffshandlung und Wucher.
          W. Köpfel, 1524 [B Luther, 1941], 1525 [B Luther,
          1942; R Nfp, 2566].

   .1.17. De Sublimiore Mundi Postestate.
          J. Herwagen, 1525 [B Luther, 1519].

   .1.18. Methodus, Quid in Evangeliis quaerendum sit docens.
          J. Herwagen, ca. 1525 [B Luther, 2002].

   .1.19. Precationum aliquot et piarum meditationum Enchiridion.
          J. Herwagen, 1525 [B Luther, 18].

   .1.20. Die Christi Jesu ex Judaeis ortu, matrisque eius Mariae
          Virginitate . . . (Johannes Lonicer, trans.).
          J. Knobloch, 1525 [S VII, 297].

   .1.21. De servo arbitrio.
          W. Köpfel, 1526 [R Nfp, 2569].

   .1.22. Ob Kriegsleüt auch in seligem stande seyn künden.
          J. Knobloch, 1527 [R BNU III, 1436].

   .1.23. Wessel, Joannes, Das die underthanen beyder geystlicher
          und weltlicher oberkeyten ettwan nit zugehorsamen
          sonder jnen zewidersteen, und sie von jren ämptern
          abzesetzen schuldig sind (M. Luther, ed.).
          W. Köpfel, 1530 [Pegg, 3882].

   .1.24. Hus, Johann, Etliche Briefe Iohannis Hus des Heyligen
          Merterers, ausz dem gefängniisz zu Constentz geschriben
          (M. Luther, ed.).
          W. Rihel, 1537 [R BNU II, 1222].

   .1.25. Treatise of the cohabytacion of the faithfull.
          W. Rihel, 1555 [R Nfp, 2573].

   .1.26. Ein Christlich Urtheyl D. Mart. Luthers von seinen
          eygen Büchern. Sampt einer Unterricht . . . wenn man in
          der heiligen Schrifft Recht studirn, und darnach gute
          Bücher schreiben will.
          No printer, 1578 [R BNU III, 1453].

     2. THE EUCHARIST.

Pl.2.1.   Von den Empfahern: Zeichen: und zusag des heyligen
          Sacraments, fleysch und blüt Christi.
          J. Prüss II, 1521 [S III B, 29].

P1.2.2.   Luther, Martin, <u>Von beider gestalt des Sacraments zu</u>
          <u>nehmen und ander neürung.</u>
          M. Schürer Erben, 1522 [B <u>Luther</u>, 1167].

   .2.3.   Luther, Martin, <u>Von anbetten des Sacraments des Heyligen</u>
          <u>Leichnas Christi.</u>
          M. Schürer Erben, 1523 [B <u>Luther</u>, 1590], 1524 [B <u>SE</u>
             <u>2</u>, 54].
          See also P3.11.13. (Bucer's Response.)

   .2.4.   Luther, Martin, <u>Das Hauptstück des . . . neuen</u>
          <u>Testaments von dem hochwirdigen Sacrament beyder</u>
          <u>gestalt.</u>
          M. Schürer Erben, 1523 [B <u>Luther</u>, 1334], 1524 [B
             <u>SE 2</u>, 56], 1524 [B <u>SE 2</u>, 57].

   .2.5.   Bucer, Martin, <u>Grund und ursach ausz gotlicher schrifft</u>
          <u>d'neüwerungen, an dem nachtmal des herren, so man die</u>
          <u>Mess nennet, Tauff, Feyrtagen, bildern und gesang.</u>
          W. Köpfel, 1525 [R Nfp, 1162], 1525 [R BNU I, 353].

   .2.6.   Oecolampadius, Joannes, <u>De Genuina Verborum Domini,</u>
          <u>Hoc est corpus meum, iuxta vetustissimos authores</u>
          <u>expositione liber.</u>
          No printer, 1525 [R Nfp, 2787].

   .2.7.   <u>Von dem brot und weyn des Herren Christlicher beriecht.</u>
          W. Köpfel, 1525 [Pegg, 162].
          See also P3.5.21.

   .2.8.   <u>Das von wegen des herren nachtmals brüderliche lieb</u>
          <u>nit soll zertrennt werden und von worem inhalt der</u>
          <u>zeychen.</u>
          W. Köpfel, 1526 [Pegg, 3304a].

   .2.9.   <u>Trostbuechlein für die klainmütigen und einfeltigen,</u>
          <u>die sich ergern, der Spaltung halb, ausz dem Nachtmal</u>
          <u>Christi erwachssen, . . . bericht, wie sich ain yede</u>
          <u>Christ in dieser Spaltung halten soll.</u>
          No printer, 1526 [R Nfp, 3373].

   .2.10. <u>Ein Christlicher Bericht von dem Brot und weyn desz</u>
          <u>Herren.</u>
          No printer, 1526 [R Nfp, 979].

   .2.11. <u>Warer verstand von des herren Nachtmal. Uff die weysz</u>
          <u>zu singen: Es ist das hayl uns komen her. . . .</u>
          W. Köpfel, 1527 [R Nfp, 3400].

   .2.12. Butzer, Martin (Martin Bucer), <u>Vergleichung D. Luthers,</u>
          <u>unnd seins gegentheyls, vom Abentmal Christi. Dialogus.</u>
          <u>Das ist, eyn freundlich gesprech.</u>
          W. Köpfel, 1528 [R BNU I, 357].

P1.2.13.   Luther, Martin, <u>Wie sich D. Martin Luther unnd Huldrych</u>
           <u>Zwinglin. In der Sum christlicher Leer, gleichformig</u>
           <u>zu sein, befunden habe.</u>
               B. Beck, 1529 [B <u>Luther</u>, 2741].

   .2.14.   Butzer, Martin (Martin Bucer), <u>Bericht ausz der heyligen</u>
           <u>geschrift von der recht gottseligen anstellung und</u>
           <u>hauszhaltung Christlicher gemeyn, Eynsatzung der</u>
           <u>diener des worts, Haltung und brauch der heyligen</u>
           <u>Sacramenten . . . Von dem H. Sacrament des leybs,</u>
           <u>unnd blüts unsers Herrn Jesu. . . .</u>
               M. Apiarius, 1534 [R BNU I, 368].

   .2.15.   Luther, Martin, <u>Vermanung zum Sacrament des Leibes und</u>
           <u>Bluts unsers Herren.</u>
               W. Rihel, 1541 [B <u>Luther</u>, 2836].
               N. Wyriot, 1584 [R Bib. Mun., 1440].

   .2.16.   Luther, Martin, <u>Kurtz bekentnis . . . vom heiligen</u>
           <u>Sacrament.</u>
               W. Rihel, ca. 1545 [B <u>Luther</u>, 3463].

   .2.17.   Westerburg, Gerhard (Gerhard Westerburch), <u>Von dem</u>
           <u>anbetten des H. Sacraments ein kurtzer Bericht.</u>
               W. Rihel, 1545 [Pegg, 3887].

   .2.18.   Westphal, Joachim, <u>Recta fides de coena domini, ex</u>
           <u>verbis apostoli Pauli & evangelistorum demonstrata ac</u>
           <u>communita.</u>
               B. Fabricius, 1555 [R BNU IV, 2456].

   .2.19.   Schnepff, Erhardus, <u>Confessio . . . de eucharistia,</u>
           <u>hanc ob causam, hoc potissimum tempore edita. . . .</u>
               B. Fabricius, 1555 [R BNU IV, 2088].

   .2.20.   Ponet, John (Bishop of Rochester and Winchester),
           <u>Diallacticon de veritate corporis et sanguinis Christi</u>
           <u>in Eucharistia.</u>
               T. Rihel, 1557 [BM 4324.aaa.2].

   .2.21.   Butzer, Martin (Martin Bucer), <u>Nova Vetera Quatuor</u>
           <u>Eucharistica Scripta Summi & acutissimi Theologi . . .</u>
           <u>M. Buceri. Joannis Sturmii, Renovatus Dolor de hoc.</u>
           <u>dissidio Eucharistico.</u>
               T. Berger, 1561 [R BNU I, 391].

   .2.22.   Eber, Paul, <u>Vom Heyligen Sacrament des Leibs und Bluts</u>
           <u>unsers Herren Jesu Christi.</u>
               Chr. Mylius I, 1562 [R BNU II, 670], 1563 [R BNU II,
               671].

   .2.23.   Marbach, Johannes, <u>Christlicher und warhaffter</u>
           <u>underricht von den worten der Einsatzung des Heyligen</u>

Abendmals. . . .
> Chr. Mylius I, 1565 [R Bib. Mun., 1458], 1566 [R BNU III, 1481].

P1.2.24.   Marbach, Johannes, Christlicher Underricht . . . Das Jhesus Christus . . . nit nur mit dem blossen Nammen, sonder warhafftig, und mit der That, erhaben und gesetzt seye.
> Chr. Mylius I, 1567 [R BNU III, 1482].

  .2.25.   Praetorius, Abdias, De discrimine sententiarum Lutheri, Sacramentariorum & Pontificiorum. In materia Dominicae Caenae. . . .
> S. Emmel, 1567 [R Nfp, 2981].

  .2.26.   Selneccer, Nicolaus, Libellus brevis . . . de Coena Domini Editus.
> Chr. Mylius I, 1568 [R BNU IV, 2112].

  .2.27.   Florus, Nicolaus, Kurtze . . . erinnerung etlicher hochwichtigen ursachen, die einen Christen bewegen sollen das H. Abendmal gern und oft zu entpfahen. Item. Gründliche Widerlegung etlicher ursachen, so vil Lëut auffhalten, das sie das Heilig Abendmal gar nicht oder ja selten entpfahen.
> T. Berger, 1579 [R Nfp, 1742].

  .2.28.   Giftheil, Joachim. In materiam de Coena Domini communefactio.
> N. Wyriot, 1580 [R Nfp, 1904].
> See also P2.3.20; P4.4.1; P4.4.2.

   3.   PHILIPP MELANCHTHON.

P1.3.1.   Die Haupt artickel, und fürnemesten puncten der gantzen heyligen schrifft durch Magister Philippem Melancthon Lateinisch gemacht, unnd volgend verteuscht. . . .
> J. Knobloch, 1522 [S VII, 252].

  .3.2.   Underscheyd zwyschen weltlicher und Christlicher Fromkeyt.
> M. Schürer Erben, 1522 [B SE 3, 11].
> J. Prüss II, 1530 [BM. 3906.d.81.3].

  .3.3.   Loci Communes seu Hypotyposes Theologicae.
> J. Herwagen, January 1523 [R BNU III, 1513], June 1523 [R BNU III, 1514].
> J. Knobloch, 1525 [S VII, 290].
> J. Albrecht, 1536 [R BNU III, 1535].

  .3.4.   Epitome Renovatae Ecclesiasticae Doctrinae.
> J. Knobloch, 1524 [R BNU III, 1517].

.3.5.   De ecclesiae autoritate et de veterum scriptis libellus.
         W. Rihel, ca. 1539 [Pegg, 3070].

.3.6.   Corpus Doctrinae Christianae.
         T. Rihel, 1580 [R BNU III, 1562].

4.   OTHER PROTESTANT THEOLOGY.

P1.4.1. Strauss, Jacob, Ein verstendige tröstlich Leer über
         das wort Sanct Paulus, Der mensch sol sich selbs
         probieren.
         M. Flach II, 1522 [Pegg, 3774].

.4.2.   Strauss, Jacob, Haubtstuck unnd Artikel Christlicher
         leer wider den wucher.
         J. Schwann, 1523 [Pegg, 3762].

.4.3.   Westerburg, Gerhard (Gerhard Westerburch), Vom fegefewer
         und standt der verscheyden selen.
         J. Schott, 1523 [Pegg, 3886].

.4.4.   Zwingli, Ulrich, Artickel so herr Vlrich zwingly uff
         Dornstag von Lyechtmessz Anno MD.xxiii. offentlich
         dispütiert.
         J. Schott, 1523 [Pegg, 3982].

.4.5.   Ein schone: geystliche: und der heyligen gschrifft
         gegründte underweisung von wegen der gelübdten.
         M. Schürer Erben, 1523 [B SE 3, 27].

.4.6.   Ein tractat in dem anzeygt würt wie der inwendig und
         usswendig mensch widereinander und bey einander sein.
         J. Schwann, 1524 [Pegg, 3807].

.4.7.   Keller, Andreas, Berycht wie Christus alleyn der voll
         Brun sey aller gnaden.
         M. Schürer Erben, 1524 [BM T.2165.111].

.4.8.   Keller, Andreas, Trachtechlin von der Barmhertzigkeit
         Gottes.
         J. Schwann, 1524 [BM T.2165.8].

.4.9.   Keller, Andreas, Ein schöner schrifftlicher bericht
         auss heyliger schrifft was der Alt und d'Neuw mensch
         sey. . . .
         M. Schürer Erben, 1524 [B SE 2, 47].

.4.10.   Keller, Andreas, Ein Kurtzer begriff deren puncte so
         yetzunder von etlichen als ein neüwe lere genent werden.
         M. Schürer Erben, 1524 [B SE 2, 46].

.4.11.   Bugenhagen, Johann, Was und weliches die sünd sey in
         den heyligen geyst davon sanct Mattheus am .xii. cap.

redt.
> M. Schürer Erben, 1524 [B SE 3, 28].

P1.4.12. Adler, Caspar (Caspar Aquila), Trostliche ermanung zu allem Evangelischen predigern.
> J. Schwann, 1524 [BM 3906.b.46].

.4.13. Bugenhagen, Johann, and Melanchthon, Philipp, Etliche Christliche bedencken von der Mess unnd andern Ceremonien.
> M. Schürer Erben, 1525 [B SE 1, 31].

.4.14. Rhegius, Urbanus, Ob das new Testament yetz recht verteütscht sey. . . .
> M. Schürer Erben, 1525 [B SE 2, 74].

.4.15. Schwebel, Johann, Hauptstück und summa des gantzen Evangeliums und war innen ein Christlich leben stet.
> M. Schürer Erben, 1525 [B SE 3, 42].

.4.16. Rhegius, Urbanus (Simon Hessus), Nova doctrina.
> J. Knobloch, 1526 [Pegg, 3463].

.4.17. Gemein reformacion und verbesserung der biszhargebrachten verwändten gotzdiensten und Ceremonien(in Bern).
> J. Prüss II, 1528 [Pegg, 169a].

.4.18. Corvinus, Antonius, Colloquiorum theologicorum libro duo.
> W. Köpfel, 1537 [Pegg, 568].

.4.19. Calvin, Ioannis, Institutio Christiannae Religionis.
> W. Rihel, 1539 [R BNU I, 404], 1543 [R BNU I, 407], 1545 [R BNU I, 409].
> J. Rihel, 1561 [R BNU I, 413].

.4.20. Corvinus, Antonius, Colloquia theologica.
> W. Köpfel, 1540 [Pegg, 567; R Nfp, 1444].

.4.21. Jacobus, Minor, Protevangelion . . . Accessit huic Dialogus quidam Christiani cum Judaeo de Christo, ex Suidae Philologia.
> J. Rihel, 1570 [R Nfp, 2139].

.4.22. Hiemeyer, David, Ernewerung der Kirchen bei den Barfüssern im Spital . . . zu Colmar.
> N. Waldt, 1575 [R Nfp, 2015].

.4.23. Heerbrandt, Jacobus, Epitome compendii Theologiae. Kurtzer Auszzug der Fürnembsten Hauptstücke heyliger, Göttlicher, Christlicher Lehr.
> N. Waldt, 1587 [R Nfp, 1969].

.4.24. Crusius, Paulus, Collatio de formis loquendi quibus utimur in descriptione peccati originalis . . . De

bonis operibus. . . .
    J. Martin, 1598 [R Nfp, 1469].

5. RELIGIOUS COUNCILS AND ATTEMPTS AT RELIGIOUS SETTLEMENT.

Pl.5.1.   Ein kurtzer bericht von einem zukünfftigen Concilio.
          J. Schott, 1522 [Pegg, 167].

.5.2.   Luther, Martin, Bekentnus Doctoris M. Luthers auff den
          yetzigen Angestelten Reychstag zu Augsburg einzulegen,
          in Siebenzehen Artickel verfasset.
          W. Köpfel, 1530 [B Luther, 2855].

.5.3.   Butzer, Martin (Martin Bucer), Furbereytung zum
          Concilio, wie alle recht Gotszfortigen von beden, yetz
          fürnemmen theylen . . . alt und new gleubige,
          Bapsttische, und Lutherische, . . . zu einigkeit
          Christlicher kirchen kommen.
          M. Apiarius, 1533 [R BNU I, 364].

.5.4.   Auszschreybung eines Heyligen Freyen Christlichen
          Concilii.
          J. Frölich, 1535 [Pegg, 531].

.5.5.   Ursachenn warumb das Concilium so bapst Paulus d'dritt
          aussgeschriben hat noch zubesuchen sei. Durch die
          Churfursten zu Schmalkalden geschriben.
          W. Rihel, 1537 [Pegg, 1228].

.5.6.   Luther, Martin, Von den Conciliis und Kirchen M.D.XXXIX.
          Cr. Mylius, 1539 [R Nfp, 2484].

.5.7.   N.N. Decanus (Martin Bucer), An statui et dignitati
          ecclesiasticorum magis conducat admittere synodum
          nationalem quam decernere bello. Epistolae duae Decani
          et Canonici cuiusdam.
          No printer, 1540 [Pegg, 3218].

.5.8.   Butzer, Martin (Martin Bucer), Vom tag zu Hagenaw, und
          wer verhinderet hab, das kein gesprech von vergleichung
          der Religion, daselbst fürgangen ist.
          No printer, 1540 [R BNU I, 374].

.5.9.   Butzer, Martin (Martin Bucer), Acta Colloquii in Comitiis
          Imperii Ratisponae Habiti. Hoc Est Articuli de religione
          conciliati, et non conciliati omnes. . . .
          No printer, 1541 [R BNU I, 377], 1542 [R BNU I, 379].

.5.10.   Butzer, Martin (Martin Bucer), Alle Handlungen und
          Schrifften, zu vergleichung der Religion . . . auff
          jungst gehaltnem Reichstag zu Regenspurg verhandlet und

einbracht.
        W. Rihel, 1541 [R BNU I, 378].

Pl.5.11.   Melanchthon, Philipp, Confession de la Foy presentée à
            Charles V à la Journée d'Augsburg.
                G. Messerschmidt, 1543 [Peter, X].

    .5.12.   Butzer, Martin (Martin Bucer), De Concilio, et Legitime
             Iudicandis Controversiis Religionis, Criminum, Quae in
             M. Bucerum Ioh. Cochlaeus ad S. Ro. Imperii . . . et
             quae Ioh. Gropperus ad Maiest. Imperatoriam perscripsit,
             Confutatio.
             Epistola Io. Cochlaei ad eosdem ordines in Mart. Bucerum.
                G. Messerschmidt, 1545 [R BNU I, 380].

    .5.13.   Butzer, Martin (Martin Bucer), Ein warhafftiger berichte
             vom Colloquio zu Regenspurg, dis jars angefangen. . . .
                No printer, 1546 [R BNU I, 387; R BNU I, 388].
                W. Rihel, 1546 [R Nfp, 1176].

    6. CATECHISMS AND OTHER BOOKS OF INSTRUCTION.

Pl.6.1.   (Brother Lukas of Prague), Ein christliche Underweysung
            der Kleinen Kinder im Glaube.
                J. Prüss II, 1523 [BM 124.a.22.2].

    .6.2.   Linck, Wenceslaus, Hie auff Gottes wort allein aller
             christen furnemen erbauwet sein soll.
                J. Prüss II, 1523 [BM 3906.g.48].

    .6.3.   Zell, Matthaeus, Frag und Antwort, auff die Artickel
             des Christlichen Glaubens . . . zu einer erklärung der
             selbigen, für die Kinder.
                B. Beck, 1525 [R BNU IV, 2516].
                J. Frölich, 1535 [R Nfp, 3622].

    .6.4.   Christlich frag und antwort den glauben und liebe
             betreffent.
                W. Köpfel, 1526 [Pegg, 1109].

    .6.5.   Capito, Wolfgang, Kinderbericht und fragstuck von
             gemeynen puncten Christlichs glaubens.
                W. Köpfel, 1527 [R BNU I, 442], 1529 [R BNU I, 443].

    .6.6.   Butzer, Martin (Martin Bucer), Kurtze schrifftliche
             erklärung für die kinder und angohnden . . . Der
             gemeinen artickeln unsers christlichen glaubens.
                M. Apiarius, 1534 [R BNU I, 370].

    .6.7.   Luther, Martin, Enchiridion Catechismi M.L. pro pueris
             instituendis.
                W. Rihel, 1536 [B Luther, 2633b].

Pl.6.8. Bucer, Martin, <u>Der kurtzer Catechismus . . . Für die</u>
         <u>schüler und andere kinder zu Strasburg.</u>
         W. Rihel, 1537 [R Nfp, 1146], 1544 [R Nfp, 1147].

  .6.9. Otter, Jacob, <u>Christliche inleytung in die erkantnus</u>
         <u>Recht geschafner leer und glaubens in frag weiss für</u>
         <u>die gar jungen kinder gestellt.</u>
         J. Cammerlander, after 1538 [B <u>Cam.</u>, 87].

  .6.10. Luther, Martin, <u>Parvus Catechismus Pro Pueris in schola.</u>
         J. Frölich, 1542 [B <u>Luther</u>, 2647], 1545 [B <u>Luther</u>,
         2651].

  .6.11. Calvin, Ioannis, <u>Catechismus Ecclesiae Genevensis, hoc</u>
         <u>est, formula erudiendi pueros in doctrina Christi.</u>
         W. Rihel, 1545 [R BNU I, 408].

  .6.12. (Martin Bucer, und die Prediger und Pfarren der Kirchen
         zu Straszburg), <u>Ein Summarischer vergriff der</u>
         <u>Christlichen lere und Religion die man zu Straszburg</u>
         <u>hat nun in die xxviii. Jar gelehret.</u>
         W. Köpfel, 1548 [R BNU IV, 2400; BM 3908.e.5.2.].

  .6.13. Marbach, Johannes . . ., <u>Ein Vermanung an die jungen</u>
         <u>Knaben und Töchterlin in der Vorbereitung, wann sie</u>
         <u>. . . das Hochw. Sacrament Jesu Christi entpfahen</u>
         <u>wöllent.</u>
         S. Emmel, 1552 [R Nfp, 2597], 1554 [R Bib. Mun.,
         2157].

  .6.14. Brentius, Johannes (Johann Brenz), <u>Catechismus pro</u>
         <u>iuventute.</u>
         No printer, 1555 [R Nfp, 1068].

  .6.15. <u>Catechismus: Christliche Underrichtung oder Lehrtafel</u>
         <u>in sechs nachfolgende stuck verfasset. . . . Für die</u>
         <u>Pfarrherr, Schulmeyster, Hauszvätter, Jugent und</u>
         <u>Lehrkinder zu Straszburg.</u>
         S. Emmel, 1559 [R Nfp, 1305].
         T. Berger, ca. 1562 [R BNU I, 467].
         Chr. Mylius I, 1564 [R Nfp, 1306].
         B. Jobin, 1578 [R Nfp, 1305a].
         A. Bertram, 1585 [R Nfp, 1307]. (includes verses by
           Fischart)
         B. Jobin, 1591 [R Nfp, 1305a]. (includes verses by
           Fischart)

  .6.16. Luther, Martin, <u>Der kleyne Catechismi für die Gemeyne</u>
         <u>Pfarrher und Prediger.</u>
         S. Emmel, 1560 [R BNU I, 468], 1570 [R Nfp, 2482].

  .6.17. <u>Etliche Christliche Frag und Antwort gestellt zu einem</u>

eingang in den Catechismus oder Kinderlehr.
Chr. Mylius I, 1565 [R Nfp, 1308].

P1.6.18. Kessler, Isaac, Kurtz Examen und underricht vom Sacrament
des heyligen Abentmals Christi . . . für die Christliche
Jugendt zu Straszburg.
S. Emmel, 1566 [R BNU II, 1308].

.6.19. Bucer, Martin, Catechismus, Christliche underrichtung.
T. Berger, 1567 [R Nfp, 1149].

.6.20. (Calvin, Jean?), ABC: ou instruction des chretiens.
N. Wyriot, 1568 [R Nfp, 722; Peter, XXXV].

.6.21. Luther, Martin, Catechismus . . . minor, latino graecus,
cum explicatione orthodoxa . . . Item praecationes et
cantiones quaedam sacrae, unà cum legibus Scholae
Argentinensis.
S. Emmel, 1568 [R Bib. Mun., 1435].

7. MARRIAGE.

P1.7.1. Luther, Martin, Das Eltern die Kinder zu der Ee nit
zwingen oder hindern.
J. Schwann, 1524 [B Luther, 1911].

.7.2. Brentius, Johannes (Johann Brenz), Wie in Ehesachen .
. . Christenlich zu handeln sey.
B. Beck, 1529 [R Nfp, 1071], 1530 [R Nfp, 1072].

.7.3. Melanchthon, Philipp, De coniugio piae commonefactiones.
A. Fries, 1551 [R Nfp, 2629].

.7.4. Spangenberg, Cyriacus, Ehespiegel.
S. Emmel, 1567 [R BNU IV, 2169].
T. Rihel, 1570 [R BNU IV, 2171], 1578 [R BNU IV, 2172].

.7.5. F. P. H., Epithalamion von der heiligkeit, nutz und
noht desz Ehestandsz.
No printer, 1579 [R Nfp, 1678].

8. STRASBOURG THEOLOGIANS.

P1.8.1. Bucer, Martin, Erhaltung christlicher Leer bitzhär zu
Straszburg gepredigt.
J. Schott, 1524 [R Nfp, 1159].
See also P2.2.1.

.8.2. Brunnfelsius, Othonis, Problemata. I. De ratione
evangeliorum. II. Quare in Parabolis locutus sit
Christus.
J. Schott, 1524 [S II B, 89].

P1.8.3.   Lambert, Francois, Farrago omnium fere rerum
           Theologicarum.
              J. Herwagen, 1525 [BM 847.L.10].

  .8.4.   Lambertus, Franciscus, De fidelium vocatione in regnum
           Christi.
              (J. Herwagen ?), 1525 [R Nfp, 2264].

  .8.5.   Capito, Wolfgang, Epistola ad Hulderichum Zuinglium.
              W. Köpfel, 1526 [R BNU I, 440].

  .8.6.   Bucer, Martin, Apologia . . . qua fidei suae atque
           doctrinae, circa Christi Caenam, qua, tum ipse, tum
           alii Ecclesiastae Argentoratenses profitentur, rationem
           simpliciter Reddit. . . .
              J. Herwagen, 1526 [R Nfp, 1144].

  .8.7.   Bucer, Martin, Praefatio in quartum tomum Postillae
           Lutheranae, continens summam doctrinae Christi.
              J. Herwagen, 1527 [R BNU I, 355].

  .8.8.   Lambertus Franciscus, Sendbrieff . . . geschrieben
           nach dem Religionsgespräch zu Marburg.
              No printer, 1529 [R Nfp, 2267].

  .8.9.   Butzer, Martin (Martin Bucer), Das einigerlei Bild bei
           den Gotgläubigen, an orten da sie verehrt, nit mögen
           geduldet werden, helle anzeyg, ausz Göttlicher Schrifft.
           . . . durch die Prediger der Kirchen Christi zu
           Straszburg.
              No printer, 1530 [R BNU I, 359; R Nfp, 1012].

  .8.10.   Butzer, Martin (Martin Bucer), Non esse ferendas in
           templis Christianorum imagines et statvas . . .
           Autoribus Ecclesiasticis Argentoraten.
              No printer, 1530 [R BNU I, 360].

  .8.11.   Lambertus, Franciscus, De symbolo foederis.
              No printer, 1530 [R Nfp, 2268].

  .8.12.   Capito, Wolfgang, Hexemeron Dei Opus explicatum a
           Vuolphgango Fa. Capitone.
              W. Rihel, 1539 [R BNU I, 444].

  .8.13.   Bucer, Martin, Von Kirchen guetern. Wes deren besitz
           und eigenthum seiei.
              W. Rihel, 1540 [R Nfp, 1166].

  .8.14.   Bucer, Martin, De vera Ecclesiarum in doctrina,
           ceremoniis, et disciplina reconciliatone & compositione.
              W. Rihel, 1542 [R Nfp, 1173].

  .8.15.   Marbach, Johannes, Von dem Bischofflichen Ampt unnd
           eines Bischoffs Tugenden . . . an die Hoch unnd

Wolgebornen Herren des Hohen Stiffts zu Straszburg da
die Wahl eines newen Bischoffs daselbst angehen solt.
J. Rihel, 1559 [R Nfp, 2600].

P1.8.16. Specker, Melchior, Vom Leiblichen Todt.
S. Emmel, 1560 [R BNU IV, 2175].

.8.17. Bucer, Martin, Von den juden Ob und wie die under den
Christen zu halten seind.
T. Berger, 1562 [R Nfp, 1165].

.8.18. Bucer, Martin, Vom Reich Christi unsers Herren.
W. Rihel, 1563 [R Nfp, 1175].

.8.19. Pappus, Johannes, Capita disputationis publicae.
A. Bertram, 1564 [R Nfp, 2814].

.8.20. Specker, Melchior, Disputatio De Justificatione
hominis coram Deo.
J. Rihel, 1567 [R Nfp, 3260].

.8.21. Marbach, Johannes, Themata de imagine Dei, cum eterna,
tum creata, de quibus disputabitur.
S. Emmel, 1568 [R BNU III, 1483].

.8.22. Bucer, Martin, Christliche Reformation. Das ist Inn
Gottes wort . . . Bericht Von Gottseliger Reformation
der Kirchen, und Pollicei. . . .
S. Emmel, 1568 [R Nfp, 1174].

.8.23. Marbach, Johann, Themata, De Natura Hominis, Eiusque
Facultate in Consequenda Salute Aeterna.
J. Rihel, 1570 [R BNU III, 1484].

.8.24. Marbach, Johann, Von Mirackeln und Wunderzeichen. Wie
man sie ausz und nach Gottes Wort, fur waar oder
falsch, erkennen soll.
No printer, 1571 [R BNU III, 1485].

.8.25. Pappus, Johannes, De auctoritate Patrum, sive Scriptorum
Ecclesiasticorum Capita Disputationis. . . .
N. Wyriot, 1579 [R BNU III, 1755].

.8.26. Pappus, Johannes, De Litera et Spiritu, Themata
Disputationis Theologicae.
K. Kieffer, 1588 [R BNU III, 1759].

.8.27. Pappus, Iohannes, Elenchus, Scriptorum doctoris Iohannis
Pappi.
No printer, 1596 [R BNU II, 677].

9. CONFESSIONS OF FAITH.

P1.9.1. (Butzer, Martin), Confessio religionis christianae,

sacratissimo Imperatori Carolo V . . . Anno M.D.XXX.
per Legatos Civitatum Argentorati, Constantiae,
Memmingae, et Lindauiae exhibita.
    G. Ulricher, 1531 [R BNU I, 362].

P1.9.2.   (Butzer, Martin), Bekandtnusz der vier Frey und Reich-
statt, Straszburg, Constanz, Memmingen und Lindaw, in
deren sie Keys. Maiestat . . . ihres glaubens und
fürhabens, der Religion halb, rechenschafft gethan
haben.
    J. Schwintzer, 1531 [R BNU I, 361].
    T. Rihel, 1579 [R BNU I, 392].

.9.3.   Garnier, Jean, Brieve et claire Confession de la Foy
Chrestiene, contenant cent articles . . . faite et
declarée en l'Eglise Françoise de Strasbourg.
    J. Poulain & R. Houdouyn, 1555 [R BNU II, 933],
       1558 [R Nfp, 1812].

.9.4.   Scriptum: Collocutorum Augustanae Confessionis.
    S. Emmel, 1557 [R Nfp, 3209].

.9.5.   (Calvin, Jean), Confession de foy faicte . . . par les
Eglises dispersés en France.
    (Chr. Mylius I), 1559 [Peter, XXII].

.9.6.   Erythraeus, Valentinus, Augustanae Confessionis, Pars
Prima, Pars Secunda . . ., Pars Tertia.
    Chr. Mylius I, 1565 – 1567 [R BNU II, 802].

.9.7.   Pappus, Johannes, Articuli Praecipui Doctrinae
Christianae: ex Confessione Augustana . . . quam
Formulam Concordiae nominant. . . .
    A. Bertram, 1591 [R BNU III, 1760].

P2.   PROTESTANT SERMONS.

   1. MARTIN LUTHER.

P2.1.1.   Sermon von dem Elichen standt.
    J. Knobloch, 1519 [S VII, 180].

.1.2.   Sermon von dem wucher.
    M. Flach II, 1520 [S VI B, 43].

.1.3.   Sermon von dem neüwen Testament das ist von der heilige
Mesz.
    M. Flach II, 1520 [BM 3906.e.115].

.1.4.   Sermon von dem bann.
    M. Flach II, 1520 [S VI B, 44; S VI B, 50].

.1.5.   Sermon von dem Sacrament der Büsz.

M. Flach II, 1520 [S VI B, 48].
M. Schürer Erben, 1520 [B SE 2, 3].

P2.1.6.   Sermon von dem Hochwurdigen sacrament des heiligen
          waren lychnams Christi, und von den Brüderschaffen.
          M. Flach II, 1520 [S VI B, 45].

.1.7.   Ein nützlich predig . . . wie sich ein Christenmensch
          . . . bereiten sol zu sterben.
          M. Flach II, 1520 [R Nfp, 2535].
          M. Schürer Erben, 1523 [B SE 2, 39].

.1.8.   Sermon von dem Gebeet und Procession yn der Crëutzwochen.
          Auch sunst von allem gebet durch dz gantz Jar. . . .
          M. Flach II, 1520 [S VI B, 53].
          also listed as: J. Knobloch, 1520 [B Luther, 385].

.1.9.   Sermon von der Betrachtung des heyligen leidens Christi.
          J. Prüss II, 1520 [R Nfp, 2561].
          M. Flach II, 1520 [S VI B, 51].

.1.10.   Sermon von dem Heiligen Hochwirdigen Sacrament der
          Tauffe.
          M. Flach II, 1520 [S VI B, 49].

.1.11.   Sermon . . . an der heyligen Drey Künig Tag, vonn dem
          Reych Christi und Herodis.
          M. Schürer Erben, 1521 [B Luther, 822].
          J. Prüss II, 1521 [B Luther, 821].

.1.12.   Nützliche Sermon . . . gepredigt am Oberisten.
          R. Beck, 1521 [B Luther, 826].

.1.13.   Viertzehen schöner christlicher Predig MDXXII zu
          Wittenberg gepredict.
          J. Schott, 1522 [BM 3905.bb.21].

.1.14.   Sermon Am Sontag nach der auffart des herren Jesu das
          Evangelium Joha. am XV. . . .
          R. Beck, 1522 [B Luther, 201].

.1.15.   Predig wie die zehen gebot getzogen werden auff die
          Syben todt sünd.
          U. Morhard, ca. 1522 [B Luther, 201].

.1.16.   Ein Sermon an dem tag des heyligen sant Iohanes des
          Tauffers Jesu Christ.
          M. Schürer Erben, 1522 [B SE 1, 15].

.1.17.   Vom Eelichen Leben.
          M. Schürer Erben, 1522 [B SE 1, 16].

.1.18.   Ein Sermon . . . vonn den Bildtnüssen.
          M. Schürer Erben, 1522 [B SE 1, 17].

P2.1.19. Eyn Sermon zu Sant Michael gethon . . . uff den tag
          d'xj. tausent junckfrauwen vom glauben und wercken.
          M. Schürer Erben, 1522 [B SE 3, 9].

  .1.20. Ein Sermon . . . Unnd darbey den verstandt, wie vil
          krafft die heyligen Evagelia über die Concilia habent.
          M. Schürer Erben, 1522 [B SE 2, 25].

  .1.21. XIII Predig.
          J. Schott, 1523 [R Nfp, 2537], 1523 [B Luther, 37].

  .1.22. XII Predigen uff etliche unser Frauwen und der Heyligen
          Fest.
          J. Schott, 1523 [B Luther, 31], 1523 [B Luther, 32].

  .1.23. Sermon von der gepurtt Marie der mütter gots, wie sie
          und die heiligen solle geert werden.
          M. Flach II, 1523 [B Luther, 1458].
          M. Schürer Erben, 1523 [B SE 2, 22].

  .1.24. Sermon von dem siben broten.
          R. Beck Erben, 1523 [B Luther, 1800].
          M. Schürer Erben, 1523 [B SE 2, 41].

  .1.25. XXVII Predig . . . newlich uszgangen Anno. XXIII.
          J. Schott, 1523 [S II B, 77].

  .1.26. Hyrin findstu Zehn nützliche Sermones.
          W. Köpfel, 1523 [R Nfp, 2568].

  .1.27. Sermon von dem weltlichen recht und Schwerdt.
          J. Schott, 1523 [S II B, 78].

  .1.28. Fyertzehen schoener christlicher predig.
          J. Schott, 1523 [R Nfp, 2538].

  .1.29. Sermon von dem fest visitationis Marie.
          M. Schürer Erben, 1523 [B SE 1, 22].

  .1.30. Eyn vast treffliche Predig an dem tag der verkündung
          unser lieben Frawen.
          M. Schürer Erben, 1523 [B SE 3, 18].

  .1.31. Ein sermon an unsers herren hymelfartstag . . . von
          der summa des Evangelii das ist der glaub.
          M. Schürer Erben, 1523 [B SE 3, 19].

  .1.32. Ein Sermon . . . uff das Evangelion Ioan x. Von dem
          gutten hirten.
          M. Schürer Erben, 1523 [B SE 3, 20].

  .1.33. Eyn Sermon uff das Evangelion von dem Reychen man und
          dem armen Lazaro.
          M. Schürer Erben, 1523 [B SE 3, 21].

P2.1.34. Ein Sermon von den heyltumen und getzierd mit
          überfluss vom heyligen Creütz in den Kirchen.
          M. Schürer Erben, 1523 [B SE 3, 23].

  .1.35. Ein Sermon von der sünd: Gerechtigkeit und urteyl.
          M. Schürer Erben, 1523 [B SE 3, 24].

  .1.36. De confessione et eucharistiae sacramento . . . De
          uso et confessione christianae Libertatis . . . Sermo
          (J. Lonicer, trans.).
          J. Herwagen, 1524 [B Luther, 1980].

  .1.37. Epistel S. Petri geprediget unnd auszgelegt.
          U. Morhard, 1524 [S IV Mor., 13].

  .1.38. Die ander Epistel S. Petri unnd eyne S. Judas gepre-
          digt unnd auszgelegt.
          J. Pruss II, 1524 [S III B, 36].

  .1.39. XXVII. predig.
          J. Schott, 1524 [R BNU III, 1424], 1526 [B Luther,
          35].

  .1.40. Sermon an dem XIII Sontag nach Pfingsten.
          M. Schürer Erben, 1524 [B SE 2, 59].

  .1.41. Ein Sermon über das Evangeliu Iohannis. iiij. Es war
          ein Kunigischer des son lag Kranck zu Capernaum.
          M. Schürer Erben, 1524 [B SE 2, 58].

  .1.42. Drey schon Sermon gepredigt zu Born.
          J. Schwann, 1524 [R Nfp, 2567].

  .1.43. Sermon von der zerstörung Jerusalem. Das Teutschlandt
          auch also zerstört werd, wo es die zeyt seiner
          heymsuchung nicht erkent.
          J. Knobloch, 1525 [S VII, 302].

  .1.44. Eyn Sermon vo der Beycht un dem Sacrament.
          M. Schürer Erben, 1525 [B SE 1, 32].

  .1.45. Conciunculae quaedam in Deiparae Virgini et Divis
          aliquot festos Dies. Nuper Latinae factae.
          J. Herwagen, 1526 [B Luther, 57].

  .1.46. Sermones aliquot sane quam Pii . . . quorum Elenchon
          proxima pagella indicabit.
          J. Herwagen, 1526 [B Luther, 55; B Luther, 56].

  .1.47. Sermon von dem Sacrament des Leibs und Bluts Christi
          wider die schwarm Geister.
          J. Knobloch, 1527 [B Luther, 2317].

  .1.48. Sermo de Fine Praeceptorum Dei, atque de vero Legis
          usu . . . ex Epistola ad Timoth. priore feliciter

explicatur. . . .
   J. Herwagen, 1527 [R BNU III, 1437].

P2.1.49. Predig . . . Das man Kinder zu Schülen halten solle.
   (H. Knobloch? or J. Prüss II?), 1531 [B Luther,
    2824].
   J. Prüss II, 1541 [S III B, 50].

.1.50. Tröstlich Predigt vor der Zukunft Christi und den
  vorgehenden Zeichen des jungstens tags.
   W. Rihel, 1536 [B Luther, 3020].

.1.51. Zwo schöne trostliche predig zu Schmalkalden getan.
   Cr. Mylius, 1537 [BM 3907.bbb.13].

.1.52. Heer-predigt Wider den Turcken.
   J. Prüss II, 1542 [B Luther, 2722].

.1.53. Homelia mire consolatoria de Fraternitabibus, habita
  in Paschae festo.
   Cr. Mylius, 1543 [R Nfp, 2510], 1545 [B Luther,
    3284].

2. LOCAL REFORMERS.

P2.2.1. Bucer, Martin, Das ym selbs niemant, sonder anderen
  leben soll. und wie der mensch dahyn kummen mög.
   J. Schott, 1523 [S II B, 75].

.2.2. Zell, Mathaeus, Ein Collation auff die einfuerung M.
  Anthonii Pfarrherrs zu S. Thomans zu Strassburg unnd
  Katherine seines eelichen gemahels.
   W. Köpfel, 1523 [R BNU IV, 2513].

.2.3. Pollio, Symphorian (Symphorian Altbiesser), Ein predig
  vom glauben wider die falschen stend, sampt einem
  sendtbrieff an die Priorin und Convent zu S.
  Katherinen zu Straszburg.
   W. Köpfel, 1525 [R BNU III, 1908].

.2.4. Hedio, Caspar, Von dem Zehenden zwu träffliche Predig,
  Beschehen in dem Münster zu Straszburg, auf den xx.
  tag Novembris.
   (W. Köpfel?), 1525 [R BNU II, 1092].

.2.5. Hedio, Caspar, Radts Predig. Wie die Oberkeit für sich
  selbs, und die Underthonen für jre Oberkeiten, in
  disser geverlichen sorglichen zeit zu bitten haben.
   J. Albrecht, 1534 [R BNU II, 1094].

.2.6. Bucer, Martin, Deri predigten aus dem Evangelii . . .
  An die Oberkeiten im Elsas auszgangen, mit einer

vermanung, nach warer Reformation der Kirchen zu
trachten.
>No printer, 1538 [R Nfp, 1167].
>See Stupperich, Bucers Deutsche Schriften 7, pp. 13-
>66, for reprint.

P2.2.7.   Marbach, Johann, Drey Christlichen Predigen, von
Christi unser Heylands himelfart. . . .
>Chr. Mylius I, 1565 [R BNU III, 1480].

.2.8.   Schadaeus, Elias, Mysterium Das ist Geheimnis S. Pauli
Röm. am II. Von bekehrung der Juden, auszgelegt und
geprediget.
>S. Meyer, 1592 [R BNU IV, 2079].

.2.9.   Pappus, Johannes, Ein Christliche Predigt, von dem
Ampt, Tugenden, und Wahl ein Christlichen Bischoffs.
Vor der Wahl desz Hochwürdigen . . . Fürsten und
Herrn, Herrn Johann Georgen . . . der Stifft zu
Straszburg . . . Gehalten zu Straszburg im Münster,
Sambstags den 20 Maii . . . 1592.
>A. Bertram, 1592 [R BNU III, 1763].

3.   OTHER SERMONS.

P2.3.1.   Nuc dimittis Oecolpamadii A. Sermon.
>M. Schürer Erben, 1522 [BM 3906.h.90].

.3.2.   Kettenbach, Heinrich von, Ein Sermon zu der loblichen
statt Ulm zu einem valete das ist zu der letse. In
welcher gemelt werden vil artickel . . . wider die
Papisten.
>M. Schürer Erben, 1523 [B SE 1, 33; R Nfp, 2233].

.3.3.   Adler, Caspar (Caspar Aquila), Eyn Sermon von der
schul Christi darin ein yetlicher lernet . . . wa es
im fället an dem weg der säligkeit.
>M. Schürer Erben, 1523 [B SE 1, 19].

.3.4.   Strauss, Jacob, Ein Sermon: in d'deutlich angezeygt
und gelert ist die pfaffen Ee.
>M. Schürer Erben, 1523 [B SE 3, 26].

.3.5.   Osiander, Andreas, Eyn eynfürung in den Passion in der
Karwochen . . . gepredigt.
>M. Schürer Erben, 1524 [B SE 2, 61].

.3.6.   Joseph Nicolaus, Eyn Sermon . . . das Fegfeür.
>M. Schürer Erben, 1524 [B SE 2, 57].

.3.7.   Otther, Jacob, Die Epistel Sancti Pauli an Titu

gepredig<u>et</u>.
  M. Schür er Erben, 1524 [B <u>SE</u> <u>2</u>, 61].

P2.3.8.   Georg von Polentz (Bishop of Samland), <u>Ein Sermon des</u>
          <u>wirdigen in Got vatters</u>.
            M. Schür er Erben, 1524 [B <u>SE</u> <u>3</u>, 32].

  .3.9.   Schweblin, Johann, <u>Ein Sermon uff Misericordia domini</u>
          <u>zu Pforthzhaim gethon</u>.
            J. Schwann, 1524 [Pegg, 3645].
            <u>Benzing lists this as:</u>
            M. Schür er Erben, 1524 [B <u>SE</u> <u>3</u>, 34].

  .3.10. Brentius, Johannes (Johann Brentz), <u>Zwo Christenliche</u>
          <u>Sermon</u>. <u>Wie das holtz des Creutzs behawen</u>. <u>Item auss</u>
          <u>was ursach gluck unnd ungluck entstee</u>.
            W. Köpfel, 1527 [R Nfp, 1092; Pegg, 341].

  .3.11. Draconites, Johann, <u>Predigt vom ewigen leben</u>.
            (W. Rihel?), 1545 [Pegg, 717].

  .3.12. Schopper, Jacob, <u>Ein Schöne ausslegunge des XVIII. und</u>
          <u>XIX. Cap. im II. Buch der Künig . . . in zwo predig</u>
          <u>getheilt</u>.
            J. Frölich, 1546 [Pegg, 3621].

  .3.13. Bugenhagen, Johann, <u>Von der jetzigen Kreigsrüstung</u>.
            No printer, 1546 [R Nfp, 1235].

  .3.14. Bullinger, Heinrich, <u>Cent sermons sur l'Apocalypse</u>.
            F. Perrin, 1558, [Peter, XIX].

  .3.15. Brunmüller, Caspar, <u>Von dem Erschrockenlichen</u>
          <u>Grausamen, Unbillichen Unchristlichen, schadlichen,</u>
          <u>Unnötigen, Gottlosen Gefährlichen und Verdamlichen</u>
          <u>laster dem Gottslesteren, ein vermanung</u>.
            P. Messerschmidt, 1560 [R BNU I, 307].

  .3.16. Rabus, Ludovicus, <u>Predig von notwendigem . . .</u>
          <u>verstandt der Sechs Hauptstück unsers Christlichen</u>
          <u>Catechismi</u>.
            Chr. Mylius I, 1560 [R Nfp, 3064].

  .3.17. Coelius, Michael, <u>Auszlegungen Predigten und</u>
          <u>Schrifften</u> (M. Ciriacus Spangenberg, ed.).
            S. Emmel, 1565 [R Nfp, 1416].

  .3.18. Brentius, Johannes, <u>Vom Hagel, Donner und allem</u>
          <u>Ungewitter</u>.
            Chr. Mylius I, 1565 [R Nfp, 1073].

  .3.19. Moll, Christoph, <u>Predig von dem Ave Maria und von</u>
          <u>anruffung der Heyligen</u>.
            Chr. Mylius II, 1575 [R BNU III, 1587].

P2.3.20. Ein Schöne . . . Predigt, vom Hochwürdigen Sacrament,
          unsers Herrn unnd Heylands Jhesu Christi h. Abendtmal.
            Chr. Mylius II, 1577 [R BNU III, 1922].

  .3.21. Giefftheil, Joachim, Predigt uber das Finsternusz des
          Monds am 31. tag Januarii im Jar 80 Geschehen, und was
          solche Zeichen weissagen.
            N. Wyriot, 1580 [R BNU II, 1013].

  .3.22. Osiander, Lucas, Predig Von Christlicher Einfalt in
          glaubens sachen.
            T. Berger, 1581 [R BNU III, 1734].

  .3.23. Miller, Georg, Ein Chrisliche Predig zu Ehren und
          Dankbarkeit der Kirchen, der Statt und Schulen inn
          Strassburg. . . .
            B. Jobin, 1585 [R Bib. Mun., 1492].

  .3.24. Graeter, Jacobus, Jubeljahrs-Predig. Auff das Jar nach
          unsers Herrn Jhesu Christi geburt tausent sechshundert.
          Welches ein rechts, Christlichs, Evangelisch
          Hunderjahrlichs Jubeljhar.
            J. Martin, 1599 [R BNU II, 1032].

    4. FUNERAL SERMONS.

P2.4.1. Luther, Martin, Zwo Predig über der Leiche des
          Kürfursten Hertzog Johann zu Sachsen.
            J. Frölich, 1533 [R Nfp, 2513].

  .4.2. Draconites, Johann, Trostpredigt über die Leich Eobani
          Hessi.
            No printer, 1541 [R Nfp, 1524].

  .4.3. Loescher, Abraham, Epicedion et narratio funebris in
          mortem venerabilis viri D. Matthaei Zeelii. . . .
            W. Köpfel, 1548 [R Nfp, 2421].

  .4.4. Regius, Ernst, De Philippo Melanchthone oratio.
          Argentorati habita anno 1561 die obitus.
            W. Rihel, 1561 [R Nfp, 3087].

  .4.5. Heldelin, Kaspar, Ein Christliche Predigt über der
          Leiche des Ehrwurdigen, hochgelerten Herrn M.:
          Matthiae Flacii Illyrici. . . .
            No printer, 1575 [R BNU II, 1122].

  .4.6. Sturm, Johannes, Consolatoria . . . epistola . . . ad
          Petrum Bilde Regii in Dania Consiliarium . . . de
          morte nepotis ex sorore Nicolai Brockii Dani . . .
          Sampt den . . . Leichenpredigt Herrn Johannis Liptitzen.
            N. Wyriot, 1579 [R Nfp, 3296].

P2.4.7.   Abschied des ehrwürdigen . . . Herrn Johann Marbachs
           . . . der christlichen Kirchen zu Strassburg für-
           nemsten Vorsteher.
           T. Berger, 1581 [R Nfp, 731].

.4.8.   Pappus, Johannes, Christliche Leichpredig Ausz dem
           Neundten Capitel der Apostel Geschichte, bey der
           Begrebnisz der Edlen . . . Frawen Veronica Stürmerin.
           N. Wyriot, 1582 [R BNU III, 1756].

.4.9.   Schadaeus, Daniel (Daniel Schade), Leichpredig Bey der
           Begräbnus des Edlen unnd Vesten Junckern Wolffgang von
           Oberkirch.
           A. Bertram, 1585 [R BNU IV, 2076].

.4.10.   Schreier, Paul, Christliche Leichpredig bey der Leich
           und begräbnusz Georg Philipsen, Grafen zu Leiningen.
           N. Waldt, 1589 [R Nfp, 3193].

.4.11.   Pappus, Johannes, Christliche Leichpredigt, Bey
           Abführung der Leiche, weyland des Edlen und
           Ehrnvehsten, Caii Rantzowe, Erbgesässen zum Kletkampff
           und Gerubou. . . .
           A. Bertram, 1591 [R BNU III, 1761].

.4.12.   Stephan, Laurentius, Leichpredigt über Albrechts
           Grafen zu Nassau Sarbruck Sarwerden . . . Tod auff
           Sontag den 11 Novembris gehalten. . . .
           J. Martin, 1593 [R Nfp, 3275].

.4.13.   Vogel, Heinrich, Predig bey der Leich Herrn Georg
           Hansen, Pfaltzgraven bey Rheyn, Hertzog in Beyern und
           Graven zu Veldentz.
           A. Bertram, 1596 [R Nfp, 3441].

.4.14.   Pappus, Johannes, Leichpredigt bey der begrabnis desz
           Ehrwürdigen . . . Herren Johannis Liptitzen.
           J. Martin, 1599 [Greiner].

P3.   ANTI-CATHOLIC POLEMIC.

   1.   MARTIN LUTHER.

P3.1.1.   Ad Leonem X. Pontificem Maximum. Resolutiones
           disputationum de virtute indulgentiarum.
           M. Schürer, February 1519 [B Luther, 4], 1519 [B
           Luther, 5].

.1.2.   Underrichtung, uff etlich Artickel, die im von seinem
           miszgünnern ussgelegt und zugemessen werden.
           M. Flach II, 1519 [B Luther, 302; S VI B, 46].
           J. Grüninger, 1523 [Pegg, 2692].

P3.1.3. An den Christlichen Adel deutscher Nation.
         M. Flach II, 1520 [B Luther, 691], 1520 [B Luther,
         692].
         R. Beck, 1520 [R Nfp, 2461].
         W. Köpfel, 1520 [R Nfp, 2462].

  .1.4. Von den Bapstum zu Rom wider den Hochberümpten
         Romanisten zu Leiptzck.
         J. Knobloch, 1520 [B Luther, 663].

  .1.5. Appelation oder berufung an eyn Christlich frey
         concilium.
         J. Prüss II, 1520 [B Luther, 778].
         M. Schürer Erben, 1520 [B SE 2, 2].

  .1.6. Von der Babylonischen gefengknuss der Kirchen.
         J. Schott, 1520 [B Luther, 712], 1520 [B Luther,
         714; S II B, 55a].

  .1.7. De Captivitate Babylonica ecclesiae.
         J. Schott, 1520 [S II B, 55].
         W. Köpfel, 1524 [B Luther, 711].

  .1.8. Antwort Auf die zedel, so under des Officials zu
         Stolpen sigel ist auszgangen.
         M. Flach II, 1520 [S VI B, 47].

  .1.9. Mancherley büchlin und tractetlin . . . Item Apologia.
         M. Schürer Erben, 1520 [R Nfp, 2577a; B Luther, 8].

  .1.10. Drey Biechlin . . . von dem Deütschen Adel. der
         heiligen Mess dem Babstumb zu Rom.
         M. Schürer Erben, 1520 [B SE 1, 4].

  .1.11. Uf das Fürhalten so durch K. Maiestat . . . dem Martin
         Luther durch den Reichs Redner zu Wormbs erzelt.
         J. Prüss II, 1521 [R Nfp, 2505].
         J. Knobloch, 1521 [B Luther, 919; R Nfp, 2504].
         J. Schott, 1522 [R Nfp, 2508; B Luther, 924].

  .1.12. Christiana & inconsternata Responsio Caesareae
         Maiestati . . . Wormatiae facta Anno M.D.XXI.
         M. Flach, 1521 [R Nfp, 2547].

  .1.13. Passional Christi und Antichrist.
         J. Knobloch, 1521 [B Luther, 1019].

  .1.14. An den Bock zu Leyptck.
         J. Knobloch, 1521 [B Luther, 828].
         J. Schott, 1521 [B Luther, 869].

  .1.15. Uff Bock Emszers Erste Antwort . . . Von vilen Bock
         Emsers lügen D.M. Luther zugeleyt. . . .
         J. Schott, 1521 [S II B, 64; B Luther, 832].

P3.1.16.   Acta et res gestae . . . in comitiis principum
           Vuormacie.
              J. Schott, 1521 [B Luther, 909].

  .1.17.   Iudicium . . . De votis. Scriptum ad episcopos et
           diaconos witembergenses.
              J. Herwagen, 1521 [B Luther, 978].

  .1.18.   Kurtz schluss rede von den gelübden unnd geystlichen
           leben des closter.
              U. Morhard, 1521 [B Luther, 983].

  .1.19.   Wider die Bullen des Endtchrists.
              M. Schürer Erben, 1521 [B SE 2, 15].

  .1.20.   Von menschen leren zu myden.
              R. Beck Erben, 1522 [B Luther, 1186].

  .1.21.   Judicium D. Martini Lutheri, de Erasmo Roterodamo.
           Philippi Melanchthonis de Erasmo, & Luthero Elogion.
              J. Schott, 1522 [S II B, 71], 1523 [Pegg, 2268].

  .1.22.   Anntwurt deütsch. Mar. Luthers auff Könnig Heinrichs
           von Engeland buch.
              J. Prüss II, 1522 [R Nfp, 2465].
              J. Knobloch, 1522 [B Luther, 1230].
              M. Schürer Erben, 1522 [B SE 2, 26].

  .1.23.   Eyn missive allen den, so von wegen des worttgottes
           verfolgung lyden tröstlych.
              W. Köpfel, 1522 [B Luther, 1169].

  .1.24.   Epistel oder undericht vonn den heyligen an die Kirche
           zu Erffurdt in Gott versamlet.
              M. Schürer Erben, 1522 [B SE 2, 23].

  .1.25.   Wider den falsch genantten geystlichen stand des Bapst
           unnd der Bischoffen.
              M. Schürer Erben, 1522 [B SE 3, 10].

  .1.26.   Wrteil D. M. Luthers und P. Melanchthonis von Erasmo
           Roterdam.
              J. Schott, 1523 [B Luther, 1486; Pegg, 2269].

  .1.27.   Den . . . lieben Freünden Gottes allen Christen zu
           Rhighe, Reuell un Tarbthe in Lieffland.
              R. Beck Erben, 1523 [B Luther, 1683].

  .1.28.   Das ein christliche Versamlung oder gemeyne: recht und
           macht habe: alle lere zu urteylen: und lerer zu
           beruffen: yn und ab zu setzen.
              J. Prüss II, 1523 [S II B, 33].
              M. Schürer Erben, 1523 [B SE 3, 15], 1523 [B SE 3,
              16].

P3.1.29. Bulla cenae domini.
          J. Knobloch, 1523 [B Luther, 1059].

   .1.30. Vom Miszbruch der Messen.
          W. Köpfel, 1523 [R Nfp, 2520].

   .1.31. Adversus Armatum Virum Cokle (Cocleum).
          J. Prüss II, 1523 [S III B, 34].

   .1.32. Keyserlich mandat jungst ussgangen zu Nurnberg über
          den Lutherischen Handel.
          J. Prüss II, 1523 [BM 3905.e.90].

   .1.33. Antwort Teütsch uff spruch so man füret menschen lere
          zu Meyden.
          M. Schürer Erben, 1523 [B SE 2, 35].

   .1.34. Ein Bepstlich Brieff dem Radt zu Bamberg gesandt wider
          den Luther. Geganantwurt.
          M. Schürer Erben, 1523 [B SE 2, 31].

   .1.35. Eyn geschicht wie got eyner erbarn Kloster jungfraue
          Florentina ausgeholfen hat (M. Luther, ed.).
          J. Prüss II, 1524 [BM 3905.e.80].
          M. Schürer Erben, 1524 [B SE 2, 55].

   .1.36. An die Herren deutschs ordens.
          J. Schwann, 1524 [B Luther, 1721].
          M. Schürer Erben, 1524 [B SE 2, 52].

   .1.37. Wider den neüwen Abgott und Alten Teuffel der zu
          Meyssen soll erhaben.
          M. Schürer Erben, 1524 [B SE 2, 60].

   .1.38. Eyn frage: ob Christus seyne gemeyn oder Kyrch uff
          Petrum und nachuolgende Bapst gebauwet hab?
          M. Schürer Erben, 1524 [B SE 3, 30].

   .1.39. Ermanunge zum fride auff die zwelff artickel der
          Bawrschafft ynn Schwaben.
          W. Köpfel, 1525 [B Luther, 2125].

   .1.40. Wider die Reubischen unnd Mördischen Rotten der
          Bawren.
          J. Prüss II, 1525 [B Luther, 2156].
          M. Schürer Erben, 1525 [B SE 2, 73].

   .1.41. Ein Brief an den Cardinal Ertzbischoff zu Mainz.
          B. Beck, 1530 [B Luther, 2805].
          J. Prüss II, 1530 [BM 3905.bbb.39].

   .1.42. Vermanung an die Geistlichen versamlet auff dem
          Reichstag zu Augsburg.
          W. Köpfel, 1530 [B Luther, 2782].

P3.1.43. <u>Wider den Meuchler zu Dresen getruckt.</u>
          J. Prüss II, 1531 [B <u>Luther</u>, 2940], 1531 [S III B,
          43].

   `1.44. <u>Warnunge. D. Martini Luther an seine lieben Deutschen</u>
          <u>. . . so die feinde Christliche Warheit diese Kirchen</u>
          <u>und Land . . . mit Krieg uberziehen und zerstören</u>
          <u>wird.</u>
          G. Ulricher, 1531 [B <u>Luther</u>, 2913].
          W. Rihel, 1546 [R BNU III, 1451].

  .1.45. <u>Auff das Vermeint Keiserlich Edict. Aussgangen in</u>
          <u>M.D.XXXI. jare nach dem Reichstage des M.D.XXX. jars.</u>
          J. Prüss II, 1531 [S III B, 42].

  .1.46. <u>Libro de la emendatione correctione diz stato</u>
          <u>christiano.</u>
          G. Ulricher, 1533 [BM 3906.aaa.125].

  .1.47. <u>Die Lügend von S. Iohanni Chrysostomo an die Heiligen</u>
          <u>Vetter in dem Concilio zu Mantua.</u>
          Cr. Mylius, 1537 [B <u>Luther</u>, 3240].

  .1.48. <u>Bapstrew Hadriani IV und Alexandri III. gegen Keyser</u>
          <u>Friderichen Barbarossa geübt.</u>
          W. Rihel, 1545 [B <u>Luther</u>, 2631; R Nfp, 2528].

  .1.49. <u>A faythfull admonycion</u> (C. Freeman, trans.).
          W. Rihel, 1554 [R Nfp, 2463].

   2. ULRICH VON HUTTEN.

P3.2.1.   <u>Clag und Vormanung gegen den übermüssigen</u>
          <u>unchristlichen gewalt des Bapstes zu Rom und der</u>
          <u>ungeistlichen geistlichen.</u>
          J. Knobloch, late 1520 [R Nfp, 2101], 1520 [R Nfp,
          2099].
          J. Schott, October–November 1520 [R Nfp, 2100],
          November–December 1520 [R Nfp, 2102].

  .2.2.   <u>Hoc in libello haec continentur: Ulrichi de Hutten .</u>
          <u>. . ad Carolum Imperatorem; . . . Conquestio . . .</u>
          <u>aliaque ad alios Epistolae.</u>
          J. Schott, after September 1520 [R Nfp, 2097], after
          September 1520 [B <u>Hut.</u>, 132], 1520 [B <u>Hut.</u>, 133].
          J. Prüss, September 1520 [B <u>Hut.</u>, 136].

  .2.3.   <u>Ein Clagschrift . . . an alle stend Deutscher nation.</u>
          <u>Wie unformlicher weise . . . Er mit eignem tyran-</u>
          <u>nischen gewalt von dem Romanisten an leib, eer und gut</u>
          <u>beschwert und benötiget werde. . . .</u>
          M. Flach, 1520 [R Nfp, 2097b].

P3.2.4.   Contenta. Ulrichi ab Hutten, Equitis germ. Exclamatio,
           in Incendium Lutheranum. Chunradi Sarctoris
           saxofranci, de eadem re ad Germanos Oratio. Carmen
           elegans & doctum, in Hieronymum Aleandrum hostem
           germanicae liberratis. Conclusiones decem
           Christianissimae, per Andream Bodenstein, de
           Carlostad. Vuittenbergae disputatae.
               J. Schott, 1520 [S II B, 56].

   .2.5.   Anzöig Wie allwegen sich die Romischen Bischoff, oder
           Bapst gegen den teutschen Kayszeren gehalten haben,
           uff dz Kürtzst uss Chroniken und Historien gezogen.
               J. Schott, 1520 [S II B, 57], 1521 [B Hut., 162].
           Also listed as:
           Lebendige abcontrafactur desz gantzen Bapstthumbsz.
           Sampt einer . . . ermanung an die freien . . .
           Teutscher Nation, das sie . . . das vatterlandt von
           disem hellsichen hundt gar erretten.
               J. Cammerlander, ca. 1535 [R Nfp, 2103].
           Ein Trewe Warnung. Wie die Päpst allwegen wider die
           Teutschen Keyser geweszt.
               J. Cammerlander, 1535 [R Nfp, 2104].

   .2.6.   Bulla Decimi Leonis contra errores Martini Lutheri et
           sequacium.
               J. Schott, 1520 [B Hut., 222], 1520 [B Hut. 223].

   .2.7.   Endtschuldigung Ulrichs von Hutten Wyder etlicher
           unwarhafftiges auszgeben von ym als solt er wider alle
           geystlicheit und priesterschafft sein. . . .
               M. Flach II, 1521 [R Nfp, 2105].

   .2.8.   Gespräch büchlin herr Ulrichs von Hutten. Feber das
           Erst. Feber das Ander. Wadiscus oder die Römische
           dreyfaltigkeit. Die Anschawenden.
               J. Schott, 1521 [S II B, 59].

   .2.9.   Hulderichi ab Hutten Eq. Germ. In Hieronymum Aleandrum
           & Marinum Caracciolum, Leonis decimi, P.M. Oratores in
           Germania. Invectae singulae. In cardinales, Episcopos
           et Sacerdotes. . . .
               J. Schott, 1521 [S II B, 61].

   .2.10. Geschicht . . . des . . . Hoh. Pfefferkorn in (Römer
           Joh.). Das ist der hoch turen Babel, id est Confusio
           Pape darinn Doctor Luther gefangen ist.
               M. Schürer Erben, 1521 [R Nfp, 2093].

   .2.11. Dialogi Huttenici Novi, perquam festivi. Bulla vel
           Bullicida. Monitor primus. Monitor secundus. Praedones.
               J. Schott, 1521 [B Hut., 161; S II B, 60].

P3.2.12.   Concilia wie man die halten sol. Und von verleyhung
           geystlicher lehenpfrunden . . . Ermanung das ein
           yeder bey dem Rechten alten Christlichen glauben
           bleiben. . . .
               J. Schott, 1521 [S II B, 58].

  .2.13.   Ein demütige ermanung an ein gemeine stat Worms.
               J. Knobloch, 1522 [B Hut., 184].

  .2.14.   Büchlin Über und gegen vergewaltigung des Papst, . .
           . Klagschrifft an Keyserliche maiestat . . . Ein
           andere Klagschrifft . . . an gemeyne Teütsch nation
           . . . Ermanung an Hertzog Friderich Churfurst zu
           Sachsen, zu vorsechtung gemeyner freyheit wider die
           Romanisten. Auch ettliche andere schrifften. . . .
               J. Schott, 1522 [S II B, 70].

  .2.15.   Vormanung an die Freien und Reich stette teutscher
           nation.
               J. Knobloch, 1522 [B Hut., 181].

  .2.16.   Ulrichi ab Hutten cum Erasmo Roterodamo . . .
           Expostulatio.
               J. Schott, 1523 [S II B, 80], 1523 [S II B, 81],
                  1523 [S II B, 82], 1524 [R Nfp, 2108].

  .2.17.   Eyn lustiger und nutzlicher dialogus . . . Hutten
           vadiscus oder die Römisch dreyfaltig genannt.
               B. Beck, 1544 [R Nfp, 2114].

   3. LAYMEN.

P3.3.1.   Gemigger von Heinfelt, Lux, Zu lob dem Luther und
           eeren der gantzen Christenhait.
               J. Prüss II, 1520 [BM T.220.4], ca. 1520 [R BNU II,
                  994].

  .3.2.   Ain guter grober dyalogus Teütsch, zwüschen zwayen
           guten gesellen, mit namen Hans Schöpfer, Peter
           Schabenhüt, bayd von Basel. . . .
               R. Beck, 1521 [S IV Beck, 34].

  .3.3.   Vadian, Joachim (J. v. Watt, psued.), Karsthans.
               J. Prüss II, 1521 [R Nfp, 3476], 1521 [R Nfp, 3478].
               W. Köpfel, 1521 [R Nfp, 3477].

  .3.4.   Eckhart zum Treubel, Ain dümietige ermanung an ain
           gantze gemayne Christenheit.
               R. Beck, ca. 1522 [R BNU IV, 2357], 1523 [R Nfp, 3368].
               M. Flach II, 1523 [S VI B, 72].

  .3.5.   Vadian, Joachim (J. v. Watt, pseud.), Judas Nazarei.

Vom alten und neuen Gott, Glauben und Lehre.
J. Prüss II, 1522 [R Nfp, 3474].
W. Köpfel, 1523 [R Nfp, 3475].

P3.3.6. Hartmuth von Cronberg, Ein treüwe vermanung an alle
Ständ auff dem Reichsstag yetz und zu Nürenburg, von
einem armen veriagten vom Adel, mit beger solliche
vermanung . . . zu hören. . . .

J. Schott, 1522 [R Nfp, 1459].

.3.7. Hartmuth von Cronberg, Schrifften . . . wider doctor
Peter Meyer, Pfarrherr zu Frankfurt . . . sein
unchristlich leer betreffendt.
J. Schott, 1522 [R Nfp, 1462].

.3.8. Hartmuth von Cronberg, Ableynung des vermeinlichen
unglimpffs so dem Andechtigen Hochgelerten und
Christenlichen vatter Doctor Martin Luther . . .
zugelegt, in dem das er unsern vatter den Babst ein
Vicari des Teufels und Antecrists genant hat.
J. Prüss II, 1522 [R Nfp, 1460].

.3.9. Argula von Grumbach, Wie eyn Christliche fraw des
Adels, in Beiern durch iren in gotlichen Schrift . . .
die Hochschül zu Ingoldstatt straffet . . . das sie
eynem Evangelischen Jüngling . . . betrangt haben;
straffet. . . .
M. Flach II, 1523 [S VI B, 71].

.3.10. Paul, Elias, Vom alten und newen Gott, Glauben und
Lere.
W. Köpfel, 1523 [R Nfp, 2846].

.3.11. (Marschalck, H.), Ein Spiegel der Blinden.
W. Köpfel, ca. 1523 [Pegg, 3716].

.3.12. Harthmuth von Cronberg, Ein schrifft und Christlich
vermanung an die Meister unnd Rath zu Straszburgk.
J. Schott, 1523 [Pegg, 579].

.3.13. Wurm von Geudertheim, Mathias, Ain Christlich
schreiben, so ain Evangelischer bruder seiner
schwestern, ainer closter iunckfrawen zugeschickt.
No printer, 1523 [R Nfp, 3567].

.3.14. Wurm von Geudertheim, Mathias, Balaams Eselin. Von dem
Bann: das er umb geltschuld . . . nit mag Christlich
gefellt werden. Und das aller geystlicher standt
schuldig ist, der weltlichen oberkeit zu gehorsamen.
No printer, 1523 [R Nfp, 3565].
M. Schürer Erben, 1525 [B SE 2, 75].

P3.3.15. Stephan von Buellheim, Ein brüderliche warnung an
          Meister Mathis Pfarrherren zu sanct Lorentzen im
          Münster zu Straszburg, sich vor seinen widersächeren
          zu verhüten und bewaren.
             J. Knobloch, 1523 [Schottenloher, 49792a].
             J. Schwann, 1523/24 [R Nfp, 1227].

  .3.16. Entschuldigung gemeyner Eydtgnossen über die artickel
          so jnen von etlichen geltsuchtigen Pfarrherrn felsch-
          lich ussgebreyt werden.
             W. Köpfel, 1524 [Pegg, 3788].
             (Ritter attributes a 1524 edition to B. Beck, not
                then printing in Strasbourg. [R BNU II, 690].)

  .3.17. Argula von Grumbach, Christliche ermanungenn an
          Hertzog Friderichen Chrufürsten zu Sachsen.
             W. Köpfel, 1524 [Pegg, 1289].

  .3.18. Sachs, Hans, Underweysung der ungeschickten vermeinten
          Lutherischen so in eüsserlichen sachen, zu ergernüss
          jres nechsten freüntlich handlen. Item ob das
          Evangelium sein krafft von der kirchen hab. H.
          Greiffenberger.
             W. Köpfel, 1524 [Pegg, 3564].

  .3.19. Eckhart zum Treybel, Christelich lob und vermanung an
          die hochberumpte Christeliche statt Straszburg, von
          wegen des heyligen worts gottes.
             M. Flach II, 1524 [S VI B, 74].

  .3.20. Zell, Katherina, Entschuldigung Katharine Schutzinn
          für M. Mathias Zellen iren eegemal.
             W. Köpfel, 1524 [BM 4888.a.3].

   3.21. Zell, Katherina, Den Leydenden Christglaubigen Weybern
          der Gemain zu Kentzingen Meinen Mitschwestern in
          Christo Jhesu zu handen.
             No printer, 1524 [Greiner].

  .3.22. Schenck, Jakob, Sendtbrieff an seyne Geschwyen.
             M. Schürer Erben, 1524 [B SE 3, 33].

  .3.23. Hartmudt von Cronberg, Drey Christliche Schrifft: Die
          erst an Bapst Leo des namens den zehendren. Die ander
          an die einwoner zu Cronenburg. Die dritte an die bet-
          tel orden. Die vierd an Jacob Robeln Wittenberg.
             M. Flach II, 1525 [S VI B, 76].

  .3.24. Was sich zu Basel uff den achten tag des Hornungs zu
          getragen.
             B. Beck, 1529 [Pegg, 149].

  .3.25. Supplication ettlicher Zunfften an ein Ersamen Rath

zu Basel abzustellen das zwispeltig predigen unnd die
Mess.
    B. Beck, 1529 [Pegg, 148].

P3.3.26.   Clarenbach, Adolph, Alle acta Adolphi Clarenbach. Was
A. Clarenbach im Landt von Berge ehe dann er zu Cöln
gefangen dess Evangeliums halben, von seinen wider-
sechern begegnet unnd zugestanden sei.
    J. Cammerlander, ca. 1531 [Pegg, 544].

   .3.27.   Rockenbach, Hans, Warhaffte entschuldigung der Neün
mannen Hannsen Rockenbachs und seiner mithafften
Burgeren der Statt Solothurn uss der selben über alles
Rechts entbieten vertiben. Was sie zu abkündigung
etliche Personen den friden verursachet.
    M. Apiarius, 1535 [Pegg, 3501].

   .3.28.   Warhafftige verantwurt unser Schulttzen, Kleyn unnd
Grossen Rates der Stat Solothurn auff das
Schandtbüchlin von unsern Fyenden ussgangen.
    W. Köpfel, 1536 [Pegg, 3691].

   .3.29.   Manuel, Nicolaus, Klag und bekanntnus der Armen Götzen
wie es inen gat mit trüwem rat, sich vor allem götzen
leben zu hüten.
    J. Cammerlander, 1538 [R Nfp, 2593].

   .3.30.   Manuel, Nicolaus, Newe Zeittung, von Bäpstlicher
vermainten Mesz, fröliche Badenfart.
    J. Cammerlander, 1545 [R Nfp, 2595].

   .3.31.   Engelhardt, Heinrich, Eyn Neüwe zeythung, wie yetzt
alle Fürsten und Herren, Stätt und Lender, alle lassen
knecht annemen.
    W. Köpfel, 1546 [R BNU II, 688].

   4.   ENGLISH POLEMIC AND STATEMENTS OF FAITH.

P3.4.1.   Edward III, Epistola Regis Angliae ad Papam contra
nimias exactiones.
    No printer, ca. 1520 [BM T.1567.7].

   .4.2.   Roy, William (and Barlowe, Jerome), Rede me and be not
wrothe.
    J. Schott, 1528 [S II B. supp., 16].

   .4.3.   Roy, William, Inter patrem Christianum et filiam
contumacem dialogus Christianus.
    J. Schott, 1528 [S II B. supp., 17].

   .4.4.   Gardiner, Stephan (Stepanus Winton), De vera obenientia.
    W. Rihel, 1536 [R Nfp, 1811; R Nfp, 3549].

P3.4.5.   Alesius, Alexander, <u>Of the autoritie of the word of</u>
          <u>god agaynst the bisshop of London</u>.
          W. Köpfel, 1537 [BM 1019.b3.4].

  .4.6.   Henricus VIII, <u>Wer Küniglicher Maiestet des Reichs</u>
          <u>stende und der Landschafft Engellandt will und meynung</u>
          <u>ist des Conciliums halb so Bapst Paulus der dryt zu</u>
          <u>Mantua auff dem xxiii tag Maij zuhalten furgeben</u>.
          W. Rihel, 1537 [R Nfp, 1987].

  .4.7.   Brinkelow, Henry, <u>The complaynt of Roderick Mors</u>.
          W. Köpfel, ca. 1548 [BM c.37.a.I].

  .4.8.   Becon, Thomas (Hugh Hilarie, pseud.), <u>the Resurrection</u>
          <u>of the Masse</u>.
          No printer, 1554 [R Nfp, 2671], 1554 [BM G.111.b.9].

  .4.9.   Sampson, Thomas, <u>A Letter to the trew professors of</u>
          <u>Christes Gospell</u>.
          No printer, 1554 [R BNU IV, 2068].

  .4.10. Foxe, John, <u>Commentarii rerum in ecclesia gestarum</u>
          <u>maximarumque persecutionum a Wiclefi temporibus</u>
          <u>usque ad annum M.D.</u>.
          W. Rihel, 1554 [R Nfp, 1758], 1556 [R Nfp, 1759],
          1564 [R Nfp, 1760].

  .4.11. Polus, Reginaldus (Cardinal), <u>Ad Henricum Octavum</u>
          <u>. . . pro ecclesiasticae unitatis defensione</u>.
          W. Rihel, 1555 [R Nfp, 2967; R BNU III, 1904].

  .4.12. <u>A supplicacyon to the quenes maiestie</u>.
          W. Rihel, 1555 [R Nfp, 3307].

  .4.13. Ponet, John, <u>An apologie fully answering by Scriptures</u>
          <u>and Auncient Doctors a blasphemose book against the</u>
          <u>Godly Marriadg of Priests</u>.
          J. & T. Rihel, 1556 [BM c.25.b.7].

  .4.14. Rydley, Nicholas, and Latymer, Hugh, <u>Certe godly,</u>
          <u>learned and comfortable conferences between D.N.</u>
          <u>Rydley and M. H. Latymer</u>.
          J. & T. Rihel, 1556 [R Nfp, 3133].

  .4.15. (Mainardo, Agostino), <u>An Anatomi, that is to say a</u>
          <u>Parting in Peeces of the Mass . . . With a sermon of</u>
          <u>the Sacrament of thankes gyuing in the end</u>.

          No printer, 1556 [R Nfp, 2586].

  .4.16. Ponet, John, <u>A shorte Treatise of Politicke Power</u>.
          W. Köpfel, 1556 [BM 1389.b.48].

5. GENERAL POLEMIC BY OTHER GERMAN AND SWISS REFORMERS.

P3.5.1. Epistola de Magistris Nostris Louaniensibus, quot,
& quales sint quibus debemus magistralem illam dam-
nationem Lutherianam.
J. Schott, 1518 [S II B, 43].

.5.2. Exustionis Antichristianorum Decretalium Acta.
M. Flach II, 1520 [S VI B, 55].
J. Knobloch, 1521 [S VII, 229].

.5.3. Die handlung der Universithet Loeuen wider Dr.
Martinus Luther.
J. Prüss II, 1520 [R BNU II, 1071].
J. Knobloch, 1520 [R BNU II, 1070].

.5.4. (S. Abydenus Corallus, pseud.), Oratio ad Carolum
Maximum Augustum et Germania principes.
No printer, ca. 1521 [Greiner].

.5.5. Oecolampadius, Joannes, Quod expediat Epistolae et
Evangelii lectionem in Missa vernaculo sermone plebi
promulgari.
U. Morhard, 1522 [Pegg, 3286].

.5.6. Schweblin, Johann, Ermanung zu den Questionieren
abzustellen überflüssigen kosten.
J. Prüss II, 1522 [Pegg, 3643].

.5.7. Mandat des Hertzogthumbs Wirtemmberg und Tech aus-
gangen zu Sturgarten.
M. Schürer Erben, 1522 [B SE 1, 18].

.5.8. Guethel, Kaspar, Schutz Rede wider etliche ungezemte
freche Clamanten weliche die Evangelischen lerer
schuldigen.
M. Schürer Erben, 1522 [B SE 3, 5].

.5.9. (Rhegius, Urbanus), Ein schöner Dialogus. Cuntz und
der Fritz. Die brauchent wenig witz.
M. Schürer Erben, 1522 [B SE 3, 12].

.5.10. (Korn, Gallus), Ein handlung wie es einem Prediger
Munch zu Nurmberg mit seinen ordens brudern von wegen
der Evangelischen warheit gangenn ist.
M. Schürer Erben, 1522 [B SE 3, 6].

.5.11. Raidbach von Feldtkirch, Johannes, Von vermessenheit
Closter regeln und statuten aller jungkfrawen Clöster
und orden.
J. Prüss II, 1523 [Pegg, 3417].

P3.5.12. Kettenbach, Heinrich, Ein practica ausz der . . . Bibel.
          J. Prüss II, 1523 [R Nfp, 2231].
          M. Flach II, 1523 [R Nfp, 2232].

.5.13.   Ursach und Handelung in d'Keyserlichen . . . statt
          Meydeburg . . . In den zweyen Pfarren S. Ioannis und
          S. Ulrichs.
          M. Schürer Erben, 1524 [B SE 2, 65].

.5.14.   Blaurer, Ambrosius, Ir gwalt ist veracht, ir kunst ist
          verlacht . . . Recht ists wiess Gott macht.
          M. Schürer Erben, 1524 [B SE 2, 44].

.5.15.   Ulrich, Herzog zu Wurttemberg, Missive an die
          Gubernator der statt Bisantz in d'ein Christlicher
          handel zu Mümpelgart verloffen . . . angezeyget wurt.
          M. Schürer Erben, 1524 [B SE 2, 64].

.5.16.   Sonnentaller, Johann, Ursach warumb der vermeint
          geystlich huff mit yren patronen das Evangelion nit
          annimpt.
          J. Schwann, 1524 [Pegg, 3693].

.5.17.   Hermann, Nicolaus, Ein Mandat Ihesu Christi: an alle
          seine getrewen Christen.
          J. Schwann, 1524 [Pegg, 1360].

.5.18.   Wider den Hauptschalck und todtfeindt des Menschen
          gewissen.
          J. Knobloch, ca. 1525 [Pegg, 1337].

.5.19.   Brenz, Johann, Von Milterung der Fürsten gegen den
          auffrurischen Baure.
          W. Köpfel, 1525 [BM 3905.b.6].

.5.20.   Gast, Hiob, Expostulatio Iustitiae cum mundo à Belial
          instigato, per dialogi modum . . . conscripta.
          J. Herwagen, 1525 [R BNU II, 935].

.5.21.   Keller, Michael (Conrad Reyss, pseud.), Antwurt dem
          . . . Doctor I. Pugenhag uff die missive so er an den
          Doctor Hesso geschickt.
          W. Köpfel, 1525 [BM 3907.bbb.2].

.5.22.   Bugenhagen, Johann, Etlich Christliche Bedencken von
          der Mess.
          J. Prüss II, 1525 [BM 3907.bbb.11].

.5.23.   Binder, Otto V., Eyn nütze Christenliche ermanung an
          die . . . Rhät und gmeynen burger der stat Nüwenburg
          . . . das sie von der . . . warheit des Evangeions
          Christi nit abwichen.
          M. Schürer Erben, 1525 [B SE 2, 64].

P3.5.24. Bader, Johann, <u>Ad illustrem Principem D. Ludovicum</u>
<u>comitem palatinum Rheni de ansere qui sacramentum</u>
<u>edisse dicitur epistola. De vero caenae dominicae</u>
<u>usu sermo.</u>
J. Knobloch, 1526 [R Nfp, 897; Pegg, 129].

.5.25. Bader, Johannes, <u>An den . . . Herren Ludwigen,</u>
<u>Pfaltzgraven bey Rheyn . . . von der Gans, die das</u>
<u>Sacrament gessen hat.</u>
No printer, 1526 [R Nfp, 898].

.5.26. <u>Ein gehapter Ratschlag Lucifers mit seinen amptleüten.</u>
B. Beck, 1529 [Pegg, 1751].

.5.27. Ludwig von Passavant, <u>Verantwortung der schmach und</u>
<u>lesterschrifft so I. Agricola genant . . . im büchlin</u>
<u>Ausslegung Teutscher spruchwort im truck assgon lassen</u>
<u>wider Ulrich Hertzog zü Wirttenberg.</u>
G. Ulricher, ca. 1530 [Pegg, 3359].

.5.28. Rhegius, Urbanus (Simon Hessus, pseud.), <u>Ernnstliche</u>
<u>erbeitunng der Evangelischen Prediger.</u>
J. Cammerlander?, ca. 1535 [Pegg, 3457].

.5.29. Vergerio, Paulus (Pietro Paolo Vergerio), and
Arcimboldo, Giovanni Angelo (Bishop of Novara,
Archbishop of Milan), <u>Catalogo . . . que egli</u>
<u>condannala magiore parte de Figiuoli de dio, con una</u>
<u>reposta.</u>
No printer, 1554 [BM 3902.aa.5].

.5.30. <u>Unterthänigs Schrifftlichs Ansuchen und Suppliciren</u>
<u>An Seine Fürstliche Durchteuchtigkeit, . . . von den</u>
<u>Einwonern und Landsassen der Niderlanden, welche</u>
<u>Protestiren und bedingen, hinfortan nach der</u>
<u>Reformation des Evangelii zuleben.</u>
No printer, 1578 [R BNU I, 66].

.5.31. Nigrinus, Georgius, <u>Gegensatz, Antithesis und</u>
<u>vergleichung der Lehr, Glaubens und Lebens Jesu und</u>
<u>der Jesuiter, d.i. Christi und Antichristi.</u>
No printer, 1581 [R Nfp, 2770].

.5.32. <u>Prognosticon Theologicum Das ist: Gaistliche grosse</u>
<u>practica ausz hailiger biblischer schrifft und</u>
<u>historien.</u>
B. Jobin, 1588 [Greiner].

.5.33. <u>Warnung: des Rohrraffens zu Strassburgs an seinen</u>
<u>unruhrigen Pasquillum.</u>
No printer, 1592 [R Nfp, 3471].

P3.5.34. Mycenius, Johannes, Tractat Teutsch. Von dem . . .
          verfluchten Schatzlein, von Wolfgango Musculo.
              B. Jobin, 1594 [R Nfp, 2748].

  6. ANTI-PAPAL POLEMIC.

P3.6.1.   Murmelius, Johannes, Anzeigung viler Päbstlicher
          missbreuch und Abgottereyen.
              J. Knobloch Erben, n.d. [R Nfp, 2735].

  .6.2.   Die Verteuschten Text aus den Bebstlichen Rechten.
              J. Knobloch, 1521 [R Nfp, 2317].

  .6.3.   Rhegius, Urbanus, Anzaygung das die Römisch Bull
          mercklichen schaden in gewissen manichen menschen
          gebracht hab und nit Doctor Luther.
              J. Prüss II, 1522 [R BNU III, 2008].

  .6.4.   Gengenbach, Pamphilius, Ein Cleglichs Gesprech . . .
          von einem Abt, Turtisanen und dem Teufel wider den
          Pabst Arianum.
              J. Prüss II, 1522 [BM 3906.g.96].

  .6.5.   Kettenbach, Heinrich, Vergleychung der Bäpstsatzung.
              J. Prüss II, 1523 [R Nfp, 2230].

  .6.6.   Was Bebstliche heyligkeyt auss Teütscher nation
          jarlicher Annata und Jedes Bistumb und Ebbtey beson-
          dern taxirt.
              M. Schürer Erben, 1523 [B SE 1, 23].

  .6.7.   Scultetus, V., Werbung Christi uff den yetzigen
          Reichstag zü Speir. Klag Christi wider den Römischen
          Bischoff.
              B. Beck, 1529 [BM 11517.c.55.5].

  .6.8.   Pol, Sebastian, Göttlicher und Bapstlicher Recht
          gleich formige zusag.
              (B. Beck?), 1529 [Pegg, 3396].

  .6.9.   Practica der Pfaffen Anfangk unnd auszganck des gant-
          zen Bapstums ausz alten Practicken und Propheceyen.
              J. Cammerlander, ca. 1535 [Pegg, 3407], ca. 1536
              [B Cam. 97], ca. 1544 [Greiner].

  .6.10. Gengenbach, Phamphilius, Der new Deutsch Bileams Esel.
          Wie die schön Germania durch argelist und zaubery ist
          zur Bäpst Eselin transformiert worden.
              J. Cammerlander, ca. 1535 [Pegg, 131].

  .6.11. Linck, Wenceslaus, Bapsts gespreng auss dem Ceremonien
          Büch. Auch etliche Ceremonien der Bischoffe.
              J. Cammerlander, 1539 [Pegg, 1704].

P3.6.12.   Gengenbach, Pamphilius, Ein Frischer Gumbisst vom
           Bapst und den seinen etwann uber Teutschland
           eingesaltzen.
              J. Cammerlander, 1540 [B Cam. 38], ca. 1545 [R Nfp,
              1868].

   .6.13.   Ein wunderbarlich . . . new geburt dess Babylonischen
           alten und jtzundt newen waldt ochsen im Herzogthum
           Braunschweig geborn, sampt den summaris seiner
           volbrachten onthaten.
              J. Cammerlander, 1544 [B Cam., 34].

   .6.14.   Des Bapst unnd der Pfaffen Badstub.
              No printer, 1546 [Greiner].
              J. Cammerlander, after 1546 [B Cam., 8].

   .6.15.   Vergerius, Paulus, Widerruff Vergerius An statt seiner
           Christlichen Bekanntnus getruckt, in wölcher der
           mehrerteil Misbreüch der Bapstlichen Bischofen
           fleissig beschriben werden, Sampt anderen noch weiter
           furnemen Abgöttereyen, die im Bapstumb, und sonderlich
           zu Rom in Schwanck seind und gehn.
              T. Berger, 1561 [R BNU IV, 2393].

   .6.16.   Flacius Illyricus, Matthias, Catalogus Testium verita-
           tis qui ante nostram aetatem Pontifici Romano eiusque
           erroribus reclamarunt.
              P. Messerschmidt, 1562 [R BNU II, 867].

   .6.17.   Maecardus, Johannes, Homiliae Duae, Quibus Purgatorii
           papistici figmentum . . . confutatur.
              Chr. Mylius I, 1565 [R BNU III, 1457].

   7.   MARRIAGE OF THE CLERGY.

P3.7.1.   Sant Ulrichs des heiligen Bischoffs zu Augspurg . . .
           antwort an Pabst Nicolaum, der sich unterstund nit mit
           recht sonder unbillich, . . . den geistlichen eeliche
           weyber wider gottes ordnung zu uerbieten.
              J. Prüss II, 1521 [S III B, 26].

   .7.2.   (Roemer, Johann), Ein schoner Dialogus von den vier
           grösten beschwernuss eins jeglichen pfarrers. . . .
              M. Schürer Erben, 1521 [B SE 1, 11].

   .7.3.   Luther, Martin, Vom Eelichen Leben.
              M. Schürer Erben, 1522 [B SE 2, 22].

   .7.4.   Luther, Martin, Von den Geystlichen und Kloster gelübte.
              M. Schürer Erben, 1522 [B SE 2, 24].

   .7.5.   Eberlin von Güntzburg, Johann, Wie gar gefehrlich sey.

So ein Priester Kein Eeweyb hat.
  J. Schwann, 1522 [R Nfp, 1530].
  M. Schürer Erben, 1523 [B SE 3, 31].

P3.7.6.   Fuchs, Jacob, Von der Ehe der Priester an den Bischof
          von Würzburg.
            W. Köpfel, 1523 [R Nfp, 1797].

 .7.7.   (Kolb, Hans), Ein Reformation nottdurfftig in der
          Christenheit mit den Pfaffen und iren Mägten.
            M. Schürer Erben, 1523 [B SE 1, 20].
            See also P3.10.3.

 .7.8.   Supplication des Pfarrers unnd der Pfarrkindern zu
          Sant Thoman, ain Ersamen Radt zu Strasbourg
          Uberantwort . . . Darausz ab zunemen, wie er die
          Christliche Ee geliebt.
            No printer, 1524 [R BNU IV, 2257].

 .7.9.   (Capito, Wolfgang, and Zell, Matthaeus), Appelatio
          sacerdotum maritorum, urbis Argentinae adversus insa-
          nam excommunicationem Episcopi
            W. Köpfel, 1524 [R Nfp, 835].

 .7.10.   (Capito, Wolfgang, and Zell, Matthaeus),
          Appelation der eelichen Priester von der vermaynten
          Excommunication des hochwirdigen Fürsten herrn
          Wilhelmen, Bischoffen zu Straszburg.
            W. Köpfel, 1524 [R BNU I, 431].
            Also listed falsely as:
            W. Köpfel, 1522 [R Nfp, 836].

 .7.11.   Lambertus, Francisus, Commentarium de sacro coniugio
          et adversus pollutissimum regni perditionis coelibatum.
            J. Herwagen, 1524 [R Nfp, 2263].

 .7.12.   Luther, Martin, An den Durchleuchtigsten . . . herren
          Albrecht Ertzbischoffen zu Meintz . . . Eyn sendbriff
          . . . sich in die ehelichen stand zu begeben.
            W. Köpfel, 1526 [B Luther, 2228].

 .7.13.   Bugenhagen, Johann, De coniugio episcoporum et diaco-
          norum.
            J. Knobloch, 1526 [Pegg, 411].

 .7.14.   Olearius, Paul, De fide concubinarum in suos pfaffos.
            J. Cammerlander, . 1540 [B Cam., 86].

 .7.15.   Melanchthon, Philippus, Defensio coniugii sacerdotum
          pia et erudita.
            Cr. Mylius, 1540 [Greiner], 1542 [R BNU III, 1539].

 .7.16.   Underricht ausz Götlichen und Gaistlichen Rechten. Ob

ein Priester ein Eheweib, oder Concubin, das ist, ein
beyschläfferin haben mog.
J. Cammerlander, 1545 [R BNU I, 574].

8. APPEALS TO THE GERMAN NATION FOR ECCLESIASTICAL REFORM.

P3.8.1. Ein Reformation des geistlichen und weltlichen stands
durch keyser Sigmundu . . . fürgenummen unnd . . .
auff dyssen tag verhindert.
M. Schürer Erben, 1520 [B SE 1, 5].

.8.2. Etlich Artickel gottes lob, und des heiligen Römischen
Reichs, und der gantzen Teutschen Nation ere und
gemeynen nutz belangend.
J. Prüss II, 1521 [S III B, 25].

.8.3. Teütscher nation beschwerd von den Geistlichen durch
der Weltlichen Reichsständ, Fürsten und Herren, Papst
Adriano schrifftlich überschickt, nechst vergangen
Reichstag zu Nürenberg im xxii. jar angefangen. . . .
J. Schott, 1523 [S II B, 83].

.8.4. Beclagung Tütscher Nation. Disz zeychen bedüt den
text des propheten Hieremie.
J. Prüss II, ca. 1526 [R BNU I, 177].
W. Köpfel, ca. 1526 [R BNU I, 178].
J. Knobloch, 1526 [R BNU I, 179].

.8.5. Ausschreiben, an alle Stende des Reichs, inn der
Christligen Religion aynnngs vorwandten nahmen. Die
Beschwerung des Keyserlichen Cammergerichts
belangende.
J. Prüss II, 1539 [S III B, 48 (misnumbered 47)].

9. DEFENSES OF MARTIN LUTHER.

P3.9.1. (Musaeus, Raphael, pseud.), Murnarus Leviathan . . .
vulgo dictus . . . Gens Prediger. Murnaris, qui et
Schönhenselin, oder Schmutzkolb, dese ipso. . . .
J. Schott, 1521 [S II B, 62].

.9.2. Verkündungs Brieff der Universitet Erdfürt zu schütz
D. Martin Luthers (W. Russ, trans.).
J. Prüss II, 1521 [Pegg, 1086].

.9.3. Marcellus, Joannes, Passion D. Martins Luthers, oder
seyn lydung.
J. Knobloch, 1521 [Pegg, 3020].

.9.4. Marcellus, Joannes, Passio Martini Lutheri.
(J. Prüss II?), 1522 [Pegg, 3022].

P3.9.5.   Hupsch Argument, Red, fragen und antwurt Dreyer
           Personen . . . Alles D. M. L. lere betreffend.
               R. Beck, 1522 [R Nfp, 840].

  .9.6.   Stifel, Michael, Lied von Luthers Lehre.
               J. Schott, 1522 [S II B, 72].

  .9.7.   Stifel, Michael, Von der christförmigen, rechtgegrund-
           ten leer Doctoris Martini Luthers, ein überusz schön
           unstlich Lyed.
               No printer, ca. 1522 [R Nfp, 3277].
               J. Schott, after 1522 [R Nfp, 3278].
               (C. Kerner), before 1525 [R Nfp, 3279].

  .9.8.   Stifel, Michael, Wider Doctor Murnars Lyed von dem
           undergang christlichs Glaubens.
               J. Prüss II, 1522 [BM 3905.d.107].

  .9.9.   Keyserlich mandat jungst uszgangen zu Nürmberg, über
           den yetzt schwebenden (so man spricht) Lutherischen
           handel. Usleg und Christlicher verstand des selbigen.
               J. Knobloch, 1523 [R Nfp, 2517].

  .9.10.   Heinrich von Kettenbach, Schutzrede yedem Christen wol
           zu wissen. Wyder das falsch anklagen der Papisten und
           Münche.
               No printer, 1523 [R Nfp, 2234].

  .9.11.   Alberus, Erasmus, Ein schöner Dialog von Martin
           Luther, unn der geschickten botschafft ausz d'Helle
           die falsche geystligkeit unn das wort Gots belangen.
               No printer, 1523 [R Nfp, 787].

  .9.12.   Brismannus, Johannes (Johann Briessmann), Ad Gasparis
           Schatzgeyri Minoritae plicas responsio per Johannam
           Brismannum pro Lutherano libello de Missis & Votis
           Monasticis.
               J. Herwagen, 1523 [R Nfp, 1096], December 1523 [B
               Luther, 1524].

    10.   PHILIPP MELANCHTHON AND OTHER WITTENBERG THEOLOGIANS.

P3.10.1.   Ernstlich handlung der Universitet zu Wittenberg an
           den Durchleüchtigsten Hochgebornen Churfürsten und
           herren Hertzug Friderich von Sachsen, Die Mesz betref-
           fend.
               M. Flach II, 1521 [R Nfp, 1953].

  .10.2.   Melanchthon, Philipp, De tribus votis monasticis
           Epistola. De Castitate. De Obedientia. De
           Paupertate.
               (J. Herwagen), ca. 1523 [R Nfp, 2661].

P3.10.3.   Jonas, Justus, Adversus Joannem Fabrum . . . pro
           coniugio sacerdotali, Iusti Ionae defensio.   Item M.
           Lutheri ad eundum Ionam Epistola.
              J. Herwagen, 1523 [B Luther, 1670].

   .10.4.   Amsdorf, Nicolaus, Die Hauptartickel durch welche
           gemeyne Christenheit bisher verfürt worden ist.
              M. Flach II, 1523 [S VI B, 70].

   .10.5.   Melanchthon, Philipp, Von dem Ampt der Fürsten.
              S. Bundt, 1540 [R Nfp, 2641].

   11.   STRASBOURG REFORMERS.

P3.11.1.   (Bucer, Martin), Gesprech biechlin neuw Kursthans.
              M. Schürer Erben, 1521 [B SE 1, 6]; 1521 [B SE 1,7].

   .11.2.   (Bucer, Martin), Ain schöner Dialogus unnd gesprech
           zwischen eim Pfarrer und eim Schultheyss betreffend
           allen übel stand der geistlichen.
              M. Schürer Erben, 1521 [B SE 1, 8].

   .11.3.   Zell, Mathaeus, Christeliche verantwortung . . . über
           Artickel im vom Bischofflichem fiscal daselbs entgegen
           gesetzt unnd im rechten ubergeben.
              W. Köpfel, 1523 [R BNU IV, 2514].

   .11.4.   Capito, Wolfgang, Entschuldigung D. Wolffgangs Fa.
           Capito.   Zeigt an ursach warumb er Burger worden,
           geprediget und ein offenliche Disputation begert habe.
              W. Köpfel, 1523 [R BNU I, 430].

   .11.5.   Butzer, Martin (Martin Bucer), Verantwortung M.
           Butzers Uff das im seine widerwertigen, ein theil mit
           der worheit, ein theil mit lügen, zum argsten
           zummessen.
              J. Schott, 1523 [R BNU I, 351].

   .11.6.   Butzer, Martin (Martin Bucer), An ein christlichen
           Rath und Gemeyn der Statt Weissenburg summary seiner
           Predig daselbst gethon.   Mit anhangender ursach seins
           Abscheydens.
              J. Schott, 1523 [S II B, 76].

   .11.7.   Pacatius, Josephus (Lucas Hackfurt or Nicolaus
           Gerbel?), Num Recte Dictum Sit a Concionatoribus Arg.
           Nihil Nobis Tribuas, Nihil Nobis Auferas.
              (J. Herwagen), ca. 1523, [R BNU III, 1749].

   .11.8.   Meyer, Sebastian, Widerrüffung an ein löblich
           Freystatt Strassburg.

No printer, 1524 [R BNU III, 1566], autumn 1524
[R BNU III, 1567].

P3.11.9. Capito, Wolfgang, Das die Pfafheit schuldig sey
Burgerlichen Eyd zuthun on verletzung jrer Eeren.
W. Köpfel, 1524 [Pegg, 477].

.11.10. Hedio, Caspar, Ablenung . . . uff B. Cunrats Tregers
Büchlin.
J. Schott, 1524 [S II B, 88].

.11.11. Capito, Wolfgang, Antwurt D. Wolffgang Capitons auff
Brüder Conradts Augustiner ordens Provincials
vermanung, so er an gemein Eidgnoschafft jungst
geschriben hat.
W. Köpfel, 1524 [R BNU I, 433].

.11.12. Capito, Wolfgang, Wasz man halten, unnd antwurten
soll, von der spaltung zwischen Martin Luther und
Andres Carolstadtt.
W. Köpfel, 1524 [R BNU I, 436].

.11.13. Bucerus, Martinus, De Caena Dominica ad obiecta, quae
contra veritatem Evangelicam Murnerus, partim ipse
finxit, partim ex Roffensi ac aliis pietatis hostibus,
sublegit. Responsio Martini Buceri.
J. Schott, 1524 [S II B, 87].

.11.14. Butzer, Martin (Martin Bucer), Bericht, von disputa-
tionen und gantzen handel, so zwischen Cunrat Treger,
Provincial der Augustiner und den predigern des
Evangelii zu Straszburg sich begeben hat. . . .
J. Schott, 1524 [S II B, 86].

.11.15. Lambert, François, Ein evangelische Beschreibung über
der Barfusser Regel.
(J. Schwann?), 1524 [BM 3905.ee.53].

.11.16. Lambert, François, In regulam Minoritarum . . .
commentarii. . . .
No printer, 1525 [R Nfp, 2265].

.11.17. Pollio, Symphorion (Symphorion Altbieser), Was man
sich gegen newen meren so teglich von den predigern
des Evangelii werden auszgeben halten soll.
W. Köpfel, ca. 1525 [R Nfp, 807].

.11.18. Lambert, François, Commentarii de causis excaecationis
multorum saeculorum.
J. Herwagen, 1525 [BM 8017.e.10].

.11.19. Sigmund von Hohenlohe, Creutz Buchlein oder Ermanunge
. . . an die Vicarien und Chorsverwandten daselbst.

W. Köpfel, 1525 [R BNU II, 1180].
B. Jobin, 1585 [R BNU II, 1181].

P3.11.20. Capito, Wolfgang and Zell, Matthaeus and Anderen,
Verantwortung auf eines Gerichteten Vergicht, jüngst
zu Zabern ausgegangen.
W. Köpfel, 1526 [R Nfp, 1287].

.11.21. Capito, Wolfgang, Dess Conciliums zu Basel satzung und
Constitution wider pfrunden händel und Curtisanen
practick.
W. Köpfel, 1530 [Pegg, 152].

.11.22. Bedrotus, Jacobus, Non esse ferendas in templis
Christianorum imagines et statuas . . . Item epistola
M. Buceri.
J. Prüss II, 1530 [Pegg, 155].

.11.23. Polliones, Simphorianus (Symphorion Altbieser),
Götlicher und Bäpstlicher Recht vergleichung. In
viler Misszbreüch ablänung.
J. Schott, 1530 [S II B, 114].

.11.24. (Bucer, Martin), Ministri Evangelii ecclesiae
Argentoratensis, Epistola apologetica ad syncerioris
Christianismi sectatores per Frisiam orientalem . . .
in qua Evangelii Christi uere studiosi, non qui se
falso Evangelicos iactant, iis defenduntur criminibus,
quae in illos Erasmi Roterodami epistola ad Vulturium
Neocommum, intendit.
P. Schöffer & J. Apronianus, 1530 [R BNU II, 698;
R Nfp 1158].

.11.25. Capito, Wolfgang, Von befridung der kirchen an den
hoch wurdigsten . . . Ertzbischoff und Churfursten zu
Mentz.
M. Apiarius, 1533 [R BNU II, 786].

.11.26. Butzer, Martin (Martin Bucer), Defensio adversus
axioma Catholicum, id est criminationem R. P. Roberti
Episcopi Abrincensis. . . .
M. Apiarius, 1534 [R BNU I, 369].

.11.27. Sturm, Johannes, Epistola de dissidio religionis.
Cr. Mylius, 1539 [Rott, 36].

.11.28. Sturm, Johannes, Epistola . . . de dissidio periculo-
que Germaniae et per quos stet quo minus concordiae
ratio inter partes ineatur.
Cr. Mylius, 1541 [Rott, 36b].

.11.29. Butzer, Martin (Martin Bucer), Abusuum
Ecclesiasticorum et Rationis, qua Corrigi Eos Abusus

oporteat, indicatio Imperatoriae Maiestati, in
comitis Reguespurgi postulanti, exhibita.
W. Rihel, 1541 [R BNU I, 376].

P3.11.30.   Butzer, Martin (Martin Bucer), Wie leicht unnd füglich
Christliche vergleichung der Religion, und des gantzen
kirchendiensts Reformation, bey unsz Teutschen zu
finden, und in das werck zu bringen.
Cr. Mylius, 1545 [R BNU I, 385].

.11.31.   Butzer, Martin (Martin Bucer), Ein Christlich onge-
fährlich bedencken, Wie ein leidlicher anefang
Christlicher vergleichung in der Religion zu machen
sein möchte.
W. Rihel, 1545 [R BNU I, 382].

.11.32.   Bucer, Martin, Wegen und mitlen Deutsche nation inn
Christlicher Religion zu vergleichen.
W. Rihel, 1545 [R Nfp, 1180].

.11.33.   Butzer, Martin (Martin Bucer), Erinnerung, an die
Keis. und Kon. Maiestaten sampt Churfürsten, Fursten
und Stende . . . jetzund zu Wurms versamlet . . . umb
vergleichung und besserung der kirchen in Teütschen
landen, sonderlich und mit ernst furzunemen.
(Cr. Mylius?), 1545 [R BNU I, 381].

.11.34.   (Bucer, Martin), Articuli. Der newe glaub, von den
Doctoren zu Löven, die sich Doctoren der Gottheit
rhumen, in xxxi Articulen fürgegeben.
No printer, 1545 [R Nfp, 1145].

.11.35.   Pappus, Johannes, Contradictiones Doctorum nunc
Romanae Ecclesiae. Indice et Teste Roberto Bellarmino
Politiano, societatis Iesu.
B. Jobin Erben, 1597 [R BNU III, 1766].

    12.   OTTO BRUNFELS.

P3.12.1.   Von dem Evangelischen anstosz. wie unnd in was
gestalt das wort Gottes uffrür mache.
J. Schott, 1523 [S II B, 79].

.12.2.   Hus, Jan, Geistlicher Bluthandel Johanns Huss, zu
Costentz verbrannt . . . (O. Brunfels, ed.).
J. Schott, ca. 1523 [BM 4650.c.19], 1525 [S II B,
97].

.12.3.   Vereum Dei multo magis expedit audire, quam missam, ad
Episocopum Basiliensem. Christus in Parabolis quare
locutus sit. Evangeliorum Ratio et authoritas.
J. Schott, 1524 [S II B, 90].

P3.12.4.   De Ratione Decimarum . . . Propositiones.
           J. Schott, 1524 [S II B, 91].

  .12.5.   Von dem Pfaffen Zehenden, hundert unnd zwen und
           fyertzig Schlussreden.
           J. Schott, 1524 [S II B, 92].

  .12.6.   Pro Ulricho Hutteno, vita defuncto, ad Erasmi
           Roterodami spongiam responsio.
           No printer, 1524 [R Nfp, 1107].

  .12.7.   Hus, Jan, De anatomia Antichristi, Liber unus . . .
           Fragmentum 1 et 2. . . . De unitate Ecclesiae . . .
           De Evangelica perfectione. De pernicie traditionum
           humanarum. . . (O. Brunfels, ed.).
           J. Schott, 1524 [S II B, 94].

  .12.8.   Hus, Jan, Locurum aliquot ex Osee, & Ezechiele
           prophetis . . . De abhorenda sacerdotum et monachorum
           Papisticorum, in Ecclesia Christi abominatione . . .
           Tomus Secundus. Commendatitia brevis M. Lutheri ad
           O. Brunfelsium de vitae, . . . doctrina et martyrio
           Jo. Huss (O. Brunfels, ed.).
           J. Schott, 1525 [S II B, 95].

  .12.9.   Sermonum Joannis Huss ad Populum, Tomus Tertius (O.
           Brunfels, ed.).
           J. Schott, 1525 [S II B, 96].

  .12.10. Processus Consistorialis Martyrii Jo. Huss, cum
           correspondentia Legis Gratiae, ad ius Papisticum, in
           Simoniacos & fornicatores Papistas. Et De Victoria
           Christi . . . (O. Brunfels, ed.).
           J. Schott, 1525 [S II B, 98].

  .12.11. Der Christen Practica, durch alle hohe und nidere
           stande, wess die sich zu irer leib und seel wolfart
           biss zu end der welt und dieses jämerlichen wesens
           zuhalten pflichtig.
           J. Cammerlander, 1540 [B Cam., 13].

   13.   POLEMIC AGAINST EPISCOPAL AUTHORITY.

P3.13.1.   Meyer, A., Mandat von eynem Ersamen Rat der stat Basel
           gegen des Bischoffs Vicari.
           J. Schwann, 1524 [Pegg, 146].

  .13.2.   Bader, Johann, Artickel und clagstuck wider Johan
           Bader von geystlichen fiskal zu Speyer . . . Antwort
           I. Baders.
           No printer, 1524 [BM 3906.e.44].

P3.13.3.   Halesius, Alexander, De authoritate verbi Dei liber
           contra episcopum Lundensem.
               Cr. Mylius, 1542 [R Nfp, 1950].

  .13.4.   Westerburg, Gerhart, Von dem grossen Gottesdienst der
           Löblichen Statt Cöllen. Eine vergleichung der statt
           Cöllen, mit den heiligen Hierusalem.
               W. Rihel, 1545 [R Nfp, 3483].

  .13.5.   Westerburg, Gerhart, An die weltliche stende, Nemlich
           Graven, Ritterschafft, Stette und gemaine Landschafft
           des Cöllschen Ertzbischtumbs, von sachen so zwischen
           dem . . . Ertzbischoffen von Cöln und dem Wirdigen
           Thumcapitel Christlichen Religion halben erhoben, und
           wem man von Rechts wegen schuldig sei zu volgen.
               W. Rihel, 1545 [R Nfp, 3482].

  .13.6.   Westerburg, Gerhart, Das der allerheiligster Vatter
           der Pabst unnd die heilige mutter die Römische Krch
           mitt ihrer aller Getrewster Dochter der Stadt Cöllen
           inn sachen des Glaubens nicht ihrren konnen.
               W. Rihel, 1545 [Greiner].

  .13.7.   Pollicarius, Johannes, Antwort auff das vergiffte büch
           des Bischoffs zu Naumburg . . . zu Erffurd im
           offentlichen truck ist auszgangen wider unsere Lehr
           und Kirchen.
               S. Emmel, 1557 [R BNU III, 1907].

  .13.8.   Pollicarius, Johannes, Von der Kirchen Wider die zwey
           Bucher des Bischoffs zu Naumburg (Julius Pflug) und
           Martini Venatorii zu Mentz und Erffurd im Truck
           auszgangen wider unsere Lehr und Kirchen andere
           Antwort.
               S. Emmel, 1557 [R Nfp, 2964].

      14.   FRENCH POLEMICAL TRACTS AND TREATISES.

P3.14.1.   Dumolin Guillaume, Traicté de l'utilité et honesteté
           du mariage et s'il est licite aux prestres de soy
           marier.
               J. Prüss II, 1527 [S III B, 40].

  .14.2.   Dumolin, Guillaume, Notable et utile traicté du zele
           et grant desir que doibt voir ung vrai chrestien pour
           garder a Jesus Christ son honneur entier.
               J. Prüss II, 1527 [S III B, 40].

  .14.3.   Dumolin, Guillaume, Tres utile traicté du vray regne
           de l'Antechrist maintenant reuelé et cogneu.
               J. Prüss II, 1527 [S III B, 40].

P3.14.4. Schuch, Wolfgang, Epistre chrestienne envoyee a
          Monseigneur le duc de Lorayne.
            J. Prüss II, ca. 1530 [BM c.37.a.22.5].

  .14.5. Guillaume de Furstenberg, Declaration faicte . . .
          touchant le querele qu'il a avec Sebastian
          Vogelspergern.
            J. Prüss II, 1539 [Peter, VII].

  .14.6. Guillaume de Furstenberg, Seconde Déclaration faicte
          . . . côtre la response publiée par ung meschant
          homme.
            B. Beck, 1540 [Greiner].

  .14.7. (Sleidan, Jean), Escript adressé aux electeurs Princes
          et aultres Estatz de l'Empire . . . comme et par quelz
          moiens s'est eslevé la papalité, la decadence
          d'icelle, ses merveilleuses practicques. . . .
            J. Knobloch II, 1542 [Peter, XIa).

  .14.8. Farel, Guillaume, Oraison tres devote en Laquelle est
          faicte la confession des pechez des fidelles qui ainsi
          crient après dieu.
            P. Messerschmidt, 1543 [Peter, XI].

  .14.9. Marcourt, Antoine, Le livre des marchans.
            (R. Guédon), 1547 [Peter, XIIb].

  .14.10. Jean de Rochefort, Livre de la Cène.
            No printer, 1548 [Peter, XV].

  .14.11. Responsio christianorum Jurisconsultorum ad Fr.
          Duareni commentarios de ministeriis ecclesiae atque
          beneficiis et alias eius declamationes.
            Chr. Mylius I, 1556. [R BNU III, 1989].

  .14.12. Hotomann, Francois (Francois Hottman), Epistre envoyée
          au Tygre de la France.
            (Chr. Mylius I), 1560 [R Nfp, 2080].

  .14.13. Traicté de la croix et affliction des enfans de Dieu,
          utile à tous pour le temps de persecution.
            (J. Neslé?), 1563 [Peter, XXVII].

  .14.14. Actes de la dispute et conference tenue à Paris . . .
          Entre deux docteurs de Sorbonne et deux ministres de
          l'Eglise réformée. (Clandestine editions.)
            (P. Estiart (?), 1566 [R BNU I, III], 1566 [Peter,
            XXX], ca. 1567 [Peter, XXXII].
            No printer, 1568 [R Nfp, 742].
            (While Estiart's name and the city of Strasbourg
            appear on the title page of the first three of
            these editions, they were clandestine editions,

probably printed in Lyons. Estiart had died by
1564. See Peter II, p. 23, pp. 39-41.).

15. POLEMIC AGAINST THE COUNCIL OF TRENT.

P3.15.1. Der Bawren Reichstag und Concilium. Wesz sich die
sieben Bawren ausz sieben Landschafften
vereynigt. . . .
J. Cammerlander, 1539 [R Nfp, 3089].

.15.2. Eins Hurenwirts, aber doch schrifftlich gesprech mit
ein unerkannten Bischoff, wie sie ungefer gen Trient
aufs Concilium zureysen, im feldt zusammen kommen.
Ein . . . Straff Büchlin.
J. Cammerlander, 1546 [R Nfp, 2087].

.15.3. Ein Gesprech Deutscher Nation mit dem alten Rolland.
No printer, 1546 [BM 8073.cc.35].

.15.4. Zwei decret des Trientischen Concili warauff die Lehre
ihrer Kirchen sthehn solle.
G. Messerschmidt, 1546 [BM 3906.cc.108].

.15.5. Melanchthon, Philipp, Recusationsschrifft in welche
alle Protestierende Religions und Eynungs verwandte
Stende ursach anzeigen warumb jr Chur und F.G. das
von Bapst Paulo dem dritten zu Trient angesetzt
Concilium zu besuchen nicht schuldig.
W. Köpfel, 1546 [Pegg, 1225].

.15.6. (Calvin, Jean) and Paul III, Responsio ad epistolam
pontificis Romani Coloniensibus missam in causa
religionis.
W. Rihel, 1546 [Pegg, 3362].

.15.7. La Response des tresillustres Electeurs et Princes du
Sacré Empire Romain à l'ambassadeur du pape Pie III,
sur la harangue . . . à eux faitte pour assister au
Concile general mandé à Trente.
(P. Estiart?), 1561 [Peter, XXVI].

.15.8. Stattliche Auszfürung der Ursachen, darumben die Chur,
unnd Fürsten, auch andere Stende der Augspurgischen
Confession, des Papst Pij IIII. auszgeschriben ver-
meynt Concilium, so er gegen Trient angesetzt. . . .
Chr. Mylius I, 1564 [R BNU I, 112], 1566 [R BNU I,
113].

.15.9. Gravamina. Adversus Synodi Tridentinae Restitutionem
seu continuationem, a Pio IIII. Pontifice indicatam,
oppositi gravamina (Laurentius Tuppius, ed.).
S. Emmel, 1565 [R BNU II, 1034].

16. JOHANN FISCHART.

P3.16.1.   Nacht Rab oder Nebelkräh. Von dem uberausz
           Jesuwidrischen Geistlosen schreiben unnd leben des
           Hans Jacobs Gackels.
               (B. Jobin?), 1570 [R BNU II, 849].

 .16.2.   Der Barfüsser Secten und Kuttenstreit. Sihe wie der
           arm Sanct Franciscus unnd sein Regel . . . Von seinen
           eignen Rottgesellen den Barfuessern und Franciscanern,
           Durch ire secten selben gemarttert, zerrissen, zer-
           bissen . . . gemacht würt . . . Anzuzaigen die Römisch
           ainigkeit. . . .
               B. Jobin, 1570 [R Nfp, 169a; WJ11].

 .16.3.   Gorgoneum caput. Ein new seltzam Meerwunder ausz den
           Newen erfundenen Inseln, von ettlichen Jesuitern an jre
           gute gunner geschickt.
               B. Jobin, 1572 [R Nfp, 1720a].

 .16.4.   Fides Jesu et Jesuitarum . . . Item Juramentum Pii
           Papae IIII continens capita Pontificiae Religionis
           cum confutatione eiusdem.
               B. Jobin, 1573 [R Nfp, 1720].

 .16.5.   Eygenwissenliche . . . Contrafeytungen oder
           Antlitzgestaltungen der Römischen Bapst von der Zahl
           28. von dem 1378. Jar, bisz auff den heut Stulfähigen,
           künstlich angebildet.
               B. Jobin, 1573 [R BNU II, 850].

 .16.6.   (Marnix, Philipp), Binenkorb Desz Heyl. Römischen
           Jmenschwarms . . . Sampt Läuterung der H. Römischen
           Kirchen Honigwaben . . . Durch Jesuwalt Pickhart, des
           Canonischen Rechtens Canonisirten . . . (J. Fischart,
           trans.).
               B. Jobin, 1579 [R Nfp, 1700], 1580 [R BNU II, 855],
                 1581 [R BNU II, 856], 1586 [R BNU II, 859], 1588
                 [R BNU II, 861].

 .16.7.   Die Wunderlichst, Unerhortest Legend und Beschreibung.
           Des Abgefuhrten Quartirten Gevierten und
           Viereckechten Vierhörnigen Hütleins . . . Alles
           Jesuwalt Pickart, den Unwürdigen Knecht der Societet
           der Glaubigen Christi.
               B. Jobin, 1580 [R Nfp, 1721].

 .16.8.   Beschläge zum Heiligthumskästlin. Heilgthumsspang
           Jesuwalti Pickhart, zu beschlagung gegenwertigs
           Heiligthumskästlinoder Brotkorbs.
               B. Jobin, 1583 [R BNU II, 857a].

P3.16.9. Der Heilig Brotkorb Der H. Römischen Reliquien . . .
          Das ist Iohannis Calvini Notwendige vermanung, von der
          Papisten Heiligthum: Darausz zu sehen, was damit für
          Abgöttery . . . getrieben worden, dem Christlichen
          Leser zu gute verteuscht (J. Fischart, trans.).
              B. Jobin, 1583 [R BNU I, 414], 1584 [R BNU I, 415],
                1590 [R BNU I, 416], 1594 [R BNU I, 417].

.16.10. Uncalvinisch Gegen Badstüblein, Oder Auszeckung des
          ungeformten dreyeckichten, auszkommenen Calvinischen
          Badstübels, so newlich ein Papist so sich Johan
          Baptista Badweiler nennt, zu hohn unnd Schmach, dem in
          Franckriech newlichsten volbrachten zug, der
          Teutschen, hat aussprengen dörfen. Darinnen
          ein Vorspieglung von unerhörter Badenfart der
          Spanischen Armadagen. . . .
              B. Jobin, 1589 [R Bib. Mun., 991].

.16.11. Wohlbedenckliche Beschreibung des an dem Konig in
          Frankreich newlich verrhäterlich begangenen
          Meuchelmords von einem Monch Prediger Ordens.
              B. Jobin, 1589 [Greiner].

.16.12. Newer creutzgang. Das ist etliche gebett, die der Bapst
          in disem lauffanden Jahr . . . wieder die Kron
          Franckreich . . . zusprechen verrodnet.
              B. Jobin, 1589 [Greiner].

  17. THE BISHOP'S WAR.

P3.17.1. Gebhard, Erzbischof von Köln, Protestationschrift . .
          . wider den angestellten Visitationtag des Key:
          Cammergerichts zu Speyer.
              No printer, 1585 [R BNU II, 939].

.17.2. Auszschreiben und Grüntlicher, Warhafftiger,
          Beständiger Bericht . . . Warumbwir uns etlicher
          unserer Mitcapitularen, der Bäpstischen Religion
          verwandten.
              No printer, 1585 [R BNU I, 117].

.17.3. Instrumentum Requisitionis ac Supplicationis Der
          Ehrwürdigen Wolgebornen Herrn Georgen von Sein . . .
          jetzigerzeit Decanats Statthalters des Hohen Stiffts
          Straszburg, Herman Adolphen Graffen zu Solms,
          Johannsen Freyhern zu Winnenberg und Beylstein,
          Ernesten Graffen . . . zu Manszfeld, der Hohen Stifft
          Cöln, Trier, Würtzburg und Straszburg respectivè
          Thumbhern.
              No printer, 1586 [R BNU II, 1246].

P3.17.4. Eines Hoch und Ehrwürdigen Thumbcapittels hoher Stifft
Straszburg, grundtliche Verantwortung und widerlegung,
deren von Graff Christoff Ladiszlaen von Thengen aus-
gegossenen unnd in offnen Truck Publicirten Calumnien
und Schmäschrifft.
No printer, 1590 [R BNU IV, 2391], 1590 [R BNU IV, 2392]

.17.5. Des Heiligen Reichs Freyen Statt Straszburg
Gegenerklärung mit warhaffter gründtlichen
Widerlegung: Der beiden Erklärungs Schrifften, so der
Hochwürdigst . . . Fürst und Herr, Herr Carolus der
Röm: Kirchen Cardinal, Hertzog zu Lottringen, Bischoff
von Metz und Herr Frantz Freyherr zu Kriechingen, zum
theyl wider sie in Truck auszgehn lassen.
No printer, 1592 [R BNU II, 946].

.17.6. Franz, Freyherr von Kriechingen, Erklerung, belangent
die . . . Bischoffliche Election, zu Strazburg. . . .
No printer, 1592 [R BNU II, 1319].

.17.7. Johann Georg, (Margraf zu Brandenburg; Postulirten
Administratoris des Stifft Strasbourg), Zwey
Auszchreiben . . . darinn J. F. G. sich gegen
deselben Stiffts Lehen und Amptleuth, auch allen
Unterthanen in gemein erbeutet, sie bey iren
wolhergebrachten Freyheiten und Gerichtigkeiten zu
Schützen und zu schirmen, und sie ermahnet, gleichfals
wider seine Widersacher treulich bey im auffzusetzen,
und in seinem gehorsam und dienst bestendig,
zuverharren.
No printer, 1592 [R BNU II, 1261].

.17.8. Instructio uff Jedes Stands so hierunter ersuchet
verbesserunge, allein zu bericht der sachen nach
dencken, und vertrawlicher Communication,
ohnvergreifflich in eil, zu vorstehender
Straszburgischer Handlung, der vonder Keys. Maiest.
sechs deputirten Chur und Fürsten verfasset.
No printer, 1593 [R BNU II, 1245].

P4. INTRA-PROTESTANT CONTROVERSY AND ANABAPTISM.

1. ANABAPTIST, SPIRITUALIST, AND SECTARIAN TRACTS.

P4.1.1. Bodenstein, Andreas (Andreas Karlstadt), Von vermügen
des Ablas wider F. Seyler.
M. Flach II, 1520 [Pegg, 280].

.1.2. Bodenstein, Andreas (Andreas Karlstadt), Von
geweychtem Wasser und Saltz wider F. Seyler.
M. Flach II, 1520 [Pegg, 275].

P4.1.3.   (Bodenstein, Andreas or Andreas Karlstadt), Von anbet-
          tung und eer erbietung der zeychen des neüwen
          Testaments.
              J. Prüss II, 1521 [Pegg, 255].

  .1.4.   Schnewyl, Johannes, Der Blinden Fürer bin ich genennt,
          dem der sich selbs blind erkennt.
              No printer, 1521 [R Nfp, 3184].

  .1.5.   Andree Boden von Carstat (Andreas Bodenstein von
          Karlstadt), Sentbrief . . .meldende seiner
          wirthschafft, Nuwe geschicht von pfaffen und munchen
          zu Wittenberg ausgangen.
              J. Prüss II, 1522 [S III B, 30].

  .1.6.   Andres Bodenstein von Carolstat, Von beyden Gestalten
          der Heilige Mysse. Von Zeichen in Gemeyn was sie
          wircken und deuten. Sie seind nit behemer oder
          ketzer, die beyde Gestalt nemen, sonder evangelische
          Christen.
              J. Prüss II, 1522 [S III B, 31].

  .1.7.   Karlstadt, Andreas, Von dem empfahern: zeichen:und
          zusag des heilige Sacraments fleisch und bluts
          Christi. Auch von anbettung und eer erbietung der
          zeichen des Neüwen Testaments.
              M. Schürer Erben, 1522 [B SE 1, 14].

  .1.8.   Karlstadt, Andreas, Ein Sermon. Vom stand der Christ
          gläubigen seelen von Abrahams schoss und Fegfeüwer.
              M. Schürer Erben, 1523 [B SE 2, 32].

  .1.9.   Karlstadt, Andreas (Andreas Bodenstein), Ayn schöner
          Sermon von Spaltung der gutten unnd böszen Engelischen
          Gaystern im Himel.
              No printer, 1524 [R Nfp, 2216].

  .1.10. Bodenstein, Andreas, (Andreas Karlstadt), Ursachen der
          halben A. Carolstatt auss den landen zu Sachsen
          vertryben.
              J. Prüss II, 1524 [Pegg, 248].

  .1.11. Bodenstein, Andreas, (Andreas Karlstadt), Von den
          Sabbat und gebotten feyrtagen.
              J. Schwann, 1524 [Pegg, 262].

  .1.12. Karlstadt, Andreas Bodenstein von, Von Engelen und
          Teuffelen ein Sermon.
              J. Prüss II, 1524 [R BNU II, 1303].

  .1.13. Karlstadt, Andreas (Andreas Bodenstein), Von den
          zweyen höchsten gebotten.
              J. Prüss II, 1524 [R Nfp, 2214].

P4.1.14. Zyegler, Clement, <u>Von der waren nyessung beyd leibs</u>
          <u>und bluts Christi . . . Und von dem Tauff wie man den</u>
          <u>sonder allen zusatz öl, saltz, oder beschwerung,</u>
          handlen sol.
            J. Schott, 1524 [S II B, 93].

  .1.15. Karlstadt, Andreas (Andreas Bodenstein), <u>Dialogus oder</u>
          <u>ein gesprechbüchlin. . . .</u>
            J. Knobloch, 1524 [R Nfp, 2213].

  .1.16. Karlstadt, Andreas (Andreas Bodenstein), <u>Auslegung</u>
          <u>diser Wort Christi.</u>
            J. Prüss II, ca. 1524 [R Nfp, 2212].

  .1.17. <u>Die scharpff Metz wider die (die sich Evangelisch</u>
          <u>nennen) und doch dem Evangelio entgegen seynd. . . .</u>
            (J. Schott or C. Kerner?), 1525 [R Nfp, 2674].

  .1.18. Huebmaier, Balthasar, <u>Von dem Christlichen Tauff der</u>
          <u>glaubigen.</u>
            No printer, 1525 [<u>Gut Jb.</u> 1963, 104].

  .1.19. Ziegler, Clemens, <u>Büchlein claren verstandt vondem</u>
          <u>leib und blut Christi.</u>
            J. Schwann, 1525 [R BNU IV, 2521].

  .1.20. Denck, Hans, <u>Vom Gesetz Gottes, wie das Gesetz auf-</u>
          <u>gehoben sei und doch erfullt werden muss.</u>
            J. Prüss II, 1526 [<u>Gut. Jb.</u> 1963, 102].

  .1.21. Cellarius, Martinus (Martin Borrhaus), <u>De operibus Dei.</u>
            (J. Herwagen), 1527 [R Nfp, 1323].

  .1.22. Buenderlin, Johann, <u>Ein gemeyne berechnung uber der</u>
          <u>heyligen schrifft inhalt.</u>
            B. Beck, 1529 [Greiner].

  .1.23. Buenderlin, Johann, <u>Ausz was ursach sich gott in die</u>
          <u>nyder gelassen un in christo vermenschet ist.</u>
            No printer, 1529 [Greiner].

  .1.24. Hoffman, Melchior, <u>Dialogus und gründliche berichtung</u>
          <u>gehaltner disputation in land zu Holsten . . . von .</u>
          <u>. . nachtmal des Herren.</u>
            B. Beck, 1529 [Deppermann, 8].
            No printer, 1530 [Krebs and Rott I, 210].

  .1.25. Schwenckfeld, Caspar, <u>Ein Christlich bedencken, Ob</u>
          <u>Judas und die ungleubigen falschen Christen, den leib</u>
          <u>und das blut Jesu Christi im Sacrament des Nachtmals,</u>
          <u>etwann empfangen oder auch noch heut empfahen und</u>
          <u>niessen mögen.</u>
            B. Beck, 1529 [R Nfp, 3205].

P4.1.26. Schwenckfeld, Caspar, Apologia und erclerung der
          Schlesier daz sy den leib und blut Christi im Nachtmal
          des herren und im geheimnisz des. h. Sacraments nicht
          verleücknen.
              B. Beck, 1529 [R BNU IV, 2105].

   .1.27. Schwenckfeld, Caspar, Bekanntnuss vom. H. Sacrament
          des leibs unnd bluts Christi, auff frag und antwort
          gestellet.
              J. Schwintzer, 1530 [R Nfp, 3206].

   .1.28. Entfelder, Christian, Von den manigfalten imm glauben
          zerspaltungen dise jar erstanden. Inn sonderheit von
          der tauffspaltung.
              No printer, 1530 [Krebs and Rott I, 204].

   .1.29. Hoffmann, Melchior, (Prophetien des lienhart jost).
              No printer, 1530 [Krebs and Rott I, 210g], 1532
              [Krebs and Rott I, 210g].

   .1.30. Entfelder, Christian, Von Wahrer Gottseligkeit.
              No printer, 1530 [Krebs and Rott I, 204 n.].

   .1.31. Buenderlin, Johann, Erklärung durch Vergleichung der
          biblischen geschrifft das der wassertauf sampt anderen
          äusserlichen gebräuchen in der apostol. Kirchen geubet
          ohn Gottes befelch und zeugniss der geschrifft von
          etlichen diser zeit wider efert wird.
              No printer, 1530 [Krebs and Rott I, 355].

   .1.32. Schwenckfeld, Caspar, Vom waren und falschen verstandt
          unnd Glauben, Sampt den ursachen desz irrthumbs und
          abfals imm Artickel von dem H. Sacrament desz leibs
          und bluts Christi. Auff. D. Johann Fabri
          calumnien. . . .
              P. Schöffer, 1530 [R BNU IV, 2106].

   .1.33. Hofmann, Melchior, Prophetische gesicht und
          Offenbarung . . . einer Gottesliebhaberin. . . .
              B. Beck, 1530 [R Nfp, 2035].

   .1.34. Hofmann, Melchior, Prophecey od weyssagung usz warer
          heiliger gotlicher schrifft.
              B. Beck, 1530 [R Nfp, 2036].

   .1.35. Hoffmann, Melchior, Warhafftige erklerung aus heyliger
          schrifft das der Satan und dy ewige verdamnuss nit
          auss gott erwachsen sei.
              J. Knobloch II, 1531 [Pegg, 1314].

   .1.36. Marbeck, Pilgrim. Clare verantwurtung etlicher
          Artickel so jetzt durch irrige geyster schrifftlich
          und mündtlich ausschweben von wegen der ceremonien

dess newen Testaments als predigern tauffen abentmal,
schrifft newlich aussgangen.
No printer, 1531 [Gut. Jb. 1963, 100].

P4.1.37. Marbeck, Pilgrim, Unterricht . . . I. das apostel
ampt, II. das bischofsampt, III. die ceremonien
Christi, IV. unterschiedt der gottheyt und menschheit
Christi, V. die sendung und worts eines newen
propheten, VI. Gebet und gut werck.
No printer, 1531 [Krebs and Rott I, 237].

.1.38. Schwenckfeld, Caspar, Vom underscheide des alten und
newen Testaments . . . Judicium: daz eyn Christ möge
ein obrer sein und wie eyn obrer möge eyn christ sein.
P. Schöffer & J. Schwintzer, 1533 [Krebs and Rott I,
299].
B. Jobin, 1589 [Krebs and Rott I, 299].

.1.39. Schwenckfeld, Caspar, Von erbawung des gewissen und
zunemen des glaubens und eines gottsäligen
christlichen lebens.
No printer, 1534 [R Nfp, 3208].

.1.40. Franck, Sebastian, Des grossen Nothelfers und
weltheiligen S. Gelts oder S. Pfennings Lobgesang
durch ein Ironey und Spotlob schimpfisch gedicht.
No printer, 1542 [R Nfp, 1763].

.1.41. Franck, Sebastian, De Arbore Scientiae Boni Et Mali,
Ex Quo Adamus mortem comedit et adhuc hodie cuncti
homines mortem comedunt.
P. Schmidt, 1561 [R BNU II, 884].

2.   POLEMIC AGAINST ANABAPTISTS AND SECTARIANS.

P4.2.1. Luther, Martin, Ein brieff an die Fürsten zu Sachsen
von dem auffrürischen geyst.
J. Knobloch, 1524 [B Luther, 1932].

.2.2. Luther, Martin, Erklerung wie Carlstat sein lere von
dem hochwirdigen Sacrament und andere achtet unnd
geacht haben will.
J. Prüss II, 1525 [B Luther, 2194].
J. Knobloch, 1525 [S VII, 303].

.2.3. Luther, Martin, Wider die hymelischen propheten, von
den bildern und sacrament.
W. Köpfel, 1525 [B Luther, 2092].

.2.4. Luther, Martin, Das ander teyl wider die himlischen
propheten, vom Sacrament.
W. Köpfel, 1525 [B Luther, 2104].

P4.2.5.   Luther, Martin, Ein Brieff an die Christen zu
           Strassburg wider den schwermer geist.
           W. Köpfel, 1525 [Greiner].

  .2.6.   Luther, Martin, Eyn Schrecklich geschicht unnd gericht
           Gottes über Thomas Münzer.
           W. Köpfel, 1525 [B Luther, 2176].

  .2.7.   Luther, Martin, Das diese wort Christi (Das ist mein
           Leib . . .) noch fest stehen widder die Schwerm
           geyster.
           J. Knobloch, 1527 [B Luther, 2422].

  .2.8.   Bader, Johann, Brüderliche Warnung für dem orden der
           Widertäuffer.
           W. Köpfel, 1527 [BM 3910.a.2].

  .2.9.   Bucer, Martin, Getrewe Warnung der Prediger des
           Evangelii zu Straszburg, über die Artickel, so Jacob
           Kautz Prediger zu Wormbs, kürtzlich hat lassen
           auszgohn, die frucht der Schrifft und Gottes worts,
           den kinder Tauff betreffend.
           No printer, 1527 [R Nfp, 1179].

  .2.10.   Alcuin, De trinitate ac Mysteriis Christi. . . .
           P. Schöffer, 1530 [Krebs and Rott I, 207].

  .2.11.   Butzer, Martin (Martin Bucer), Handlung inn dem
           offentlichen Gesprech zu Straszburg . . . gegen
           Melchior Hoffman.
           M. Apiarius, 1533 [R BNU I, 365], 1533 [Krebs and
              Rott II, 111].

  .2.12.   Butzer, Martin (Martin Bucer), Quid de Baptismate
           Infantium Iuxta Scripturas Dei sentiendum,
           excussis. . . .
           M. Apiarius, 1533 [R BNU I, 367].

  .2.13.   Capito, Wolfgang, Eine wunderbare Geschichte, so sich
           an einem Widertäufer genannt Claus Frey zugetragen.
           M. Apiarius, 1534 [R Nfp, 1288].

  .2.14.   Calvin, Johannes (Jean Calvin), Vivere apud Christum
           non dormire animis sanctos, qui in fide Christi decedunt.
           W. Rihel, 1542 [R BNU I, 406].

  .2.15.   Calvin, Iohannes (Jean Calvin), Psychopannychia.
           W. Rihel, 1545 [R BNU I, 410].

  .2.16.   Calvin, Johannes (Jean Calvin), Brevis Instructio
           muniendis fidelibus adversus errores sectae
           Anabaptistarum.
           W. Rihel, 1546 [R BNU I, 411].

P4.2.17. Calvin, Johann (Jean Calvin), <u>Adversus fanaticam et</u>
<u>furiosam sectam Libertinorum</u>.
W. Rihel, 1546 [R Nfp, 1268].

3. REPORTS ON THE ANABAPTISTS.

P4.3.1. Odenbach, Johannes, <u>Eyn sendbrieff und Ratschlag an</u>
<u>verordnete Richter uber die armen gefangen zu Altzen,</u>
<u>so man nent Widerteuffer</u>.
No printer, 1528 [R Nfp, 2784].

.3.2. Blarer, Thomas, <u>Wie Ludwig Hetzer zu Costentz mit dem</u>
<u>Schwert gericht usz diser zyt abgeschieden ist</u>.
No printer, 1529 [R Nfp, 1018].

.3.3. <u>Warhafftiger bericht der wunderbarlichen Handlung der</u>
<u>Teüffer zu München</u>.
No printer, 1535 [BM 4661.aaaa.35].

.3.4. Dorpius, Henricus, <u>Wahrhafftige historia wie das</u>
<u>Evangelium zu Münster angefangen, und darnach durch</u>
<u>die Widertauffer verstört, wider auffgehört hat</u>.
Cr. Mylius, 1536 [R Nfp, 1523].

.3.5. Rhegius, Urbanus, <u>Ein bedencken der Lüneburgeschen,</u>
<u>Ob einer Oberkeyt gezijmmen die widerteüffer, oder</u>
<u>andere ketzer, zum rechten glauben zu dringen</u>. . . .
J. Frölich, 1538 [R BNU IV, 2013].

4. THE STURM-PAPPUS CONTROVERSY AND THE SPANGENBERG-PISTORIUS
CONTROVERSY.

P4.4.1. Sturm, Johannes, <u>Crontra D. Ioannis Pappi Charitatem</u>
<u>et Condemnationem Christianam</u>.
No printer, 1579 [R BNU IV, 2232].

.4.2. Pappus, Johannes, <u>Defensio IIII</u> . . . <u>contra Sturmium</u>.
No printer, 1580 [R Bib. Mun., 1620].

.4.3. Spangenberg, Cyriacus, <u>Gegenbericht auff Doctorn</u>

<u>Joann. Pastorii Sieben Bose Geister</u>.
B. Jobin Erben, 1596 [R Bib. Mun., 1959].

P5. PROTESTANT DEVOTIONALS, PRAYERBOOKS, AND SERVICE BOOKS FOR
LAY USE.

P5.1.1. Luther, Martinus, <u>Kurtze Form das Pater noster zu</u>
<u>verston und zu betten. Für die jungen Kinder im</u>
<u>Christen Glauben</u>.
M. Flach II, 1520 [S VI B, 52].

P5.1.2.   Luther, Martinus, <u>Underwisung Wie man beichten sol</u>.
          M. Flach II, 1520 [S VI B, 54].

  .1.3.   Rhegius, Urbanus, <u>Underricht Wie ein Christen mensch</u>
          <u>got seinem herren teglich beichten soll</u>.
          M. Flach II, 1522 [S VI B, 66].

  .1.4.   Lonicerus, Johannes (Johann Lonitzer), <u>Bericht</u>
          <u>buchlin</u>. <u>Wie das ein yegklich Christen mensch gewisz</u>
          <u>sey der gnaden, huld und guten willen Gottes gegen</u>
          <u>ym</u>.
          J. Schott, 1523 [S II B, 74].

  .1.5.   Spalatin, Georg, <u>Etliche Christliche gebett und</u>
          <u>underweysung</u>.
          W. Köpfel, 1524 [R Nfp, 3246].

  .1.6.   Johannes Eberlin von Günzburg, <u>Ein Schoner Spiegel</u>
          <u>eins Christlichen lebens</u>.
          J. Schwann, 1524 [R Nfp, 1531].

  .1.7.   <u>Von der Evangelischen Messz. Mit schönen Gebetten,</u>
          <u>vor und nach der entpfahung des Sacraments</u>.
          M. Flach II, 1524 [S II B, 75].

  .1.8.   Bugenhagen, Johann, <u>Was un welches die sund sey in</u>
          <u>den heyligen Geist</u>. <u>Von lesung der Psalmen</u>.
          J. Prüss II, 1524 [BM 3406.c.27].

  .1.9.   <u>Eyn schön neuw Lied vom glauben unnd Testament auch</u>
          <u>von der bereytung zu dem tysch Gottes</u>. . . .
          Schürer Erben, 1524 [B <u>SE</u> , 1960].

  .1.10. <u>Enchiridion: oder eyn Handbüchlein, eynem yeglichen</u>
          <u>Christen fast nutzlich bey sich zu haben</u> . . . <u>Der</u>
          <u>ander theyl. Straszburger Kirchengesang</u> . . . <u>Das</u>
          <u>dritt theyl. Straszburger Kirchenampt</u>.
          W. Köpfel, 1525 [R Nfp, 1544].

  .1.11. Luther, Martin, <u>Christliche vorbetrachtung so man will</u>
          <u>betten des heylig Vatter unser</u>.
          M. Schürer Erben, 1525 [B <u>SE</u> 3, 39].

  .1.12. Gast, Hiob, <u>De Toleranda cruce paraclesis seu exhor-</u>
          <u>tatio in gratiam infirmioris cuiuspiam amici</u>.
          J. Herwagen, 1526 [Greiner; Pegg, 1149].

  .1.13. Melanchthon, Philipp, <u>Ein büchlin für die leyen unnd</u>
          <u>Kinder</u>.
          J. Prüss II, 1527 [R BNU III, 1525].

  .1.14. Eckhart zum Truebel, <u>Ein vetterliche gedruge gute</u>
          <u>zucht lere und bericht Christliche zuleben unnd</u>

sterben an meine kynder und alle frumme Christen.
R. Beck, 1528 [R BNU IV, 2358].

P5.1.15. Otther, Jacobus, <u>Christliche leben und sterben. Wie
sich des Herren nachtmals zu brauchen mit gewisser
Conscienz und frid.</u>
B. Beck, 1528 [R Nfp, 2803].

.1.16. Brunnfels, Otto, <u>Biblisch Bettbuchlin Der Altvätter,
und herrlichen Weibern, beyd Alts und Newes
Testaments. Ermanung zu dem Gebett, und wie man
recht Betten sol.</u>
J. Schott, 1531 [S II B, 121].

.1.17. Otther, Jacob, <u>Ein kurtzer bericht, wie man sich bey
den krancken und sterbenden halten soll.</u>
M. Apiarius, 1534 [R BNU III, 1736].

.1.18. Eckhart zum Truebel, <u>Bericht und anzeyge zu lob und
eeren und preiss Gottes, aller menschen und Creaturen.</u>
J. Frölich, 1539 [R Nfp, 3370].

.1.19. Bader, Johannes, <u>Ein gottsälige Anleytung und kurtze
underweysung zum Reich Gottes.</u>
J. Frölich, ca. 1540 [R Nfp, 899].

.1.20. <u>Enchiridion Christianismi: de vita et passione Jesu
Christi.</u>
J. Schott, 1541 [BM 551.e.40].

.1.21. Otter, Jacob, <u>Bettbüchlin für allerley gemeyn anligen
der Kirchen.</u>
W. Rihel, 1546 [Pegg, 3336].

.1.22. Cordier, Maturin, <u>Quatre epistres chrestiennes en
Ryme françoise.</u>
(R. Guédon), 1547 [Peter, XIIIa].

.1.23. <u>Der Psalter in gebett gestellt, sampt anderen ange-
henckten und zugethanen gebetten, an vil orten
gebessert mit Titelen und eynem Register.</u>
W. Rihel, 1550 [R BNU III, 1956].

.1.24. Ratz, Jacobus, <u>Vom Fastenn. Welches das Recht,
Christlich, unnd notwendig, auch das falsch und
onchristlich Fasten sey. . . .</u>
J. Frölich, 1554 [R Bib. Mun., 1783].

.1.25. Rodt, Mathias, <u>Das Salve Regina verteutscht . . . Mit
anzeygung wie die H. Junckfraw Maria und die lieben
Heyligen recht zu ehren seyen.</u>
S. Emmel, 1555 [R BNU III, 2022].

.1.26. <u>Tischgebete für die Kinder Uber und Ab disch.</u>

Heylsame und Tröstliche Sprüch, ausz Göttlicher
Heyliger geschrifft . . . auszzeichnet. . . .
S. Emmel, 1557 [R BNU IV, 2329].

P5.1.27.   Luther, Martin, Ein sehr christlich . . .
Bettbüchlein.
S. Emmel, 1560 [R Nfp, 2473].

.1.28.   Cherlerus, Paulus, In natalem Jesu Christi, Salvatoris
nostri Dei patris & Mariae virginis.
Chr. Mylius I, 1562 [R BNU I, 475].

.1.29.   Nuber, Vitus, Ettliche sehr nötige und tröstliche
Gebett.
T. Berger, 1562 [R Nfp, 2776].

.1.30.   Luther, Martin, Beteglöcklin Doctoris Martini Lutheri,
ausz allen des Mannes Gottes gedruckten Büchern
zusammengestellt durch M. Petrum Trewer.
B. Jobin, 1571 [R Nfp, 2474], 1579 [R Nfp, 2475],
1580 [R BNU III, 1454], 1591 [R Nfp, 2477].

.1.31.   Poppius, Georgius, Elegia in natalem Jesu Christi
salvatoris nostri diem de lapsu, primorum parentum
& reparatione humane generis scripta.
Chr. Mylius II, 1572 [R Nfp, 2973].

.1.32.   Habermann, Johannes, Wöchentlich Christliche Gebeten
. . . lateinisch geordnet . . . Num aber auf ein neues
nach der letzten lateinischen Mehrung . . .
verdeutscht.
B. Jobin, 1575 [R Nfp, 1947].

.1.33.   Neuheuser, Samuel, Ein Christliches Trostbüchlein in
zwolfe unterschidliche Capitel abgetheylet.
B. Jobin, 1575 [R Nfp, 2756], 1580 [R Nfp, 2757],
1585 [R Nfp, 2758], 1593 [R Nfp, 2759].
B. Jobin Erben, 1595 [Greiner].

.1.34.   Avenarius, Johannes (Johann Habermann), Precationes in
singulos septimanae Dies.
B. Jobin, 1582 [R Nfp, 892], 1591 [R BNU I, 120].

.1.35.   Handbüchlein darin der Psalter Davids, die Sprüche und
Prediger Salomonis sampt den gebruchlechsten
Christlichen Lobgesängen.
B. Jobin, 1593 [R Nfp, 1952].

P6.   PROTESTANT HYMNALS AND DEVOTIONAL SONGS.

1.   COLLECTIONS OF HYMNS FOR CONGREGATIONAL SINGING.

P6.1.1.   Luther, Martin, Enchiridion geistlicher gesenge, so
           man yetzt . . . yn den Kirchen syngt.   Gezogen ausz
           der heyligen geschrifft des waren und heyligen
           Evangelions. . . .
               W. Köpfel, 1525 [R Nfp, 2491].

.1.2.   Walther, Johannes, Wittenbergische Gesangbüchli.
               P. Schöffer & M. Apiarius, 1534 [R Nfp, 3463], 1537
               [R Nfp, 3464; B Luther, 3674].

.1.3.   Weisse, Michael, Von Christo Jesu unserem säligmacher
           . . . etlich Christliche Kostliche lobgesäng ausz
           einem vast herrlichen Gsangbuch gezogen (Katharine
           Zell, ed.).
               J. Frölich, 1534 [R Nfp, 3481], 1534 [R Nfp, 2408],
               1535 [R Nfp, 2409], 1536 [R Nfp, 2410], 1536 [R
               Nfp, 2411].
           Also listed as:
           Byechlin der geystlichen gesang. . . .
               J. Frölich, 1536 [R Nfp, 1209].

.1.4.   Gesangbuch darinn begriffen sind, die aller für-
           nemisten und besten Psalmen, Geistliche Lieder und
           Chorgeseng, aus dem Wittenbergischen, Strasburgischen
           und anderer Kirchen Gessängbuchlin. . . .
               G. Messerschmidt, 1541 [R Nfp, 1885].

.1.5.   Ein New Auserlesen Gesangbüchlin in das die besten
           verteudschten Psalmen, Hymni, und ander Chorgesenge
           und Geistliche Lieder, aus den bewertisten Kirchen
           Gesangbuchlin (preface by Martin Bucer).
               W. Köpfel, 1545 [R Nfp, 1888], 1547 [R Nfp, 1889].

.1.6.   Das Newer und gemeret Gesangbüchlein, Darinn Psalmen,
           Hymni, Geistliche Lieder, Chorgesenge, Alte und newe
           Festlieder, sampt etlichen Schrifftsprüchen und
           Collect gebetlin. . . .
               T. Berger, 1559 [R Nfp, 1890], 1560 [R Nfp, 1891],
               1562 [R BNU III, 1892], 1566 [R Nfp, 1893].

.1.7.   Das gros Kirchen Gesangbuch, darinn begriffen sind die
           aller furnemisten und besten Psalmen, Lieder, Hymni,
           und alte Chorgesenge . . . Hat mehr bei L. stücken
           jetzund mehr, dann das erste Kirchen Gesangbuch anno
           XLI. allhie ausgegangen.
               G. Messerschmidt, 1560 [R Nfp, 1886].
               T. Berger, 1572 [R Nfp, 1887].

P6.1.8.   Ein new ausserlesen Gesangbüchlin fur die Kirchen.
           Von newen übersehen.
               P. Acker, 1568 [R Nfp, 1894].

  .1.9.   Gesangbüchlin von Psalmen, Kirchengesängen und
           Gaistlichen Liedern. D. Mart. Luthers. Auch viler
           anderer Gotseligen Leut. . . .
               B. Jobin, 1576 [R Nfp, 1895].

  .1.10.   Geistliche Gesänge, Mit vier Stimmen zu singen in den
           Kirchen und Schulen zu Straszburg.
               N. Wyriot, 1577 [R Nfp, 1884].

  .1.11.   Reinigius, Paschasius (Paschasius Reinicken), Hausz
           Kirchen Cantorei.
               No printer, 1595 [R Nfp, 3091].

  .1.12.   Habermann, Johannes, Christliche Gebett in Gesänge
           auff bekandte Melodien gestellt.
               B. Jobin Erben, 1595 [R Nfp, 1948].

  .1.13.   Habermann, Johannes, Bettbüchlein Gesangweisse, in
           artige inn Kirchen und Schulen bekandte und gebreuch-
           liche Reumenbundt und Melodias.
               B. Jobin, 1595 [R Nfp, 1949].

     2. CHURCH MUSIC FOR CHOIRS.

P6.2.1.   Dietrich, Sixtus, Magnificat octo Tonorum.
               P. Schöffer & M. Apiarius, 1535 [R Nfp, 1510], 1537
               [R Nfp, 1511].

  .2.2.   Orlando di Lasso, Theatrum musicum aliorumque
           praestantissimorum musicorum selectissimae cantiones
           sacrae, quatuor quinque et plurium vocum.
               N. Wyriot, 1580 [R Nfp, 2800].

  .2.3.   Maior, Georgius, Cantica ex sacris Literis, in eccle-
           sia cantari solita cum hymnis et collectis.
               J. Rihel, 1594 [R BNU III, 1465].

     3. POPULAR SPIRITUAL SONGS.

           See also P3.9.6.; P3.9.8.

P6.3.1.   Lied . . . Wie allweg die geystlichen hon Die krancken
           in der letsten not Gefuret hand so ferr von Gott. Mit
           erschröcklichen worten vil.
               U. Morhard, n.d. [S IV Mor., 15].

  .3.2.   Lied vom glauben unnd Testament, auch von der

bereytung zu dem tysch Gottes.
U. Morhard, n.d. [S IV Mor., 14].

P6.3.3.   Zwey Lieder Das erst, was wöllen wir aber heben an .
. . Das ander, Frölich so wil ich singen, und dancken
meinem Gott.
T. Berger, n.d. [R Nfp, 2380].

.3.4.   Zwey . . . Geistliche Lider, Das erst, Es ist ein
schaffstal und ein Hirt . . . Ein ander . . . nun
hörend zu jhr Menschen Kindt, wölt ihr recht selig
werden.
T. Berger, n.d. [R Nfp, 2383].

.3.5.   Geistlich Lied von der frommen witfrawen Judith.
T. Berger, n.d. [R Nfp, 2366].

.3.6.   Zwey . . . Lieder, Das erst, Hilff Gott das mir
gelinge du Edler schöpffer mein, Das ander Lied, Die
Weiszheit Gottes Vatters zart.
T. Berger, n.d. [R Nfp, 2382].

.3.7.   Von Evangelischer Lehr, ein neüw Lied. . . .
T. Berger, n.d. [R Nfp, 2285].

.3.8.   Zwey . . . Lieder, Das erst, Hör zu du Stoltzer
madensack . . . Das ander . . . Ach Gott wem soll ichs
klagen.
T. Berger, n.d. [R Nfp, 2384].

.3.9.   Zwey . . . Lieder, Das erst, Von deinet wegen bin ich
hie, Herr Gott vernimm mein wort . . . Das ander . . .
Christum von himmel ruff ich an, in disen grossen
nöthen mein.
T. Berger, n.d. [R Nfp, 2387].

.3.10.   Meyenlied von dem gnadenreichen lieblichen Meyen
Christum am Creütz hangende.
T. Berger, n.d. [R Nfp, 2678].

.3.11.   Zwey . . . Lieder, Das erste, Wacht auff in Gottes
namen   Das ander . . . Nun hörend zu on allen
spot.
T. Berger, n.d. [R Nfp, 2379].

.3.12.   Meistergesang. Ein schön neüw weinacht Lied, Gott
schöpffer ich ruff dich an. . . .
T. Berger, n.d. [R Nfp, 2616].

.3.13.   Lied, gezogen aus dem H. Evangelisten Mattheo, am
zwentigsten Capitel von Arbeiterm im Weinberg.
T. Berger, n.d. [R Nfp, 2368].

.3.14.   Zwey . . . Lieder, Das erst, Die Son die steht am

höchsten, die welt hat sich verkert . . . Das ander,
von diser trübsalen letsten zeit.
   T. Berger, n.d. [R Nfp, 2394].

P6.3.15. Zwey . . . Lieder, Das erst, Ach Gott lasz dich erbar-
men . . . Ein ander Lied ausz dem 32. Psalmen Davids,
Es sey dem wol des überschirt.
   T. Berger, n.d. [R Nfp, 2385].

.3.16. Zwey . . . Lieder, Das erst, So will ich aber heben an
und singen in Gottes eer . . . Dz ander Lied, Nun
heb ichs an zu dieser frist, Gott wöll das mir
gelinge.
   T. Berger, n.d. [R Nfp, 2388].

.3.17. Zwey schöne newe Geistliche lieder. Das erste Es ist
vil wunders in der Welt . . . Dz ander . . . Ihr
lieben Christen frewt euch nun.
   T. Berger, n.d. [R Nfp, 2396].

.3.18. Zwey . . . Lieder, Das erst von der usserwwölten Braut
Christi . . . Das ander . . . vom wesen und leben eins
waren Christen.
   T. Berger, n.d. [R Nfp, 2389].

.3.19. Zwey . . . Lieder, Das erst, Ich danck dir lieber
Herre . . . Das ander. Bedacht hab ich und wundert
mich.
   T. Berger, n.d. [R Nfp, 2386].

.3.20. Zwey Lieder, Das erst, von der liebe Gottes . . . Das
ander . . . Ausz den Evangelio Mathei am XX. Cap. wie
unns Gott in seinen Weingarten berufft.
   T. Berger, n.d. [R Nfp, 2390].

.3.21. Zwey . . . Lieder, Das erst, Kumpt her zu mir spricht
Gottes son, Das ander. Ich armer Sünder klag mich seer.
   T. Berger, n.d. [R Nfp, 2392].

.3.22. Zwey . . . Lieder, Das erste, Ich ruff dich
Himmelischer Vatter an, wölst meinen Glauben stercken
. . . Das ander Lied. O Herr und Gott, von Sebaoth,
zu dir schreien wir Armen.
   T. Berger, n.d. [R Nfp, 2393].

.3.23. Zwey . . . Lieder, Das erst, Ungnad beger ich nit von
dir, O Gott . . . Das ander . . . Soltu bey Gott dein
wonung han und seinen Himmel erben.
   T. Berger, n.d. [R Nfp, 2395].

.3.24. Lied, von dem Reichen mann und armen Lazaro . . . Ein
ander geistlich Lied, Von den Siben worten.
   T. Berger, n.d. [R Nfp, 2320].

P6.3.25.   Lied, Ach Gott lasz dichs erbarmen doch.
           T. Berger, n.d. [R Nfp, 2319].

  .3.26.   Drey . . . Lieder, Das erste, Ich habs gewagt gantz
           unverzagt, ausz göttlicher Liebe und trewe. Das ander
           . . . Es giengen drey Gespielen ausz zu dienen der
           heiligen Gottes Braut . . . Das dritt Lied. Mein Gott
           wie lang sol ich warten.
           T. Berger, n.d. [R Nfp, 2399].

  .3.27.   Lied, Die weisheyt des Fleischs wirdt hoch berümpt .
           . . Ein ander . . . O Reicher Gott.
           T. Berger, n.d. [R Nfp, 2321].

  .3.28.   Drey Lieder. Das erst, von dem Heydnischen frewlein
           und der Hochzeit zu Cana Galilea . . . Das ander, Ein
           schön Frawen lob . . . Das dritt . . . Der gnaden
           brunn thut fliessen.
           T. Berger, n.d. [R Nfp, 2400].

  .3.29.   Ein schön neuw Lied, von einem Christlichen Prediger
           Wie er von des Wort Gottes, ist verfolgt unnd getödt
           worden . . . Ein ander Lied, Gottes gnad und sein
           Barmhertzigkeit.
           T. Berger, n.d. [R Nfp, 2358].

  .3.30.   Ein Lied vonn dem frommen Joseph, wie er umb seiner
           tröumen willen von seinen Brüdern verhaszt unnd inn
           Egypten verkaufft ward.
           T. Berger, n.d. [R Nfp, 2316].

  .3.31.   Lied von der gemeinschaft Christi und vom Brotbrechen
           des Herren nachtmal . . . Ein ander . . . darin dz
           gantz leben Unsers Herren Jhesu Christi begriffen.
           T. Berger, n.d. [R Nfp, 2347].

  .3.32.   Lied, von einer Jungfrawen die mit dem bösen Geist
           bessessen was. Ein ander Geistlich Lied, O Got wir
           dancken deiner güt durch Christum Unsern Herren.
           T. Berger, n.d. [R Nfp, 2326].

  .3.33.   Lied. Von der welte lauff, Mit hilffe Gott des Herren
           . . . Ein ander . . . O Jesu zart Gottlicher art, ein
           rosz an alle dornen.
           T. Berger, n.d. [R Nfp, 2328].

  .3.34.   Christenlich Lied, desgleichen vor nie gesehen,
           Begreiffend mit einem Kurzen inhalt das gantz Neuw
           Testament.
           T. Berger, n.d. [R Nfp, 2341].

  .3.35.   Ein new schön Evangelisch Lied . . . Ein ander . . .

Und Gebett umb ein gute stund des todes.
T. Berger, n.d. [R Nfp, 2342].

P6.3.36. Lied, Ewiger Gott in deinem Reich . . . Ein ander
Geistlich Lied, wie Christus den Lazarum von dem Tode
aufferweckt hatt.
T. Berger, n.d. [R Nfp, 2346].

.3.37. Lied, Wacht auff ihr Christen alle, . . . Ein ander
geystlich Lied zu dieser trübsäligen Zeit.
T. Berger, n.d. [R Nfp, 2348].

.3.38. Lied, von dem Reichen Mann und armen Lazaro.
T. Berger, n.d. [R Nfp, 2349].

.3.39. Lied, von Abgott Bell unnd seiner Priesterschaft, und
von ihrem Diebstal.
T. Berger, n.d. [R Nfp, 2351].

.3.40. Lied, O Herre Gott gib den verstaud. . . .
T. Berger, n.d. [R Nfp, 2367].

.3.41. Lied, von der frommen und Gottseligen Junckfrawen
Esther.
T. Berger, n.d. [R Nfp, 2353].

.3.42. Lied von dem Künig Pharon. Hort zu so will ich heben
an.
T. Berger, n.d. [R Npf, 2357].

.3.43. Lied von der vertreybung der Juden zu Rotenburg a.d.
Thawber und von irer Synagog.
M. Schürer Erben, 1521 [B SE 1, 9].

.3.44. Lied, Die Krancken in der letsten not, gefüret hand so
ferr von Gott.
M. Schürer Erben, 1524 [B SE 1, 26].

.3.45. Heyden, Sebald, Der Passion oder das Leiden Jhesu
Christi inn gesangweise gestelt, inn der melodey des
Psalmen Es sind doch selig alle die.
J. Frölich, ca. 1530 [R Nfp, 2012].

.3.46. Vogel, Nicolaus, Lied, von dem verlornen Sun, Luce am
fünfzehenden capitel.
J. Frölich, ca. 1540 [R BNU IV, 2441].

.3.47. Zwey schöne geistliche Lieder.
No printer, 1550 [R Nfp, 2391].

.3.48. Lied, Wie die Predicanten der stat Augspurg geurläubt
und abgeschafft seind, den XXVI. Augusti, A.D. M.D.Ll.
geschehen.
T. Berger, 1551 [R Nfp, 2330].

P6.3.49. Lied, von dem Leiden unnsers Herren Jhesu Christi,
          ausz den vier Evangelisten gezogen . . . Ein ander .
          . . von dem verlornen Son.
               T. Berger, ca. 1555 [R Nfp, 2369].

  .3.50. Gut, Wendelin, Lied . . . die klein Bibel genant von
          glauben liebe, mit sampt der hoffnung.
               P. & P. Köpfel, 1555 [R Nfp, 1946].

  .3.51. Gletting, Benedict, Zwey . . . Lieder. Das erst, Von
          dem Frewlein von Samaria bey Sanct Jacobs Brunnen . .
          . Das ander, von der Bilgerfahrt.
               T. Berger, ca. 1560 [R Nfp, 1906], ca. 1564 [R Nfp,
               2398], 1570 [R Nfp, 2322].

  .3.52. Lied, vonn dem fall Adam und Eve . . . Ein ander . . .
          Lied in meines Herren garten, wachsen der blumlein
          vil.
               T. Berger, 1560 [R Nfp, 2370].

  .3.53. Lied, von dem Göttlichen wort Gottes.
               T. Berger, ca. 1561 [R Nfp, 2371].

  .3.54. Zwey . . . Lieder, Das erst, Ach Gott thu dich
          erbarmen, durch Christum deinen Son . . . Das ander,
          von dem Wolckenbruch geschehen den XX. tag Aprilis
          Im 1562 jar.
               T. Berger, 1562 [R Nfp, 2397].

  .3.55. Geystliche Kriegsrüstung Wider den Turcken, Gebett,
          Psalmen . . . zu Gott um Victori und Sieg wider des
          Christlichen Namens Erbfeind, Denturcken, Allen
          Christen . . . zu gebrauchung.
               Chr. Mylius I, 1566 [R Nfp, 2255].

  .3.56. Dry . . . Lieder. Das erst, ein Klaglied von dem
          absterben . . . Joh. Brentzen . . . Das ander vom
          Herrn D.M. Luthers sterben . . . Das dritt von des
          Herrn D. Justus Jonas seliger abschied.
               T. Berger, ca. 1570 [R Nfp, 2403].

  .3.57. Schrot, Martin, Zwey Hubsche newe Geistliche Lieder,
          Das erst, O Got in dem hochsten thron, . . . Die welt
          die hat ein thummen mut. . . .
               T. Berger ca. 1570 [R Nfp, 3201].

  .3.58. Heymairin, Magdalene, Das Buch der Apostolischen
          Geschichten Gesangweiss gestellt.
               No printer, 1586 [R Nfp, 2014].

  .3.59. Lied, Uff das geschrey so man uff des Bischoffs Grab
          soll horen Ein Requiem aeternam.
               No printer, 1592 [R BNU III, 1365].

P6.3.60. Lantz, Hans, <u>Ein Lustig Glossierendt Liedt, Uff das</u>
          <u>Babstlich Gedicht, von der Statt Strasburg, Anfangent,</u>
          <u>Ir Kirchen rauber alle, Allen Römische Cortisanen und</u>
          <u>Poetischen Babstfreunden zugefallen gesungen, jhe zwey</u>
          <u>Gesätz uff eines.</u>
          No printer, 1592 [R BNU III, 1334].

  .3.61. Suderman, Daniel, <u>Nun höret zu ihr Christen leut, ich</u>
          <u>wil euch warlich sagen.</u>
          No printer, 1596 [R Nfp, 3300].

P7. PROTESTANT MANUALS FOR THE CLERGY.

  1. PROTESTANT POSTILS.

P7.1.1. Luther, Martin, <u>Enarrationes Epistolarum et</u>
         <u>Evangeliorem, quas Postillas vocant</u> (in Latin).
             U. Morhard, 1521 [B <u>Luther</u>, 851].

  .1.2. Luther, Martin, <u>Postil. Oder uszleg der Epistel und</u>
         <u>Evangelien</u> (in German).
             J. Schott, 1521 [R Nfp, 2533].
             J. Knobloch, 1525 [S VII, 299].
             W. Köpfel, 1527 [B <u>Luther</u>, 1128], 1529 [B <u>Luther</u>,
                 1129], 1531 [B <u>Luther</u>, 1130; R BNU III, <u>1442</u>],
                 1544 [B <u>Luther</u>, 1132; R BNU III, 1450].
             W. Köpfel, 1537 [B <u>Luther</u>, 1131]. (Volume I.)
             W. Köpfel, 1539 [B <u>Luther</u>, 1131]. (Volume II.)
             W. Köpfel, 1542 [B <u>Luther</u>, 1131]. (Volume III.)

  .1.3. Bugenhagen, Johannes, <u>Postillatio in Evangelia.</u>
             J. Knobloch, 1524 [R Nfp, 1237], 1524 [R Nfp, 1236].

  .1.4. Luther, Martin, <u>Enarrationes quas Postillas vocant</u>
         <u>in Lectiones Illas quae ex Evangelicis historiis.</u>
             J. Herwagen, 1525 [R Nfp, 2488], 1527 [B <u>Luther</u>,
                 1148]. (Volumes I and II.)
             J. Herwagen, 1526 [R Nfp, 2489]. (Volumes III and IV.)
             J. Herwagen, 1528 [B <u>Luther</u>, 1149].
             G. Ulricher, 1530 [R BNU III, 1441], 1535 [R BNU
                 III, 1444].

  .1.5. <u>Libellus Militantis: Postillationes Paucas et pias</u>
         <u>super Epistolas et Evangelia, quae . . . in diebus</u>
         <u>Dominicis super Missam faciendum recitantur.</u>
             J. Cammerlander, 1536 [B <u>Cam.</u>, 60], 1538 [R Nfp,
                 2283].

  .1.6. Corvinus, Antonius, <u>Postilla in Evangelia Domincales</u>
         <u>totius anni. . . .</u>
             W. Köpfel, 1536 [R Nfp, 1440], 1537 [R BNU I, 592].

P7.1.7.   Corvinus, Antonius, Loci in Epistolas et Evangelia,
          Quae dominicis diebus ac in divorum feriis per totius
          anni. . . .
             W. Köpfel, 1537 [R BNU I, 590].

   .1.8.   Corvinus, Antonius, Loci in Evangelia cum Dominicalia
          tum de Sanctis.
             W. Köpfel, 1537 [R BNU I, 591].

   .1.9.   Hedio, Kaspar, Epitome in Evangelia et Epistolas, quae
          legentur in Templis per circuitum anni. . . .
             Cr. Mylius, 1537 [R BNU II, 1096].

   .1.10. Butzer, Martin (Martin Bucer), Von der waren Seelsorge
          unnd dem rechten Hirtendienst . . . den pfarrern und
          obren seer nutzlich zu wissen.
             W. Rihel, 1538 [R BNU I, 372].

   .1.11. Corvinus, Antonius, Kurtze Auszlegung der Evangelien
          so auff die Sontag von Ostern bis auff den Advent
          gepredigt werden.
             W. Köpfel, 1539 [R Nfp, 1445].

   .1.12. Corvinus, Antonius, Postilla in Epistolas et Evangelia
          cum de Tempore, tum de Sanctis.
             W. Köpfel, 1540 [R BNU I, 593], 1543 [R Nfp, 1441],
             1548 [R Nfp, 1442].

   .1.13. Weller, Hieronymus, Brevis explicatio Epistolae
          dominicalium per totum annum.
             Cr. Mylius, 1546 [R BNU IV, 2453].

   .1.14. Corvinus, Antonius, Postilla. Oder auszlegung Aller
          Sontags Evangelien und Epistelen.
             W. Köpfel, 1553 [R Nfp, 1443].

   .1.15. Schenck, Conradus, Evangelia Dominicorum, Festorumque
          dierum carmine Hexametro reddita.
             N. Wyriot & P. Hugg, 1560 [R Nfp, 3172].

   .1.16. Evangelia und Episteln sampt den Summarien und Gebett
          auff alle Sonntag und die fürnembste Feste durchs
          gantze Jar.
             Chr. Mylius II, 1580 [R Nfp, 1673], 1581 [R BNU II,
             829].

   1.17.   Fabricius, Georgius, Summae Evangeliorum dominicalium,
          eorumque praecipuis festis solent in Ecclesia explicari.
             B. Jobin, 1583 [R Nfp, 1683].

   2.   LITURGIES.

P7.2.1.   Form und Gebet zu dem Ehe einsegen, Heyligen Tauffe,

> Abendtmal des Herren, Krancken besuchen und Begräbnüsz
> der Abgestorbnen, wie es zu Straszburg unnd anderszwa
> gehalten wirdt.
> No printer, n.d. [R Nfp, 1749], n.d. [R Nfp, 1751].
> W. Köpfel, n.d. [R Nfp, 1750].

P7.2.2.   Teütsch Kirchenampt, mit lobgesengen und götlichen
          psalmen wie es die gemein zu Straszburg singt und
          halt.
          W. Köpfel, n.d. [R Nfp, 2237], n.d. [R Nfp, 2238],
              1525 [R Nfp, 2239].

.2.3.   Luther, Martin, Formulae Missae et communionis pro
          ecclesia Wittenbergensi.
          W. Köpfel, 1523 [R Nfp, 2519].

.2.4.   (Rappolt, Wolfgang), Ordnung: wie es sol mit dem
          Gottes dienst und des selben dienern in
          d'Pfarrkirchen der Stat Elbogen gehalten werden.
          M. Schürer Erben, 1523 [B SE 3, 25].

.2.5.   Luther, Martin, Die weyse und Ordenung der Mess, und
          wie man das Hochwirdig Sacrament niessen soll.
          W. Köpfel, 1524 [B Luther, 1710].

.2.6.   Teutsche Mess und Tauff wie sye yetzung zu Straszburg
          gehalten werden.
          W. Köpfel, 1524 [R Nfp, 2669].

.2.7.   Deutsche Mess wie sye yetzundt zu Straszburgk gehalten
          wurt. Item Betbüchlein sampt vil andren.
          No printer, 1524 [R Nfp, 2670].

.2.8.   Das Tauffbüchlin nach rechter Form uff Teutsch zu
          Tauffen.
          W. Köpfel, 1524 [R Nfp, 3311].
          M. Schürer Erben, 1524 [B SE 3, 35].

.2.9.   Ordenung und innhalt Teütscher Mesz, so yetzunt im
          gebrauch haben Evangelisten unnd Christlichen
          Pfarrherren zu Straszburg.
          W. Köpfel, 1524 [R Nfp, 2794].

.2.10.   Ordenung und ynnhalt Teutscher Mess und Vesper, So
          yetzund im gebrauch . . . zu Straszburg. Mit etlichen
          Neüwen geschrifftlichen introit, Gebet, Vorred oder
          Prefation und Canon.
          W. Köpfel, ca. 1524 [R Nfp, 2795].
          M. Schürer Erben, 1524 [B SE 3, 31].

.2.11.   Ordenung des Herren Nachtmal: so man die Messz nennet
          sampt der Tauff und Insegung der Ee Wie yetzt die
          diener des wort gots zu Straszburg Erneüwert und

nach Götlicher gschrifft gebessert haben. . . .
> J. Schwann, 1525 [R Nfp, 2796; R BNU III, 1674],
> 1525 [B Luther, 3635].
> W. Köpfel, 1525 [B Luther, 3633].

P7.2.12. Strassburger Kirchenampt, nemlich von Insegnung der
Eelüt, vom Tauf und von des herren nachtmal, mit
Psalmen.
> W. Köpfel, 1525 [R Nfp, 2240].

.2.13. Das ander theyl. Strassburger kirchengesang. Das
vatter unser, Der glaub. Die zehen gepott. Das Misere.
Das Misere. . . .
> W. Köpfel, 1525 [R Nfp, 2241].

.2.14. Das dritt theyl Straszburger kirchen ampt.
> W. Köpfel, 1525 [R Nfp, 2242].

.2.15. Psalmen gebett. und Kirchen übung wie sie zu
Straszburg gehalten werden.
> W. Köpfel, 1526 [R Nfp, 3002], 1526 [R Nfp, 3003],
> 1530 [R BNU III, 1935], 1533 [R Nfp, 3004].

.2.16. Ordnung und Kirchengebreuch für die Pfarrin unnd
Kirchen Dienern, zu Straszburg, und der selbigen
anhörigen, uff gehabten synodo fürgenommen.
> J. Prüss II, 1534 [R BNU III, 1676].

.2.17. Psalter mit aller Kirchenübung die man bey der
Christlichen Gemein zu Straszburg und anders pflägt
zu singen.
> W. Köpfel, 1539 [R Nfp, 3036].

.2.18. Hymni, Psalmi, Versiculi et Benedicamus proparuulis
ecclesiasticis.
> J. Frölich, 1540 [BM 3425.aa.9.2].

.2.19. (Calvin, Jean and Marot, Clément), La manyere de faire
prieres aux eglises Francoyses tant devant la predica-
tion comme apres, ensemble pseaulmes et cantiques
francoys qu'on chante aus dictes eglises. . . .
> J. Prüss II, 1542 [S III B, 51].

.2.20. (Calvin, Jean and Marot, Clément), La forme des
prieres et chantz ecclesiastiques avec la maniere
d'administrer les sacremens et consacrer le mariage.
> G. Messerschmidt, 1545 [Peter, XI I].

.2.21. Dietrich, Veit, Die Deudsche Lytania mit etlichen
angehengten Gebetlein. Auch wie die eltern ire
kindlein . . . sollen betten lernen.
> W. Köpfel, 1546 [R Nfp, 1513].

P7.2.22.   Missa latina quae olim ante Romanum circa 700 Domini
            annum in usu fuit, bona fide ex vetusto authenticoque
            Codice descripta.
               Chr. Mylius I, 1557 [R Nfp, 2693].

   .2.23.   Kirchenordnung der Graue und Herrschaften Mümpelgart
            unnd Reichenweiler, auch wie es derselben anhangenden
            sachen und verrichtungen, mit verleihung Göttlicher
            genaden, hinfüro gehalten und volnzogen werden soll.
               No printer, 1571 [R BNU II, 1309].

   .2.24.   Kirchenordnung, Wie es mit der Lehr und Ceremonien,
            in der Graffschafft Hanaw und Herrschafft Lichtenberg,
            sol gehalten werden.
               Chr. Mylius II, 1573 [R BNU II, 1310].

   .2.25.   Kirchenordnung, Wie es mit der Lehre Göttliches Worts
            und den Ceremonien . . . in der Kirchen zu
            Straszburg biss hie her gehalten worden.
               J. Martin, 1598 [R BNU II, 1311].

P8.   PROTESTANT MARTYROLOGIES.

P8.1.1.   Ein warhafftig geschicht wie Caspar Tawber. Burger
           zu Wien . . . für ein Ketzer zu Todt verurtaylt
           worden ist.
              R. Beck, 1524 [R Nfp, 1899].

   .1.2.   Luther, Martin, Das warhaftig geschicht, des leydens
           und sterbens Lienhart Keysers seligen . . . von das
           heyligen Evangelii und Götlicher warheyt wegen zu
           Passau verurteylt, und zu Scherding verbrant.
              J. Prüss II, 1527 [B Luther, 2448].

   .1.3.   Rabus, Ludovicus, Tomus I. De S. Dei Confessoribus vet
           erisque ecclesiae Martyribus ex sacris literis, . . .
           Ecclesiae patrum scriptis, ad . . . hodiernae
           Ecclesiae consolationem . . . collectus.
              B. Beck Erben, 1552 [R Bib. Mun., 1772].

   .1.4.   Rabus, Ludovicus, Historien der Heyligen Auszerwolten
           Gottes Zeügen, Bekennern und Martyren, so in
           Angehender ersten Kirchen, Altes und Neuwes
           Testaments zu jeder zeyt gewesen seind. . . .
              S. Emmel, 1554 [R BNU III, 1962], 1555 [R Bib. Mun.,
              1773], 1555-1557 [R Bib. Mun., 1774].

   .1.5.   Wahre Historia und Geschicht, wie Valentin Paceus
           Prädicant weiland zu Leipzig, einen Tod und ein End
           genommen, welcher von der wahren Erkenntnis des heili-

gen Evangelii ist abgefalen
  B. Fabricius, 1558 [R Nfp, 2604].

P8.1.6. Historia vera: de vita obitu, sepultura, accusatione
         haereseos, condemnatione, exhumatione, combustione,
         honorificaque tandem restitutione beatorum atque
         doctiss. Theologorum, D. Martini Buceri & Pauli
         Fagii, quae intra annus XII. in Angliae Regno accidit.
         P. Messerschmidt, 1562 [R BNU II, 1173].

  .1.7. Ein ware histori Vom leben, sterben, begrebnuss,
         anklagung der ketzerey, verdammung, ausgraben,
         verbrennen, und letslich ehrlicher wider ynsetzung
         der saligen und hochgelehrten Theologen D. Martini
         Buceri und Pauli Fagii, die sich in zwolff jaren in
         dem Engelendischen Reich begeben hat.
         P. Messerschmidt, 1562 [R BNU II, 1174].

  .1.8. Rabus, Ludovicus, Historia de S. Abele Ecclesiae
         militantis in veteri testamento Protomartyre.
         S. Emmel, 1568 [R Nfp, 3065].

  .1.9. Rabus, Ludovicus, Historien der Martyrer. Erste
         Theil.
         J. Rihel, 1571 [R BNU III, 1964; R Bib. Mun., 1776].

  .1.10. Rabus, Ludovicus, Historien der Martyrer. Ander
         Theil.
         J. Rihel, 1572 [R Bib. Mun., 1776].

Abstemius, Laurentius (Lorenzo Astemio) H1.3.56

Abul Hafsan al Mukhtar S1.13.6

Accolti, Benedetto V9.3.6

Accursius, Franciscus C9.1.5

Ackermann, Johann V5.2.3a, V5.2.3b, V5.2.3c, V5.2.3d, V5.2.3e

Adelphus, Johannes: see Muling

Adler, Caspar (Caspar Aquila) P1.4.12, P2.3.3

Adrianus, Cardinal (Adriano Castellense) C4.2.13

Aegidius, Petrus H1.1.27

Aepinus, Johann B7.6.19

Aeschines A2.2.24a, A2.2.24b

Aesop A2.1.1, A2.1.2a, A2.1.2b, A2.1.2c, A2.1.2d, A2.1.2e, A2.1.3, A2.1.4a, A2.1.4b, A2.1.4c, A2.1.5a, A2.1.5b, A2.1.6, A3.1.1a, A3.1.1b, A3.1.7, A3.1.20

Aesop, Goudanus, et al H2.1.7a, H2.1.7b, H2.1.7c, H2.1.7d, H2.1.7e, H2.1.7f, H2.1.7g, H2.1.7h, H2.1.7i, H2.1.7j, H2.1.7k, H2.1.7l, H2.1.7m

Agerius, Nicolaus S1.15.13, S1.15.14

Agricola, Johann H1.1.101, V4.1.10

Agricola, Rudolphus T1.6.5

Agrippa, Henricus Cornelius (Heinrich von Nettesheim) H1.1.37a, H1.1.37b

Alanus de Insulis (c. 1120-1202) C1.2.12, C1.2.22, C2.1.14, C7.2.6

Albert von Eyb H1.1.5a, H1.1.5b

Albert, Cardinal, Archibishop C10.1.25

Alberti, Leone Battista S11.9.1

Alberus, Erasmus P3.9.11

Albrecht (Meister) S9.1.1a, S9.1.1b

Albucasis (Abu al-Qasim Khalaf ibn Abbas al-Zahrawi) S1.13.4, S1.5.5

Alciati, Andrea: see Alzati

Alcuin C2.1.2, P4.2.1

Aleander A2.2.7

Alesius, Alexander (Alexandar Halesius) P3.4.5, P3.13.3

Alexander VI, Pope C9.1.12

Alexander de Villa Dei (Alexandre de Villedieu) T1.1.4a, T1.1.4b, T1.1.4c, T1.1.4d, T1.1.4e, T1.1.4f, T1.1.4g, T1.1.4h, T1.1.4i, T1.1.4j, T1.1.4k, T1.1.4l, T1.1.4m, T1.1.4n, T1.1.4o, T1.1.4p, T1.1.4q, T1.1.4r, T1.1.4s, T1.1.4t

Alexandre de Parme (Alessandro Farnese, Duke of Parma) L1.7.3

Alfonso of Naples H2.1.1a, H2.1.1b

Altbiesser, Symphorian: see Pollio

Altenstaig, Joann T1.4.4a,
    T1.4.4b, V5.3.2

Althamer, Andreas B7.6.8

Alveld, Augustin C10.1.5

Alzati, Andree L1.2.15

Amadis de Gaulis (Amadis von
    Frankreich) V6.2.15a, V6.2.15b

Amerbach, Vitus (Viet Amerbach)
    H1.1.40, H1.1.51, H1.1.53,
    H1.1.54a, H1.1.54b

Amis der Pfaffe V2.2.1

Amsdorf, Nicolaus P3.10.4

Andernach: see Guenther von Andernach

Andreae, Joannes C9.1.2a, C9.1.2b,
    C9.1.11

Andreas Hispanus (Andres de
    Escobar) C4.1.20a, C4.1.20b

Andrelinus, Publius Faustus H1.3.19a,
    H1.3.19b, H1.3.19c, H1.3.19d,
    H1.3.19e, H1.3.19f, H1.3.19g,
    H1.3.19h, H1.3.23, H1.3.41a,
    H1.3.41b

Angelus de Clavasio C1.3.14a,
    A1.3.14b, C1.3.14c, C1.3.14d,
    A1.3.14e, C1.3.14f, C1.3.14g,
    C1.3.14h, C1.3.14i

Anianus S5.1.2

Anselmus de Canterbury C1.2.11,
    C1.2.16

Anthonius de Bitonto C3.1.37a,
    C3.1.37b, C3.1.37c

Antoninus C4.1.10a, C4.1.10b,
    C4.1.10c

Antoninus Florentinus C1.3.6a,
    C1.3.6b, C1.3.6c, C1.3.6d,
    C1.3.6e, C1.3.6f, C1.3.16a,
    C1.3.16b, C1.3.17

Antonius de Rampegolis (Antonio
    Rampegolo) C4.1.28, B7.1.4

Apuleius, Lucius A1.5.5, A3.1.3a,
    A3.1.3b, A3.1.3c

Aquinas, Thomas C1.2.14a, C1.2.14b

Arator B7.1.7

Arcimboldo, Giovanni Angelo
    (Bishop of Novara, Archbishop
    of Milan) P3.5.29

Argula von Grumbach P3.3.9,
    P3.3.17

Arietulus, Kilianus V7.2.6

Aristotle S4.6.1, S5.3.2a,
    S5.3.2b, S7.1.12a, S7.1.12b,
    S7.1.14, S7.1.15, S7.1.19,
    A2.5.1a, A2.5.1b, A2.5.1c,
    A2.5.1d, A2.5.1e, A2.5.1f,
    A2.5.2a, A2.5.2b, A2.5.3,
    T1.2.12a, T1.2.12b

Arnobius Afer the Elder B7.2.3

Arnoldus de Villa Nova S1.3.2,
    S1.12.16, S2.1.2a, S2.1.2b,
    S2.1.2c, S2.1.2d, S2.1.2e,
    S2.1.2f, S2.1.2g, S2.1.6a,
    S2.1.6b

Asconius Pedianus, Quintus A1.5.9

Athanasius, Bishop of Alexandria
    C1.1.12

Bollanus, Dominicus C7.1.13

Bonaccialo, Ludovico (Luigi
    Bonacciuoli) S1.2.3, S1.2.4

Bonaventura C1.2.7a, C1.2.7b,
    C1.2.10a, C1.2.10b, C3.1.38

Borkowski, Petrus L1.8.18, T4.1.46,
    T4.1.48, T4.1.49, T4.1.50, T4.1.51

Borrhaus, Martin: see Martin
    Cellarius

Bosch, Michael H3.1.27, T4.1.7,
    T4.2.8

Bosso, Matteo (Mathaeus Bossus)
    C3.1.52, H1.3.17, H1.3.22

Boterus, Johannes (Giovanni Botero)
    L1.3.9

Botlam, Ibin (Ibn Butlan) S1.13.5

Boulay, Edmond V11.1.12

Brack, Wenceslaus H4.1.1a, H4.1.1b,
    H4.1.1c, H4.1.1d, H4.1.1e, H4.1.1f

Bramer, David V5.2.10

Brant, Sebastian C7.1.8, L1.3.5a,
    L1.3.5b, L1.3.5c, L1.3.5d, L1.3.5e,
    L1.3.5f, L1.3.5g, H1.2.3, H1.2.5,
    H1.2.6, H1.2.27, H1.2.30, V3.1.13a,
    V3.1.13b, V3.1.13c, V3.1.13d,
    V6.1.4, V6.2.1a, V6.2.1b, V6.2.1c,
    V6.2.1d, V6.2.1e, V6.2.1f, V6.2.1g,
    V9.1.5

Brassicanus, Joannes H1.1.25,
    H1.1.28, H1.1.31, T1.1.22a,
    T1.1.22b, T1.1.22c, T1.1.22d,
    T1.1.22e, T1.1.22f, T1.1.22g

Brentel, Jorgen V6.3.6

Brenz, Johann (Johannes Brentius)
    B7.6.8, B7.6.23, P1.6.14, P1.7.2a,
    P1.7.2b, P2.3.10, P2.3.18,
    P3.5.19

Brescia, Albertano da (Albertanus
    Causidicus Brixiensis) C5.1.13a,
    C5.1.13b

Brinkelow, Henry P3.4.7

Brismannus, Johannes (Johann
    Briessmann) P3.9.12a, P3.9.12b

Brother Lukas of Prague P1.6.1

Brundelsheim, Conrad von C3.1.17a,
    C3.1.17b

Brunfels, Otto S1.2.5, S1.7.8,
    S1.7.9, S1.7.10, S1.7.11,
    S1.7.12a, S1.7.12b, S1.8.5,
    S1.9.2, S1.9.3, S1.9.8, S1.9.12,
    S1.9.14, S1.9.15, S3.1.8a,
    S3.1.8b, S3.1.8c, S3.1.8d,
    S3.1.8e, S3.1.9a, S3.1.9b,
    S3.1.9c, S14.1.3, H3.1.9,
    H3.1.10, H3.1.14, H3.1.17a,
    H3.1.17b, B7.8.1a, B7.8.1b, B7.8.2
    B7.8.3a, B7.8.3b, B7.8.3c,
    B7.8.3d, B7.8.4, B7.8.5a,
    B7.8.5b, B7.8.5c, B7.8.5d,
    B7.8.6, B7.8.7, B8.4.2, B8.4.3,
    P1.8.2, P3.12.1, P3.12.3,
    P3.12.4, P3.12.5, P3.12.6,
    P3.12.11, P5.1.16

Bruni, Leonardo Aretino (Leonardus
    Aretinus, L. Brunus Aretinus)
    H3.1.11a, H3.1.11b, V2.1.5

Brunmüller, Caspar P2.3.15

Brunner, Leonhart B8.2.12

Bruno, Giordano S7.1.20

Gruelich, Martin S11.7.2a,
   S11.7.2b, S11.7.2c

Gruenpeck, Joseph S15.1.7

Grynaeus, Simon S6.2.7

Guarinus, Baptista H3.1.8

Guarna, Andreas T1.1.25a,
   T1.1.25b

Guenther von Andernach, Johann
   (Johann Guentherius, Johannes
   Andernacus Guinterius) S1.4.11,
   S1.4.12, S1.4.14, S1.4.15,
   S1.4.16, S1.7.21, S1.8.8

Guethel, Kasper P3.5.8

Guevara, Antonio V5.1.5, V5.7.2a,
   V5.7.2b, V5.7.2c

Guido de Monte Rotherii C4.1.6a,
   C4.1.6b, C4.1.6c, C4.1.6d,
   C4.1.6e, C4.1.6f

Guilelmus Parisiensis (Guillermus,
   Bishop of Paris) C3.1.6a,
   C3.1.6b, C3.1.6c, C3.1.6d,
   C3.1.6e, C3.1.6f, C3.1.6g,
   C3.1.6h, C3.1.6i, C3.1.6j,
   C3.1.30, C8.1.3a, C8.1.3b

Guilelmus Peraldus (Paraldus)
   C3.1.31

Guilhelmus de Gouda C6.4.1a,
   C6.4.1b, C6.4.1c, C6.4.1d

Guillaume de Furstenberg
   P3.14.5, P3.14.6

Gunther Ligurinus (Gunther of Pairis)
   H5.3.5

Gunther, Peter H1.1.8

Gut, Wendelin P6.3.50

Gwalther, Rudolphus (Rudolph
   Walter) T3.2.5

Habermann, Johann P5.1.32,
   P6.1.12, P6.1.13

Hartlieb, Jacob H1.1.13

Hartmuth von Cronberg P3.3.6,
   P3.3.7, P3.3.8, P3.3.12,
   P3.3.23

Hawenreuter, Johann Ludwig (Johann
   Ludwig Hauvenreuter) S1.15.3,
   S1.15.9, S1.15.16, S5.3.5a,
   S5.3.5b, S5.9.3, S5.9.4, S5.9.9,
   S5.9.10, S5.9.12, S5.9.13,
   H1.2.49, H1.2.53, T1.8.6, T4.1.3,
   T4.1.27, T4.1.29, T4.1.36, T4.1.37

Haymonis (Haymo, Bishop of Halberstadt)
   B7.1.12

Hebenstreit, Johann S12.1.53

Heckel, Wolfgang V7.3.1a,
   V7.3.1b, V7.3.2a, V7.3.2b,
   V7.3.3

Hedio, Caspar C2.1.10, H1.2.43,
   H5.1.9, P2.2.4, P2.2.5, P3.11.10,
   P7.1.9, V9.1.9a, V9.1.9b,
   V9.1.17a, V9.1.17b, V9.4.1a,
   V9.4.1b, V9.4.1c, V9.4.2a,
   V9.4.2b

Heerbrandt, Jacob P1.4.23

Hegesippus A5.2.5a, A5.2.5b,
   A5.2.14a, A5.2.14b, A5.2.14c,
   A5.2.14d, A5.2.14e, A5.2.14f,
   A5.2.14g

Heinerer, Adam T4.1.24

P3.1.21b, P3.1.22a, P3.1.22b,
P3.1.22c, P3.1.23, P3.1.24,
P3.1.25, P3.1.26, P3.1.27,
P3.1.28a, P3.1.28b, P3.1.28c,
P3.1.29, P3.1.30, P3.1.31,
P3.1.32, P3.1.33, P3.1.34,
P31..35a, P3.1.35b, P3.1.36a,
P3.1.36b, P3.1.37, P3.1.38,
P3.1.39, P3.1.40a, P3.1.40b,
P3.1.41a, P3.1.41b, P3.1.42,
P3.1.43a, P3.1.43b, P3.1.44a,
P3.1.44b, P3.1.45, P3.1.46,
P3.1.47, P3.1.48, P3.1.49, P3.7.3,
P3.7.4, P3.7.12, P4.2.1, P4.2.2a,
P4.2.2b, P4.2.3, P4.2.4, P4.2.5,
P4.2.6, P4.2.7, P5.1.1, P5.1.2,
P5.1.11, P5.1.27, P5.1.30a,
P5.1.30b, P5.1.30c, P5.1.30d,
P6.1.1, P7.1.1, P7.1.2a, P7.1.2b,
P7.1.2c, P7.1.2d, P7.1.2e,
P7.1.2f, P7.1.2g, P7.1.2h,
P7.1.2i, P7.1.4a, P7.1.4b,
P7.1.4c, P7.1.4d, P7.1.4e,
P7.1.4f, P7.2.3, P7.2.5, P8.1.2

Lutz, Reinhard C10.1.59

Macropedius, Georgius H1.1.86,
    V8.2.17

Maecardus, Johannes P3.6.17

Magninus S1.3.5

Magnus, Albertus C1.2.6, C1.2.13,
    C3.1.35, C7.1.3a, C7.1.3b,
    C7.1.3c, S1.2.1a, S1.2.1b,
    S1.7.23a, S1.7.23b, S1.7.23c,
    S1.7.23d, S3.1.3, S3.1.5a,
    S3.1.5b, S3.1.5c, S7.1.1, S7.1.4,
    S7.1.5, S7.1.6

Magnus, Olaus S6.5.4

Maillardus, Oliverius (Olivier
    Maillard, ca. 1430-1502) C3.1.49a,
    C3.1.49b, C3.1.49c, C3.1.58

Mainardo, Agostino P3.4.15

Major, Georg (Georgius Maior)
    B2.1.18a, B2.1.18b, P6.2.3

Malleolus, Isaak S13.1.6

Mallinius, Caspar Polonus H1.6.1

Manardus, Johannes (Giovanni Manardo)
    S1.7.7

Mancinello, Antonio H1.3.6, H1.3.27,
    H1.3.28a, H1.3.28b, H1.3.28c,
    H1.3.40, H2.1.4a, H2.1.4b

Mantuanus: see Joannes Baptista
    Mantuanus

Manuel, Nicklaus V8.2.1, P3.3.29,
    P3.3.30

Manutius, Paulus (Paolo Manuzio)
    H1.3.60

Marbach, Erasmus B7.7.11, T4.1.22

Marbach, Johann H1.2.47, P1.2.23a,
    P1.2.23b, P1.2.24, P1.6.13a,
    P1.6.13b, P1.8.15, P1.8.21,
    P1.8.23, P1.8.24, P2.2.7

Marbach, Philipp T4.2.10

Marbeck, Pilgrim P4.1.36, P4.1.37

Marcellus, Joannes P3.9.3, P3.9.4

Marchesinus, Joannes B7.1.3a,
    B7.1.3b, B7.1.3c, B7.1.3d,
    B7.1.3e

Marcourt, Antoine P3.14.9

Mark von Lindau C5.1.23

Mark von Weiden C5.1.24

Note: Last publications of a printer were often posthumous. These editions reflect work in process at the time of death or reprints where the name was not changed. In either case the name still appeared on the title page or on the colophon.

Similarly, one or two books may appear before a printer opened his shop. These were probably printed while he was serving as a journeyman and he was permitted by the master of the shop to issue a book or books under his own name.

Acker, Paul
1568 P6.1.8

Albrecht, Johann
1532 S4.4.1
1533 A4.1.8,B6.1.7,L1.3.5D,
S1.7.11,S15.2.4C,T1.3.5
1534 H1.3.58,H1.4.22,P2.2.5,
S15.2.4D,T1.8.3D
1535 A1.5.9,B7.6.15,H3.1.18,
S1.7.14
1536 B7.4.13,L1.3.4K,L1.3.5E,
P1.3.3E,S15.2.4E
1538 L1.3.4L,L1.3.5F

Anshelm, Thomas
1488 C4.1.9A

Attendorn, Peter
1489 L1.2.3
1492 V5.2.2A

Baldus, Elias
1592 V11.5.2,V11.5.3

Beck, Balthasar
1525 P1.6.3A
1527 S3.1.1E
1528 P5.1.15,S3.1.4E
1529 B8.5.1,B8.5.2,P1.2.13,
P1.7.2A,P3.3.24,P3.3.25,P3.5.26,
P3.6.7,P3.6.8,P4.1.22,P4.1.23,

P4.1.24A,P4.1.25,P4.1.26,
S1.2.2D,S1.7.6E,S1.9.7,S3.1.1F,
V11.2.1
1530 B8.5.3,B8.5.4,P1.7.2B,
P3.1.41A,P4.1.33,P4.1.34,S3.1.4F
1531 A5.2.4A,B6.1.6,V9.1.7
1532 A5.2.5A,C2.1.4,S1.7.6F,V9.1.8
1533 V5.6.2
1535 A5.2.4B
1536 A3.1.14A
1537 A5.2.5B
1539 A5.2.4C
1540 A3.1.14B,C2.1.7,P3.14.6,
S1.9.16A
1541 S1.1.4,S1.7.18A,S1.7.19A,
S1.7.19B,S1.7.19C,S1.9.17A,
S1.10.7,S1.10.8,S1.10.9,S2.1.6B
1542 C5.1.37,S1.5.7A,S1.7.20A,
S1.9.16B
1543 B8.2.14A,S1.7.20B
1544 A5.2.4D,P3.2.17
1545 A3.1.14C,B8.2.14B,S8.1.5A
1546 S7.1.11,V1.1.11

Beck, Balthasar Erben
1551 S1.5.7B,S15.3.2
1552 P8.1.3,S1.7.19D,S1.9.16C,
S1.9.17B

Beck, Reinhardt
1510 S3.1.1C
1511 C6.2.14,C6.2.15,H1.1.19,

H4.1.7C,L1.4.2
1512 C6.2.6C,H1.1.20A,H5.2.4
1513 C1.3.14F,C4.1.16C,H4.1.7D,
L1.2.14,T1.1.27A,V2.3.3J,V5.3.1A
1514 C6.2.6D,H1.1.20B,H4.1.6C,
H4.1.7E,S5.3.1,T1.1.27B,T1.2.2A
1515 H1.3.9J,H5.3.3,S3.1.4C
1516 C7.1.9B,H4.1.6D
1517 H1.3.9K,T1.1.22G
1518 T1.2.2B,T1.4.7A
1519 B2.1.5,B7.1.12,L2.1.9
1520 B4.1.1C,C6.2.19,P1.1.3C,
P3.1.3C
1521 P2.1.12,P3.3.2,S3.1.4D,V5.3.1B
1522 P2.1.14,P3.1.20,P3.3.4A,P3.9.5

Beck, Reinhardt Erben
1523 C10.1.25,P2.1.24A,P3.1.27,P3.3.4B
1524 P8.1.1
1528 P5.1.14

Berger, Theobald
(undated popular songs were given
estimated dates)
1541 V8.1.9,V10.5.1,V10.5.2
1551 P6.3.48
1552 V7.1.31
1553 V7.1.32
1554 V4.1.15A,V10.6.6
1555 P6.3.40,P6.3.49,V7.1.5,
V11.1.15
1556 P6.3.3,P6.3.5,V10.9.1
1557 P6.3.4,P6.3.6,P6.3.7,
V7.1.6,V7.1.33,V7.1.34,V7.1.35,
V10.4.5
1558 P6.3.8,V7.1.36,V8.1.18
1559 H1.1.63,P6.1.6A,S14.1.5C
1560 P6.1.6B,P6.3.9,P6.3.51A,
P6.3.52,V1.1.12,V2.1.16E,
V2.1.19B,V2.1.19C,V5.2.1,V7.1.37
1561 P1.2.21,P3.6.15,P6.3.10,
P6.3.11,P6.3.53,V11.1.16
1562 P1.6.15B,P1.8.17,P5.1.29,
P6.1.6C,P6.3.12,P6.3.13,
P6.3.54,S14.1.5D,V4.1.16,V8.1.10C
1563 P6.3.14,P6.3.15,V7.1.7,
V7.1.38A,V7.1.39,V10.5.3,

V10.5.4,V10.5.5,V10.5.6,V10.6.9,
V10.10.1,V11.4.3
1564 P6.3.16,P6.3.51B,S12.1.52,
T1.8.5,V6.1.2,V7.1.9,V8.1.21,
V10.3.3,V10.6.10
1565 P6.3.17,P6.3.18,V7.1.10,
V7.1.40,V10.3.4,V11.2.7
1566 P6.1.6D,P6.3.19,P6.3.20,
V7.1.11,V8.1.22,V8.2.14A,
V10.6.11,V11.2.9,V11.2.10
1567 P1.6.19,P6.3.21,V10.2.5
1568 P6.3.22,V4.1.15B,V8.2.13,
V10.12.1,V11.3.1C,V11.3.2
1569 S12.1.54A
1570 A4.4.1,P6.3.24,P6.3.51C,
P6.3.56,P6.3.57,S1.7.28,
V2.1.33,V7.1.8,V7.1.41,V7.1.42,
V7.1.43,V7.1.45,V7.1.46,
V7.1.47,V7.1.48,V7.1.49,V7.1.50,
V7.1.51,V7.1.52,V7.1.53,V7.1.54,
V7.1.55,V8.1.25,V8.2.14B,V9.1.23
1571 P6.3.26,V7.1.12,V7.1.57,
V7.1.58,V7.1.60,V10.12.2B
1572 P6.3.27,P6.3.28,V8.1.26,
V11.3.3
1573 P6.3.29,V7.1.13
1574 P6.3.30,V8.2.15
1575 P6.3.31,P6.3.32,V7.1.14
1576 B5.1.8B,B8.4.7,P6.3.33
1577 P6.3.34,S12.1.54B
1578 P6.3.35,V7.1.15
1579 P1.2.27,P6.3.36
1580 P6.3.37,V10.9.6
1581 P2.3.22,P2.4.7,P6.3.38,
S12.1.54C
1582 P6.3.39,V7.1.16,V10.5.7
1583 P6.3.41
1584 P6.3.42,V10.2.9
1585 V10.1.9

Bertram, Anton
1564 P1.8.19
1581 S15.1.11
1584 H1.1.81,S5.9.8,S14.1.5F,
T3.2.10A,T4.1.16,T4.1.18
1585 H1.1.83,L1.7.3,L1.8.2,
P1.6.15E,P2.4.9,S15.1.12,

S15.2.6D,V4.1.14B,V6.1.3D,V6.2.1E,
V6.2.5C
1541 A5.2.6C,S11.9.1,S12.1.37A,
S15.2.4G
1542 S5.4.7,S10.1.4,S12.1.18C,
S12.1.38,V11.2.4
1543 B7.6.19,S1.11.5A,S11.6.3,
S12.1.40,S12.1.41A,V5.2.8,
V6.1.1F,V10.6.1
1544 P3.6.9C,P3.6.13,S12.1.18D,
S12.1.37B,S12.1.41B,S16.1.4C,
V9.3.5
1545 A3.1.17A,P3.3.30,P3.6.12B,
P3.7.16,P3.12.11,S1.7.23A,
S1.11,5B,S12.1.18E,S12.1.41C,
S17.1.5,V6.1.3E,V6.2.1F,V8.2.5
1546 P3.6.14B,P3.15.2,S1.7.17B,
S12.1.37C,V2.3.1M,V10.4.2
1547 S12.1.43A
1548 S1.7.23B,S1.8.6C,S4.3.2

Carthusian Press
1533 C7.1.22

Dumbach, Friedrich von
1497 C6.2.5
1499 C4.1.15

Eber, Johann
1481 H3.1.1
1483 C5.1.3

Eber, Johann
1481 C1.1.1A

Egenolff, Christian
1528 S4.2.1A,S5.4.3
1529 C9.1.26,H1.3.57,H3.1.16,
H3.1.17B,H5.4.3,S3.1.6,S4.2.1B,
S5.4.4,S5.5.2,S11.3.1,S12.1.28,
T1.2.6A,T1.2.7,T1.8.3C,
V4.1.11,V4.1.12,V6.1.8
1530 A1.1.4B,A2.2.21,A4.1.7,
H1.1.15B,H1.1.33,L1.3.7,
L1.5.3,S1.5.4,S2.1.1G,S3.1.7,
S6.5.1,S9.1.3,S10.1.3,S11.1.2A,
S11.1.2B,S11.4.1,S12.1.29,

S15.2.4B,S15.2.5,V9.1.6A,
V9.1.6B
1531 S1.4.10

Eggestein, Heinrich
1480 C4.2.1K

Emmel, Samuel
1549 S7.1.12A
1552 P1.6.13A
1553 A5.2.4E
1554 H1.1.59,P1.6.13B,P8.1.4A
1555 B8.2.14C,B8.4.5,P5.1.25,
P8.1.4B
1556 A5.2.4F,H5.1.9,P8.1.4C
1557 B7.6.22B,P1.9.4,P3.13.7,
P3.13.8,P5.1.26
1558 H1.1.62,S1.11,8B,S15.3.3A,
1559 P1.6.15A,S1.7.18B,S1.9.16D,
T1.3.9F
1560 B2.1.15,B7.6.23,B8.6.1,
P1.6.15A,P1.8.16,P5.1.27,S16.1.5
1561 S8.1.5C
1562 A5.2.4G,B8.6.2A,B8.6.3,T1.3.9G
1563 P1.7.4A,V8.1.20
1564 A5.2.4H,B7.6.22C,B8.6.2B,
B8.6.4A,B8.6.5,T1.3.9J
1565 P2.3.17,P3.15.9
1566 B8.6.6,H1.1.66,P1.6.18,
S15.3.3B,S16.1.6,T1.3.9M
1567 A1.6.31,A1.6.32,H1.2.38B,
L1.2.21,P1.2.25,P1.7.4B,
S16.1.7,T1.3.9H,T1.3.9N
1568 A2.2.34,H3.1.25,L1.1.14,
P1.6.21,P1.8.21,P1.8.22,
P8.1.8,S1.14.6,S7.1.15
1569 B8.6.4B,B8.6.7,B8.6.8,
T1.3.9K,V9.2.11,
1570 P1.6.16B

Estiart, Pierre
1566 P3.14.14A,P3.14.14B,V9.1.21
1567 P3.14.14C

Faber, Nikolaus
1575 V10.6.14,V10.6.15
1582 V10.12.4
1583 V11.3.7

Frölich, Jacob
(undated songs and plays were
given estimated dates)
1530 P6.3.45
1533 P2.4.1,V8.1.3
1534 P6.1.3A,P6.1.3B,V2.1.6C,
V8.2.2
1535 H1.1.36,H5.1.5,P1.5.4,
P1.6.3C,P6.1.3C,V8.1.4
1536 P6.1.3D,P6.1.3E,P6.1.3F,
V5.5.3,V11.1.11
1537 H1.1.38,T1.8.2F,V8.2.3
1538 P4.3.5,V2.1.6D,V8.1.5A,
V8.1.6,V10.3.1
1539 P5.1.18,V2.3.1N,V2.3.2G,
V6.3.3A
1540 A5.2.10,H1.2.39,P5.1.19,
P6.3.46,P7.2.18,T1.3.4D,V2.1.6E,
V6.3.3B,V7.1.3,V8.1.1
1541 T1.6.9A,V8.1.10A
1542 H3.1.20,P1.6.10A,T3.2.2,V7.1.4
1543 S11.6.1D,T1.7.2B,V6.2.9B
1544 S1.10,4B,S11.8.1C,T1.7.5A,
V6.3.4A
1545 P1.6.10B,S11.6.1E,V2.3.2H,
V5.2.9
1546 P2.3.12,T1.7.5B,V8.1.8B,
V10.1.3
1547 V10.6.2,V10.6.3
1548 V2.3.9B,V6.3.3C,V6.3.6
1549 S11.4.3,S11.7.2A,T1.8.4
1550 A1.6.24A,A5.1.15,H5.4.12,
V6.3.3D,V6.3.5,V8.1.11A,V8.2.7
1551 S1.10.6C,V6.2.9C,V6.3.4B,
V6.3.4C,V8.1.10B,V8.1.12
1552 V8.1.13,V8.1.14
1554 P5.1.24,V2.1.6F,V6.3.3E,
V6.3.7A,V8.2.8,V10.8.1
1555 S11.7.2B,V5.3.6B,V8.1.11B
1557 V2.1.18B,V2.3.9C,V6.3.14,
V10.6.8A
1558 A2.1.5A

Gillotte Le Pords
1587 L1.7.4

Götz, P.
1514 V4.1.1F

Greff, Hieronymus
1502 V1.1.5

Grimm, Hans
1545 S11.5.2

Grüniger, Johann
1483 B1.1.1B,C1.2.3C,C5.1.2,
S12.1.2
1484 C3.1.13,C3.1.16,C3.1.17A,
C3.1.17B,C9.1.3A,L1.1.1
1485 B1.1.2,C4.1.8,C6.1.2,
L3.1.1A,T1.1.4A
1486 H4.1.1A,L3.1.1B,T1.1.5A,
T1.1.6A,T1.2.1
1487 C1.3.9,C6.1.3A,C6.1.4A,C6.2.2
1488 A1.1.1B,C6.1.5A,V2.3.1B
1489 B2.1.1,B7.1.3E,C3.1.30,
C3.1.31,C5.1.7A,C6.1.6A,C6.1.7A,
C6.1.8,C9.1.9A,V2.3.1C
1490 B3.1.1A,C1.3.1,C1.3.16A,
C1.3.17,C5.1.7B,C6.1.9A,C6.1.10,
C6.1.11,C9.1.9B,L3.1.1C,S12.1.6,
T1.1.6B
1491 C5.1.7C,C6.1.12A,C9.1.11,
L1.2.5
1492 B1.1.1C,S12.1.7
1493 C5.1.70,S3.1.3,S7.1.1
1494 C5.1.7E,C6.1.4B,C6.1.13,
C6.3.3,V6.2.1A
1495 B3.1.2A,C3.1.36,C3.1.37A,
C6.1.5B,C6.1.14,C6.1.15,L1.2.7,
T3.1.2
1496 A4.1.1A,B3.1.2B,C1.3.16B,
C1.3.19,C3.1.37B,C3.1.37C,C3.1.39,
C4.2.10,H3.1.3A,L1.2.8,S12.1.10,
V6.2.1B
1497 B1.1.1D,C1.2.12,C1.3.20,
C3.1.22C,C4.2.1B,C6.1.7B,H1.1.6,
C1.2.5,H3.1.3B,S1.5.1A,S1.6.1,
T3.1.3A,V6.2.1C
1498 A1.2.1,C4.1.9C,C5.1.9A,
C7.1.8,H1.2.6,H1.2.6,H1.4.1,
H3.1.3C,T1.3.1B,T3.1.3B
1499 A3.1.4,A4.1.1B,C1.3.22,
C6.1.16,S12.1.13,V2.3.1D
1500 C3.1.18H,C4.1.9D,C4.2.6,
C4.2.7,C5.1.9B,C6.2.7,L1.3.1,

S1.4.2,S2.1.3A,S15.2.1,T1.1.4P,
V2.1.12A,V2.1.12B,V2.1.13A,
V3.1.11A,V3.1.11B,V5.2.5A
1501 C1.1.4B,C5.1.9M,V2.3.2B
1502 A1.3.1A,C4.1.17,C5.1.13A,
C9.1.17,H1.1.8,V3.1.14A
1503 A4.1.1C,C5.1.7F,C5.1.9N,
H1.1.3,H1.1.10A
1504 C7.1.13,C9.1.18A,C9.1.18B,
H1.1.11,S5.1.3D
1505 C4.2.10,C5.1.9C,H1.1.14,
H1.3.11,S2.1.3B,T1.1.16
1506 C4.1.9E,C9.1.20,H1.1.10B,
V9.2.3
1507 A5.2.1A,A5.2.2A,B7.1.7,
C1.1.8,H1.3.14A,H1.3.14B,S6.3.2,
V3.1.15A
1508 A4.2.1,A5.2.1B,B7.1.8,
C7.2.2,H1.1.17A,H1.1.18,H2.1.1A,
H5.2.3,H5.3.1,S2.1.3C,S5.1.3E,
T1.1.21,V2.1.12C,V2.1.13B,
V2.1.17,V3.1.14B
1509 C3.2.4,H1.1.17B,H1.2.19,
H1.3.15B,H1.3.21,H2.1.1B,S1.9.4,
S2.1.3D,S6.2.4,S6.3.1B,S6.3.3,
S6.3.4,S12.1.20,V1.1.6D,V6.2.2A
1510 A1.5.2B,C3.1.55,C4.1.22,
C5.2.5,V3.1.14C
1511 A2.2.3,A4.1.3,A4.2.3,
S6.4.1,V6.2.3A
1512 C3.2.13,C3.2.14,C3.2.16A,
C6.2.16,S2.1.4A,S5.1.3F,S5.2.1,
T1.4.5,V2.1.20
1513 C3.2.17,C4.1.9F,C5.1.7G,
S1.5.1B,S6.2.5,V8.1.2,V9.3.1A
1514 B7.1.10,C3.1.57,C3.2.8B,
C3.2.8C,C3.2.16B,C3.2.19A,S2.1.4B,
V1.1.8,V2.1.21,V2.2.4,V3.1.14D,
V6.2.3B,V9.3.1B
1515 A3.1.9,B3.1.2C,C3.2.19B,
C3.2.22A,S2.1.4C,S5.1.3G,V2.1.22,
V6.2.7A
1516 C3.2.23A,C3.2.24A,C5.1.23,
C5.1.24,H1.3.50,V3.1.15B,V6.3.2
1517 C3.2.22B,C3.2.23B,C3.2.24B,
C3.2.25,H1.1.24,S2.1.4D,S3.1.1D
1518 C1.3.36,C3.2.15B,C3.2.26,
C3.2.27A,L1.1.5,S1.4.7,S1.7.6A,

S1.9.5A,V6.2.3C
1519 C3.2.19C,S1.6.3,S1.7.6B,
S1.8.4,S1.9.5B,S2.1.4E,V6.2.2B,
V6.2.7B
1520 C3.2.28,C3.2.29,C5.1.27,
C10.1.1A,C10.1.2,C10.1.3,C10.1.4,
S15.1.3,V9.3.2A,V9.3.2B
1521 C3.2.27B,C3.2.30,C10.1.1B,
C10.1.6,C10.1.7,C10.1.8,L1.3.6,
S2.1.4F
1522 C3.2.22C,C10.1.9,C10.1.10,
C10.1.11,C10.1.12A,C10.1.12B,
C10.1.13,C10.1.14,S6.3.7,S6.4.2,
V6.1.6A
1523 C1.1.13,C7.1.19,C10.1.16,
C10.1.17,C10.1.18,C10.1.19,
C10.1.20A,C10.1.21,C10.1.22,
C10.1.23,C10.1.24,C10.1.26,
C10.1.27A,C10.1.28,L1.1.9,
P3.1.2B,S1.1.2B,S1.1.2C,S12.1.27A
1524 C5.1.32,C7.1.20,C10.1.20B,
C10.1.27B,C10.1.29,C10.1.30,
C10.1.31A,C10.1.32,C10.1.33,
C10.1.34A,C10.1.34B,C10.1.35,
C10.1.36,C10.1.37,C10.1.38,
C10.1.39,C10.1.40,C10.1.41,S15.2.4A
1525 C10.1.31B,C10.1.44,S6.3.8,
S12.1.27B,V2.3.2C,V11.1.6,V11.1.7
1526 S1.7.6C,S16.1.2A
1527 B5.1.5E,C7.1.21,C10.1.45,
C10.1.46,C10.1.47,H5.3.4,S6.4.3,
S6.4.4A,S16.1.2B,V9.3.3
1528 C10.1.48,S2.1.4G,S16.1.2C,
V5.3.2
1529 B5.1.5F,C10.1.50,S1.6.4B,
S1.7.6D,S3.1.4G,S16.1.3A,V2.3.2D
1530 S6.4.4B,S12.1.27C,S16.1.3B,
V2.1.27A,V9.3.2C
1531 S2.1.4H,S16.1.3C

Grüninger, Bartholomäus
1531 S2.1.4I
1532 B5.1.5G,S2.1.4J,
1533 V6.1.6B
1535 S1.9.5C,V2.3.9A,V6.1.6C
1536 V2.3.2E
1537 S2.1.4K,V2.1.13C
1538 S1.8.6D,V6.1.6D

1516 C4.2.15A,L1.3.5A,T1.1.20C,
V2.3.7
1517 C4.2.15B,S12.1.24
1519 S1.3.7,V6.1.3C
1520 H1.3.53B
1522 H1.3.19H

Husner, Georg
(estimated dates were assigned to
undated editions)
1479 C4.2.1A
1480 C1.2.1A,C3.1.2,C4.1.1A,
C4.2.1B
1481 C3.1.6A
1482 C3.1.8
1483 C1.2.1B,C1.3.5,C3.1.6B,
C3.1.11,C4.2.1C
1484 C1.2.1C,C3.1.12,C9.1.4A
1485 B7.1.2B,C1.2.3B,C1.2.4,
C1.3.7,C3.1.3,C3.1.6C,C3.1.18A,
C4.2.1D,C9.1.7A,S5.1.1A
1486 C1.2.1D,C3.1.6D,C4.2.1E,
C9.1.3B,H5.1.1B,L1.2.1A,S8.1.2,
V2.3.3A
1487 B7.1.2C,C1.3.10,C1.3.11A,
C3.1.1G,C3.1.25A,C3.1.27A
1488 C1.2.1E,C3.1.6E,C3.1.18B,
C3.1.21B,C3.1.29A,C7.1.4B,C9.1.4B,
H4.1.3A,L1.2.2A
1489 C1.2.5A,C3.1.6F,C4.2.1F,
C9.1.3C,H5.1.1C,V2.3.1E,V2.3.3B
1490 C3.1.6G,C3.1.14C,C3.1.25B,
C3.1.33,C4.1.6E,L1.2.1B,L1.2.2B
1491 C1.2.9,H3.1.2A,H4.1.1E,
H4.1.3B,H4.1.4,S1.3.2,S5.1.1B
1492 C4.2.1G,C8.1.2
1493 C1.2.1F,C3.1.6H,C3.1.18C,
C3.1.21C,C3.1.26B,C3.1.29B,
C4.1.6F,C7.1.4C,C9.1.3D,C9.1.4C,
C9.1.3D,C9.1.4C,C9.1.7B,H4.1.3C,
L3.1.1E,V2.3.1F
1494 C3.1.18D,C3.1.25C,C3.1.34C,
C3.1.35,H5.1.1D,L1.2.1C,
L1.2.2C,T1.1.11A,V2.3.3C
1495 B7.1.1,C1.2.7B,C1.2.10B,
C1.3.2H,C1.3.11B,H3.1.2B,
H4.1.3D,T1.1.11B

1496 C1.1.5,C1.2.11,C3.1.38,
C4.2.1H,C7.1.6A,C9.1.8B,H4.1.3E
1497 H1.1.2B,H1.3.4
1498 C3.1.4,C3.1.44,C4.2.1I,
C5.1.10,C9.1.4E,H4.1.2D,T1.1.11C
1499 C9.1.3E,C9.1.15,V2.3.1G
1500 C1.2.3A,C3.1.46A,C4.1.1B,
H5.2.2A,L1.2.1D
1501 C3.1.46B
1502 C4.2.1J
1505 S5.1.1C

Jobin, Bernard
1566 V10.11.1
1568 V10.8.2
1570 P3.16.1,V10.8.4,V10.8.5A,
V10.8.6,V11.1.18,V11.4.4
1571 P3.16.2,P5.1.30A,V10.8.3,
V10.8.7A,V10.8.8,V10.8.9,
V10.8.10,V10.8.11A,V10.8.7B
1572 P3.16.3,S1.14.12,S4.4.5A,
S4.4.5B,S12.1.55A,V6.2.9E,
V7.3.4,V10.8.12,V10.9.3,V10.10.2,
V10.14.2A,V11.4.5A
1573 B4.1.11I,H5.3.13,P3.16.4,
P3.16.5,S1.14.14,S4.4.6,S6.5.5,
S12.1.55B,V2.3.13A,V5.1.5,V6.2.11A,
V7.3.5,V9.4.4,V10.1.5A,V10.8.13A,
V10.9.4,V10.9.5,V10.14.2B
1574 H1.1.70,H5.3.14,S1.14.15,
S1.14.16,S1.14.17,S4.7.1,
S6.5.6,S12.1.55C,T1.3.25A,
V7.3.6A,V7.3.7A,V10.8.14,V10.8.15,
V10.8.16,V10.8.17,V10.8.18,
V10.8.19,V10.8.20,V10.11.2A,
V10.11.3A,V10.11.3B,V10.11.3C
1575 B4.1.11J,H1.2.50,H1.6.1,
H5.1.12,P5.1.32,P5.1.33A,
T1.3.26,V6.2.12A,V10.1.5B,
V10.8.21,V10.10.3B,V10.11.2B,
V11.4.5B,V11.4.5C,V11.4.8A,
V11.4.8B
1576 B4.1.11K,B7.6.25,P6.1.9,
S1.4.18,S1.12.16,T1.2.15,
T1.3.25B,T1.8.7,V6.3.22,V6.3.23,
V7.1.63,V10.11.4A,V10.11.5A,
V10.14.1,V11.4.4D

Rusch, Adolf
 1481 B1.1.1A,C3.1.5A

Schaffner, Wilhelm
 1498 C5.1.9D
 1508 C3.1.50A
 1513 C3.1.50B
 1514 H4.1.7F
 1515 C3.1.50C

Schmidt, P.
 1561 P4.1.41

Schöffer, Peter (Schaeffer, Scheffer)
 1529 V7.2.1A
 1530 B7.6.10,P3.11.24,P4.1.32,
 P4.2.10,V7.2.2
 1531 S5.4.5
 1532 S6.3.9,S6.5.2
 1533 P4.1.38A
 1534 P6.1.2A
 1535 H1.1.37A,H1.1.37B,P6.2.1A,
 T1.7.3,V7.2.3
 1537 P6.1.2B,P6.2.1B
 1539 V7.2.1B

Schott, Johann
 1500 A3.1.5,C1.1.4D,H1.2.10,
 L1.2.9,V3.1.2D,V5.2.3A
 1501 C7.1.11A,S2.1.2C
 1502 H1.3.7A,H1.3.8
 1503 S5.1.3A
 1504 S5.1.3B
 1505 H1.1.12
 1508 S5.1.3C
 1509 H1.2.20A
 1510 A1.5.2A,A2.3.2,C9.1.21,
 H1.3.9L,H3.1.5,L1.2.12
 1511 C9.1.22,L1.2.13,S1.7.4
 1512 C9.1.23
 1513 H1.2.24,H1.3.32C,H1.3.43,
 H1.3.46A,S6.3.5,S14.1.1
 1514 B7.1.9,H1.3.46B,S1.6.2
 1515 A1.7.3A,A2.2.8,A2.2.11,
 H1.1.22,L1.2.15,T1.5.3
 1516 A2.3.3,C1.3.35,C4.1.19B,
 C9.1.25,H1.3.1
 1517 C6.4.4D,S1.5.2A,S17.1.4B

 1518 H1.2.27,P3.5.1,S8.1.3D
 1519 S2.2.16,A2.2.17,C6.2.18,
 H1.1.27,H1.2.20B,H1.2.29, H3.1.9,
 H3.1.10,L1.1.6
 1520 H1.2.30,P3.1.6A,P3.1.6B,
 P3.1.7A,P3.2.1C,P3.2.1D, P3.2.2A,
 P3.2.2B,P3.2.2C,P3.2.4,P3.2.5A,
 P3.2.6A,S6.3.6
 1521 H1.1.30,P3.1.14B,P3.1.15,
 P3.1.16,P3.2.5B,P3.2.8,P3.2.9,
 P3.2.11,P3.2.12,P3.9.1A,P3.9.1B,
 P7.1.2A,S12.1.25A,S12.1.25B
 1522 B5.1.5A,B8.2.2,C3.2.16C,
 C3.2.31,C4.2.16,P1.5.1,P2.1.13,
 P3.1.11C,P3.1.21A,P3.2.14,
 P3.3.6,P3.3.7,P3.9.6,P3.9.7A,
 S15.2.3A
 1523 P1.4.3,P1.4.4,P2.1.21A,
 P2.1.21B,P2.1.22A,P2.1.22B,
 P2.1.25,P2.1.27,P2.1.28,P2.2.1,
 P3.1.21B,P3.1.26,P3.2.16A,
 P3.2.16B,P3.2.16C,P3.3.12,P3.8.3,
 P3.11.5,P3.11.6,P3.12.1,P3.12.2A,
 P5.1.4,S15.2.3B
 1524 B8.2.4,P1.8.1,P1.8.2,
 P2.1.39A,P3.2.16D,P3.11.10,
 P3.11.13,P3.11.14,P3.12.3,
 P3.12.4,P3.12.5,P3.12.7
 1525 P4.1.14,B7.04,9,P3.12.2B,
 P3.12.8,P3.12.9,P3.12.10,P4.1.17
 1526 P2.1.39B,S1.5.2B,S14.1.3
 1527 B7.6.8,B7.6.8,B7.8.1A,
 B7.8.2,B7.8.3A
 1528 B7.8.1B,B7.8.3B,B7.8.4,
 B7.8.5A,B7.8.6,P3.4.2,P3.4.3,
 S1.5.2C,S1.5.3
 1529 B7.8.3C,B7.8.5B,B8.4.2,
 B8.4.3,H3.1.17A,S1.4.8,
 S1.7.7,S1.9.9
 1530 B7.8.5C,C2.1.1C,H1.2.35,
 P3.11.23,S1.5.2D,S1.7.8,S3.1.8A
 1531 H5.3.5,P5.1.16,S1.13.2,
 S15.2.3C
 1532 B7.8.5D,S1.5.5,S1.11.2,
 S1.13.5,S3.1.8C,S3.1.9A
 1533 S1.9.13,S1.13.6A,S1.13.6B
 1534 A3.1.12A,B7.8.3D,S1.7.12A,
 S3.1.9B,S15.2.3D